CITROEN CX

Road Test Portfolio

Compiled by
R M Clarke & A G Powell

ISBN 9781855209312

BROOKLANDS BOOKS LTD.
P.O. BOX 146, COBHAM,
SURREY, KT11 1LG. UK
sales@brooklands-books.com

CICXRP

www.brooklands-books.com

LS/6T1/2119

Contents

Contents continued

Acknowledgements

We have had portfolios on Citroen's most prestigious models in our list for over 30 years and we currently have titles on the Traction Avants, the DS & IDs, the SM plus the ubiquitous Deux Cheveaux. We are now delighted to report on the next range of Citroens used by French Presidents - the CX, which brings the story up to 1991.

Our "reference portfolios" are produced in small numbers for owners and enthusiasts and their existence is only possible because of the understanding and generosity of the original publishers of the stories that we reproduce. In compiling this book we have drawn on copyright articles and features which first appeared in: *Autocar, Auto International, Asian Auto, Autosport, Car, Car and Driver, Car South Africa, Classic Cars, Classic and Sportscar, GTS, Modern Motor, Motor, Motor Sport, Motor Trend, Road & Track, Sports Car World* and *What Car?* To the writers, photographers and managements of these magazines we extend our grateful and ongoing thanks. We are also indebted to the Citroen Car Club* and, in particular, to Robert Draper, Chairman of the CX section, who wrote the informative introduction which follows and also to Paul Noon who, at short notice, supplied a splendid range of photographs of his cars - one of which graces the front cover and the second is the top left hand picture on the back cover.

R.M. Clarke

The CX was introduced in 1974 to replace the aged but much loved DS. The car was well received and was voted European Car of the Year in 1975. Often referred to as the last 'real Citroen' the CX was designed by a team led by Robert Operon prior to Citroen becoming merged with Peugeot to create the PSA group. Unfortunately the CX had a rather troubled gestation even by Citroen's standards. The car was developed from the Projet L prototypes that were originally planned as a replacement for the BMC 1800 Landcrab. One of the Projet L cars survives in the Citroen conservatory and is powered by a watercooled version of the GS flat four engine. The original plan was to use a tri-rotor Comotor Wankel unit but a six cylinder air cooled unit was also tried. Ultimately the Wankel engine option failed through issues of reliability, excessive fuel consumption and Citroen/NSU/Comotor agreement breaking down. Unfortunately the lack of a suitable engine came very late in the day for the CX's development and the engine bay was too small to allow anything larger than a four cylinder engine. While the body and interior were extremely stylish and modern the mechanicals were a pretty humdrum (by Citroen standards) carry over from the DS. Early cars were plagued with heavy, unassisted steering and the 2.0 litre petrol engines were also rather underpowered, ironically these early cars are now extremely sought after.

The steering was quickly changed for the self-centering, variable power assisted Diravi system from the SM. This change transformed the character of the car making low speed manoeuvres finger-tip light but also giving exceptional stability on high speed motorways. While the 2000 plodded on, the larger engine sizes were increased with the 2200 engine being replaced by the 2400 and the 2200 diesel being replaced with a 2500.

The estate was introduced soon after the saloon and proved a very popular car due to its huge load area and carrying capacity. The Safari was the plain estate form and the Familiale offered three rows of seats as an early people carrier. The estate form saw the wheelbase being extended by 23cm (9 inches) and this allowed the creation of the most prized of the CX variants, the Prestige saloon. Originally the Prestige kept the same roof line as the standard car but this was soon raised, reputedly at the demand of President Mitterand. Again, the early, low roof, cars are most sought after.

Strangely for an executive saloon there was no fully automatic gearbox until 1980. Until then the closest thing was the C-matic, effectively a hydraulically automated 3 speed manual gearbox with torque convertor and an electrically operated clutch. This was no Citroen special as similar gearboxes were offered by other manufacturers e.g. Hondamatic and Vauxhall's Easytronic. The engineering in the C-matic system is relatively simple but adjustment can be complex and the lack of a torque-convertor lock up makes them very fuel inefficient. In 1980 the 2400 Pallas was offered with a ZF three speed automatic transmission. This is much more in keeping with the relaxed nature of the CX but the automatic is more noted for its durability than its smoothness.

The first of the more sporting variants was the 1977 2400 GTi with Bosch L-Jetronic fuel injection boosting power to 128bhp. This engine was also used in the higher specification saloons and estates. In 1981 the 2400 was increased to 2500 and then in 1984 the first of the GTi turbo models was introduced along with a restyled dashboard and other improvements. The Turbo cars were fast and refined, they offered high levels of equipment and performance albeit at the expense of the traditional 'magic carpet' ride. They had a dedicated following in Germany as autobahn cruisers capable of taking on the high performance Mercedes and Porsches of the day. The Turbo II of 1986 offered improved performance by way of intercooling.

In more mundane models the long serving 2.0 litre motor from the DS was finally replaced in 1982 by a new aluminium-block OHC engine jointly developed by Peugeot and Renault. The Douvrin engine was also available in 2.2 form. This engine offered substantial improvements due to reduction in weight, greater power and lower fuel consumption. This change also saw an increase in the front track and the flaring of the front arches. Pallas models and above were fitted with metric TRX wheel rims. TRX fit tyres are now exceedingly expensive and many owners replace them with almost identical imperial rims that accept standard tyres.

The Series 2 was introduced in late 1985 bringing larger, plastic bumpers and a more conventional interior layout. The revolving drum speedometer and rev counter were replaced with conventional style clock and needle design as previewed in the Series 1 GTi Turbo.

While there is no doubt that the Series 2 cars were better built, better rustproofed and have higher specification it is the Series 1 cars that are most sought after. The CX saloon was replaced in 1989 by the XM but the estate lived on until 1991 albeit built by Heuliez rather than Citroen.

Robert Draper

*Citroen Car Club - www.citroencarclub.org.uk

Citroën introduce the CX

Larger and faster than the GS, the new CX shows a resemblance to the SM.

In the engineering world, the work of the Citroën *bureau d'études* is highly respected; an entirely new car from this source is, therefore, something of an event. The latest Citroën, the CX, is altogether larger and faster than the GS, but more compact than the immortal DS. Some of the technique of the ultra-advanced SM has also rubbed off on the newcomer.

Compared with the DS, the wheelbase is nearly a foot shorter, the overall length 1 ft 5 in less, but the width is down by only 3 in. However, the interior space is not much less than that of the bigger model, partly due to the more compact engine installation. The big news is that Citroën have gone transverse. Whether or not this is a legacy of the short liaison with Fiat one does not know, but the very efficient Fiat-type transmission, in which the gearbox pinions double for transfer gears, is employed. The gearbox has four-speeds and the unit is conveniently placed for a floor-mounted gearlever.

The four-cylinder engine derives from that of the DS and has inclined valves operated by short pushrods, the light-alloy cylinder head carrying a twin-choke Weber carburetter. Alternative engines of 1985 cc and 2175 cc develop 102 and 112 bhp respectively. A special economy version of the car is deliberately over-geared to reduce petrol consumption at high cruising speeds.

In France, the autoroutes tend to be high and exposed, making front-wheel drive almost obligatory for really fast travel in gale-force winds. Many of the other roads are very bumpy, so the softest possible suspension is desirable. For such conditions, the well-known Citroën hydropneumatic constant-height suspension is ideal, with engine-driven pump and driver-controlled ride-height. The geometry gives a progressive rate, notably at the rear, with anti-dive in front. The suspension is by upper and lower transverse links in front, with light-alloy trailing arms at the rear.

The power-operated suspension and brakes are perhaps too well known for a full technical description to be necessary. The front brake discs have gone outboard, because the transverse engine makes inboard mounting almost impossible. The rear disc brakes have a separate circuit and the mechanical calipers are independently mounted in front, operated by a hefty orthodox lever between the seats (cheers !). The Michelin ZX tyres are 185 SR 14 in front and 175 SR 14 at the rear (HR 14 XVS on the 2200).

Citroën have for years been the masters of aerodynamics, which is why their cars go so fast with only a moderate power output. The engineering term CX indicates the co-efficient of air penetration, which is a suitable symbol for the new car, as it has 11 per cent less drag than the DS, which was itself outstanding in this field. The result is that the CX 2200 will maintain 111 mph on only 112 bhp. An efficient shape pays off at much lower speeds, too, the fuel consumption being 28 mpg at 75 mph or 36 mpg at 56 mph.

Very important is the power-assisted steering, with powered return, derived from the SM. However, the steering is not quite so quick as that on the Maserati-engined car, with 2.5 turns from lock to lock instead of two turns, in deference to those unaccustomed to racing cars. Without power assistance, the cheaper version needs 4.5 turns and is, of course, unavoidably heavier to operate with so much weight concentrated in front.

It is extremely interesting that Citroën have, in effect, gone back to using a separate box-section steel frame, from which the rigid steel body is insulated at some 16 mounting points. The current practice of having separate front and rear sub-frames was abhorrent to the design team, because if you mount them softly enough to absorb road and engine noise, directional stability must suffer and steering response be blurred. To join the two frames together, for rigidity, and insulate the body from them, is the logical answer.

Ergonomic switch controls.

The car has many safety features, to which must be added the excellent all-round view to which the large screen contributes, with a single wiper blade to clean it all over.

The CX is fully equipped and the 2200, being the high-performance model, has a rev counter and an oil pressure gauge among its more elaborate furnishing. The heating and ventilation system is especially schemed so that its operation is not affected by differences in car speed or engine revs.

For years, the Citroën DS has demonstrated remarkable speed and economy as a result of its efficient body shape. Yet, other manufacturers still make cars with high noses and square lines that squander precious petrol and reduce maximum speed. Let us hope that the even more effective CX will at last teach them the practical advantages of scientific body design.

JOHN BOLSTER

SPECIFICATION AND PERFORMANCE DATA

Car described: Citroën CX2000 and CX2200 four-door saloon.

Engine: Four cylinders inclined forward at 30 degrees, 86 x 85.5 mm (1985 cc), 102 bhp at 5500 rpm, 90 x 85.5 mm (2175 cc), 112 bhp at 5500 rpm; compression ratio 9 to 1; pushrod-operated inclined valves in light-alloy head; Weber twin-choke downdraught carburetter.

Transmission: Single dry plate clutch; four-speed all-synchromesh gearbox, ratios 0.8, 1.133, 1.833 and 3.166 to 1 (economy 2000 fourth gear 0.75 to 1); helical spur gear final drive, ratio (2000) 13/62, (economy 2000) 14/61, (2200) 12/55.

Chassis: Box-section steel frame reinforcing, but insulated from steel body shell; hydropneumatic self-levelling suspension with engine-driven high-pressure pump and nitrogen-filled spheres plus integral dampers for each wheel, with upper and lower transverse front links, light-alloy rear trailing arms, and anti-roll bars fore and aft; rack and pinion steering with power assistance an option; power-operated disc brakes all round, ventilated at front; bolt-on steel disc wheels, fitted Michelin tyres (2000) front 185 SR 14 ZX/rear 175 SR 14 ZX, (2200) front 185 HR 14 XVS/rear 175 HR 14 XVS.

Equipment: 12-volt lighting and starting; speedometer; clock; voltmeter; fuel gauge (rev counter and oil pressure gauge on 2200); heating, demisting, and ventilation system; single two-speed wiper and washers; flashing direction indicators; reversing lights.

Dimensions Wheelbase 9 ft 4 in; track (front) 4 ft 10 in, (rear) 4 ft 5½ in; overall length 15 ft 1 in; width 5 ft 8 in; weight 2,788 lb.

Performance: 2000, Economy 2000, 2200—Maximum speed, 108, 104, 111 mph. Standing quarter-mile, 18.5, 18.7, 18.[illegible] s. Acceleration, 0-62 mph 13.1, 13.3, 11.7 s.

Fuel Consumption: 27, 30, 28 mpg (makers' figures).

Driving impressions ...

Earlier this month I was given the opportunity to try both the CX2200 and the CX2000 over 200 miles of varying road surfaces in Lapland. None of the roads could really have been described as good and a great deal were glorified cart tracks, but how superbly the new models coped with them! The well-proven hydropneumatic suspension soaked up the potholes and ridges with no complaints whatever. The CX2200 with the excellent power-assisted steering was the more preferable of the two in these conditions, especially on the loose surfaces, there being virtually no violent feedback through the wheels of the poor surfaces, which made for very pleasant, tireless driving. It was, however, firm enough for the driver to be in the picture at all times.

The smaller model, without the assistance, was certainly no handful and was, in fact, still surprisingly light to handle. In comparison to its market competitors in the range it, of course, cannot be equalled — only its sister can be compared and one is then talking about near perfection.

Despite the difference in engine size there appears to be very little in the performance of the two models and the manufacturer's claimed maximum speeds of 111 and 108 mph are quite conservative.

The engine never strains — indeed one can hardly hear it even under the harshest acceleration — and 100 mph comes up smoothly and quickly. Once the car is running at near maximum speed it will happily stay there for mile upon mile.

One of the most pleasing aspects of the new model is its speed, coupled with economy, on all the models. The 2000 and 2200 both averaged around the 26 mpg mark while be-

Citroën CX

New 2-litre car, smaller than D-series,

Medium-large car of great promise uses existing 2-litre engine in transverse installation. Well-tried hydropneumatic suspension, chassis reinforcement for unitary-type body, excellent aerodynamics. In production now for French market first, in Britain next year.

CITROËN ARE unique in their devotion to advanced engineering. Each of their cars is designed to be ahead of its time, thus ensuring a long production run so that tooling costs may be amortised at a much lower rate than is general. This in turn means that despite their advanced features, the cars may be offered at competitive prices.

Citroën succeeded first in the field both of very small cars – the 2CV and its enormous family of derivatives – and of large cars. They then turned their attention to the middle of the market and produced the GS, which was acclaimed just as the DS had been before it. The GS made the range much better-balanced, but a great gulf still yawned between it and the DS. This gap has now been at least partly closed by the introduction of another completely new car, the CX.

Our table shows how much closer is the CX, in size and performance, to the DS than to the GS. This is inevitable given the decision to use the existing 2-litre engine as the basic power plant. The only alternative would have been to develop an entirely new engine, and this one imagines the company were in no position to do so soon after breaking new ground and investing heavily in the air-cooled GS flat-four.

However, the CX is usefully smaller than the DS, which some people have always found a handful especially in town and in confined situations. Its wheelbase, though long by absolute standards, is shorter by 11in. and this is reflected in the smaller turning circle. Disappointingly, it is hardly any lighter than the bigger car, but this is due to the much superior crashworthiness of the CX structure.

Main features

Although the D-series engine is used in the CX, it is turned sideways-on and inclined forward at 30deg to the vertical. The four-speed, two-shaft gearbox is driven via the diaphragm-spring clutch, its input shaft in line with the crankshaft centreline. Drive is taken from the inboard end of the output shaft through a massive helical spur to the final drive unit, which is therefore well off-centre (offset to the left as viewed from the driving seat). Rather than use drive shafts of unequal length, Citroën employ an intermediate shaft to take the right-wheel drive across the back of the engine, with a steady bearing attached to the sump.

The wheels are smaller than Citroën have used before on a car of this size (or even on the GS), their diameter being 14in.; slightly larger-section tyres are used at the front than at the back, the spare being of the smaller size. Steering is by rack and pinion, the rack neatly tucked away behind the engine and thus very well protected in a frontal collision. Power steering, based on that of the SM but with less extreme gearing, is available as an option on all but the top model in the range, where it is standard.

The suspension is Citroën's well-tried hydropneumatic spring-damper units, with transverse arms at the front and trailing arms at the rear. At the front, the units act on the upper suspension arms, which are also linked to a massive anti-roll bar. The front suspension also uses anti-dive geometry.

Disc brakes are used all round, though the transverse engine demands the use of outboard discs at the front, in contrast to previous Citroën practice. The front discs are ventilated. Brake application is by the same high-pressure hydraulic system which feeds the suspension, with separate front and rear circuits and a proportioning valve operated by a small torsion bar from the front anti-roll bar.

It is, however, the structure which is the greatest point of interest. In it, Citroën have united a unitary body which is in itself very strong, with a longitudinal frame which ensures geometrical accuracy as well as transmitting crash loads, and affording better suppression of road and engine noise.

2000/2200

with transverse engine and gearbox

by J. R. Daniels, B.Sc.

Engine and transmission

Those who regard the Citroën 2-litre engine as old-fashioned forget that it was only introduced in 1966, to supplement and eventually replace the really old, long-stroke engine which dated back to before the war. It was a change which went almost unnoticed, yet the new engine was a great advance and is a perfectly acceptable basis for the CX power unit. Though it has no overhead camshaft, it is modern enough in other respects. The camshaft is high-set, rather as in the Hillman Avenger, and driven by a duplex chain. Short push-rods in a crossover pattern operate valves set in a 60deg vee – so the combustion chamber is hemispherical and the layout crossflow. In the CX the carburettor is mounted on the back of the engine, so to speak, while the exhaust is carried down the front face and through the gap between the sump and the final drive – another reason why the intermediate drive shaft, fixed relative to the engine, had to be employed.

	GS 1220	CX 2000	D Special
Engine, c.c.	1,220	**1,985**	1,985
Power/rpm	60/6,500	**102/5,500**	99/5,500
Torque/rpm	64/3,250	**112/3,000**	106/2,500
Wheelbase, in.	100½	**112**	123
Length overall	162	**181**	193
Width overall	63½	**68**	71
Empty weight, lb	1,885	**2,788**	2,815
Final drive	4·125	**4·77**	4·857
mph/1000	15.25	**19.3**	20·2
Tyres	145–15	**F 185–14** **R 175–14**	185–15
Fuel, gallon	9·5	**15·0**	14·3

Skew gears from the camshaft drive the oil pump and the distributor, and a pulley on the opposite end of the shaft from the drive sprocket carries a belt drive to the water pump, and thence to the alternator. The fuel pump is mechanical, and a further drive serves the position-displacement hydraulic pump to provide pressure for braking, suspension and, where applicable, power steering.

In its basic form, at 1,985 c.c., the engine is just over-square and gives an output of 102 bhp at 5,500 rpm. In this version the claimed maximum speed is 108 mph with the normal gearing, which is 19·3 mph per 1,000 rpm in top. This speed corresponds closely with peak power. There is also an economy version of the CX2000 with a higher final drive and also a higher top gear; in this case the maximum is a claimed 104 mph at a leisurely 4,600 rpm.

The larger-capacity engine achieves its 2,175 c.c. capacity by boring-out, as in the D Super 5 of which it is also the power unit. For the CX2200 it produces 112 bhp at 5,500 rpm, giving a claimed maximum speed of 111 mph.

The 2000 and 2200 share the same gearbox, though the 2200

The CX bears a strong family resemblance to both the GS and the SM, and like them is exceptionally good from an aerodynamic point of view. Note the clean nose entry, steeply-raked and curved screen and faired rear wheel arches

uses a clutch of slightly larger diameter as well as a higher final drive ratio. As already mentioned, the gearbox is of two-shaft, all-indirect design; top gear is an overdrive ratio. The intermediate drive shaft across the back of the engine, a technique used also in the Lancia Beta, adds a certain degree of complication but at the same time avoids any possible problem of vibration of a long drive shaft and simplifies production in that the outer shafts, with one-piece joints inboard and constant-velocity joints outboard, are identical left and right.

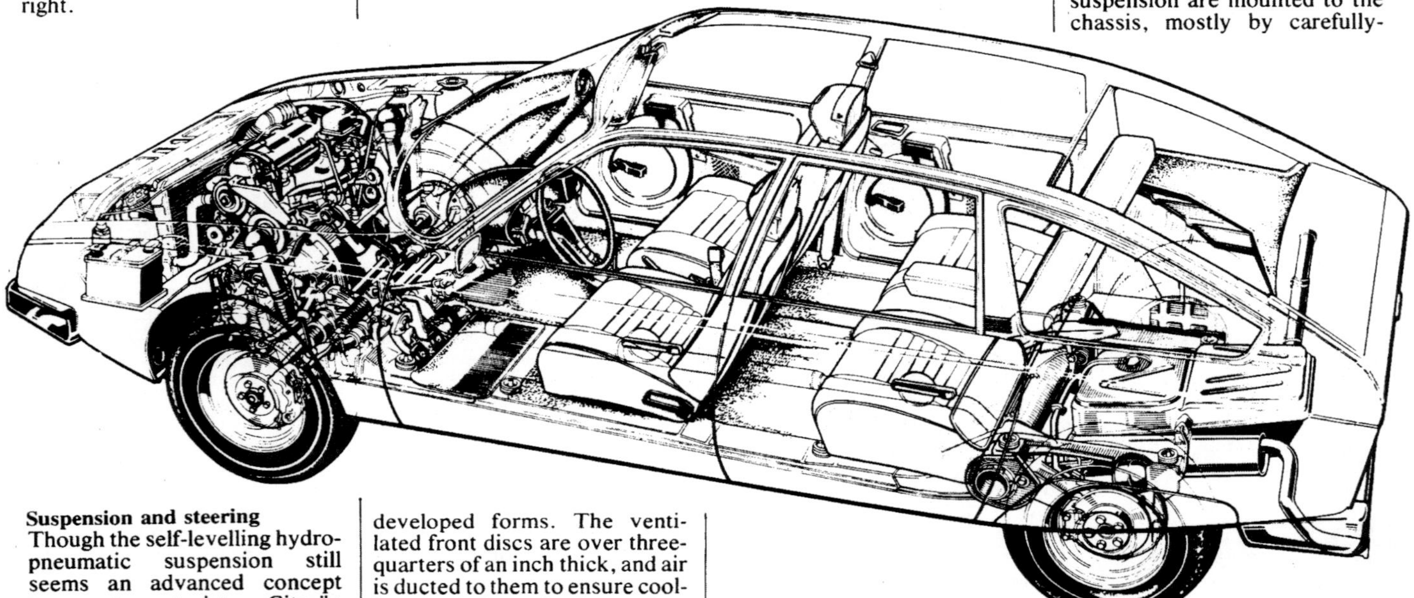

Citroën cutaway shows basic mechanical layout with DS-derived 2-litre engine turned sideways and inclined forward at 30deg. Hydropneumatic suspension units are clearly seen, but the separate chassis is not evident in this view

Suspension and steering

Though the self-levelling hydropneumatic suspension still seems an advanced concept to most motorists, Citroën point out that they have developed the system over 20 years, first on the D-series, and then on the GS. They have not only developed it to a high degree of reliability, but have also worked hard to eliminate some of its early, less desirable features. The anti-dive front end geometry is one result, helping the CX to maintain a constant ride height under braking and acceleration; the familiar ride-height adjustment is retained.

Front and rear anti-roll bars are evidence of Citroën's determination to cut roll, which affects the handling even of the SM, to a practical minimum. In the CX, the front bar is nearly an inch in diameter, while that on the rear, connecting the trailing arms, is 0·69in. diameter.

Although the wheels are smaller than those of the DS and GS, they are wide-rimmed. For both the 2000 and the 2200, the standard size is 5½J–14, with five-stud fixing. The tyres, remarkably, are different sizes front and rear, those at the front being of 185 section compared with 175 at the back (and on the spare). Quite why this was done is not clear; one is driven to suspect that bigger tyres were needed to achieve a sufficient load rating at the front, but that there was not enough room in the rear arches to clear 185 tyres – the rear arches are faired in for the sake of aerodynamic efficiency.

Despite the smaller-diameter wheels, the CX brakes are very large. The use of 10·2in. discs at the front, backed up by 9·2in. discs at the rear, indicate that Citroën have no intention of letting the CX run out of brakes in either its present or in future developed forms. The ventilated front discs are over three-quarters of an inch thick, and air is ducted to them to ensure cooling. Each front disc is acted on by two sets of pads, one operated by the main braking system with a separate piston for each independent hydraulic circuit; the other, smaller set of pads is operated by the parking brake lever. As in the DS, a pad-wear indicator is fitted, lighting a facia warning when the main pads are reduced to a certain thickness.

Apart from the front/rear pressure proportioning valve already mentioned, pressure in the rear brake line is limited by a load-sensing valve on the rear suspension.

Rack and pinion steering is used in the CX, drawing on all the experience gained with the DS and SM. The basic, non-powered system is relatively low-geared, with 4½ turns of the wheel from lock to lock for a claimed turning circle between kerbs of 36ft. The steering wheel itself is an average 16in. in diameter. The powered system, offered as an option on all models and as standard on the 2200, is essentially that of the SM. It has the same self-centring and speed-related "feel", but has 2½ turns from lock to lock instead of only two. The steering wheel is an inch smaller in diameter, and the servo unit has been isolated from the steering itself and installed in the passenger compartment.

Structure

The body shell of the CX, especially the passenger compartment, is as strong and stiff as those of many contemporaries. The main floor is a massive single pressing, to which are added cross-members for local stiffening in the seat-mounting areas, and which also give added resistance to sideways impact. The main sideways-impact strength, however, comes from the sill members which are box-sections of considerable size. They provide a footing for three very strong roll-over hoops formed by the main pillars of the six-light structure, which in turn form a complete "cage" by linking up with the roof side rails which run in a smooth arc from the windscreen base to the extreme rear of the fastback-styled body. At the front of the passenger compartment, a single bulkhead pressing crosses the structure; at the rear, a second diaphragm isolates the boot and its contents, ensuring that luggage does not burst into the passenger compartment in a severe frontal collision.

Citroën's engineers presumably started with the idea of using front and rear subframes to obtain better engine and road noise insulation, but the idea was taken one stage further. In effect the subframes are there, but they are linked beneath the body by two longerons which complete a chassis frame to which the entire body is mounted by sixteen flexible couplings. The longerons are wide but not very deep, so the chassis is not particularly strong in torsion; but it does resist any tendency to "lozenge" in a horizontal plane. This ensures accurate suspension geometry and improves the handling; while body and chassis together are quite adequately stiff in torsion.

The chassis performs two other functions. It is a noise filter, and also the first line of defence against front or rear impact. Because the engine/transmission and the suspension are mounted to the chassis, mostly by carefully-designed flexible attachments, and the body is then flexibly mounted to the chassis, both engine and road noise has to pass two barriers to reach the interior. The front part of the frame is the most massive of all, the longerons being joined by two cross-members, one close to the extreme front and the other just forward of the passenger compartment. An arch-frame is built up on this second cross-member, with outward extensions at the top to house the front suspension units. The engine sits immediately *ahead* of the arch, attached low down by flexible couplings and high up by two massive steady-bars picking up on built-up brackets. The front anti-roll bar, and the steering rack, pass *behind* the arch-frame and the suspension link attachment points are housed within it.

The rear subframe is much simpler. The longerons are continued rearwards, becoming much deeper to provide protection for the fuel tank which sits between them. The single cross-member is a very large tube, to the ends of which are attached the rear suspension trailing arms. While the front hydropneumatic units are housed vertically in the arch-frame, those at the rear lie almost horizontally, nested within the deepest section of the longeron.

The front and rear bumpers are, naturally, attached to the extreme ends of the chassis frame. While they are not claimed to be American-style 5 mph bumpers, there is no doubt they could be made so with little extra effort, since the second function of the chassis frame is to transmit and absorb the first force of any front or rear impact. Because it is a continuous structure, it is able to distribute loads widely, while keeping them clear of the passenger compartment. Once the impact exceeds a certain severity, the compartment does of course become involved, but by that time the frame and then (in a frontal accident) the engine/transmission assembly will have played their part in absorbing loads and reducing the deceleration. Citroën claim that after a 31 mph crash into a barrier at 60deg angle – a more difficult case to meet, in many ways, than an absolutely "square" collision, and also perhaps more realistic – three of the four doors could still be opened.

Left: Back view of the CX shows careful aerodynamic treatment with concave rear window and boot lid. Spoilers, front or rear, are notable for their absence. Boot lid has short upper deck, but extends right down to rear bumper, giving a low sill for easy loading

Aerodynamics and Equipment

It is depressing to spend too much time talking about the crashworthiness of a new car, for crashing is not after all its prime function. Safety is a good thing to have, but it costs weight, and weight costs money and economy. Citroën have done their best, as always, to regain as much as possible by seeking to design the most aerodynamically efficient body consistent with practical requirements.

All the hallmarks of proper aerodynamic design are there. The nose entry is smooth, the headlamp lenses blended into the contour. A smooth undertray attached to the bottom of the chassis frame runs back as far as the front axle line. The windscreen is steeply raked and also curved, but it is interesting that Citroën have not seen fit to do away with conventional gutter rails. At the rear, there is a distinct break where the roof ends, and the rear window is concave, as is the (very short) upper deck of the boot lid. The lid curves smoothly over and is then undercut slightly to provide a number-plate housing. The rear wheel arches, but not the front ones, are faired; the 2200 also has wheel trims which virtually turn the wheels into plain, flat discs.

The result of all this, and of attention to detail in such things as sealing and exterior door handle design, is a claimed drag coefficient of 0·30, a figure unrivalled by any large saloon other than Citroën's own DS. Low drag does not of itself guarantee exceptional fuel economy, as Citroën themselves proved with the GS; but in alliance with sufficient power and high enough gearing it promises a substantial advantage.

Given the very long wheelbase, it is not surprising that there is plenty of room inside the car. There is no evidence of the back seat design being skimped, either in cushion size or in the rake of its backrest. The CX is a full four (or five) seater in every sense of the word. The boot, too, is large and very reminiscent of the GS, being an almost perfect box-shape with no sill at all. The spare wheel is stowed under the bonnet, and needs to be removed to gain proper access to most engine components; but once it is out, access is certainly much easier than in the DS or the GS.

Inside, all the instruments and minor controls are grouped on a binnacle which looks for all the world like a small, sectioned flying saucer hovering above the rest of the facia. The switches ranged round its edge are all within finger-reach of the steering wheel rim; the indicators, in Citroën tradition, are not self-cancelling. Because of the limited space in the binacle, Citroën have retained their drum-type speedometer rotating behind a magnifying porthole, as used in the home-market GS. The same arrangement is also used for the rev counter where one is fitted. Other instruments comprise a clock, fuel gauge and voltmeter. The only water temperature indica-

Engine and transmission cutaway shows crossflow engine layout, with exhaust taken beneath the engine from the front face. Two-shaft, all-indirect gearbox and helical spur transfer gear take drive to offset differential; an intermediate shaft takes drive across the back of the engine with a steady bearing attached to the sump

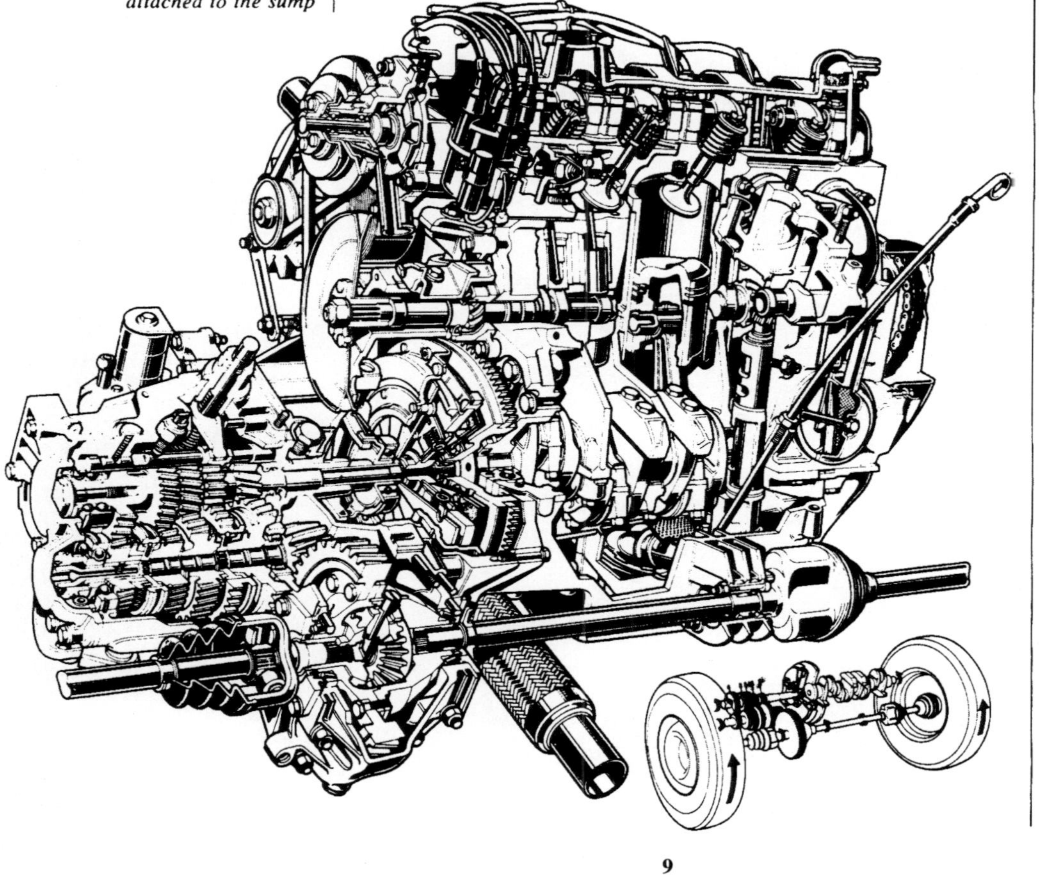

tion is a warning light. A centre console carries other minor controls, including those for the heater. The heating and ventilation system is of the true air-blending type, with a permanently-hot matrix.

One very noticeable feature is the use of a single very large wiper blade, centrally pivoted, sweeping the whole screen. This gives a simplified system, while Citroën claim that since the blade is always parallel to the airflow over the screen, there is no risk of lifting-off.

The front seats, which move fore and aft through a range of 220mm (over 8½in.) have reclining backrests. The driver's seat is adjustable for height, though not on the move, but head restraints are offered only as an option. Where the optional inertia-reel belts are ordered, they are (for the French market, at least) neatly concealed within the centre door pillars, the reels at the base.

Production and Development
The CX is now in production at the new Citroën factory at Aulnay near Paris, which opened only recently and "cut its teeth" on a small run of the DS. It will unfortunately be some time before the British motorist has a chance to buy the car, since right-hand-drive production is not scheduled until late spring of 1975.

While the CX is for the time being available in only three very similar forms –2000, 2000 Economy and 2200 – there is clearly scope for considerable development. The engine could easily be uprated to the standard of the 2·3-litre Pallas, with or without fuel injection. A five-speed gearbox, however, is unlikely because a fifth speed would add to the width of the engine/transmission package and there appears not to be room. Undoubtedly, work is going ahead on an automatic transmission for the CX, to be offered as an option.

The front-drive layout of the car lends itself to alternative body styles, of which an estate – the CX Safari? – is the most obvious. Like the DS Safari, it would offer considerable volume and easy loading.

At the time of the introduction, the price of the CX had not been decided. Since it is a smaller car than the DS, it will presumably sell at a lower price; but since it embodies more advanced engineering, that price may not be *much* lower. There remains the question of what will eventually fill the gap which still exists between the GS1220 and the CX2000. It cries out for a car of 1,500–1,600 c.c., and the eventual answer may be found in the form of a GS with a bigger engine. As to where that engine may come from, one should perhaps consider the implications of the recently-announced agreement between Citroën and Peugeot.

Driving impressions
Europe these days is getting to be a difficult place to launch a new car without attracting a blaze of local publicity. Citroën took their journalists to Swedish Lapland, there to face a wide variety of roads, the unpredictable nature of the reindeer and the sadly, wholly predictable attitude of the mosquitoes.

My driving started with the plain 2000 (the Economy version not being available), with a half-way change to the 2200. The total route covered some 260 miles in a loop from Gallivare, north and then east to the Finnish border and back. The roads varied from semi-sealed Swedish country track to fast, modern trunk road.

The immediate impression of the CX was that it was an easier car to get used to than the DS, or even the GS. All the controls feel more conventional – especially the brakes, which do not operate in the same load-sensitive, no-movement manner as in the earlier cars. One could very quickly drive with confidence, and no feeling of strangeness.

The next very firm impression was one of comfort and stability. By any standard, let alone that of the older Citroëns, the CX rolls very little and feels a great deal more predictable and reassuring as a result. If the firm control of roll has affected the ride, one is scarcely aware of it. In fact the ride feels slightly harsh at low speed on bad surfaces, but that is the only loss. At higher speed there is no sign of the "float" which afflicted the DS in its early days, and reaction to single sharp humps and badly-spaced undulations, while still marked, does not have the sometimes-spectacular violence of the bigger car.

Again, one might have expected 4½ turns from lock to lock to make the steering feel uncomfortably low-geared, more so on a route which included many tight corners, some of them entered while braking down from high speed. Yet at no time did I feel unable to apply lock as quickly as I needed it, except when doing a three-point turn in a fairly narrow road. For the most part the CX's handling is remarkably neutral for a nose-heavy, front-drive car. Certainly the understeer increases if corners are taken very fast, but one expects that and the behaviour is always

Structural drawing shows rigid body structure, including strongly caged passenger compartment. Separate chassis, essentially front and rear sub-frames joined by two longeron members, carries the engine and suspension units, and also mounts the body on 16 flexible joints. Note the front-end undertray

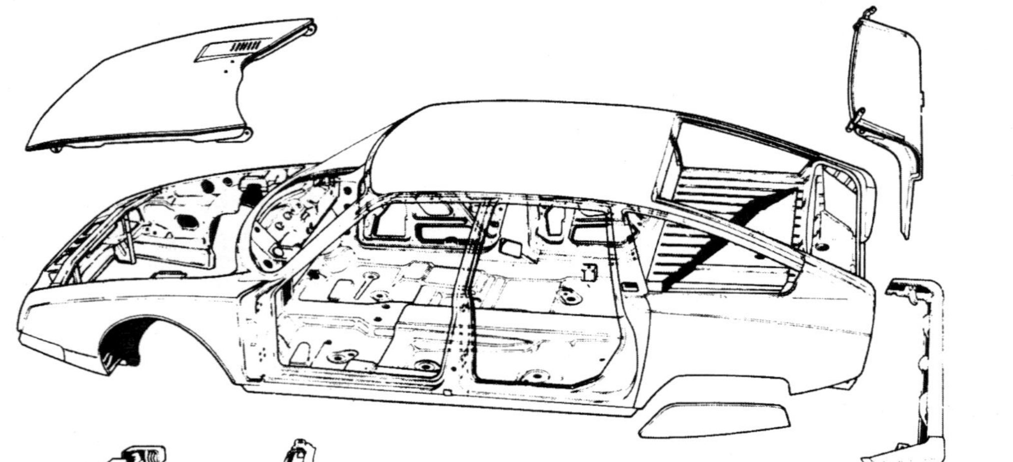

Above: Interior treatment is futuristic, with instruments and minor controls in "flying saucer" in front of the driver. Centre console is a standard feature, with provision for mounting radio and cassette player vertically. Fabric seats are standard, head restraints optional

Opposite page: Because of restricted space, both speedometer and rev counter are of the revolving-drum type, viewed through a magnifying glass..Clock, fuel gauge and voltmeter are remaining instruments. Other functions are taken care of by warning lights. All minor controls are within finger-stretch of wheel rim

predictable. On a loose surface, the tail will readily drift outwards and in this case the movement is easier to control with the throttle than with opposite lock. Inevitably there is some reaction to sudden opening or closing of the throttle, but much less than in, say, a BLMC 1800.

The engine feels entirely different from the great mechanical lump it seems in the DS, partly no doubt because it is farther away and partly because of the way it is mounted. The chassis succeeds less well in damping out road noise, which is still noticeable at times on most surfaces.

Because of the quietness of the engine and exhaust, the performance seems less than spectacular. Citroën actually claim a time of about 13sec to 60 mph for the 2000, and about 11·5sec for the 2200, but we had no chance to verify these figures more than very approximately. But the claimed maximum speeds seemed to be about right, if not actually modest. The 2200 would hold an indicated 180–185 km/hour (112–115 mph) for long periods, even on slight gradients and through bends.

Though the engine is over the power peak at maximum speed, there is no sign of any falling-off of power, no valve-bounce or sudden strangulation. The 2200 in particular was driven very much on the rev-counter, and I found the Cyclops-eye type of instrument much better as a rev-counter than as a speedometer.

I am more than ever convinced, after driving the SM and now the CX, that steering can be over-geared and too responsive for the average driver. The effect is much less obvious in the CX, but I am inclined to think three turns from lock to lock would be a better compromise between ease of control and rapid steering response. In other respects the system has much to recommend it, especially the servo-centring.

During the drive it rained considerably, giving a chance to try the single-wiper in earnest. Citroën's anti-lifting claim seems well justified, though the blade appears to leave a large unwiped area at both top corners of the screen instead of just one as would be the case with a two-blade system.

The CX is generally a quiet car, although some wind rush is added to the degree of road noise already referred to, so perhaps the gutter rails do play a part. When a side window is opened, the noise becomes spectacularly worse, so it is as well that the new ventilation system is so good.

The seats, upholstered in nylon, proved excellent except that I felt a slight lack of lumbar support after four hours. I also tried riding in the back, and was very impressed by the comfort there: since I am well over six feet, this is something I find all too rarely.

As for economy, the 2000 (which was taken on by somebody with less regard for fuel consumption) achieved over 27 mpg, which must be regarded as good on an exercise of this kind. The 2200 which was driven much harder both by the first incumbent and by me, still managed 24·5 mpg which is, relatively speaking, even better.

There can be no doubt that the CX, the second big European car to be launched since the fuel crisis, is as well placed as anything in its class to make good use of precious fuel. In other ways it marks a considerable advance for Citroën. It is less idiosyncratic, easier to drive (without, as far as one can see, sacrificing any of the traditional Citroën virtues) and much improved in handling and mechanical noise. The bold decision to use a transverse engine installation in a car this size has paid off well in terms of safety and use of space, and the CS must surely succeed in winning the favour of a large part of the European middle-class market. □

SPECIFICATION (CX2200)

FRONT ENGINE, FRONT-WHEEL DRIVE

ENGINE

Cylinders	4, in line, transversely mounted, 30deg forward inclined
Main bearings	5
Cooling system	Water; pump, electric fan and radiator
Bore	86·0 mm, 3·39in. (90·0 mm, 3·54in.)
Stroke	85·5 mm, 3·37in.
Displacement	1,985 c.c., 121·2 cu. in. (2,175 c.c. 132·7 cu. in.)
Valve gear	Overhead; pushrods and rockers
Compression ratio	9·0 to 1; min. octane rating 97RM
Carburettor	Weber 34DMTR25 twin-choke
Fuel pump	Mechanical
Oil filter	Full-flow, replaceable cartridge type
Max. power	102 (112) bhp (DIN) at 5,500 rpm
Max torque	112 (123) lb. ft. at 3,000 (3,500) rpm

TRANSMISSION

Clutch	Diaphragm-spring, 8·5 (8·9) in. dia.
Gearbox	4-speed, all-indirect, all-synchromesh
Gear ratios	Top 0·80 Third 1·13 Second 1·83 First 3·17 Reverse 3·15
Final drive	Helical spur, ratio 4·77 (4·58) to one
Mph/1,000 rpm in top	19·3 (20·0)

CHASSIS AND BODY

Construction	Steel body mounted on twin-longeron main frame at 16 points

SUSPENSION

Front	Independent, upper and lower transverse arms with anti-dive geometry, hydropneumatic spring/damper units, anti-roll bar
Rear	Independent, trailing arms, hydropneumatic spring/damper units, anti-roll bar

STEERING

Type	Rack and pinion (power-assisted)
Wheel dia.	16 (15) in.

BRAKES

Type	Disc brakes front and rear, front discs ventilated, dual independent hydraulic high-pressure circuits
Servo	Hydraulic
Dimensions	F 10·2in. dia. R 9·2in. dia.
Swept area	F 235 sq. in., R 162 sq. in. Total 397 sq. in. (232 sq. in./ton laden)

WHEELS

Type	Pressed steel disc, 5-stud fixing, 5½in. wide rim
Tyres—make	Michelin ZX (Michelin XVS)
—type	Radial-ply tubeless
—size	F 185–14in., R 175–14in.

EQUIPMENT

Battery	12 volt, 50Ah
Alternator	63 (83) Amp AC
Headlamps	4-lamp system, tungsten-halogen main beam, 90/190 watt (total)
Reversing lamps	Standard
Electric fuses	12
Screen wiper	Two-speed
Screen washer	Manual trigger-type
Interior heater	Standard, air-blending type
Heated rear window	Standard
Safety belts	Static standard, inertia-reel optional, back seat belts optional
Interior trim	Nylon seats, pvc headlining
Floor covering	Carpet
Jack	Screw pillar type, assisted by suspension height adjustment
Windscreen	Thick-interlayer laminate

DIMENSIONS

Wheelbase	112in.
Front track	58in.
Rear track	53½in.
Overall length	181in.
Overall width	68in.
Overall height	53½in.
Frontal area	26·4 sq. ft.
Kerb weight	2,788 (2,822) lb
Max. permitted weight	3,836 (3,880) lb
Max. towing weight	29·6 cwt
Max. internal payload	1,048lb
Fuel tank	15 gallons
Coolant	19·4 pints
Engine sump	10 pints
Gearbox/final drive	2·8 pints

TEST Citroen CX 2000

1,985 c.c.

New Citroën sets high standards of ride, handling and braking. Steering heavy and too low-geared. Disappointing level of wind noise, but quiet in other respects. Very airy and spacious interior with outstanding passenger comfort. Only average fuel economy. A slight disappointment as the "Car of the Year"

Opposite page: Side view best shows true aerodynamic shape of Citroën CX; front view is dominated by big headlamp lenses. Interior design includes futuristic "flying saucer" instrument and minor control binnacle. Single-spoke wheel is in true Citroën tradition

Below right: Rear view emphasizes shrouded rear wheels and concave, sloping window. Boot opening extends down to bumper level

ONE has come to expect much of new cars from Citroën and should expect exceptional things from a Citroën that is "The Car of the Year." Thus if some reservations are necessary over the Citroën CX it is, perhaps, because too much can be expected of any company, especially in these times of rapidly escalating cost.

For the CX is by no means as radical as were the DS or GS at the time of *their* introduction. Other manufacturers have more than caught up in areas where Citroën were at one time pre-eminent, and although the design is clearly capable of lasting a long time, the CX is not as significantly better than its rivals as were its predecessors.

In terms of other models in the Citroën range, the CX falls closer to the DS series than to the GS. Although the wheelbase falls exactly between the two, the transverse mounting of the engine allows the front seat passengers to be positioned usefully further forward than in the DS and the amount of rear seat space rivals the bigger car. The other thing that puts the CX closer to the DS is its use of the same engine, which even tilted 30 deg forward, is still bulky enough to demand a large car round it. However, the CX, at 15ft 1in., is exactly 12in. shorter than the DS.

Compared to its rivals in world markets, the CX shows a useful gain in wheelbase and therefore interior room without the penalty of extra length. In other areas that bear comparison, the CX gives away power output to most. It makes up for this, in part, by superior aerodynamic shape, but not by any inherent lightness, since the very strong body and separate base chassis unit take the kerb weight up to 25·2cwt – higher than most competitors. It follows that fuel consumption should show gains at the expense of performance and indeed this proves to be the case, partly because the gearing is chosen with economy in mind.

In these times of ever more expensive petrol, Citroën obviously could not forsake their tradition of good aerodynamic design, and like all their earlier post-war designs, the CX has an extremely low drag coefficient. "CX" is in fact the (French) engineer's notation for drag coefficient – hence the car's designation.

It is usually the case, though, that wind-cheating design means compromises between shape and accommodation and the CX is no exception. Headroom is limited for tall people, especially in the front. In other respects there are no such compromises and despite the low overall height, the cabin is light and airy with generous glass areas all round. This is especially so in the back of the car where the rear quarter windows reach almost to the tail, giving the driver and passengers a commanding view all round. As usual with "two-box" designs that fall away to a saloon car tail, and have a low entry point for the nose, the extremes of the car to front and rear are out of sight. A driver does well to remember the frontal overhang, which causes a two-foot difference between the kerb and wall turning circles.

Performance and consumption

The engine used in the CX 2000 is the same 1,985 c.c. in-line four-cylinder unit introduced into the DS series in 1966. It is a modern design with a high-mounted camshaft working conventional pushrod and rocker-operated valves. The combustion chamber is hemispherical in shape and a crossover arrangement of the rockers enables the valves to operate in a 60 deg vee to provide a crossflow layout. Maximum power from the slightly oversquare engine is 102 bhp (DIN) at 5,500 rpm, and maximum torque of 112 lb. ft. is developed at 3,000 rpm. In its transverse location in the engine bay, the carburettor is placed on the rearward face of the engine with the exhaust pipes sweeping down the front face before turning rearwards alongside, and protected by the sump.

Drive from the five-bearing crankshaft is taken via an 8·5-in. dia clutch to the all-indirect two-shaft gearbox which has synchromesh on all gears. The gear ratios are high, calling for a low final drive ratio to give a speed in top gear of 19·3 mph per 1,000 rpm.

With this ratio, the mean maximum speed of 110 mph takes the engine some 200 rpm over the peak power point, suggesting that a further gain in economy is possible with a slightly higher final drive, without significant loss of all-round performance.

In the event, the CX 2000 gives acceleration that is at least average for its class with a 0-60 mph time of 12·2sec and a respectable time to 80 mph of 22·1sec. Maximum acceleration through the gears reveals a gap between second and third gear with their respective maxima of 51 and 81 mph. The acceleration in each gear does not reveal any flat spots and the engine and transmission show their flexibility by allowing smooth, if leisurely, acceleration from 10 mph in third gear.

Although the steady-speed fuel figures show the consumption is as good as 28·4 mpg at a steady 80 mph, the overall figure was only 23·2 mpg. The compound carburettor spends a lot of time with both chokes open if all the performance potential is used, and only on a leisurely long-distance run can consumptions in the high twenties be expected. The petrol tank providing a range approaching 350 miles and with some restraint, 400 miles could be covered without need for replenishment.

Brakes

In contrast to the D series, the CX 2000 has outboard-mounted ventilated disc brakes at the front with big scoops to ensure adequate cooling. Although on paper the all-disc braking arrangement appears marginal, in practice it proves fully capable of meeting all demands. In typical Citroën fashion, the brakes are served by the car's high pressure control hydraulic system and the brake pedal is in effect a pressure-bleed control. Unlike the D series, the CX employs a conventional brake pedal which most drivers preferred. The handbrake, operating on the front wheels, produced a laudable 0·5g retardation on its own and proved easily capable of holding the car up or down a 1-in-3 gradient.

On the CX 2000 *without* power-steering, the pump for the hydraulic system is a single cylinder unit which can no longer be heard making the high-speed "clackety" sound so characteristic of other Citroën models.

Ride and Handling

The CX 2000 employs the familiar Citroën hydropneumatic suspension system that ensures constant ride height irrespective of load, together with provision for changing the ride height. As usual, it is noticeable that the ride is much harder on the high ground clearance setting. It would be no exaggeration to say that the hydropneumatic suspension system has created a legend in its own time and in the CX it gives its usual exemplary per-

Citroën CX 2000

formance. Only sharp undulations, or a hump-backed bridge can catch out the system as the wheels fail to drop fast enough but this is not a great failing. Some drivers felt that there was too much roll, while others were unaffected, but there is certainly much less roll than in the D series. Anti-dive geometry is used in the front suspension layout and the car remains nicely stable under braking.

With exactly two-thirds of the car's weight over the front wheels, the CX 2000 is inevitably prone to understeer. This fact, allied to heavy low-geared steering through a large diameter steering wheel, means that it is hard work to drive fast on a twisting road, or in town. With 185SR14 section tyres at the front, steering effort is high all the time, especially so at low manoeuvring speeds. Parking the car calls for a lot of effort. There is a tendency for the steering to stick on full lock when reversing, and care is needed to place the car accurately.

Comparisons

MAXIMUM SPEED MPH

BMW 520i	(£3,898)	114
Citroën CX 2000	**(£3,195)**	**110**
Volvo 244GL	(£3,785)	106
Austin 2200HL	(£2,424)	104
Triumph 2500TC	(£2,907)	104

0–60 MPH, SEC

BMW 520i	10·5
Volvo 244GL	11·4
Triumph 2500TC	11·8
Citroën CX 2000	**12·2**
Austin 2200HL	13·5

STANDING ¼-MILE, SEC

BMW 520i	17·5
Volvo 244GL	18·0
Triumph 2500TC	18·7
Citroën CX 2000	**18·8**
Austin 2200HL	19·2

OVERALL MPG

Triumph 2500TC	24·1
Citroën CX 2000	**23·2**
BMW 520i	22·4
Volvo 244GL	21·3
Austin 2200HL	20·7

Performance

ACCELERATION

True speed mph	Time in Secs	Car Speedo mph
30	3·9	31
40	6·3	41
50	8·7	52
60	12·2	61
70	16·8	71
80	22·1	81
90	31·1	91
100	46·7	102

Standing ¼-mile
18·8sec 73 mph

Standing kilometre
34·7sec 93 mph

Mileage recorder:
1·8 per cent under-reading

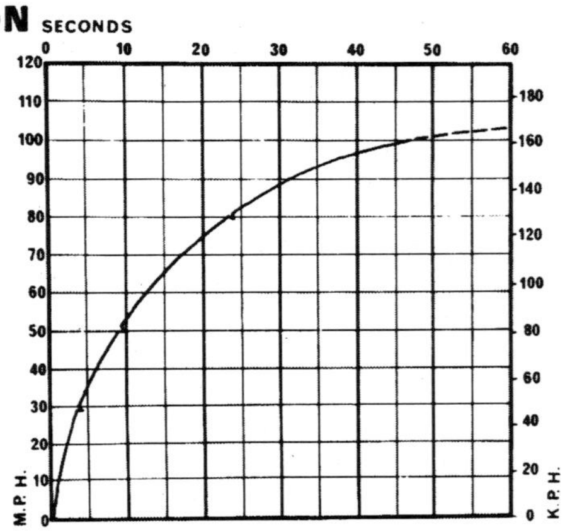

GEAR RATIOS AND TIME IN SEC

mph	Top (3·82)	3rd (5·40)	2nd (8·74)
10–30	—	8·8	4·8
20–40	13·4	8·1	4·6
30–50	12·5	7·5	4·9
40–60	12·7	7·5	—
50–70	12·6	8·8	—
60–80	14·3	10·6	—
70–90	18·8	—	—
80–100	27·0	—	—

GEARING
(with 185SR-14in. tyres)

Top	19·3 mph per 1,000 rpm
3rd	13·5 mph per 1,000 rpm
2nd	8·4 mph per 1,000 rpm
1st	4·8 mph per 1,000 rpm

MAXIMUM SPEEDS

Gear	mph	kph	rpm
Top (mean)	110	177	5,700
(best)	112	180	5,800
3rd	81	130	6,000
2nd	51	82	6,000
1st	29	47	6,000

BRAKES

FADE (from 70 mph in neutral)
Pedal load for 0·5g stops in lb

1	30	6	35–40
2	30–35	7	35–40
3	35	8	35–40
4	35	9	35–40
5	35	10	35–40

RESPONSE (from 30 mph in neutral)

Load	g	Distance
30lb	0·35	86ft
40lb	0·55	55ft
50lb	0·73	41ft
60lb	0·88	34·2ft
70lb	0·92	32·8ft
Handbrake	0·50	60ft
Max Gradient	1 in 3	

CLUTCH
Pedal 40lb and 5¼in.

Consumption

FUEL
(At constant speed – mpg)

30 mph	39·2
40 mph	37·4
50 mph	35·1
60 mph	31·5
70 mph	28·4
80 mph	25·0
90 mph	21·9
100 mph	18·4

Typical mpg 26 (10·9 litres/100km)
Calculated (DIN) mpg 25·8 (10·9 litres/100km)
Overall mpg 23·2 (12·2 litres/100km)
Grade of fuel Premium, 4-star (min 98RM)

OIL
Consumption (SAE 20W/50) Negligible

TEST CONDITIONS:
Weather: Fine and dry
Wind: 0–6 mph
Temperature: 16deg C (60deg F)
Barometer: 29·6in. Hg
Humidity: 58 per cent
Surface: Dry concrete and asphalt
Test distance 780 miles

Figures taken by our own staff at the Motor Industry Research Association proving ground at Nuneaton.

Dimensions

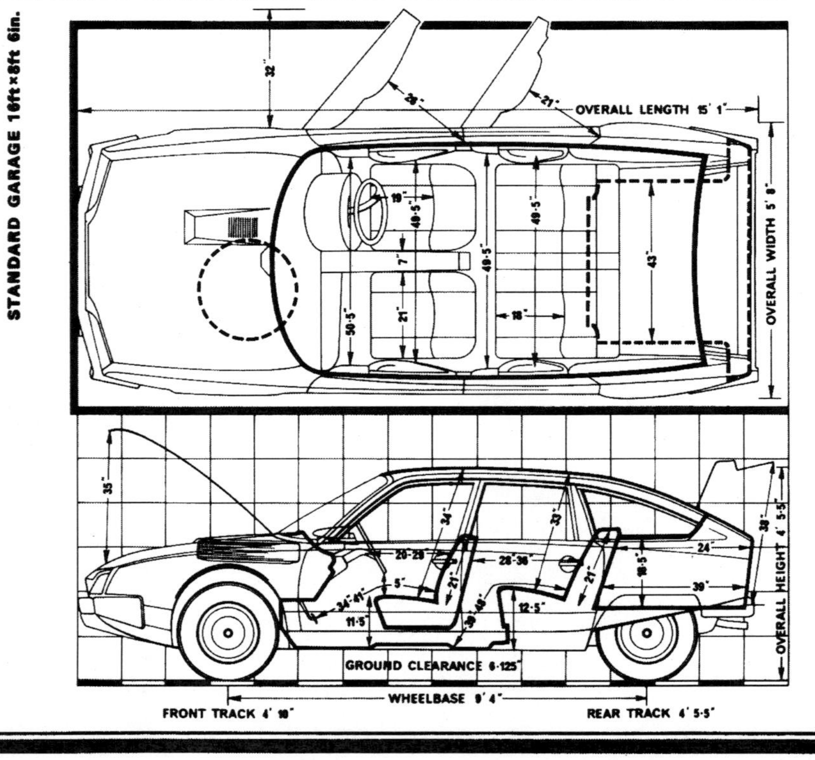

TURNING CIRCLES:
Between kerbs
L, 35ft 9in.; R, 35ft 4in.
Between walls
L, 38ft 8in.; R, 38ft 6in.
Steering wheel turns, lock to lock 4½

WEIGHT:
Kerb Weight 25·2cwt (2,823lb–1,282kg) (with oil, water and half full fuel tank)
Distribution, per cent F, 67; R, 33
Laden as tested: 28·7cwt (3,214lb–1,459kg)

Although the CX understeers heavily, the grip of the Michelin ZX tyres is excellent in all conditions and the front end weight bias ensures good traction. However, one needs to enter corners consciously early to avoid running unexpectedly wide; there is only limited tuck-in if the accelerator is released in mid-corner.

Fast progress is possible on winding roads to the accompaniment of body roll, some tyre squeal and also a noticeable lurching if moving from one lock to the other, for instance in an S-bend. However, the soft, deep seats locate passengers and driver well and the effect is rather more alarming from the outside than it is to the occupants.

Natural stability is excellent with no noticeable deflection by changes of camber of road surface. There were no appreciable sidewinds during the period of the test but from past experience, there should be no qualms in this context.

Noise

The basis of the CX body/chassis unit is a pair of linked sub-frames, the front one supporting the engine/transmission unit on a cantilever while at the back a large-diameter tube and a pair of short extension arms locate the rear suspension. The engine/transmission is rubber-insulated from this base frame, which itself is rubber-insulated from the unitary construction body. Thus there are two insulating barriers to any vibration reaching the passenger

Specification

Citroën CX 2000

FRONT ENGINE, FRONT-WHEEL DRIVE

ENGINE

Cylinders	4, in-line
Main bearings	5
Cooling system	Water; pump, thermostat, electrically-operated fan
Bore	86mm (3·39in.)
Stroke	85·5mm (3·37in.)
Displacement	1,985 c.c. (121 cu. in.)
Valve gear	Pushrod operated overhead valves
Compression ratio	9 to 1. Min octane rating: 98RM
Carburettors	Weber 34 DMTR 25/200 Compound 2-choke
Fuel pump	AC Delco – mechanical
Oil filter	Disposable canister
Max power	102 bhp (DIN) at 5,500 rpm
Max torque	112 lb. ft. (DIN) at 3,000 rpm

TRANSMISSION

Clutch	Single dry plate, diaphragm spring
Type	Cable operation, 8·5in. dia
Gearbox	4-speed, all synchromesh
Gear ratios	Top 0·80 Third 1·13 Second 1·83 First 3·17 Reverse 3·15
Final drive	4·77 to 1
Mph at 1,000 rpm in top gear	19·3

CHASSIS and BODY

Construction	Unitary body rubber mounted to interconnected front and rear subframes

SUSPENSION

Front	Single top and bottom links, wide-based at inner end, hydropneumatic spring/damper units, anti-roll bar (0·9in. dia)
Rear	Light alloy trailing arms, hydropneumatic spring/damper unit, anti-roll bar (0·7in. dia)

STEERING

Type	Rack and pinion – 24·5 to 1 ratio
Wheel dia	16in.

BRAKES

Make and type	4-wheel discs, ventilated at front. 4 piston calipers front, 2 piston rear. Load sensitive valve for rear divided circuit
Dimensions	F 10·235in. dia R 9·230in. dia
Swept area	F 34 sq. in., R 15 sq. in. Total 49 sq. in. (34 sq. in./ton laden)

WHEELS

Type	Pressed steel disc 5½in. J wide rim
Tyres – make	Michelin ZX
– type	Radial ply tubeless
– size	185SR-15/175SR-15in.

EQUIPMENT

Battery	12 Volt 50 Ah.
Alternator	53 amp a.c.
Headlamps	Quartz halogen main beam 80/110 watt (total)
Reversing lamp	Standard
Electric fuses	9
Screen wipers	Two-speed
Screen washer	Standard electric
Interior heater	Standard air-blending type
Heated backlight	Standard
Safety belts	Extra
Interior trim	Fabric seats, pvc headlining
Floor covering	Carpet
Jack	Screw-type
Jacking points	2 each side beneath sills
Windscreen	Thick inter-layer laminate
Underbody protection	Bitumastic on all underbody surfaces; Tectyl in all other vulnerable areas

MAINTENANCE

Fuel tank	15 Imp gallons (68 litres)
Cooling system	18·7 pints (inc heater)
Engine sump	10 pints (5·7 litres) SAE 20W/50. Change oil every 3,000 miles. Change filter every 12,000 miles
Gearbox and Final drive	2·8 pints. SAE 80EP. Change every 12,000 miles
Grease	No points
Valve clearance	Inlet 0·006in. (cold) Exhaust 0·008in. (cold)
Contact breaker	0·016in. gap; 55deg dwell
Ignition timing	10deg BTDC (static) 10deg BTDC (stroboscopic at 850/900 rpm)
Spark plug	Type: AC 42FS or Bosch W225T 35 or Champion L87Y. Gap 0·026in.
Tyre pressures	F 28; R 30 psi (all conditions)
Max payload	1,116lb (506kg)

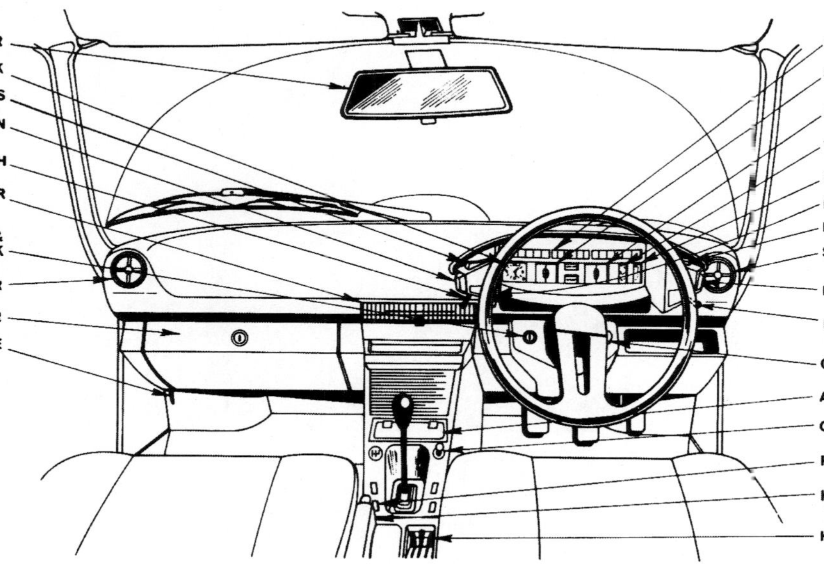

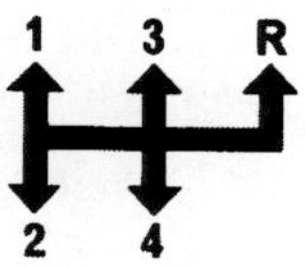

Servicing

3,000 miles	6,000 miles	12,000 miles

Times for servicing and routine replacements not finalized

Parts prices unavailable

Citroën CX 2000

compartment, and little mechanical noise reaches the inside of the car. Any engine noise that can be heard is induction noise only; at tickover, the engine is inaudible inside the car.

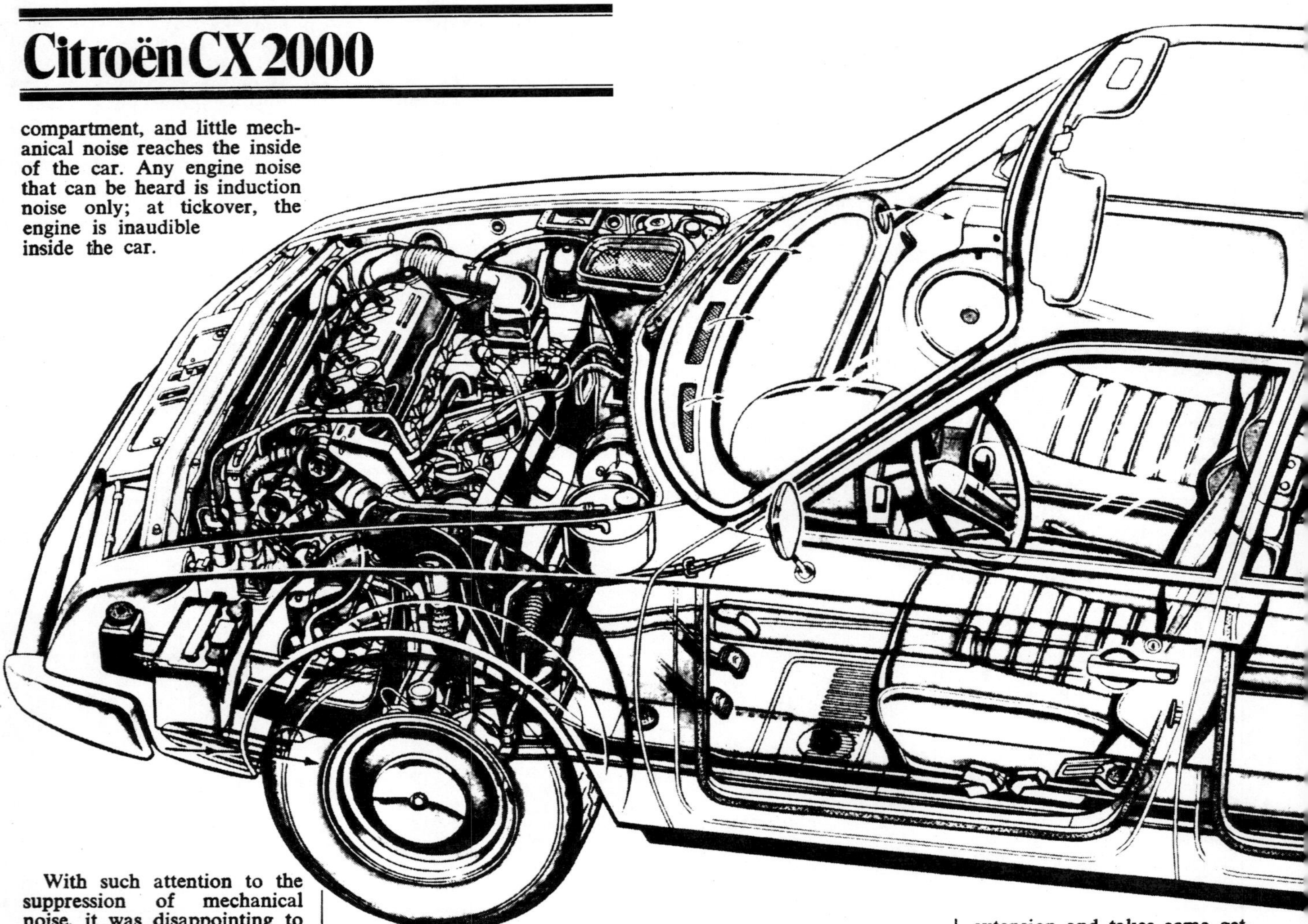

With such attention to the suppression of mechanical noise, it was disappointing to find considerable wind noise which increases at speed. The noise insulation of the bottoms of the doors could be a culprit here as on wet roads, a good deal of swishing can be heard from the tyres. Another noisy item is the gearchange which makes a distinct clonk each time the lever is pushed into gear; but there is no discernible noise from the gearbox or final drive.

Comfort and controls

There is a distinctly futuristic atmosphere inside the CX 2000; it is almost reminiscent of the ideas of twenty years ago as to what today's cars would look like – somewhat over-stylized, with much use of shape and apparently needless sculpturing of panels. As a result, opinions varied widely on the overall effect, though most were guardedly in favour.

In typical innovative Citroën fashion, fingertip controls have been made exactly that by the provision of extensions from the facia, almost to the wheel rim, with all the major controls on them. It takes a little time to become accustomed to the controls themselves as most operate in an unfamiliar way. The twin indicators control is, for instance, a rocker switch on the top of the left-hand control extension and takes some getting used to.

Above: Plenty of room around transverse 2-litre engine for minor adjustments, and spare wheel stowed under the bonnet. Note single-blade wiper

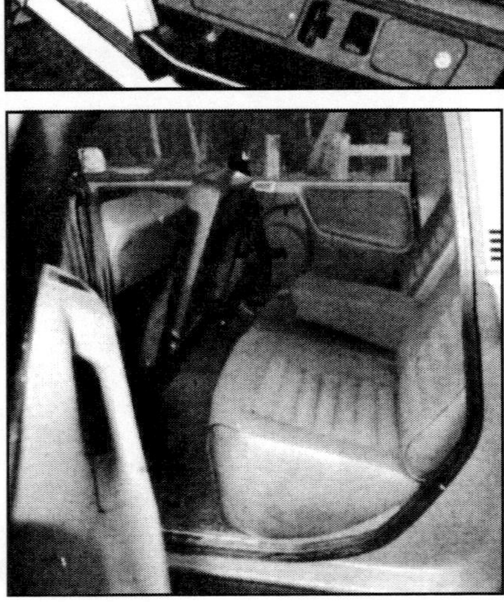

Left: Plenty of room in back seat too, thanks to long wheelbase. Doors and arches are wide enough to make access easy. Centre armrest is standard

The instruments themselves are also different with permanently-lit drums showing only the actual speed or engine revs to the driver. Above the instruments there is a comprehensive display of warning lights, the critical ones of which can be checked for function by depressing a small button in the water temperature warning light.

The large diameter single-spoke steering wheel has a pleasant self-skinned polyurethane rim that is warm and soft to the touch. Its size does, however limit the amount of knee-room available to the driver, and even with the height of the front seat adjusted to its lowest position, there is little room to pass the hands between the wheel and the thighs. Adjustment of the front and rear heights of the seat is best done when one is not seated in the car; the comfortable front seats can both be adjusted for rake.

The upholstery of the test car consisted of a brushed nylon covering for the wearing surfaces with pvc material for the sides and bases. The same pvc is used for the door trim panels but a slightly different colour of the same material is used for the door-cum-arm pull. The

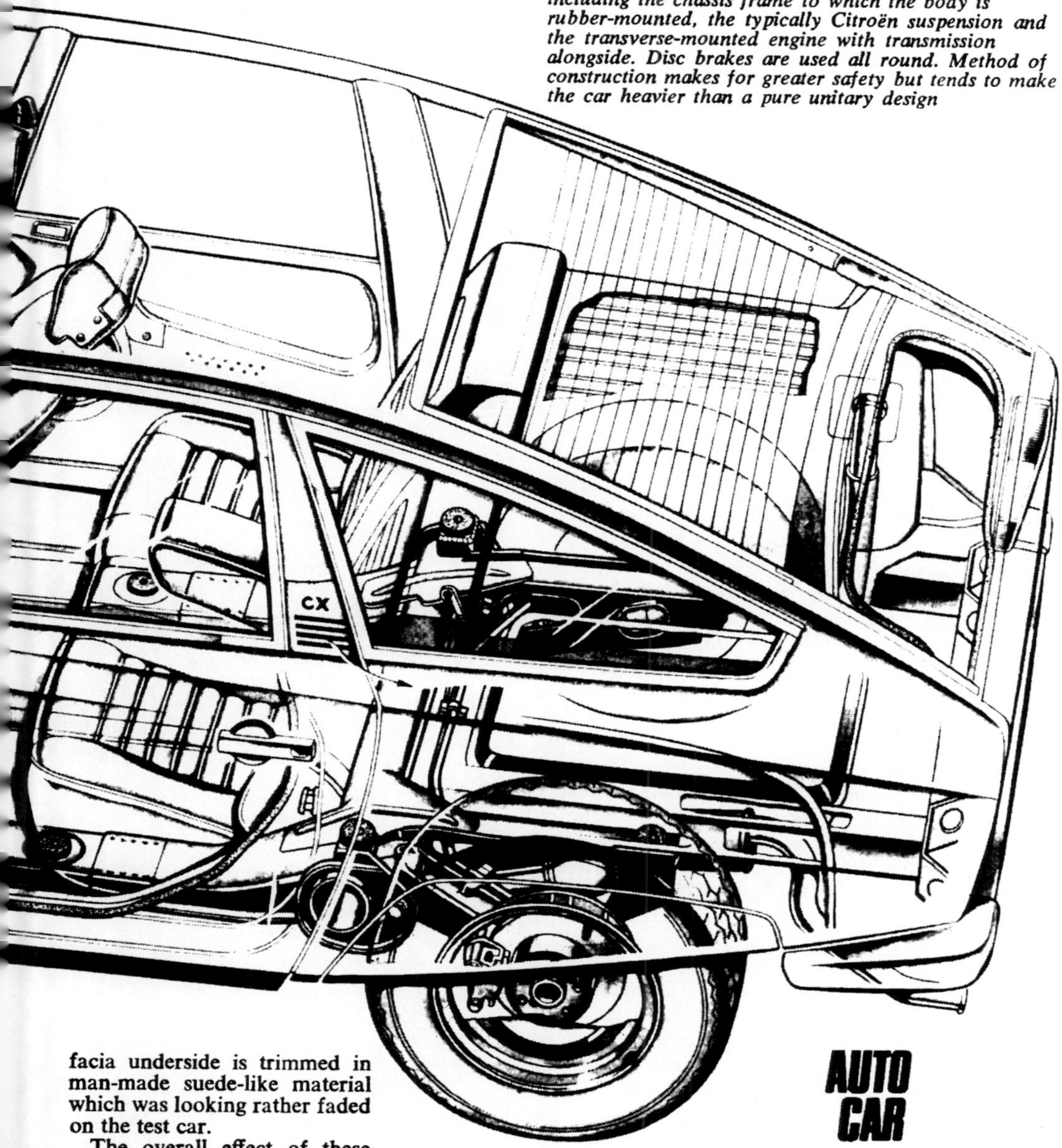

Cutaway shows major features of the Car of the Year, including the chassis frame to which the body is rubber-mounted, the typically Citroën suspension and the transverse-mounted engine with transmission alongside. Disc brakes are used all round. Method of construction makes for greater safety but tends to make the car heavier than a pure unitary design

facia underside is trimmed in man-made suede-like material which was looking rather faded on the test car.

The overall effect of these different fabrics and materials was not unpleasant, but the interior had a rather worn look that belied the youth of the car.

In the centre of the facia is a built-in console which can house an optional radio and which has the gearlever and gaiter set in it. Behind the gear-lever between the front seats are the controls for the heater, air distribution and also the three-speed boost fan. Stowage space is limited to elastic-fronted pockets in each door and a roomy, lockable glove-compartment.

As the spare wheel is stowed under the bonnet, there is no interruption in the shape of the roomy boot, which as in the GS is regular and tall, with the lid opening well out of the way.

Living with the Citroën CX 2000

Starting from cold is instantaneous and the mixture enrichment control can be quickly dispensed with. When the engine is hot, it requires a short period of churning before it fires. The clutch action on the test car was smooth and progressive, but the take-up point was too close to the floor, requiring full disengagement for each gearchange. Provided that the clutch clears completely, the gearchange is clean but rather ponderous with long fore-and-aft movements.

It takes rather less time to familiarize oneself to the CX than to other Citroën models, and once the function of the fingertip controls is learned, they too work well. The single-arm windscreen wiper leaves symmetrical unwiped areas in the top corners of the screen which create blind spots for really tall drivers and result in some loss of visibility when driving on rising and falling twisty roads. In all other directions visibility is good. At night the powerful lights give good illumination on dipped and main beam and the shaped headlamp glasses seem to resist the collection of road dirt, as does the deep, heated rear window.

The function of the heater controls is graphically displayed and the controls are lit at night. The fresh air system feeds through eyeball vents at the extremities of the screen and through a flap vent in the centre of the car. The air-blending heater allows good control of temperature, irrespective of car speed.

The seats are most comfortable in either front or back and the doors open wide to give good access to them, despite the low overall height of the car.

Underneath the bonnet, access is good to all items needing routine maintenance. The distributor is mounted on the top of the engine and the coil is tucked away from points that might admit water. The aluminium-cored radiator is cooled, when necessary, by a thermostatically-controlled fan which is noisy in operation. The spare wheel, which is of the same size as the rear tyres, rather than the front, is easy to remove from its position against the bulkhead. A neat piece of thinking here is that the jack and wheelbrace are stowed in a container that fits into the spare wheel centre where they keep clean and dry.

Citroën servicing requirements for the CX 2000 involve an oil change every 3,000 miles but the filter requires changing only every 12,000 miles. Servicing costs may well be higher as a result of the relatively frequent oil changes, but on the other hand, there are no greasing points.

Conclusions

The Citroën CX 2000 may possibly have been chosen as the "Car of the Year" more because of its novelty than for its virtues. There is no doubt that it would be a much more likeable car with lighter steering, and in fact, this is to be an optional extra later this year. The system will be like that of the Citroën SM but with a slightly lower ratio.

While on paper the insulation of the interior from noise and harshness looks effective, in practice there is more noise than one might expect. However, there is no doubt that the ride and handling are significantly better than anything else in its class and with some attention to a limited number of areas, the CX could be even nicer. Its existing virtues, which include the amount of space and the degree of comfort offered, more than justify the price which is in any case competitive with its European mainland rivals. □

MANUFACTURER:
S.A. André Citroen, quai André-Citroen 133, 75747 Paris XVe, France
UK CONCESSIONAIRES:
Citroen Cars Limited, Mill Street, Slough SL2 5DE

PRICES	
Basic	£2,731.00
Special Car Tax	£227.58
VAT	£236.69
Total (in GB)	**£3,195.27**
Inertia reel seat belts	f.o.c.
Licence	£40.00
Delivery charge (London) approx	£20.00
Number plates approx	£7.00
Total on the Road (exc insurance)	**£3,262.27**

Insurance	Group 5
EXTRAS (inc VAT)	
Metallic paint	t.b.a.
Power steering	t.b.a.
Headrests	t.b.a.
**Fitted to test car*	
TOTAL AS TESTED ON THE ROAD	**£3,262.27**

Through the snow forests, the Cx is fast and smooth

A smooth ride and fast, quiet cruising are striking capabilities of the Citroën Cx models — and the manufacturer claims a high safety rating for this new car, both active and passive.

Passive safety is evident in basic passenger cell construction, and such details as the carefully recessed interior handles, the seat belt inertia reels concealed inside the door pillars, and the seats — which provide proper lateral and lumbar support under Citroën's usual soft surface, and are also designed to prevent the occupants from slipping out of the harness in an impact.

After an experimental 50 km/h crash into a barrier at 60 degrees, Citroën say three of the four doors will open, though regulations only stipulate one.

Report and pictures:
GORDON WILKINS

Apart from good ride and road holding, responsive steering and an advanced braking system, active safety is promoted by good all round vision and well-thought-out controls. The big, steeply-raked windscreen is swept by a single wiper in racing style. The near-horizontal rear window is concave to ensure rapid drainage of surface water.

Instruments extend the principle introduced on the GS with magnifying lenses to project the figures from illuminated revolving drums on both speedometer and tachometer. Braking distances from each speed are also shown on the speedometer. Extensions to the instrument binnacle bring all minor switches to reach without taking a hand off the wheel; on the left, town and country horns, wiper/washer, hazard warning and direction indicators; on the right, main light switch, dipper, flasher and rheostat for instrument lighting.

13 PILOT LIGHTS

Along the top is an impressive array of 13 warning lights, all clearly identified, plus a check button. They include monitors for brake pad wear, hydraulic system pressure, engine oil temperature, engine oil pressure and water temperature.

On the centre console are controls for the electric front windows, (optional on 2000) heater-ventilation and suspension ride height.

Seats are trimmed in soft fabrics or synthetics. Front seats have reclining backrests, and there is height adjustment for the driving seats. Headrests are optional, with a simple height adjustment by moving the cushion which is attached by press studs. Extra equipment on the 2200 includes tachometer, handbrake reminder light, inertia reel belts, electric front windows, more luxurious upholstery, carpet, and roof lining, pneumatic oil level indicator, full wheel trim instead of nave plates, and stainless steel exhaust trim.

Basically the same as the DS unit, the engine has a cast-iron block with removable wet liners, and five-bearing forged steel crankshaft. The valves, operated by pushrods and rockers, are set at 60 degrees included angle in hemispherical combustion chambers in a light alloy

The Cx embodies the latest Citroën advances in aerodynamics, and has a classic bullet shape.

The raked rear window is concave to encourage water drainage.

Interesting interior features include an instrument binnacle with extensions for minor controls.

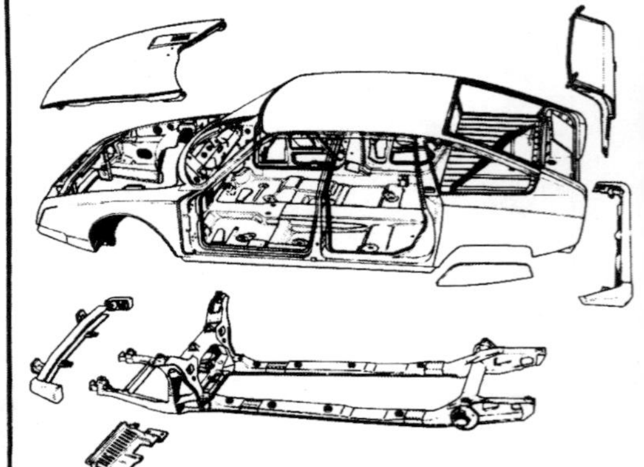

Major coachwork components exploded to show the safety structure.

head. The carburettor is a twin-choke Weber.

Bore and stroke of 86 x 85,5 mm give the basic engine 1 985 cm^3 and on a 9:1 compression it produces 75 kW DIN at 5 500 r/min. Bore goes up to 90 mm to give 2 175 cm^3 for the 2200 version, which delivers 78 kW at 5 500 r/min.

GEARING DIFFERENCES

On the economy 2000, fourth gear is 0,75:1 instead of 0,8 — and final drive is 14/61 against 13/62, giving a top gear speed of 36 km/h per 1 000 engine r/min, against 31. This is said to improve fuel consumption at a steady 100 km/h from 34 to 37 mpg, for an extra fifth of a second on the acceleration times over the standing 400 m or up to 100 km/h, and a loss of 6 km/h in maximum speed.

The Cx 2200 has the same gear ratios as the standard 2000, but with a 12/55 final drive giving 32 km/h per 1 000 r/min. DIN kerb masses are 1266 kg for the 2000, and 1285 kg for the 2200. As on the DS, tyres of different sizes are used at front and rear: 185 SR 14 ZX and 175 SR 14 ZX on the 2000: same sections but HR XVS on the 2200.

Steering is manual on the 2000, needing 4,5 turns lock to lock; 2200 has power-assisted steering with variable return power as on the SM, but geared for 2,5 turns lock to lock instead of 2,0.

Brakes are ventilated discs, with separate circuits for front and rear. Large ducts take air to the front discs, which have two-piece light alloy calipers with four pistons. Rear discs are smaller and have two-piston calipers attached to the light alloy suspension arms.

Unlike the DS, the Cx has a small grille for the cross-flow radiator and its thermostatically-switched electric fan, but a smooth line is given to the nose by the sloping, rounded bonnet and the curved glasses over the headlights. Height adjustment on the seat enables the driver to see well forward along the sloping nose; vision all round is good.

Interior space, width, legroom and headroom is very generous — I found the driving position excellent; the finger-tip controls make driving easy, and the instruments in their binnacle are highly legible through the unobstructed arc of the wheel.

At low speeds over the rough forest tracks of Lapland, where I tried the car, the hydropneumatic suspension gives a fairly firm ride; at high speeds the car rushes ahead with a majestic indifference to the disturbances going on below. This shows the system at its best.

Road noise is very low, but over really bad surfaces a high-frequency vibration made me wonder whether the determination to insulate the body from road noise may have entailed some reduction in overall torsional stiffness. However, insulation from road shocks is very efficient: bumps are heard rather than felt.

170-PLUS TOP SPEED

The engine is agreeably smooth and quiet at medium speeds, becoming more audible from 110 km/h upwards. Gear changing was easy and quick. At an indicated 6 000 r/min in third the 2000 was showing 127 km/h on the speedometer, and 160 in top was equivalent to 5 250. Citroën claims 0-400 m in 18,5 seconds and 0-100 km/h in 13,1 with a maximum of 173 km/h.

Without power assistance the steering was light enough even when parking, but with a wheelbase of 2845 mm the turning circle is in proportion: 10,97 m.

As its reaction was not quite so quick, the power steering did not require the time to get accustomed to it which many people find with the SM. The ratio is about right for fast driving.

On the car I drove it had a slight tendency to wander on the straight, possibly due to tyre pressures or wheel balance. Other cars behaved normally.

The 2200, which was not to go into production until later, is naturally faster and more flexible, showing 180 km/h on the speedometer. Citroën's figures are 178 km/h maximum, with 0-400 m in 18 seconds and 0-100 km/h in 11,7.

This is a car for quiet and effortless motorway cruising at 160 km/h. Driven more gently it need not consume much more fuel than the 2-litre; in fact, works figures show a consumption of 7,8 litres/100 km at a steady 100 km/h, against only 8,3 litres/100 km for the standard 2-litre, thanks to the higher gearing.

The advantage continues at 120 km/h with 10 litres/100 km against 10,5 and the two draw level at 140 km/h with 12,3 litres/100 km. Equivalent figures for the economy 2-litre are 7,6; 9,7 and 11,7 litres/100 km, respectively.

On a 420-km circuit comprising main roads and forest tracks, I got 11,3 litres/100 km on the 2000 and 10,1 on the 2200. The average of several drivers was 10,4 litres/100 km for the 2000 and 10,2 for the 2200, but the figures varied widely according to driving style. ●

by John Bolster

The Citroen CX2200 is completely functional in its styling.

CX2200: setting standards

As regular readers are aware, we tested the Citroën CX 2000 in the summer of this year and the present subject, the CX 2200, is a more luxuriously equipped version of the same car, with a slightly larger engine. It has been the policy of the manufacturers to bring out the cheaper models first, and we still await the ultimate CX with the highly sophisticated power steering that was developed for the SM.

Compared with the 2000, the 2200 has an extra 4mm in the cylinder bores, increasing the piston-swept volume by 190cc and adding 10bhp to the output, plus a little more torque in the middle ranges. However, the final drive ratio has been changed from 4.769 to 4.583 to 1, top gear remaining an overdrive of 0.8 to 1. The result is that the larger-engined car can beat the 2000 on both acceleration and maximum speed, but only by a very small margin, though there is a feeling of rather more power in reserve during normal driving.

Instruments lack proper round dials but heating, ventilating and minor controls are well-arranged.

What is much more interesting is the question of fuel economy, for I found that the bigger-engined model was the better of the two in this respect. There are individual variations in cars, of course, but I would put down the improved economy to the fractionally higher gearing and greater torque. One expects good figures with a car such as the CX, which has phenomenally low wind-resistance, but my overall consumption included a great deal of driving in London, in addition to lots of 6000rpm motoring when taking acceleration times and a fair bit of travelling at well over 100mph. That I averaged almost exactly 25mpg under these conditions is more than praiseworthy and I am sure that many owners will beat 30mpg when driving with a little moderation. Constant speed figures, claimed by the makers, are 36mpg at 56mph and 28mpg at 75mph.

Where this Citroën excels its predecessor, the DS, is in flexibility and silence. I often drive cars with fairly large four-cylinder engines that will not run comfortably at less than 30mph in top gear. This is quite unacceptable in these economy-conscious days, but I am unable to fathom how Citroën have persuaded their ancient power unit to pick up cleanly and smoothly from 8 (yes eight) mph in top. With such flexibility, why pay extra for automatic transmission?

I have no expensive apparatus for measuring sound levels, but I have evolved a simple method which has the advantage of costing nothing. I set the radio so that the programme is enjoyable, but not loud, at 30 mph in top gear. I then cruise at 100mph, without altering the volume. If I can still enjoy the music and follow the news bulletins in their entirety, I know I am driving a quiet car. That may seem a severe test but the Rolls-Royce, the Jaguar, and now the Citroën, have passed it.

The CX is a big, spacious car with exceptional leg room in the back, so its weight is quite substantial. It is therefore necessary to employ the gearbox when rapid acceleration is required. Obviously, it does not have quite the surge of power for overtaking that those French cars with the V6 engine possess, but it keeps up with them surprisingly well at high speeds and the Citroën driver is laughing all the way to the filling station.

I analysed the engineering reasons behind the CX in my article on the 2000, so I shall be brief. Its makers have been building front wheel drive vehicles for 40 years and their system of hydropneumatic suspension and power-operated disc brakes has been on the market for 20 years.

Though the CX has ultra-modern styling and is more compact than the DS their is nothing untried about it.

Garage men no longer burst into tears when asked to work on a Citroen.

The car is more complex than a cart-sprung horror, of course, but complexity need not mean unreliability. A four-cylinder car is more complicated than a single-cylinder moped, but is it any less reliable? I trow not!

Its difficult to put the advantages of the very soft, self-levelling suspension into words but perhaps I can express it in this way. If you make a long journey in the Citroën, so that you take its ride for granted, you should then jump into one of those ordinary cars and drive smartly up the road. Its ten to one that you will soon stop, get out, and walk round the car kicking the tyres, for something seems terribly wrong. The power saved in not flinging a ton of car up and down over every bump is one reason for the petrol economy, for the amount of power used in levelling the car is negligible.

Whether or not its worth paying extra for the larger-engined model is a matter of opinion, but I must admit that I go for the electrically-operated windows, the rev-counter, and the luxurious interior. I adore really stark sports cars, devoid of all creature comforts, but when I am in a saloon, I like to be as comfortable as possible.

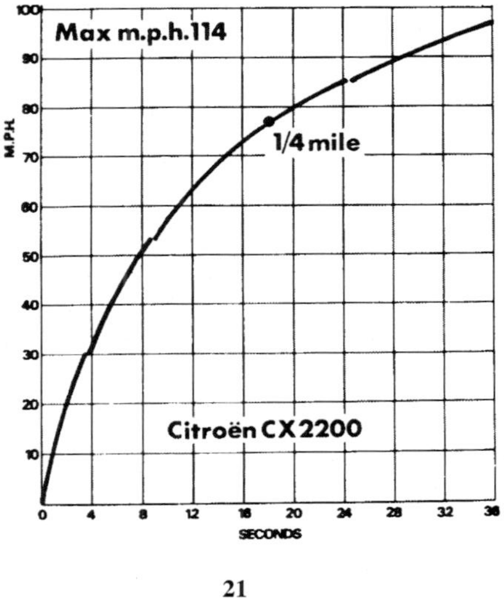

The 2200 has all the best features of the 2000, such as its excellent heating and ventilation system, its well-arranged switches and controls, and its accessible transverse engine. It also has those things that I don't like, including direction indicators that don't self-cancel and instruments lacking proper round dials, though I must admit that the warning lights are well arranged and easy to understand. I would certainly prefer to have the optional power steering, not so much for its lighter operation as its much higher gearing, which is 13.5 to 1 compared with the standard 24.5 to 1, or 2.5 turns instead of 4.5. That would make all the difference on a winding road.

Twenty years ago, when the DS first appeared, its many advanced features filled some prospective buyers with dread. Though the CX has ultra-modern styling and is more compact than the DS, as befits present traffic conditions, there is nothing untried about it. Time was when garage men burst into tears when asked to work on a DS, but nowadays they are just as happy to wipe their greasy hands on the seats of a Citroën as on those of any other car.

The Citroën CX 2200 offers a standard of comfortable, fast, and economical travel for four or five people that is perhaps unobtainable elsewhere. Its a civilised car which is good-looking because its so completely functional. Nevertheless, as I have said before, I still wish that it would wiggle its headlights round corners, as the dear old DS used to do.

Car Tested: Citroen CX 2200 4-door saloon, price £3,775 including car tax and VAT

Engine: Four-cylinders 90 x 85 5mm (2175cc). Compression ratio 9 to 1. 112bhp at 5500rpm. Pushrod-operated overhead valves in hemispherical combustion chambers. Weber twin-choke down-draught carburetter.

Transmission: Single dry plate clutch, 4-speed synchromesh gearbox with central remote control, ratios 0.80, 1.13, 1.83 and 3.17 to 1. Final drive by helical-toothed spur gears, ratio 4.583 to 1.

Chassis: Steel monocoque with full-length sub-frame. Independent hydropneumatic self-levelling suspension of all four wheels, powered by engine-driven pump, with front wishbones and rear light-alloy trailing arms, plus anti-roll bars both ends. Rack and pinion steering. Fully power-operated dual-circuit disc brakes, ventilated in front, with compensation for weight transfer. Bolt-on steel wheels, fitted Michelin 185/175 SR-15 tyres.

Equipment: 12-volt lighting and starting. Speedometer. Rev-counter. Fuel and temperature gauges. Clock. Heating, demisting and ventilation system with heated rear window. 2-speed windscreen wipers and washers. Front door windows with electric control. 2-speed windscreen wipers and washers. Flashing direction indicators. Reversing lights. Cigar lighter.

Dimensions: Wheelbase 9ft 4in. Track 4ft 10in/4ft 5.5in. Overall length 15ft 1in. Width 5ft 8in. Weight 1 ton 4½ cwt.

Performance: Maximum speed 114mph. Speeds in gears: Third 85mph, second 53mph, first 30mph. Standing quarter-mile 18.0s. Acceleration: 0-30mph 3.6s, 0-50mph 7.8s, 0-60mph 11.5s, 0-80mph 20.2s, 0-100mph 41.2s.

Fuel consumption: 25 to 30 mpg

Overall, the Citroen CX body is a brilliantly efficient design.

CX2200 Pallas: exceptional

Perhaps the most important technical breakthrough of recent years has been the VariPower steering of the Citroën SM. The SM, alas, is no more, because its Maserati engine is no longer available. It is excellent news, however, that the highly sophisticated steering is now available on the CX 2200. Admittedly, it can only be obtained on the up-market Pallas version, and the extra cost is considerable. Nevertheless, the difference is so great that it must pay for itself in terms of driving pleasure.

This difference may be expressed numerically as 2½ turns from lock to lock instead of five turns, but there's much more to it than that. The five turns of the standard car are fairly heavy at parking speeds, but the steering of the Pallas is fully powered. Even if the vehicle is stationary, the driver has only to release the steering at full lock when the power centering will spin it back to the straight-ahead position. Such steering is ideal for parking and town work but it could be far too light and insensitive for high-speed driving — owners of some American cars will know what I mean.

Here, the most essential feature of VariPower comes into play. As the car goes faster, the fully-powered steering first becomes merely power-assisted and then, at the highest speeds, virtually manual. It is manual steering with a difference, however for the hydraulic power is in reserve to prevent the wheel from being snatched from the driver's hands by a vast bump or pot-hole. At high speeds, the very quick steering feels rather like that of a racing car, permitting the driver to alter the line, or dodge a slippery patch of road, with merely a flick of the wrist.

Such quick steering feels perfectly natural to

the man who used to own a Frazer-Nash or a Bugatti. To those accustomed to the more villainous manifestations of modern technique, a period of acclimatisation may be necessary. Let me say, though, that the Pallas steering will seem far less tricky than that of the SM. The SM required only two turns of the steering wheel to go from lock to lock, but the Pallas asks for 2½, that small increase causing the response to be far less daunting to the uninitiated. There were those who never felt fully in control of the SM, but I think that the most insensitive driver would eventually get the message with the Pallas.

What this steering does is to make a large and luxurious saloon handle like a light single-seater. Personally, I am terrified to drive fast in cars with soggy, low-geared steering, because I know that in an emergency one has no hope of dodging and must meet the obstacle head-on. VariPower is the best steering yet and certainly the safest; I make no excuse for devoting so much space to this very important feature. Incidentally, the steering can be fixed on full lock for parking on a hill, by removing the key.

The other control which is typically Citroën is the brake pedal. This has the very short movement with which addicts are familair, from the old 'button' of the DS. Though an ordinary pedal is now used, the response is still that of the ancient arrangement, but few people find much difficulty in coping with this nowadays, perhaps because the long-travel, spongy brake pedal is less common than it once was on other cars.

The expression CX is the term used in equations by French technicians, to denote the drag coefficient. It is therefore a logical label for a car with extremely low drag characteristics. What is so pleasing about the Citroën is that it achieves this result, plus exceptional stability, without the use of unsightly dams and spoilers. Much of its efficiency comes from the smooth underside. Beneath the nose, an air intake is concealed which feeds the radiator, and this draws off much air that would otherwise be forced underneath, causing both drag and lift.

More important is the shape of the upper part of the nose, which gently encourages laminar flow of the air over the top surface of the body, thereby rendering obstruction of the passage underneath less necessary. It will also be noticed that the nose is rounded in plan, this persuading some of the air displaced to join the general airflow pattern along the sides. This is done with great care, for with ordinary, square-nosed cars, the cross-flow combines with the overall flow to form vortices parallel with the sides of the car, producing lift in addition to drag.

If the shape of the nose is of paramount importance, so is the underside at the rear of the car. It is well known that any car, travelling at speed, draws a turbulent wake behind it. Most cars have a high-pressure area underneath, which tends to lift the back of the car, but if the rear under-panel of the car slopes away from the ground, the increasing clearance can put this normally high-pressure region in full communication with the low-pressure wake.

This is the reason for the raised tail of the Citroën, which gives a downward pressure on the rear tyres instead of the lift that causes instability in less intelligent designs. The upswept rear panel under the car could not be used effectively if the Citroën had a back axle, but it doesn't. Nor could it be employed if a large spare tyre had to be carried low down beneath the luggage boot. However, the spare has been accommodated under the front bonnet, in spite of its downswept nose. Thus, there is a big duct of steadily increasing volume beneath the car, which prevents a high-pressure build-up and reduces drag by increasing the pressure of the turbulent wake.

This brief analysis of the body shape of the CX only touches on a few aspects of a brilliant design. It is a car of our times because it is a large and spacious saloon with unusually comfortable rear seats, yet it is as fast as some cars of two or even three times its engine size and, when driven with moderation, its fuel consumption may be compared with that of the popular 1.6-litre class.

The front seats are adjustable for height as well as in a fore and aft direction, so drivers of all sizes may be accommodated, the generous glass area giving a good all-round view. All the seats feel luxurious and they also locate the occupants well against lateral forces. I have travelled in the rear seats and found them exceptionally comfortable. The controls are well placed, notably the switches for the direction indicator and the lights, the windscreen wipers and washers, and the town and country horns — far more convenient than the usual flimsy stalks.

The engine accelerates smoothly from 500rpm in top gear and one may make numerous local journeys without ever exceeding 3000rpm. However, this is a big car with only 2175cc to pull it, so it pays to go up to 6000rpm in the gears when rapid overtaking is required. The engine can then be heard and felt, but it is normally exceptionally quiet, as is the transmission. The gearchange is easy but it is most pleasant when handled gently rather than snatched.

The maximum speed of a Citroën is always difficult to assess and it seems to go on building up when the car is driven on full throttle for a considerable distance. I timed it at 114mph after holding it flat for a couple of miles, but it might well have registered a little more with a longer run. Though I have greatly enjoyed a 5-speed box on the DS, I did not consciously miss the extra ratio. As the permitted maximum revs, 6000rpm, would be equivalent to 120mph, the car is sufficiently high geared to render over-revving impossible.

All four tyres stick to the road, thanks to the hydro-pneumatic suspension. The angle of roll is not excessive but the car is at its best on the faster bends, where it feels exceptionally stable, and has roadholding to spare if a sudden emergency enforces a change of line or panic braking. The understeering characteristic is more noticeable on the sharper corners and the stability in side-winds is outstanding. The brakes are easy to apply violently without locking the wheels, in spite of the short pedal travel; they stand up well to hard driving.

The ride is very smooth without any up and down movement or pitching. A single sub-frame for both front and rear suspensions ensures that

Controls are well placed for finger-tip operation on binnacle behind wheel.

The luggage boot has a flat floor, with no lips over which heavy objects must be lifted.

Low frontal aspect and wide-track is evident. Nose shape also encourages air-flow to the sides.

Crowded under-bonnet scene. Most routine check items, however, are readily accessible.

the precision of the steering shall not be marred by relative movement. It carries the engine and transmission as well as the suspension anchorage points and is insulated from the steel body shell by 16 flexible mountings. The luggage boot has a flat floor, with no lips over which the heavy objects must be lifted. The self-levelling suspension ensures that the car maintains the same height, irrespective of load.

Accurate focusing of the powerful headlights avoids dazzle in the dipped position. The heating system works effectively in a remarkably short distance after a cold start. The separate duct for cool breathing air can be pressurised by the three-speed fan, and air admission is through proper eyeball-type ventilators.

It is difficult to express in words the effortless movement of the Pallas and the pleasure that even a *blasé* motorist obtains from handling it. The steering seems so exactly right and driving is just as enjoyable whether one floats along country lanes or cruises at over 100mph. The torque of the engine encourages early changing up, to the benefit of fuel economy. Even including stops and starts and town work, the car seems reluctant to consume more than a gallon of petrol for 25 miles, while the man who sticks to the limits may see a full 30mpg on a long run.

The Pallas can be identified by a full length rubbing strip and rubber inserts in the bumpers, plus stainless steel window trim and attractive *enjoliveurs* on the wheels. "My" car was finished in a dark metallic colour called Grey Vulcain, with upholstery in caramel jersey velour. It was so good-looking that several strangers commented on it when I parked it. In the past, I would perhaps have been more excited by the sort of car that sets its tyres on fire when the lights go green, but nowadays such driving is scarcely realistic. I have been testing cars for AUTOSPORT for a quarter of a century and in that time well over a thousand vehicles must have shared my journeys with me, but I shall remember the miles I enjoyed in the company of the Citroën CX 2200 Pallas for a long time.

SPECIFICATION AND PERFORMANCE DATA

Car tested: Citroen CX 2200 Pallas 4-door saloon, price £4,360 including car tax and VAT.

Engine: Four-cylinders 90 x 85.5 mm (2177 cc). Compression ratio 9 to 1. 112bhp at 5500rpm. Pushrod-operated overhead valves in hemispherical combustion chambers. Weber twin-choke down-draught carburettor.

Transmission: Single dry plate clutch. 4-speed synchromesh gearbox with central remote control, ratios 0.80, 1.13, 1.83 and 3.17 to 1. Final drive by helical-toothed spur gears, ratio 4.583 to 1.

Chassic: Steel monocoque with full-length sub-frame. Independent hydro-pneumatic self-levelling suspension of all four wheels, powered by engine-driven pump, with front wishbones and rear light-alloy trailing arms, plus anti-roll bars both ends. VariPower steering with fully-powered rack and pinion having variable assistance in inverse ratio to car speed and powered centering giving 2½ turns lock to lock. Fully power-operated dual circuit disc brakes, ventilated in front, with compensation for weight transfer. Bolt-on steel wheels, fitted Michelin 185/175 SR 15 tyres.

Equipment: 12-volt lighting and starting. Speedometer. Rev-cõunter. Fuel and temperature gauges. Clock, Heating, demisting and ventilation system with heated rear window. Electrically-controlled door windows. 2-speed windscreen wipers and washers. Flashing direction indicators. Reversing lights. Map light. Cigar lighter.

Dimensions: Wheelbase 9ft 4in. Track 4ft 10in/4ft 5.5in. Overall length.15ft 1in. Width 5ft 8in. Weight 1 ton 4½ cwt.

Performance: Maximum speed 114 mph. Speeds in gears. Third 85 mph, second 53 mph, first 30 mph. Standing quarter-mile 18.0s. Acceleration 0.30 mph 3.6s, 0.50 mph 7.8s, 0.60 mph 11.5s, 0.80 ph 20.2s, 0.100 mph 41.2s.

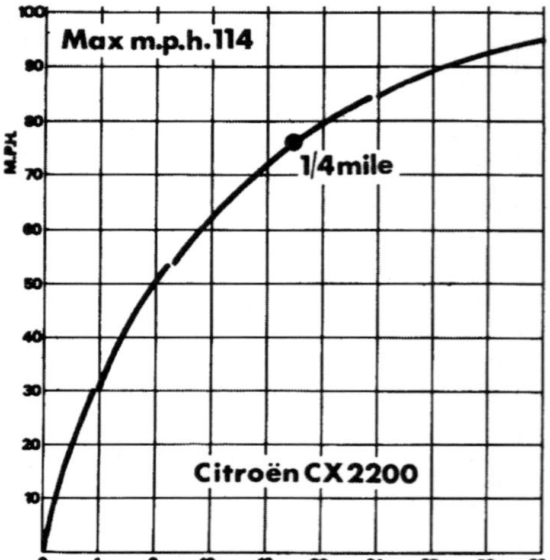

ROAD TEST

CITROEN CX 2200 PALLAS MATIC

Most expensive CX fitted with optional semi-automatic transmission which smooths and quietens engine and compensates for its inherent lack of low-speed torque. Handsome and roomy body. Ride good, but disappointing for a Citroen; handling clumsy. Poor heating and ventilation.

THE REVOLUTIONARY Citroen DS became a familiar sight on the roads of Britain following its introduction in 1955, endearing itself to many with its undoubted virtues, the foremost being a standard of ride comfort which for many years remained radically superior to that of any other car. In the view of its enthusiastic owners, these virtues easily outweighed the car's equally marked faults, such as excessive wind noise, sluggish acceleration, the asthmatic, rattly behaviour of its engine and a collection of idiosyncrasies including a highly sensitive braking system.

It is perhaps partly through the force of this enthusiasm and through Citroen's reputation for successful technical innovation—deserved on the whole—that its successor, the CX, has in its turn been appearing in increasing numbers on our streets and lanes during the past few months. The new model's handsome lines, though, must also be important to its success, and it is certainly more refined than its predecessor, with a vastly superior standard of interior trim and design.

After testing the basic 2000 version last year (*Motor*, May 17, 1975), we confessed to certain feelings of disappointment. We accepted the value of its roomy body and of its ability to cruise quietly at high speeds, but felt that its ride, though good, did not justify the complexity of its hydropneumatic suspension, and that its refinement, though raised above the level of its predecessor, still lay below the standard expected of a car of its price. In particular, we complained of engine, wind and road noise. And further experience with a number of CX models has highlighted a further shortcoming common to them all; a distinctly poor heating and ventilation system and an interior which becomes very stuffy in warm weather.

To verify our evaluation of this important and technically interesting new car, we have been running a staff CX Pallas — on which we shall be commenting in due course—while the subject of our test is another example of this model fitted with Citroen's semi-automatic transmission system. In addition, we report briefly on a manual-transmission version elsewhere in this issue.

All CX models are powered by Citroen's venerable four-cylinder water-cooled engine, mounted transversely at the front, canted 30 deg forwards, and driving to the front wheels. The gearbox—whether manual or semi-automatic—is mounted directly on the end of the engine and drives to an integral final drive and differential assembly immediately behind it, but the drive-shafts are not unequal in length, as is usual with a layout of this sort. Instead, the near-side drive-shaft is driven directly, but the off-side shaft is driven indirectly through a jackshaft running across the car to a support bearing. At the front the wheels are located by equal-length parallel links, at the rear by trailing arms. The hydropneumatic springing system uses exceptionally soft gas springs, working in conjunction with a hydraulic self-levelling system which maintains a constant ride height regardless of load, and so prevents the suspension travel from being used up on bumps. The disc brakes, ventilated at the front, are fully powered by a system that automatically apportions effort between the front and the rear to compensate for changes in load distribution.

In Britain the range of cars available begins first with the CX 2000 previously tested, which is powered by the 1985cc, 102 bhp version of the basic engine. An estate version of this model has recently been introduced, the CX 2000 Safari Super, and this has as standard equipment Citroen's special "Vari Power" steering system. Above the 2000 comes the better-equipped 2200 Super, fitted with the 2175 cc 112 bhp version of the engine, and above that, in turn, there is the more luxuriously appointed CX 2200 Pallas with the same engine and Vari Power steering as standard. Our test car was also fitted with Citroen's optional (for £230.49 extra) semi-automatic transmission system. The fittings of the Pallas additional to those of the 2200, comprise; a handbrake warning light, an interior oil level gauge, a map reading light, a pocket at the rear of each front seat, rear courtesy/reading lights, velour rather than plain cloth upholstery, and a height adjuster for the driver's seat. Reclinable front seats, a cigar lighter, clock, tachometer, a backlight heater, a roof aerial and a pair of speakers built into the front doors and two-speed wipers also form part of the standard specification. Externally, the car is distinguished by stainless steel brightwork and is available in metallic green or grey at no extra cost.

Despite this long list of equipment, the Pallas faces formidable competition in Britain, a recent increase having raised its price to £4765.41. The 3-litre Ford Granada Ghia, for instance, costs a good deal less, yet is even better equipped, having a sliding roof, a radio and tinted glass as part of its standard specification. It is also superior to the Citroen in performance, handling, roadholding, refinement, instrumentation, heating and ventilation, while being its equal in accommodation and nearly its equal in ride. The Princess HLS, too, matches the CX in many respects but costs well over £1000 less.

The character of our test car was greatly influenced by the semi-automatic transmission system fitted to it. This system uses a hydrokinetic torque converter through which the engine drives to an essentially normal clutch and gearbox. But the clutch is actuated by hydraulic pressure from the transmission pump which lubricates the system and keeps the torque convertor filled. This pressure is in turn controlled by electric switches operated by gearlever movement. And the box has three gears only, first having a special high ratio while second and top have the same ratios as the third and top gears of the manual transmission. To describe this arrangement, Citroen have introduced the curious new word "Matic" to the English language, though the badge on the tail of the car is inscribed C Matic, the C presumably standing for the French word Convertisseur.

This transmission system has two important effects: it makes the car quieter and more refined than its manual - gearbox equivalent and does much to compensate for the lack of low-speed torque which is an inherent fault of the breed. Even with the bigger 2175 engine, for instance, the maximum torque value of 123 lb ft is developed rather high in the rev range at 3500 rpm. But the multiplication of effort provided by the torque converter improves the top gear acceleration very considerably, the 20-40 mph acceleration time, for example, being 8.1 sec compared with the 11.8 sec of the 2000 and 11.3 sec of the manual-transmission Pallas, while the 30-50 mph time is 9.7 sec compared with 11.7 sec and 10.6 sec for the two other cars.

Brake pedal is wide enough to be operated with either foot. Pallas seats are large and well upholstered in brushed nylon

Nevertheless, the CX Matic remains rather slow compared with other cars of similar size and price. Thus the Renault 30's 30-50 mph acceleration time is only 7.8 sec, while for the Ford Granada Ghia with its fully automatic transmission the time is as low as 3.7 sec. And the car gets to 60 mph from a standstill in a distinctly leisurely 14.7 sec, even when using all three gears (it's not necessary to do so, as the torque converter allows the car to start in top).

In these days of almost universal speed limits, however, the 107.7 mph maximum is quite adequate, and the car's ability to cruise quietly at 90-100 mph is one of its major virtues. Perhaps partly because of the cushioning effect of the torque converter, the engine vibrations apparent in other CX models are largely absent from the Matic version, though the power unit still becomes noisy between 5000 rpm and the 6000 rpm limit.

But the churning or fluid friction losses associated with a torque converter inevitably worsen the fuel consumption. The overall figure obtained was 20.2 mpg compared to the 22.9 mpg of the manual-gearbox car, while even the touring figure was only 22.4 mpg, suggesting that few owners would be likely to do better unless they seldom drive faster than 60 mph. Even so, a consumption of 20.2 mpg is about average for the class and not bad for a large and roomy car.

Changing gear in the Matic is a clutchless and theoretically easy operation which merely requires the lever to be pushed from one slot to the next. There is no clutch pedal to be depressed—the electrically controlled hydraulic system takes care of all the decoupling required. In practice, as with other systems of this kind like the NSU Ro80's, the arrangement is a little tricky to use at first, and some careful timing is required, especially for smooth downward changes. But the Matic system worked well enough, and has the advantage that the change switch is triggered by gearlever movement only, not by pressure on the gearlever knob alone, so that those in the habit of resting their hand on this knob will not declutch the engine. First gear is located opposite reverse, to the left and to the rear, so the change to second involves a dog-leg movement and could be a little notchy and obstructive, especially at full throttle or if rushed. If taken carefully, though, it became light and slick, while the change from second to top never presented any difficulties. But in any case the system allows many changes to be dispensed with entirely. In town the transmission can be left in second gear, a ratio good for over 80 mph. It is perhaps just a little sluggish in this gear for the first few feet away from the lights, but accelerates with more than adequate vigour thereafter. The car will also pull away in top, though very sluggishly, getting to 60 mph in 24.7 sec.

Our test staff expressed mixed views about this system: some held it to combine most of the advantages of manual with those of automatic transmissions; others regarded it as being a half-hearted attempt at automaticity, neither one thing nor the other. A modern fully automatic gearbox, however, would confer additional advantages while allowing the same degree of manual control if required.

If the performance and refinement of the car are dominated by the semi-automatic transmission, the handling is dominated by the Vari Power steering. This is essentially the system introduced on the SM, but it is less direct for the CX, requiring 2½ rather than 2 turns to move the front wheels from lock to lock. It hydraulically locks the front wheels into the position set by the steering wheel, an auxiliary sub-system providing an artificial self-centring torque which increases as speed rises.

In parking manoeuvres and at low speeds this system certainly makes the Pallas exceptionally effortless to drive compared with nearly all other cars, and especially the standard CX 2000 with its heavy and low-geared manual steering. And as it is less direct, the steering is also much less "twitchy" and more easy to adjust to than the SM's system. After a brief period of familiarisation, therefore, it is also fairly easy to use when motoring briskly down a twisty road. But it is sometimes difficult to avoid cornering in a series of jerks, and it can be difficult to place the car accurately at high speed if a rapid change of direction is called for. On the limit, this steering system is less satisfactory still, as it is always the front wheels that lose adhesion first, and the total absence of genuine "feel" gives the driver no warn-

Moving the gearlever operates the clutch. We like the minor control layout but not the instruments

ing when that limit has been reached and makes the car difficult to correct if it has. Hence we continue to believe that the best power steering systems are the conventional types with feedback, as used by Mercedes and others.

As for the CX 2000, the important thing about the roadholding of the Pallas is not so much what it does but the way it does it. Although the car can be put off line by bumps when trying really hard, its grip on both wet and dry surfaces is generally good. But it lurches into corners with so much roll, tyre squeal and understeer that it is not a pleasant car to drive quickly.

The Pallas is identical to the standard CX in several other ways, two obvious ones being accommodation—which is excellent—and visibility—also good, though it's difficult to see the extremities of the rounded aerodynamic body. The brakes are the same too: very powerful, very reassuring and progressive but highly sensitive with an exceptionally short pedal travel. The ride is excellent, but not as good as that of some other cars with conventional springing such as the Peugeot 604. It tends to be harsh and stiff at low speeds over small irregularities of cobblestone size, and to be a little jerky over short and shallow undulations.

But the Pallas Matic was quieter than the 2000 we tried: not merely is there less engine noise and vibration as already mentioned, but wind noise is lower too, being moderate even at 100 mph. As before, though, there was plenty of bump-thump and road roar.

We also found the heating system most unsatisfactory. It is slow to warm up, admits little heated air under ram pressure alone, and no more than a trickle to the footwells even with the booster fan at full—and noisy—blast. A fair amount of warm air is emitted by the two eyeballs, special to the Pallas model, which are mounted on the cenral console, but these are located just where they create the most stuffiness. In warm weather the flow of fresh air just doesn't begin to dispel the car's inherent stuffiness.

Most of our test staff found the driver's seat comfortable, and well shaped, but few could take advantage of its height and tilt adjustment due to the proximity of the steering wheel. The throttle pedal travel is too long in our view, but we found the minor controls—an array of rocker and other switches in pods on either side of the steering wheel—very pleasant and easy to use. Equally, we have grown to dislike the permanently illuminated revolving drum speedometer and tachometer; the convex front surfaces of their lenses create irritating reflections and there are large gaps between the numbers displayed, the speedometer being calibrated only at 10 mph intervals with the even rather than the odd numbers emphasised.

The Pallas is well equipped, but the potentially luxurious appearance of its interior was spoilt on our test car by some detail faults. The plastic front door mouldings (blue on our test car, linked to a white exterior) were discoloured, for example, and the driver's door pull fitted badly. The finish of the manual-gearbox car, however, was considerably better.

In conclusion, we consider the CX Pallas Matic to be an excellent car in several important respects. It has a handsome, comfortable and roomy body, for example, and cruises in a relaxed way at high speeds. Its ride is good, too, though we find it disappointing in view of the potential of the hydropneumatic springing system. But the car needs more refinement, has mediocre performance and handling and a poor heating and ventilation system.

MOTOR ROAD TEST No. 22/76

Citroen CX 2200 Pallas Matic

PERFORMANCE

CONDITIONS

Weather	Cold. Wind 0-15 mph
Temperature	50-54° F
Barometer	29.15 in Hg
Surface	Dry tarmacadam

MAXIMUM SPEEDS

	mph	kph
Banked circuit	107.7	173.2
Best ¼ mile	115.2	185.5
Terminal speeds :		
at ¼ mile	71	114
at kilometre	89	143
at mile	99	159
Speed in gears (at 6000 rpm) :		
1st	48	77
2nd	82	132

ACCELERATION FROM REST

mph	sec	kph	sec
0-30	4.9	0-40	3.6
0-40	7.2	0-60	6.5
0-50	10.4	0-80	10.3
0-60	14.7	0-100	15.5
0-70	19.3	0-120	22.3
0-80	26.0	0-140	33.0
0-90	36.6		
Stand'g ¼	19.5	Stand'g km	35.8

ACCELERATION IN TOP

mph	sec	kph	sec
20-40	8.1	40-60	5.3
30-50	9.7	60-80	6.6
40-60	11.5	80-100	7.5
50-70	13.2	100-120	9.0
60-80	15.3	120-140	13.1
70-90	20.0		

ACCELERATION IN 2ND

mph	sec	kph	sec
20-40	6.2	40-60	3.0
30-50	7.1	60-80	5.1
40-60	7.7	80-100	6.0
50-70	8.7	100-120	8.0
60-80	11.7		

FUEL CONSUMPTION

Touring*	22.4 mpg 12.6 litres/100 km

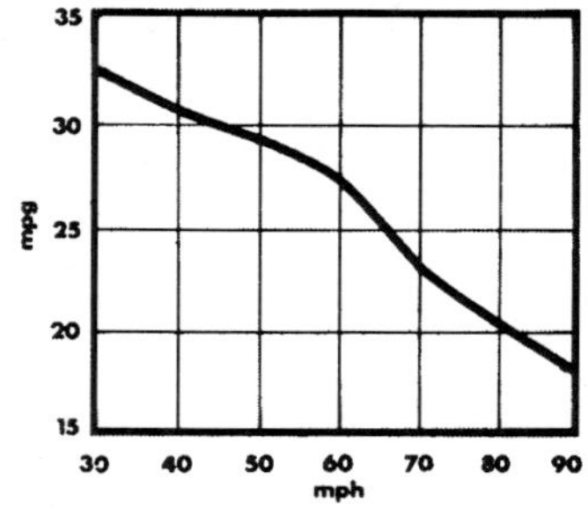

Overall	20.2 12.2 litres/100km
Fuel grade	97 octane 4 star rating
Tank capacity	14.9 galls 68 litres
Max range	334 miles 538 km
Test distance	1200 miles 1920 km

* Consumption midway between 30 mph and maximum less 5 per cent for acceleration.

SPEEDOMETER (mph)

Speedo	30	40	50	60	70	80	90
True	29.5	40	49	58.5	68	78	89

WEIGHT

	cwt	kg
Unladen weight*	25.4	1295
Weight as tested	29.2	1485

*with fuel for approx 50 miles.

Performance tests carried out by Motor's staff at the Motor Industry Research Association proving ground, Lindley.

GENERAL SPECIFICATIONS

ENGINE

Cylinders	4 in line
Capacity	2175 cc (132.73 cu in)
Bore/stroke	90 x 85.5 mm (3.54 x 3.37 in)
Cooling	Water
Block	Cast iron
Head	Aluminium
Valves	Pushrod ohv
Valve timing	
inlet opens	½° btdc
inlet closes	42½° abcd
ex opens	38½° bbdc
ex closes	4½° atdc
Compression	9.0 : 1
Carburetter	Weber 34 DMTR 28
Bearings	5 main
Fuel pump	Mechanical
Max power	112 bhp (DIN) at 5500 rpm
Max torque	123 lb ft (DIN) at 3500 rpm

TRANSMISSION

Type	Semi automatic with torque converter and hydraulically operated clutch
Internal ratios and mph/1000 rpm	
Top	0.800 1/19.3
2nd	1.133 : 1/13.6
1st	1.944 : 1/8.0
Rev	2.389 : 1
Final drive	4.770 : 1

BODY/CHASSIS

Construction	Unitary construction body with perimeter chassis attached by 16 flexible mountings.
Protection	Electrophoretic dip, undersealant and tectyl in sills.

SUSPENSION

Front	Equal length parallel transverse links with anti-roll bar and hydropneumatic self-levelling springing.
Rear	Trailing arms with anti-roll bar and hydropneumatic self-levelling springing.

STEERING

Type	Rack and pinion
Assistance	" Varipower " varying assistance
Toe in	1-4 mm
Camber	0° +13′ −29′
Castor	0°40′—1°
Rear toe in	1-4 mm

BRAKES

Type	Discs, ventilated at the front.
Servo	Fully powered by engine-driven hydraulic pump.
Circuit	Two
Rear valve	Compensation for bad distribution.
Adjustment	Self-adjusting

WHEELS

Type	5.5 in steel
Tyres	185 SR 14 front ; 175 SR 14 rear
Pressures	28/30 psi F/R

ELECTRICAL

Battery	50 Ah
Polarity	Negative earth
Generator	1008W alternator
Fuses	10
Headlights	55/45/40 W trapezoidal halogens.

Make: Citroen **Model:** CX 2200 Pallas Matic
Makers: Societe Anonyme Automobiles Citroen, 117-167 Quai Andre Citroen 75747—Cedix 15
Concessionaires: Citroen Cars Ltd, Mill Street, Slough SL2 5DE
Price: £4073.00 plus £339.42 car tax plus £352.99 VAT, £4765.41.

ROAD TEST

CITROEN CX 2000 SAFARI

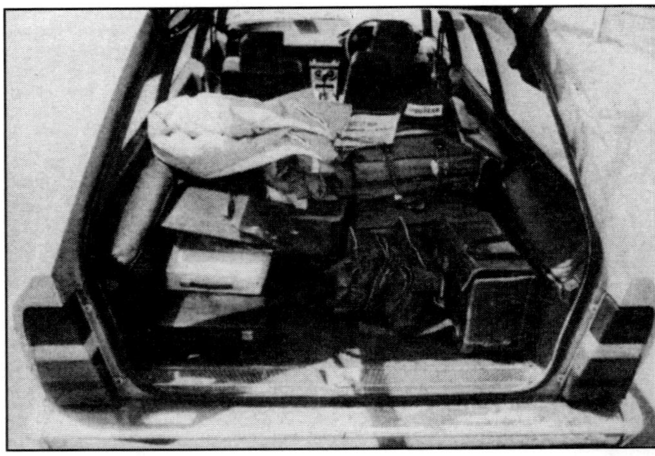

Estate version of Citroen's biggest model is a capacious hold-all. Hydropneumatic suspension leaves ride and handling barely affected by load. Consumption reasonable but performance, apart from top speed, indifferent. Ventilation inadequate in hot weather. Very comfortable: excels as a long-distance cruiser

THERE IS ONE THING CITROEN cannot be accused of: slavishly following fashion. Their engineers have always tended to go their own way almost to the point of idiosyncrasy, from the Light Fifteen or "traction avant" of the Thirties through the ugly duckling but immensely practical 2CV to the DS of 1955 which was staggeringly advanced for its day. Their latest model, the CX, is not quite so advanced as the DS was at its introduction, but is nevertheless still more complex than most of its competitors, and in some respects superior in design.

If there is one feature that can be singled out to demonstrate Citroen's approach it must be the high pressure hydraulic system that operates the steering, brakes and hydropneumatic self-levelling suspension. It is above all the last of these that makes the version tested here, the Safari, so good, for it is a real asset in that the car will take quite enormous loads without any deleterious effect on either ride or handling. And thanks to the excellent use of interior space coupled to an extra 11.4 in of overall length compared with the saloon with an increase in wheelbase of 9.8 in the sheer volume behind the front seats is cavernous. As some indication it took four people plus luggage for a week to Le Mans and back again with room to spare and without any noticeable effect on comfort levels. However, it is not a light car: unladen it weighs 27 cwt and with a load on board it is distinctly sluggish when accelerating, although it seems happy enough to cruise flat-out all day when road conditions permit.

The body structure is similar to that of the saloon, with a low-drag shell mounted via a number of rubber bushes to a perimeter frame which takes all the running gear. The engine and transmission are identical to those installed in the CX 2000 saloon (for the time being there is no 2200 Safari available), with a four-cylinder 1985 cc engine (which features hemispherical combustion chambers in its light alloy head) placed transversely in the nose, canted forwards 30 deg, and driving the front wheels via a four-speed manual gearbox and equal length drive-shafts, the latter made possible by a bearing-supported jackshaft running across from the differential to the off-side.

At the front the suspension is by equal-length parallel links whose geometry incorporates anti-dive properties, with trailing arms at the rear. The springing medium is the well-known hydropneumatic system with soft gas springs working in conjunction with a hydraulic self-levelling system, and there are anti-roll bars at both ends. The "Vari-Power" steering system is standard on the Safari and is similar to that employed on the sporting SM and provides both automatic self-centring and a reducing assistance as speed rises, while the fully powered (not merely power assisted) brakes incorporate ventilated discs at the front and rear.

Although the 2-litre engine gives a healthy 102 bhp (DIN) at 5500 rpm there is only a mediocre 112 lb ft (DIN) torque at 3000 rpm (the Peugeot and the Volvo, for example, give 118 and 125 lb ft respectively but with less than 100 bhp maximum power in both cases) and this shows up in the distinctly sluggish acceleration.

Top gear performance in particular is poor, the quickest 20 mph increment (from 50 to 70 mph) taking a languid 14.6 s, while the 30-50 mph time was no less than 15.4 s, a figure that can be beaten by almost all the cars in the "How good" section that follows this test: even the Hillman Imp, for example, is quicker, as is the Citroen GS Estate. Third gear, though good for over 80 mph, doesn't feel all that much quicker either while getting away from traffic lights under normal road conditions is also a leisurely process. However, the performance did not drop off noticeably when the Safari was fully laden, and given a long and level straight it will run happily at between 90 and 100 mph (indicated), although, of course, any obstruction—other traffic, for example—slows you down more than usual, while the lack of acceleration makes overtaking a ponderous manoeuvre and it is a long time before a respectable cruising speed is attained again. We recorded a top speed of 103.2 mph and a 0-60 mph time through the gears of 15.1 s, somewhat worse than Citroen's claim of 106 mph and 13.7 s respectively.

If performance is poor, fuel consumption is reasonably good. Including a trip across France where the performance was used to the full the Safari recorded a useful 23.0 mpg overall, while the touring consumption, 26.6 mpg, is excellent. The fuel consumption curve in fact doesn't drop below 30 mpg until 60 mph is reached, while at a steady 40 mph (corresponding to 2000 rpm) it will give 36 mpg: for those drivers who are not bothered about performance, economy should be excellent.

In addition the huge (15 gallon) tank gives a remarkable range: using the touring consumption figure this works out at over 400

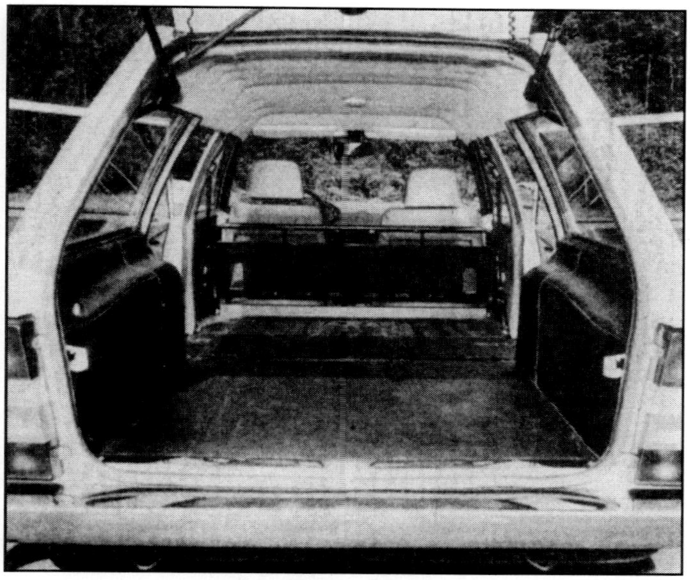

Motoring equivalent of the screenplay " Jaws " (top right). Citroen's Safari gobbles up luggage with ease and took our team and its luggage (left) to Le Mans with room to spare. Below: the back seat folds completely flat

miles, and on more than one occasion we saw well over 300 miles before the gauge indicated that a stop for refuelling was required.

The clutch on the Safari was particularly smooth and progressive, and smooth changes were not difficult, helped, perhaps, by the engine's apparently considerable rotary inertia—its revs neither build up or die down very quickly. But the gearchange itself is rather rubbery, notchy, and strangely imprecise. Reverse, however, was almost invariably obstructive and usually grated loudly when selected. The ratios are reasonably spaced, first being good for 29 mph, second for 50 mph and third for over 80 mph.

In order to judge the handling it is really necessary to spend some time with the car, since the steering requires acclimatisation. The Safari is fitted with the Citroen developed VariPower steering system geared to give 2½ turns lock to lock with a hydraulic locking arrangement to hold the wheels in the position set by the steering wheel so that they are not deflected by bumps, and a self-centring device which varies the load felt according to vehicle speed and steering wheel angle. The good points of the system are that it makes parking very easy and that it is direct without the twitchiness of the higher-geared (two turns lock to lock) SM system. The less pleasant aspects include a "dead" portion about the straight ahead, so that keeping the car on a straight line is a little tricky and long fast curves tend to be taken in a series of bites. In addition a combination of the directness and the considerable roll which the suspension allows makes it difficult to prevent an initial lurch into a corner and the self-centring coming out of a corner is abrupt as well, while the artificial "Feel" of the system means that, on the limit, there is no warning to the driver that the front wheels are about to lose adhesion —and makes it awkward to correct when they do.

Under more normal driving conditions, however, and once you are used to these characteristics, you tend to find the steering of other cars stodgy, heavy and low-geared, while the handling (provided you don't go near the limit) is safe and predictable. Understeer builds up with cornering speeds, accompanied by considerable roll (in spite of anti-roll bars front and rear). Tyre squeal disguises the fact that the cornering powers of the Michelin ZX 185 SR 14s (the Safari has equal sized tyres front and rear, unlike the saloon) are high in either the wet or the dry. If the handling is not such as to appeal to the enthusiast the hydropneumatic suspension does give one enormous benefit: it doesn't matter whether the car is empty or laden, the characteristics barely alter, and there is none of the usual "pendulum action" whereby the car becomes tail-happy with a load on board, nor does it adopt a nose-up attitude.

Like the saloon the Safari has the Citroen fully-powered braking system, but with ventilated discs and a control which compensates for load distribution. Unlike the DS the CX has a normal pedal arrangement for the brakes, although it does still operate the same type of valve. The change from the DS's button-on-the-floor makes braking much more progressive, although pedal travel is still limited and loads very light so that a gentle caress rather than a definite shove is required. Once you get used to this sensitivity (rather like the steering) the brakes lose their abruptness and smooth stops are easy. In action they are formidably powerful, and in conjunction with the anti-dive properties of the suspension, the car feels absolutely rock-steady and stable even during panic stops.

Accommodation is the name of the game when it comes to estates, and the Safari must be one of the most commodious around. The length of the floor with the rear seats folded (83 in) is the longest of all the European cars we have tried, and only exceeded by some of the American monsters. But length is only one of the factors: the roof line has been raised at the rear to give more height, the floor is perfectly flat, there is no lip at the back (although the door doesn't include the rear bumper as it does on the GS) and the padded wheel arch covers still allow 46in of width; thus the space available is not only huge but of a very useful shape as well. Most of the extra length of the Safari comes within the wheelbase, and there is very little overhang so that most of the load is ahead of the rear wheels —perhaps another reason why the Safari is less tail-happy laden than most estates.

Citroen have also taken advantage of the extra length to increase the length of the rear side doors, which not only makes entry for passengers easy but provides usefully large apertures as well.

Because of its sleek lines the CX Safari is actually 4 in shorter than the DS Safari but doesn't look it: the transverse engine layout has thus been used to retain not only a long and aerodynamic nose but to give better accommodation within a more compact layout as well. It is unlikely that anyone will complain about passenger room in the CX, for there is more than enough room in all the important dimensions, and only the tallest of passengers sitting behind a tall driver may find leg room restricted.

Twenty years ago the ride of the DS was regarded as almost miraculous: the hydropneumatic system of the CX is the same in principle, but in the meantime the ride of some more conventionally sprung cars has more than caught up. The Citroen ride is still very good, and copes well with the more turbulent, potholed and uneven road surfaces so often encountered in France, for instance, but there is more than a trace of low-speed harshness and the car is not as resilient, smooth and quiet as some other modern saloons like the Jaguar XJ6. Nevertheless, helped by the soft and sumptuous seats, comfort levels are high, and, perhaps because of the somewhat greater weight of the Safari, we found the ride of this model to be a slight improvement over the others we have tried.

With an extensive fore-and-aft range, a tiltable backrest and height adjustment, most drivers easily achieve a comfortable driving position, although some taller drivers found that, if the seat was raised at the front, their

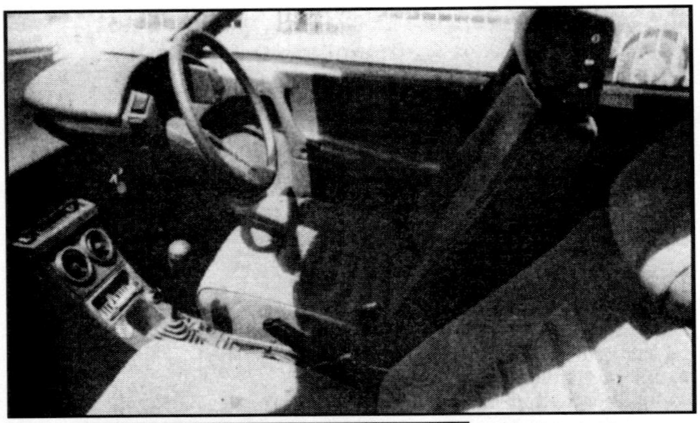

The interior is as sumptuous as it looks. Comfort levels are high, though the ventilation system can't cope with really warm weather

Rear seat comfort is good. The doors open wide, there's plenty of legroom for tall passengers and there are useful elasticated pockets in the back of each front seat

knees fouled the steering wheel. Because the seats are so soft they tend to hold you in quite well, but could still do with a little more lateral support in view of the large roll angles the car can adopt. Most of the major controls are well laid out, although the clutch pedal is too high and close to the transmission tunnel, while the handbrake is close to the passenger's seat. When you get to them, most of the minor controls —switches mounted on pods either side of the steering column —are ergonomically correct and very definitely under fingertip control; most impressive. The only complaint we have is that the indicator switch is not self-cancelling. The novel instrument display, with revolving drum speedometer and tachometer permanently illuminated, was less popular since it has to be read rather than just glanced at and the glasses reflected badly. In addition there are more normal gauges for fuel level and charge plus a matching clock: again they tend to reflect. Above these is a row of no less than 15 warning lights, some of which are blanks, however.

The recent spell of very warm, sunny weather plus a trip to one of the hottest Le Mans races in memory didn't give us much chance to assess the heating but did reveal some of the shortcomings of the ventilation system. Perhaps because of the huge expanse of sloping glass in the windscreen the interior soon became almost unbearably hot, and even with the noisy fan on the fastest of its three speeds it was necessary to open the windows to get a sufficient throughput of cooling air, at the expense, of course, of peace and quiet.

Citroen have been introducing running changes to the mounting points of the body to the perimeter frame and of the engine in the interest of refinement, and the Safari was the best of the CXs we have tested in this respect. The engine is still fussy in the lower two gears over about 4000 rpm, while tyre roar and suspension thump are noticeable as well, but once you are on a motorway or cruising at speed the engine sounds much less obtrusive and wind noise is very low indeed (when the windows are closed) so that it is under these conditions that the Safari is at its best, and high speed long-distance travel could be said to be its forte.

The Safari is finished and equipped to the same standards as the Super saloon models, which means that it comes with such items as electric window lifters for the front doors, a driver's seat adjustable for height, a roof aerial and door-mounted loudspeakers, an oil-level indicator on the dash, a tachometer, a handbrake warning light and (for the Safari only) a rear window wiper. The interior decor is plush and pleasant, and the finish in general is good.

Thanks to the considerable glass area, visibility all round is excellent, while the slender rear pillars and huge rear window make reversing into tight spots particularly easy. The edges of the CX are much better defined than the bulbous sides of the DS, and it is really only the nose that is invisible over the long sloping bonnet.

MOTOR ROAD TEST No 30/76
Citroen CX 2000 Safari Super

PERFORMANCE

CONDITIONS

Weather	Hot, sunny: wind 0-10 mph
Temperature	78°-82° F
Barometer	29.7 in Hg
Surface	Dry tarmacadam

MAXIMUM SPEEDS

	mph	kph
Banked circuit	103.2	166.0
Best ¼ mile	103.4	166.4
Terminal speeds:		
at ¼ mile	69	111
at kilometre	87	140
Speed in gears (at 6000 rpm):		
1st	29	47
2nd	50	80
3rd	82	132

ACCELERATION FROM REST

mph	sec	kph	sec
0-30	4.4	0-40	3.7
0-40	7.2	0-60	6.3
0-50	10.1	0-80	10.0
0-60	15.1	0-100	16.0
0-70	20.1	0-120	23.0
0-80	26.7		
Stand'g ¼	19.8	Stand'g km	36.8

ACCELERATION IN TOP

mph	sec	kph	sec
20-40	16.0	40-60	9.3
30-50	15.4	60-80	9.8
40-60	14.9	80-100	8.8
50-70	14.6	100-120	10.1
60-80	17.9		

FUEL CONSUMPTION

Touring*	26.6 mpg 10.6 litres/100 km
Overall	23.0 mpg 12.3 litres/100 km
Fuel grade	98 octane 4 star rating
Tank capacity	15 galls 68 litres

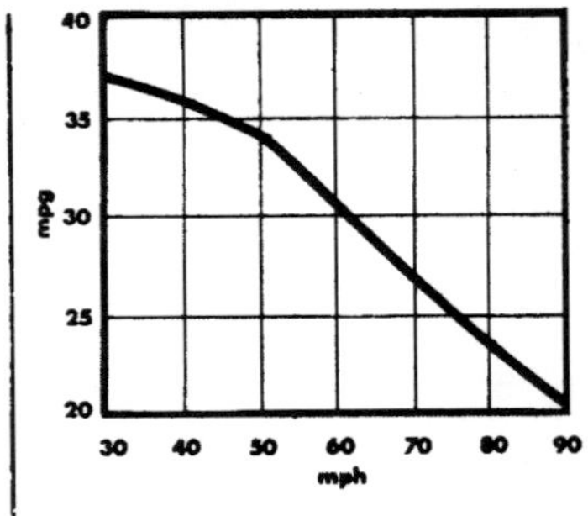

Max range	400 miles 642 km
Test distance	2117 miles 3406 km

*Consumption midway between 30 mph and maximum less 5 per cent for acceleration.

SPEEDOMETER (mph)

Speedo	30	40	50	60	70	80	90
True	28	38	47.5	57	67	77.5	87.5

WEIGHT

	cwt	kg
Unladen weight*	27.0	1371.7
Weight as tested	30.7	1554.6

*with fuel for approx 50 miles.

Performance tests carried out by Motor's staff at the Motor Industry Research Association proving ground, Lindley.

GENERAL SPECIFICATIONS

ENGINE

Cylinders	4 in line
Capacity	1985 cc (121.2 cu in)
Bore/stroke	86/85 mm (3.386/3.366 in)
Cooling	Water
Block	Cast iron
Head	Light alloy
Valves	Pushrod ohv
Valve timing	
inlet opens	0° 30′ btdc
inlet closes	42° 30′ abdc
ex opens	38° 30′ bbdc
ex closes	0° 30′ atdc
Compression	9.0 : 1
Carburetter	Weber twin-choke
Bearings	5 main
Fuel pump	Mechanical
Max power	102 bhp (DIN) at 5500 rpm
Max torque	112 lb ft (DIN) at 3000 rpm

TRANSMISSION

Type	4 speed, manual
Clutch	Sdp diaphragm spring
Internal ratios and mph/1000 rpm	
Top	0.800 : 1/19.2
3rd	1.133 : 1/13.6
2nd	1.833 : 1/8.4
1st	3.166 : 1/4.9
Rev	3.153 : 1
Final drive	4.77 : 1

BODY/CHASSIS

Construction	Unitary construction shell with perimeter frame
Protection	Electrophoretic dip, undersealant and Tectyl in sills

SUSPENSION

Front	Equal length parallel transverse links with anti-roll bar and hydropneumatic self-levelling springing
Rear	Trailing arms with anti-roll bar and hydropneumatic self-levelling springing

STEERING

Type	Rack and pinion
Assistance	Full power
Toe in	1 to 4 mm
Camber	0° + 13′ – 29′
Castor	–0° 40′ to –1°
Rear toe in	1 to 4 mm

BRAKES

Type	Discs all round
Servo	Fully powered
Circuit	Twin
Rear valve	Yes
Adjustment	Self-adjusting

WHEELS

Type	Pressed steel, 5.5J x 14
Tyres	Michelin 185 SR 14 ZX
Pressures	32/35 psi F/R

ELECTRICAL

Battery	12V 50 Ah
Polarity	Negative
Generator	Alternator
Fuses	10
Headlights	55/45/40W trapezoidal halogens

Make: Citroen
Model: CX 2000 Safari Super
Makers: Societe Anonyme Automobiles Citroen, 117-167 Quaie Andre Citroen, 75747-Cedix 75, France
Concessionaires: Citroen Cars Ltd, Mill Street, Slough, Bucks SL2 5DE
Price: £3760 plus £313.33 Car Tax and £325.87 VAT totals £4399.20.

Other possible competitors which we have not tested in their latest form include the Triumph 2500 S Estate, the Toyota Crown 2600 Estate and the Datsun 260C Estate.

CITROEN CX 2000 SAFARI £4399

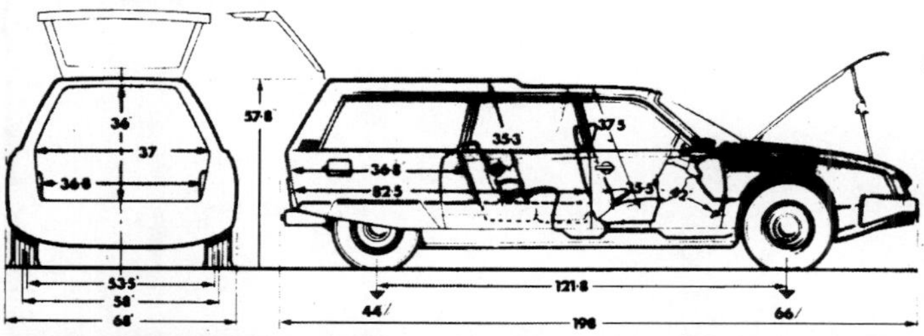

Estate version of Citroen's biggest model, equipped to the same standard as 2200 Super but with 2-litre engine from 2000. Huge luggage and passenger space, while hydropneumatic suspension means that handling and ride are barely affected by loads. Sluggish acceleration (notably in top) but excellent cruiser and reasonably economical. Handling safe but unexciting. Ventilation cannot cope with very hot conditions.

Power, bhp/rpm	102/5500
torque, lbft/rpm	112/3000
tyres	185 SR14
weight (cwt)	27.0
max speed (mph)	103.2
0-60 mph (sec)	15.1
30-50 mph in 4th (sec)	15.4
overall mpg	23.0
touring mpg	28.6
fuel grade (stars)	4

VOLVO 245 DL £4255

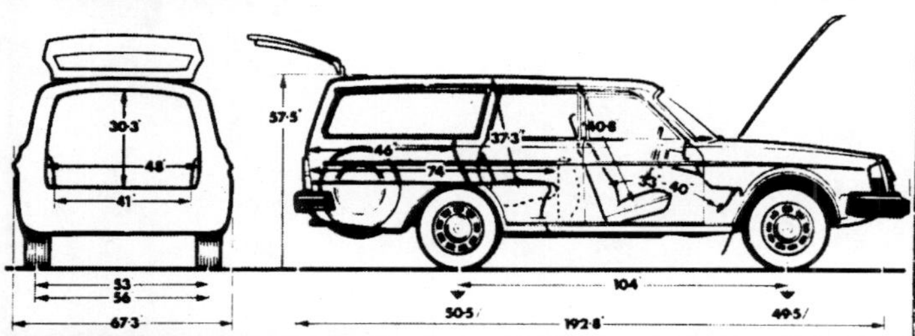

Along with Citroen and Peugeot one of the leaders in interior space. Also versatile — a third row of seats facing backward in the tail is an optional extra. Has a reputation for being well-built and reliable, while safety is strongly emphasised. Heating, ventilation, finish and layout of facia are superb. Performance only modest and engine unrefined at high revs. Peculiar steering characteristics.

Power, bhp/rpm	97/5000
torque, lbft/rpm	178/3000
tyres	185 SR14
weight (cwt)	26.2
max speed (mph)	94.7
0-60 mph (sec)	13.1
30-50 mph in 4th (sec)	9.7
overall mpg	21.3
touring mpg	25.4
fuel grade (stars)	3

PEUGEOT FAMILIALE £3580

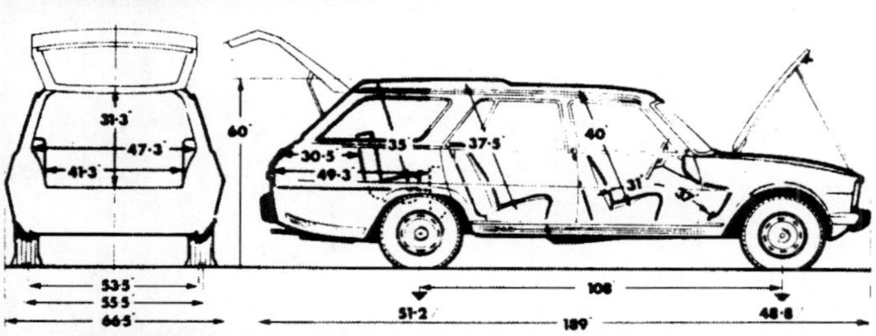

Passenger-carrying rather than load-carrying version of Peugeot's 504 estate — it has three rows of seats, the rearmost collapsible. Standard estate, though, should compete closely with the Citroen on interior volume. Has typical Peugeot characteristics — an excellent ride from the long-travel, supple suspension and good noise suppression. Performance and economy about average, steering low-geared but roadholding good.

Power, bhp/rpm	93/5200
torque, lbft/rpm	178/3000
tyres	185 SR14
weight (cwt)	25.6
max speed (mph)	96.7
0-60 mph (sec)	13.7
30-50 mph in 4th (sec)	10.3
overall mpg	23.6
touring mpg	24.6
fuel grade (stars)	4

OPEL REKORD DIESEL AUTO £3880

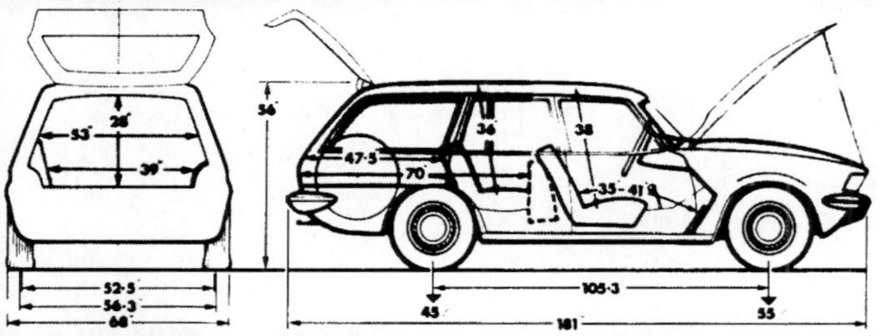

An anachronism: in terms of refinement one of the best diesels we have ever tested, but surprisingly thirsty — the automatic transmission obviously didn't help. Also typically diesel in being slow. Doesn't really compare when it comes to load space, but has many usual Opel virtues — good roadholding and handling, an impressive finish, attractive and clear instruments, comfortable seats and driving position.

Power, bhp/rpm	60/4400
torque, lbft/rpm	87/2500
tyres	175 SR14
weight (cwt)	25.1
max speed (mph)	75.3
0-60 mph (sec)	30.8
30-50 mph in 4th (sec)	10.6
overall mpg	24.4
touring mpg	30.4
fuel grade (stars)	Diesel

FORD FAIRMONT £4506

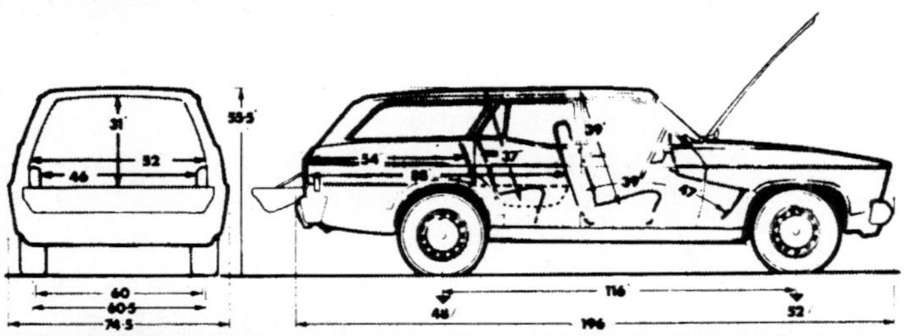

Vast American-designed, Australian-built estate with enormous load space and longest and widest platform with rear seats lowered. Tailgate folds down (once rear window has been dropped electrically into the door) to give yet more length — or can be opened sideways like a normal door. Five-litre V8 makes it fastest (but not by much) and thirstiest. Quiet and relaxed at speed, comfortable with good ride

Power, bhp/rpm	230/5000
torque, lbft/rpm	300/2800
tyres	185 SR14
weight (cwt)	31.7
max speed (mph)	106.3
0-60 mph (sec)	10.0
30-50 mph in k'down	4.1
overall mpg	15.0
touring mpg	18.1
fuel grade (stars)	4

FORD GRANADA 3000 GL £4517

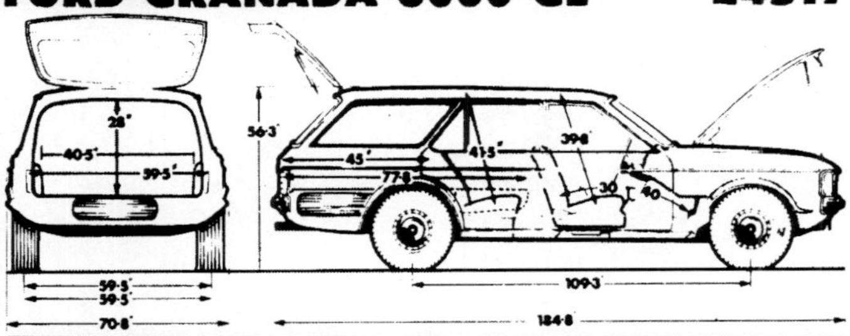

Probably the best of the British estates — comfortable, quiet, refined but doesn't really compare with the Continentals when it comes to load space. Handling badly affected by load — becomes very tail happy. Three-litre V6 engine gives effortless performance although maximum speed not all that much more than more aerodynamic Citroen, and consumption does suffer in the process: auto transmission doesn't help.

Power, bhp/rpm	138/5000
torque, lbft/rpm	174/3000
tyres	185 SR14
weight (cwt)	28.6
max speed (mph)	105.1
0-60 mph (sec)	12.2
30-50 mph in k'down	4.4
overall mpg	16.8
touring mpg	20.8
fuel grade (stars)	4

Shazam! Citroën Cx!

An extraterrestrial auto
for cosmic
cruising on the roads of France.

BY DAN COZZI

• Buck Rogers and Flash Gordon weren't there when the doors swung open to reveal the 1955 Paris Automobile Show, but their presence was felt. Citroën selected that show to debut a car that seemed more at home in the 21st century than in crotchety old 1955; a car manufactured in a grimy art-deco factory on the left bank of the Seine that was yet a radical glimpse of the future.

But if Buck and Flash weren't among the hoard that elbowed its way into the shimmering presence of this clairvoyant anticipation of the automobile's future, it didn't really matter—the Citroën DS achieved instant popularity anyway. The 749 cash deposits taken by Citroën representatives during the first half-hour

grew to 12,000 orders for the DS by the end of the first day.

For 19 years, Citroën perpetuated the legendary DS. They built almost a million and a half copies of their outlandish car before the legend wore out. So when the time came to at last "invent" a successor to the fabulous DS, Citroën adhered to the formula unveiled at the 1955 Paris Auto Show: The car's appearance would be updated just enough to squelch the mutterings of Citroën's critics, and some minimal concessions to 20 years of changing tastes would be made.

The new embodiment of Citroën's peculiar vision was designated the Cx, the European symbol for an object's aerodynamic coefficient. After an auspicious presentation at the Paris Motor Show of 1973, the Cx finally hit the cobblestones in August 1974. Citroën touted their new car as the final solution to the problems of fuel economy, safety and ride. The French public seemed satisfied that the Cx represented a suitably elitist image in the Citroën tradition. The factory soon reported hundreds of orders per day, and the Cx went on to win numerous awards for safety and styling, including a prize for European "Car of the Year."

In 1970, when the specifications for what emerged as the Cx were first drawn up, Citroën visualized a front-engine, front-drive car with a centralized hydraulic system operating the four-wheel self-leveling suspension, steering and disc brakes. The DS engine, however, would be turned 90 degrees and coupled transversely to a new transmission and final-drive unit. The major suspension and chassis parts would be redesigned, and a fully stressed chassis/body unit, including a stressed roof panel, would be added to the five-passenger, four-door configuration.

As with the DS, styling is . . . well, unique. A dreamy mixture of lines and creases and curves. Still, some people seem to prefer Simcas.

Inside the car, one also discovers evidence of the same resolutely independent, ivory-tower thinking that is so apparent on the outside: All the instruments and control switches have been grouped on the steering column or on the dash immediately in front of the driver. Everything is in plain sight and readily available to the whim of a finger . . . once you discover—and commit to memory—the relationship between function and form for each control.

One small concession to modern thinking—to stubbornness, the engineers at Citroën might say—has been made in the interior. The petite, mushroom-shaped brake button so dear to the hearts of former DS owners has been replaced by a conventional pedal more typical of our modern age.

But if many of the mechanical and styling features of the Cx seem peculiar, the sensations associated with driving this car are no less eccentric. Above all, the Cx driver must have patience: bringing the engine to life illuminates a bright orange indicator light that flashes a cryptic "Stop." As you glare back at the instrument panel's angry command, the horizon suddenly changes position as the car jacks itself up to ride height, first at the rear, and then at the front.

Finally, the orange light blinks out. After releasing the parking brake (extinguishing yet another light) and selecting a gear, you are ready to "Go." When you engage the clutch, the engine rocks on its supports as axle-shaft torque tries to wind the block around the final drive gear. And then with an elastic lurch, you're off—if not really running, at least you're moving.

At first, you may be disturbed to learn that Citroën's engineers, not wishing to burden you with the mundane task of steering, have disconnected the steering wheel from the rest of the car. But then you begin to learn about the steering: 2.5 turns lock to lock, with full power assist. With a flick of the wrist you can crank huge steering angles into the front

Shazam! Citroën Cx!

wheels. The French simply assume that you wish to dispense with that nonsense about "feedback."

As a mad bicyclist dashes across your path, you fumble for the horn. But where is the horn button? Not on the steering wheel. No (swish), those are the wipers. And (squirt), that's the washer. That one is (owoooo) the heater. The headlights. The (click-click) turn indicators? Here. Up on top! At last. *Honk-Tweet*! Would you believe it . . . a two-tone horn.

. . . Flail the gear lever and stomp sadistically on the pedals—the Cx leisurely gains speed. The Cx is a 21st century spaceship gliding effortlessly toward the horizon without a jounce or a tremor, as if scornful of the road. Well, there does seem to be a familiar engine vibration at certain speeds, and the windows don't quite keep all the wind noise out. And the seats are so soft that they can cause a few aches, and the high forward cowl reduces forward vision . . . but only a constipated non-French journalist would stoop to quibbling about all that.

Through dips and curves, the Cx responds with stability, though at the expense of large steering/slip angles at the front wheels. Thanks to the soft, friction-free suspension system, the tires are in touch with the road no matter how rough the surface. On the other hand, the pitch and roll of the car can approach nautical dimensions. The limit of adhesion is difficult to approach, but because the Cx will let go in a terminal way once you get there, it's just as well. Also, the sedate acceleration of the Cx can lead to an imperious refusal to brake for any road hazard or obstacle—like a bread riot among the rabble in the streets—for fear of wasting precious time getting up to speed again. To maintain a good average speed, you must avoid the brakes and rely on good vision, sharp reflexes and total concentration to keep you out of trouble. But then, that's part of the Citroën formula.

As it begins to rain, the Cx's unusual single wiper blade slashes across the vast, deeply-curved windshield . . . leaving a large part of the glass unwiped. The upper left corner grows opaque with road grime. Well, Alfonse, the magnetostrictive hovercraft that Flash Gordon kept outside his townhouse only had a single wiper; why should the Cx grant any special dispensation to your unworthy complaints? Slide down in the seat if you want better visibility, peasant.

The benign masters at Citroën have learned to be patient with the poor bourgeoise who drives other brands of automobiles. A Citroën requires that its driver discard his plebeian habits and learn the Truth. The engineers and management at the factory along the Seine firmly believe that only they can lead the Republique of France into the Automotive Utopia. Their gentle but insistent touch has transformed everything about the Cx into something that whispers Citroën at every opportunity. Indeed, when you consider that the Cx is both a French car—a peculiar entity onto itself—and a Citroën, you begin to realize how beyond your humble comprehension this automobile really is.

The Cx strides with futuristic ease along the cosmic superhighways of eternal France, its occupants smothered in comfort, immersed in imperious indolence. Although it does practically anything that can be reasonably asked of an automobile with unshakable competence, the Cx is most at home on smooth, straight, endless roads. Perhaps Louis XIV knew the grace of traveling unmolested in a self-contained environment of dignity, rank and luxury, gazing idly at the simple peasants at work in the fields.

If Buck Rogers were French and living in Paris, he would understand perfectly. •

CITROËN Cx2200

Manufacturer: S.A.A. Citroën
133 Quai Andre Citroën
75747 Paris, France

Vehicle type: transverse front-engine, front-wheel-drive, 5-passenger

Price as tested: Nf 34,460 ($7750)

ENGINE

Type: 4-in-line, water-cooled, cast iron block and aluminum head, 5 main bearings
Bore x stroke . . . 3.55 x 3.46 in, 90 x 85.5 mm
Displacement . . . 135 cu in, 2175 cc
Compression ratio . . . 9 to one
Carburetion . . . 1x2-bbl Solex
Valve gear . . . pushrod-operated overhead valves
Power (SAE net) . . . 110 bhp @ 5500 rpm
Torque (SAE net) . . . 124 lbs-ft @3500 rpm
Specific power output . . . 0.815 bhp/cu in, 50.5 bhp/liter
Max. recommended engine speed . . . 6000 rpm

DRIVE TRAIN

Transmission . . . 4-speed, all-synchro
Final drive ratio . . . 4.76 to one

Gear	Ratio	Mph/1000 rpm	Max. test speed
I	3.166	4.84	26 mph (5500 rpm)
II	1.833	8.40	46 mph (5500 rpm)
III	1.133	13.6	75 mph (5500 rpm)
IV	0.8	19.2	110 mph (5700 rpm)

DIMENSIONS AND CAPACITIES

Wheelbase . . . 112 in
Track, F/R . . . 58/53.5 in
Length . . . 184 in
Width . . . 68 in
Height . . . 53.5 in
Ground clearance . . . 5 in
Curb weight . . . 2830 lbs
Weight distribution, F/R . . . 67/33%
Battery capacity . . . 12 volts, 50 amp-hr
Alternator capacity . . . 1008 watts
Fuel capacity . . . 18 gal
Oil capacity . . . 5 qts
Water capacity . . . 11 qts

SUSPENSION

F: . . ind. control arms, hydropneumatic springs, anti-sway bar
R: . . . ind. trailing arms, hydropneumatic springs

STEERING

Type . . . rack and pinion, power assisted
Turns lock-to-lock . . . 2.5
Turning circle curb-to-curb . . . 36 ft

BRAKES

F: . . . 10.2-in ventilated disc, power assisted
R: . . . 9.3-in solid disc, power assisted

WHEELS AND TIRES

Wheel size . . . 5.5 x 14-in
Wheel type . . . stamped steel, 5-bolt
Tire make and size . . . Michelin 185HR-14 front, 175HR-14 rear
Tire type . . . steel-belted radial

TRAGEDY OF A GREAT CAR

Citroen's CX 2200 Super is a superb touring car that would satisfy even the most jaded of Australian drivers yet it costs more than twice as much here as it does in France. So, some of its buyers aren't going to use it as they should. We drove it 1100 kms in one day and, though it has its shortcomings, we fell under its spell.

IT'S LIKE YOUR first lesson in the realities of fast driving; where your mentor takes you aside and explains that suburban road-racing circuits don't exist and 60 km/h road signs mean what they say . . . the rest is between you and the highway patrol. You are told you have to realise there is a lot to consider before you decide to drive your car quickly — and that there are places where you can go quickly and fully use the potential of your car without having to think about rounding a nicely-banked corner and collecting three kids playing ball, a woman with her shopping basket and a dogfight.

The only difference with the Citroen CX 2200 is that the car itself and the unmistakable influence of its creator, Andre Citroen, are your mentors and the open road teaches you the rest. All three teach you with subtlety. Yet the car won't show you what it can really do until you are on the open road. Schizophrenia, if you like.

Around town it looks good, sure, but performs almost like a slug — 1280 kg of car is a lot for a 2175 cm^3 four-cylinder engine to get up a push, or in the case of the Citroen, pull. The lesson really begins when you unleash the car on the open road and its aerodynamics take over. It literally becomes a different car — a marvellous, floating, touring machine that will eat kilometre after kilometre at 160 km/h without flinching.

We put 1100 km on a CX 2200 Super in one day — Sydney to Parkes and back — and learned a lot about the car that is replacing Citroen's ubiquitous D series.

There was talk around the office before we left about it not being a sports car in the true sense of the term but any doubts were forgotten by the time we'd hit Bell's Line of Road. Aerodynamics are excellent and, coupled with the hydro-pneumatic-type suspension, give the car that very rare thing in a mass-produced car — handling. Steering in our car wasn't power-assisted — though power steering is virtually standard equipment now — and some testers felt it was too heavy in such a weighty car. But it's very much a question of personal taste, with some of our drivers feeling the unassisted steering was light and accurate at speed.

The car's basic handling characteristic is understeer and it can be frightening in the wet. The engine, the DS in-line, water-cooled four, and transmission unit are mounted transversely between the front wheels and inclined 30 degrees towards the front to lower bonnet height. This means 70 percent of the car's weight is cantilevered out over the front wheels — and that's something you should be thinking about when the car lulls you into absolute security at 160 km/h.

The car's aerodynamics help in the sweepers but, as one of our drivers found, fairly tight corners can be a handful. But the same driver attributed this partly to the car's unassisted steering — he was adamant that the CX lacked two things, a fifth gear and power-assisted steering.

Aerodynamics play a big part in the car's economy and slipperiness is carried through right down to detailing features, like flat hub caps. Driving around 130-140 km/h all day, we got around 26 mpg. But it's in the way you drive the car that economy and performance figures start to juggle around. The accelerator has a very long travel and lends itself to two distinct ways of driving the car: For around-town economy you tend to use the first part of the accelerator's travel only — accelerate more and the second throat of the twin-choke Weber 34 carburettor comes in, the car starts to perform more like a sports car and fuel economy goes down. Around town, using the first throat of the carburettor, consumption is about 30 mpg.

It seems almost incredible at times but very rough bumps don't throw the car off its line. The Citroen's self-levelling system and soft gas springs absorb bumps rather than telegraph them back through the steering wheel and through the body as a series of sharp bangs. You still feel bumps and severe ruts in the road but you feel them softly. And the CX still stays on line.

The fact that it doesn't bounce around makes the CX very much suited to Australian roads. And it has that great Citroen device, the suspension height adjustment, which is both individual and extremely versatile for Australian conditions.

Yet you only really appreciate this on the open road. And it comes as a surprise that Andre Citroen himself disliked driving on the open road. But the man's cars eat miles.

Brakes are discs all round — all operating off the main hydraulic pressure system, front and rear operated on independent circuits, and the front pair ventilated for better cooling. There is even a warning light to tell the driver when brake pads need replacing. The brake pedal itself is, in appearance, as close to conventional as Citroen has come. It's not the half tennis ball shape of the D series cars but works just as well. The system is still fully powered and very sensitive to short travel. It operates more off the pressure you apply rather than downward force.

Like the rest of the car, the brakes took some getting used to. But we found them fade-free and damned near perfect for the car.

On wet roads it is possible to lock up the front wheels, under hard braking, and produce heart-stopping slides. One tester found backing off the pedal led to a momentary delay before the brakes disengaged completely — he got a fright.

The transverse setup of the engine/transmission goes a long way towards making the CX a much quieter car at speed than the D series cars, which had the engine conventionally mounted but protruding into the cabin. Wind noise was low and we found you can open one of the electrically-operated front windows and still hear your passenger talking to you when 140 km/h is showing.

Citroen obviously placed ergonomics before styling fancies when it came to instrument and switches layout. The steering wheel is single-spoked — it would hardly be a Citroen if it wasn't — but there are no stalks protruding from the column. Instead, everything is located on a single module, at finger-tip reach, directly in front of you.

Blinkers, lights, wipers, horn . . . the lot, can be operated merely by extending your fingers to the rocker switches. There is no need to release your grip on the wheel.

In front of you are two square magnifying glass-type lenses which magnify the upright, revolving cylinders which are the tachometer and speedometer. A stationary pointer below each shows you what is happening. Both lenses are illuminated day and night — they have to be, as reflection off the magnifying surface makes it almost impossible during daytime to read the instruments. They are flanked by a fuel gauge and clock, with a tripmeter in the centre.

But it's on top of the main instruments that the fun begins. There is a bank of no less than 14 warning lights

Interior is pure Citroen — comfortable as well as functional. The half-moon shaped instrument pod takes some getting used to but is in many ways a superior system once you get the hang of it.

which, thankfully, we didn't have to puzzle out. Heater/demister controls are on the centre console along with the radio and controls for the front-only electrically-operated windows. The gearshift is also on the console.

There is an effectiveness in the transmission that is another of those Citroen characteristics which come out on the open road. The car needs a good transmission because of the Citroen philosophy of relatively heavy cars and small engines. And this one worked well. But, by the time we had reached Forbes, the same tester was still sticking with his belief that the car needed a fifth gear.

First is relatively low and close to second but there is a large gap between second and third. Fourth gear is an overdrive but with only 31 km/h (19.3 mph) per 1000 rpm it is capable of reaching the engine's 6000 rpm redline. We saw the redline at 192 km/h after a long run-up but felt the engine would go higher. Even at that speed, the CX was completely stable.

Visibility is extremely good as the dashboard slopes at a low angle away from the passenger and keeps the dash height very low. At each end of the dashboard there are circular fresh air vents with two additional circular vents in the console and a small grille at the top of the dashboard.

Seats are polyurethane foam cushions and, while not as soft as those on the larger Citroens, they are firm and provided good support. And the driver's seat is adjustable for height, fore and aft movement, and it tilts and rakes.

True, it looks like a long GS. But it is a lot larger, while still having a wheelbase much shorter than the D's. The car was a well-kept secret before its official release two years ago and Peugeot's takeover at the time had helped take eyes away from what was a big thing for Citroen — a completely new model. Pre-release speculation did have it, though, that the car would have a Maserati-based V6, a GS engine with two cylinders added to make a flat-six, or a good rotary. They were wrong.

The DS in-line, water-cooled four it did get is a good engine and is much quieter than it was in the bigger cars. Citroen's flair for aerodynamics and penchant for the avant garde has made sure that the car is a superb tourer — and we could have driven it for a week and still been learning about it, and from it. But in the form we drove it it *was* undergeared.

The finish is good and exceeds anything produced here. Yet in France, the CX is a $5000 car — and its finish, ride and performance are what the French expect for that much money. In Australia the same car costs more than twice that much and is classed as an exotic car, with all the status implications attached. So, instead of appealing to the broad cross-section of people it should, it will be bought by the very few. But that is an anomaly all the harping in the world isn't going to fix.

WHEELS Editor, Peter Robinson, who took the CX after SPORTS CAR WORLD, summed things up nicely when we next saw him: "The great tragedy of the car is that people will buy it for its looks, only drive it around the city, and never realise its full potential." We couldn't have put it better ourselves. □

The Citroën CX2400 . . . even more handsome than its illustrious forbear, the DS.

CITROEN CX2400

road test

Fast, safe and outstandingly smooth

Some months ago, I tested the Citroën CX2200, my report including a technical analysis of the car's aerodynamics. Now, the slightly larger engine of the long-chassis Prestige model has become available in the normal-wheelbase saloons, and it is with one of these that the present road test is concerned. As the body shape is unchanged, those readers requiring an explanation of the low-drag airflow characteristics might care to look up the AUTOSPORT issue of March 25.

That report concerned the Pallas version, but this differs from the Super only in luxury furnishing. Both cars have the advanced but somewhat expensive Vari-power steering, which gives diminishing assistance as the speed rises and only half the number of steering wheel turns from lock to lock, compared with the plain steering of the standard model.

The larger engine develops an additional 5bhp which is scarcely enough to make the car appreciably faster. It also gives a very useful torque increase in the lower and middle ranges, which is at once noticeable in terms of improved liveliness and responsiveness, the 2400 picking up speed remarkably quickly after a check, with no need to change out of top gear. This is very pleasant, but it may also pay dividends in fuel economy by reducing gearchanging, a subject which concerns the French deeply. If the car is driven absolutely flat-out, the extra 170cc could cause a very small increase in petrol consumption, but during normal road motoring the opposite is the case.

This is a remarkably quiet car, the usual boom periods of a four-cylinder engine being absent. It is also outstandingly smooth, which may partly be due to the use of a heavy flywheel, noticeable as the engine slows for an upward gearchange. Nevertheless, it may be wondered whether or not the retention of a four-cylinder power unit is justified in a car of this class. The answer is that the Citroën gives an extra 5mpg compared with the two French V6-engined cars, yet its maximum speed is superior to that of the Peugeot 604 and of the same order as that of the Renault 30 TS. It cannot quite equal the six-cylinder machines for acceleration, but with the ever-rising cost of fuel one might accept that.

Obviously, it is the advanced aerodynamics of the Citroën that render such performance possible with a relatively modest power output. Here, the old firm still leads the world, for no sacrifices have to be made to obtain a low drag factor. Indeed, the remarkable space available for the rear passengers is outstanding and the flat boot floor, with no lip to obstruct the loading of luggage, is a feature that the owner will appreciate over and over again. The stability in side winds is another advantage, but the superb appearance of the car is one of its most endearing characteristics. This is functional streamlining at its best, like a greyhound compared with ordinary dogs.

In the past, some people have found the highly individual character of Citroëns a bit hard to take. The famous brake button of the DS has been replaced by a normal-looking pedal, though the fully-powered operation is the same, but few drivers find the brakes of the CX unusual nowadays. What they will find odd at first is the powered self-centring of the Vari-power steering.

The famous brake button of the DS has been replaced by a normal-looking pedal.

This makes manoeuvring delightfully easy, but the rapid straightening-up after a corner can be disconcerting at first. Let me assure my readers that one does become accustomed to the unusual response quite quickly, and the advantages are then so apparent that it's worth a little perseverance. Like the DS, the CX is a car of character, which makes no concession to people brought up on soggy, unresponsive vehicles, but we Citroën addicts know that with quick steering you can dodge the accident, which is a pretty good definition of safety.

The self-levelling suspension system is too well known to require any description. It gives an absolutely level ride that is incomparable, but there are circumstances when its very softness proves its undoing and the bumpstops come into play. This never happened during the present test, for which the suspension gets ten out of ten, but I did produce the effect on the hump-backs of the Montlhéry road circuit during a recent test. The extremely powerful brakes are so well compensated that the wheels do not tend to lock, even in the wet. I dislike hard seats, but the luxuriously soft ones of the CX are marvellously comfortable.

The gearchange works best when not excessively hurried. The particular car that I had for this test suffered from some vagueness of selection, but it was merely due to a loose bolt in the linkage, which was tightened in a matter of seconds. The heating and ventilation system worked well, but the heat was reluctant to be turned off once it was really going. This again may be a matter of simple adjustment, but I must speak as I find.

Whenever I think of Citroëns, I am reminded of many long, fast journeys that I have made over the years in the various versions of the DS. I think of bucking gales on the *autoroutes*, rushing up and down mountains, and flying over the ice and snow, always faster and more safely than I could have done it in almost any other car. I look forward to doing all those things in the CX in the future, and it is even more handsome than its illustrious forbear.

SPECIFICATION AND PERFORMANCE DATA

Car Tested: Citroën CX2400 Super 4-door saloon, price £4529 including car tax and VAT.
Engine: Four-cylinders 93.5 x 85.5mm (2347cc). Compression ratio 8.75 to 1. 115bhp at 5750rpm. Pushrod-operated overhead valves in hemispherical combustion chambers. Weber twin-choke down-draught carburettor.
Transmission: Single dry plate clutch. 4-speed synchromesh gearbox with central remote control, ratios 0.80, 1.13, 1.83, and 3.17 to 1. Final drive by helical-toothed spur gears, ratio 4.583 to 1.
Chassis: Steel monocoque with full-length sub-frame. Independent hydro-pneumatic self-levelling suspension of all four wheels, powered by engine-driven pump, with front wishbones and rear light-alloy trailing arms, plus anti-roll bars both ends. VariPower steering with fully-powered rack and pinion having variable assistance in inverse ratio to car speed and powered centring giving 2½ turns lock to lock. Fully power-operated dual-circuit disc brakes, ventilated in front, with compensation for weight transfer. Bolt-on steel wheels, fitted Michelin 185/175 SR15 tyres.
Equipment: 12-volt lighting and starting. Speedometer. Rev-counter. Fuel and temperature gauges. Clock. Pneumatic engine oil level gauge. Heating, demisting and ventilation system with heated rear windows. Electrically controlled front door windows. 2-speed windscreen wipers and washers. Flashing direction indicators. Reversing lights.
Dimensions: Wheelbase 9ft 4in. Track 4ft 10in/4ft 5.5in. Overall length 15ft 1in. Width 5ft 8in. Weight 1 ton 4½cwt.
Performance: Maximum speed 114mph. Speeds in gears, third 85mph, second 53mph, first 30mph. Standing quarter-mile 17.8s. Acceleration: 0-30mph 3.5s, 0-50mph 7.7s, 0-60mph 11.3s, 0-80mph 20s, 0-100mph 40.2s
Fuel Consumption: 24 to 30mpg.

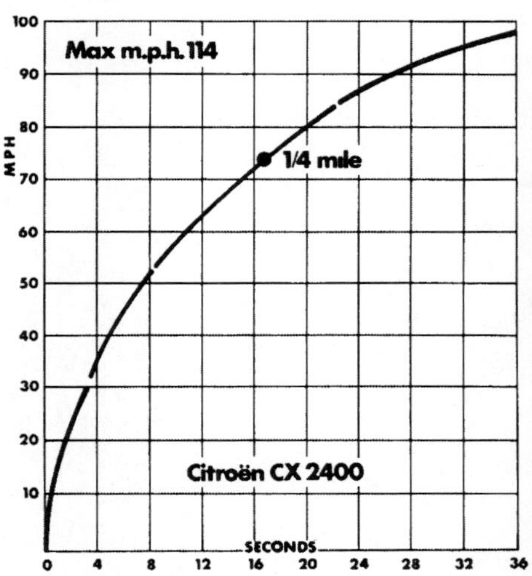

Above: The larger engine gives a very useful torque increase in the lower and middle ranges. Below: The flat boot floor, with no lip to obstruct the loading of luggage, is a feature that the owner will appreciate over and over again. Bottom: The superb appearance of the car is one of its most endearing characteristics.

Citroen CX2000 Safari *(17,000 miles)*

By Stuart Bladon

Long-suffering camion

IF EVER there was a year when it suited me personally to have a spacious estate car, 1976 was the one. With a move of house tackled in mid-summer, and all the subsequent constructional works which resulted, the Citroen Safari proved its worth over and over again. If it wasn't the occasion for moving the enormous mountain of debris that results when you dismantle a fireplace, it was on the countless other operations when cumbersome materials such as three-metre lengths of pipe had to be carried, that it came into worthy service over and over again.

When the needs of the weekend were not too space-demanding, the Safari was quickly wrested from me, frequently by Andrew Shanks to use as support car for his racing activities, and on one occasion by photographer Peter Cramer to use as a sort of motor caravan. Would you believe that two adults and four children of varying ages up to 11 can and did sleep in the back of the Safari?

We took delivery in April 1976, and the first trip of any length was a drive over to Droitwich for the launch of the new Rover 3500 a couple of months ahead of its introduction. A rare sight in those days, the enormous body of the Citroen Safari was source of considerable interest, as it has been ever since although many more of them are now to be seen around.

Running-in restrictions limited it to 4,000 rpm, which meant that 75 mph was permissible, but the loss of that quite important span from 4,000 to 5,500 rpm made it very difficult to overtake anything. I confess to being rather dismayed in those first few weeks at the lack of performance confronting me for the next few months. Partly, I think, it was the abrupt transition from my BMW 528, and partly, too, it was that I had not then adapted to Safari motoring. You soon learn that you have to build the speed up where you can, and are then able to keep it going quickly by making the best of its outstandingly reassuring and manageable cornering. Also, if the occasion calls for a burst of acceleration to overtake, it is surprising how well the Citroen responds once you get the right gear, rev the engine and give it a chance for the second choke to open.

Sensibly spaced gear ratios help one to make the best of the available power, but two litres really is not sufficient for such a big car. In all other respects it served admirably as a tow-car when used to pull a Bessacarr Denaby caravan to France in the summer, but the falling-off of speed on every gradient and an accumulation of frequent strings of vehicles wishing to go faster, was an embarrassment I have not previously suffered. At the time, only the 2000 Safari was available, but since then, the diesel

and the 2400 petrol versions have been added. The 2400 costs getting on for £500 extra, but is to be recommended.

Fairly high gearing and a good aerodynamic shape contribute to very good economy. The CX 2000 Safari has frequently returned more than 27 mpg on a run, even when cruising at more than 80 mph as we did on a September trip to Germany and France. Even when towing a caravan or large trailer, it gives better than 20 mpg.

In conjunction with a 15-gallon fuel tank, this gives a terrific range. It has proved an everyday occurrence to do well over 300 miles without refuelling, and on a few occasions we even stretched the distance between fill-ups to over 400 miles.

Standard modification when the Safari is equipped for towing is to duplicate the electrically-driven cooling fan. After this was done one was rather conscious of the roar from the front on the odd moment when low-speed work caused the fans to cut in, but they certainly deal with the heat build-up very competently. In all the hard work to which the Safari has been subjected, there has been no problem with overheating, nor has a single drop of water had to be added to the cooling system.

Its oleo-pneumatic suspension system with automatic self-levelling is one of the most outstanding features of the car. The ride is magnificent in all conditions, and the suspension is never caught out by any sudden dip in the road or hump back bridge taken fast. One of the joys of Citroen driving is that one can treat those sleeping policemen with the contempt they deserve, noting that the disturbance reduces the faster they are crossed!

Only two slight problems emerged with this suspension system, both concerned with the way in which the level collapses to its minimum position when the engine is switched off. The first is that if one is parked with the tail hanging over a high kerb or other protrusion one returns to the car to find it firmly aground, as though the tide had gone out while you were away. It takes about 15 seconds of fast idle to pump everything up again. The second snag is that when towing, the slight collapse of the rear end, on switching off the engine, can make it difficult or impossible to disconnect the trailer. One soon remembers to leave the engine ticking over for unhitching. These are small snags to set against the advantage of superb, level ride comfort in all conditions and regardless of load — in fact, the greater the weight, the more impressive is the car's behaviour.

Former colleague Michael Scarlett gave us this amusing account of a family outing in the Safari: "I say," said his father, "I'm terribly sorry about all this smoke coming from my pipe." A minute or two passed before someone made the obvious comment: "But you're *not* smoking your pipe!" They stopped to investigate the cause of large quantities of white smoke entering the car from somewhere underneath, and pinpointed a hydraulic leak dripping slowly on to the exhaust pipe. Inspection of the fluid reservoir showed the level well up, so they pressed on hopefully; but ir

In September the Safari was used for transport to Germany and then across to the Charles de Gaulle Airport at Paris, during which it performed faultlessly and impressed with its good economy. Opportunity was taken to photograph it with Concorde in the background

Long Term Report

due course the central row of warning lights, including the big one labelled "STOP", came on.

Citroen do not mean you to be unaware that the fluid level has dropped dangerously low, because loss of pressure would obviously affect the brakes as well as the suspension and power steering. A check button enables the driver to test the four important warning tell-tales, including that for engine temperature. There is also a check button to the right of the steering column which enables the fluid level to be registered while driving along; when pressed, it allows the hydraulic fluid to run into a little glass tube indicator, showing the level.

The fluid leak was repaired by Citroen under warranty. We were informed that it had come from one of the numerous suspension-related pipes under the car, which, as the French service manager told us, was "not well orientated".

In view of the hard work the Citroen has been put to in its nine months with us and the high mileage covered, now nearing 20,000, its reliability has proved fair enough but we have experienced some silly minor faults. The first of these was at 2,100 miles, when the right hand sidelamp and indicator unit fell out of its bumper housing and dangled on a single wire in front of the wheel. On refitting and reconnecting, the indicator did not work at first, as though still suffering from shock at the narrow escape from being trodden on by the wheel; but it soon recovered and gave no further trouble. Another, later on, was the bonnet release, which came undone and fell on to the floor (at 4,400 miles).

At the same time it was noticed that petrol was being lost from the fuel filler when the tank was full. A new filler cap was fitted, and provided it is fully tightened, this has given no further trouble.

Once or twice when submitting the Safari for service, I drew attention to a tiresome squeak, apparently coming from the rear seat. The Citroen service department were evidently unable to rectify it, and eventually as a two-man effort – one to drive and the other to explore – we tracked it down to the tailgate. Simple adjustment of the catch made the door close a little tighter, and stopped the squeak. But what Citroen *did* rectify unasked, was a faulty pressure limiting valve in the line to the rear brakes.

I had commented in an earlier report that we were experiencing premature brake locking. Citroen said it was only the third failure of this valve they had experienced on a CX, and the repair certainly transformed the braking performance – no more sliding on with locked wheels and attempting on and off footwork with the pedal; it has always stopped very well indeed since this attention. The brakes are generously big – discs front and rear–even for a car of this carrying capacity and pedal response is vigorous and not too abrupt. The handbrake is also beefy and used to be appreciated when I lived at a house with a sloping driveway. It works on the front discs.

In recent months the little amber warning light showing a drawing of a brake pedal tended to flash on. Handbook check showed it to mean "brake pads worn", not "brake fluid low" as had been suspected but a service check showed the pads to be not then ready for replacement. The light again came on with regularity though still not to any discernible pattern such as after hard braking, or when it's wet. It is still not time to renew the pads, however; at the last service a short-circuit in the warning system was repaired.

With a personal interest in car radios and tape players I tend to be a little pernickety about the ICE in my own car, and was rather horrified at the standard provision of a vertical radio slot in the CX. How do you see the tuning scale when it's mounted there, and what cassette player will work standing on its back? One or two do, it's true; but the majority don't.

We threw the problem at the Car Music Centre of 122 Shepherds Bush Centre, London W12 8PP, and were highly delighted at the original solution they evolved – as bizarre as the rest of the Citroen's interior stying. The radio – a Blaupunkt Essen – was fitted in an

Citroen CX2000 Safari

Maximum speeds

Gear	mph		kph		rpm	
	Staff	Saloon	Staff	Saloon	Staff	Saloon
Top (mean)	98	110	157	177	5,450	5,100
(best)	99	112	159	180	5,500	5,150
3rd	80	81	129	130	6,000	6,000
2nd	50	51	80	82	6,000	6,000
1st	28	29	45	47	6,000	6,000

Acceleration

True mph	Staff	Saloon	Staff	Saloon
30	5.1	3.9	33	31
40	7.7	6.3	44	41
50	11.6	8.7	54	52
60	16.8	12.2	64	61
70	22.9	16.8	75	71
80	37.3	22.1	88	81
90		31.1	96	91

Standing ¼-mile: 20.3 sec, 69 mph (staff); 18.8 sec, 73 mph (saloon)
Standing kilO: 37.0 sec, 79 mph (staff); 34.7 sec, 93 mph (saloon)

mph	Top		3rd		2nd	
10-30	--	--	10.2	8.8	5.6	4.8
20-40	17.3	13.4	9.3	8.1	5.3	4.6
30-50	16.7	12.5	9.0	7.5	6.1	4.9
40-60	16.0	12.7	9.7	7.5	--	--
50-70	18.1	12.6	12.0	8.8	--	--
60-80	24.5	14.3	15.4	10.6	--	--

Consumption

Overall mpg: 23.6 (12.0 litres/100km (staff); 23.1 (12.2 litres/100km) Saloon.

Note: *"Saloon" denotes performance figures for Citroen CX 2000 saloon tested in* Autocar *of 10 May, 1975 (Safari not tested so far).*

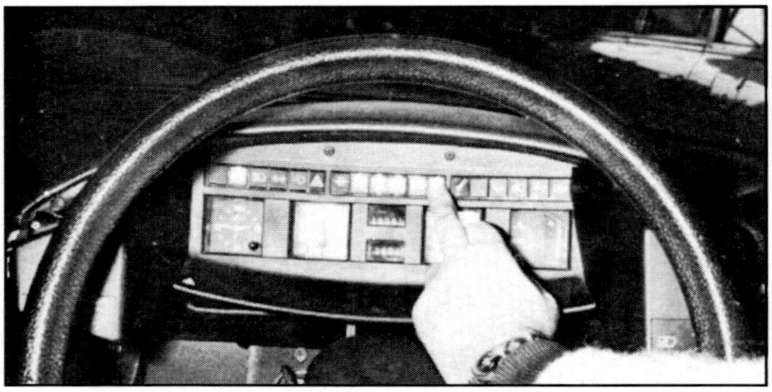

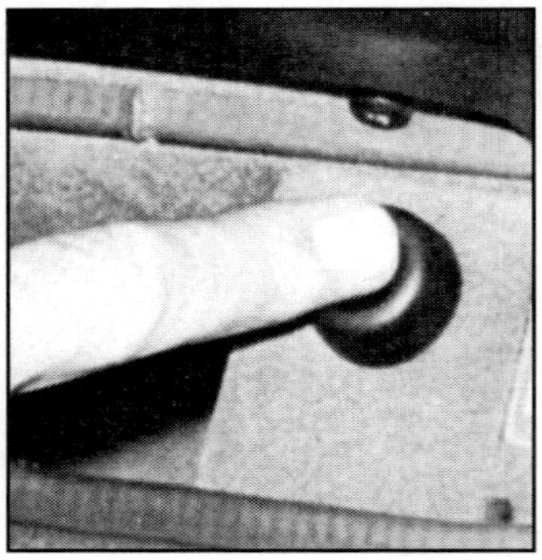

Test check button (above), allows the four main warning tell-tales to be tested, and hydraulic fluid level can be checked while driving along (right)

Left: The engine has kept reasonably clean although it is not an easy unit to wash down. Access to routine attention points is unexpectedly good

The standard Citroen tow hitch is very sturdy, and picks up on the main chassis members

enclosed box attached to the side of the instrument nascelle. It has proved a very convenient position for it, and the slight tremor of the set at tickover does not seem to have any ill effects.

The CX already comes with front door-mounted apertures for speakers, and we had two more speakers neatly installed on the rear quarters, with a front-rear balance control. The result was impressive and has given great pleasure throughout our use of the car.

However, we landed in trouble with Citroen, who said that removal of the console to house the radio's separate stereo unit, had resulted in disconnection of the ventilator outlets. Our complaint about lack of output from the central vents resulted in a bill for £20 for putting it all back together correctly.

Quite apart from this, I must confess that I find the ventilation the least pleasing aspect of the Safari – and, indeed, of any CX. In

Right: Just part of the maze of pipework related to suspension and brakes

Vertical vanes at the front (far right) channel cooling air into a scoop which leads it to the front disc brake on each side

Below: Looking rather like a police evidence picture of "where the body was found," this view of the Safari shows the scene after one of our staff used the car for a sans-tent family camping trip

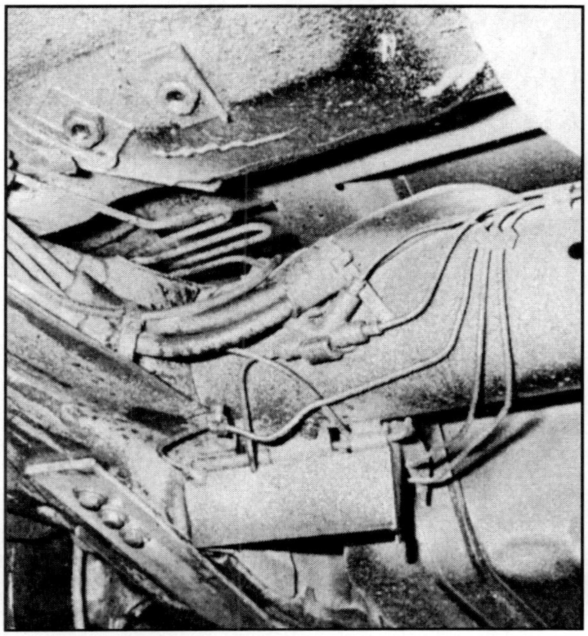

the long hot summer it was always a difficult car to keep cool enough without opening the side windows, which results in a lot of noise at speed; and too much heat always seemed to seep through the console. Now that winter is with us it is a car that is slow to warm up and needs the heater full on most of the time. Also, hardly any air at all comes through the heater unless the fan is kept on at least at its low-speed setting.

The electric windows have been appreciated and it seems a logical economy to mix electric front windows with manually-wound rear ones. The electric motors have a cut-out to prevent overload, such as when the windows have become frozen; and there has been no trouble with their operation. The electrical problem we did experience resulted from a short-circuit in the line to the roof lamp switch. Andrew Shanks was using the Safari as tender for a race meeting at Snetterton at the time, and in endeavours to isolate the fault, which kept blowing the fuse, he plucked more and more switches out, trapping their wires with loops of paper so that they did not disappear beyond recall into the bowels of the car.

You get two wipers with the Safari, and with typical Citroen logic they are positioned one at each end. The front wiper copes extremely well and although it leaves quite large areas unswept in the upper corner of the screen on each side, they are unimportant, and wet weather view is good. On its vigorous second speed, it clears heavy rain adequately well. Sometimes embarrassingly, sometimes conveniently, it chucks the water off sideways on to the adjacent car if the washers are used while waiting in traffic.

On my first journey with the Safari I used the rear window wiper, and then spent several miles trying to switch it off. I had not learned then that it automatically ends after 15 sweeps, and in attempting to switch off I kept re-energising the "on" switch. However this system does not work well. On wet roads, even if it's not raining, there is so much spray blowing up in the swirl at the back of the car that the rear wiper is needed continuously and it should have a positive on/off switch for constant running. Both front and rear washers operate on a pulse system (the rear one at the same time as the wiper is activated), and this works well and tends to conserve the water in the reservoirs.

Power steering is also standard with the Safari, and helps to make it very easy to berth this great length of car at the end of a run. Like the suspension, it takes a little while to get going fully after the first start of the day. At speed on the straight there is some trace of fidgety movement out of line, but the lesson here is not to be tempted to correct it. If the wheel is held straight, the car holds its course very well. I have often been astonished to step out of the car at the end of a run and find a strong wind blowing, when the good stability and aerodynamic shape had left the Safari almost totally unaffected.

It has always been part of my motoring upbringing that it was wrong to force the steering round while the car was not moving, so it comes as a contradiction of this way of life to run a Citroen CX, whose Varipower steering automatically self parks in the central position, even after you have switched off. The moment you release the wheel, if the steering is locked over, it promptly self-centres. The car thus always looks tidy, with its wheels pointing straight ahead – but is it good for tyres, steering linkages, and so on?

An early misadventure with the Safari left me glad to have a laminated windscreen as standard fitting. Accelerating away from a roundabout into a curving dual carriageway, I saw an oncoming lorry shed a load of stones which bounded across the rigid centre strip. Most of them I managed to avoid, but one caused a large star at the base of the screen. At first it looked as though we might get away with it, but during the heat of the day a large crack spread remorselessly across the glass. Owners would be wise to check that their insurance covers windscreen breakage, since a new one for the Safari costs some £100.

Opinions vary about the highly original layout of the CX facia. Personally, I don't like the digital speedometer and rev counter in which the figures move through a little window. It reminds me of the 1937 Morris 8 on which I did much of my early driving, and the speed cannot be gauged without looking at the instrument, in the way that is possible out of the peripheral vision with a large needle-on-dial speedometer. A small thumb wheel is located just under the nascelle on the right, for varying the "always on" illumination of rev counter and speedo.

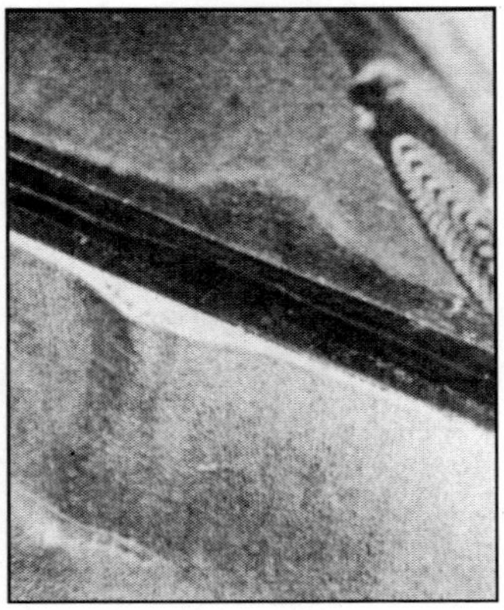

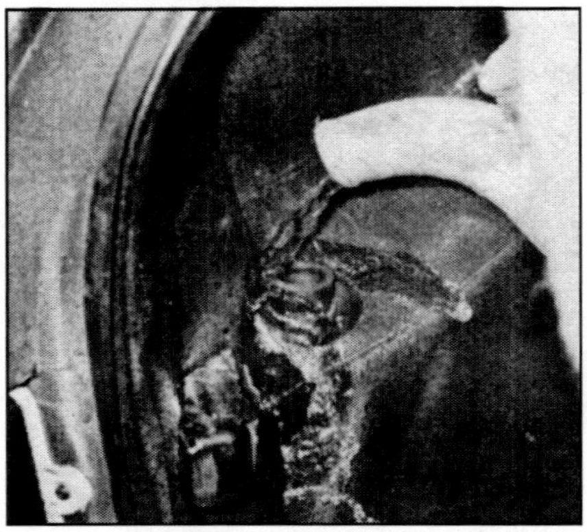

A few of the little snags with the Citroen Safari: ashtray that will no longer stay closed because the spring has gone (above, left); trim pulling away from the side seal in the load compartment (above); awkwardly placed filler for the rear window washer reservoir (left); and glove box awkward to close (below). As explained, these details did not spoil the overall enjoyment of the car's many good features

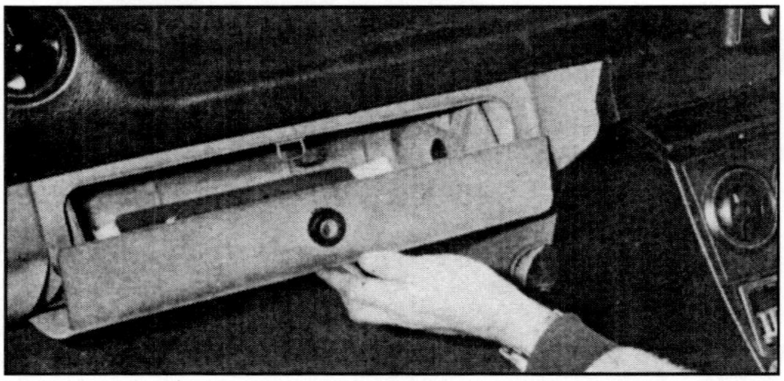

I value greatly the finger-tip controls for lamps, wipers and washers, all within easy reach of a hand still holding the wheel. The lighting arrangement is good, using the dipswitch to give choice of dipped or side lamps for urban streets, when the main lighting switch is at the side lamp position. They are halogen lamps and give good range but are restricted when dipped. Indicators which do not self cancel are an old Citroen tradition which I find no hardship. At least they don't self-cancel when you don't want them to, in response to some small movement of the wheel.

A detail dislike is its ashtray which proves difficult to empty and is almost designed to lose its little spring so that the lid won't stay closed. Cold weather also drew attention to a problem with the door locks, that they are prone to freeze up and become very difficult to turn without risk of breaking the key. It's a nuisance, also, that the front passenger door can't be locked from outside without using the key.

These are all minor points which detract little from the overall impression of a sturdy, reliable and long-suffering workhorse which asks to be driven hard. Chafing marks on the floor mat in the back tell of the amount of load carrying we have done with the Safari; but the car has stood up well, and the lack of underbody corrosion noted is most impressive. For any potential buyer who needs the space, my advice would be that the CX Safari is a choice that certainly will not be regretted – but, you *do* need the extra power of the 2400. □

Cost of ownership

Running costs	Life in miles	Cost per 10,000 miles (£)
One gallon of 4-star fuel, average cost today 80p	23.6	338.98
One pint of top-up oil, average cost today 38p	1,000	3.80
Front disc pads (set of 4) at £16.90 inc VAT	20,000	8.45
Rear brake linings (set of 4) at £11.55 inc VAT	20,000	5.78
Michelin XVS tyres (front pair) at £37.64 each (average)	35,000	32.26
Michelin XVS tyres (rear pair)	See note	nil
Service (main interval and actual cost incurred)	3,000	40.62
Total		429.89
Running cost per mile:	**4.3p**	
Approx. standing charges per year		
***Insurance**		76.40
Tax		40.00
Depreciation		
Price when new		4 231
Trade in cash value (approx.)		3,800
Typical advertised price (current)		4,000
Total cost per mile (based on cash value)	**9.8p**	

**Insurance cost is lowest figure obtainable from Quotel for average driver of clean record paying £25 excess, and after deduction of full no claims bonus, and with car garaged in Hertfordshire. The spread of insurance quotes given by Quotel is narrow, with a maximum after-NCB payment of £88.*

Tyres were measured at 15,600 miles and found to be still reading over 8mm at the rear, against the original new depth of 8.7mm. Rear tyre wear can, therefore, be regarded as negligible and it would be logical to alternate them with the front tyres, effectively doubling the life there.

Specification

Engine: 4-cyl, 86.0 x 86.0 mm (3.39 x 3.39 in), 1985 c.c. (121.8 cu. in.); CR 9.0 to 1; one Weber carb, 102 bhp (DIN) at 5,500 rpm; max torque 112 lb. ft. (15.5 mkg) at 3,000 rpm.

Transmission: Front engine, front drive. Manual overall ratios 3.82, 5.39, 8.73, 15.12. Top gear mph/1,000 rpm 19.2.

Suspension: ifs, transverse arms, oleo-pneumatic. Rear, independent, trailing arms, oleo-pneumatic. Steering, rack and pinion (power assisted).

Brakes: Disc front and rear (servo), 10.2 in. front discs 9.3 in. rear discs.

Dimensions: Wheelbase, 10 ft. 1.75 in. (309.25 cm); front track 4 ft. 10in. (147.3 cm), rear track 4 ft. 5.5 in. (133.4 cm). Overall length, 16 ft. 2 in. (492.8 cm), width 5 ft. 8 in. (172.7 cm), height 4 ft. 9.75 in. (146.7 cm),. Turning circle 36 ft (109 m). Unladen weight 3053 lb. (1388 kg); max. payload 1510 lb. (686 kg).

Others: Tyres 185SR-14 in.; 5.5 in. rims; fuel 15 galls (68 litres).

CITROEN CX DIESEL

SCORNING BOTH FLYING machines and high-powered road transport, we opted for a diesel Citroen CX to take us on the 1500mile London-Turin-London journey. We had to go to Turin for the Salon (see CAR January '76) and we wanted to do it economically; we also had had little experience using diesels over long distances. Citroen gave us the choice of saloon or estate, but we chose the saloon for its more comfortable rear seat and for the simple fact that nicking visitors' possessions from parked cars is practically the national sport in Italy and estate cars leave you rather naked in that respect.

The CX diesel specification matches that of the Super saloon. Nothing has been trimmed off, so that electric windows and power steering are standard. The differences are restricted to under-bonnet matters and a label on the cabin window above the filler neck that warns: diesel only. Even under the bonnet there's not a great deal of difference; the transverse engine looks very much as it does in petrol versions until you notice the absence of a carburettor and distributor. A formidable fuel injection system is a predominant feature, adding a few more tubes and pipes to the spaghetti that winds its way around the compartment.

There is nothing complex about starting the diesel from cold. You simply turn on the ignition and wait until the red light that inhabits the slot normally reserved for the tachometer extinguishes itself. You then turn the key the rest of the way and the big battery turns the engine over; that combustion-chamber pre-heating ritual ensures that it fires quickly, even if it does take a few miles before the traditional diesel clatter subsides as the components reach their working temperatures. I always find it rather ironical that one of the main reasons the steam car failed was that potential customers objected to waiting a couple of minutes while the boiler got up steam. Yet I have never heard the cold-start delay being held against diesels.

The compression-ignition CX's performance is not startling. Nevertheless, it managed the sort of acceleration that one would expect to find in, say, a 1.3litre saloon. So with four occupants and luggage, overtaking must be planned with care, for there is not a sufficiently large margin of acceleration in third and top to play traffic games. Once on the autoroutes of France, however, the diesel was pacey enough, being capable of reaching its cruising/maximum speed in the early nineties and holding it for long periods in both silence and comfort. Once the CX is into third and top gears there is never any real indication that the power is courtesy of Diesel and not Otto. It is just the same relaxed feeling that's common to all CXs and which is one of their really great virtues. Diesels, of course, are very common in France because they are cheap to run, which was the purpose of our exercise.

The CX was topped-up in Slough, driven into London and from there to Dover, then Calais, Arras, onto the autoroute, leaving it to go on to Nantua where we stayed at France's answer to Fawlty Towers but with the advantage of a marvellous restaurant. From Nantua to the Mont Blanc Tunnel and down to Turin via Aosta. The return was just about a repeat performance with a diversion back to the Mont Blanc Tunnel because the Mont Cenis pass was closed, and another in France while we found suitable food and accommodation at Bourg-en-Bresse: very suitable on both counts as it happened, thanks again to the seemingly infallible Michelin Guide.

Now the startling thing in all this was that taking the CX diesel saved us £28 over a petrol-engined vehicle giving the same fuel consumption. There is a massive differential between diesel and petrol prices in Italy, a substantial one in France and minimal advantage in the UK. If we were making regular visits to France and Italy to sell UK-made wares, then nothing on earth would talk us out of a diesel car, be it Peugeot, Opel or Citroen. The economic facts are simple and speak for themselves, but there are some hidden advantages as well as expenses. For example, diesel engines require far more frequent oil changes than their petrol counterparts and in fact we had to top up the CX when the sump ran low after about 1000miles of motoring. This is apparently normal, for there is an under-bonnet compartment specially designed to take a Total engine-oil container; the garage-man was so surprised not to find one already in place that he went to pains to point out what it was for and to insert the appropriate container. On the other hand, a plus feature is that diesel engines last longer than petrol engines and the time between major overhauls is subsequently markedly reduced. And that, in a way, is what diesel-engined cars are all about. To get the full advantage of both the fuel economy and the engine longevity you really need to do either a very big mileage or plan to keep the vehicle for a very long time.

RON WAKEFIELD

Citroën Cx 2200 Diesel

Manufacturer: Société Anonyme Auto. Citroën
133 Quai André Citroën
75747 Paris, France

Vehicle type: front-engine, front-wheel-drive, 5-passenger

Price as tested: $7500 f.o.b. Paris (approx.)

Engine type: 4-in-line, water-cooled Diesel cast-iron block and aluminum head, fuel injection

Displacement	133 cu in, 2175cc
Power (SAE net)	66 hp @ 4500 rpm
Transmission	4-speed manual, all-synchro
Wheelbase	112.0 in
Length	183.5 in
Curb weight	3020 lbs

• How do you describe a Citroën adequately? Unique, stubbornly different, defiantly French—all apply. The Cx, top of the current line, is all that and more. All the traditional Citroën elements are there: front drive, hydropneumatic suspension, fully powered brakes, aerodynamic body and strange controls that force you to learn driving all over.

Now the Cx can be had with a Diesel engine. Strangely, the Diesel itself is conventional; it clatters like the others, actually a bit more. Acceleration is sleepy, but fuel economy is great. Good aerodynamics help it to a respectable top speed, and it will cover nearly 400 miles per fillup.

Superb riding comfort and the semi-plush, ultra-modern interior make the Cx a real passenger's car. Wind noise is low, and even with the self-igniter the high-speed cruising is quiet. But the driver, on the other hand, suffers. For all the high-flying and worthwhile technicalities, he has to shut off the directional signals after a turn. The gearbox is recalcitrant, and the fancy brakes grab.

Power steering is new, and the Cx certainly needed it. Like the old SM's system, it assists less as you steer away from center position or drive faster. But at that center position, it is too sensitive, even at high speed. Lane changes on the freeway are hair-raising, a sort of combination between old Cadillac and old Corvair, complete with rear-end swings and body rolls. In the city, you have to learn to restrain the wheel from its power-assisted return action; otherwise, it may overshoot.

Perhaps it's just as well that Citröen is inactive in the American market now. The Cx, Diesel or no, is probably too eccentric for its own good. •

Citroen CX 2200 Diesel

Equivalent model to CX2200 Super, with 2.2-litre diesel engine.
Little noise or refinement penalty; valuable gains in economy; reasonable performance.
Good stability and steering, predictable cornering and superb ride comfort.
Excess nose weight gives slight tendency to lock up in heavy braking, but brake response very good.
A potentially long-life low cost car of great comfort and spaciousness

OUR RECENT foreign touring number revealed the tremendous difference between petrol and diesel prices on the Continent, particularly in France where diesel costs only about half as much as derv. With this discrepancy in its favour, as well as the potentially better economy, it is astonishing that almost every Frenchman does not run a diesel car, and even more surprising that it was only last year — following a preliminary announcement at the 1975 Frankfurt Show — that Citroen added diesel cars to their range.

Only one diesel unit is available, known as the M22.621, and it is offered for the Safari estate car as well as the saloon tested here. Derived from a Citroen commercial unit first launched in the C35 van in 1975, the engine is an in-line four-cylinder unit with capacity of 2,175 c.c. It has exactly the same bore and stroke as the 2200 petrol engine, but compression is raised from the normal 9-to-1 of the petrol unit to 22.25-to-1. It is a pushrod ohv engine, with high-mounted side camshaft driven by pinion. As for all the CX range, the engine is mounted transversely at the front, driving the front wheels, and leans forward at an angle of 30 deg to the vertical.

In diesel form, the engine produces 66 bhp instead of 112 bhp (both figures DIN), and reaches peak output 1,000 rpm lower, at 4,500 rpm. The reduction in peak torque is much less marked, with 93 lb. ft. available at 2,750 rpm, against the 123 at 3,500 rpm value for the 2200 petrol unit.

Bare comparison of performance figures for the diesel give a false impression that it is a lot slower than it proves to be on the road. An acceleration time of over 20 sec to reach 60 mph from rest is on a par with some of the bigger motor caravans, and is getting on for twice as long as the 2200 petrol car takes. By the time the diesel has accelerated through the gears to 80 mph, the petrol version would have reached well over 100 mph.

For many buyers, however, all out acceleration is not a topic for major concern, and we should emphasize that all the time we had the Citroen diesel we were impressed by its relative liveliness, rather than despondent at the sluggishness implied by the acceleration figures.

To a great degree this is due to the sensible spacing of the gears, which allows the best use to be made of the engine. The indirect ratios are all the same as for the petrol car, but a slightly lower overall ratio is produced by use of 13/62 reduction gears to give a 4.77-to-1 final drive against the

2200's 4.58. Top gear is a slightly geared-up indirect ratio to give a 3.81 overall ratio in top, and an effective 19.3 mph at 1,000 rpm.

Maximum speeds in the indirect gears are 24 (which is on the high side for a diesel car's first gear), 42 and 66 mph. By the time these limits are approached one can sense that further revving is of no avail and that a change up is due, and this does mean that one can sometimes feel the engine is running out of revs rather early when overtaking in third. If so, the gear change is so good and positive that no effective time is lost in a quick change up to top.

There is a popular misconception of diesels that they produce a great deal of torque at low revs. This is perhaps owed to the type of vehicle for which diesel engines are usually developed, and in a high speed diesel for car use the reverse is true: response at low speeds is somewhat lacking. The car calls for free use of that very sturdy and easily manageable gearbox to get the best out of it. What is noticed is the effect of the heavier flywheel, whose great inertia enabled the car to surprise the testers with a shriek of wheelspin when making its full power starts from the line. It helps, for smooth progression through the gears, to keep the throttle partly open.

Diesel cars generally have improved greatly in terms of control simplicity in recent years, and the old days of separate start and stop controls have passed. The Citroen is right up to date in this respect, having just a single key control for the engine combined with a steering column lock. For a cold start it is turned first to the warm-up position, which activates the glow plugs in the cylinder head for initial starting. A red warning light comes on to reveal that the pre-heater plugs are switched on, and the key can be left at this position until the warning light goes out.

On one morning of bitter frost, we left the key at this warm-up position while de-icing the windows, and by the time this operation was completed in four minutes, the light was still showing, yet an immediate start was possible and no doubt would have been much earlier. The tell-tale soon goes out once the engine starts, and in more normal weather we found that a 20-second warm-up spell with the pre-heater plugs was adequate for a first time start. It seemed to help, also, to use the starter without opening the throttle at all. The engine would begin to fire after about three or four seconds' running on the starter motor, and was then ready for full power almost immediately. There seemed none of the usual delay associated with a cold petrol engine, and when driving off one notices the lack of water vapour from the exhaust.

On switching off, the key is just turned to the off position, locking the steering, and the engine stops with a slight convulsion as it comes to rest against the heavy compression.

Above: The engine itself is very different in appearance from that of the petrol CX and has different air intake arrangements, but otherwise under the bonnet is the same crowded but surprisingly accessible scene

Only an extra "D" on the name plate instantly tells this is a diesel car, so prominent notices on and above the filler flap are necessary

One's neighbours will soon be aware that one is running a diesel car, and they will hear every departure since the engine is very noisy to anyone outside, especially when it is cold and has not had time for the clearances to reduce with metal expansion. Inside the car, the noise level is extremely well suppressed and is certainly not objectionable. It is a little more noisy than the equivalent Citroen petrol car, but the difference is not very great, and is certainly not sufficient for an unknowledgeable passenger to notice any difference. When passing between buildings, especially with a window open, the clatter echoed back reminds one that the quietness inside is owed to excellent insulation of the bulkhead, and that for outside observers it is very noisy indeed.

Ahead of its competitors in many respects, this Citroen diesel is exceptionally smooth; it pulls strongly over a reasonably wide rev range, and there is no snatch or abrupt loss of power when it is taken up to the governed rev limit at 5,000 rpm in the indirect gears. On motorways the Citroen diesel proved well able to sustain the sort of 80-85 mph which is the norm for today's business car traffic, and its ultimate maximum speed on the level of 89 mph can be exceeded downhill without over-revving since the governor allows a 5,000 rpm maximum engine speed.

Fuel consumption

Whoever buys a diesel car will do so primarily for its potential economy, and they will certainly not be disappointed. The 2200D returned an overall fuel consumption of 31.8 mpg for the full test, which is very creditable for a car of this size, including a lot of town work plus fast cruising on motorways. Several intermediate checks, including the one which covered performance testing at MIRA, returned over 33 mpg.

Because of the limited performance available we suspect that the normal consumption obtained by owners will be closer to our hard driving test figures than is usually the case. One should therefore regard 35 mpg as a normal target consumption. Derv in Britain currently costs about 2-3p per gallon less than petrol, but its relationship can be, and indeed is, altered by the Government's fuel tax structure with regularity and without apparent rhyme or reason. Comparative overall consumption for the 2200 petrol was 23.5 mpg.

The same fuel tank is fitted, with a capacity of 15 gallons, so the 2200D has a phenomenal range. A full tank would take the car easily from London to Glasgow (420 miles). A fuel warning light is fitted among the row of tell-tales, and of course it is important not to run out because of potential difficulty in priming the injectors. No drop in oil level was noticed during the test. Engine oil must be of special grade for diesel engines; the level can be checked from inside the car using the pneumatic test button to the right of the facia.

Handling, ride and steering

Inevitably we have concentrated in this test on the differences due to the engine, since the rest of the car is very much the same as for the CX2000, as far as equipment is concerned. The 2200D must set some sort of new record in having nearly 70 per cent of the total weight on the front wheels, yet there is no direct awareness of this for the driver. The Varipower steering gives ample assistance to take the hard work out of pulling the nose of the car through corners, and the Michelin XVS tyres give such good grip that there is no tendency to slide straight on when cornering, even when braking. The exception is when driving on snow, when the nose-heavy handling calls for some caution.

Steering effort remains largely consistent, since the assistance given reduces as speed goes up. It is extremely accurate, coupled with the prominent directional stability resulting from such forward weight distribution, and the result is that the car is easy to hold straight at speed even in strong cross winds. With such sensitive steering, any slight movement off line tends to be noticed and it is best to avoid the temptation to do too much correction, or a weaving motion can result.

At low speeds the steering becomes noticeably heavier even with this varying rate of assistance, but still little effort is needed for acute changes of lock when parking. What one is having to overcome is not so much the resistance of the wheels, as the strong self-centring action of the steering. If the wheel is released, it spins rapidly back to the central position, and this happens even with the car at rest and the engine switched off.

Ride comfort afforded by the oleo-pneumatic suspension has been a Citroen legend for years and is equally impressive on the CX diesel. It is self-levelling to compensate for load and absorbs undulations magnificently. Sharp bumps or potholes produce a slight jolt and thump, but the suspension is generally above criticism and is an outstanding feature of this most comfortable car. A lever between the seats allows the ride height to be altered, chiefly to give extra ground clearance when needed for rough ground.

Upper part of facia panel is moulded in polyurethane, with the separate instruments and control panel mounted on it. Fingertip controls on the flying saucer-shaped panel are for indicators, horn, windscreen wipers / washers, and hazard warning on the left-hand extension and headlamps, flasher, dipswitch and panel rheostat on the right-hand one. Instruments are (from left to right) clock, speedometer, total and trip mileage recorders, pre-heater telltale, battery condition and fuel tank contents gauges, and there is a comprehensive row of warning lamps set above the instruments. On the right of the cubby hole alongside the steering column is a check gauge for engine oil level. The centre console houses a fresh air grille, the radio, directional fresh air vents, ashtray, cigarette lighter and controls for electric window lifts, heated rear window, and interior lamp. The heater controls are fore and aft slide levers set alongside the handbrake (behind the gearlever)

Specification

ENGINE	Front, front drive
Cylinders	4 in line, transverse
Main bearings	5
Cooling	Water
Fan	Electric
Bore, mm (in)	90 (3.54)
Stroke, mm (in)	85.5 (3.37)
Capacity, c.c. (in)	2,175 (132.7)
Valve gear	ohv
Camshaft drive	Gears
Compression ratio	22.25-to-1
Fuel	Derv
Carburation	Bosch Rotary or Roto Diesel injection
Max power	66 bhp (DIN) at 4,500 rpm
Max torque	92.6lb. ft. at 2,750 rpm
TRANSMISSION	
Type	Four-speed, all synchromesh
Clutch	Single plate, diaphragm

Gear	Ratio	mph/1000 rpm
Top	0.8	19.3
3rd	1.13	13.6
2nd	1.83	8.4
1st	3.17	4.8

Final drive gear	Helical spur
Ratio	4.77-to-1
SUSPENSION	
Front—location	Independent, upper and lower transverse arms
springs / dampers	Hydropneumatic units
anti-roll bar	Yes
Rear—location	Independent, trailing arms
springs / dampers	Hydropneumatic units
anti-roll bar	Yes
STEERING	
Type	Rack and pinion
Power assistance	Varipower standard
Wheel diameter	14in.
BRAKES	
Front	10.2in. dia disc
Rear	8.6in. dia disc
Servo	Hydraulic
WHEELS	
Type	Pressed steel
Rim width	5½J
Tyres—make	Michelin
—type	XVS radial
—size	185 (front), 175 (rear), 14in.
EQUIPMENT	
Battery	12 volt 88Ah
Alternator	72 amp
Headlamps	4 lamp halogen, 90/190 watt (total)
Reversing lamp	Standard
Hazard warning	Standard
Electric fuses	10
Screen wipers	2-speed
Screen washer	Electric
Interior heater	Water valve
Interior trim	Jersey seats, PVC headlining
Floor covering	Carpet
Jack	Screw pillar
Jacking points	2 each side under sills
Windscreen	Laminated
Underbody protection	Tectyl
MAINTENANCE	
Fuel tank	15 Imp. galls (68 litres)
Cooling system	12.5 pints (inc heater)
Engine sump	7.7 pints SAE
Gearbox and final drive	2.8 pints SAE
Grease	No points
Valve clearance	Inlet 0.006in. Exhaust 0.008in. (cold)
Contact breaker	None
Ignition timing	N/A
Spark plug	N/A
Tyre pressures	F29; R 29 psi (normal driving)
Max payload	1,034lb (470kg)

Maximum Speeds

Gear	mph	kph	rpm
Top (mean)	89	143	4,600
(best)	90	145	4,650
3rd	66	106	4,850
2nd	42	68	5,000
1st	24	39	5,000

Acceleration

True mph	Time (sec)	Speedo mph
30	**5.9**	32
40	**9.3**	43
50	**14.6**	53
60	**20.8**	63
70	**30.8**	74
80	**50.8**	84
90	—	96

Standing ¼-mile:
21.9 sec, 61 mph
kilometre:
40.7 sec, 74 mph

mph	Top	3rd	2nd
10-30	—	9.4	5.6
20-40	14.2	9.2	6.2
30-50	14.7	9.6	—
40-60	22.4	11.1	—
50-70	29.3	—	—
60-80	30.1	—	—

Consumption

Fuel
Overall mpg: 31.8
(8.9 litres/100km)
Calculated (DIN) mpg: 33.3
(8.5 litres/100km)

Constant speed:

mph	mpg
30	60.3
40	55.3
50	49.6
60	41.8
70	36.6
80	30.4

Autocar formula
Hard driving, difficult conditions
28.6 mpg
Average driving, average conditions
35.0 mpg
Gentle driving, easy conditions
41.3 mpg

Grade of fuel: Derv
Mileage recorder: 2 per cent over reading

Oil
Consumption (SAE 30/HD3C) negligible

Regular Service

	Interval		
Change	**3,000**	**6,000**	**12,000**
Engine oil	Yes	Yes	Yes
Oil filter	No	Yes	Yes
Gearbox oil	No	No	Yes
Spark plugs	None	None	None
Air cleaner	No	Clean	No
C/breaker	None	None	None
Total cost	**£2.75**	**£12.92**	**£25.85**

(Assuming labour at £5.50/hour)

Brakes

Fade *(from 68 mph in neutral)*
Pedal load for 0.5g stops in lb

	start/end		start/end
1	30/35	6	35
2	30/35	7	35
3	35	8	35
4	35	9	30
5	35	10	30

Response *(from 30 mph in neutral)*

Load	g	Distance
20lb	0.40	75ft
40lb	0.75	40ft
50lb	0.85	35ft
60lb	0.95	32ft
Handbrake	0.35	86ft

Max gradient 1 in 3

Clutch

Pedal 40lb and 5½in

Test Conditions

Wind: 8-10 mph
Temperature: 3 deg C (38 deg F)
Barometer: 28.7in Hg
Humidity: 100 per cent
Surface: wet asphalt and concrete (dry for final brake test)
Test distance 781 miles

Figures taken at 5,400 miles by our own staff at the Motor Industry Research Association proving ground at Nuneaton

Parts Cost

(including VAT)

Brake pads (2 wheels) —front	£15.65
Brake pads (2 wheels) —rear	£10.69
Silencer(s)	£23.94/18.96
Tyre—each (typical advertised)	£37.64
Windscreen	£82.08
Headlamp unit	£50.78
Front wing	£35.34
Rear bumper	£84.11

Warranty Period
12 months unlimited mileage

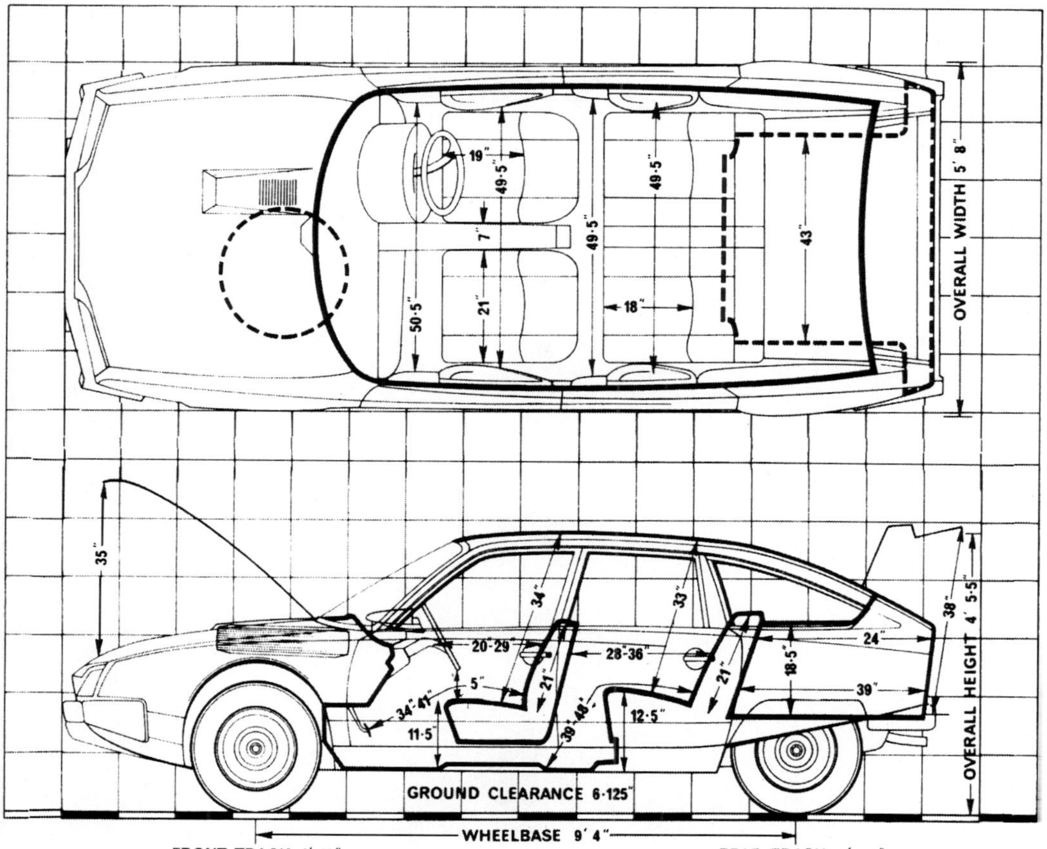

FRONT TRACK 4' 10"　　REAR TRACK 4' 5·5"

Weight

Kerb, 28.0cwt/3,140lb/1,426kg
(Distribution F/R, 67.9/32.1)
As tested,
31.57cwt/3,536lb/1,605kg

Boot capacity: 16.8cu.ft.

Turning circles:
Between kerbs
L, 35ft 9in; R, 35ft 4in
Between walls
L, 38ft 8in; R, 38ft 6in
Turns, lock to lock, 2.5

Test Scorecard

(Average of scoring by *Autocar* Road Test team)

Ratings: *6 Excellent*
5 Good
4 Better than average
3 Worse than average
2 Poor
1 Bad

PERFORMANCE	3.35
STEERING AND HANDLING	4.25
BRAKES	4.40
COMFORT IN FRONT	3.75
COMFORT IN BACK	4.57
DRIVER'S AIDS *(instruments, lights, wipers, visibility, etc)*	4.00
CONTROLS	3.63
NOISE	4.17
STOWAGE	3.67
ROUTINE SERVICE *(under-bonnet access: dipstick, etc)*	3.56
EASE OF DRIVING	3.72
OVERALL RATING	**3.93**

Comparisons

Car	Price (£)	max mph	0-60 (sec)	overall mpg	capacity (c.c.)	power (bhp)	wheelbase (in.)	length (in.)	width (in.)	kerb weight (lb)	fuel (gal)	tyre size
Citroen CX2200D	**4,699**	**89**	**20.8**	**31.8**	**2,175**	**66**	**112**	**181**	**68**	**3,140**	**15.0**	**185/175HR14**
Citroen CX2000 Super	3,956	110	12.2	23.2	1,985	102	112	181	68	2,788	15.0	185/175HR14
Mercedes-Benz 300D (A)	7,600	90	20.8	25.7	3,005	80	110	186	70.3	3,290	17.2	175SR14
Opel Rekord 2100D (A)	3,988	81	27.4	27.0	2,068	60	105	180	67.8	2,773	15.4	175SR14
Peugeot 504D	4,042	84	21.7	31.1	1,948	56	108	177	66.5	2,607	12.3	165SR14

Brakes

Ventilated disc brakes are fitted all round, and there is a pressure limiting valve in the line to the rear brakes. There is very strong servo assistance, such that only 40 lb load on the pedal, which is little more than is needed to work the clutch, gave 75 per cent efficiency. When first tested, on wet roads, this proved almost the maximum obtainable before the car began to skid. On dry roads, a 95 per cent stop is obtainable. Fade tests at three-quarters of maximum speed (68 mph) produced consistent, unaffected results.

A sturdy pull-up handbrake to the left of the driving seats holds the car securely and coped easily with the 1-in-3 test hill. Surprisingly, in view of the limited power and fairly high bottom gear, the car proved able to restart on this very testing gradient.

Comfort, fittings and equipment

Comments in our recent Citroen Safari *Long Term Report* need to be repeated in respect of the 2200D, concerning the unsuitability of the car for cold weather. The door locks are so prone to freeze up that it proved almost essential to leave the car unlocked at night, and the output of the heater is slow to build up and is inadequate for a frosty morning. Best delivery is from the central vents on the console, though most people prefer to have the warm air blowing directly on to their feet.

In other respects, the Citroen is a generously equipped, well-appointed and very comfortable car. There is a lockable drop-down glove box beneath the facia in front of the passenger, plus an open pigeon hole to the right of the steering column. All instruments and switches are neatly grouped in and around the broad hooded nascelle, and the single spoke steering wheel (a Citroen tradition dating back to the original DS of 1955) gives an unobstructive view of the instruments.

The speedometer is digital, its figures being enlarged by a lens in the face of the instrument. A thumb wheel protruding beneath the finger-tip switch block on the right controls its illumination, which is independent of the side lamps. No rev counter is fitted, and the space normally occupied by this on petrol models houses the pre-heater telltale. The background features Citroen's chevron trademark, and it seems rather pointless for this to be illuminated as well. A clock with second hand is fitted to the left of the speedometer, and a fuel gauge and battery capacity indicator are in the matching square on the right.

The single wiper blade, centrally mounted, clears a large area of the screen, and its switch control is so conveniently placed for trigger operation by the driver's left hand on the wheel that the lack of any intermittent action or linked wash/wipe system is not a nuisance.

Distinctive and aerodynamically efficient shape has marked the bigger Citroens for over 20 years. The streamlining is proportionately more advantageous with 66 bhp of diesel instead of 112 bhp of the outwardly identical petrol 2200

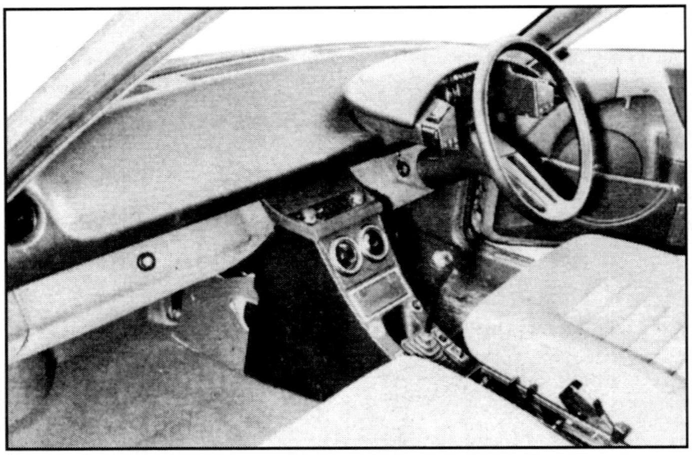

Unuausl and futuristic style extends to the interior, where seats front and rear provide great comfort. Matching of moulded door handles with one piece door mouldings is not the neatest feature. Windows on this version are electrically operated at front, manual at the rear; absence of winders on front doors provides extra pocket space

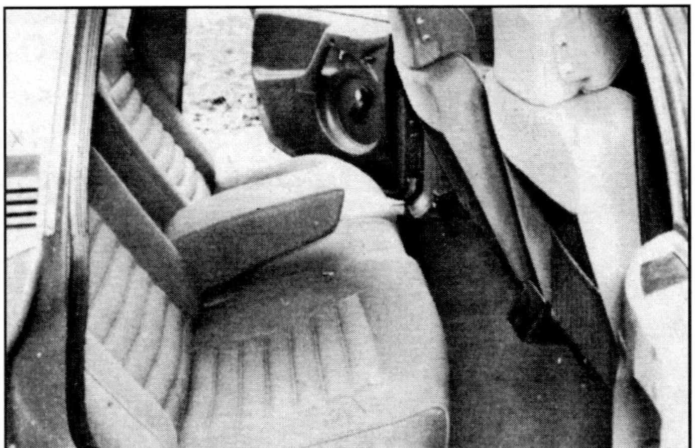

Boot is deeper than CX's exterior appearance might suggest, and the sill is down at the bumper line making loading of heavy objects easy. Floor is flat and unimpeded by spare wheel, which lives under the bonnet

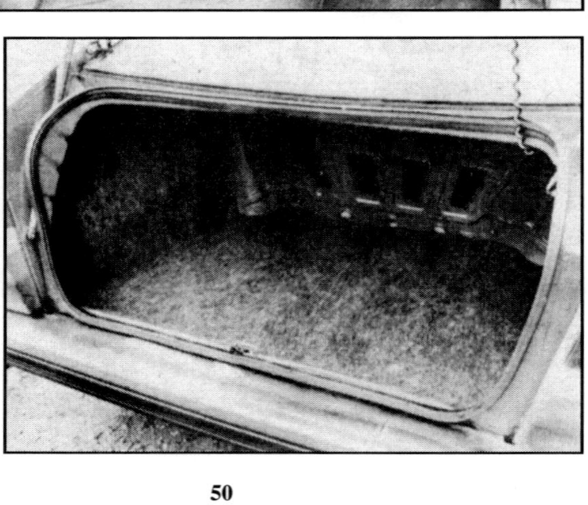

The seats are extremely comfortable, well-shaped, and have a measure of vertical adjustment as well as a lever to provide notched settings of the backrest. The front windows are electrically operated by a switch either side of the gear lever. Matching switches farther back control the heated rear window and interior lamp, which is adequately bright for map-reading at night.

Wind noise level is excellently low, so is the amount of road noise from the wheels on coarse surfaces. We do not consider these assessments to be influenced in relation to the rather higher than usual degree of engine noise.

Where it fits in

In all important respects, the equipment and furnishing of the diesel are the same as for the CX2400 Super; the CX2200 petrol is no longer listed. Exceptions are deletion of the rev counter and (obviously) the choke with its related warning light, and automatic (C-matic) transmission is not available. It is priced between the Super and Pallas versions of the 2400.

Conclusion

As well as producing a major saving on fuel bills, one would reasonably expect a much longer life without overhauls to be provided by the engine. Because the equivalent petrol version is a rather lusty and not particularly refined unit, the penalty of the diesel in terms of extra noise and reduced power is not as marked as it might be, and the whole package is a satisfyingly efficient and still impressively pleasing car. We feel it right to end this test by emphasizing how impressed we are with the Citroen Diesel, and there is perhaps no better way to do this than to declare our intention to take one on to our staff fleet for long-term assessment. □

MANUFACTURER:
SA Andre Citroen
quai Andre Citroen 133
Paris XV, France

UK CONCESSIONAIRES:
Citroen Cars Ltd
Mill Street
Slough, Berkshire

PRICES:	
Basic	£4,016.00
Special Car Tax	£334.67
VAT	£348.05
Total (in GB)	**£4,698.72**
Seat Belts, inertia reel	standard
Licence	£40.00
Delivery charge (London)	£27.00
Number plates	£5.50
Total on the Road (exc insurance)	**£4,771.22**
Insurance	Group 6
EXTRAS (inc VAT)	
Motorola radio*	£42.75
* Fitted to test car	
TOTAL AS TESTED ON THE ROAD	**£4,813.97**

Citroen CX 2200 Pallas

Tony Curtis reports on a car which "still seems in good condition" but also "has off days"

SINCE I last reported on my Citroen CX — at the end of February — it has covered a further 2000 uneventful and essentially trouble-free miles, bringing the total to nearly 26,000. The car still seems in good condition — the engine continues to use little oil, for example, and the faulty electric window I complained of in my previous Running Report was soon fixed by my local dealer.

At the moment, though, the car is so wildly overdue for its 24,000-mile service that I fear it will skip an interval completely before I finally get it to the garage. I've always found it difficult to fit a car service into my timetable, which is generally a rather complicated mixture of trips abroad, work at MIRA, visits to factories and days on which I *must*, as far as is humanly possible, be in the office. For the CX the problems are compounded by the shortness of the intervals which are only 3000 miles long. But at least by having the car serviced near my home in Potters Bar, rather than near our offices in Sutton, I'm able to deliver and collect it without any significant wastage of time. It's all too easy, I've often found in the past, to waste an hour delivering a car in the morning and more than that collecting it in the evening — and by Murphy's Law it always seems to happen on occasions when I need every minute I can grab. But it's time, I think, that Citroen stretched their service interval to 6000 or at least 5000 miles.

At around 23,500 miles I began to worry about replacing the front tyres the treads of which were beginning to wear below 2 mm. For a front-wheel drive car on its first set of boots this is usually a fairly painless operation financially speaking, since the front tyres generally wear at about twice the rate of the rear tyres. So you buy a single new tyre and fit it to one front wheel, fit the unused spare to the other and use one of the old tyres as the spare. This should keep you going for several thousand more miles until the rear tyres begin to wear out.

But for the CX life is not quite so simple, since the rear tyres and the spare are of 175 section and the front tyres are of 185 section. (Is it legal, I ask myself, to drive about with a 175 section tyre on one side of the car and a 185 section tyre on the other?) The replacement operation, therefore, involves the purchase of a pair of tyres. After ringing a few dealers however, to obtain the necessary two Michelin radials of the XVS type — the high-performance alternative to the XAS recommended in this application — I was somewhat alarmed to find them in short supply, not wishing to collect a couple of endorsements. Eventually, though, I was able to find a pair with the help of Chris Rogers, Michelin's Press Officer in this country. But other CX owners in the same position are advised to order their new tyres in advance.

Although the old tyres retained good grip in the wet right to the end, the new ones have noticeably improved the handling, cornering with less squeal and reducing the basic understeer.

While remaining essentially troublefree, my CX has not done so well in one or two respects. The black paint which coats the window surrounds is beginning to flake off, for example, and the metallic green body panels are becoming chipped by stones at the front and sides. The various buzzes I complained of in my last report remain — they seem less conspicuous but this is probably because my ear has developed a filter to cut them out.

Much more important, though, is the fact that the car definitely has its off days — especially when it hasn't been used for a little while — when it misfires and runs roughly. The cause could be something as simple as a loose connection to one of the sparking plugs, but it is difficult to tell, as these live in deep wells beneath the rockerbox cover. Whatever the cause, the problem is having its effect on fuel consumption, now down to about 21 mpg instead of the 25 mpg it should be. And it is the same trouble, I'm almost convinced, which creates the occasional slight clutch judder when moving off from rest. My local dealer, however, and the Citroen HQ at Slough, are not quite so sure, and are contemplating removing the clutch for inspection and possible replacement.

IN BRIEF

Model: Citroen CX 2200 Pallas
When bought: January 1976
Total Mileage: 24,777
Price when bought: £4361
Price now: replaced by 2400
Value now: £3925
Overall mpg: 21

Faults and failures

0-6000: ill-fitting glovebox lid. Clutch replaced on warranty after persistent judder.
6000-12000: body mountings modified under warranty to eliminate engine vibration periods. Faulty wheelbearing replaced on warranty.
12000-18000: brake pads replaced at 12,000 miles. Fresh air inlet duct modified under warranty; improved engine mountings fitted under warranty; rev-counter buzz cured.
18000-24000: brake pads replaced at 19,000 miles. Persistent misfire, ticking speedo and buzz under facia. Nearside electric window not working.
24000-30000: Front tyres replaced at 24,900 miles.

By Stuart Bladon

Top Flight Citroens

Injection and five-speed gearbox provide the missing punch for CX

SOME TIME ago it was known that Citroën planned a new model introduction this month, and it was interesting to speculate whether this meant the long-rumoured arrival of the V6, 2.6-litre engine, which is built in France for Peugeot - Renault - Volvo, as a new power unit for the CX. In the event, it is nothing so radical; but this is no cause for disappointment. The new model, called the Citroën CX2400 GTi, offers really good performance — at least a match for the Renault 30TS — and is almost its equal in terms of smoothness.

Bosch L-Jetronic fuel injection is used in the GT for the larger of the two petrol engines (the 2200 is now available only as a diesel). Compared with the former, carburettor 2400 engine, which continues in production, the new injection version offers 13 bhp more, with a new peak of 128 bhp. Maximum power is developed appreciably lower in the rev range — at 4,800 rpm instead of 5,500 — and there is a useful gain in torque. Maximum value is 145 lb. ft. against the carburettor engine's 132 lb. ft.

As well as electronic fuel injection, the new engine has Ducellier electronic ignition; there are no mechanical contact points, and the spark is triggered magnetically. The new model is available only in manual transmission form, and has a five-speed gearbox as standard. There are no plans to make the GT available in the future with C-Matic transmission.

All five gears are indirect, both fourth and fifth effectively increasing the gearing. In fifth gear, car speed at 1,000 rpm is 21.1 mph, compared with 19.2 mph for fourth gear of the ordinary 2400. One would have felt that an appreciably higher ratio could have been used for fifth to justify the extra cost of a five-speed gearbox, but Citroën have evidently been anxious to retain this as a performance gear rather than just a cruising ratio. The final drive unit is the same (4.77-to-1) as in the ordinary CX2400, but it should be pointed out that the former CX2200 used to have a 4.58-to-1 final drive.

Direct comparison of the overall gearing is provided in the following table:

	Existing CX2400		New CX2400 GT	
Gear	Overall ratio	Mph/ 1,000 rpm	Overall ratio	Mph/ 1,000 rpm
1st	15.11	4.89	15.11	4.89
2nd	8.72	8.45	8.72	8.45
3rd	5.39	13.50	5.96	12.40
4th	3.81	19.20	4.48	16.50
5th	—	—	3.50	21.10

Other mechanical details of the new GTi are the same as for the 2400. The engine has bore of 93.5 mm and stroke of 85.5 mm, to give 2,347 c.c. capacity. The engine is mounted transversely at the front, inclined forwards at an angle of 30 deg. It drives the front wheels, the gearbox being in line with the engine, on the left-hand side of the car as seen from above.

Suspension is hydropneumatic, all-independent, with self-levelling provision, and the steering is Citroën Varipower, with powered

Far left: Special wheels identify the CX GT; they were not fitted on cars made available for road impressions in France

Left: A badge showing stylised GTi letters appears on the C-post on each side

Below: As installed, the injection pipes and trunking are adapted neatly to the available shape. The gearbox is in line with the engine, and in front of it is the pump for the hydraulic systems

Below: The additional air trunking and fuel injection system is neatly installed, making good use of available space. The sensor unit is hidden away at the front, on the right of the car (left of picture here)

return to the central position even after stopping the engine. Disc brakes are used front and rear, ventilated at the front.

As well as the more powerful engine and five-speed gearbox, the CX GT has special wheels with centre pressings in the form of a large five-pointed star. Michelin XVS 185 HR 14 tyres are standard. The surrounds of the side and rear windows are finished in matt black, and there are black side stripes. Embellishing panels along the door sills and a GTi badge on the C-post finisher strip help to identify this top performer in the CX range. There is also an outside mirror on the driver's door, electrically adjustable from inside.

Chief interior change is the surprising use of leather for the seat upholstery and map pockets front and rear. The seats are in black or linen coloured. Interior roof trim is in Taragon, and there is a special loop-pile carpet claimed to give added sound-deadening.

Other features special to the GT are a leather gaiter for the gear lever, illumination for the front ashtray and the ignition lock, carpet in the glove compartment(!), and black trim for the facia, steering wheel, and centre console. A water temperature gauge — omitted from the standard CX instrumentation — is added below the main instrument cluster, and the two-speed wiper has intermittent action as well as continuous wiping. A roof aerial and door-mounted loudspeakers with trim covers as for the Prestige are fitted as standard.

On the road

Opportunity for driving impressions was provided by Citroën on an interestingly varied route in southern France, with GTs devoid of all badges and without the special wheels, so that other French motorists would not notice the then-unannounced car.

As well as the over-riding impression of a far more eager engine, devoid of that slight trace of hesitance which tends to be noticed with the carburettor versions, the new unit impressed with its much greater refinement. It is appreciably smoother, and has no noticeable rough periods.

Fifth gear is not high, of course, and the lazier kind of driver will appreciate the way in which the car accelerates strongly in this ratio. Yet it also provides a very low level of noise at 100 mph cruising. The car tried tended to have an unusually high wind noise level especially on the driver's side, suggesting a faulty seal, and this was the more dominant feature when driving fast.

Citroën claim a top speed of 118 mph for the GT (against 113 mph for the standard 2400). There was no opportunity to make timed test runs, but 193 kph indicated on what seemed an unusually accurate speedometer (still the strange Citroën digital type) certainly supports the claim.

As seen from our table of gear speeds, fourth falls about midway between third and top of the standard car, and proves a really good performance gear giving the CX GT the sort of mid-range acceleration for fast overtaking which it has always lacked. The gearchange is strongly spring-loaded towards the third-fourth plane of movement and, if one forgets to move the lever firmly to fifth, it is likely to finish up back in third. When this happens, the driver is well aware that the wrong gear slot has been taken before releasing the clutch, so the only problem is the need to try again.

Reverse gear is found by pushing the lever down against the safety spring, and bringing it back, parallel with fourth gear. Fifth gear is offset, in the position taken by reverse on the four-speed car.

Any driver finds the handling of the CX, and particularly the ultra-sensitive and varying-assisted steering, a little unsettling at first acquaintance. It is a unique conception of car steering which takes some getting used to, but with familiarity it gives precision and ease of control with low effort. This aspect of the car, though, is the same as on all the CX range.

The only disappointing aspect on this preliminary assessment of the car was the lack of support provided by the new leather seats. They have inadequate rounding of the sides of the squabs, so the driver finds himself using the steering wheel for lateral location, and the passenger tends to slide from side to side on the seat. The appearance of the seats is impressive, but in other respects the standard nylon-cloth-upholstered ones are both more comfortable and give better support. Perhaps Citroën will be persuaded to offer these as an alternative to the new leather ones.

In other respects the GT brings new appeal to the CX by adding the performance element, and taking away the former impression of a car that is desperately under-powered. The GT gives such better response that the driver no longer feels he is having to row the car along. It should also prove more economical, since the engine is more efficient and the gearing a little higher. Unfortunately, although now on the market in France, the GT will not become available in this country until September. Potential buyers of a CX2400 will find it difficult to decide whether the extra refinements of the GT are worth the added wait. □

AutoTEST

Citroen CX2400

Larger engine and slightly lower gearing make latest CX smoother and more responsive to drive.
Performance and fuel consumption little altered from former CX2200.
Superb comfort except for poor ventilation; exceptional steering, needs a lot of familiarization.
Good, relaxed cruising with restrained wind and mechanical noise levels.
An excellent car in all but a few respects

DEVELOPMENT OF THE Citroen CX range has moved rapidly. Although it is still less than three years since the new model first appeared, there have already been three engine options added (including the diesel), while the Safari estate car has joined the range. The CX2200, which only last year we described as the "flagship of the CX range", has already been replaced.

Now the CX2400 is top model, but even this has been overtaken in France by introduction of the GTi, with fuel injection and a five-speed gearbox; this model is not yet available in the UK. Even when it comes there should be a strong position in the sales league for the 2400, which has effectively taken the place of the 2200 in the Citroen line-up, and that engine size is now offered only as a diesel.

Main difference between the two is the increase in bore diameter, from 90 to 93.5 mm. The capacity of the transversely-mounted four-cylinder engine goes up from the former

Well-packed and highly unorthodox, the engine bay houses not only the forward-inclined engine, with gearbox behind, but also the spare wheel. Despite the congestion, there is good access to sparking plugs, distributor and carburettor

2,175 c.c. to 2,347 and compression ratio is reduced slightly, from 9.00-to-1 to 8.75. As before, there is a twin-choke Weber carburettor, only its size has changed.

These differences are fairly small in percentage terms and the power increase is a mere 5 bhp, to the new DIN value of 115 at 5,750 rpm. Torque shows a bigger gain, going up from 123 lb.ft to 135, and the peak comes lower in the rev range at 2,800 rpm instead of 3,500. These figures lead one to expect the main improvement to be noticed in better low-speed response rather than in any dramatic gain at the top end. So it is no surprise to find that the CX2400's performance through the gears is almost exactly the same for the CX2200 Pallas which we tested in March last year. Acceleration from standstill to 60 mph took 11.8 sec against 11.6 for the 2.2-litre model, and 100 mph was reached in an equally close 40.1 sec instead of 40.8. Similarly, a standing quarter-mile time of 18.1 sec for the CX2400 is almost identical with the 18.2 sec of the former car.

As the CX is not particularly high-geared, it is capable of being over-revved in top on a motorway descent — a point which the driver could well need to watch on a fast trip through Germany. On the level it readily reached 111 mph, with the rev counter beginning to move into the red zone at 6,100 rpm. The top speed is thus the same as that of the CX2200.

The extra torque available shows itself in improved response in the gears, rather than through them where power plays a greater part. Direct comparison with the 2200 shows useful gains in all gears in the respective 20 mph increments. It is this extra punch which is greatly appreciated on the road; it is not very tangible in terms of seconds saved in full throttle acceleration, but it makes the 2400 seem much more responsive. The difference is particularly marked in the better low-speed pulling in top gear and there seems less need for frequent gear changing.

All models are now slightly lower geared, having a final drive ratio of 4.77-to-1 instead of 4.58. This undoubtedly adds to the impression gained that the car is much more eager and flexible. It has the effect of lowering the maxima in the gears from 30, 52 and 85 mph to 29, 50 and 81 mph. Again, the changes are too small to quibble about, although a reduction in gearing is contrary to the current trend in the interests of economy.

We are sufficiently familiar with other CX models to be convinced that the 2400 engine is appreciably smoother than either of its smaller counterparts. To recall chief features of the design, the engine has five main bearings and the overhead valves are inclined, opening in hemispherical combustion chambers. For a four-cylinder unit the Citroen engine had an unusually large swept volume, but in this case big does not mean rough or harsh. It is very smooth right through the rev range and although there is a fair amount of throaty engine noise, it does not sound harsh or thrashy when revved hard.

Cruising at around 85 mph calls for only 4,400 rpm, which the CX sustains with a subdued and not obtrusive power roar. At the lower end of the rev range the engine pulls without snatch down to about 20 mph in top gear, although a change down to third becomes normal driving habit with the CX once the speed drops below about 30 mph.

Starting is always prompt, with use of the choke when cold; but the engine is surprisingly reluctant to fire when hot, calling for tedious churning on the starter motor. Warm-up is quick and the choke control can be pushed in halfway almost at once. It will pull without enrichment after about the first mile.

Transmission

In first gear, the clutch takes up very smoothly from rest, but there is severe judder if any attempt is made to get away in second. A restart on the 1-in-3 test hill proved possible, but was achieved only with controlled clutch slip which produced a strong smell of burnt linings. Standing start acceleration tests were best done with abrupt clutch engagement at about 3,500 rpm sufficient to produce front wheelspin for the first few yards, and crisp getaway. Too many revs lost time with excessive wheelspin. These techniques are in any case of rather academic interest for the average owner.

The gear change has sturdy precise movement; it's very much a gear *lever*, rather than a gear stick. Synchromesh is effective on all gears but sometimes baulks for an instant. Care is needed to get the clutch fully down before engaging reverse to avoid a crunch of gears. Reverse gear position is parallel with third, and has strong check spring loading. The lever is also spring-loaded firmly to the third-fourth plane, and slips almost without need to guide it from second to third.

Fuel consumption

Since the gearing has been lowered and engine size increased, it is commendable that fuel consumption has not suffered. The CX2400 returned 23.5 mpg overall — exactly the same as the figure for the CX2200 Pallas. The body's excellent aerodynamic form obviously pays great dividends on a long, fast run, while in contrast, London traffic running brings more than the usual penalty because of the considerable weight of the Citroen.

During the test we readily achieved 24-25 mpg from the CX2400 saloon, while a recent opportunity for a long journey with the CX2400 Safari was even better, giving 25.9 mpg. Tank capacity of 15 gal means that 300 miles can be covered after filling up, still leaving a useful surplus of 30-50 miles before a refuelling halt.

After our 1,200-odd test miles a pint of oil was needed to restore the sump level. The dipstick is buried away at the back of the engine, and when the bonnet is open, care is needed to avoid rubbing clothing against the heavily-greased spring assister in the centre of the bonnet support strut.

An oil check button to the right of the facia gives a reading of oil level in a little glass tube; and to remind the driver to check it, a little light comes on in the indicator each time the ignition is turned on. It remains lit until the engine is started.

Steering and handling

Many people confess to feeling decidedly uneasy with the steering when they drive a CX for the first time, and there is no doubt that this highly sensitive, strongly assisted and powered self-centring system takes a bit of getting used to before one can feel at ease with it. On the straight it gives the impression of poor directional stability if the driver tries to correct the slight lateral movements of the car. It is almost a necessary discipline to learn that, if the steering is held steady, the car runs straight.

On corners, the power assistance still leaves need for a fair amount of effort to turn the wheel and the feel of the steering is very satisfactory — not over-assisted, yet not objectionably heavy. The assistance reduces progressively as speed increases and it makes very light work of parking or turning the car.

Unless the ignition key is taken out, locking the steering, the wheel automatically self-centres to line up the front wheels, even with the engine switched off, as soon as the wheel is released. Those who don't like the idea of the front wheels being turned in this way with the car at rest find themselves trying to avoid finishing up with the wheels on lock when parking the CX.

Unladen, the front wheels carry twice the weight of the rear ones and inevitably there is strong understeer which the power assistance disguises to a great extent. In spite of this, there is little tendency for the front end to feel nose heavy and prone to slide straight on when cornering hard; indeed, the handling generally is excellent. The driver feels very confident of the response of the car and there is excellent grip on slippery roads. The only slight disappointment is the rather excessive degree of roll that occurs when cornering hard, but this is perhaps a safety factor, reminding the driver how hard he is pushing the car.

Brakes

Disc brakes are fitted all round, ventilated at the front, and the servo is powered by the central hydraulic system. Pedal load is unusually light, taking only 50 lb for maximum efficiency and response is always very reassuring. A pressure-limiting valve in the line to the rear brakes prevents them from locking up until the stage at which heavy braking on a slippery surface has caused the front ones to lock first. Generally, the adhesion under braking is very good and the car is not prone to slide on with locked wheels.

Fade testing produced a slight initial increase in pedal load, but by the fifth application from 70 mph, the effort had stabilized. The handbrake works on separate pads on the front discs, and really can serve as an emergency brake, capable of 45 per cent efficiency. It holds securely, and without need for specially hard application, on the 1-in-3 test hill. As well as the central warning tell-tale marked "STOP", to warn of loss of hydraulic pressure, there is an amber warning lamp for front pad wear.

Ride and comfort

All the elaboration of self-levelling, hydro-pneumatic suspension on the CX is justified by the magnificent ride which results. The car absorbs undulations, humps and bumps superbly well and the resultant very resilient ride is also firmly damped. There is no swaying or wallowing and hump-back bridges taken quickly do not catch the suspension out. The only weak point of the system is the slight delay taken to recover normal ground clearance after the car has stood for a while.

Initial movement of the suspension is very firm, evidently with little rubber in the mountings and, as a result, a lot of harshness is transmitted on certain surfaces and there is a sharp report if a wheel hits a road cat's eye.

The ability to increase the ground clearance by means of the control lever beside the driving seat was useful on more than one occasion, and enabled us to negotiate flood water that would otherwise have been impassable.

As well as a high standard of ride comfort, the CX has well-shaped, softly upholstered and extremely comfortable seats. A lever to the right of the driving seat, centrally pivoted, allows the tilt of the cushion to be altered, having the effect of providing vertical height adjustment. Another lever farther back gives rake adjustment for the backrest (similarly for the passenger seat) and a very comfortable driving position can be achieved.

Headrests are standard, with detachable cushions; the headrests themselves can be removed, but this has to be done with care otherwise the splayed nylon feet tend to tear the top of the support tubes away from the seat.

Although so much of the car has been well designed, the ventilation remains one of the chief weak points. Through-flow is poor and delivery from the eye-ball vents is dependent on having the decidedly noisy blower

The clock, with second hand, is in the left of the four instrument squares. Fuel gauge and voltmeter are in the matching one on the right. The "travelling numbers" speedo and rev counter are plain to read, but only after the driver has taken his eyes from the road; they are illuminated automatically and brightness is adjustable by a thumb-wheel control beneath the right-hand control block. Finger-reach switches control horn, indicators (which are non-self-cancelling), wipers and washers on the left; and lights, including dip and flash, on the right. The choke control to the right of the steering column has its own warning tell-tale just beneath and there is an illuminated oil-level check to the right below the eyeball ventilator. A formidable row of warning lights covers every function. Electric window switches are to either side of the gear lever

Specification

ENGINE	
Cylinders	4 inline
Main bearings	5
Cooling	Water
Fan	Electric
Bore, mm	93.5
Stroke, mm	85.5
Capacity, c.c.	2,347
Valve gear	ohv
Camshaft drive	Chain
Compression ratio	8.75-to-1
Octane rating (minimum)	97 RM
Carburettor (make & type)	Weber twin choke 34 DMTR 35/250
Max power	115 bhp (DIN) at 5,500 rpm
Max torque	131 lb.ft. at 3,000 rpm
TRANSMISSION	
Clutch	Single disc dry type
Gear	Ratio
Top	0.8
3rd	1.133
2nd	1.833
1st	3.153
Final drive gear	Helical spur
Ratio	4.77-to-1 13/62
SUSPENSION	
Front — location	Independent, double wishbone
— springs, dampers	Hydropneumatic units
— anti-roll bar	Yes
Rear — location	Independent, trailing arms
— springs, dampers	Hydropneumatic units
— anti-roll bar	Yes
STEERING	
Type	Rack and pinion with power self-centring
Power assistance	VariPower standard
BRAKES	
Front	10.23in. dia. ventilated discs
Rear	9.17in. dia. discs
Servo	Yes, Hydraulic
WHEELS	
Type	Pressed steel disc
Rim width	5½in. J
Tyres — make	Michelin
— type	Radial tubeless XVS
— size	Front 185-14 Rear 175-14
EQUIPMENT	
Battery	12 volt 55 Ah
Alternator	72 amp
Headlamps (dipped/full beam wattage)	4-lamp halogen, 90/190 watt (total)
Reversing lamp	Standard
Hazard warning	Standard
Electric fuses	2 fuse boxes, 10 fuses
Screen wipers	Two-speed
Screen washer	Electric
Interior heater	Water valve
Interior trim	Cloth seats, vinyl headlining
Floor covering	Carpet
Jack	Screw type
Jacking points	4, below front and rear doors
Windscreen	Laminated
Underbody protection	Paint system and wax
MAINTENANCE	
Fuel tank	15 Imp galls (68 litres)
Cooling system	18.5 pints (inc heater)
Engine sump	8 pints SAE 20W50
Gearbox and final drive	3 pints SAE 80
Grease	No points
Valve clearance (cold)	Inlet 0.006 in. Exhaust 0.008 in.
Contact breaker	0.016in. gap 55° dwell angle
Ignition timing	10 deg BTDC (static or 00 deg BTDC (stroboscopic at 850 rpm)
Spark plug - type	AL42 FS
— gap	0.028 in.
Tyre pressure	F 28; R30 psi (normal driving)
Max payload	1,080 lb (490 kg)

Maximum Speeds

Gear	mph	kph	rpm
Top (mean)	113	182	5,870
Top (best)	116	187	6,025
3rd	81	130	6,000
2nd	50	80	6,000
1st	29	47	6,000

Acceleration

True mph	Time (sec)	Speedo mph
30	**3.6**	30
40	**5.8**	41
50	**8.1**	51
60	**11.8**	61
70	**15.7**	71
80	**21.0**	82
90	**28.9**	92
100	**40.1**	103

Standing ¼-mile:
18.1 sec, 78 mph
kilometre:
33.5 sec, 92 mph

mph	Top	3rd	2nd
10-30	—	6.9	4.0
20-40	9.9	6.2	4.0
30-50	9.2	6.0	4.4
40-60	9.4	6.4	—
50-70	10.6	7.4	—
60-80	11.7	9.3	—
70-90	14.1	—	—
80-100	19.2	—	—

Consumption

Fuel

Overall mpg: 23.5
(12.0 litres/100km)

Calculated (DIN) mpg: 23.7
(11.9 litres/100km)

Constant speed:

mph	mpg
30	39.9
40	37.1
50	32.5
60	28.6
70	26.0
80	22.5
90	19.7
100	16.4

Autocar formula
Hard driving, difficult conditions
21.1 mpg
Average driving, average conditions
25.9 mpg
Gentle driving, easy conditions
30.6 mpg

Grade of fuel: Premium, four-star (98 RM)

Mileage recorder: 1 per cent over reading

Oil

Consumption (SAE 20W/50): negligible

Brakes

Fade *(from 70 mph in neutral)*
Pedal load for 0.5g stops (lb)

	start/end		start/end
1	25	6	40/50
2	30/35	7	40/55
3	35/40	8	40/55
4	35/40	9	40/55
5	40/50	10	40/55

Response *(from 30 mph in neutral)*

Load (lb)	g	Distance (ft)
20	0.35	86
30	0.55	55
40	0.72	42
50	0.95	32
Handbrake	0.45	67

Max gradient: 1 in 3

Clutch

Pedal 40lb and 5½in.

Test Conditions

Wind: 0-5 mph
Temperature: 17 deg C (63 deg F)
Barometer: 30.2 in. Hg
Humidity: 40 per cent
Surface: dry asphalt and concrete
Test distance: 1,200 miles

Figures taken at 10,000 miles by our own staff at the Motor Industry Research Association proving ground at Nuneaton

Regular Service

Interval (miles)

Change	**3,000**	**6,000**	**12,000**
Engine	Yes	Yes	Yes
Oil filter	No	No	Yes
Gearbox	Check	Check	Yes
Spark plugs	Clean	Check	Check
Air filter	No	Clean	Clean
C/breaker	No	Check	Check
Total cost	**£2.80**	**£10.64**	**£27.72**

Assuming labour at £5.60/hour

Parts Cost

(including VAT)

Brake pads (2 wheels— front	£16.90
Brake pads (2 wheels) — rear	£11.54
Exhaust system, complete	£75.41
Windscreen (laminated)	£88.65
Headlamp unit	£42.98
Front wing	£38.17
Rear bumper	£104.03

Warranty period
12 months/12,000 miles

Weight

Kerb, 26.7cwt/2,990lb/1,357kg
(Distribution F/R, 67.4/32.6)
As tested, 30.2cwt/3,390lb/1,540kg

Boot capacity: 16.8 cu. ft.

Turning circles:
Between kerbs
L, 35ft 9in; R, 35ft 4in.
Between walls
L, 38ft 8in.; R, 38ft 6in.
Turns, lock to lock: 2.5

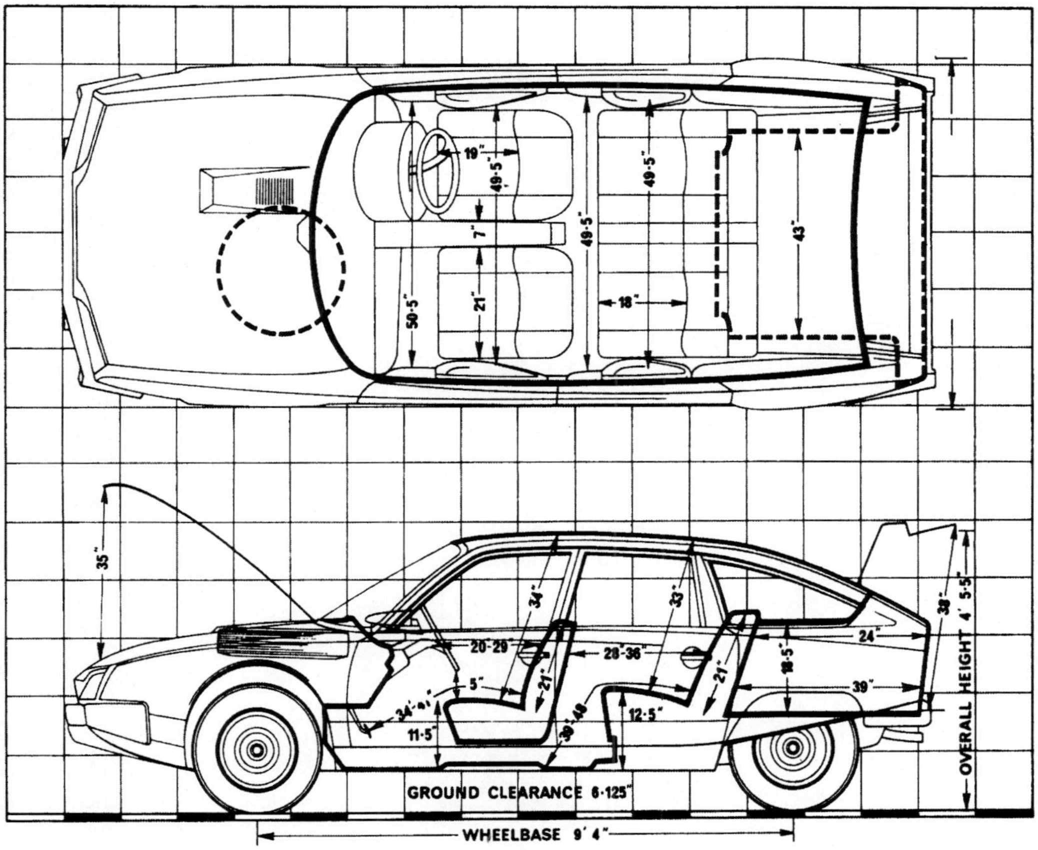

Test Scorecard

(Average of scoring by *Autocar* Road Test team)

Ratings: *6 Excellent*
5 Good
4 Above average
3 Below average
2 Poor
1 Bad

PERFORMANCE	4.17
STEERING AND HANDLING	5.08
BRAKES	5.00
COMFORT IN FRONT	3.92
COMFORT IN BACK	4.86
DRIVERS AIDS *(instruments, lights, wipers, visibility, etc)*	4.88
CONTROLS	4.63
NOISE	4.17
STOWAGE	4.00
ROUTINE SERVICE *(under-bonnet access: dipstick, etc)*	4.00
EASE OF DRIVING	4.64
OVERALL RATING	**4.53**

Comparisons

Car	Price (£)	Max mph	0-60 (sec)	Overall mpg	Capacity (c.c.)	Power (bhp)	Wheelbase (in.)	Length (in.)	Width (in.)	Kerb weight (cwt)	Fuel (gal)	Tyres size
Citroen CX2400	**£4,991**	**113**	**11.8**	**23.5**	**2,347**	**115**	**112**	**181**	**68.0**	**26.7**	**15.0**	**185/175 HR-14**
Audi 100 GLS	5,286	107	10.9	21.4	1,984	115	105.5	184	69.5	22.6	13.2	165-14
BMW 520	5,729	114	10.5	22.4	1,990	130	104.0	182	67.0	24.6	12.5	175HR-14
Ford Granada 3000GL	5,147	113	9.4	17.4	2,664	138	109.0	180	71.0	27.8	14.3	175HR-14
Renault 30TS	5,458	111	11.7	20.2	2,664	131	105.0	178	68.0	25.5	14.7	175HR-14
Rover 3500	5,983	123	8.4	20.5	3,528	155	110.5	185	69.0	27.2	14.5	185-14

in use. In hot weather, the air coming through the ventilators tends to get warmed above ambient on its way through the system, making the car very hot inside. In contrast the heater is slow to warm up and is of the water-valve type, giving little if any progression between full on and full off.

Controls and equipment

For simplicity and convenience, the layout of minor controls in the CX is one of the best there is. Switches for wipers, indicators and horn are within finger reach when holding the wheel normally with the left hand; and matching controls for the right hand operate the three lighting switches — off, side, head below the finger block, flasher switch on the side, and dip switch on the top. First pressure on the horn switch sounds a gentle "beep" suitable for town, and a firmer press fires up very effective air horns mounted under the bonnet.

Electrically-operated front windows are standard, their switches being to either side of the gear lever, on the lower part of the central console. Adjacent, farther back, are switches for the interior light, which is adequately bright for map reading, and for the heated rear window. There is a lockable, drop-down compartment to the left of the facia and an open cubbyhole on the right.

Instruments are digital, with variable light intensity controlled by a thumb-wheel beneath the right-hand control block. The markings are clear and the speedometer and rev counter proved accurate, but there is no denying that the driver has to take his eyes from the road to be able to read them clearly; they cannot be seen out of the corner of the eye, as can the normal analogue type.

Minor instruments are confined to a vertically-reading fuel gauge and voltmeter, with clock having sweep second hand on the left. Across the top of the instruments is a row of warning lights, all individually labelled with symbols. The important central ones, for hydraulic pressure, brake line pressure, oil pressure and water temperature, can all be tested by a touch on a button in the right-hand lamp of this central group.

The front doors cannot be locked from outside before closing, but the locking catches are at the leading edge of each door and it is easy for the driver to lock the three passenger doors before getting out. There are child safety catches for the rear doors. The boot has an interior light, operated by raising the lid and the boot lid can be left unlocked when required.

The Citroen's huge windscreen is well swept by the single, centre-pivoted wiper, though we have noticed before that the Citroen CX windscreen tends to get very smeary, perhaps as a result of the unobstructed wind flow over the front of the car.

An irritating detail is that the rather crude door-mounted mirror tends to blow back in the wind at speed, despite efforts to tighten it; and the interior mirror, which is bonded to the windscreen, fell off and defied all attempts to stick it back on. The seat belt inertia reels tended to be very sensitive and reluctant to unlock on the test car, so it was important to fasten belts before driving off.

The headrests have detachable cushions and they can also be removed altogether for better visability or out of consideration for rear-seat passengers

As well as the usual adjustment to-and-fro for the seat and its backrest angle, there is vertical adjustment to tilt the front of the seat cushion

The appearance of the facia is neat, but the vertical mounting for the radio/tape unit is totally unsatisfactory, making it dangerously difficult for the driver to see its tuning scale

Rear-seat comfort is as sumptuous as in front, and there is a folding centre armrest. Air from the heater is channeled through to the rear compartment

Removal of tools and spare wheel to the engine compartment leaves the boot pleasantly clear, with a low floor. A boot light is standard

Where it fits in

With the 2,347 c.c. engine, the CX is available as Super (subject of this test) Pallas, Prestige and Safari estate car, so it can be seen that the CX2400 Super is the bottom model of the range other than the CX2000. However, it is so well equipped and furnished as to seem more like a luxury version. Pallas specification adds two rear door lights and courtesy lights operated by all four doors, Jersey cloth upholstery, carpeted rear parcels shelf, map light, chromed door mirror and the option of air conditioning. Leather upholstery is also available for the Pallas, but not for the Super.

Luxury model is the longer-wheelbase Prestige, which adds rear fog lamps, air conditioning as standard, electric window lifts for rear as well as front, Vinyl roof and metallic paint. The diesel versions automatically take the same specification as the Super.

Conclusion

Citroën motoring is a rather different way of life from the ordinary run of cars and it may not be to everyone's taste to have so potentially-complicated a machine and such sensitive steering. Yet as a formula for comfort, spaciousness and speed with good fuel economy it has few rivals. The larger engine certainly adds much more responsive performance to these attributes; it **feels** decidedly livelier, with less awareness that it is only a four-cylinder engine under the bonnet. □

MANUFACTURER:
Societe Anonyme Automobiles Citroen
177 A167 Quai Andre Citroen
75747 Paris Cedex 15

UK CONCESSIONAIRES:
Citroen Cars Ltd
Mill Street
Slough SL2 5DE

PRICES	
Basic	£4,266.00
Special Car Tax	£355.50
VAT	£369.72
Total (in GB)	**£4,991.22**
Seat belts (inertial reel, front only)	standard
Licence	£50.00
Delivery charge (London)	£37.50
Number plates	£6.00
Total on the road (exc insurance)	**£5,047.22**
Insurance	Group 6
EXTRAS (inc VAT)	
Metallic paint	£62.01
TOTAL AS TESTED ON THE ROAD	**£5,109.23**

Prestige is Indulgence

Impressions of the Citroen CX Prestige

What one must bear in mind when he is driving a limousine, especially the long wheel based ones, is that the vehicle is developed and built as such for the rear passengers (presumably the bosses and towkays), indeed uncompromisingly so. Rear seats would thus seem to be extra comfortable, legroom and headroom plus all the amenities would also be generous and well located for the rear passengers. This indeed was the general impression coveyed to us by the Citroen CX Prestige. When we first laid eyes on the Prestige, we were immediately aware that the car looked extra long. It was. The Prestige is almost 8 inches longer than its stablemate the Pallas (16' 1¼" vs 15' 3½"). This extra length is not superficial as the Prestige wheelbase is also an extra 8 inches longer. All this extra space is used to pamper the rear passengers, and the rear legroom space has to be seen to be believed (the only cars with similarly impressive legroom is the Mercedes 600, the Rolls and the 1wb Jaguars). There is so much space both in terms of legroom and headroom that the only passengers who may complain would be Harlem Globetrotters. All this space is, moreover, reserved only for the rear. The front is roughly similar to the Pallas, except for the driving position as the seat rollers have been retarded. After all, one can't have the chauffeur encroaching into the boss's space. If the driver is on the tall side he may also find his head too close to the padded ceiling for comfort.

But comfortable is what all Citroens are, and the Prestige has the same excellent ride as the Pallas, which is well damped, incredibly comfortable (sort of floaty feel) and with tolerable body-roll. We can certainly affirm that the famed hydropneumatic suspension really works. This superb system is mated to the tremendous seats (only word that can describe them), all covered and finished in soft leather and toped by four comfortable leather bound headrests. We suspect that it would require 4 cows to sacrifice their hides, so generous is the expanse of leather found in the Prestige. Things such as the dash and interior door trim are all leather, too. (definitely not for those allergic to leather). Practically whatever else which is not leather bound is covered with high quality carpeting, including the two footrests located in the rear. The Prestige pampers its occupants to such an extent (especially the rear occupants) that it actually borders on indulgence; all windows are electrically operated, two separate cigar lighters in the rear in addition to the one located in front. Items such as rear hinged on sun visors, side visors and twin rear interior lights all compliment the very luxurious nature of the car. And we thought the CX 2200 Pallas we tested some time ago was luxurious! Which just goes to show that even the "Palace" i.e. Pallas can be improved upon. All these improvements only serve to make owners and drivers (even test drivers) feel superior and even arrogant, knowing they are owning or driving a car which is exclusive and rather unique.

However if you should feel the urge to dismiss your chaffeur for the day and sample the other qualities of the car (other than its ride and luxury) you would not be disappointed. In fact you may enjoy driving the Prestige to the extent of dismissing your chauffeur permanently. The item we found to be extra enjoyable (and unique to Citroens alone) is the superb power assisted and self-centering steering. First feel and looks alone (single spoke and deliciously padded) already conveys the right impression. But beauty is only skin deep and it is only when you drive the long

Prestige is Indulgence

limousine, or should it be steer the 'mobile palace' that you would fully appreciate an item which is as unusual as Citroens are to the ignorant. A gentle twirl would mean instant correction, it is that sharp as only a mere 2½ turns is necessary to bring about full lock to lock. The steering is also self-centering hence after any steers it will always (as if by magic) self center and return the front wheels to the straight ahead position, enabling easy parking and relaxed long distant drives. Here the Prestige (as will all other Citroens having this feature) will steer arrow straight and is practically impervious to crosswinds and road undulations.

However all in not perfect for the driver as space as mentioned is rather limited for the tall driver. Seats are however adjustable is rather limited for the tall driver. Seats are however adjustable for height as well as the normal reach/distance. Nevertheless if you happen to be 6 feet or over you would still find your head disconcerting close to the well padded ceiling. Clutch effort is on the heavy side and we would have liked to find an automatic transmission in a vehicle of the Prestige's nature. For those who would rather let the transmission do most of the work a C-matic (semi-automatic) is available on order. The normal gearshift found in the Prestige is a four-speed affair, and while the planes are sufficiently defined they tend to have rubbery movements.

Instruments are similar to the other CXes with all the vital functions housed in the "space-age" binnacle. And fittingly enough for a model which is at the top of an exceptional range of cars the Prestige has an extra temperature gauge which while being informative (and confirms our belief that the CX doesn't overheat even in mid-day traffic jams) looked a bit like an extra tag-on and doesn't quite blend harmoniously with the general architecture. Vinyl top is also standard and the paintwork is glaze finished to give it that extra sparkle and class making the CX stand out like a rose in a field of cherry blossoms. A generous amount of felt is also used for the underbonnet. Firewall insulation is also generous, effectively reducing the engine noise to a pleasant hum most of the time. An electric wing mirror which works with a satisfying buzz completes the driver's aids. Other general equipment complimenting its limousine tag are four speakers (one on each door) and

special quality control to make sure that each Prestige would come out of the assembly line in tip-top condition.

While the Prestige doesn't overheat (thanks to the twin radiator fans), the electric fans do produce some noise especially when the second one is activated. Noise level is however still well suppressed within the cabin and the occupants would only be able to detect a mere humming sound with the three-speed air-conditioner on. Nevertheless we had the distinct impression that the 2400cc 4 cylinder could do with an extra 2 cylinders thereby endowing it with the silky smoothness a car of this class should possess. As it is we would have to make do with the present four, with does have to its credit flexibility and adequate performance. Bearing in mind the Prestige is a gentleman's limousine we would think its power output of 115bhp adequate but not generous for a car loaded with such a lot of luxuries. As the vehicle we tested was a brand new vehicle, and also because we respected its price tag, we did not put the car through our full range of acceleration tests. Citroen claims its acceleration to 100 kilometers from rest to be 11.9

seconds, a time which if accurate (as most Citroen claims are) would be good. Top speed is said to be 109 mph and having driven the 2400 Pallas we have no reason to doubt these claims. What is difficult to convey on paper is the deceptive sense of speed. The speed would creep up unobstrusively but rapidly given an empty stretch of road. And of course like all Citroens the Prestige is an excellent cruiser, a vehicle par excellence on highways. Byways would reveal the good handling and tenacious roadholding of the car. However in spite of all these inherent excellent qualities it is best not to hustle the Prestige around corners as the extra length of the car, while providing acres of space, does tend to let you know you are driving a very long car indeed. However if you should make the mistake of entering a sharp "S" bend too fast, a dab on the excellent brakes (both front and rear are ventilated to prevent fade) would quickly eliminate its tail wagging tendencies. But in order to make the car break its chosen line you would have to be travelling very fast indeed and under most normal fast driving the behaviour of that 16-foot vehicle proved to be exemplary. As is to the expected the hydropneumatic suspension, while providing a host of valuable benefits, does tend to make the car roll excessively on corners though through experience we can verify that its roll does not enroach on its roadhandling properties.

For those miserly ones who count cents, and we doubt that Prestige owners would be miserly) the Prestige will return a very creditable 22.5 miles to a gallon, befitting its very aerodynamic shape.

To recap on what we said in the beginning, the Prestige is built uncompromisingly as a luxurious and spacious limousine and the fact that it has succeeded in its goal so admirably must be the best form of moving advertisement for Citroens. Ride is simply marvelous and the interior of the car reeks of luxuries and practically every imaginable amenity for the discerning bosses. We would reccommend anyone (those rich enough) who is looking for a luxury car to include the Prestige in their shortlist, as the price tag is exclusive enough at $57,649.73 Finish and trim are excellent and other than for a few minor reservations (as opposed to a long list of positive points) the Prestige impressed us as few other cars have. ●

CX PRESTIGE

Brief specifications

Engine:

No. of cylinders	:	4 cylinders, in-line, transversly mounted
Bore and stroke	:	93.5 × 85.5 mm (3.68 × 3.37)
Capacity	:	2347 cc
Compression ratio	:	8.75 : 1
Max. power	:	115 bhp (DIN) at 5,750 rpm
Max. torque	:	136 lb. ft. (DIN) at 3,500 rpm
Carburettors	:	Single Weber down draught twin barrel

Transmission:

Driving wheels	:	front
Type	:	4-speed, fully synchronized

Gear ratios:

First	:	3.166
Second	:	1.833
Third	:	1.133
Fourth	:	0.800
Rev	:	3.153
Final drive	:	4.769

Suspension:

Front	:	Independent, wishbones, hydropneumatic suspension, anti-roll bar, automatic levelling control.
Rear	:	Independent, swinging trailing arms, hydropneumatic suspension, anti-roll bar, automatic levelling control.

Steering:

Type	:	rack and pinion, variable power assisted
Lock to lock	:	2.5 turns

Brakes:

Type	:	disc/disc, ventilated front and rear, servo assisted.

Performance:

Acceleration 0 – 100 kmh in 11.9 seconds
Top speed 109 mph
Fuel consumption 22.5 mpg

GIANT TEST

Citroen CX2400 GTi
Ford Granada 2.8S

SOMEWHERE IN MOST OF THE POPULAR CAR MAKERS' RANGES you'll find a saloon in receipt of GT badges, which shows how distorted the term has become since, in its original Italian connotation, it was applied (and still is) only to two-plus-two coupes. But the marketing men have long since learned not to worry about such minor details; often as not, they don't even care enough to let the engineers go beyond badges, black paint and, if they're very lucky, stiffer shock absorbers in the creation of said GT saloons. The Cortina GT is a prime example of the 'minimum' GT, a car that emerges as rather less satisfactory and capable than its softer GL sister; on the other hand, Ford themselves have from time to time come up with the real thing. For instance, the old Australian Falcon GTs of the late '60s and early '70s were the sort of cars that create legends: fast, furious and finely balanced, capable of blowing an Aston Martin of the same era into the weeds and able to acquit themselves well enough with the better Italian GT cars. So, to be charitable, perhaps Ford have paid their dues and redressed the balance. General Motors too – the Commodore GS/E, for instance, was hardly a proper grand tourer but it was a damned good car. Anyway, to get to the point: Ford are still firmly in the game with not just the Cortina GT but the Granada, except that the car concerned isn't called a GT anymore: for the new model, the four-door express has been dubbed the 2.8S. Citroen, on the other hand, have taken to calling their version of the same ideal a GTi, whereas the corresponding DS was simply called the EFi. As it stands at the moment, there isn't much choice beyond the two cars tested here if you're really hankering after a four-door car in the 2.0 to 3.0litre region with just such 'GT' overtones. The Saab EMS only has two doors, the new Commodore has not yet arrived in any form, the Triumph 2500S is on its last legs and entirely out of the race and the BMW 523 (no badges but the right sort of car) hasn't arrived; the 528i, which has, is too expensive. Do the new Rover 2600 and R30TS, whatever their capabilities, fit the image? The list says that the Ford is notably the cheaper at £5910, but add in the sort of goodies that our test car carried – like central locking system, headlight washers, electric sunroof and electric aerial – and you have a price within striking distance of the £6350 Citroen – £6264 to be exact.

STYLING, ENGINEERING

Having just been down at Pininfarina's in Italy and looking again at the old BLMC Berlina Aerodinamica prototype of 1967, one realises once more just how much the Citroen CX (and the GS, and Lancia's Gamma) owe to that car. It began a trend that is hardly in full swing even now. But wherever Citroen's inspiration came from, they certainly got the CX right and now that it's well into its fourth year it looks as fresh as a spring chicken. It's low, clean, sleek and still futuristic, and has more ability to stop people in the street than any other family saloon. For the GTi, there aren't many body changes: a special regatta blue joins the other standard colours, the window surrounds are blacked-out, specially-designed alloy wheels replace the normal steel ones, there are two fog lights hung below the front bumper (along with rubber air scoops) and GTi badges lurk on the tail and C-pillars. Effective enough. As we said last month, Ford's re-skin of the Granada is simply brilliant and most people will never suspect that its inner panels are just as they were for the old car. The styling of the new model is as elegant as you'll probably find in a classic three-box family saloon; in its own way, it's as clean as the Citroen and just as tasteful. But is it a trifle *too* ordinary-looking for mass production? We think not; others apparently find it all too tame, but if there is a real problem it's that the car looks smaller than it is and can be confused with the Cortina. The body of the Granada S is just the same as that of the basic Granada L, which has so much matt black paint in the obvious areas that there's no room left to add more for the S. The give-aways are really only the special alloy wheels and their Michelin TRX tyres and two foglights mounted in front of the grille. And somehow that's enough to make the S look a little more purposeful than its sisters.

The Citroen, of course, has an in-line four-cylinder engine – that familiar old-plodder! – driving the front wheels, and the weird and wonderful high-pressure hydraulics system for its steering, brakes and suspension that sets the CX apart from just about everything else except its own sisters and the odd Maserati. The engine capacity stays the same as that for the other top-line CXs: 2347cc, fairly oversquare, with a tame 8.75 to one compression ratio and nothing more modern than pushrod-operated overhead valves. But, along with the Prestige, it has Bosch L Jetronic fuel injection so that its power is lifted from the 115bhp at 5500rpm in the normally-aspirated 2.4litre engine to 128bhp at a low 4800rpm. Not surprisingly, it's a torquey old beast, providing a bit over 145lb/ft – but the peak is developed at a relatively high 3600rpm (it's 132lb/ft at 2750 in the carburettor 2400). The Ford engine has more cylinders as well as more capacity; for the new Granadas, however, the Essex V6 has been ditched and the German version takes its place – 2.3 and 2.8litres instead of 2.5 and 3.0. For the S, it's the 2.8litre, with the benefit of fuel injection (optional in the GL and Ghia) but this time its the Bosch K Jetronic system. Compared with the Citroen, the Ford V6 is a real revver, generating its 160bhp at 5700rpm and its 162lb/ft of torque at 4300. The Ford sends this power through a normal four-speed transmission; the GTi one-ups it and the other Citroens by having a five-speed transmission with top heavily over-driven, and yet, because it has a very low final drive ratio it ends up with an mph/1000rpm figure only marginally higher than that of the Ford.

You run into bigger differences in the suspension. The Ford is conventional but not altogether basic: at the front it has wishbones, coil springs and an anti-roll bar and the S has the advantage of gas-filled shock absorbers. At the rear, the suspension is independent with BMW-like semi-trailing arms, variable rate coil springs, anti-roll bar and another set of those Bilstein dampers. Rather more development has gone into the tune of its suspension than that of the other Granadas; it had to – the Granada S is the first production car to carry Michelin's new TRX low profile tyres. Ford's suspension experts worked long and hard with Michelin to sort out harshness and vibration problems and perfect the handling. They believe passionately in the qualities and the future of the TRX and expect it to be fitted to scores of cars within the next two years. The CX also runs on Michelins, but they're the familiar XVSes, and somewhat narrower at 185HR14 (on 5.5in rims) than the Ford's 190/65HR390 TRXs (which are mounted on unique 15.35in wheels so that they cannot possibly be fitted to ordinary, unsuitable rims). Tranverse arms locate the front wheels, working as parallelograms, with connecting rods running from the upper arms to the piston and cylinder units of the hydropneumatic system, interconnected front to rear. There's an anti-roll bar too. At the back, there are long trailing arms made of alloy, again linked by small connecting rods to the hydropneumatic units. Another anti-roll bar finishes it all off (uprated, along with the damping for the GTi). The hydraulics system, driven by an engine pump, also powers the all-disc brakes, and the unique steering. It's called VariPower and what it means is that the steering progressively loses its assistance with speed; and with a 13.5 to one ratio, it's quick enough to require only 2.5 turns lock to lock. The Ford's power steering is far more conventional, but the Germans have worked hard on it and it is now much better than in the old Granadas; as we'll see later, the Michelins bring some extra benefits to the steering too. The Citroen has the longest wheelbase (112in) against 109in for the Ford, but it's the Granada that consumes the most space by measuring 187in from nose to tail against the tidier Citroen's 184in. They're both heavy cars, but the 2965lb CX has a slight edge over the 3003lb Ford.

PERFORMANCE

The Citroen might have a five-speed gearbox and a modest weight advantage, but you don't overcome a power discrepancy of 32 horses so easily; and the Granada will spurt away from it in the traffic lights derby any day of the week. Indeed, the Granada is a properly quick car if you rev it hard, sprinting to 60mph in 8.8sec. Against, that the Citroen – after a fairly chirpy start as it loses traction because of transference of weight – is a full second slower. And yet out on the road there isn't a penneth's worth between them. The Citroen's engine is quite incredibly

Unorthodox Citroen dash (top) brings futuristic feel to the cabin, controls on 'horns' are very good. For GTi wheel gets brush alloy strip down spoke. Jersey seats look sumptuous, do their job well, in league with an excellent ride (second down). Self-levelling suspension also copes with whatever you care to load into cavernous boot (third down). Bosch L Jetronic injection endows 2.4litre four with incredible flexibility (above). Details, top to bottom: Air flow through eyeball vents is feeble, headlights should have washers but air horns back up lesser city bleeper and moveable map light is a good touch.

flexible, happily pulling away from 700rpm – or as low as it will go – in fifth gear. You constantly find yourself working down to 5mph in third around town, and fourth will deliver the goods from 10mph or so. So you have plenty of low-down oomph in the gears in the CX to make lazy driving a fact of life, and overtaking an easy mid-range matter when you want to get on with it. You then tend to change up early, and there is no point whatsoever in going much beyond 5000rpm. On the other hand, while the Ford is smooth down low (though nothing like as flexible as the CX), you need to take it beyond 6000rpm to get the best from it. So one ends up with two rather different ways of reaching similar ends; so similar in fact, that if the two cars are run in convoy they will end up being very, very close over a long distance. At the very top end, just for the record, the Granada has a 2mph advantage over the Citroen. Neither engine is the sort to have you falling head over heels in love with it. The Citroen might be staggeringly flexible, but it's quite noisy and a bit of a shaker up high; and nor is the Ford as smooth as one would like beyond 5500rpm, even if it will rev to 7000 very briskly. There's nothing in it for economy: both range between 20 and 24mpg.

HANDLING, ROADHOLDING

And here we reach the most fascinating part of this test. The sheer grip of the Citroen CX has been one of its best features since the day it was introduced, earning it a position near the top of the saloon car roadholding ladder. The Granada, too, has always been fairly good; and given the benefit of its dramatically different new Michelins looked set to push the standard up a rung. But it transpires that the handling marks the main difference in their cornering ability. Both feel stable and reliable on the road, with the sort of grip that people could only dream about years ago. But put them on a track where their precise limits can be determined and – surprise! – it's the Citroen that has the strongest sheer grip. Where the Ford will begin to break away – at the rear of course – at 75mph in a given bend the CX is hanging on at 80 before nudging into understeer. In such an instance, driver skill becomes important in the Ford, for it gets into oversteer and no mistake about it, requiring positive action at the wheel. It then answers with impeccable manners and can then be hustled through in a full tail-out attitude. In a tight bend, this truly superb handling can take the Ford to an advantageous position against the Citroen. A stretch of twisty road will have the Citroen pushing into sufficient understeer to wash off speed unless the entry pace is trimmed, and once it's in understeer it takes a moment or two with the throttle shut down to return the nose to the chosen line. The Ford can be flung in, pushed easily into oversteer and balanced around carefully on the throttle, and if the revs are kept high, its greater power will enable it to sprint more quickly between the bends. In short, it handles absolutely magnificently, sitting flat and giving the driver all the information he needs for accuracy as well as pleasure. It really is a driver's sort of car, and if you don't know how to deal with oversteer and, even more, how to enjoy it, you'd be better off staying away from the Granadas. When the tail end break away begins, there is sufficient warning from the Michelins, for they have a gentleness not unlike that of the Pirelli P6s and P7s, and they're full of information. If the Michelins' performance on the Granada is anything to go by, the Pirellis are better, having both more grip and a longer 'transition' period. But since the Granada is still inferior to the CX in roadholding, one must assume that more development work can be done to raise the limits; it's early days yet for the TRX, and Granada S.

It does, of course, take a long time to get to know the CX. That steering is so different, the reaction to it so swift, that most drivers lurch from side to side on the road until they learn to use the finest possible movements, both as they apply lock and as they wind it off. Steering the car is more of a mental process than a physical one, and once you've adapted to that you will sail along in a state of considerable relaxation. And yet, even when you know the car, you can have an off day with it: you only need to be slightly heavy handed or abrupt with it to jerk it about, jiggling your passengers' heads from side to side. Should you get it really wrong with the CX by entering a bend far too fast, it tries hard to sort itself out and remain stable. It'll be rolling a lot and understeering, and if you keep on pulling it tight the tail will flick out. But even then the car is trying to get itself back in line and the merest touch of opposite lock and a little power will have it shipshape in short order, even if the body action is a bit messy. Overall, however, the Citroen is at its best in long, fast bends or for storming down motorways (whence it will move very slightly from side to side, and you should let it). In town, the speed and effortlessness of the steering are huge boons.

DRIVER APPEAL

The Ford is strictly conventional in the cabin; its facia something of a cross between American and German styles and perhaps with a touch of British traditionalism thrown in by way of its wood veneer instrument panel. The panel is deeply shrouded and neatly-styled. The speedo and tachometer (redlined at 6500rpm) are directly ahead of the driver, with the fuel and temperature guages between them. Oil pressure and battery guages are high up on either side of this panel-within-a-panel, and lined up symmetrically with them are minor switches (round, flat knobs) like the rheostat, intermittent wiper control and so on. The rest of the auxiliary functions are controlled by the three stalks now standard in European Fords. There are big vents in the centre of the dash as well as at its edges and the heater controls are both easy to use and understand. The reach to the handsome four-spoke wheel is very good. Its angle is just right too, and the vision is excellent in all directions. Unfortunately, the throw of the clutch is too long, upsetting one's seating balance, and the gearshift is too far forward for comfortable action. As in all the rear drive Fords, however, it shifts lightly and precisely. The feel of the steering and the smoothness of its action is beyond reproach; it is also very quick when coupled to the Michelins, almost as quick at changing the Granada's direction at speed as the Citroen's high-powered system but far more conventional at lower speeds. We'd rate the Ford's steering as absolutely first class and its handling is as good, if not better than, the BMW Seven Series. Its brakes aren't up to the same standard though. There's a slight sponginess, and if they're pushed hard the Granada will dodge about too much, trying hard to lock a rear wheel and calling for some correction at the wheel.

While the strength of the Citroen's brakes is impressive, especially in high speed stops, we found ourselves feeling somewhat disenchanted with the set-up in the GTi. The pads seem to be a lot harder than they are in the other CXs, calling for higher pedal pressure (and yet with the minimal pedal movement that is part and parcel of the Citroen system). The idea of the system is to demand as little by way of effort as the steering does: just a gentle squeeze with the toes. But with the heavier pressures required in the GTi, the brake/steering balance is disrupted. Was it that inconsistency that made the action of the clutch seem more annoying in city traffic than we'd remembered from other CXs too? Certainly it does not take up very smoothly, the angle of the pedal itself is very awkward and it is well out of line with the brake and throttle. There is also a long throw, and not enough space between the floor and the underside of the dash for a size nine foot to travel vertically. Again, this is entirely out of phase with the theory and the action of the steering. As LJK Setright has so often asked, why on earth don't Citroen do the logical thing and use high pressure hydraulics for the clutch too? The gearshift is fractionally too far forward, and while it's not a bad shift it's not a very good one. The fact that we happened to have the CX Familiale with its C-matic transmission in our clutches while we had the GTi only helped to show up the deficiencies of the clutch/shift of the manual car, not so much because they are especially bad but just because they are out of phase with the steering and the overall, very special character of the CX.

The dash is as unorthodox as the suspension, the steering and the body styling. There are the two 'horns' that sweep back either side of the one-spoke wheel, thus locating the minor controls precisely at the finger tips. There are also the strange rotating drum instruments in their TV-like windows; we like them, many people don't. The CX does without the Ford's multi-variable intermittent wiper sweep and there's no sunroof even if you want one, but there are electric front windows and a detachable map light, dual tone horns, a push-button check on the dash for the engine oil level, built-in rear foglights as well as the front ones. The foglight switch hides up under one of the 'horns'.

COMFORT

French cars in general and Citroens in particular are renowned for their comfort. Step inside the GTi and you're in an even plusher world than even the CX usually provides. The upholstery is a mixture of jersey and cord cloth (some spectacular leather schemes are optional) and looks quite irresistible; not only are the seats so sumptuous looking, but the cabin as a whole really looks finished off, with nicely moulded door panels which incorporate properly usable arm rests as well as radio speakers, and carpeting that extends up the sides of the central console; in the back there are even blinds that can be pulled up to shut the sun off tender necks. The seats themselves are soft foam, and apparently well-shaped; but while they certainly are comfortable, they don't have quite enough lateral support to fully locate you at the sort of cornering forces the GTi can generate so easily. While one of our number had a mild grumble about insufficient lumber support as well, the rest of us found the seats as pampering as ever. In the back, the shape of the seats makes up for only fair legroom and the overall level of comfort is sufficient to put passengers to sleep in very short order. The ride is fairly firmly damped, so that at low speeds over cobbles, for instance, it can actually feel a little joggly, but at any sort of cruising speed it is really superb; fluid and very relaxed. Crests are really the only things that can catch the CX out – it just doesn't like to have its nose lift high, and it will wobble in objection as it drops its wheels back down again. The engine is on the raucous side when it's revved, but it's unobtrusive enough at cruising speeds unless you're well over 100mph. Windnoise is low, but even that's too much for our liking; the car isn't as quiet as it deserves to be. At 80mph, the Granada is discernibly quieter, with almost no engine noise and very little by way of rushing wind. But the Ford doesn't ride nearly as well as the CX; to achieve such a high level of handling, its suspension has been set quite firmly. It is not uncomfortable though; in fact, we prefer the feeling of control it has to the softer arrangment in the Granada Ghia, which sometimes has

Ford's dash is neatly-styled and ergonomically efficient, vision is very good in all directions and ventilation excellent (top). Seats are not as good as they look, lacking adequate leg and lumbar support (second down). Boot is conventionally shaped but holds a lot (third down). Injection unit gives engine good visual appeal, power up high is very good (above). Details, top to bottom: one key works doors, boot and ignition (central locking is an extra), Michelin TRXs transform steering and handling but gearshift is too far forward and back seat squab is far too upright and uncomfortable

wayward handling. The S feels to have more integrity, more character; and whether it's simply the tyres or not we don't know, but there is less road noise than in the more expensive model. The driveline vibration is still there though. What lets the Granada down most, however, is its interior. When it comes face to face with something like the CX, it looks too basic, well-equipped and tasteful though it may be. It's essentially just another interior; and as you might have gathered from our story last month, we are singularly unimpressed with Ford's new seating arrangements. The front buckets are too short in the cushion and there isn't enough lumbar support in the squabs. The back seat is a nightmare: a cushion that lacks any sort of positive support and a squab that not only lacks lower back support but is too upright. During this test, we had a number of people who hadn't sampled the Ghia earlier in the back seat of the S; they grumbled as much as our Ghia passengers had, even the children among them. So, if it was a question of carrying four or five, the Ford was left behind in favour of the Citroen every time. Boots on both cars are very good, the Citroen's deep, low-level box being especially useful (and with the self-levelling suspension to take care of any weight you might care to emburden it with). Finish is about equal on both cars; fair. Lights are poor on the Granada on low beam, very good on high beam; the Citroen's aren't as good as they look or as they should be for fast, long distance night work. Ventilation is awful in the Citroen. If you can afford it, order the optional air conditioning.

CONCLUSIONS

Despite the absolutely superb handling of the Ford – and one can gain tremendous pleasure from driving it, so it's a real GT car in that sense – we'd plump for the Citroen every time. It won't accelerate as quickly, but it's every bit as fast point-to-point and because of its ride and its seats it is going to get both driver and passengers there in considerably more comfort than the Ford. Once you've learned how to drive it properly – and if you've not driven a CX or SM before, it really does take you a good many days to feel at ease – you find that it can be hurried along give and take roads at consistently high and safe speeds. Rushing into bends with it is no good: enter them relatively slowly and you will find that you can then simply build up speed as you go through to exit at a very rapid rate of knots (so fast, sometimes, you'll be hoping there isn't another bend in quick succession!). If you do get it wrong, the car does its level best to keep everything under control, eventually doing the right thing, when all else has failed, by going into oversteer. It is an immensely safe car. We love the CX's shape, we always enjoy its comfort; and yet we left this, the fastest CX yet, with less enthusiasm than we expected. It's time for Citroen to tread the refinement path again (has it suffered at the hands of the company's financial problems?) ditching that mechanically-operated clutch in favour of a hydraulic unit with as little movement as the brakes and steering require; at the very least, the angle of the pedal and the space available for the foot in front of it needs attention. The gearchange could also be improved, the windnoise should be despatched altogether, and the ventilation made much better. What the car really needs is not just an injection engine nor a five-speed gearbox; it still deserves a good rotary engine, or the Renault/Peugeot/Volvo V6 and a proper automatic transmission. Until something like that happens, however good the CX may already be, we don't think its real promise will be fulfilled. The Ford? If you're into handling and not much else it's simply terrific; otherwise, it feels too under-developed, too cold and crude, something of a boy-racer machine. The drive-line vibration and why Ford won't cure it you know about (*CAR* Nov); there's no excuse for getting the seats wrong though, and they let the car down as a long-distance four seater. For a driver alone the Ford can be a very nice car; beyond that, it doesn't seem to offer enough for the money just yet.

Four years on, CX still looks modern as tomorrow. GTi has matt black window surrounds, alloy wheels

Clean Ford is elegant rather than handsome, well-proportioned Optional headlight washers mount in big over-riders

	Citroen	Granada
Capacity	2347	2792
Bore (mm)	93.5	93.0
Stroke (mm)	85.5	68.5
Compression (to one)	8.75	9.2
Valve gear	OHV	OHV
Aspiration	Bosch injection	Bosch injection
Power (DIN/rpm)	128/4800	160/5700
Torque (DIN/rpm)	145.4/36	162/4300
TRANSMISSION		
Type	FWD, five-speed	RWD, four-speed
Ratios and mph/1000		
First	3.16/4.9	3.16/6.5
Second	1.83/8.4	1.95/10.6
Third	1.25/12.4	1.41/14.7
Fourth	0.94/16.5	1.00/20.7
Fifth	0.73/21.1	
Final drive ratio	4.76	3.45
CHASSIS AND BODY		
Construction	Front subframe, unitary	Unitary
Front suspension	Parallel arms, hydropneumatic unit, anti-roll bar	Wishbones, coils, anti-roll bar
Rear suspension	Independent, trailing arms, hydropneumatic units, anti-roll bar	Independent, semi-trailing arms, variable rate coils, anti-roll bar
Steering	Varipower rack and pinion	Powered rack and pinion
Turns lock to lock	2.5	3.5
Turning circle	38ft 8.5in	34ft
Wheels	Cast magnesium 5.5J x 14	Alloy 6J x 15.35
Brakes, type	Servoed discs	Servoed discs and drums
DIMENSIONS (inches)		
Wheelbase	112	109
Front track	58	59.3
Rear track	53.5	60.5
Length	183.75	187
Width	68.25	70.5
Ground clearance	6	7
Fuel tank (gals)	15	14.3
CABIN DIMENSIONS (inches)		
Front headroom	38.5	38
Front legroom (seat forward/back)	34/41	35.3/41
Rear headroom	36	36
Rear legroom (seat forward/back)	39/32	33/26.3
Front shoulder room	54.5	56.7
Rear shoulder room	53.5	56.7
Luggage capacity (cu ft)	16.8	13.2
MAINTENANCE		
Major service time	4hrs 57min	2hrs 36min
Sump (capacity/oil grade)	9.25/20W50	7.48/10W30
Oil change intervals	3000miles	6000miles
Grease points/intervals	None	None
Time for removing/replacing engine/gearbox	17hrs 24min/ 12hrs 36min	3hrs 30min/ 2hrs
Time for replacing clutch	12hrs 6min	2hrs 12min
Time for renewing front brake pads	1hr 18min	36min
Time for renewing exhaust system	3hrs 30min	1hr
Number of UK dealers	211	1200
MECHANICAL SPARES PRICES		
Engine	605.92exch	497.40 new
Gearbox	456.91exch	N/A YET
Differential	N/A YET	252.40
Clutch unit	50.5	53.06
Brake disc	32.08	12.73
Set brake pads	16.90	13.72
Set drum linings	—	14.12
Fuel pump	92.11	—
Damper (front)	35.31sphere	13.85
Exhaust system	82.23	104.22
Oil filter	4.30	3.29
Alternator	50.98exch	61.34
Starter motor	61.71exch	N/A YET
Speedometer	56.45	N/A YET
BODY PART PRICES		
Front door (primer)	57.41	58.22
Front bumper	37.36	21.54
Bonnet (primer)	71.76	90.54
Windscreen	136.47	19.95
Headlamp unit (each)	42.98	21.75
Grille	23.27	22.21
TOTAL COST, INCLUDING CAR TAX AND VAT		
Price without extras	£6350	£5910
Price as tested	£6350	£6264
Model range price span	£4495-£8250	£2830-£6974
GUARANTEE		
Length and conditions	12months/ unlimited mileage	12months/ unlimited mileage

ACCELERATION	0-30	0-40	0-50	0-60	0-70
Citroen	3.4	5.0	7.2	9.8	13.4
Ford	2.9	4.6	6.5	8.8	11.0

SPEED IN GEARS	FIRST	SECOND	THIRD	FOURTH	FIFTH
Citroen	0-30	0-50	5-75	10-99	15-118
Ford	0-43	0-69	10-96	20-120	

Fuel consumption (on Elf): Citroen 20-24mpg, Ford 20-24mpg

The last of its kind

MOTOR Test

Will anyone ever build another car as complex as Citroen's CX series?

THE Citroen CX series has always resided on a pedestal in the minds of most motorists — including the staff of Modern Motor. For some reason or other, our staffers have never spent any real time behind the wheel of a CX, but we have had a clear preconception of how its progress would be quiet, quick and delightfully easy on the occupants.

But just as there are some people you like better by not getting to know them too well, we rather wish now that our acquaintance with the CX GE 2200 had remained a distant one. It is never nice to have your dreams shattered.

Perhaps we expected too much, or perhaps we should have allowed a practical outlook to be overawed by the sheer complexity of the device. Either way, we found little of the magic we expected.

There is a saying that "there are cars, and there are Citroens", and we suppose we can understand why some people are diehard enthusiasts for the marque.

Certainly, in terms of one-upmanship, the CX has absolutely no equal. Its styling, even amongst contemporary wedges, is still unique and carries a considerable "presence". For some buyers, that's very important.

We think we can understand, too, how the car might come into its own on an undulating autoroute in its home country, or even bashing across a dusty plain out here.

In many ways, the CX is well-suited to country use, and in fact the cars coming to Australia are "distant export" versions modified for rough going.

The modifications include additional gussets in the body, reinforced front and rear suspension frames, extra dust-sealing and filtering and even such rally tweaks as a flexible alternator mounting.

The radiator is also larger than the domestic version.

One modification which is largely unwarranted here is a smaller rear roll bar, presumably because Citroen France imagines we spend most of our time on loose surfaces.

For most users, in fact, the CX could do with considerably less understeer and more control of the roll movement. We found the CX to be not a particularly pleasant car to drive in any way fast on a twisty road.

As cornering speed increases, so does the understeer, in a pretty dramatic way. At the same time, the front tyres protest loudly.

The unique feature of the CX — its interconnected hydraulic suspension system — does not really like being hurried into changing its pressures and fluid flows to cope with repeated changes in direction.

Through a set of S-bends, the CX lurches from one roll angle to the other and defies attempts at smooth cornering.

Where it does show up well is through long, fast curves where the self-levelling suspension can get down to the business of balancing everything up.

The unusual power assistance employed by Citroen does not make it any easier to come to terms with the handling. The effort input from the steering wheel goes into the power assistance control unit, which then actuates the rack.

A mechanical link exists in case of hydraulic failure, but the system effectively damps out any real road feel. It compensates for this by varying the force felt at the wheel according to road speed.

This artificial "feel" is produced by a cam linked to the wheel, and the force felt increases with the angle of the wheel and with speed through a centrifugally-operated governor. It is extremely clever, but we can't help asking why. Less complicated power-assisted racks are nicer to use.

Another failing is that, in parking manoeuvres, it is possible to move the wheel more quickly than the power assistance can cope, so you must adapt to using slow and deliberate movements of the steering.

The system does have the advantage of having foolproof self-centering. It would be possible to lock up the brakes with one flat tyre and no hands on the wheel, and the Citroen would stop in a straight line, which is very handy if you happen to want to try that trick.

The hydraulic suspension system has some endearing traits. For instance, when you brake for a set of lights it keeps the nose from dipping, and then when you stop everything subsides gently until you drive off.

The principle of the suspension system is that each

The CX GE 2200 Citroen. Our colour picture is a time-exposure showing the extremities obtainable through the adjustable ground clearance. At its highest point, the car is 275 mm above the ground, at its lowest, 155 mm.

wheel is interlinked by hydraulics. The actual springing is largely provided by gas contained in a sphere attached to each wheel.

Between the membrane containing the gas and an actuating piston in the unit is a quantity of fluid which can be varied in volume by a central pump to adjust the ride height at that particular wheel.

Plunk a whole lot of luggage in the tail, more fluid is pumped to the stern and everything is levelled up again. The same applies from side to side.

Its other characteristic, which could be of enormous value in the scrub, is that it allows the height of the suspension to be varied at will.

A lever in the centre console allows the driver to select low, normal, high or emergency position. Fully extended, the suspension gives 275 mm of ground clearance. In this position, speed must be limited, but in the next slot, which still gives more clearance than the average car, you can run at full stream.

The self-levelling does guarantee a complete absence of pitch, but it doesn't give a magic carpet ride. You can still feel the bumps when they come, and the ride is about the equivalent of a reasonably sorted-out conventional system.

The brakes are also unique to Citroen in their mode of operation, but they really do work and if there is any one area of the car that is outstanding, it is the stopping department.

Anyone who has driven a truck with air brakes will understand the feel of the CX brakes. You don't depress a pedal in the ordinary way. Instead, you apply pressure to a control button, which looks like a pedal.

The first stop inevitably results in violent overbraking, but it is surprising how quickly your foot can be trained to hold itself in check, rather like adapting to ping pong after lawn tennis.

Once you have the knack the braking is brillian , helped by the anti-drive provided by the self-levelling suspension.

The four-wheel discs went on stopping our test car with no sign of fade despite some very hard use. Which is just as well because the system is such that you are unlikely to detect any change in effort as a more conventional system might provide before the brakes go on holiday. There was no sign of any lock-up at the rear, but any attempt at left-foot braking to reduce understeer would need a lot of practice.

The hydraulic plumbing does add apparent confusion to the Citroen's under-bonnet scene, but closer inspection shows that the general level of accessibility is good.

The Citroen's powerplant is a 2175cc overhead valve four-cylinder which develops 82 kW at 5500 rpm. It is mounted transversely and, naturally, drives the front wheels.

Carburation is by dual-choke downdraught 34 mm Weber, and the engine is fairly lively, if a little noisy.

Power comes on fairly strongly from about 3000 rpm, and the redline shows up at 6000 rpm. Keeping the engine

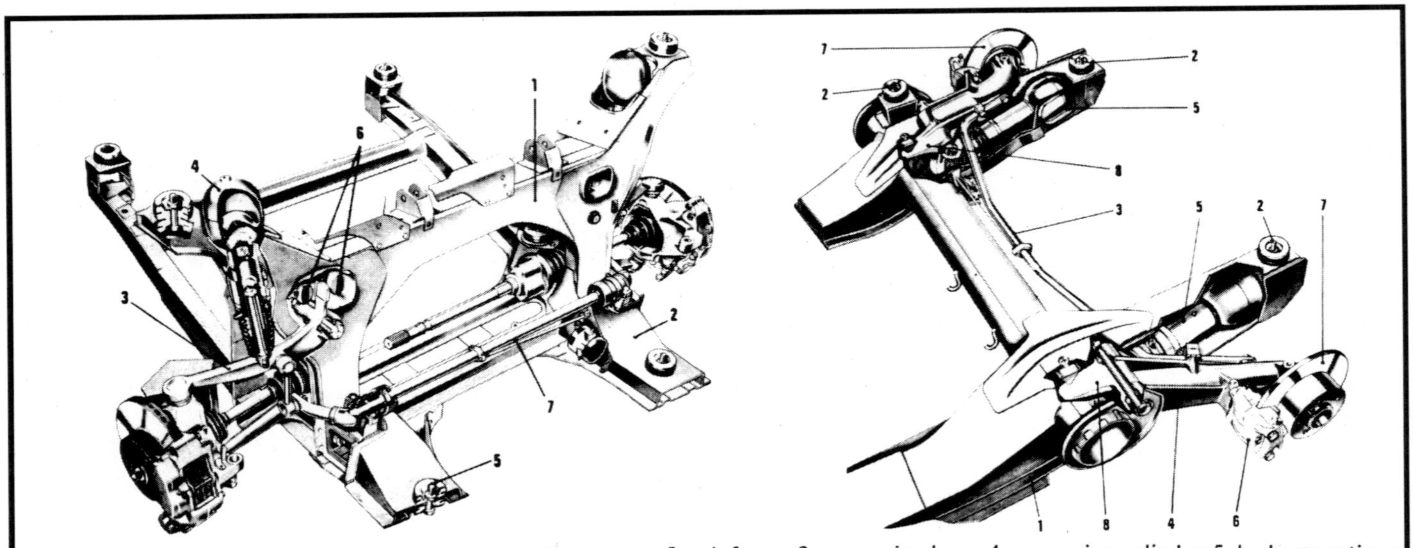

The CX suspension set-up. Left, the front: 1, front unit structure; 2, sub-frame; 3, suspension lever; 4, suspension cylinder; 5, body mountings; 6, bump and rebound buffers; 7, anti-roll bar. Right, the rear: 1, sub-frame; 2, flexible mountings; 3, anti-roll bar; 4, wheel arm; 5, suspension cylinder; 6, braking unit; 7, disc; 8, bump and rebound stops.

between these limits is fairly easy with the four well-spaced ratios. The gearshift, though, is rather long and cumbersome.

The mechanical noise level is higher than we expected (again maybe we expected too much). But what's even more startling is the unbelievably rowdy electric fan which is thermostatically controlled. It cuts in with a wail that turns even the heads of passers-by.

Economy in terms of a 2-litre engine is not exceptional but — rated against the size of the car, its passenger and luggage capacity and the number of ancillary power systems employed — it's probably quite reasonable at 13.1 litres per 100 kilometres.

The flight deck of the CX is most impressive with the instrument pod housing a dozen warning lights and half a dozen instruments.

If anything major is amiss, a large red "stop" signal lights up, and minor lights indicate the source of the problem.

The bank of warning lights covers everything from worn brake pads to low hydraulic fluid level. There is even a low-beam warning light but, strangely, there did not seem to be one for the choke, even though the literature lists one.

The speedometer and tachometer display their readings in magnifying windows. The idea isn't new and we find it hard to justify.

With the speedometer, the read-out is reasonable, though it does require you to actually read the number rather than register a position, as with a normal instrument.

The tachometer, however, is a nuisance and does not compare with being able to glance at a needle position when the instrument is being used to provide a guide to maximum revs.

A clock, water temperature, fuel gauge and odometer read-out complete the panel.

In aircraft style, minor controls are placed on the extremities of the pod and are arranged so that more than one finger can be used to operate them.

However, in terms of ergonomics, the system tends to assume the hands are always in the straight-ahead position.

Dipping the headlights in the middle of a corner requires a more precise hand movement than flicking a normal steering column stalk.

Another quirk is that the Citroen has no self-cancelling system for the turn indicators. They are controlled by a simple rocker switch and with practice you get into the habit of flicking the switch to off after a corner. But it's just one more thing you have to remember in traffic.

The test CX had optional air conditioning, which the large area of steeply raked glass would make almost mandatory in the Australian summer. The system had a good output, but you can detect its effect on the car's performance.

The front windows are electrically operated, while the rear use a normal manual winding system.

The single windscreen wiper is one huge blade which sweeps an impressive area of the sloping screen. It's fast enough to cope with heavy rain and fast touring speeds, but there is no provision for an intermittent mode.

The rear window has an effective electric demist.

The seats, which are upholstered in a pleasant velour, are very comfortable and have a good range of adjustment.

In the rear, there is an enormous amount of legroom, and the flat floor resulting from the front-wheel-drive layout adds to the general spaciousness.

The boot is huge and must be the easiest of any car to load. This is because the whole of the car's vertical face forms part of the lid, and there is no lip at the extremity of the luggage area.

The general level of finish, both inside and on the exterior, is excellent. One could imagine that the person who will buy the Citroen will get pleasure out of keeping it looking good.

Obviously, any owner would need to have some mechanical enthusiasm to desire a Citroen in the first place. In this respect, the CX GE 2200 has loads of appeal.

Judged against its competitors, though, we find it hard to justify the overall complexity with its inherent cost penalty.

PRICE

Dollars x 1000

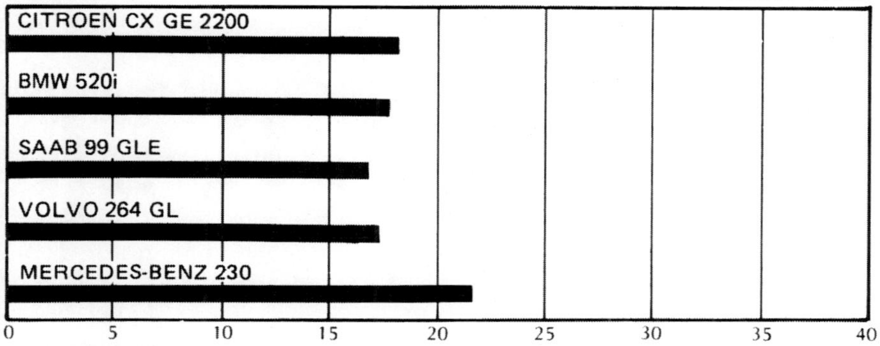

FUEL CONSUMPTION

Litres per 100 kilometres

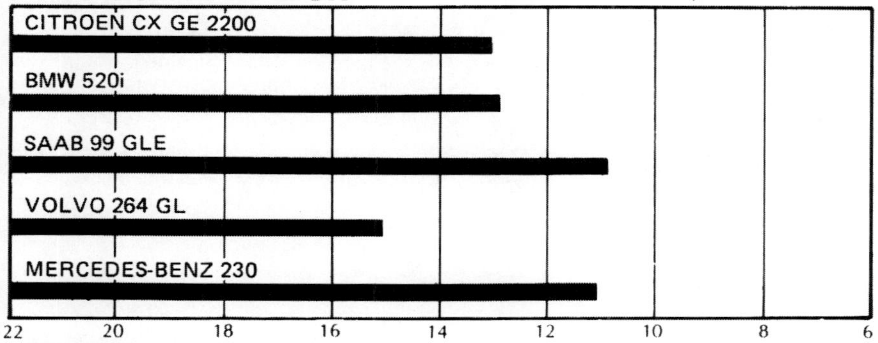

ACCELERATION

0-100 km/h, seconds

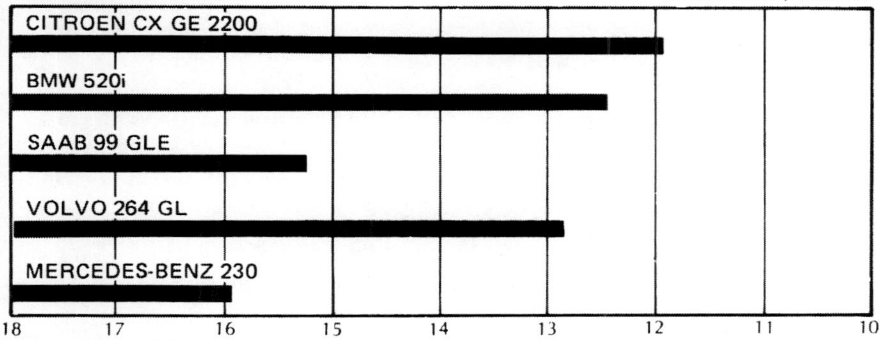

WEIGHT TO POWER

Kilograms per kiloWatt

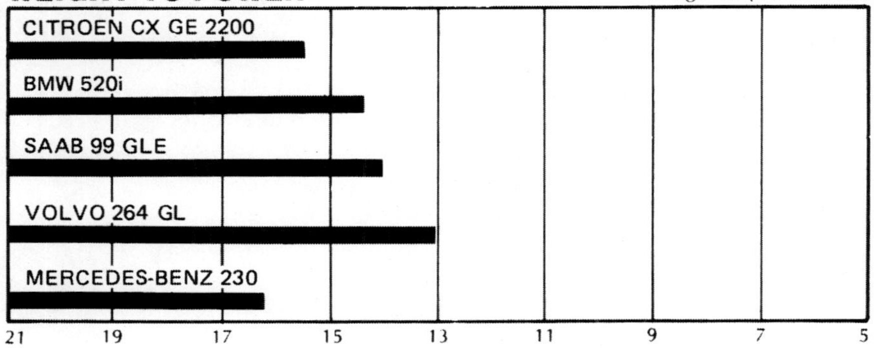

THE FIVE-STAR TEST

Comfort	★★★★
Handling	★★★
Brakes	★★★★★
Performance	★★★
Quietness	★★★
Luggage capacity	★★★★

CHECKLIST

Adjustable steering	No
Carpets	Yes
Cigarette lighter	Yes
Clock	Yes
Day/night mirror	Yes
Hazard flashers	Yes
Heated rear window	Yes
Laminated screen	Yes
Petrol filler lock	Yes
Radio	Yes
Tachometer	Yes
Intermittent wipers	No
Rear window wiper	No

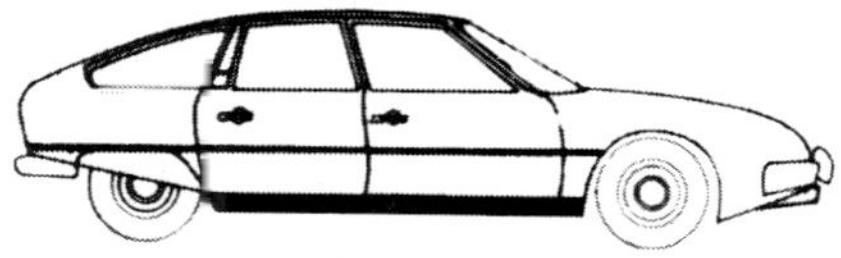

CITROEN CX GE 2200 ROAD TEST DATA

As tested

ENGINE

Location	Front
Cylinders	4
Bore x Stroke	90 x 85.5 mm
Capacity	2175cc
Carburation	Dual downdraught 34 mm Weber
Compression Ratio	9:1
Fuel Pump	Mechanical
Valve Gear	OHV
Maximum Power	82 kW at 5500 rpm
Maximum Torque	167 Nm at 3500 rpm

TRANSMISSION

Type	Four-speed manual
Driving Wheels	Front
Clutch	Single dry plate
Gearbox ratios	
First	3.166
Second	1.833
Third	1.133
Fourth	0.800
Final Drive Ratio	3.153

SUSPENSION

Front	Independent, upper and lower transverse arms, anti-roll bar
Rear	Independent, trailing arms' anti-roll bar
Shock Absorbers	Hydropneumatic
Wheels	5J x 14
Tyres	185HR x 14

BRAKES

Front	260 mm discs
Rear	233 mm discs

STEERING

Type	Rack and pinion
Turn, Lock to Lock	2.5
Turning Circle	10.9 metres

DIMENSIONS AND WEIGHT

Wheelbase	2845 mm
Front Track	1474 mm
Rear Track	1360 mm
Overall Length	4630 mm
Overall Width	1730 mm
Overall Height	1360 mm
Ground Clearance	155-275 mm
Kerb Weight	1265 kg

CAPACITIES AND EQUIPMENT

Fuel Tank	68 litres
Cooling System	11 litres
Engine Sump	5.7 litres
Battery	12 V 50 Ah
Alternator	72 A

CALCULATED DATA

Weight to Power	15.43 kg/kW
Specific Power Output	37.70 kW/litre

FUEL CONSUMPTION

Average for Test	13.1 litres/100 km
Best Recorded	12.5 litres/100 km

ACCELERATION

0-60 km/h	5.0 seconds
0-80 km/h	7.5 seconds
0-100 km/h	11.9 seconds
0-110 km/h	15.0 seconds

OVERTAKING TIMES

	3rd	4th
50-80 km/h	4.2s	6.9s
60-100 km/h	7.7s	13.5s
80-110 km/h	5.2s	8.1s

STANDING 400 METRES

Average	19.0 seconds
Best Recorded	18.9 seconds

SPEED IN GEARS

First	61 km/h
Second	79 km/h
Third	122 km/h
Fourth	163 km/h

Citroën CX 2400 GTi

The fastest, most powerful CX yet. Incorporating Bosch L-jetronic petrol injection and five-speed transmission. Good, safe handling and excellent ride comfort. A superb car, let down by rather poor ventilation.

EVER SINCE the appearance of the corrugated-iron 2CV immediately after the War, it would be fair to say that Citroën have never built a conventional car. Indeed, in many ways, Citroën have done everything that was, at the time, against all engineering tradition.

In 1955, they stood the motoring world on its head with the introduction of the ID/DS range, a car which was said to be 10 years ahead of its time. Now, some 22 years later, no other manufacturer has quite caught up with the French revolution.

The CX, which appeared, in its 2-litre form, in 1974, was not perhaps such a surprise. Although its long, smooth shape continues in the DS tradition, it was nothing like as startling as the SM. With the new car, Citroën were able to pick the best of the bunch from their previous ideas. Naturally, front-wheel drive was retained, but the engine was transverse, canted forward, with the transmission behind it. The oleo-pneumatic, self-levelling suspension was retained, and the self-centering, power steering came from the SM.

In May of this year, the GTi was launched in continental Europe, and last month it became available in Britain. The engine, with bore and stroke dimensions of 93.5 × 85.5mm, is one of the largest four-cylinder units in use today, with a capacity of 2,347 c.c. The biggest change is the use of petrol injection in place of the twin-choke Weber used on the normal CX2400; the system is Bosch's L-jetronic, electronically controlled. This, with a marginal increase in compression ratio from 8.75 to 9.10-to-1, brings about an 11.5 per cent increase in power, from 115 bhp (DIN) at 5,500 rpm to 128 bhp, developed at only 4,800 rpm. Torque too is up, by 10 per cent, to a

Citroen's unique shape for the CX is unmistakable, a blend of curves and sweeps. On the GTi, the front fog lamps are standard, as are the light alloy wheels and black surrounds to the side and rear windows. There are GTi badges on the boot panel and quarter pillars

useful 145 lb.ft. at 3,600 rpm. To maintain tune and to reduce servicing costs, the GTi is fitted with contactless electronic ignition.

There are major changes, too, in the transmission. The four-speed, manual gearbox of the carburettor-engined car is replaced by an all-indirect, five-speed one; the tyre size and sections are unchanged, using Michelin XVS 185HR14 covers, but mounted on lightweight alloy wheels.

First gear is marginally lower than on the carburettor car (3.17 compared to 3.15-to-1) but top is now a true overdrive, pulling 21.1mph per 1000 rpm on the same 4.77-to-1 final drive ratio. This high gearing means that the GTi tends to be far more comfortable when cruising really fast on motorways, but even so, at the mean maximum speed of 118 mph the revs are well past the peak of the power curve, at nearly 5,600 rpm.

Front-wheel-drive cars always tend to look and sound slightly "hooligan" when moving off under full power but, with its big section tyres, the GTi managed to retain some of its dignity, with just a few yards of wheelspin when the clutch was engaged at around 3,500 rpm. The extra power and torque by comparison with the CX2400 show up immediately in terms of times taken in acceleration, with 40 coming up in 5.1sec against 5.8sec, 60 in 10.1 (11.8) and 80 mph in 18.2 sec, 2.8 sec better than the CX2400.

It took a certain amount of experimenting to get best times for, with the power being developed low in the rev range, there was a tendency to hang on in the gears up to the 6,000 rpm red line. We eventually settled for changing at 5,500 rpm. The difference is shown by the times recorded — 10.1sec to 60 mph changing at 5,500, against 10.6sec at 6,000 rpm. But the really remarkable feature about the GTi is the extraordinary flexibility of the engine, especially when it is remembered that it has only four cylinders. In top (fifth) gear it would pull away cleanly from 20mph — that is under 1,000 rpm — without any fuss. This is a real credit to the combination of engine design and the efficiency of the L-jetronic injection.

In the lower gears, the GTi will reach 29, 51, 74, and 99 mph at 6,000 rpm; these figures are rather academic, however, as it pays to change up 500 rpm earlier, no matter what the circumstances.

Ride and handling

There can be little doubt that, for the first few days of ownership, the GTi can be a rather disconcerting car to drive. The VariPower steering seems to have a mind of its own, the brake pedal no apparent travel, and the drive line can snatch and jerk. It takes time to come to terms with it, but once you have altered your method of driving, the GTi becomes a thoroughly rewarding car to use.

There are just 2.5 turns from lock to lock on the steering, which has power self-centering. Newcomers will drive the car in a series of lurches, until they realize that it must be steered every inch of the way. Let the steering wheel run back of its own accord on the exit from a corner and it will snap back to the centre position. But if the wheel is fed back smoothly, the car responds in a similar manner and one soon learns the technique required for comfortable driving.

The GTi has very nearly 70 per cent of its 26.8 cwt over the front wheels, and this gives it inherent understeer characteristics. The power steering gives just the right amount of assistance, so that it feels heavier as more lock is applied. This in turn gives the driver a good *sense* of the understeer and prevents the car from being put into attitudes from which it cannot recover. The steering is also speed-sensitive, with less assistance being given the faster the car is travelling. On motorways, this means that it feels very heavy but, as you never want to turn at right angles at this sort of speed, it gives the car a very high degree of stability. We have found that all the CX range tend to wander very slightly at speed; left to their own devices, they are happy but if the driver tries to correct, a weaving motion will set in.

The original oleo-pneumatic, self-levelling suspension system used on the DS has been considerably refined and is no longer, as we once described it, "heave and sigh for the open road. . . ." The ride comfort is good, with ample wheel and "spring" movement to absorb humps, undulations, and potholes with ease. Yet the damping effect is on the firm side, which cuts out any tendency to wallow or pitch. It is only on coarsely-surfaced roads (concrete sections of motorway especially) that any harshness is transmitted into the passenger compartment. Running over cats' eyes will also produce a sharp bang.

Between the front seats is a control to adjust ride height. There are two "on the move" positions: normal and high. The very high, wheel-changing position can be used at low speeds on very rough tracks.

Despite the apparently packed underbonnet area, access around the transverse engine is fairly good. The injection control equipment is behind the four induction pipes. The rectangular unit to the left of the spare wheel is the heater/ventilation intake. The wheel changing equipment is stowed on top of the spare, with the central hydraulic reservoir tucked in the right-hand rear corner of the bonnet opening. The bonnet is propped open by an over-centre strut

Fuel consumption

Our fuel measurement equipment does not yet allow us to tackle cars with petrol injection but, overall, the GTi returned 21.6 mpg, compared with the 23.5 mpg of the CX2400 carburettor car which we tested in July of this year. Our best figure, using the car for normal running about and keeping off motorways and high-speed driving, was 23.1mpg, while a really fast run dropped the brim-to-brim figure to 19.4mpg. So, with reasonable use, the 15 gallon tank should give a range of about 320 miles. A good feature is that the fuel filler has a big neck, so there is no blowing back.

Brakes

Full power braking, using the high-pressure hydraulic system which also serves the suspension and steering, is used on the CX GTi. As we said earlier, this tends to be a bit disconcerting at first because the pedal has hardly any travel. A progressive spring bias is built in to give the feel. Pressures are light, with just 20lb needed for check braking and 50lb giving a maximum of 0.95g. Because the CX GTi has anti-dive suspension the nose does not dip, even under heavy braking, and this can give the impression that the brakes are not working properly. From cold there is a tendency for some initial fade, but this stabilizes after five stops from 70mph at 0.5g.

The parking brake works, unusually, on the front discs, using its own separate pads. With so much weight over the front wheels it is highly effective, giving 0.45g, which means that it could be useful in an emergency. It held the car easily on the 1-in-3 hill, from which it was able to move off again with just a scrabble of front wheelspin.

Fittings and comfort

Like the rest of the car, Citroën like to be different from everyone else when it comes to the interior. They have managed to break away from the traditional layout; their facia panel looks more like a piece of modern sculpture than the product of a car factory.

In their own perverse way, they have also stuck to their rotating drum speedometer and rev counter. While these may fit the company's futuristic image, they cannot be read quickly; dials with needle pointers would be very much better. For the fuel gauges and voltmeter, vertical scale displays are used; the fuel gauge is not a hot wire type, and lurches up and down in corners or under acceleration. The GTi has the usual CX press-button oil level sight glass tucked away beneath the right-hand side of the facia, and only this model has the temperature gauge on the opposite side.

The main controls and switches are carried on two "horns" which flank the instruments and are within finger-tip reach when the hands are on the steering wheel. The group on the left include a rocking switch for the indicators which, as in all Citroëns, are not self-cancelling. A loud repeater and clear warning lamp ensure that the driver does not forget, and after a few miles one starts to appreciate this system. Beneath the indicators is the wiper switch with intermittent sweep position. All the CX range have a single, huge blade, pivoted centrally. This is effective enough up to about 70mph, but beyond that there is a tendency for it to lift off at the top of the blade, right in the driver's line of vision. A light pressure on the horn button produces a polite noise; more pressure and a pair of strident air horns join in. On the opposite side, matching switches control the headlamp dip/main beam, main lighting switch and the headlamp flasher.

The headlamps are not particularly good, producing a woolly pattern on dip beam and a rather uncontrolled blast of light on main beam. On the GTi, a pair of very effective front foglamps are standard, as are the built-in rear foglamps, controlled by press-button switches hidden away under the control panel. Lighting for the speedometer and rev counter comes on with the ignition, the remainder of the instrument lighting being controlled by the main lighting switch. A dimmer controls the intensity.

A central console carries the radio (an extra), ashtray and cigarette lighter, controls for the electric front windows, and press button switches for the heated rear window and really good interior lamp. Tucked between the seats, alongside the suspension height control, are the group of three heater and ventilation controls.

For a car which started on a virtually clean sheet of paper, the ventilation is something of a disappointment. There is little ram effect, and the blower is needed virtually all the time. A water-valve heater control is used, and this takes a long time to

This facia could only be on a Citroën. The "drum" speedometer and rev counter flank the total and trip mileage recorders, with the clock on the left and combination fuel and battery condition gauges on the right. The temperature gauge is alongside the ignition lock. The row of warning lamps monitor all usual functions, plus the central hydraulic system. Finger-tip controls on the left are for indicators, wash/wipe and horn, and on the right, main lighting switch, dip and flash. Switches around gear lever are for electric front windows, heated rear window and interior lamp. Heater, ventilation and suspension ride height controls are out of this picture, alongside the handbrake

Specification

ENGINE	Front, front drive
Cylinders	4, in-line transverse
Main bearings	5
Cooling	Water
Fan	Electric
Bore, mm (in.)	93.5 (3.68)
Stroke, mm (in.)	85.5 (3.37)
Capacity, c.c. (in³)	2,347 (143)
Valve gear	ohv
Camshaft drive	Chain
Compression ratio	9.1-to-1
Octane rating	98 RM
Injection	Bosch L-jetronic
Max power	128 bhp (DIN) at 4,800 rpm
Max torque	145 lb. ft. at 3,600 rpm
TRANSMISSION	
Type	Five-speed, all-synchromesh,

Gear	Ratio	mph/1000rpm
Top	0.73	21.1
4th	0.94	16.5
3rd	1.25	12.4
2nd	1.83	8.5
1st	3.17	5.0

Final drive gear	Helical spur
Ratio	4.77-to-1
SUSPENSION	
Front—location	Double wishbones
—springs	Hyrdopneumatic
dampers	units
—anti-roll bar	Yes
Rear—location	Trailing arms
—springs	Hydropneumatic
dampers	units
—anti-roll bar	Yes
STEERING	
Type	Rack and pinion, with power self-centering
Power assistance	VariPower
Wheel diameter	15.0 in.
BRAKES	
Front	10.24 in. dia disc
Rear	9.20 in. dia disc
Servo	Hydraulic
WHEELS	
Type	Light alloy 5 studs
Rim width	5½ in.
Tyres—make	Michelin XVS
—type	Radial ply, tubeless
—size	185HR14
EQUIPMENT	
Battery	12 volt, 60 Ah
Alternator	80 amp
Headlamps	Halogen, 90/190 watts total
Reversing lamp	Standard
Hazard warning	Standard
Electric fuses	4
Screen wiper	Two-speed, plus intermittent
Screen washer	Electric
Interior heater	Water valve
Interior trim	Cloth seats, pvc headlining
Floor covering	Carpet
Jack	Screw pillar
Jacking points	4, under sills
Windscreen	Laminated
Underbody protection	Paint and wax
MAINTENANCE	
Fuel tank	15.0 Imp gal (68 litres)
Cooling system	18.5 pints (inc heater)
Engine sump	8.2 pints SAE 20W/50
Gearbox and final drive	2.8 pints SAE 80EP
Grease	No points
Valve clearance	Inlet 0.006 in. (cold) Exhaust 0.008 in. (cold)
Contact breaker	Electronic ignition
Ignition timing	25 deg BTDC (at 2,500 rpm)
Spark plug—type	Champion L87Y
—gap	0.025 in.
Tyre pressures	F30, R32 psi (normal driving)
Max payload	1,025 lb (466 kg)

Maximum Speeds

Gear	mph	kph	rpm
Top (mean)	118	190	5,590
(best)	117	188	5,545
4th	99	159	6,000
3rd	74	119	6,000
2nd	51	82	6,000
1st	29	47	6,000

Acceleration

True mph	Time (sec)	Speedo mph
30	**3.5**	28
40	**5.1**	40
50	**7.4**	51
60	**10.1**	61
70	**13.7**	72
80	**18.2**	82
90	**24.3**	92
100	**34.4**	103
110	—	114

Standing ¼-mile: **17.4 sec,** 75 mph
kilometre: **32.3 sec,** 97 mph

mph	Top	4th	3rd	2nd
10-30	—	8.8	5.9	3.8
20-40	10.9	7.8	5.4	3.6
30-50	10.9	7.5	5.1	3.9
40-60	11.0	7.8	5.0	—
50-70	11.6	8.3	6.4	—
60-80	11.7	10.8	—	—
70-90	13.4		—	—
80-100	15.7	—	—	—

Consumption

Fuel
Overall mpg: 21.6
(13.1 litres/100km)

Calculated (DIN) mpg: 21.2
(13.4 litres/100km)

Constant speed:
Measuring equipment not compatible with petrol injection.

Autocar formula
Hard driving, difficult conditions
19.6 mpg
Average driving, average conditions
23.8 mpg
Gentle driving, easy conditions
28.1 mpg

Grade of fuel: Premium, four-star (98 RM)

Mileage recorder: 3.0 per cent over-reading

Oil
Consumption (SAE 20/50)
3,000 miles per pint

Regular Service

Interval (miles)

Change	3,000	6,000	12,000
Engine oil	Yes	Yes	Yes
Oil filter	—	—	Yes
Gearbox	—	—	Yes
Spark plugs	—	—	—
Air Cleaner	—	—	Clean
Total cost	**£5.62**	**£10.57**	**£31.95**

(Assuming labour at £5.50/hour)

Brakes

Fade *(from 70 mph in neutral)*
Pedal load for 0.5g stops (lb)

	start/end		start/end
1	25/25	6	40/50
2	30/35	7	40/50
3	35/40	8	40/55
4	35/40	9	40/55
5	40/50	10	40/55

Response *from 30 mph in neutral*

Load (lb)	g	Distance (ft)
20	0.35	86
30	0.55	55
40	0.72	42
50	0.95	32
Handbrake	0.45	67

Max gradient: 1 in 3

Clutch

Pedal 40lb and 5½in.

Test Conditions

Wind: 4-10 mph
Temperature: 13 deg C (55 deg F)
Barometer: 29.8 in. Hg
Humidity: 72 per cent
Surface: Damp asphalt and concrete
Test distance: 1,137 miles

Figures taken at 3,000 miles by our own staff at the Motor Industry Research Association proving ground at Nuneaton.

Parts Cost

(including VAT)

Brake pads (2 wheels) — front	£16.90
Brake pads (2 wheels) — rear	£11.55
Exhaust system	£83.58
Tyre — each (typical advertised)	£46.22
Windscreen	£136.48
Headlamp unit	£42.98
Front wing	£42.07
Rear bumper	£66.29

Warranty Period
12 months/unlimited mileage

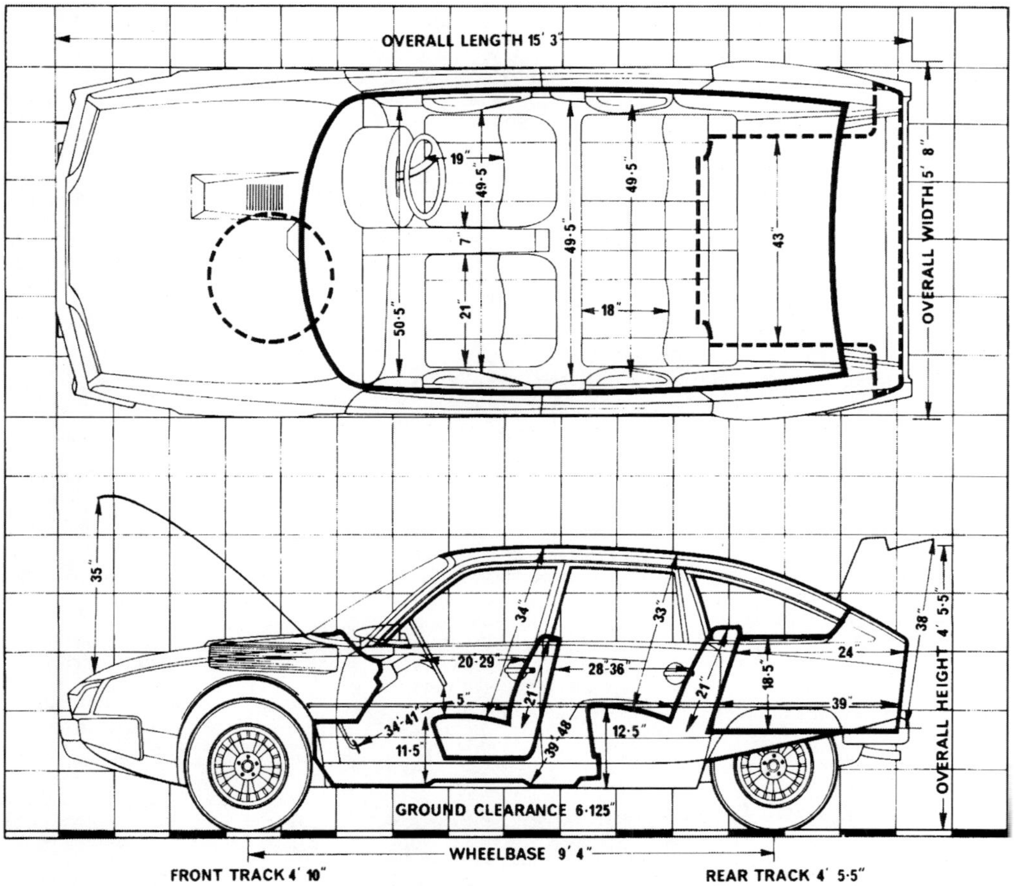

Weight

Kerb, 26.8 cwt/3,000 lb/1,364 kg
(Distribution F/R, 69.5/30.5)
As tested, 30.0cwt/3,361lb/1,528kg

Boot capacity: 16.8 cu ft

Turning circles:
Between kerbs L, 35ft 9in; R, 35ft 4in.
Between walls L, 38ft 8in; R, 38ft 6in.
Turns, lock to lock: 2.5

Test Scorecard

(Average of scoring by *Autocar* Road Test team)

Ratings: *6 Excellent*
5 Good
4 Above average
3 Below average
2 Poor
1 Bad

PERFORMANCE	4.67
STEERING AND HANDLING	4.92
BRAKES	4.40
COMFORT IN FRONT	4.17
COMFORT IN BACK	4.00
DRIVERS AIDS *(instruments, lights, wipers, visibility etc)*	4.00
CONTROLS	3.75
NOISE	4.17
STOWAGE	3.67
ROUTINE SERVICE *(under-bonnet access, dipstick etc)*	4.50
EASE OF DRIVING	4.36
OVERALL RATING	**4.30**

Comparisons

	Price (£)	Max mph	0-60 (sec)	Overall mpg	Capacity (c.c.)	Power (bhp)	Wheelbase (in.)	Length (in.)	Width (in.)	Kerb weight (cwt)	Fuel (gal)	Tyre size
Citroën CX2400 GTi	**6,530**	**117**	**10·1**	**21·6**	**2,347**	**128**	**112.0**	**181.0**	**68.0**	**26.8**	**15.0**	**185HR14**
Audi 100-5E	5,599	109	11·8	23·3	2,144	136	105.5	184.5	69.5	23.5	13.2	185/70-14
Lancia Beta 2000	4,513	110	10·1	24·0	1,995	119	100.0	169.0	66.5	21.8	11.4	175/70-14
Princess 2200 HLS (A)	4,320	98	14·2	21·8	2,227	110	105.0	175.5	68.0	23.9	16.0	185/70-14
Renault 30TS (A)	6,185	111	11·7	20·2	2,664	131	105.0	178.0	68.0	25.5	14.7	175HR14

Citroen CX2400 GTi

Left: The front seats are very comfortable, upholstered in a mixture of jersey and cord. The head restraint cushions are detachable
Above: In addition to the deep door pockets, there is a locker with a drop-down lid in front of the passenger
Right: This neat map reading light, with a flip-up magnifier, has a built in switch

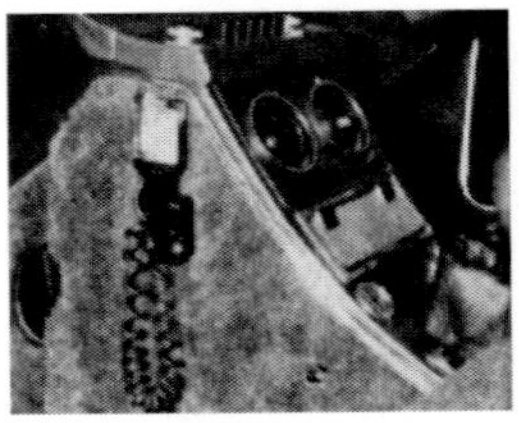

Left: The rear seats have ample head and leg room, and the armrest gives good location

Right: The door mirror is electrically adjustable by means of the small control on the sill

Below: In bright sunlight or for modesty perhaps, there are "net" blinds behind the seats, and sideways mounted sun vizors

respond, so that it tends to be difficult to achieve a comfortable climate within the cabin.

To complement the excellent ride, the seats in the GTi are very comfortable, trimmed in a wide-ribbed corduroy material. For the driver, the seat cushion can be adjusted for tilt, while both front seats have reclining backrests, although the lever controls do not give the same precise adjustment that can be achieved with a wheel control. If there is criticism, it is that there is not quite enough lateral support from the backrests. At the sort of speeds at which the GTi can be cornered the driver tends to have his body rolled off the seat. Head restraints are standard, with soft, clip-on cushions.

Rear-seat passengers have ample head and leg room, with a drop-down armrest to provide some extra location. The seating is again very comfortable. The rear windows are controlled by normal handles, and the doors are fitted with childproof catches. Neither front door can be slam locked, and a separate key is used for these and the boot.

Visibility is really superb and, despite the long, sloping bonnet line, which disappears from the driver's vision, the GTi is really a very easy car to place. The pillars are slim and the quarter window, behind the rear passengers, ensures that there are no serious blind spots. Noise levels too are low, with a gentle rush of wind over the smooth lines. Under full-throttle acceleration, the big four-cylinder engine tends to be a bit thunderous, yet even this noise is subdued once cruising speed has been reached and held.

Boot space is generous, and the almost-vertical rear panel lifts well clear to make loading easy. With the spare wheel and jacking equipment stowed away under the bonnet, the space is totally uncluttered. An interior lamp is provided and there is the additional light, with the parking lamps on, from the number plate lamps, which have a window in the rear of their housings.

With the spare wheel and tools under the bonnet, the boot is free to take a great deal of luggage. It has its own lamp and the sides and floor are fully carpeted. The low sill makes it easy to load

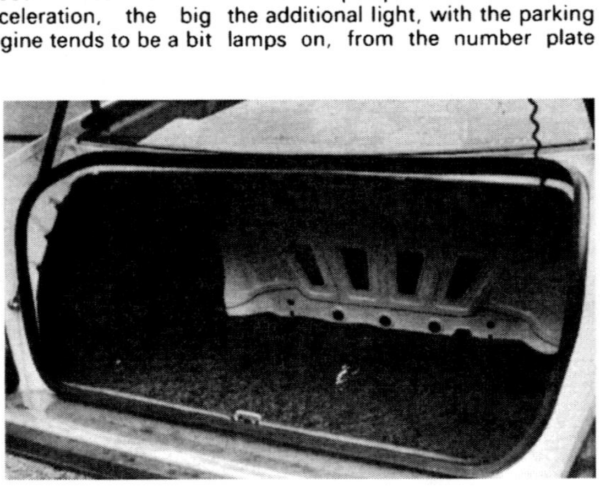

Under the bonnet, the transverse engine and its neat layout of petrol injection equipment is fairly easy to work on, and the spare wheel, stowed flat at the rear of the compartment, does not need to be removed. But getting it out is quite a job, and care has to be taken not to knock off the various electrical connectors which surround the wheel.

The only slightly difficult item to check is the battery, buried in the left-hand front wing, ahead of the wheel. The "heart" of every CX is the high-pressure pump for the hydraulic supply, but this is located so that changing the drive belt is a very simple task.

Where it fits in

At £6,350, the GTi is the second most expensive CX in the range, which starts with the 2000 Confort, at £4,461. The two 2400s are the Super and Pallas, at £4,991 and £5,498, while the Prestige, the top model in terms of trim, with metallic paint, tinted glass, air conditioning and Citroën's own C-matic three-speed, semi-automatic transmission all standard, runs out at £7,770. C-matic is available as a £270 extra on all the 2400s, except the GTi.

Conclusion

This is the fastest of the Citroën CX range, a car perfectly capable of being cruised all day long flat out, carrying its passengers in near-perfect comfort. There can be little doubt that, as always, you either get on with the Citroën way of life, or you do not; there is no half-way house.

It takes time to learn your way about a CX. If you have never driven one before, do not be put off too quickly. In a world where convention and standardization have been imposed on practically everything we use, the GTi comes as a great gust of fresh air to blow away the cobwebs. □

MANUFACTURER:

Automobiles Citroën
133 Quai André Citroën, 75747
Paris, France

UK CONCESSIONAIRES:
Citroen Cars Ltd,
Mill Street, Slough,
Buckinghamshire SL2 5DE.

Basic	£5,427.00
Special Car Tax	£452.25
VAT	£470.34
Total (in GB)	**£6,349.59**
Seat belts	Standard
Licence	£50.00
Delivery charge (London	£59.40
Number plates	£7.00
Total on the road	**£6,465.99**
(exc insurance)	
Insurance	Group 7
TOTAL AS TESTED ON THE ROAD	**£6,465.99**

Citroen CX Pallas C-matic Injection

Three speed semi-automatic transmission suits CX character, giving surprisingly good and very relaxed performance. Superb ride and leech-like road holding is matched by handling that needs getting used to. A very sophisticated and aerodynamically efficient car that suffers from poor ventilation.

THERE ARE manufacturers who have developed the conventional car into an art form, but there is one that has also consistently committed itself to a path of innovative suspension design and aerodynamic efficiency. Citroen's often revolutionary approach allows (and demands) very long production runs. The 2CV is of course still going strong, while the CX range only began to replace the ID/DS after nearly 20 years' production. Admittedly the SM proved a little too adventurous to become popular, but it did serve as a watershed for the CX series.

The CX Pallas C-Matic Injection competes in the growing market for executive and up-market family cars, and while it comes near the top of the CX range in trim specification, engine tune, and price, it still falls between the cost of its most expensive competitor — the Lancia Gamma, and say the Renault 30TS or Rover 2600. Only the Lancia shares the CX's fastback, non-hatchback concept.

Semi-automatic transmissions have been around for some time. The C-Matic simply goes one stage further by incorporating a torque converter behind the electrically triggered, but conventional clutch. Earlier C-Matic cars annoyingly had the switching gear in the gearlever knob, leaving one with no drive if the gearlever was inadvertantly touched. The switching system has now been moved to the base of the gearlever and is only sensitive to any movement toward neutral — a much more satisfactory arrangement.

Mechanically the CX 2400 Pallas C-Matic Injection shares the most powerful all-electronic Bosch L Jetronic injected version of the 2,347 c.c. 93.5 × 85.5mm inclined four, with the GTi five-speed manual car. On a compression ratio of 8.75 to 1 it gives 128 bhp (DIN) at 4,800 rpm, and a hefty 145 lb. ft. torque (DIN) at 3,600 rpm. In fact an ideal power curve to mate to a semi-automatic three speed transmission.

Our Pallas C-Matic tipped the scales at 27.4 cwt at the kerb, a 0.6 cwt increase over the GTi tested in October last year. This is probably due to the higher standard of trim and heavier transmission. However the excellent aerodynamic qualities of the CX remain constant. A drag co-efficient of 0.34 is untouchable by any other manufacturer, and mention is seldom made of the way in which Citroen use their "total concept" to obtain aerodynamic downforce without the aid of "add on" devices. Self levelling suspension enables a constant shaped venturi or low pressure area to be formed between the road and the very clean underside of the car, thereby creating some speed sensitive downforce — incidentally comfortably anticipating the Lotus 79 Grand Prix car by nearly four years. How much down force is not revealed, but it is characteristic of the company to turn what would normally be unwanted airflow to its advantage.

Interestingly we were able to conduct a rough back-to-back coasting test against a Lancia Gamma Berlina saloon (claimed drag co-efficient 0.37) and found that the Pallas took a mean 1.5 sec longer during the decay in velocity from 80 mph to 40 mph.

Performance and economy

We have yet to come across a Bosch L Jetronic injected engine that does not start easily and run well from cold. The CX Pallas C-Matic Injection was no exception to the rule. Because of its torque converter, the C-Matic transmission has the advantage of allowing starts to be made in any gear, and with a total lack of fuss. Around town it becomes natural to select 2nd gear and leave well alone. Therein acceleration is adequate from rest, and yet up to 80 mph is available for overtaking or climbing steep slopes.

Comparison of performance with the manual five-speed CX 2400 GTi is difficult because the three gears on the C-Matic fall neatly between the five on the GTi. In spite of two fewer gears, the constant speed acceleration figures for the Pallas C-Matic suffer very little compared with those of the GTi, and lower down are actually improved thanks to the effectiveness of the torque converter, and well chosen ratios. For example while the manual GTi will accelerate from 30-50 mph in top in 10.9 sec, the C-Matic Pallas only takes 9.1 sec, and it is not until over 60 mph that the admittedly slightly higher-geared GTi can manage any improvement. Without labouring over times too much, it suffices to say that on the road it would take a very enthusiastic driver in a GTi to outperform the C-Matic Pallas. Only in straight line acceleration does the C-Matic show any real disadvantage. The manual GTi will accelerate from rest to 60 mph in 10.1 sec, and to 100 mph in 34.4 sec, while the C-Matic Pallas manages figures of 12.1 sec and 39.7 sec respectively. The flat power curve tails off significently over 5,500 rpm, and we found it best to change up at 5,800 rpm just as the engine was beginning to sound rather busy and harsh. Below 5,000 rpm it is happy, and still refined by four cylinder standards.

Interestingly, accelerating from rest to 60 mph using second gear only took 14.9 sec, a time comparable with the new 2-litre O-series Princess, and only 2.8 sec longer than when using the gearbox to the full. Just for fun we also tried a standing start in top and still managed to fit 100 mph into the 1-mile horizontal timing straights at MIRA, this time in 52.4 sec. In so doing the quarter-mile post passed by in 24.1 sec at a fraction over 60 mph.

On the road there are certainly no quirks involved with using C-Matic; quite the contrary, the system fits in well with the soft, well-damped suspension and general aura of the car. Changing gear is as fast as you can make it, and we were quite unable to beat the clutch or confuse it in any way. Whilst not outstanding, acceleration is relaxed right through to a maximum speed of 111 mph which corresponds to 5,750 rpm, 250 rpm beyond peak power — a calculation that assumes no torque converter slippage.

Throughout our testing the relatively heavy CX Pallas C-Matic Injection was rarely driven with economy in mind. An overall fuel consumption of 20.9 mpg reflects this. It encompassed figures ranging from 16.6 mpg while testing at MIRA to more representative averages around 23 mpg in more normal use — figures that compare remarkably well with the GTi and milder tuned carburettor CX 2400 which managed 21.6 mpg and 23.5 mpg respectively. In practice all three types would return very similar figures, giving an absolute range of something over 300 miles from each 15-gallon tankful of fuel.

Steering

The system was justifiably criticised when it first appeared on the SM, as being over-responsive, with a mere 2 turns from lock to lock, and out of sympathy with suspension frequencies. The CX Pallas retains the Varipower power assisted rack and pinion, but thankfully it is lower geared with 2.5 turns from lock to lock. As on the SM, the degree of assistance diminishes as speed rises and there is the same servo self-centering action that would be of great assistance if a front tyre blew. It is accurate and responsive, but the driver needs as before to "grow into" its character for a couple of days. Any attempts at correcting what appeared to be a slight endemic high speed straight line wander tended to make matters worse. Likewise those converting from more conventional cars will find that the steering has to be unwound just as methodically on the exit of a corner as it is applied on the entry. Cross country and town driving cannot be accomplished by letting the steering unwind through castor action that centres the wheel mechanically, unrelated to road speed or corner radius. However thanks to sensibly low but not over-direct gearing one rarely has to cross one's hand on the steering wheel, and with a little familiarisation and relaxation, the CX Pallas behaves rewardingly. There is then time to assess some of the system's qualities. High gearing and servo self-centering makes parking and low speed manoeuvring a pleasure; the absence of kickback, or transmission of any road shocks through the steering wheel might suggest a lack of feel, but surprisingly the carefully tuned system that loads up mechanically on lock, in sympathy with roll and cornering g would be difficult to fault for predictability and *sense* of the amount of spare tyre adhesion available.

Ride, Handling and Roadholding

Citroen hydropneumatic suspension is as unique as its self-levelling and bump absorption characteristics. Load the rear of the CX Pallas down with the engine stationery and it will sag sadly. Pressurise the hydraulic nitrogen-filled suspension units with a running engine and the rear soon pumps itself into the correct attitude. There is provision, via a lever between the front seats, to raise the ride height in two stages, the highest for changing a wheel, and the other which leaves a little droop travel available, for running slowly over rough terrain.

Under normal fast driving conditions the suspension's ability to soak up large undulations and yet damp out rough surfaces is extraordinary; as remarkable as the consistency of ride, empty, or fully laden. There seems to be no limit to the amount of suspension travel, and the impression at the limit of bump is only of a rapid rise in spring rate, rather than the bang that would accompany the conventional car's suspension hitting the bump stops. Even *in extremis* control is there and steering unaffected, no doubt helped by zero camber change front and rear.

Although road noise levels are subdued, there are occasions when one wheel drops into a pothole or hits a sharp bump that can catch the springing out, producing thump through the bodyshell. Also it is occasionally possible to confuse the self-levelling correctors by taking a hump or brow rather too fast. On landing the front of the car will tend to stay on droop or pumped up for a

Specification

ENGINE	Transverse front; front wheel drive
Cylinders	4
Main bearings	5
Cooling	Water
Fan	Electric
Bore, mm (in.)	93.5 (3.68)
Stroke, mm (in.)	85.5 (3.37)
Capacity, cc (in.³)	2,347 (143)
Valve gear	Ohv
Camshaft drive	Chain
Compression ratio	8.75-to-1
Octane rating	97 RM
Fuel injection	Bosch L-Jetronic
Max power	128 bhp (DIN) at 4,800 rpm
Max torque	1,45lb ft (DIN) at 3,600 rpm
TRANSMISSION	
Type	3-speed C-Matic (two-shaft) with torque converter and manual gear selection
Gear Ratio	mph/1000rpm
Top 0.80	19.2
2nd 1.13	13.6
1st 1.94	7.9
Final drive	Helical spur
Gear ratio	4.77 to 1
SUSPENSION	
Front—location	Double transverse arm
springs and dampers	Hydropneumatic spring damper units
anti-roll bar	Yes
Rear—location	Trailing arms
springs dampers	Hydropneumatic spring damper units
anti-roll bar	Yes
STEERING	
Type	Rack and pinion
Power assistance	Yes plus power self-centering
Wheel diameter	15.0 in.
BRAKES	
Front	10.2 in. dia. disc
Rear	9.2 in. dia. disc
Servo	High pressure hydraulic system
WHEELS	
Type	Pressed steel
Rim width	5½ in. J
Tyres—make	Michelin
—type	XVS radial ply
—size	185 HR 14
EQUIPMENT	
Battery	12 volt 60 Ah
Alternator	80 amp
Headlamps	Halogen 110/120 watts (total)
Reversing lamp	Standard
Hazard warning	Standard
Electric fuses	6
Screen wipers	2-speed plus intermittent
Screen washer	Electric
Interior heater	Water valve
Interior trim	Cloth seats, pvc headlining
Floor covering	Carpet
Jack	Screw pillar
Jacking points	2 each side under sills
Windscreen	Laminated
Underbody protection	Paint and wax
MAINTENANCE	
Fuel tank	15.0 Imp. galls (68 litres)
Cooling system	22.0 pints (inc. heater
Engine sump	8.0 pints SAE 20/50
Gearbox and final drive	2.8 pints SAE 80EP
Grease	No points
Valve clearance	Inlet 0.006 in. (cold) Exhaust 0.008 in. (cold)
Contact breaker	Electronic breakerless
Ignition timing	25 deg BTDC (stroboscopic at 2,500 rpm)
Spark plug—type	Champion L87 Y or equivalent
—gap	0.026 in.
Tyre pressures	F 30; R 32 psi (normal driving)
Max payload	1,047 lb (475 kg)

The distinctive Citroen interior is typified by the facia. The instrument panel reaches forward to house the minor controls at fingertip level. On the left are the indicator, horn and wiper switches. On the right are the dip/main beam, headlight flasher, and light switches. The instrument panel has a row of warning lights underneath which are from left to right; a clock, the speedometer, trip and normal mileage recorder, revcounter, fuel guage, and battery condition gauge. The oil level sight glass is next to the right hand facia pocket, and the water temperature gauge alongside the ignition switch. The console itself houses the radio and the "eyeball" ventilation outlets, map reading light, electric window switches, heated rear window and interior light switches. Behind the gearlever are the heating/ventilation and ride level controls

Maximum Speeds

Gear	mph	kph	rpm
Top (mean)	111	179	5,750
(best)	113	182	5,875
2nd	82	131	6,000
1st	48	77	6,000

Acceleration

True mph	Time (secs)	Top	Inter	Speedo mph
30	4.1	7.8	5.0	30
40	5.9	12.1	8.3	41
50	8.8	17.0	11.4	52
60	12.2	22.6	14.8	62
70	15.9	28.3	18.8	72
80	21.7	34.5	25.1	83
90	29.2	41.9	—	94
100	39.6	52.4	—	105

Standing ¼-mile:
18.7 sec, 75 mph
kilometre:
33.9 sec, 95 mph

mph	Top	2nd	1st
10-30	6.7	5.0	3.2
20-40	8.3	6.2	3.6
30-50	9.1	6.4	—
40-60	10.7	6.5	—
50-70	11.7	7.4	—
60-80	12.5	10.3	—
70-90	14.6	—	—
80-100	19.2	—	—
90-110	—	—	—
100-120	—	—	—

Consumption

Fuel
Overall mpg: 20.9
(13.6 litres/100km)

Constant speed:
Measuring equipment not compatible with fuel injection.

Official fuel consumption figures
(ECE laboratory test conditions; not necessarily related to *Autocar* figures)

Urban cycle	19.0 mph
Steady 56 mph	31.0 mpg
Steady 75 mph	24.6 mpg

Autocar formula
Hard driving, difficult conditions
18.8 mpg
Average driving, average conditions
23.0 mpg
Gentle driving, easy conditions
27.2 mpg

Grade of fuel: Premium, 4-star (97 RM)
Mileage recorder 1.5 per cent over-reading

Oil
Consumption (SAE 20/50)
1000 miles/pint

Brakes

Fade *(from 75 mph in neutral)*
Pedal load for 0.5g stops in lb

	start/end		start/end
1	26-29	6	38-70
2	28-34	7	38-52
3	30-40	8	40-55
4	35-55	9	40-50
5	35-65	10	40-50

Response *(from 30mph in neutral)*

Load	g	Distance
10lb	0.20	150ft
20lb	0.43	70ft
30lb	0.59	51ft
40ft	0.82	37ft
50lb	0.97	31ft
Handbrake	0.42	72ft

Max. gradient 1 in 3

Test Conditions

Wind 10-12 mph
Temperature 27 deg. C. (80 deg. F.)
Barometer 29.8 in. Hg
Humidity 40 per cent
Surface dry asphalt and concrete
Test distance 1,251 miles

Figures taken at 6,947 miles by our own staff at the Motor Industry Research Association proving ground at Nuneaton.

Regular Service

Interval

Change	5,000	10,000	30,000
Engine oil	Yes	Yes	Yes
Oil filter	Yes	Yes	Yes
Gearbox oil	No	No	Yes
Spark plugs	No	Yes	Yes
Air cleaner	No	No	Yes
C/breaker	N/A	N/A	N/A
Total cost	**£11.38**	**£61.58**	**£83.84**

(Assuming labour at £6.50/hour)

Parts Cost

(including VAT)

Brake pads (2 wheels) — front	£16.90
Brake pads (2 wheels) — rear	£12.91
Exhaust system complete	£60.50
Tyre — each (typical advertised)	£46.00
Windscreen (laminated)	£94.90
Headlamp unit	£42.98
Front wing	£32.41
Rear bumper 3 parts	£76.57

Warranty Period
12 months/unlimited mileage

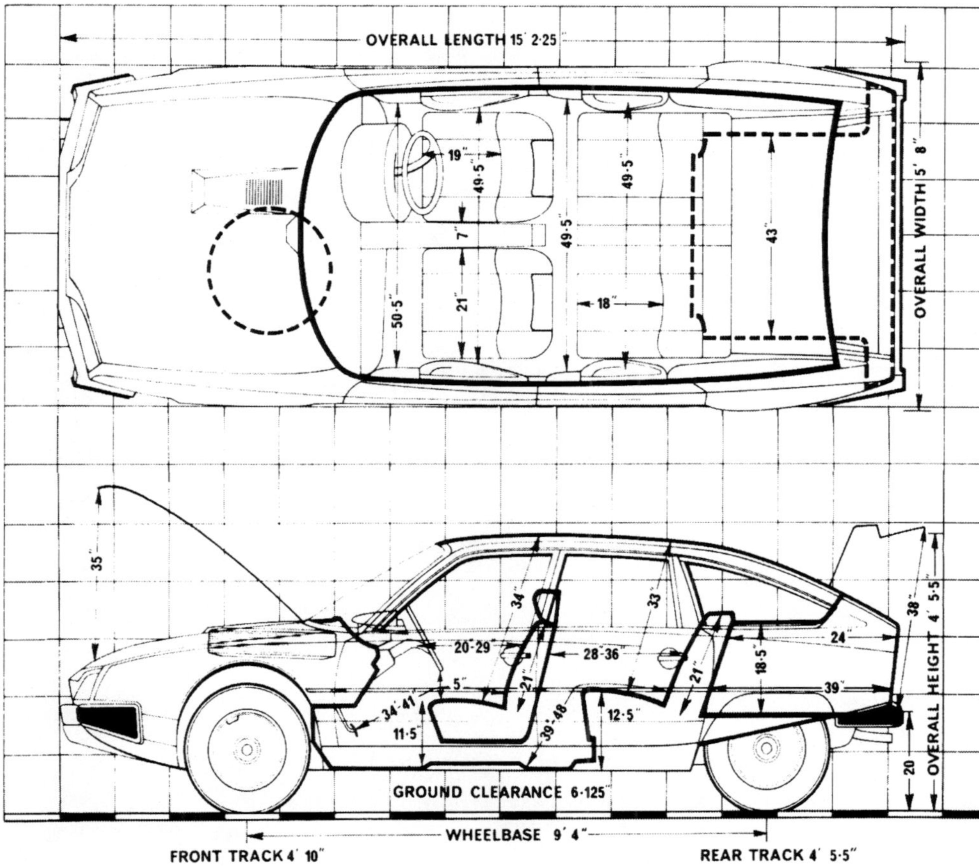

Weight

Weight
Kerb 27.4 cwt/3,073 lb/1,395 kg
(Distribution F/R, 68.5/31.5)
As tested, 30.8 cwt/3,452lb/1,568 kg

Boot capacity: 16.8 cu. ft.

Turning circles:
Between kerbs
L, 35ft 9in. R, 35ft. 4in.
Between walls L, 38ft 8in.; R, 38ft. 6in
Turns lock to lock 2.5

Test Scorecard

(Average of scoring by *Autocar* Road Test team)

Ratings: *6 Excellent*
5 Good
4 Above average
3 Below average
2 Poor
1 Bad

PERFORMANCE	4.7
STEERING AND HANDLING	4.7
BRAKES	4.4
COMFORT IN FRONT	4.4
COMFORT IN BACK	4.4
DRIVERS AIDS *(instruments, lights, wipers, visibility etc.)*	4.3
CONTROLS	4.3
NOISE	4.5
STOWAGE	4.0
ROUTINE SERVICE *(under-bonnet access: dipstick etc.)*	4.3
EASE OF DRIVING	4.4

Comparisons

	Price (£)	max mph	0-60 (sec)	overall mpg	capacity (c.c.)	power (bhp)	wheelbase (in)	length (in)	width (in)	kerb wt (lb)	fuel (gal)	tyre size
Citroën CX Pallas C/matic Inj	**6,797**	**111**	**12.2**	**20.9**	**2,347**	**128**	**112.0**	**181.0**	**68.0**	**3,073**	**15**	**185HR 14**
Lancia Gamma Berlina	7,136	118	10.1	19.1	2,484	140	105.0	180.5	68.0	3,052	13	185/70HR14
Audi 100 5E	6,020	109	11.8	23.3	2,144	136	105.5	184.5	69.5	2,632	13.2	185/70-14
Rover 2300	5,645	111	11.9	22.0	2,350	123	110.5	185.0	69.0	2,954	14.5	175/14
Renault 30TS (A)	6,476	111	11.7	20.2	2,664	131	105.0	178.0	68.0	2,853	14.7	175/14HR
Princess 2200(A)	4,871	98	14.2	21.8	2,227	110	105.0	175.5	68.0	2,677	16.0	185/70-14
Ford Granada 2.3 GL (A)	5,734	98	14.5	20.6	2,293	108	109.0	187.0	70.5	2,932	14.3	185-14

moment or two. However you have to go looking for this sort of thing and at sensible speeds ride can hardly be faulted.

Despite having nearly 70 per cent of its weight over the front wheels, the CX Pallas does not suffer unduly from understeer. On the one hand one never feels the desire to go rushing into corners, and yet considerable roadholding reserves are there if required, especially in the wet. Unlike some front-wheel drive cars that have a tendency toward total front end washout, the CX Pallas goes on responding to the steering once mild understeer has been established, and claws its way through the corner. Pouring on too much lock in itself scrubs off speed and in turn mitigates the understeer. Alternatively lifting off will restore matters to a more neutral state.

Roll as always with a Citroen is considerable, but not offputting, because it gives the driver warning of imminent loss of adhesion, and progressive breakaway.

Unaided, hydropneumatic suspension offers little in the way of roll stiffness, consequently anti-roll bars do most of this work, which naturally leads to a rapid rise in cornering spring rates. This and the normal wheel-to-wheel interference that anti-roll bars produce can cause a rocking motion while cornering hard over undulating surfaces. Once again it is hardly discernable on the road and is neither upsetting nor leads to any apparent loss in the very high cornering power.

During the maximum speed runs at MIRA we felt that the steering was still a little too responsive in relation to the complient suspension. The transition from running straight ahead to turning into the banking producing a floating motion until the car was settled into the corner. Perhaps the speed involved makes criticism of this kind seem irrelevant, but it is as if the low frequency response of the chassis still gets out of synchronisation with small quick corrections to the steering.

Overall the CX Pallas's ride handling and roadholding qualities far outweigh the niggles. It is a responsive car that insulates the occupants commendably from the outside world, and feels directionally more stable the faster one travels.

Brakes

The high pressure hydraulic system not only serves the suspension and steering, but also the brakes. Conventional braking systems depend on operating the brake pedal to build up pressure at the wheel cylinders, with or without the assistance of a servo. Citroen have fluid already under very high pressure for the steering and suspension, and can simply tap it for braking. Naturally this results in rapid response to driver action. Pedal pressures are perhaps over-light, and because of the concept, there is absolutely no "spare" pedal movement. Like the rest of the car it takes a little time to acclimatise, and learn the art of smooth braking. Initially very responsive, the brakes are nevertheless progressive, with pedal pressure ranging from only 10lb giving 0.2g retardation, to 50lb for the optimum 0.97g stop.

Fortunately C-Matic transmission renders heel-and-toe gearchanges less relevant, whereas with the manual GTi, uneven braking can result from using the overlight brake pedal as a pivot for opening the throttle.

Throughout our 10 fade-searching stops from 75 mph, pedal pressures rose slightly and there was some pad smell during the last five runs. However, there was no suggestion of fade, and almost no pitch thanks to anti-dive front suspension geometry. The remarkably effective handbrake operates on the front wheels. It managed an almost unbeatable 0.42g deceleration and easily held the CX Pallas C-Matic on a 1 in 3 slope, from which a restart could be made with contemptuous ease.

The front seats are upholstered in excellent quality tough and "breathing" cloth. Anti dazzle blinds unroll from behind the rear seats which are as luxurious as those in the front. Notice the detachable cushions on the head restraints, and the knee "holes" in the back of the front seats.

Comfort and controls

The interior is as positive in design as the outside. Replacing the more conventional dash and minor controls is a semi-circular moulding that not only houses the, to us, irritating rotating drum speedometer and rev-counter, warning lights, clock and fuel gauges, but reaches forward toward the steering wheel. At its outer ends sit, on the left, the horn button, wiper switch, and non self-cancelling indicator rocker switch. On the right are the headlamp flasher button, dip/main beam rocker switch, headlight switch and panel light dimmer. With one's hands on the steering wheel at "ten to two" all these can be operated by fingertip but only with the steering pointing straight ahead. By the time one has become familiar with the other unu-

Citroen Pallas details from left to right: The distance between the steering wheel rim and minor controls is about three inches. The indicator switch on the top of the "horn" is not self-cancelling. The heater/ventilation and ride level controls (centre) are between the front seats. Moving the single lever forward raises the car, and back lowers it. The Pallas has an electrically operated driving door mirror as standard. It is operated from the toggle switch on the door sill

sual features of the CX Pallas the minor controls have fallen into place, and their operation becomes second nature. The press button oil level sight glass proved accurate enough, and opposite it under the left-hand side of the instrument panel is the water temperature gauge.

The facia itself comprises an expanse of curved moulded plastic, with unfortunately no provision for retaining travelling paraphernalia. Reflections in the screen (thankfully laminated) might have prompted this, and it is left to a fairly large glove box and small semi-circular door pockets to provide stowage. Electric front door windows and driving door mirror are standard fitments.

The driver sits well positioned, and over the sloping bonnet forward visibility is good. However when manoeuvering in a tight space it can be difficult to judge accurately how much front bodywork is out of sight. Some thought the sumptuous herringbone pattern cloth-covered front seats a little soft but there were no actual complaints of driving fatigue. Although there is plenty of headroom, leg room in the rear is only just adequate for a tall person unless your knees are low enough to fit into the thoughtfully provided hollows in the back of the front seats.

Although five can survive for a long journey, the CX Pallas is far more suited to carrying four people very comfortably with the rear seat centre armrest folded down; comforably that is, but for a surprisingly poor ventilation system. Three levers between the front seats, control heat, fresh air, and the fan. Whilst there is no shortage of heat, the amount of fresh air available is disappointing (the test period was hot). Even at motorway speeds little ram airflow is available, and considerable noisy fan assistance is needed to push enough fresh air through. Naturally running with open windows disturbs otherwise serene cruising, and on balance we found it was better to suffer in silence.

Ventilation aside, living conditions are well up to standard, and include some nice practical touches, like the soft detachable head restraint cushions, rear side window sun visors, rear blinds, and excellent courtesy and map reading lights. On full beam the halogen headlights too are entirely up to the performance of the car, but illumination tends to be rather diffused when they are on dip beam.

Living with the CX 240 Pallas injection

The potential CX Pallas C-Matic Injection owner who already knows the type is usually as committed as the people who make it. Those sitting on the sidelines will always ask what happens if the hydraulic electrically operated clutch or electronic fuel injection go wrong? Citroen guarantee the hydropneumatic suspension for two years or 65,000 miles, while the rest of the car is covered by a 12 month, unlimited mileage guarantee. Citroen have a good record for customer service, and service intervals,

A crowded underbonnet is nevertheless neatly laid out. The injection control equipment is behind the four injection pipes. The air intake to the left of the spare wheel is to serve the heating / ventilation. Battery aside, day to day maintenance items are easy to check, and the all-important drive belts easy to reach. The central hydraulic reservoir is just out of the picture to the right rear of the bonnet opening. The wheel changing equipment is housed in the centre of the wheel itself. The battery is covered and under the two right hand inner wing mounted air horns, which makes it awkward to check.

apart from an interim oil change at 5,000 mile intervals, are every 10,000 miles. Day-to-day maintenance is straighforward — in fact the bonnet hardly needs to be opened, since the oil level can be checked from inside the car. Only the battery buried in the left-hand wing is awkward to check.

The spare wheel site between the engine and bulkhead under the bonnet, which must help in the provision of a large uncluttered boot (larger than a Lancia Gamma but 2 cu. ft. smaller than a Ford Granada), and clean rear underbody.

The heart of any Citroen CX is of course the high pressure hydraulic pump. It is driven from the front of the engine by a conventional and very substantial V belt. Should it fail, there is enough pressure in the hydraulic accumulator to steer and stop safely. In fact a priority valve dictates that the suspension sags first followed by the steering becoming very heavy — neither disastrous, and both giving plenty of warning of hydraulic failure, over some miles. However, it would seem sensible for the high mileage owner to carry a spare belt and the necessary tools to change it, because life being what it is, such a failure would be bound to occur in the early hours of the morning miles from civilisation.

Where it fits in

The CX Pallas C-Matic Injection is almost the most expensive CX available at a little under £7,000 on the road, compared with the most basic 2-litre four-speed manual carburettor model at nearly £5,000. Comparing like with like is difficult because only the more expensive (£7,136) and far less sophisticated Lancia Gamma shares the same conception. On the other hand the Rover 2300/2600 and Renault 30TS have the advantage of being dual purpose hatchback vehicles and less expensive (then the "up market Pallas" at least). In fact, by specifying C-Matic transmission at £176 extra on the CX 2400 Super the price remains well under £6,000 which makes the car far more competitive in the class. It's a question of how much value one puts on luxury trim.

Conclusions

As we have suggested the CX Pallas 2400 C-Matic Injection is outstanding aerodynamically whether you like its appearance or not. We do. It has the positive style that we have come to expect from Citroen and which one is likely to love or dismiss. The C-Matic semi-automatic transmission's smoothness compliments the CX character exactly and gives a unique combination of driver control and all the benefits of clutchless operation. Those who are sympathetic to its extraordinary ride/roadholding/braking combination are unlikely to be put off by the lack of equally good ventilation (a shortcoming receiving attention at the moment), the instruments or the short period of acclimatisation required in the driving seat. However humans, or the car buying variety, are conservative by nature. When hard earned cash has to be spent, secondhand values have to be considered. Citroen's complexity and sophistication has traditionally frightened the market, consequently it is in this area if anywhere, that some sacrifice might have to be made by the potential Citroen CX Pallas C-Matic Injection owner. □

For a non-hatchback the boot is usefully large and uncluttered, thanks to the spare wheel being housed under the bonnet. The boot is illuminated, and the door is held open by a gas strut. A low sill makes loading luggage relatively easy.

MANUFACTURER:
Automobiles Citroen
133, Quaie Andre Citroen
75015 Paris
France

UK CONCESSIONAIRES:
Citroen Cars,
Mill Street,
Slough,
Buckinghamshire,
SL2 5DE.

PRICES	
Basic	£5,809.00
Special Car Tax	£484.08
VAT	£503.45
Total (in GB)	**£6,796.53**
Seat Belts	Standard
Licence	£50.00
Delivery charge (London)	£68.04
Number plates	£10.00
Total on the Road	**£6,924.57**
(exc. insurance)	
Insurance	Group 7

EXTRAS (inc. VAT)	
Electric sun roof	£315.90
Air conditioning	£407.16
Leather upholstery	£360.36
*Radio / Cassette player	£98.00

**Fitted to test car*

TOTAL AS TESTED ON THE ROAD	**£7,022.57**

by John Bolster

The CX is an expensive car, but for luxurious riding comfort, silence, and safety it is unbeatable at any price.

CITROEN CX 2400 PALLAS INJECTION

A luxurious beauty

I had been looking forward to testing the Citroën Prestige. I adore the sinful luxury of long-wheelbase limousines, even if I can't afford to employ 'James', or perhaps 'Gaston' in this case, *Hélas*! Some rotter dented it at the critical moment and I had to make do with a normal-wheelbase CX Pallas. However, it was a CX with a difference, for it had fuel injection and C-matic transmission, and this last-minute substitute turned out to be one of the best cars I've driven this year.

When the Pallas arrived, long, low, and dark red, I realised once again that there is nothing more beautiful than an efficient aero-dynamic shape. The CX has a lower drag-factor than any other saloon and it employed ground-effect long before the Formula 1 boys got the message. It's slippery, stable, and glued to the road, yet it has no ugly spoilers or other excrescences.

The normal CX is perhaps short of power to exploit its aerodynamic advantage. With Bosch L-Jetronic fuel injection the story is entirely different, for not only does the engine produce a useful increase in horsepower at lower revs, but it hands out a massive 145lb ft of torque at 3600rpm.

The test car was fitted with the C-matic torque converter transmission, for which the engine's characteristics are admirably suited. This is similar in principle to the Porsche 'Sportomatic', in which a fluid torque converter is in series with an automatic clutch. There is no clutch pedal, withdrawal taking place when movement of the gearlever makes an electrical contact, and a three-speed gearbox sufficies.

The term Pallas covers a luxury specification with various extras included, such as electric window operation. The interior is most luxuriously appointed with no vulgar decoration, and the single-spoke steering wheel gives an excellent view of the instruments. In this connection, I would remark that although the speedometer and rev-counter are most ingenious and perfectly legible, I would still prefer proper round dials, perhaps because you can't teach an old dog new tricks. The driver has a good all-round view and the soft seats are blissfully comfortable, especially after some hard Teutonic ones. The boot is very roomy, with no sill to impede loading, and the big spare tyre is in the proper place — under the bonnet.

Nobody should form an opinion of the Vari-power steering without trying it over a fair distance; one needs to become acclimatised, but the benefits are so great that it is worth acquiring the knack. Let me say, straight away, that there are some people with extrem-

It's slippery and stable without needing any ugly spoilers.

Above: The CX instrument panel; the spherical object on the left is an ash-tray. Above right: The concave rear window can be seen clearly in this rear view. Right: The fuel-injected 2347cc engine produces 128bhp. Far right: The boot is very roomy with no sill to impede loading.

ely slow reactions who actually prefer soggy, low-geared steering with four or five turns from lock to lock. The Citröen has two and a half turns, with full power operation so that the wheels can be flicked from lock to lock during parking manoeuvres.

As the car gathers speed, a centrifugal governor makes the operation heavier, so that the driver feels in full control and does not cause the car to wander, which is all too easy to do with excessively light steering. The Citroën steering feels rather like that of a racing car or even a motorcycle, but at low speeds the power assistance renders such high gearing practicable. The CX has a preponderance of weight on the driven front wheels and though I have driven one with non-assisted steering, the Varipower absolutely makes the car.

As for the C-matic transmission, one can use it as a sporting manual box, going up to 47 and 81mph in the gears. However, very little acceleration is lost if all starts are made in second and top is engaged around 50mph. For that matter, rather more gradual starts can be made in top, but perhaps the most comfortable method is to use second in traffic or on winding roads and top at cruising speeds. The lever can be pushed into any slot without shock, but the mechanically sensitive can still double-declutch or use heel and toe, though of course it isn't necessary.

The first impression of the test car was of its amazing silence. It was so much quieter than any previous CX I have driven that I must assume the extra padding of the Pallas to be responsible. The engine can scarcely be heard at cruising speeds and makes only a mild buzzing when pressed, while the transmission is totally silent. This is most agreeable, and allowed the excellent stereo equipment to be enjoyed to the full.

There is no tyre roar, but an occasional thump can be heard over joins in the road surface. This, like the very moderate wind noise, would be inaudible if the engine made the usual amount of commotion.

The performance is distinctly brisk, as the figures show. The actual getaway is well below the wheelspin level but the car does not hang about, like some automatics, and the acceleration in the middle ranges allows rapid and safe overtaking. As with all very slippery cars, it's difficult to determine the absolute maximum because speed keeps on building up. In this case, I got the speedometer past 120mph with the rev-counter touching the red at 6000rpm, which my stop-watch called an honest 115mph, a satisfactory result.

Very high cornering power, especially for a car that is by no means a featherweight, is a feature. There is naturally some understeer but this is not sufficient to reduce the crisp responsiveness of the steering. The stability in side winds is outstanding and the handling remains excellent and entirely predictable on wet roads. This is the result of the close relationship between Citröen and Michelin, the CX and its tyres having been developed together. It is remarkable what tight curves the car will negotiate at speeds above 100mph, which would hardly be expected of so luxurious a carriage.

Luxury is the right word with the Pallas. The hydro-pneumatic suspension irons out all the bumps and though there is some roll on corners, the seats give good lateral location, including the rear ones. The back doors allow easy access and the rear passengers have plenty of space in every direction. The disc brakes, ventilated in front, cope easily with the weight and speed.

While the passengers enjoy exceptional riding comfort, it is a pity that the heating and ventilation have not been better thought out. It seems impossible to obtain adequate cool breathing air while keeping the lower part of the car warm, and this should receive attention. My only other complaint concerns the lights, which are excellent on full beam but cause some angry flashing from other motorists when dipped, though I couldn't see why.

The interior is most luxuriously appointed.

The Citroën CX is a car which has been improving all the time and with fuel injection it's exceptional road-going properties can be really exploited. It combines riding comfort for the passengers with pleasure for the driver to an extraordinary extent, and much of that enjoyment comes from handling a steering gear with only two and a half turns, lock to lock. One steers more by a thought process than by consciously turning the wheel, and after a very sharp corner the powered self-centring straightens the steering at once. If released, it will come back too quickly, but personally I brake the wheel with the palms of my hands, so that it straightens up at the right pace.

In Pallas guise, the CX is an expensive car, but for luxurious riding comfort, silence, and safety it is unbeatable at any price. To some extent, the big Citroëns have always been an acquired taste, but what marvellous enjoyment they give when one has become an addict! ■

Specification and performance data

Car Tested: Citroën CX 2400 Pallas Injection (C-matic) 4-door saloon, price £6,997.
Engine: Four-cylinders 93.5 x 85.5mm (2347cc). Compression ratio 8.75 to 1. 128bhp DIN at 4800rpm. Pushrod-operated inclined-valves. Bosch L-Jetronic fuel injection.
Transmission: Transverse engine and C-Matic tramsmission, with fluid torque converter, automatic clutch, and 3-speed gearbox, ratios 0.80, 1.13, and 1.94 to 1. Helical spur final drive, ratio 4.77 to 1.
Chassis: Combined steel body and chassis. Hydropneumatic self-levelling suspension with manual height control, operated by high-pressure, engine-driven pump and accumulators, equal-length front wishbones and rear trailing arms. Vari-power fully-powered speed-conscious steering. Anti-roll bars both ends. Disc brakes, ventilated in front, fully-powered by high-pressure hydraulic system, with dual circuits and rear limiting valve. Bolt-on steel wheels, fitted 185 HR 14 tyres.
Equipment: 12-volt lighting and starting. Speedometer. Rev-counter. Fuel, water-temperature, and sump level guages. Voltmeter. Clock. Heating, demisting, and ventilation system with heated rear window. Electrically-raised windows, 2-speed and intermittent wipers and washers. Flashing direction indicators with hazard warning. Reversing lights.
Dimensions: Wheelbase 9ft 4in. Track 4ft 10in/4ft 5.5in. Overall length 15ft [illegible].25in. Width 5ft 8in. Weight 1ton 7.4cwt.
Performance: Maximum speed 115mph. Speeds in gears, second 81mph, first 47mph. Standing quarter-mile 18.3s. Acceleration: 0-30mph 4.0s, 0-50mph 8.4s, 0-60mph 11.5s, 0-80mph 21.5s, 0-100mph 36.2s.
Fuel Consumption: 20 to 26mpg.

Auto TEST

Citroen CX2500 Diesel Super

Not electrifying, but more pleasing

Citroen CX2500 Diesel Super

Latest diesel version of Citroen's unique CX series. Replaced original 2,175 c.c. CX 2200 diesel (itself introduced with engine developed from same-capacity 1973 van autumn 1975) with larger bore and stroke engine) 2,500 c.c. version giving 75 bhp at 4,250 rpm in February 1978 mated to five-speed gearbox.

PRODUCED BY:
S. A. Automobiles Citroen,
133 Quai Andre Citroen,
75747 Paris 15,
France

SOLD IN THE UK BY:
Citroen Cars Ltd,
Mill Street, Slough,
Berkshire (SL2 5DE)

LIKE MERCEDES, the diesel for Citroen is its bread and butter. It was not always so as far as the cars were concerned; there was no DS diesel, and the development of the Citroen G35 diesel van unit used in the CX did not appear until 1975. Peugeot's long-established domination of the French diesel car market must have been a spur to Citroen, and however late they responded to it, the change has been spectacular. Of course the growing importance of fuel economy and the more favourable price of diesel in France has helped greatly — but the fact that the production of CX diesels at the Aulnay plant is now around 50 per cent of the total speaks for itself.

With derv still taxed more heavily than petrol — at 42 pence per gallon against petrol's 37p — the case for running a diesel in Britain is not so clear-cut. Taking the excellent 31.5 mpg overall test consumption of "our" 2500 D against the comparable 23.5 mpg of the CX 2400 tested in July 1977, and bearing in mind that the petrol car (CX2400 Super) now costs £253 less, it would be a matter of at least 30,000 miles before the British owner of the diesel would start to save money. But the advantage is there; and regular readers of *Autocar* Road Tests will need no reminder that our overall fuel consumption generally reflects near-enough the worst possible consumption obtainable from any test car. The average owner will do much better — we would expect at least 35 mpg as a bottom limit for most owners.

Performance
Most acceptable for a diesel

The 93x92mm, 2,500 c.c. engine is transversely mounted like its petrol brothers, and produces 75 bhp (DIN) at 4,250 rpm, with a hefty 111 lb ft maximum torque at 2,000 rpm. The five-speed gearbox is arranged so that fifth is a normal top gear rather than an overdrive. With overall gearing of just over 22 mph per 1,000 rpm, the highly creditable (for a diesel of this size) 97 mph maximum speed corresponds to 4,400 rpm, suggesting that the car is if anything a little under geared. The difference is in fact too small to matter, and one can understand why the makers have gone to the bother of fitting what sounds like a sports sort of gearbox to a homely diesel. It's done, paradoxically enough, for the same reason that one fits such a box to a sports car — because of a rather narrower-than-usual power band. 4,250 rpm is not high as power peaks go, and although it is possible to rev at 4,750 before the usual diesel governor cuts in, there is little point in revving that high. At the other end, the engine will pull, academically speaking, from 800 rpm, but one does not like to use it below 1,200 rpm. You need the five-speed to make best use of the fat middle part of the diesel power curve; the engine is not inflexible by diesel standards — provided the speed does not drop below 35 mph, you are happy to stay in top. But for best acceleration, the range of the box is welcome, and its ratios well chosen, as the revs to which the engine falls after changing up through the box at 4,250 rpm demonstrate — 22 mph in first corresponds to 2,500 rpm in second, 37 in second is 2,900 in third, 55 in third is 3,200 in fourth, and 73 in fourth is 3,300 in fifth.

The low first gear is necessary for much of the work which the car is likely to do. Re-starting on 1-in-3 was achieved, but with some hot lining smells from the clutch, even though the engine had to be revved only a little. In pure performance, the 2500 is really very acceptable for a diesel — and by that we mean that it is not really a sluggard by petrol engine standards. In fact that performance parameter beloved of the enthusiast, the 0-60 mph time (of 17.0 sec), is only made as slow as it is by the fact that one is beginning to feel the slowing effect of the governor as one approaches 60, so that it is better to change up to fourth beforehand. Gearchanging is easy — the change is light, a little rubbery, yet precise enough. We did however notice some weak synchromesh, surprising on this low mileage car, both loudly during the acceleration runs and not so loudly during ordinary driving. It is important not to be impatient about selecting first from rest, and one does well to make fairly accurately matched downchanges — an unusual requirement nowadays.

Like all big Citroens, the car is very much at its best — a quite delightful best — on the open road. It cruises easily at up to 90 mph, and its other virtues (and vices) combine to make it very relaxing on a long run. It isn't annoying in town — just rather harder work than some other cars.

How many of the usual diesel irritations does it have? The answer is "Not many." You get used to the power, which as we have said already is more than enough. It makes those seemingly undisguisable diesel taxi noises on tickover and remains undeniably diesel up to around 55 mph in top (2,500 rpm); thereafter it is beautifully smooth in sound and feel, apart from a surprising over-run rasp from the exhaust on changes up. Its diesel-ness is very obvious at up to 40 in top (1,800 rpm). On the other hand, Citroen (and presumably CAV going by the test car) have joined the narrow band of manufacturers headed by VW (and Bosch who incidentally are alternative suppliers to Citroen) who have succeeded in mellowing the diesel characteristic most annoying to the smooth driver — that abrupt cut in power when you lift off the accelerator (it isn't really a throttle on a diesel) during and, more important, as one approaches a change-up. The car is correspondingly easier to drive smoothly. One suspects that the credit is partly Citroen's, in providing the right sort of engine mounting characteristic, always more difficult with a transverse engine like this. Those of us who recall the 2500's predecessor (which wasn't good in this respect) are especially impressed. Once warm, diesels start marvellously quickly, but from cold there is the small penalty of time spent waiting for the cold start ignition glow plugs to warm up; in fairly chill "summer" weather, the car took only 12 sec before it would run, which is slighly better than our much-admired Volkswagen Golf diesel in the same temperatures.

Noise
Not too much of it

The car's engine noise has been mentioned already; it is a little tiresome in traffic, at slow speeds, but gets much better as you go faster. On the test car there was a surprising amount of wind noise, demonstrating once again that wind noise heard inside is not a function so much of shape as of sealing. The ride is superb, but the suspension is surprisingly noisy — bump-thump is rather higher than average.

Economy
Very frugal

As is proper for such a car, we began this *Autotest* by discussing the overall fuel economy — which is outstanding for a car of

Spare wheel under bonnet saves a lot of boot space, and is easily removeable; inclined engine is relatively easy to get at, notably on induction side

this size. The extra capacity has seemingly done no harm to this compared with the figure returned by the original CX diesel (31.8 mpg overall). With the help of our TransFlo fuel flow metering equipment we are now able to measure steady speed consumption on most fuel injection cars; the figures for the 2500 D are fascinating — nearly 60 mpg at a steady 30 mph in top gear, over 40 mpg at a steady 60 mph, and only a little under 40 at a steady 70 mph. We kept the meter going for a flat-out maximum speed lap, when the car returned 23.2 mpg — just for the record.

Filling diesels to the brim is always made difficult by derv's habit of frothing; the Citroen filler helps as much as possible by being very close to the tank, and of unusually large diameter. The 15-gallon tank gives a most useful range of never less than 450 miles — which is around half as much again as on most petrol cars — and up to close on 600 if driven gently.

Citroen's almost lone attention to aerodynamics makes for a still-very-distinctive shape whose penalties may include some awkwardness due to length, but whose advantages in economy are undeniable

On the road
Superbly stable

Citroen's thinking on steering and ride are well known. The steering is powered, very high-geared — only 2½ turns lock to lock for a turning circles which at 35½ft between kerbs are remarkable for such a long (15ft 2in.) car — and has the added peculiarity of powered self-centreing, which straightens the wheels whenever you let go, even when stationary.

The high gearing, once you have got used to its almost over-twitchiness, is delightful, and is just what such a long car needs in tight places. With even more front-heaviness than before (nearly 71 per cent of the unladen mass is on the front wheels in contrast to 68½ per cent on petrol CXs and 61½ per cent on the more orthodox front-drive Princess), the car is of course an excellent straight runner. Citroen claim very high side-wind stability; we found it very good compared to most rear-driven cars, and not noticeably better than the better contemporary front-drive competitors. It is if anything a bit of a handful in strong winds, needing more than usual concentration because of the responsiveness of the steering. All cars, even the most stable, move in side winds; and although the CX moves much less than most, its steering is rather too responsive in slight corrections. You are reminded that for once, there is no direct mechanical connection between steering and front wheels.

This is a small criticism, because one gets used to it. The same applies to the total lack of any feel in the steering — feel is nice to have, but not nearly as essential as purists say, since accuracy is far more important, and a sensitive driver of experience "feels" what the car is doing through his organs of balance as much as through his hands. We are not so sure about the powered self-centreing. The few times it is wanted are when parking, and even then the car's power assistance — in the normal sense — is all that is really necessary. There are more frequent times, when one finds oneself stuck in a traffic jam on a corner of any sort, when it is a small but noticeable nuisance. Let go of the wheel while you wait, and the steering unwinds, so that before moving off again you must re-apply some lock — the right amount of lock if cars are close on each side. We would rather do without it.

In spite of its front heaviness, the car does not understeer as much as one might expect, although generally speaking that is its ultimate fate if cornered to its limit. Decelerating in mid-bend generally has little effect, except on some occasions when cornering very fast when what may be an effect due to the car's suspension system can induce a surprise moment of oversteer. We only encountered this once on a closed track; it does not occur at any time in normal driving. There is some roll, but not too much.

Ride is generally superb, as ever. The car soaks up bumps in a fashion that is almost totally unknown to most other cars, and in this it will give the owner the greatest satisfaction. It has that most valuable attribute which ought to be found on all cars by now — self-levelling. It does the usual Citroen party tricks, sinking when you switch off, rising on re-starting, and of course has a really useful range of suspension height adjustment if the going gets really awkward. You learn to remember the sinking when parking beside a high kerb; it is possible to find that the driver's door of the Citroen you parked is impossible to open widely enough to get in again on your return. The ride is not perfect; it is arguable that the simpler system used by Peugeot is a better all-round compromise which does not suffer from the hydropneumatic system's occasional embarrassment, such as its now well-known sharp unreadiness over a hump — the front wheels, pushed up into the wheelarch, don't come down again quickly enough on the other side. The car is also surprisingly harsh over very sharp-cornered bumps. Overall however, it is magnificent; the ride is one of the principal joys of Citroen motoring.

Brakes are live-power assisted, and very responsive, almost too much so on first acquaintance; you get used to them however, and in most respects they are satisfactory. Being inboard, one suspects that they have cooling problems if used hard and often. Our fade test showed up a not unacceptable rise in pedal pressures needed, which is made more noticeable by the relatively small size and

The improved (and more conventional) position of the radio is obvious here. All important minor controls are cleverly grouped at the fingertips of hands placed on the steering wheel rim — indicators, horn and wipe / wash on the left, and all lamp controls on the right. Instruments are limited to the rolling drum type speedometer, fuel and battery volts gauges (on right) and a clock. Oil level sight glass is low on right, window switches, rear glass heater and interior lamp controls are all beside gearlever, in front of heater / ventilation controls and height control lever

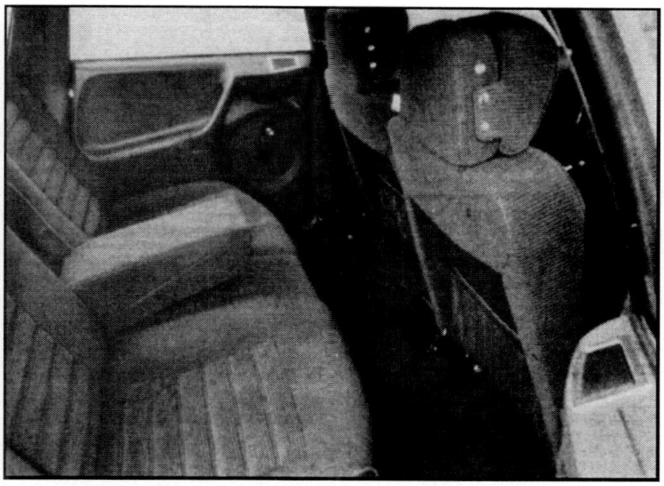

Portraits of comfort — CX seating is as good as it looks, and there is tolerable oddment space. As well as rake and fore and aft position adjustment, front seats also have height variation (controlled with the large lever)

rather too rounded profile of the brake pedal, which accentuates apparent pedal pressure. There is also the comparatively small pedal movement too, which exaggerates the feeling of fade.

Working on the front wheels, the handbrake is an unusually powerful one. You can't lock the front wheels — not surprisingly — and up to over 0.4g is obtainable, depending for once more on the strength of the driver than anything else. The car can be held easily on 1-in-3 slopes, pointing either way, which is more than can be said for front-drive cars with rear handbrake systems.

Behind the wheel
Commandingly relaxed

The seats seem at first rather too soft, but go on a decent journey and you come to appreciate them enormously. They are most relaxing and comfortable, giving most people a subtle amount of what feels like the right support at all times. Passengers appreciate the head restraints, saying that one can snooze in the car very easily. Tall drivers might be glad of a little more legroom; our six-footers found themselves a little knees-up, short of some thigh support. You tend to adopt a fairly reclined attitude if tall, which, these criticisms aside, is very comfortable.

Driving position is generally good, and one is made to feel very much in command of this large and bulky car. As the number of Citroen CXs (and DSs) with dented mid-sections suggests, it is a car whose length must be respected and remembered; it *has* got that excellently generous lock, compensating one for any awkwardness due to size, but that lock means more sideways displacement on tight turns, so care and judgement are needed. Luckily, for once here is a manufacturer who has almost always provided little obstruction to view in any direction, at any rate on his bigger cars, so that visibility is good. It needs to be, because the extremities of the car are invisible from the driving seat. The big central wiper is a bold design feature which works pretty well on the effectively half-square proportions of the screen, but there is a large unswept "triangular" area in each top corner of the screen which is irksome for the tall driver.

The finger-tip driving minor controls work very well, with delightfully positive switching and that very sensible Citroen preference for non-self-cancelling wipers — which don't cancel when you don't want them to, and which can be switched off so easily thanks to the position of the switch.

There is the usual CX rolling drum speedometer — a 1970s version of an 1929 Morris Minor idea — which works well enough, saving dashboard area. It is lit at all times, and we found the brightness too great, even in daylight when one could be distracted. On their petrol CXs, an electronic revcounter is available, occupying the other window in front of the driver. Since diesel engines don't use electric ignition (and probably because most diesel owners would not want one anyway), no revcounter is available for the 2500D — but the window is still there, filled with the Citroen chevron — and lit as brightly as the speedometer. We would welcome a rheostat lighting control for this.

Boot is of very handy size and proportions, and has ideally low sill

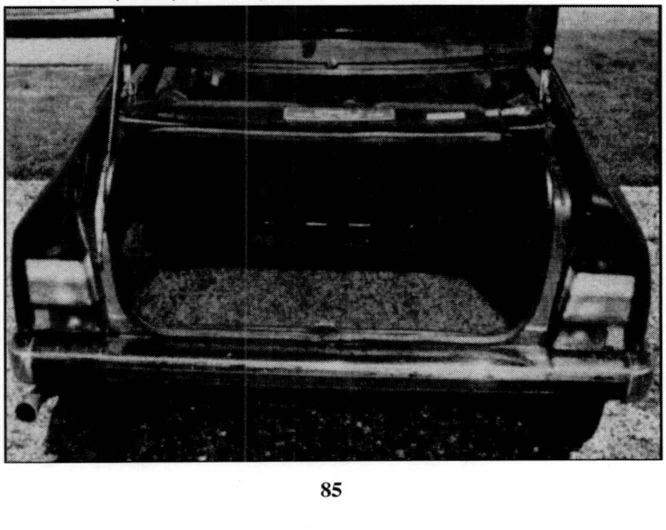

Living with the CX 2500 diesel

On the subject of brightness, we as before applaud the superb interior lamp, which gives all the light one so often needs inside a car — other manufacturers please note. The car's air-blending heating system works superbly, and ventilation is good too.

As you should expect with such a long wheelbase, there is a proper amount of rear room; this is a true family car in the best senses of the phrase. The superb boot has that usual Citreon freedom from any intrusion, bags of space, and a shape that is ideally squared.

There are anomalies; the trip mileometer has an old-fashioned twiddle-and-push type of zeroing arrangement. One would welcome more instruments and less warning lamps — there are 16 of the latter on the test car, plus one blank, and only a fuel and a battery volts gauge to back up the speedometer. Elaborate air horns are fitted — very effective. There is the excellent oil level gauge, a thing like an old-fashioned oil sight glass which gives a plausible reading when you are driving but which you are only meant to take seriously ten minutes after stilling the engine. The radio is now better mounted, in front of the dash instead of between the seats; there is an ashtray on top of it, whose spherical shape suggests anything but its actual purpose to first-time CX riders. We would find nothing in the handbook about how you are supposed to empty this; a vacuum cleaner may be the best way, since it doesn't seem to be removable.

Oddment space is provided by putting a thin wall across the circular spaces left for the absent window winders — the car has electric windows as standard — plus a small pocket on the right beside the oil sight glass, and a lockable swing-down glove bucket on the left.

The bonnet is self-propping, opening to reveal a beautifully tidy engine layout which is refreshingly accessible in most respects.

The CX range

In order of price, the CX 2500 Diesel Super comes second in the CX heirarchy, above the base CX 2000 Super four-speed (£5,796) and below the CX 2400 Super five-speed (£6,480).
After that comes the CX 2400 Pallas five-speed (£7,131), the CX 2400 Pallas injection C-matic (semi-automatic gearbox £7,799), the fastest example which is the CX GTi five-speed (£7,776) and finally the CX Prestige injection which can be had in five-speed manual or C-matic two-pedal versions both priced at £10,416. For anyone interested, there are four estate cars, all of them remarkable machines — two CX Safari and two Familiales, all with four-speed manual boxes only and with either 2400 petrol or 2500 diesel engines.

HOW THE CITROEN CX 2500 DIESEL SUPER PERFORMS

Figures taken at 1,200 miles by our own staff at the Motor Industry Research Association proving ground at Nuneaton

TEST CONDITIONS:

Wind: 10-20 mph
Temperature: 14 deg C (58 deg F)
Barometer: 29.4 Hg (997 mbar)
Humidity: 60 per cent
Surface: dry asphalt and concrete
Test distance: 755 miles

MAXIMUM SPEEDS

Gear	mph	kph	rpm
Top (mean)	**97**	156	4,400
(best)	**99**	159	4,500
4th	**79**	127	4,600
3rd	**61**	98	4,750
2nd	**42**	68	4,750
1st	**24**	39	4,740

ACCELERATION

FROM REST

True mph	Time (sec)	Speedo mph
30	**4.5**	31
40	**7.3**	42
50	**12.0**	53
60	**17.0**	63
70	**23.7**	74
80	**35.3**	84
90	**53.3**	96

Standing ¼-mile: 20.7 sec, 66 mph
Standing km: 37.6 sec, 81 mph

IN EACH GEAR

mph	Top	4th	3rd	2nd
10-30	—	—	7.5	4.6
20-40	12.6	9.0	6.8	5.0
30-50	12.3	9.3	7.2	—
40-60	13.2	10.4	10.1	—
50-70	16.3	13.3	—	—
60-80	21.0	—	—	—
70-90	30.8	—	—	—

FUEL CONSUMPTION

Overall mpg:
31.5 (9.0 litres/100km)

Constant speed:

mph	mpg	mph	mpg
30	57.1	70	37.2
40	51.9	80	31.7
50	45.7	90	26.1
60	41.8		

Autocar formula:
Driving and conditions: Hard 28.4 mpg, Average 34.7 mpg, Gentle 41.0 mpg

Grade of fuel: Derv
Fuel tank: 15 Imp galls (68 litres)
Mileage recorder reads 2.7 per cent long

Official fuel consumption figures
(ECE laboratory test conditions; not necessarily related to Autocar figures)
Urban cycle: 31.8 mpg
Steady 56 mph: 46.3 mpg
Steady 75 mph: 34.9 mpg

OIL CONSUMPTION

(SAE 20W/40) Negligible

BRAKING

Fade *(from 66 mph in neutral)*
Pedal load for 0.5g stops in lb

	start/end		start/end
1	26/30	6	38/65
2	28/35	7	38/60
3	30/40	8	40/52
4	35/45	9	40/50
5	35/55	10	40/50

Response *(from 30 mph in neutral)*

Load	g	Distance
10lb	0.20	150ft
20lb	0.43	70ft
30lb	0.59	51ft
40lb	0.82	37ft
50lb	0.97	31ft
Handbrake	0.42	72ft

Max. gradient: 1-in-3

CLUTCH

Pedal 28lb; Travel 6in.

WEIGHT

Kerb, 26.4 cwt/2,960 lb/1,342 kg
(Distribution F/R, 70.8/29.2)
Test, 29.9 cwt/3,350 LB/1,519 kg
Max. payload 1,036 lb/470 kg

DIMENSIONS

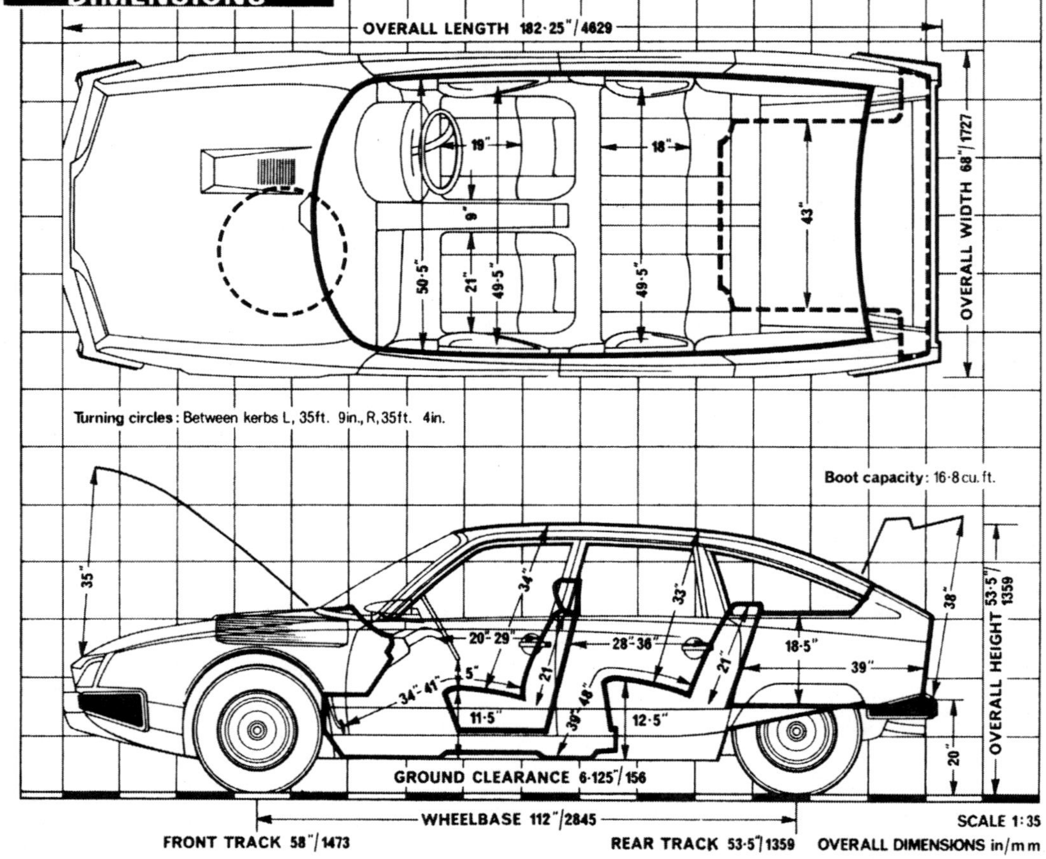

PRICES

Basic	£5,404.00
Special Car Tax	£450.33
VAT (15 per cent)	£878.15
Total (in GB)	**£6,732.48**
Seat Belts	Standard
Licence	£50
Delivery charge	£75.60
Number plates (approx.)	£10
Total on the Road (exc. insurance)	**£6,868.08**
EXTRAS (inc. 15 per cent VAT)	
Metallic paint	£97.17
Tinted glass	£125.83
*Radio (dealer fitted, approx.)	£60.00

**Fitted to test car*

TOTAL AS TESTED ON THE ROAD	**£6,928.08**
Insurance	Group 5 or 6

SERVICE & PARTS

Change	Interval 3,000	6,000	9,000
Engine oil	Yes	Yes	Yes
Oil filter	No	Yes	Yes
Gearbox oil	No	No	Yes
Spark plugs	No	No	No
Air cleaner	No	No	No
C/breaker	No	No	No
Total cost	**£10.20**	**£15.89**	**£56.99**

(Assuming labour at £8.00/hour)

PARTS COST *(including VAT)*

Brake pads (2 wheels) — front	£24.58
Brake pads (2 wheels) — rear	£18.63
Exhaust complete	£86.67
Tyre — each (typical)	£35.95
Windscreen (laminated)	£118.91
Headlamp unit	£53.51
Front wing	£46.25
Rear bumper	£63.51

WARRANTY

12 months/unlimited mileage
(but suspension & hydraulics 24 months/65,000 miles)

SPECIFICATION

ENGINE

ENGINE	Front; Front drive
Head/block	Al. alloy/cast iron; transversely mounted
Cylinders	4, cut in block
Main bearings	5
Cooling	Water
Fan	Electric
Bore, mm (in.)	93 (3.66)
Stroke, mm (in.)	92 (3.62)
Capacity, cc (in³)	2,500 (152.5)
Valve gear	Ohv
Camshaft drive	Chain
Compression ratio	22.25-to-1
Fuel injection	CAV Roto Diesel
Max power	75 bhp (DIN) at 4,250 rpm
Max torque	111 lb ft at 2,000 rpm

TRANSMISSION

Type: Five-speed
Clutch: Diaphragm spring

Gear	Ratio	mph/1000rpm
Top	0.73	22.07
4th	0.94	17.14
3rd	1.25	12.89
2nd	1.83	8.80
1st	3.17	5.08

Final drive gear: Helical spur
Ratio: 4.54 to 1

SUSPENSION

Front—location	Independent, double transverse arms, Hydropneumatic
springs & dampers	Hydropneumatic
anti-roll bar	Yes
Rear—location	Independent, trailing arms, Hydropneumatic
springs & dampers	Hydropneumatic
anti-roll bar	Yes

STEERING

Type	Rack and pinion
Power assistance	Yes
Wheel diameter	15 in.
Turns lock to lock	2.5

BRAKES

Front	10.24 in. dia. disc
Rear	8.83 in. dia. disc
Servo	power hydraulics
Handbrake	Centre lever, front disc

WHEELS

Type	Steel
Rim Width	5½ in.
Tyres — make	Michelin
— type	XZX radial ply
— size	185 SR 14 in.
— pressures	F: 30; R: 30 psi (normal driving)

EQUIPMENT

Battery	12V 88Ah
Alternator	84A
Headlamps	120/110W
Reversing lamp	Standard
Hazard warning	Standard
Electric fuses	5
Screen wipers	2-speed
Screen washer	Electric
Interior heater	Air blending
Air conditioning	Not available
Interior trim	Cloth seats, PVC headlining
Floor covering	Carpet
Jack	Screw
Jacking points	2 each side
Windscreen	Laminated
Underbody protection	Tectyl

HOW THE CITROEN CX 2500 DIESEL SUPER COMPARES

Citroen 2500 Diesel Super £5,404

Front engine, front drive

Capacity 2,500 c.c.

Power 75 bhp (DIN) at 4,250 rpm

Weight 2,960 lb / 1,342 kg

Autotest 7 July 1979

Ford Granada 2100 Diesel £5,655

Front engine, rear drive

Capacity 2,112 c.c.

Power 63 bhp (DIN) at 4,500 rpm

Weight 2,935 lb / 1,344 kg

Autotest 30 September 1978

Mercedes-Benz 240D £8,982

Front engine, rear drive

Capacity 2,399 c.c.

Power 65 bhp (DIN) at 4,200 rpm

Weight 3,035 lb / 1,375 kg

Test Extra 29 March 1975

Mercedes-Benz 300D £11,147

Front engine, rear drive

Capacity 3,005 c.c.

Power 80 bhp (DIN) at 4,000 rpm

Weight 3,290 lb / 2, kg

Autotest 25 December 1976

Peugeot 504 Diesel £5,320

Front engine, rear drive

Capacity 1,948 c.c.

Power 80bhp (DIN) at 4,500 rpm

Weight 2,607 lb / 1,184 kg

Autotest 21 December 1974

Peugeot 604 Turbo Diesel £7,170*

**Price in France, no GB price yet*

Front engine, rear drive

Capacity 2,304 c.c.

Power 80 bhp (DIN) at 4,150 rpm

Weight 3,168 lb / 1,437 kg

Driving impressions 31 March 1979 (car not yet available in Britain)

MPH & MPG

Maximum speed (mph)

Peugeot 604 Turbo Diesel	*98
Citroen 2500 Diesel Super	97
Mercedes-Benz 300D	93
Ford Granada 2100 Diesel	85
Peugeot 504 Diesel	84
Mercedes-Benz 240D	83

Acceleration 0-60 (sec).

Citroen 2500 Diesel Super	17.0
Peugeot 604 Turbo Diesel	*17.4
Mercedes-Benz 300D	20.8
Mercedes-Benz 240D	21.3
Peugeot 504 Diesel	21.7
Ford Granada 2100 Diesel	27.2

Overall mpg

Citroen 2500 Diesel Super	31.5
Peugeot 504 Diesel	31.1
Ford Granada 2100 Diesel	30.1
Mercedes-Benz 240D	29.0
Mercedes-Benz 300D	27.2
Peugeot 604 Turbo Diesel	—*

** Manufacturer's claims; therefore no overall* Autotest *consumption available*

The limited range of the diesel market in Britain (or rather British cars) and the corresponding interest abroad is obvious from our lists of possible Citroen rivals. In the case of the most recently announced contender — Peugeot's very interesting and remarkably satisfactory 604 Turbo — it is not to be made available in this country until January — but we do have the experience of the manufacturer's launch driving impressions to draw upon (which included a check of maximum speed which corroborated the maker's performance claims quoted). Performance is not of first importance to the diesel buyer — but it makes a great difference to even the most patient driver if he has something approaching petrol urge to draw upon. The figures speak for themselves, and they point up once again the well-deserved and increasingly important of a *properly-designed,* more truly aerodynamic shape. To come virtually top in performance *and* economy is almost unknown in our *Autotest* comparisons — but, pending a test of that Peugeot, the Citroen does it.

ON THE ROAD

All of these are large-ish cars by European standards, and all are independently suspended on all corners. Ride is therefore at least good in all cases, and outstandingly good as far as the Citroen is concerned — and in the Peugeot cases; in fact it could be argued that the Peugeot overall rides better than the CX because its simpler suspension is a better general compromise which does not get seriously caught out by any bump combination. For many applications, the Citroen is the only car here with the considerable advantage of true self-levelling suspension (the very long wheelbase special versions of the Mercedes are so equipped, but not the standard car). Only the 504 is not available with power steering. Being the only front-drive car, the CX is both the most stable and, to a lesser extent, the one which understeers most. Ford, Mercedes and Peugeot all use semi-trailing arm rear ends which will ultimately break away — but you must be driving in most un-diesel style to find this out. Thanks to its superb power steering, the Merc just has the advantage in pleasure of handling terms, but only just — but one cannot complain about the CX.

SIZE & SPACE

Legroom front / rear (in)

(Seats fully back)

Mercedes-Benz 240D	43/38
Mercedes-Benz 300D	43/38
Ford Granada 2100 Diesel	41/40
Citroen CX 2500 Diesel Super	41/39
Peugeot 604 Turbo Diesel	38/41
Peugeot 504 Diesel	37/40

With the 504 as the mildly odd-one-out in size — it is the only truly medium-size saloon amongst this bevy of larger cars — it naturally takes bottom of the list here. But it should be remembered that none of these cars are mean in space; that includes rear accommodation which in all cases is generous enough for a full average-family load. Compared with the others, the Citroen user will revel in an unusually generous and uncluttered boot, and he will not be disappointed by the ease of driving of the car compared with the others — that last qualification is important, because nearly all Citroens, and certainly the CX need much more familiarity than other cars before one is able to feel at home. Once this has been achieved, the very great comfort of CX motoring becomes obvious, and its virtues as a long distance cruising machine of great relaxation are almost indispensable.

VERDICT

Economy is of course the strongest card in the diesel's hand, and all of these are mean cars by any standards. Economy is tremendously important today — but human nature being what it is, if an economical car can also be made pleasing to drive, it becomes doubly attractive. This combination has until recently been rare in diesel cars, simply because performance was so limited, and the response of the engine was characteristically demanding, at any rate for the driver normally used to petrol cars. The arrival of the five-cylinder 300D Merc marked the beginning of better diesels, although many would say that Daimler-Benz already made the most pleasant examples of the type in the shape of the similarly bodied 240D. Volkswagen's brilliant Golf diesel was the real turning point however — and in our opinion the Peugeot 604 Turbo and the subject of this text, the superb CX 2500 keep the new standard up. Pending a full *Autotest* of the 604, we would put the Citroen on top today — it merits a word you don't often hear applied to diesels — delightful. □

Road Test

CITROEN CX ATHENA

The Douvrin-built 2 litre engine (as fitted to the Renault 20) has given the CX a new lease of life. Performance is as before, but economy has improved dramatically and refinement is now one of the car's strong points. Other CX virtues — comfort, ride, high-speed cruising — and faults — instrumentation, steering and brakes — remain.

A FEW years ago the idea of a Citroën fitted with a Renault engine would have been unthinkable to the two French companies who compete strongly both at home and abroad. Yet, thanks to rationalisation and mergers, the power plant that appears under the bonnet of the recently announced Citroën CX Athena first appeared in the Renault 20: the rest of the car is pure CX.

The combination is a result of French pragmatism. The engine is made by a company called "Française de Mecanique" in a large factory at Douvrin in North-West France. The company is half-owned by Renault, half by PSA-Peugeot-Citroën-Chrysler, and makes engines for both companies. Among them is the so-called 829 unit: it is this which apears in both the Renault 20 and the CX Athena — and the Peugeot 505, yet to be seen in the UK. It replaces Citroën's own 2-litre engine, though the bigger 2400 cc version continues for the time being.

In fact the 829 appears in two versions of the CX, the other being named the Reflex. They both replace the CX 2000 Super. The Reflex is the "base" model, though it comes quite well equipped, and the Athena is the more "up-market" car, the most important differences being a five-speed gearbox, electric-lift windows, tinted glass and higher levels of trim. The engine apart, both cars share the well-known CX mechanical features including all-independent hydro-pneumatic suspension, full power steering and brakes, and a stylish and aerodynamic bodyshell.

At £6,229, the Athena is competitively priced in the 2-litre executive car class. BL products fall either side, with the Princess 2200 HLS at £5,788 and the Rover 2300 at £6,384. Ford's Granada 2.3GL is rather more expensive at £6,839, the Peugeot 504 Ti is quite a lot cheaper at £5,858 (and no doubt it will fairly soon be supplemented by the new 505), while probably the most competitive car is another French model, the Renault 20TS at £6,167. The Audi Avant CD5E is another similar type of car but is far more expensive at £9,466: even the ordinary 100 GL5E costs £7,390.

The most important feature of the new cars is the engine. Like other Douvrin power plants the 1995 cc 829 uses an alloy block with pressed-in wet cylinder liners and an alloy head. The valves are arranged

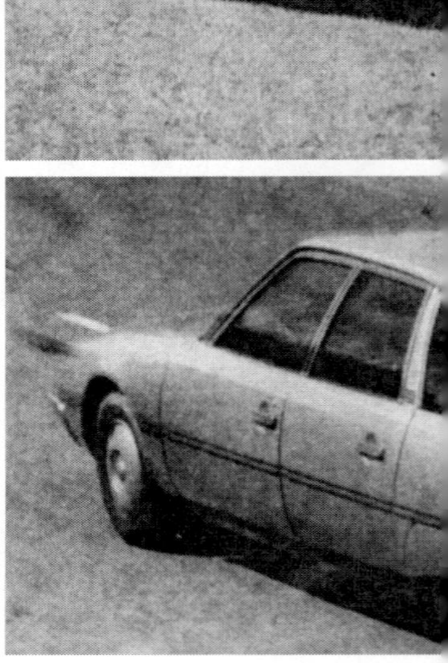

in a narrow vee in the cross-flow head, and the camshaft runs between them and operates them via rockers: it is driven by a toothed belt which also drives an accessory jackshaft. As installed in the CX, the 829 is fitted with a Weber twin-choke DMTR 46/250 carburetter and develops 106 bhp (DIN) at 5500 rpm and 122 lb ft torque (DIN) at 3250 rpm. This is slightly less than Renault (who also fit a Weber, but of another type) and Peugeot (who use Bosch K-Jetronic fuel injection) claim, the output in both cases being 110 bhp.

On paper, the new engine shows a distinct improvement over its predecessor. The performance it gives the CX is very similar, while fuel consumption has measurably improved. The CX 2000 had a top speed of 109.2 mph, while the Athena lapped MIRA's banked circuit at 106.8 mph — but the latter was tested under quite adverse wind conditions. It is significant that the fastest quarter mile on Mira's banked circuit was covered at 112.5 mph in the Athena, 112.3 mph in the CX 2000, so there is very little between the two. Acceleration, too, shows that the performance differences are marginal. The Athena took 11.8 secs to reach 60 mph from a standing start, the CX 2000 11.9 secs. The top gear acceleration times are not strictly comparable, since the Athena has a five-speed gearbox, and there is thus a greater choice, while the CX 2000 had a four-speed. However, the 30-50 mph increment in top in the CX 2000 took 11.7 secs, almost exactly half-way between the Athena's 13.0 secs in fifth and 8.8 secs in fourth — the latter figure very respectable indeed for the class.

Where the new engine scores is in economy. It gave 25.3 mpg overall, and an impressive 29.9 mpg touring:

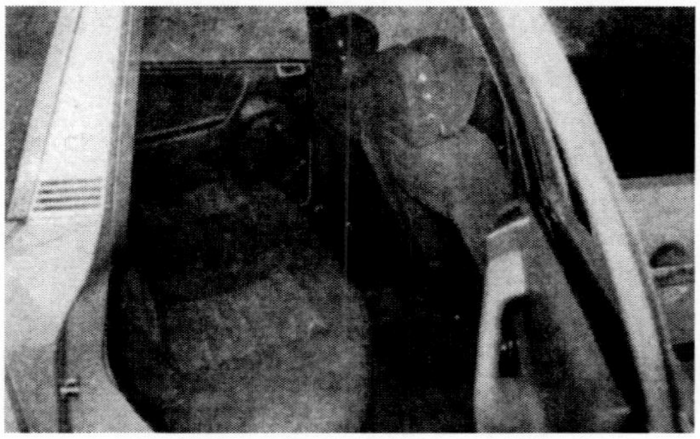

Above: the soft but well designed front seats are superbly comfortable and have substantial head restraints. Left: those in the rear are no less comfortable and there is generous leg room. Below: futuristic and unmistakably Citroen, the Athena's facia styling is not to everyone's taste

the CX 2000 gave 21.6 mpg and 26.8 mpg respectively, so the improvements are well worthwhile. Perhaps even more startling are the steady-speed figures in fifth. At 30 mph the Athena recorded 42 mpg, at 40 mph 41 mpg, at 60 mph 33.2 mpg. At the legal limit it still gives a very good 31.1 mpg.

Compared to the opposition, too, the Athena shows up well. Only the Rover 2300 is faster on top speed and acceleration to 60 mph: the Princess can match the Athena, and the Peugeot 504 Ti is slightly quicker to 60 mph. When it comes to economy, the re-engined Citroën is considerably more miserly than any of the competitors we have chosen: none can match it on either overall or touring consumption.

The new engine scores in yet another area — refinement. All who drove it commented on how much smoother and quieter it is compared to the smaller versions of Citroën's own engine. When cruising at any speed it is little more than a muted hum, contributing less than other sources to overall noise levels. It is at all times smooth, and revs eagerly, unlike the previous engine which had a discernible "heavy flywheel" effect — it felt reluctant to rev quickly, and revs died relatively slowly when the accelerator pedal was released. When accelerating however, it becomes a little more

"Eyeball" rotating drum speedometer and rev counter are difficult to read at a glance; supplementary dials are few

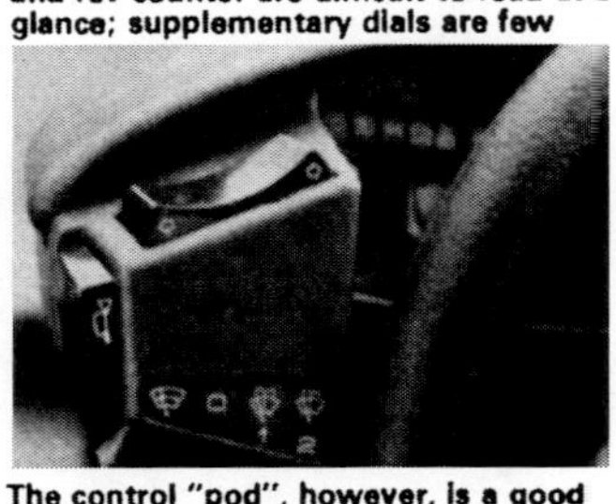

The control "pod", however, is a good idea allowing operation of the major functions without taking your hand from the steering wheel

What looks like a propriatory air freshener is, in fact, a swiveling ash tray

obtrusive. Boom periods appear at about 4000 rpm, and above 5000 rpm on up to the 6000 rpm red line it can be quite raucous. The new engine starts easily, warms up rapidly, and shows only minor temperamental quirks until fully warmed.

The five-speed gearbox is mounted on the end of the engine and driven directly via a diaphragm-spring clutch. On really fast, snatched changes the synchromesh can become baulky, but at all other times the change is light, precise, and smooth, aided by excellent spring biasing. Matching the gearchange is a nicely weighted and progressive clutch. One slight flaw from previous models remains, however: because of the long-travel, soft suspension, changes can be jerky as the car pitches from a nose-up attitude during acceleration, through nose-down during the change, to nose-up again. The ratios are well spaced, with maxima of 31, 53, 78 and 103 mph available in the intermediates. Fifth, at 22 mph/1000 rpm, is a relaxed cruising gear, yet can give reasonably lively acceleration above about 50 mph.

The rest of the car follows previous Citroën CX practice, and thus many of our earlier comments still apply. To recap briefly, the suspension at the front is by equal-length parallel transverse links and hydropneumatic struts, with more struts and trailing arms at the rear. Full power steering is standard, by Citroën's unique system which is light, very direct and has a self-centring set-up which gives artificial feel.

With nearly 70 per cent of the weight on the front wheels, and front-wheel-drive, the handling characteristics are fairly predictable: understeer, mild at low speeds and growing stronger as cornering speeds increase. Grip from the Michelin XVSs (185 HR 14 at the front, 175 HR 14 at the rear) is good in the dry, but does accentuate the understeer in the wet.

Even after a lengthy acquaintance, we do not care for the CX's power steering. It is excellent for parking, with one-finger effort and one turn lock-to-lock, but the rest of the time it is unpleasant. The power steering set-up is such that you have to "steer" the car all the time, even when unwinding lock — if you let the wheel run back through your hands it simply whips back to the central position — and it is nervous at high speed, so that concentration is required, for example, to keep the car on a straight course on a motorway. It is direct and light at low speeds which is useful around town, however.

Like the steering, the brakes are fully powered from the central hydraulic system. As before, the arrangement is let down by the limited and abrupt action of the brake pedal. It is possible to get used to the action, however, and over the years Citroën have managed to introduce a little more progression, but the car could do with yet more. As compensation the brakes themselves, with discs all round, are immensely powerful and reassuring.

The hydropneumatic springs (in essence soft gas springs working in conjunction with a hydraulic self-

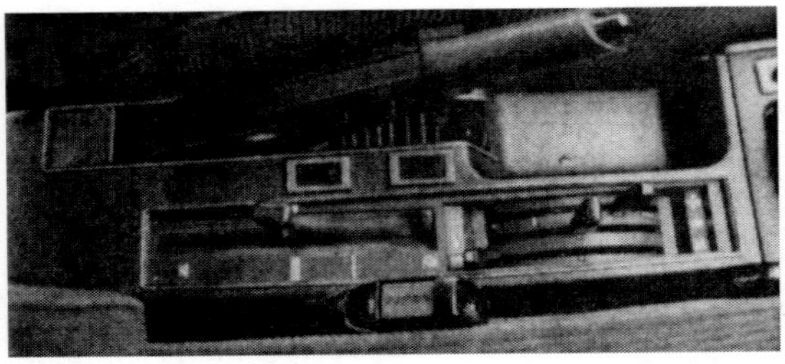

Left: although easy to operate, the heater controls are awkwardly positioned between the front seats

levelling arrangement) are even today fairly rare, and when found are usually on much more expensive cars. There is no doubt that, on the whole, they do provide a near magic-carpet ride, but other manufacturers using conventional springs are catching up — the Renault 20 is a good example. And the springs can be caught out by potholes, which cause a loud thump and a jerk. Nevertheless, ride is one of the Athena's best features: the roll which accompanies spirited cornering, and pitch under acceleration and braking, are not.

Passengers seem to love the CX range, not only for its smooth ride but also for the excellent interior accommodation: the seats are superbly comfortable, and there is plenty of legroom both fore and aft, though there was a minor criticism that headroom in the back is marginal for tall people. All doors open wide, the boot is spacious, the lid opens right down to floor level so there is no lip, and there is plenty of storage space inside for odds and ends.

Like the others, the driver's seat is excellent. Soft and large, you tend to sit in rather than on it, and it provides plenty of support in all the right areas. There is plenty of adjustment too, so that a good driving position is easy to achieve.

The major controls are well placed, but the minor ones are more confusing. Some, like the finger-tip rocker switches on the ends of the instrument pod, are beautifully sited (though most who drove the car would have liked self-cancelling indicators) and work extremely well, but others — like the heater levers — are placed down between the seats where they are awkward to find and mean taking your eyes off the road if you want to adjust them. However, owners may find that, with experience, they can operate them by touch alone.

There is a considerable amount of glass area in the CX, so general visibility out is good. However, the nose slopes away quite markedly so the tip is not visible, which makes parking and slotting into narrow gaps quite difficult.

One other "futuristic" feature of the CX that was consistently disliked by testers was the "eyeball" instrumentation. The speedometer and tachometer consist of illuminated yellow drums which rotate past a fixed line. Their markings are reasonably clear (large numerals at 20 mph intervals, smaller figures in between) but they do require to be read rather than absorbed at a glance.

The awkward positioning of the heating controls has been mentioned, but, once that is accepted, they proved to be easy to operate and gave reasonably fine control. Early CX's appeared with just eyeball vents at each end of the facia. These are still retained but are not very effective in most circumstances and that on the driver's side at least is masked by the instrument pod. On ram their throughput is meagre, likewise when fan boosted. The latest CXs boast additional vents in the centre of the facia, and these are powerful on ram alone and even more so when fan boosted. However, a fault somewhere in our car's system allowed warm air to seep into the flow, so that they never really gave out cool air and this made the interior stuffy.

Noise suppression in the Athena is generally good, and particularly so when cruising at high speed, for then the engine is barely audible and, though there is perceptible wind noise from about 60 mph on, it doesn't get any worse. In fact the noisiest part of the car comes from the suspension and heavy tread tyres: the former can lead to thumps on some potholes, the latter to roar on some coarse surfaces.

To sum up, the new Douvrin engine has answered the major criticism made of previous CXs — that the power unit was old-fashioned, noisy and harsh. In addition, it has kept the performance, yet radically improved the fuel consumption with better refinement. Otherwise the Athena is like the rest of the CX range, with all its faults and virtues.

Above: the Athena's transverse engine sits ahead of the spare wheel and major ancillaries are easy to get at

MOTOR ROAD TEST NO 40/79 ● CITROEN CX ATHENA

PERFORMANCE

CONDITIONS

Weather	Damp: wind 10-20 mph
Temperature	58-64°F
Barometer	29.2 in Hg
Surface	Damp tarmacadam

MAXIMUM SPEEDS	**mph**	**kph**
Banked Circuit	**106.8**	**171.8**
Best ¼ mile	112.5	181.0
Terminal Speeds:		
at ¼ mile	75	121
at kilometre	94	151
at mile	100	161
Speed in gears (at 6000 rpm):		
1st	31	50
2nd	53	85
3rd	78	125
4th	103	166

ACCELERATION FROM REST

mph	sec	kph	sec
0-30	3.8	0-40	3.1
0-40	5.7	0-60	5.0
0-50	8.2	0-80	8.1
0-60	11.8	0-100	12.4
0-70	15.8	0-120	18.3
0-80	21.6	0-140	26.6
0-90	29.5		
Stand'g ¼	18.1	Stand'g km	33.5

ACCELERATION IN FIFTH

mph	sec	kph	sec
20-40	13.6	40-60	8.2
30-50	13.0	60-80	8.2
40-60	13.4	80-100	8.3
50-70	13.4	100-120	11.1
60-80	15.1	120-140	11.5
70-90	19.2		

ACCELERATION IN FOURTH

mph	sec	kph	sec
20-40	9.1	40-60	5.5
30-50	8.8	60-80	5.5
40-60	9.3	80-100	5.9
50-70	9.5	100-120	6.7
60-80	11.2	120-140	9.0
70-90	14.1		

FUEL CONSUMPTION

Touring*	29.9 mpg 9.5 litres/100 km
Overall	25.3 mpg 11.2 litres/100 km
Govt tests	23.3 mpg (urban) 39.8 mpg (56 mph) 31.4 mpg (75 mph)
Fuel grade	97 octane 4 star rating
Tank capacity	15 galls 68 litres
Max range	450 miles 722 km
Test distance	1530 miles 2461 km

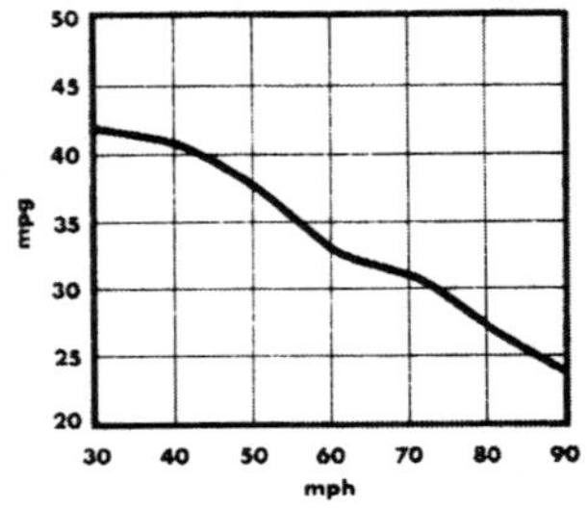

*Consumption midway between 30 mph and maximum less 5 per cent for acceleration.

NOISE

	dBA	Motor rating*
30 mph	60	8
50 mph	66	14
70 mph	72	18
Max revs in 2nd (1st for 3-speed auto)	81	34

*A rating where 1 = 30 dBA and 100 = 96 dBA, and where double the number means double the loudness.

SPEEDOMETER (mph)

Speedo	30	40	50	60	70	80	90
True mph	27	37	46	55	66	76	86

Distance recorder: 3 per cent fast

WEIGHT

	cwt	kg
Unladen weight*	24.2	1229
Weight as tested	27.9	1417

*with fuel for approx 50 miles

Performance tests carried out by Motor's staff at the Motor Industry Research Association proving ground, Lindley.

GENERAL SPECIFICATION

ENGINE

Cylinders	4 in line
Capacity	1995 cc (121.6 cu in)
Bore/stroke	88/82 mm (3.46/3.23 in)
Cooling	Water
Block	Light alloy
Head	Light alloy
Valves	Sohc
Cam drive	Belt
Compression	9.2:1
Carburetter	Weber 34 DMTR 46/250
Bearings	5 main
Max power	106 bhp (DIN) at 5500 rpm
Max torque	122 lb ft (DIN) at 3250 rpm

TRANSMISSION

Type	5-speed manual,
Clutch dia	228.6 mm
Actuation	Cable

Internal ratios and mph/1000 rpm

Top	0.733:1/22.07
4th	0.939:1/17.23
3rd	1.250:1/12.94
2nd	1.833:1/8.83
1st	3.166:1/5.11
Rev	3.153:1
Final drive	4.54:1

BODY/CHASSIS

Construction	Unitary all-steel
Protection	Electrophoretic dip, undersealant, Tectyl treatment in sills

SUSPENSION

Front	Independent by equal length parallel transverse links, anti-roll bar, hydropneumatic springs.
Rear	Independent by trailing arms, anti-roll bar, hydropneumatic springs.

STEERING

Type	Rack and pinion
Assistance	Full hydraulic Vari-Power

BRAKES

Front	Disc, 10.2 in dia
Rear	Disc, 8.8 in dia
Park	Front
Servo	Fully powered by high pressure hydraulics
Circuit	Split front/rear
Rear valve	Control valve
Adjustment	Automatic

WHEELS/TYRES

Type	Pressed steel 5½J × 14
Tyres	Michelin XVS 185 HR 14 Front, 175 HR 14 Rear
Pressures	27/27 psi F/R (normal) 30/30 psi F/R (full load/highspeed)

ELECTRICAL

Battery	12V, 45 Ah
Earth	Negative
Generator	Alternator 1kW
Fuses	5
Headlights	
type	Halogen
dip	90 W total
main	110 W total

Make: Citroen
Model: CX Athena
Makers: Automobiles Citroen, 133 Quai Andre Citroen, 75747 Paris, France
Concessionaires: Citroen Cars Ltd, Mill Street, Slough, Bucks SL2 5DE
Price: £5,000.00 basic plus £416.67 car tax plus £812.50 VAT equals £6,229.17

The Rivals

The CX Athena is in a busy sector of the market, though some competitors such as the Audi Avant GL 5s (£6,969), the BMW 520 (£7,772), and the Saab 900 GLS (£6,655) cost a lot more.

CITROEN CX ATHENA £6229

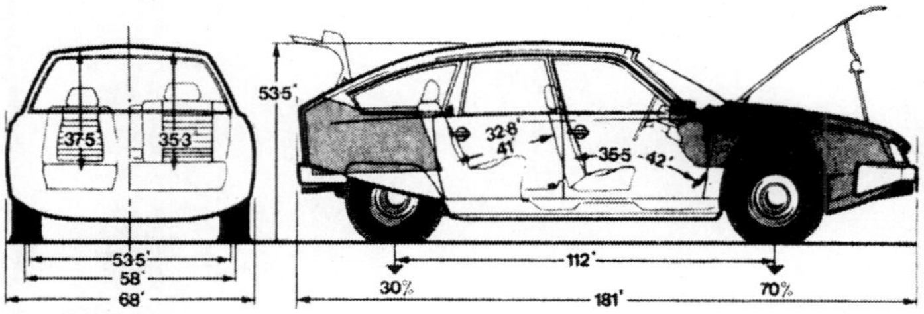

Power, bhp/rpm	106/5500
Torque, lb ft/rpm	122/3250
Tyres	185 HR 14 front, 175 HR 14 rear
Weight, cwt	24.2
Max speed, mph	106.8
0-60 mph, sec	11.8
30-50 mph in 4th, sec	8.8
Overall mpg	25.3
Touring mpg	29.9
Fuel grade, stars	4
Boot capacity, cu ft	10.2
Test Date	September 15, 1979

The Athena and Reflex models are now fitted with the 2 litre Douvrin-built all-alloy engine as used in the Renault 20 and Peugeot 505. Performance is almost unchanged, but fuel consumption and refinement have improved dramatically. Other CX virtues including a comfortable ride, spacious interior and good high-speed cruising, remain, as do faults — poor instruments, unpleasant steering and brake feel.

AUSTIN PRINCESS 2200 HLS £5788

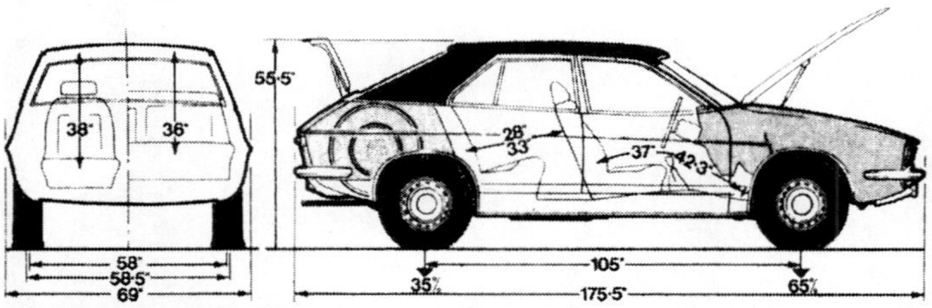

Power, bhp/rpm	110/5250
Torque, lb ft/rpm	126/3500
Tyres	185/70 SR 14
Weight, cwt	22.9
Max speed, mph	105.4
0-60 mph, sec	11.8
30-50 mph in 4th, sec	9.8
Overall mpg	22.2
Touring mpg	28.4
Fuel grade, stars	4
Boot capacity, cu ft	12.4
Test Date	July 26, 1975

Tested by us as a Wolseley 2200, but only name and nose changed since. Version assessed was a manual but automatic versions available. Hydragas suspension gives safe handling (aided by good power steering) and smooth ride. Comfortable and refined with multi-adjustable seat and low noise levels. Very roomy but boot is difficult to load and the instrument faces reflect. One of Leyland's best efforts for years.

FORD GRANADA 2.3 GL £6839

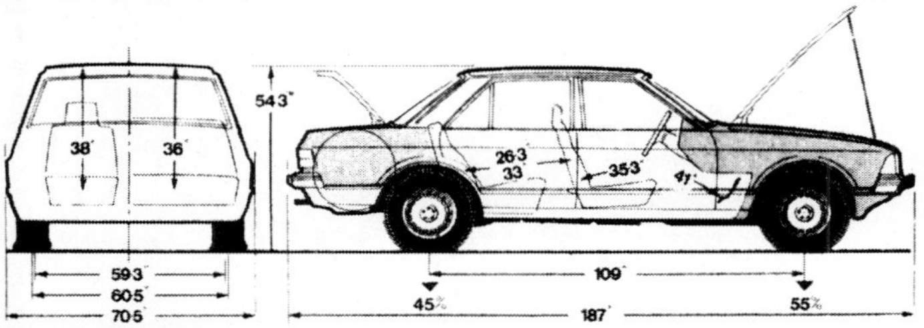

Power, bhp/rpm	108/5000
Torque, lb ft/rpm	130/3000
Tyres	185 SR 14
Weight, cwt	25.3
Max speed, mph	100.1
0-60 mph, sec	13.5
30-50 mph in 4th, sec	11.7
Overall mpg	19.5
Touring mpg	25.7
Fuel grade, stars	4
Boot capacity, cu ft	13.2
Test Date	September 16, 1978

Smaller version of the Cologne V6 in Ford's biggest saloon. Performance and economy both below par; excellent ride, good handling despite rather lifeless power steering; brakes lack feel. Perhaps not the outstanding car in its class, but nevertheless an extremely well conceived package, with no major faults and plenty of virtues, not least its generous accommodation and excellent refinement.

PEUGEOT 504 Ti £5858

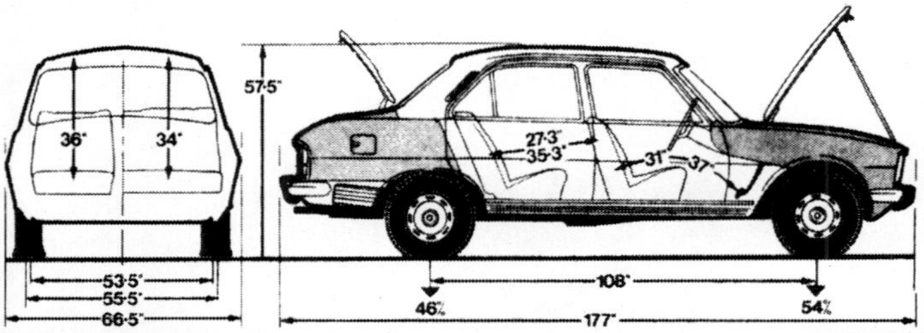

Power, bhp/rpm	106/5200
Torque, lb ft/rpm	124.4/3000
Tyres	175 HR 14
Weight, cwt	23.8
Max speed, mph	103.9
0-60 mph, sec	11.4
30-50 mph in 4th, sec	9.9
Overall mpg	23.1
Touring mpg	—
Fuel grade, stars	4
Boot capacity, cu ft	11.9
Test Date	January 28, 1978

Power steering, now standard on Ti, combines with smooth engine and transmission to make the 504 a pleasant and relaxed car in town as well as on the open road. Respectable performance and economy, and still good ride and refinement though no longer top of its class. Comfortable, spacious and well equipped (sliding sun roof and electric windows standard); it also has good ventilation. Feeble heating and ugly facia remain weak points.

RENAULT 20TS £6167

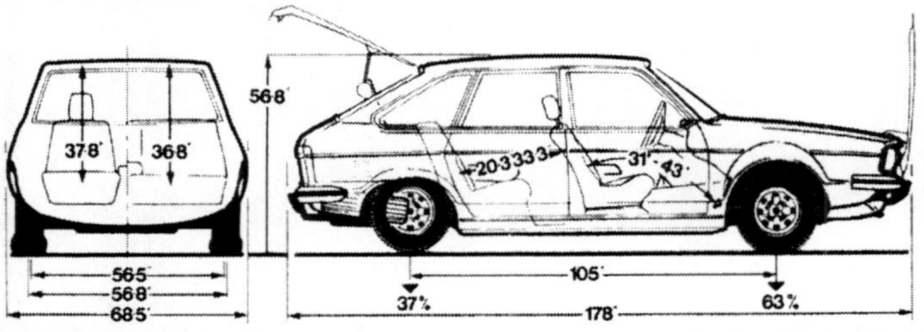

Power, bhp/rpm	110/5500
Torque, lb ft/rpm	125/3000
Tyres	165 SR 14
Weight, cwt	24.2
Max speed, mph	103.8
0-60 mph, sec	12.2
30-50 mph in 4th, sec	11.9
Overall mpg	22.1
Touring mpg	26.8
Fuel grade, stars	4
Boot capacity, cu ft	11.8
Test Date	December 3, 1978

Excellent addition to Renault's executive car line-up. New 2-litre engine gives fair performance and average fuel consumption. Pleasant power steering enhances very good handling, and the ride is excellent. Comfortable seats, commodious interior, very high level of equipment. Too much noise from engine and the ventilation. Well finished. Now with five-speed gearbox as standard though not tested by us in this form.

ROVER 2300 £6384

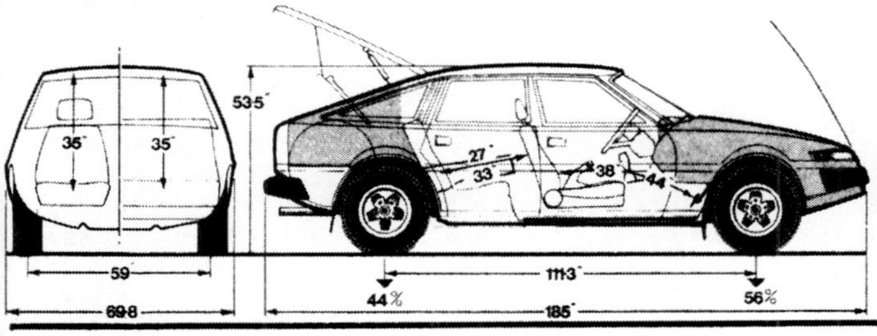

Power, bhp/rpm	125/5000
Torque, lb ft/rpm	134/4000
Tyres	175 HR 14
Weight, cwt	25.7
Max speed, mph	114.1
0-60 mph, sec	10.8
30-50 mph in 4th, sec	10.0
Overall mpg	21.5
Touring mpg	24.0
Fuel grade, stars	4
Boot capacity, cu ft	12.7
Test Date	September 16, 1978

An excellent car, fitted with the smallest version of Rover's new in-line six. Performance very good and consumption, therefore, reasonable. A comparative rarity in this class in being a versatile hatchback — the Renault 20/30 is another. Roadholding excellent, but ride can be bumpy at times. High gearing makes it a very good high-speed cruiser as well. It has a reputation for poor quality, though.

MINI TEST

Different styles and different engineering solutions – but who makes the best use of the Douvrin 2.0litre engine, Renault with their 20TS or Citroen with the new Athena?

WHAT A FORMIDABLE GALLIC TRIO IT IS. And what a perfectly timed entree. Just when the fuel guzzlers at the top end of the executive market are beginning to get the thumbs down, even from business buyers, Citroen reinforce the French onslaught on the attractive upper 2.0litre sector with their Reflex and Athena. With the helping hand of OPEC, the Douvrin co-op engine, already powering the Renault 20TS/LS and Peugeot 505, has become an even greater moving force than might have been envisaged when the big three French manufacturers embarked on their common engine programme. It was originally economies of scale that motivated the project: the demand for fuel economy has since given it fresh impetus and importance.

The Peugeot 505 arrives in Britain in the next few weeks but the new Douvrin-powered Citroens are already here, tackling the well entrenched Renault (among others) for a much bigger slice of the 2.0litre market than that captured by the superseded CX2000 which accounted for only 11percent of all CX sales here. Most of the big Citroens favoured in Britain have hitherto been up-market ones, but the emphasis now is likely to swing towards the four-speed £5697 Reflex and, in particular, the better equipped five-speed Athena. This, at £6229, costs £62 more than the Renault 20TS but nearly £500 more than the new 20LS which has the same engine and five-speed transmission.

It's a good measure of the new all-alloy overhead cam engine that it can achieve with 2.0litres what the CX2400 (dropped from the range) managed on 2.4. What's more, it does so with superior refinement and economy. Compared with the old 2000, the Athena is a major advance. With 106bhp (against 102) and 122lb/ft of torque (112), it has a higher top speed of 110mph (108), a better 0-60mph time of 11.5 sec (12.8) as well as significantly better fuel consumption. Pussy-foot drivers could well see returns of up to 35mpg, though nearer

30 – respectable enough – would be more normal. Such frugality is of course in part due to clean aerodynamics and high gearing (22.1mph/1000rpm in fifth against the CX2000's 19.3) in the best Citroen tradition. The superiority of the new engine over the old is nevertheless clear cut, as the performance of the cheaper Reflex – as fast as the Athena but inevitably a little fussier and thirstier – clearly indicates.

According to Citroen, the small disparity in quoted torque and power outputs between the Reflex/Athena and the Renault 20TS/LS is accounted for by different measuring techniques rather than different specifications, though the engines are not identical. Both have Weber carburation but the Renault has an automatic choke, the Citroen a manual one with a red-alert light in the facia-mounted pull which has to be fairly carefully set to avoid stalling or excessive revving. Apart from their installation and the position of certain ancillaries – for accessibility reasons the Citroen has a forward-facing distributor with a revised camshaft-drive – the engines and their outputs can be regarded as the same. Only the injected version of the Peugeot differs significantly. There's little in it on kerb weight either – both the Athena and 20TS scale about 24cwt – so they are predictably pretty evenly matched on performance. The Renault *feels* the more lively because of its lower gearing (20.8mph/1000rpm in fifth), but in an all-out sprint through the gears unruly tramp and wheelspin makes it slower off the mark than the Citroen which, assisted by wider 185 section front tyres (the Renault is on 165s, the Citroen on 175s at the back), has markedly superior traction off the line. According to our stopwatch both cars will accelerate to 60mph from rest in about 11.5sec, which is brisk going for big 2.0litre five-seaters. Both cars pull strongly and cleanly without stutter from low revs, though delicate throttle control is needed to avoid

MINI TEST

Douvrin 2.0litre four is largely same in both Athena and Renault though installations are very different. Engine is mounted transversely in the Citroen (this page); also has forward facing distributor and revised camshaft drive. Higher gearing and better aerodynamics give Athena 5mph on top speed and better fuel consumption. Cabin is CX; ventilation still poor despite mods

snatching in the Citroen's poorly cushioned drivetrain. The Renault is much more forgiving and the easier of the two cars to drive smoothly. In the low and mid-speed ranges, lower gearing makes the Renault's pickup in fourth and fifth brisker than the Citroen's, but this advantage is offset at higher speeds by the Athena's superior aerodynamics which give it a clear 5mph advantage on top speed.

More to the point, higher gearing and better streamlining make the Citroen significantly less thirsty. All three DoE tests – at 56mph it is doing 40mpg – show the Athena to have a clear-cut advantage which our own measurements confirm. Longer legs mean less mechanical fuss and noise too, though the Athena's superior engine refinement does not stem entirely from higher ratios. Citroen have all but eliminated the boom period around 4000rpm that was quite obtrusive in the Peugeot 505 we drove in France, and plainly evident in the Renault tested here. You can certainly hear and feel the Athena's engine throb when it's extended in the lower gears towards the 5700rpm red sector, but at its natural 90mph cruising gait – about 4000rpm on the vague revolving drum rev counter – the Citroen is a very quiet car and demonstrably more relaxed and peaceful than the Renault in which engine, wind and road roar (plus gear whine in fifth) merge as one prominent whoosh at speed. In short, Citroen have utilised the co-operative engine rather better than Peugeot and Renault – not that they've done a bad job.

Improvements to the Citroen are not confined to its performance. The lighter (by 110lb) engine/cooling system has allowed the use of even softer front suspension, and the awkward and obstructive gearchange of early CX five-speeders has given way to a lever that slips cleanly and easily through a rather floppy gate with minimal baulking. The clutch has a smoother, more progressive action than before too. With the acquisition of a respectable gearchange the flaw that marred the manual CX as a driver's car *par excellence* has been eliminated. The super-responsive powered steering may be initially unnerving to anyone unused to such sharp reactions from small inputs: powered self-centring and very high gearing demands an extremely sensitive touch, particularly when unwinding, to avoid zig-zag cornering and over correction. The long wheelbase also calls for a wide-angle approach to sharp turns and driveways. But live with VariPower steering for a bit and that of all other cars will feel by comparison cumbersome and lethargic.

The unyielding wooden feel of the pressure-sensitive all-disc powered brakes also needs acclimatisation to prevent head-snapping jerks both on application and release, particularly at low speeds. But what fantastic brakes! They arrest this big car without dive or deviation from high speed with an almost uncanny sense of poise and power.

Poise: yes, that's the secret to the Citroen's ride too. It is not so much that the hydropneumatic suspension eliminates jars and jolts. It doesn't: you can feel and hear the big Michelins thumping over bumps and troughs, though the noise is well muffled and the disturbance small. It is more the car's stability over awkward cambers and dips rather than its handling of surface irregularities that gives the Citroen such remarkable balance and composure. Its roadholding is outstanding and the grip seemingly as tenacious under braking on bumpy corners as it is when the going's good. It is a brave driver who pushes on towards the very high limit of adhesion, and a foolhardy one who

Engine sits north/south in Renault bay, gives 20TS more lively feel than Athena, but wheelspin makes it slower off the mark. Same Weber carburation is used, though Renault has auto choke against Athena's manual. Cabin and body (same as J6's) are restrained, bit dowdy. Room is good though, and driving position better than Citroen's. Renault also has higher level of spec

explores beyond it: recovering a 'lost' big Citroen is for aces only.

Although outclassed, the Renault is far from disgraced. By normal standards, its power steering is one of the best, well weighted and fabulously responsive, yet it feels a bit vague compared with the Citroen's. But then everything else does. Held on lock, especially through a long roundabout or motorway cloverleaf, the valving squelches and hisses irritatingly, adding to the noise of squealing tyres if you're in a hurry. The big Renault will hustle through corners safely and quickly but it doesn't have the roadholding reserves of the Citroen and the body tends to heave and roll a bit under spirited cornering, especially on poor roads when the ride can lose some of its generally superb composure. The smooth disc/drum brakes, easier to feather on and off than the CX's, are strong and reassuring.

The Renault is a very comfortable car. You sit tall in plush, embracing armchairs, looking down from a good vantage point over the bonnet. Not that visibility is impaired by the much lower, more reclined driving position in the Citroen: its low sills and concave facia, which creates a feeling of great spaciousness though it is in fact a bit wasteful of space, ensures a commanding view over the long, raked nose. Not everyone will feel completely at home in the Citroen however. Even though the seat is (awkwardly) adjustable for height as well as reach and rake, the one-spoke steering wheel tends to rub against your thighs, and tall drivers could do with more rearward movement. There is no convenient resting place for your left foot in the rather narrow footwells either. The Renault's driving position, pedal layout and four-spoke steering wheel – if not its hand controls – are on the whole preferable. The gearchange is a little more notchy and clonky than the Citroen's though, and the minor switches nothing special. Reaching for the ignition key often means inadvertently operating the adjacent wiper stalk. The Citroen's unique switchgear – rockers and toggles strategically arranged at each end of the 'rainbow' instrument cowl within finger-stretching reach – is quite outstanding, arguably the best devised until the Visa came along despite the non-self-cancelling indicators. The same cannot be said of the controversial drum type instruments which are permanently illuminated (a rheostat regulates intensity) beneath a battery of warning lights. The conventional instrument panel of the 20TS will arouse no strong feelings, and there's no question about the superiority of the Renault's excellent ventilation system. Strong throughput can be boosted to a hair-blowing gale, whereas the Citroen will deliver no more than a poorly directed and noisy breeze. The CX's ventilation is better than it was – but it's still not good enough.

Both cars are well appointed and equipped: electric front windows and tinted glass are standard and the Renault also has central locking – but no head restraints. Both cars have cloth-and-plastic trim, although the interior decor – restrained in the Renault, characteristically futuristic in the Citroen – is very different. With its five doors and multi-position seating, the Renault is clearly the more versatile carrier. For many buyers the innate advantages of this packaging concept will outweigh the streamlined Athena's more striking appearance, superior driving qualities and better economy. But the space-age Citroen, at first more demanding to drive, is the more rewarding once you have come to terms with its unique character and controls. And for the money, it is very good value indeed.

Road on the

Citroen 2400 Prestige

THE charge is often made that cars today are all boringly similar, but to Citroen this somewhat sweeping statement would be a dreadful slander.

Citroen have, since the mid-thirties, steadily evolved a concept which proves that advanced engineering, driver satisfaction, and reliable good service *can* go hand in hand; in 45 years they have produced but three upper range model families — they need long production runs to cover high investment costs. But this is good for the customer from the point of view of spares availability and familiarity among servicing staffs. We hope that Peugeot will allows Citroen to retain their individuality even if a certain rationalisation of components (which is already happening) makes corporate economic sense. There must be room in the eighties and beyond for individualists like the Citroen CX — especially as the product is such a satisfying one.

The Citroen CX is one of the most distinctive, attractive and aerodynamically efficient vehicles on our roads today, with a drag coefficient of only 0.34 and stability "designed in" without afterthought spoilers. The key to much of the Citroen's character is the high pressure hydraulic network which controls steering, suspension and brakes. So too they contribute to the unique "feel" of a Citroen CX which requires considerable familiarisation — say at least 200 miles, whereas an average driver may settle into other cars quite happily within 50 miles or so. In the event of an hydraulic failure which could affect brakes, steering and suspension Citroen engineers have designed an accumulator which acts as a reserve while a priority valve deflates the suspension first and then makes the steering gradually heavier — all over a sufficient period of time (and with mechanical back-up) for there to be absolutely no danger. Power steering employs rack and pinion — favoured by Citroen since the Light 15 — geared at a pretty responsive 2·5 turns lock to lock. This makes town manoeuvring much easier than might be imagined, but a stranger to the car is likely to start up the road in a series of zig-zags. You soon learn to use very light touches to steer by and gradually these deft "course corrections" become second nature. The steering also has a powered self-centring action — thus one has to learn to unwind the steering smoothly or let it unwind itself in a controlled way. One has to remember not to let go of the wheel if lock has been applied, when stationary at a traffic light filter, say, because the steering wheel will unwind all its lock. On the road the system is delightfully free from kickback and road shock and no doubt the sophisticated suspension contributes here too. The Citroen has a certain amount of artificial "feel" designed into its steering and indeed a centrifugal regulator applies more pressure to the cam to make the steering slightly heavier on lock at higher road speeds. While it would be true to say that the "feel" is not that which one would find on a good orthodox system, nonetheless the messages which a sensitive driver will expect to be conveyed to him are all there.

Similarly the suspension is unique by virtue of its hydraulically pressurised nitrogen-filled suspension units. The Citroen's ability to glide over rough terrain as though it were not there is legendary, and there is additional height adjustment, from the cockpit. As a bonus the CX has self-levelling provision which smooths the ride still further and takes care of light adjustment maladies caused by a heavily laden boot. Whilst movement is commendably restrained, bad surfaces do transmit sound through the bodyshell, and the suspension can be caught out, by a hump-back bridge for instance, if one is travelling quickly. So much for up and down movement — Citroen do seem to have a penchant for roll when pushed hard. Viewed away from the car the angles can sometimes look excessive but inside one is rarely made uncomfortable by them. And the roll helps when cornering by converting understeer — almost 70 per cent of the car's weight is over the front wheels — into roll oversteer. What happens in practise is that the two virtually cancel each other out and that the tenacious grip of the driven front wheels is able to take pretty well anything you care to give in the way of steering movement or power. Thus one is able to pilot an undeniably large car like the Prestige (at over 16ft long and nearly 6ft wide) incredibly quickly and with consumate ease on cross-country journeys — indeed this is a thoroughly enjoyable car to use in these conditions and gives pleasure almost bordering on the sensual. For with this suspension and steering the overall sensation is of smooth fluidity.

The third "arm" of the high pressure hydraulic triumvirate is the Citroen's braking system, used to activate 10·2 inch diameter ventilated disc brakes up front and 8·8 inch rears incorporating a load-sensitive limited valve. The hydraulics have a dual system for safety, while the handbrake is operated separately on the front wheels and is a truly effective emergency brake as well. Again a stranger needs to acclimatise to its "peculiarities" — the first touch of the rather "dead" pedal will often stand the car on its nose, so a practice away from other road users is a good idea! But again familiarisation proves that really effective, progressive braking can be yours from the merest touch of the pedal, while the anti-dive suspension greatly reduces passenger discomfort during stop/start town driving.

The example we tried was the top of the range Prestige which is a long wheelbase (the same as the estate Safari and Familiale 8 seater) four seater car with more than ample legroom at the rear. Thus it is really superb as a businessman's express and we find it baffling that so few manufacturers offer something similar — indeed Great Britain, once so rich in such motor cars, has only a number of rather costly conversions to offer the company chairman. This car retails for £10,416.41 for which one has the 2400cc four cylinder fuel injected engine developing 128bhp (DIN) at 4800rpm; a choice of either the five-speed manual box or the three-speed C-matic semi-automatic gearbox without cost difference; electrically operated windows; central locking; metallic paint finish; and air-conditioning as standard. The only option on the Prestige is leather upholstery which is another £733.79 and which we had on the test car — this brings the grand total to £11,150.20. Jolly expensive one might think for a four cylinder motor car and in competition with say the BMW 728 automatic at £11,711, the Jaguar 3·4 automatic at £12,509, and the Mercedes Benz 280 at £12,351 — all six cylinder motor cars — and the Rover V8S, at £10,929, with two more still. What's more they are all somewhat quicker at the top end and through the gears. But they are all more expensive, bar the Rover, have larger engines similar or poorer fuel consumptions and certainly less space. And none of them has the Citroen's dynamic personality.

Our test car was fitted with the C-Matic semi-automatic gearbox — a normal gearbox coupled to a torque converter and an automatically operated internal clutch. The clutch pedal is banished and there is a normal-looking floor mounted gearlever. This has three positions: left and back for first, right and forward for second, and back for third. Beyond third and back is a Park position which locks the gearbox for extra safety, while forward of first position is reverse — the lever being required to be pushed down to engage. Linked to the lever is an electric solonoid which engages the clutch electrically when the lever is moved. But the real beauty of the system is that you are seldom required to use the lever if you do not wish to. First is reserved for starting on steep slopes, or when cold, or if you want a rapid getaway and has a maximum speed of 44mph. Second can be selected for most normal driving, i.e. from rest to 77mph. Top is naturally for high speed cruising up to 110mph or a little less than the manual version, and such is the flexibility of the system that it is even possible to start in top. Alternatively a driver can use the gearbox normally changing up and down without having to use a clutch pedal. Again the newcomer has to remember for the first few miles to discipline the left foot, because the brake pedal on the C-matic cars has been arranged to be more conveniently used by that foot and the forgetful might try to do a rapid clutch-assisted gearchange and find themselves notching-up some pretty impressive deceleration figures instead! That said the system is easier to use than to describe and it suits the car so well that I honesty wonder why anyone specifies the manual box. Taking things a stage further still — how nice it would be if Citroen could arrange this transmission to be operated by a tiny lever on the side of the instrument pod with one's finger tips, rather in the manner of the pre-war Cotal electric gearboxes. Thus delicacy of control would be a continuous feature throughout the car.

The engine can be heard but never intrudes unduly right up to the car's maximum. Again there is no kick-in-the back acceleration but neither is the car slow — there is just a steady progress right through the torque band. Much of this smoothness is attributable to the Bosch L-Jetronic fuel injection which is fitted to the Prestige and which improves its fuel consumption over the normally aspirated engine.

From the driver's seat is a panoramic view through the windscreen but even so the sharply raked A-posts are a bit on the thick side and can hide pedestrians and cyclists momentarily in built-up areas. A single wiper contrives to wipe this large curved pane of glass and parks out of sight. A traditional Citroen single spoke steering wheel allows full view of the instruments and warning lamps contained within the futuristic "pod" behind it. Directly in front of the driver are a permanently illuminated speedo and rev counter of the revolving drum variety behind convex screens — which incidentally pick up stray reflections inspite of copious shrouding. The extreme ends of the ovaloid instrument pod are given over to everyday controls — there are no confusing-to-use stalks on *this* Citroen. On the extreme left-hand end is a flat push-in pad which operates the strident horns. Above this is the rocker switch which operates the direction indicators for which there is no self-cancelling mechanism. One remembers to cancel them manually but around town when a series of street corners have to be negotiated in quick succession there is often insufficient time to cancel them whilst twirling the steering wheel from lock to lock. It does, however, mean that slight steering wheel movement in the opposite direction does not immediately cancel the signal — something which can happen with other cars when manuoevring at certain junctions. The bottom surface of the left-hand ovaloid apex has the two speed plus intermittent wipe control working in a left to right plane, with powerful washers being brought in by pulling the pendant switch back toward the driver. Curiously the hazard warning control has been carefully hidden beneath this control cluster.

Moving over to the right-hand side of the instrument pod, we find the horn's opposite number is the headlamp flasher, and the direction indicator's twin is the headlamp dipswitch, while that of the windscreen wiper is the main lighting switch. It must be said, with the possible exception of the indicator's lack of self-cancelling, that these controls work beautifully. Everything is within finger tip reach of the steering wheel and whilst this layout is unique to Citroen, it is so logical one wonders why other manufacturers persist with alternative arrangements. Another useful aid is an oid level indicator which registers when the ignition is turned on. Between the seats live the hearing and ventilating slides, height control slide and handbrake of an almost disappointingly orthodox pull-up type. Then comes the gear selector with window lift switches around, cigarette lighter, cubby-hole, ventilation grilles and finally the radio which brings us back up to dashboard level. Perched on top of this is a spherical object looking like a certain proprietory air-freshener — in reality the ashtray. The passenger has a somewhat depressing dished area of moulded plastic in front and below this a knee level lidded compartment for odds and ends. Overall, though, the Prestige boasts the most luxurious, stylish and light and airy interior imaginable. The seats were sumptuously trimmed in beige leather with square panelling and buttoning and the doors were likewise trimmed in the same leather. The roof lining came in a matching perforated suedette and the carpets were of high quality and deep pile. Old-world touches came in the form of moquette upholstered foot rests, padded sunblinds for the rear door windows and see-through pull-up sunblinds behind the seats. There are headrests for all four passengers of course and each rear passenger has an individual cigar lighter. Air-conditioning keeps the interior fresh, and the rear passengers can really stretch their legs out and relax after a gruelling business lunch. The Prestige has a wheelbase $9\frac{1}{2}$ inches longer than the saloon, a body $9\frac{3}{4}$ inches longer and wider rear doors (7 inches), while headroom also benefits by 2 inches. Surprisingly the car has a conventional boot and is not hatchback as its shape might suggest. Inside the boot there is ample space for most requirements but the sharp corner edge of the boot lid when raised is directly at eye level which can be dangerous. Another grouse concerns the doors which have no effective keeps, and surprisingly, for this class of car, no rear warning lamps. A further irritation was the map reading light at the front attached to the side of the radio/air vent console and designed to illuminate when pulled down — it kept unclipping itself, bathing the interior with unwanted light.

However this car gave excellent service during a spell in the Midlands and Yorkshire and charmed me with its fine manners, style and finish. A great many CX's were noted on the M1 motorway which is not surprising because they make excellent long distance cruisers, while this long wheel base car seemed even happier than the saloon at swishing through the byeways on cross-country trips. Overall fuel consumption came out at a little over 18mpg which demonstrates more how it was driven than what is possible, for this can go up to the late twenties on gentler driving, while the petrol economy minded can make further gains using the manual gearbox — but for me (and uncharacteristically at that) it would be the C-Matic every time. What a super motor car! ●

B.P.

Above, the Citroen CX in long wheelbase Prestige form is sleek and aerodynamically efficient. Below left, futuristic driver controls are no mere gimmicks.

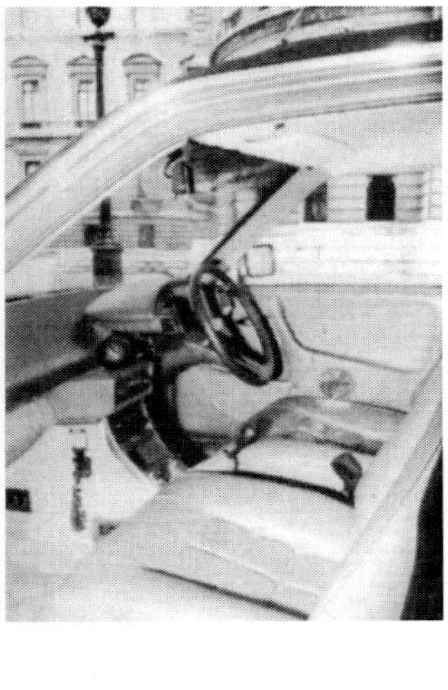

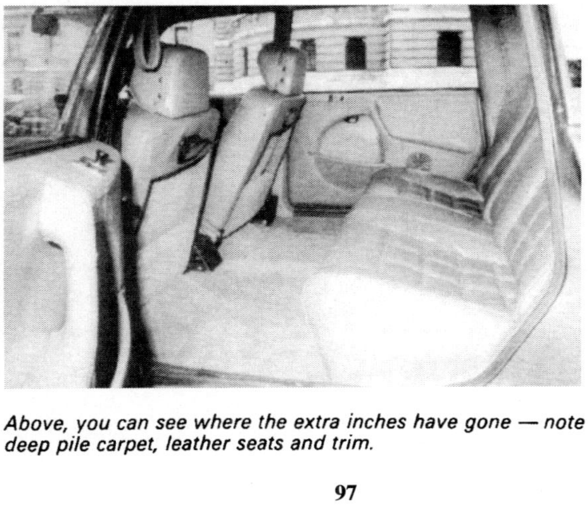

Above, you can see where the extra inches have gone — note deep pile carpet, leather seats and trim.

DRIVING IMPRESSION by Jim McCraw

THE DIESEL FROM SPACE

We now know for sure that there are superior beings who can transmit thoughts and shapes across galactic distances with pinpoint accuracy. We know not who these aliens be, but we are sure they can implant thoughts and shape the actions of mere men, and we are grateful. For they have caused the Citroen CX Pallas 2500D, and it has come from another dimension somewhere to bring us peace, quiet and transcendental transportation.

We know that these aliens must have visited our Earth or examined it from afar with telemicroscopic instruments because the plans were ultimately transmitted to Citroen, in France, the exact and only spot on the planet where the CX Pallas could have been built by men.

And then, with yet another fantastic

divination, the aliens must have looked at all 22 million people in California and selected Al Mardikian as the one man who could bring his own mystical forces together to federalize the car for sale to the grateful ones. The CX Pallas has landed in its preordained spot in Hermosa Beach, California, and behold! it meets all applicable federal standards for all 50 states. The Diesel From Space has arrived.

Al Mardikian's Trend Imports Sales, Inc., specializes in exotic, expensive, hard-to-get cars brought up to federal specs one by one. Some need and get only slight modifications; others get a turbocharger; still others get two turbochargers. Mardikian is still working the bugs out of a twin-turbo Ferrari Boxer Berlinetta that will sell for $125,000 or more. In the meantime, he busies himself with federalizing the aliens' gift to the Americans, the Citroen CX Pallas diesel, starting at a mere $17,500. The timing couldn't have been more perfect.

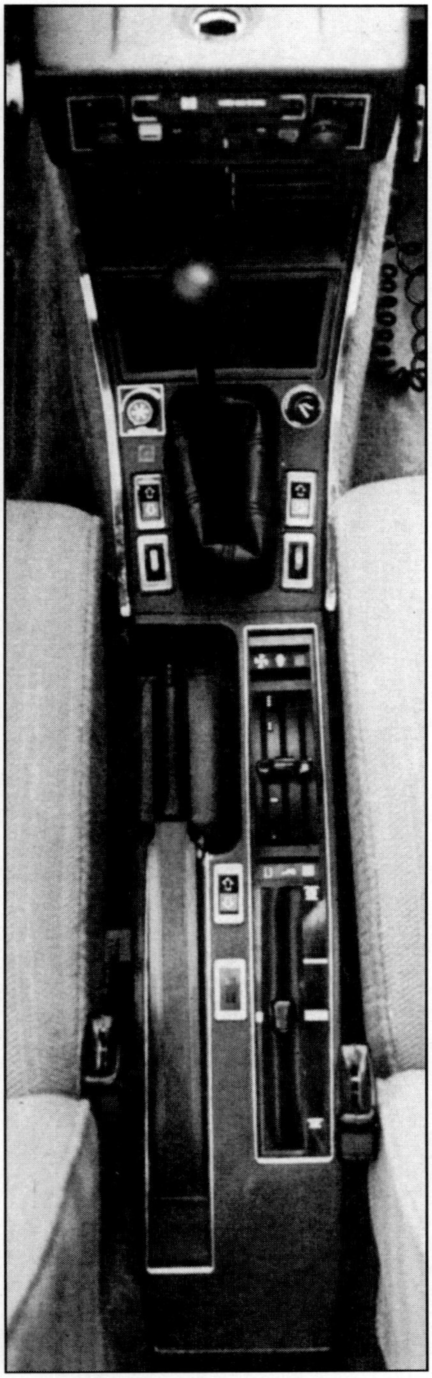

The Citroen CX Pallas is a most extraordinary automobile. It uses a monocoque body shell, full frame and subframes to isolate drivetrain, suspension and people from each other. The 2500cc diesel engine mounts transversely and drives the front wheels through a 5-speed manual transaxle and a 4.77:1 final drive. Each wheel has its own disc brake, and each wheel has its own hydropneumatic suspension unit. There are upper and lower arms for the front wheels and trailing arms for the rear wheels, and the four individual units are plumbed together to provide automatic level control, fantastically long travel and complete shock absorption. The system, with integral pump, reservoir and manual override control inside the car, has been refined and developed by Citroen for over 20 years, and it yields a ride almost too smooth and quiet to believe. The one-spoke steering wheel is tied to a rack-and-pinion system with variable ratio and variable assist as well as a power-return feature. No matter how slight or severe the steering wheel input, the wheel always comes back to center when released. The boosted all-disc braking system uses a foot pedal in the car with only a quarter-inch of total travel. Severity of deceleration depends on how hard the pedal is attacked and not on total length of pedal stroke, and this translates into enormous braking power, instantly, with the brush of a toe. And there is much, much more.

For instance, the CX Pallas' gyro-like stability. The front wheels, which drive and steer the car, are 4.5 inches wider apart than the rear wheels. The front tires are 185s, the rears 175s, and the combination of Michelin XZX tires and the odd track arrangement makes the car far more neutral than a front-engine front-drive car should be. The whole car seems a little twitchy and ungainly at low speeds, with its super-sensitive steering and brakes, but once the little diesel has pulled to 25 mph, the CX Pallas calms down, smoothes out, and rigs for silent running all the way to 100 mph. In that 75-mph band, the car is a chariot from the gods.

The exterior design led directly to the name for the series. It's an expansion of the term "CX" used in Europe as the abbreviation for "coefficient of drag" (over here it's usually CD). The CX car is flat-bottomed and very slippery, with acres of tinted glass, a drooping hoodline and severely chopped-off tail section. The unity of its shape is somewhat marred by the large electrically operated mirror on one side, but you've got to have mirrors, even in space. Other than that single large projection and the roof-mounted flying antenna, each panel blends perfectly with the next, front to rear, with everything tucked and trimmed to work with the wind. Wind noise, even with windows or sunroof fully open, is remarkably low at normal road speeds. The extended bumpers and inset side markers added by Al Mardikian's company do very little to upset the inherent harmony of the Citroen's lines.

The interior has none of the coldness or hardness we've been conditioned to accept in space vehicles. The door panels are sculptured to provide elbow room, and each is equipped with a recessed radio speaker at chair height and a pistol-like trigger and grip to open the latch. Both front bucket seats are built like couches, covered with fine cloth and triple-adjustable. The console starts at the center of the dash and extends rearward between the seats, housing emergency brake, air conditioning controls, the 4-position manual override stick for the suspension, window and sunroof controls, lighter, storage bin and main air outlets. The Pacific cassette system at top center is crowned by a globular ash receiver. The dash panel on the right side of the car is scooped out on its top side for passenger safety and fitted on the bottom side with an enormous glovebox.

The dash panel on the left is topped by a housing containing 17 different varicolored warning lights, clock, speedometer, odometer, tripmeter, fuel gauge and ammeter. The outer corners of the housing are arrayed with all controls for horn, wipers, lights, directionals and flashers, and each one can be operated without removing a hand from the single-spoke steering wheel. On the lower left is another storage bin and a pneumatic engine oil level gauge with its own light. The only thing missing was a tach to match the drum-type speedometer, not supplied on low-revving diesel models.

The rest of the interior is at least as interesting and feature filled as the left front seat area in the CX Pallas. The headliner is all suede. The sunroof fits perfectly into the padded headliner center strip. There are sun visors for each rear side window, and a set of perforated sunshades stowed in the rear shelf that lock onto hooks in the roof. The shades are black on the inside and white on the outside to manage the sunlight. There is a fold-down rear armrest that effectively makes the CX a 4-person car, and a speaker in each rear door. There is an excellent set of seatbelts for each person, three dome lights altogether, and a dash-mounted mini-light with a coil-cord. There's not a bad seat in the car. Usable empty space is everywhere, and there is 16.8 cubic feet of it in the flat-floored trunk.

Well, if the look of the shape is less important than the shape itself, and if what it has is less important than what it does, where is the CX Pallas 2500D from space? Where is it relative to all of the other, ordinary cars that were created right here, without extraterrestrial guidance? We think it is way out there. Not just out there, or out there in left field, but out there in the lead. Why? Because with all of its tricks in suspension, aerodynamics, steering, luxury and controls, it is powered not by a nuclear engine or antigravity field generator, but by a 2500cc diesel engine. The Citroen diesel started easily, warmed quickly and smoked very little. With the advantage of a horrendously low 4.77:1 final drive ratio and the slightly sticky 5-speed transaxle, the 75-horsepower engine makes the CX Pallas alarmingly quick. It will get to 60 mph in less than 18 seconds, and it will do a full 100 mph on level ground in 5th gear. Over the course of a week, the CX Pallas barely put a dent in the load of its 18-gallon fuel tank and achieved an overall economy of 33.1 mpg. That combination of performance and economy, wrapped in a shape like that of the CX Pallas, puts it, as we said, way out there.

Unfortunately, the aliens who planted the idea for the CX Pallas diesel seem powerless and unimaginative when it comes to dealing with earthbound laws of supply and demand. Mardikian the Federalizer can only bring them in and shape them into conformity a few at a time, with no cooperation whatsoever from Citroen. And he can only chip away at the already long waiting list. But The Diesel From Space is indeed here, and we are still grateful. Now we wait, and carefully watch the skies.

SPECIFICATIONS

GENERAL	
Vehicle type	Front-engine, front-drive, 4-door, 4-pass. sedan
Base price	$17,500
Options on test car	Air conditioning, AM/FM stereo cassette, power sunroof, power steering, power windows, tinted glass
Price as tested	$19.500
ENGINE	
Type	Inline 4-cyl. diesel, water cooled, cast iron head and block, 5 main bearings
Bore & stroke	93 x 92 mm
Displacement	2482cc (151 cu. in.)
Compression ratio	22.2:1
Fuel system	Mechanical fuel injection
Recommended fuel	No. 2 diesel
Emission control	None
Valve gear	Overhead valves
Horsepower (DIN)	75 at 4250 rpm
Torque (DIN)	111 lb.-ft. at 2000 rpm
Power to weight ratio	N.A.
DRIVETRAIN	
Transmission	5-speed manual transaxle
Final drive ratio	4.77:1
DIMENSIONS	
Wheelbase	112 in.
Track, F/R	58/53.5 in.
Length	183.5 in.
Width	68 in.
Height	53.5 in.
Ground clearance	6.0 in.
Curb weight	2950 lb.
Weight distribution, F/R	N.A.
CAPACITIES	
Fuel capacity	18 gals.
Crankcase	4 qts.
Cooling system	5 qts.
Trunk capacity	16.8 cu. ft.
SUSPENSION	
Front	Fully independent hydropneumatic, one unit per wheel
Rear	Fully independent hydropneumatic, one unit per wheel
STEERING	
Type	Rack and pinion, variable ratio power assist
Turns lock-to-lock	2.5
BRAKES	
Front	10.2-in. power-assisted discs
Rear	9.2-in. power-assisted discs
WHEELS AND TIRES	
Wheel size	14 x 5 in.
Wheel type	Steel disc
Tire make and size	Michelin XZX 185SR14
Tire type	Steel-belted radial
Recommended pressure, F/R	36/36 psi
FUEL CONSUMPTION	
EPA city	None
MT 73-mile test loop	33.1 mpg

IMPORTER

Trend Imports Sales, Inc.
612 Pacific Coast Highway
Hermosa Beach, CA 90254

BUYING SECONDHAND

Citroen CX

THERE IS no doubt that, even today, ownership of a big Citroen is something of an acquired taste. Way back in the 1930s, when the famous *traction-avant* models were introduced, Citroens were right out of the ordinary. They caused a huge sensation in 1955 with the launch of the futuristic DS19 car, and the current CX range progressively replaced them in 1974 and 1975. To the then existing (but reliable) complication of self-levelling hydropneumatic suspension was added that of a transverse engine front-wheel-drive installation. Production of the well-loved DS range ran for 20 years, and all the signs are that the CX models will follow suit.

CXs have now been on sale in Britain for more than five years, and have already been sold with several different engines, and in more than one body derivative. Due to its price levels, its complexity, and its sheer size, the CX is not as numerous as many other cars. In Britain's rather restricted big-car market, the CX has had to compete for attention with cars as varied as the Audi 100, the Lancia Gamma, the Renault 20 and 30 and the BL Princess 2200 (all of which have front-drive), not to mention the Volvo 244s, Ford Granadas, Rover 2300/2600s, and the Peugeot 604. On that basis, presumably, the big Citroens have something rather special to offer.

Defining the pedigree

All CX Citroens are based on the same structure which — rarely for a current model — includes a separate chassis frame, but it is not a self-supporting structure. The body shell, on the other hand, is almost as strong as a conventional unit-construction item. The frames, however, also incorporate front and rear subframes for the suspension components.

All cars have front and rear independent suspension, by high-pressure hydro-pneumatic units (with pressure supplied from an engine-driven pump), which incorporates self-levelling. Four-wheel disc brakes are also a feature, with high-pressure hydraulic circuits also powered by the same engine-driven pump.

Top left: The CX2000 Safari estate with long, 121.9in., wheelbase. Left: Current 1,995 c.c. Douvrin-engined Athena. Below left: Introduced at the same time as the Athena, in August 1979, was the cheaper Reflex model

Below far left: The CX2000 was the most basically equipped version but even so cloth seats were standard. Below centre: Light alloy wheels (top) are a distinguishing feature of the 128 bhp CX 2400 GTi, while see-through sun blinds (bottom) to shield rear passengers are now a Citroen feature. Below: A mixture of jersey and cord upholstery is used on the CX GTi and head restraints are detachable

Left: Interior of the CX2500 Diesel which has the Super trim level with cord upholstery. Note the single-spoke steering wheel which is a Citroen feature, as are the finger-tip switches flanking the instruments

All cars have transversely-mounted four-cylinder engines, but in five years a surprising variety and combination of units, and transmissions, has already been used. Depending on the model, it might have a petrol or a diesel engine, a four-speed, five-speed, or a semi-automatic gearbox.

Although the mechanical packages are all basically similar, they are hidden by two different lengths of four-door saloon, and a selection of even more bulky estate cars.

Engines

Although all the CX models have transversely-mounted four-cylinder engines, they are of several different pedigrees. Not only are there two distinctly different types of petrol engine, but there is a diesel engine family only loosely related to the others.

The most numerous engine family is that used in all CX petrol-powered models except the Reflex and Athena. It is an overhead valve unit with part-spherical cylinder head and opposed valves, first seen in the old Citroen DS models in 1965. Not only is it (or was it — for the CX2200 was only an interim model in the scheme of things) available in 1,985 c.c., 2,175 c.c. and 2,347 c.c. sizes (CX2000, CX2200 and CX2400 respectively), but at the top of the range the 2,347 c.c. engine is available as a 115 bhp unit with a Weber carburettor, or as a 128 bhp unit with Bosch injection. All these engines are based on the same cylinder block casting and are externally all the same size. It is worth noting that although they were always thought to be a touch rough when installed (lengthways) in the obsolete DS models, they are smooth and acceptable in the transverse layout of the CX.

The other petrol-powered engine, still rather rare on the secondhand market as it only became available in August 1979, is the 1,995 c.c. overhead-camshaft Renault-Peugeot unit, fitted to the Reflex and Athena models. This unit, uncidentally, is also fitted by Peugeot in the 505 model, and by Renault in the 20TS model. It

Typical underbonnet layout of the CX range. This is actually the 2-litre ohc Athena. Note the transverse engine installation and the horizontally mounted spare wheel behind it

is slightly more powerful than the CX2000 which it replaced, but (on the evidence of our test car) noticeably more economical.

Finally, there are the diesels — the 2,175 c.c. unit available from 1976 to 1978, and the 2,500 c.c. unit which replaced it with no overlap. The 2,175 c.c. engine has the same bore, stroke, and general cylinder block dimensions as the CX2200 petrol engine, though the conversion to diesel power was not as simple and straightforward as all that. It was originally developed for the Citroen G35 diesel van. The 2,500 c.c. unit is merely a larger version, with increased bore *and* stroke. Naturally, neither diesel is as powerful as the petrol engines — the CX 2500D having a mere 75 bhp.

There are three different transmissions — two manual and one semi-automatic unit. The base transmission is a four-speed all-synchromesh transmission mainly found on the cheaper down-market models, and the estate cars. A five-speed all-synchromesh gearbox, which always gives higher overall gearing, to aid economy, is standard on Athena, CX2400 (except 1977 models), CX2400GTi, CX Prestige and CX2500D saloons, and is optional on all the various Safari estate car models.

Finally there is the C-Matic semi-automatic transmission, which has a three-speed synchromesh transmission linked to a torque converter, and where gear-changing is by a conventional floor-mounted gear-lever. Movement of the lever triggers a micro-switch in the linkage, which disengages a conventional clutch in the drive line. This transmission is only standard on the CX Pallas Injection (really the plushy automatic alternative to the CX2400GTi), and optional on all other

APPROXIMATE SELLING PRICES

Price range	CX2000 Confort	Reflex	Athena	CX2200 Super	CX2200 Pallas	CX2400 Super	CX2400 Pallas	CX2400 GTi	CX2400 Prestige	CX2200 Diesel	CX2500 Diesel
£1,400-£1,500	1975										
£1,900-£2,100	1976			1976							
£2,300-£2,500	1977				1976						
£2,500-£2,700						1977					
£2,800-£3,000	1978						1977			1977	
£3,200-£3,400						1978					
£3,500-£3,700	1979						1978			1978	
£3,700-£3,900											1978
£4,000-£4,200						1979			1977		
£4,200-£4,400								1978			
£4,500-£4,700							1979				
£4,700-£4,900									1978		1979
£5,000-£5,400		1980						1979			
£5,300-£5,700			1980								
£6,200-£5,400								1980	1979		

Note: *Safari Estate cars may be worth between £400 extra (1976 models) and £700 extra (1979 models) compared with equivalent saloons. Add an extra £400 on top of this for Familiales. C-Matics add between £100 (1977) and £300 (1980) to values.*

SPECIFICATION AND PERFORMANCE

	CX2000 Manual 4-speed	CX2200 Pallas Manual 4-speed	CX Athena Manual 5-speed	CX2400 Manual 4-speed	CX2400GTi Manual 5-speed	CX2400i Pallas Auto.	CX2200 Diesel Manual 4-speed	CX2500 Diesel Manual 5-speed
Tested in *Autocar* of:	10 May 1975	20 March 1976	8 Sept 1979	16 July 1977	15 Oct. 1977	5 Aug. 1978	22 Jan. 1977	7 July 1979
Specifications:								
Engine size (c.c.)	1,985	2,175	1,995	2,347	2,347	2,347	2,175	2,500
Engine power (DIN bhp)	102	110	106	115	128	128	66	75
Car length				All saloons 15ft 2.3in.				
width				All saloons 5ft 8.1in.				
height				All saloons 4ft 5.5in.				
Boot capacity (cu. ft.)	16.2							
Turning circle (kerbs)	35ft 6in.							
Unladen weight (lb)	2,823	2,918	2,713	2,990	3,000	3,073	3,140	2,960
Max. payload (lb)	1,116	1,050	1,058	1,080	1,025	1,047	1,034	1,036
Performance:								
Mean maximum speed (mph)	110	112	109	113	118	111	89	97
Acceleration (sec):								
0-30mph	3.9	3.6	3.7	3.6	3.5	4.1	5.9	4.5
0-40mph	6.3	5.8	5.9	5.8	5.1	5.9	9.3	7.3
0-50mph	8.7	8.1	8.7	8.1	7.4	8.8	14.6	12.0
0-60mph	12.2	11.6	12.5	11.8	10.1	12.2	20.8	17.0
0-70mph	16.8	15.6	17.0	15.7	13.7	15.9	30.8	23.7
0-80mph	22.1	19.8	22.6	21.0	18.2	21.7	50.8	35.3
0-90mph	31.1	28.4	31.2	28.9	24.3	29.2	—	53.3
0-100mph	46.7	40.8	43.7	40.1	34.4	39.6	—	—
Standing ¼-mile (sec)	18.8	18.2	18.2	18.1	17.4	18.7	21.9	20.7
Consumption:								
Overall mpg	23.2	23.5	26.2	23.5	21.6	20.9	31.8	31.5
Typical mpg — easy driving	30	31	34	31	28	27	41	41
— average	26	26	29	26	24	23	35	35
— hard driving	21	21	24	21	20	19	29	29
Mpg at steady 70 mph	28.4	30.0	27.9	26.0	—	—	36.6	37.2
Fuel grade	4-star	4-star	5-star	4-star	4-star	4-star	Derv	Derv
Oil consumption (mpp)	Nil	Nil	3,000	Nil	3,000	1,000	Nil	Nil

CHASSIS IDENTIFICATION

2-litre and 2.2-litre models	Series	Chassis No.
July 1975: CX2000 and CX2200 saloons first sold in UK (Announced in France in August 1974). Both with transverse engines, front drive, hydro-pneumatic suspension, self-levelling, etc. From: CX2000	MA/MB	04MB0001
CX2200 Super	MA/MC	02MC3001
January 1976: CX2200 Pallas introduced; no Pallas version of CX2000.	—	—
April 1976: CX2000 Safari Super estate announced, with long-wheelbase five-door body shell, but no CX2200. Opening chassis number: CX2000 Safari	MA/MD	00MD0081
Summer 1976: CX2200 Super and Pallas saloons both dropped, at: CX2200 Super	MA/MC	05MC2546
CX2200 Pallas	MA/MC	07MC4829
August 1976: CX2000 named Confort, with power steering standard. From: CX2000 Confort	MA/MB	10MB0001
CX2200 Diesel version of saloon and Safari announced, from: CX2200 Super Diesel	MA/MG	01MG0001
CX2200 Super Safari Diesel	MA/MH	00MH5001
April 1977: CX2000 Safari discontinued, at: CX2000 Safari	MA/MD	0MD4009
September 1978: CX2200 Diesel models dropped (replaced by CX2500 Diesels), at: CX2200 Diesel saloon	MA/MG	05MG0659
CX2200 Diesel Safari	MA/MH	01MH3491
1979 models of CX2000 continue with new chassis series:	—	16MB2501
August 1979: CX2000 models withdrawn at	MA/MB	18MB0466
Replaced by new CX Reflex and Athena models, with same structure, but with transverse-mounted Peugeot Douvrin 1,995 c.c. overhead camshaft engine. Reflex with four-speed gearbox, Athena with five-speed gearbox. Opening chassis number: Reflex/Athena	MP	00MP1713
2.4-litre models		
August 1976: First imports of CX2400 series saloons and estates, replacing the CX2200 cars. Opening chassis numbers: CX2400 Super and Pallas	MA/MJ	00MJ0001
CX2400 Prestige (L.W.B.)	MA/MK	00MK2001
CX2400 Super Safari	MA/MF	00MF0001
October 1977: Changes for 1978 model year, including 5-speed box on saloons, plus electrical and equipment improvements. From: CX2400 Super and Pallas	MA/MJ	03MJ7501
CX2400 Super Safari	MA/MF	00MF4001
Prestige with carburettor engine dropped, and replaced by 128 bhp injection engine. From: CX2400 Prestige	MA/ML	00ML0001
Introduction of new derivative of normal-wheelbase saloon, with fuel injection engine, from: CX2400GTi	MA/ME	01ME2001
January 1978: Introduction of injection version of CX2400 Pallas, called CX2400i Pallas, from: CX2400i Pallas	MA/ME	00ME2001
2.5-litre Diesel model		
April 1978: New range of diesel-engined models, effectively replacing original 2.2-litre diesls. From: CX2500D Saloon	MA/MM	00MM0001
CX2500D Safari	MA/MN	00MN0001

CX2400s. It is not available on Reflex/Athena/CX2000/CX2200 or diesel models.

Suspension and steering

All cars have the self-levelling all-independent hydro-pneumatic suspension, with power provided by an engine driven pump. This explains why the CX range (like the old DS range) gradually "sits down" after the engine has been switched off, and "stands up" when the engine is first started up because it is a function of the loss or re-gaining of pressure in the system.

There are two types of steering. The standard manual steering, found only on 1975 and 1976 CX2000s, was low geared. On all other models, the Varipower power-assisted system, very high geared, and requiring almost complete driver attention due to its powered-self-centring habits, is standardized.

Body choice, model range, availability

There are two types of saloon — normal and long wheelbase — and an estate car based on the long-wheelbase version. These three different body shells, however, have to be permutated with the formidable number of engines and transmissions, and with several different trim levels. The normal body shell is commodious enough, but in long-wheelbase form (only available in Prestige guise with the 128 bhp 2.4-litre injection engine) there is a considerable gain in rear seat lounging room.

The Safari estate is built on the longer-wheelbase under frame, and again is available in several mechanical guises, but although there is only one steel shell there are two types of accommodation. Normal Safaris have the useful estate car type seating, but the Familiale derivatives have an extra, third, row of folding seats behind the line of the rear wheels, which face forward, and can be completely folded away when not needed: Familiales therefore can carry up to eight people at the expense of very limited luggage space left over. Either Safari, however,

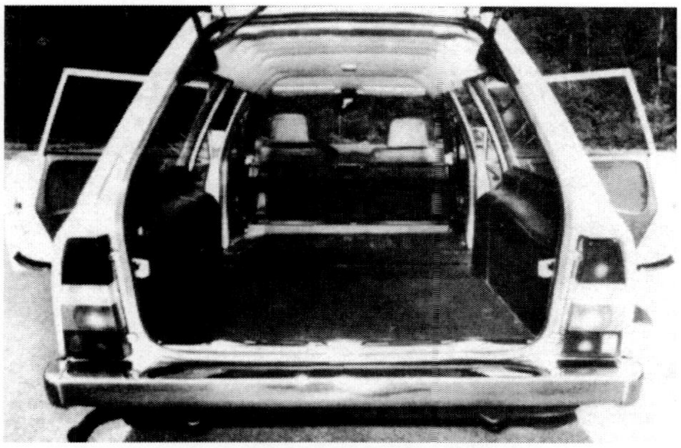

The load-carrying capacity of the CX Safari is enormous and there is a flat floor 84in. long when the seats are folded down

SPARES PRICES

	Reflex/ Athena	CX2000/ 2200	CX2400	CX2500 Diesel
Engine assembly-bare (exchange)	£586.40	£648.13	£691.74	£1,038.70
Gearbox assembly (exchange)	£456.61R £694.00A	£404.74	£404.74	£404.51
Clutch pressure plate (new)	£29.81	£32.29	£32.29	£32.29
Clutch driven plate (new)	£24.53	£25.93	£25.93	£39.17
Automatic gearbox with convertor (exchange)	NA	£773.77	£773.77	NA
Brake pads — front (set, new)	£25.10	£25.10	£25.10	£25.10
Brake pads — rear (set, new)	£18.97	£18.97	£18.97	£18.97
Suspension spring dampers — front (pair)	£75.81	£87.58	£87.58	£87.58
Suspension spring-dampers — rear (pair)	£88.80	£87.58	£88.80	£88.80
Radiator assembly (new)	£69.82	£63.27	£63.27	£113.32
Alternator (exchange)	£62.47	£70.59	£70.59	£82.60
Starter Motor (exchange)	£72.76	£72.76	£72.76	£72.76
Front wing panel	£51.11	£51.11	£51.11	£51.11
Bumper, front (new)	£84.57	£84.57	£84.57	£81.12
Bumper, rear (new)	£89.01	£89.01	£89.01	£89.69
Windscreen, laminated	£44.60R £129.64A	£94.60	£129.64	£94.60
Exhaust system complete	£82.77	£83.63	£83.63	£100.74

All the above prices include VAT at 15 per cent. Where prices for Reflex and Athena models differ, the letter R or A appears after the prices to identify the model. NA indicates the item is not applicable to that model

ENGINE AVAILABILITY

Model	1,985c.c. Ohv Petrol 102 bhp	1,995c.c. Ohc Petrol 106 bhp	2,175c.c. Ohv Petrol 110 bhp	2,347c.c. Ohv Petrol 115 bhp	2,347c.c. Ohv Petrol 128 bhp	2,175c.c. Ohv Diesel 66 bhp	2,500c.c. Ohv Diesel 75 bhp
saloons, 112in. Wb.	1975-1979	1979-1980	1975-1976	1977-1980	1978-1980	1976-1978	1978-1980
Prestige saloon, 121.9in. Wb	--	—	—	1977	1978-1980	—	—
Safari estates, 121.9in. Wb	1976-1977	—	—	1976-1980	—	1976-1978	1978-1980

Note: *Normal wheelbase CX models are available in three trim-equipment packs. The most basic of these is the Confort, followed in acending order of equipment by the Super and the Pallas. The Prestige specification is only available on the long wheelbase floorpan.*

Familiale versions of the Safari estate have an extra row of seats so that up to eight people can be accommodated. With the seats folded down load space is similar to the normal Safari

with all rear seats folded, has a loading space no less than seven feet (84 in.) long.

There are several trim levels, starting with the base, or Confort level, then the Super, next the even more plushy Pallas, and finally (for the long wheelbase model only) the Prestige. All Safaris are trimmed to the equivalent Super standard of the saloons from which they and their engines are derived.

Our charts make it clear as to which cars were on the British market at what times. The CX2200 models were only sold between 1975 and 1978, and the CX2400s only became available in the autumn of 1976 CX2000s were completely replaced by the Reflex/Athena models in the summer of 1979. The CX2500 Diesel was a direct replacement for the CX2200 Diesel in 1978.

Our Buyers' Guide still lists eight different CX saloons, and four different Safari estates, and the range is still in full scale production. Getting on for 30,000 CXs of all types have now been sold in this country, and many secondhand examples may be found at Citroen dealerships, of which there are 260 in the UK.

What to look for

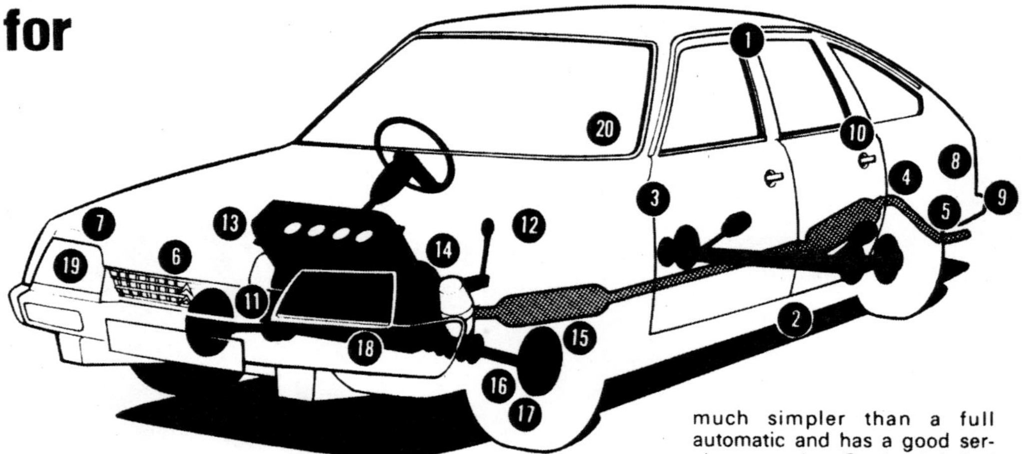

Body and Trim

YOU WILL FIND a fair spread of second-hand CXs in the British market, ranging from high-mileage examples of 1975 vintage, to some of the first re-sold Reflex/Athena models. It follows that there will be an equally wide spread of condition. Early cars will be rusting in several places if they have not been looked after. Special points to study are the tops (1) and bottoms (2) of the doors, where paint can be removed by the widespread door-fitting and sagging (3) problems of early cars; the front edge of the rear wings (4); and especially the detachable rear spats (5) which take a pounding from thrown-up gravel. Front wheel mudflaps, where fitted, cut down the gravel "spray" and save the aft of the car from its worst effects. The smooth front end (6) of the CX seems to offer a larger area than most for stone-chip damage. The front wheel arches and wings on the other hand are notably rust-free. A particular rust spot to look for in Estate CXs occurs at the lower edge of the tailgate. In general, rust problems and interior paint finish have been less frequent since 1979 when a new paint shop was commissioned at Aulnay. Current cars have anti-gravel primer beneath, and a clear-lacquer finishing coat. Up to 1978, CX paint finish tended to be worse than average for the 2-litre class, so don't regard poor-looking paint with undue suspicion.

It is well worth looking out for body damage on used CXs. The curved front wings (7) are good at collecting glancing blows, and the long wheelbase has caught out many a driver entering a narrow gateway, so check the rear doors and wings (8) with extra care. Bumper contact is less of a problem, though if they have been thumped the rear bumpers (9) can be tricky to realign perfectly. Internally, the worst problem is one of splitting door trims (10) — so have a push-check in case it's not obvious.

On a more serious note, the longerons of the CX semi-chassis (11) tend to buckle in any major front-end thump, and such crinkles are well worth looking for. The car will almost certainly not run straight if such damage exists.

Mechanical

The innocent always fear the seeming complication of the CX high-pressure hydraulic system, though in fact it is not that involved. A single reservoir, high-pressure pump and accumulator serve the needs of power steering, suspension and brakes. A worthwhile bonus is that unlike conventional springs and dampers, those in the CX never wear or sag. When hydraulic system trouble does occur, it is usually the result of fluid contamination. Check, therefore, that the LHM fluid in the main reservoir (12) is a clean green. *Any* sign of dirt must be treated with suspicion. Watch also for fluid weeping from system joints. Another known CX trouble is radiator leakage, so regard low coolant level (13) as a possible warning.

All the CX engines and transmissions are noted for their durability with the possible exception of the clutch (14) in hard-driven examples — watch for any suggestion of slippage or late take-up. The gearchange was never one of the best, and apparently slow synchromesh is not a sign of trouble. The drive shafts and constant velocity joints so often a source of trouble in front-driven cars, are exceptionally tough in the CX and have a long service life. The brakes are light in operation and have a very short pedal travel. Some Citroen drivers seem to spend their lives treating them harshly and it is worth checking the condition of the four brake discs (15). Remember that in Citroen tradition, the parking brake acts on the front wheels.

Hard-driven CXs place a heavy load on the front suspension, and a critical point is the lower ball-joint (16) which must be checked for wear. The lower front suspension arms (17) may also be bent by "kerbing". The result is uneven tyre wear — a good check point. Bent arms also make the front end of the car appear to jump slightly sideways when it is driven over a hump. More serious derangement of the steering geometry is obvious from any need to apply effort to the steering (with its powered self-centring) to hold the car straight.

The special versions of the CX pose few extra problems. The diesel engines are reckoned to be even stronger and longer-lived than the petrol units. The Bosch fuel-injection system used in the higher-performance versions has a good reputation, except for some troubles caused by road dirt fouling the terminals of the large relay under the left headlamp (18). The C-Matic semi-automatic transmission is much simpler than a full automatic and has a good service reputation. On the electrical equipment side, there are few consistent faults. Headlamp reflectors in older cars are often dulled (19) by the long-term effects of condensation inside the lens. Another visibility problem may be caused by yellowing of the lower corners of the windscreen (20) resulting from separation of the laminations — all CXs have laminated screens. So far, there have been no recall campaigns on the CX.

In theory, the lower-powered CXs run 185-14 in. tyres at the front and 175-14 in. at the back, an awkward mix. However, the CX GTi and Prestige as well as the estates have 185s all-round, so there can be little objection to standardizing on the larger size. Bear in mind that Citroen stalwartly refuse to approve the use of anything but Michelin tyres. As in all front-driven cars, the front tyres wear much quicker than the rears — at least twice as fast — but the average wear rate is good, with an easy 25,000 miles obtainable from a set if the fronts and rears are switched half-way.

It (almost) goes without saying that the CX is an unusual car to drive, to the point where someone trying one for the first time might assume there is something wrong with the steering and brakes. Some drivers grow to love the CX and feel awkward in anything else; others never come to terms with it. Make sure you can feel the former attitude coming on before you commit yourself.

The CX complex

We investigate whether the used car market needs to be so wary of Citroën's complicated design

NO CAR company exhibits a more individualistic approach to car design than Citroen. It comes as a slight jolt, for instance, to realise that the GS model is almost a decade old, yet it still looks more like a car of the 80s than most of its rivals.

The same is true of the big CX, which replaced the 20-year-old DS in 1974. Rival companies which dismissed the curves, droopy nose and sloping rear screen as mere eccentricities are now having to come to terms with them as serious aids to fuel economy.

Neither is it simply the styling which sets Citroens apart from other models. Conventional springs and shock absorbers are dispensed with, replaced by a system known as hydropneumatic. There is no travel in the brake pedal — the merest touch brings the car to a juddering halt.

The power steering has such strong self-centring action that it will do so on its own when the car is stationary. Then there are the finger-tip controls, the revolving drum instruments and the non-cancelling indicators.

They all add up to a car that delights Citroen enthusiasts, and which leaves non-believers totally perplexed. Even now, chief among the doubters are the garage trade in general. Their scepticism of the adventurous mechanical components is reflected in the secondhand value they place on the cars.

For instance, a CX bought new in 1976 would have cost in the region of £3800. So, too, would an Audi 100LS, Volvo 244DL and Ford Granada GL estate. Today, a garage would offer in the region of £1700 on part exchange for the CX, and that is some £100 less than for the Audi, £500 less than the Volvo and £800 less than the Ford.

In the UK, where it was first imported in July 1975, it has been a steady rather than sensational seller. From sales of 1618 in that first half-year they rose to 7068 in 1978. In the nine months to the end of September 1979, a total of 5727 units had been sold, a total to that point of 24,573. During the period the number of Citroen dealers rose from fewer than 200 to nearly 250. Their market share overall went up from 1.8 percent to more than 2 percent.

Evolution

How could any company follow the amazing DS? Citroen's answer was to use most of that car's mechanical components and to give it a new body with more space. Of course, it was a bit more complicated than that, but what emerged at the Paris Motor Show in 1974 was a body with a distinctly GS look, over suspension, brakes, engine and transmission that had been evolved with the DS. The engine had been moved through 90 degrees for a mounting across the chassis, and the unique DS swivelling headlights had been ditched.

But it really was a very unusual machine. The space-age style scooped out interior, the finger tip controls mounted on a separate pod in front of the driver, the single windscreen wiper and the concave rear screen — it was as if the makers had taken their stylists fresh from college, full of original ideas and free from previous conceptions of what had been the automotive norm.

Two models were initially imported, the 2000 with 102 bhp and the 2200 with 112 bhp and the option of the unusual VariPower steering that had been used on the Citroen-Maserati grand touring car. This steering is very direct and provides plenty of assistance at low speed and practically none at high speed.

These pioneers for the CX range were joined in the Spring of 1976 by two more models. The 2200 received the Pallas treatment, which meant extra brightwork and higher quality interior, as well as power steering and electric front window lifts as standard. The C-matic semi-automatic transmission became an optional extra. Effectively, this three-speed unit amounts to a clutchless manual transmission. There is no clutch pedal, but there is a torque converter which means the car can be driven around town, say, left in second gear.

The other new model was the Safari, or estate. It had a raised rear roof section, and was said to be even more aerodynamically efficient than the saloon. It used the 2000 engine.

A few months later, in August 1976, numerous changes were introduced to the range. For a start, the 2200 engine was dropped in favour of the 2400. This was essentially the same unit but taken out to 2347 cc. It produced a little more power — 115 bhp — but showed much better pulling power. It was adopted for all the larger-engined models, including the Super in saloon and estate form and the Pallas.

By that time the Pallas was not the top model. It had been ousted by the Prestige, an exceedingly luxurious model using the long wheelbase chassis of the estate. This gave country club-type leg room in the back, where special floor cushions were even provided to allow the weary businessman to rest his feet.

At the same time, Citroen joined the diesel club, the CX becoming the first passenger car from the company to have the compression ignition engine. Three years later, the diesel was accounting for 48 per cent of all CX production.

Just over one year later, in October 1977, Citroen had another batch of CX changes. None was fundamental, illustrating that the designers' concept after three years in production had grown few warts. Instead, development concentrated on widening the appeal of the model.

At the one end, a more sporty version known as the GTi was introduced. This had a fuel injection engine equipped with electronic ignition and producing 128 bhp; other refinements included a five-speed gearbox, light alloy road wheels and fog lights. Naturally, the injection engine also went into the Prestige.

Other versions retained the carburetter engine, but they did eventually benefit from the addition of the extra gear.

The estate car range was

Performance figures

Model	Speed (mph)	0-60 mph (secs)	Mpg	Insurance group
2200 carb	110	11.4	24-28	6
2200 diesel	90	18.6	33-37	6
2400 carb	112	10.6	21-26	6
2400 injection	115	10.1	20-25	6

Secondhand prices

Model	1975	1976	1977	1978	1979
Saloons					
2000	£1500-2200	£1700-2400	£2200-3000	£2800-3700	£3600-4600
2200	£1600-2600	£1800-3100	—	—	—
2400 Super	—	—	£2600-3500	£3200-4300	£4100-5300
2400 GTi	—	—	—	£4000-5200	£5100-6100
2400 Prest	—	—	£3700-5000	£4600-6100	£6000-7600
2200D	—	—	£2300-3300	£3000-4100	—
2500D	—	—	—	£3200-4300	£4100-5300
Estates					
2000	—	£2200-3000	£2600-3600	—	—
2400	—	£2200-3000	£2600-3600	—	—
2400	—	—	—	£3600-4900	£4500-5900
2400 Fam	—	—	£2600-3700	£3300-4400	—
2500D	—	—	—	£3400-4600	£4300-5600

Spare parts prices and fitting times (All prices less VAT)

Front wing	£39.34 (8.10 hrs)	Alternator	£54.32 (0.45 hrs)
Front bumper	£62.42 (2.50 hrs)	Exhaust (petrol)	£71.17 (2.70 hrs)
Headlamp unit	£36.96 (0.80 hrs)	Gearbox	
Front brake pads	£19.32 (1.30 hrs)	2400 petrol	£311.28 (12.6 hrs)
Windscreen	£99.76 (2.00 hrs)	engine: 2400	£532.31 (17.0 hrs)
Clutch unit	£44.81 (12.1hrs)	2200 D	£830.09 (17.0 hrs)

Above: the comfortable and roomy interior styling matches the exterior looks of the CX
Below: the fingertip controls and drum-type instruments combine to form a unique fascia

broadened with the addition of the Familiale. This was like the Safari, but with an extra row of seats in the "boot" to enable it to carry up to eight people.

To give the diesels a little more appeal, the power output was raised to 75 bhp in April 1978. This was achieved by taking the capacity to 2500 cc and fitting the revised engine to the saloon and estate cars in both Safari and Familiale versions. Six months later the diesel saloon received the overdrive five-speed gearbox as standard — something which was essential for long motorway journeys.

The only other change to the range came in the Summer of 1979, when the basic 2000 model was replaced by models known as the Reflex and Athena. These featured the light-alloy overhead camshaft engine of 1995 cc capacity and 106 bhp output. The engine was the joint development by Peugeot and Renault, made at a specially constructed factory at Douvrin in northern France. The Reflex features a four-speed gearbox, and the Athena is a rather better equipped version with five-speed gearbox and electric window lifts.

In action

It has a reasonable turn of speed taking weight and engine size into consideration. Naturally, the diesels lack the throttle response of even the least powerful 2-litre models, and they are something of an acquired taste.

Where all CX versions are equally at home are motorways. All are capable of cruising at speeds around the legal limit for hour on end, especially when a five-speed gearbox reduces engine noise and improves fuel consumption.

The truly impressive aspect of the car in these conditions is its directional stability. The power steering really does want to run straight ahead, pulling the car with it. High speed motorway curves make the point: the CX driver hardly needs to alter the steering, for the car seems to go round locked into its lane and as solid on the road as a battle tank. It is smooth and effortless into the bargain, which makes it a relaxing car for long journeys.

The CX's ride is smooth, the seats soft and well shaped. For anyone unused to the Citroen approach to road comfort, a ride in a CX is a revelation. The rear seats offer good support as well — and that is not always the case with luxury cars — and all round passenger space is generous. The boot is of large dimensions, too, and has a sensibly low loading height.

But any amount of left-right-left and stop-start-stop town driving may not endear the CX to the driver and passengers. This is not the model's forte, for it exhibits a lot of body roll. Its nose dips under braking and it squats when accelerating hard.

Without power assistance its steering is intolerably heavy. With power assistance, which most models seem to have, the steering requires considerable acclimatisation. It is direct to the extent that a newcomer will steer round a corner in three-penny bit fashion, applying and taking off lock.

When these peculiarities are combined with an indifferent gearchange, indicators that have to be cancelled manually, and a brake pedal that has virtually no travel in it, then the newcomer to the car can be put off.

It is almost like learning how to drive all over again, but if the driver perseveres he will not be disappointed.

Conclusion

To put the CX in perspective it is essential to compare prices. For the cost of a new Allegro, Fiesta or Sunbeam — around £3500 — a buyer could have an S-registered CX2400 Super. It is a car with masses of room, unequalled ride comfort and such niceties as power steering, adjustable ride height suspension and electric window lifts.

The minus points are that it will not return such good mpg (though it is on a par for its own course), and it will cost more to service and insure. While routine items like brake pads and filters are no more costly than average, items like the headlamp units are. So, too, is matching the metallic paintwork with which many are finished.

We could find no concrete evidence that a secondhand CX is any more unreliable than a secondhand anything else. Judging by used prices, the garage trade does not agree. However, there is a lot of prejudice among dealers over what is and is not considered a good used buy.

A used CX with full service history bought from an appointed Citroen agent should be safe. You should get a guarantee as well, but check whether it includes parts and labour.

Our choice would be a late model 2400 Super with the extra gear — a sort of loss leader in the range. The 2-litre ones, especially without power steering, are a little too slow and basic. The others amount to more money for what is basically the same car. The Pallas treatment is purely cosmetic, the specialist Prestige and GTi are a lot more expensive. Diesel models are economical for their size, and surprisingly refined, but the present price of diesel fuel still does not render them economic.

What to look for

The garage trade may not like them much, but Citroen's representation has steadily grown in this country. Nevertheless, secondhand CX prices seem to be that bit lower than for equivalent executive cars.

Owning any secondhand car is more of a risk than owning a factory-fresh new one. The question the would-be owner has to answer is whether paying less is worth the risk of paying for a vehicle that is more complicated than usual.

"A lot of emotion is talked about secondhand Citroens," says Paul Buckett, the importers' technical training officer. "But really they are no more difficult — just different."

Certainly we could find no evidence of great problems with the hydropneumatic suspension which seems to frighten most people, including mechanics. Of course, it can corrode or develop leaks, but it should last the lifetime of the car.

According to the makers, some six-year wear tests on the suspension system of the DS — from which the CX's evolved — showed that it cost one-sixth in maintenance of a conventional metal and shock absorber system. When new, the makers guarantee the hydropneumatic for two years, twice as long as the rest of the car.

But, and this is possibly the most important aspect of CX maintenance, the system may only be topped up with the bright green liquid hydraulic mineral known as LHM. Girling's Universal brake fluid is unfortunately the same colour. But it is very definitely not the same substance, and if it is added it can attack the seals.

To check the system the ride height lever should be put into the maximum position. With the engine running, the whole car will gently whirr and click until it is sitting well clear of its wheels. If it is sound the car will remain in its elevated position; if it is not it will sink slowly.

A further test comes with riding in the car. If the suspension spheres are leaking, the ride becomes firmer, sharper. But unless the would-be owner is used to hydropneumatic he may not notice and it would be advisable wherever possible to take an existing owner with you for advice.

So, if the hydraulic is any colour but bright green, do not consider buying the car. The LHM requires replacement every 30,000 miles because it ages, and obviously a car with a full service history by an authorised agent is a safer bet.

A word of warning here on a safety aspect of checking the suspension: when the car is raised on its suspension, never get underneath to check other items like exhaust, brake lines, etc. When looking at mechanicals underneath, use the jack as well. That system could have a leak . . .

Corrosion has so far not proved to be a particular problem, though obviously inspection of the door sills and for stone chips will have to be made. Rust can also set in where stainless steel brightwork meets bodywork. However, in general Citroen's Tectyl treatment at the modern factory appears to be sound.

One area that does oxidise is the aluminium of the rear brake calipers. This can result in the pads siezing on, though a cure for the problem is quite simple.

According to one Citroen mechanic, a far greater annoyance than corrosion and hydraulics concerns a ticking on the speedometers of some right-hand-drive models. "We spend more time correcting this fault under warranty than anything else," he said. The cure is to pump grease into the cable and make sure it follows the easiest route inside the binnacle.

A relatively recent modification was an increase in the size of the lower steering ball joint.

The Citroen's VariPower steering should run straight ahead, but if it unaccountably pulls to one side, don't worry too much. The system can be manually adjusted to self-centre accurately.

Early models exhibited a boom at certain speeds in the passenger compartment. This was cured early in 1976 by removing two of the body mounting points, and models after this period should show no such problems.

Similarly, early models had a troublesome engine vibration problem. The rubber mountings were subsequently changed to a different compound, and these were marked with green (or possibly blue) to distinguish them from the plain earlier mounts.

Because of the engine's crossways location — the old DS had the unit virtually in the driver compartment — it seems altogether less obtrusive. It is now an exceedingly well proven unit, having been in the DS since the early days.

A tinkling sound at idle from the rear of the engine can mean that the timing chain needs adjustment. There is a tensioner that usually does the job automatically, but occasionally it sticks. In high mileage models it could also be a warning note that a new chain is required, but it is more likely to be a simple case of manual adjustment.

The gearbox is largely free from vices, though the change has always been a bit slack and imprecise. If it becomes excessively so, a pinch bolt on top of the linkage where it enters the box may be loose. Tightening it is a two minute job, and later models with increased thread length are unlikely to show the problem. On a very limited number of early models, the cones for first gear synchromesh were under size, which resulted in noisy gearchanges after a short period.

Brake and drive shaft wear do not seem to be particular problems. Because of the unusual nature of the high pressure braking system, air in the lines does not manifest itself in the same way as it does in conventional systems — a soggy brake pedal. Instead, the brake pedal retains its firm feel, but the braking reaction is delayed by a second or so.

Tyre wear is average at the front. Depending on the type of driving, they can last anywhere between 20,000 and 50,000 miles.

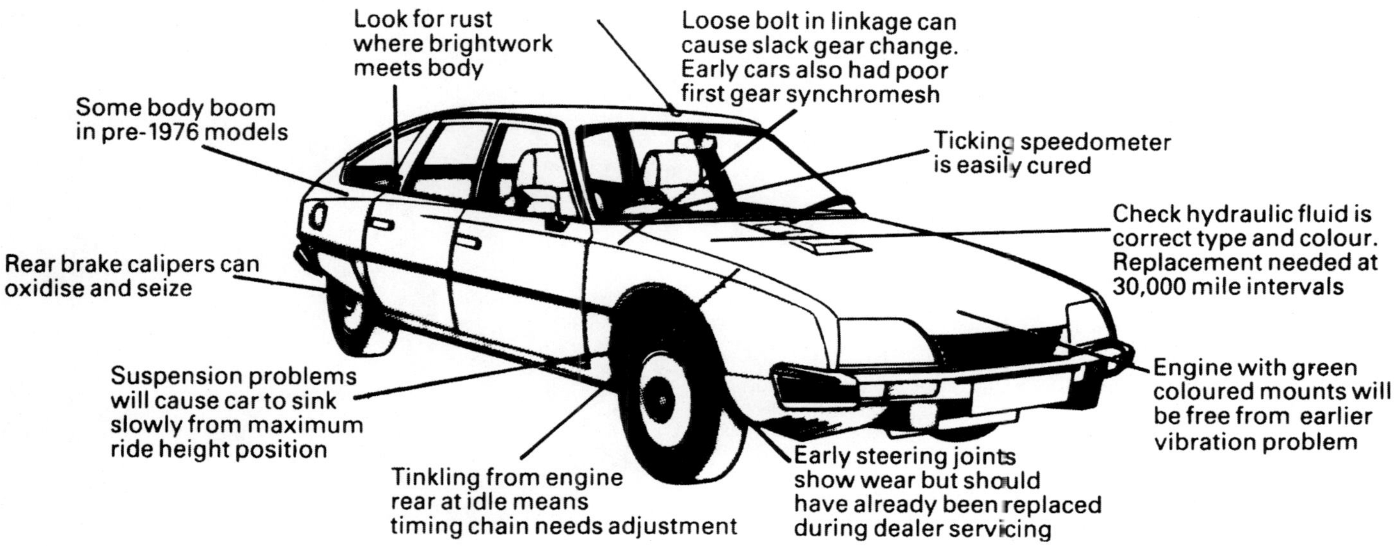

Road Test

CITROEN CX 2500 D PALLAS

The fastest and most economical big diesel car we have tested also scores high marks for refinement; in other respects, judgment of the car depends on one's personal taste for the comfortable but idiosyncratic CX range.

THERE IS some evidence that motor manufacturers with diesels in their model range are faring relatively well through the present period of industrial gloom; certainly, diesel cars are currently taking a larger portion of the UK market than was the case a year ago.

Although there is little likelihood that diesel-engined cars will ever dominate the market, it is probable that the compression-ignition engine will continue to increase its share of sales for some years to come.

The UK is only now beginning to open up to diesel sales. Although we do not have the benefit of the lower purchase price for DERV which exists in some countries, the diesel does have other benefits which are beginning to be appreciated in a time of rising costs: better fuel consumption, cheaper insurance, the probability of cheaper maintenance costs for high-mileage users, and a higher re-sale value. The main reason for this greater acceptance by the public, however, is that the new generation of diesels performs much better than was once the case.

Citroen has been making diesel engines since before World War II, and a diesel CX appeared within a year of the range's introduction in 1975. Since then, the capacity has been increased from 2,175 cc to 2,500 cc, giving considerably greater power and torque at lower engine speeds.

In this country, no less than 20 variants make up the CX range. Six of the CXs are diesels, ranging in price from the 2500S (£7,494) to the luxurious Pallas (£8,149) which is the subject of this test. In between these two in price are the Estate and Familiale (which has an extra row of seats) with either four or five gears.

Apart from its engine, the Pallas Diesel is virtually identical to the 2,400 cc petrol-engined Pallas (£7,524), except that there is no C-matic alternative to the five-speed manual gearbox, and the tyres are SR-rated (185-section

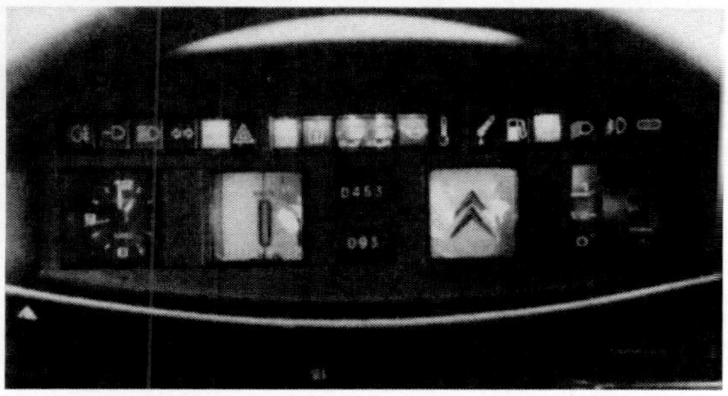

Above: apart from giving insufficient lumbar support CX Pallas seats are well shaped. The head restraints are detachable and adjustable, and the driver's seat height may be altered by means of the lever at the side of the seat. Above right: the spacious rear seats. Right: unattractive instrument display beneath a confusing array of warning lights

Above: style rather than function prevails in the design of the CX facia; though there are some useful cubbies, the large "shelf" on the passenger's side serves no purpose. Note the shrouded vent outlet on the driver's side

at the front and 175 at the rear) compared with the petrol model's HR-rated 185s all round.

As in all CX models, the transversely-mounted engine drives the front wheels, and the suspension is by equal-length wishbones with anti-dive geometry at the front and trailing arms at the rear, springing and damping being provided by Citroen's hydropneumatic system which is designed to maintain a constant ride height. Anti-roll bars are fitted at each end. The steering is power-assisted and the brakes are fully power-operated.

The Pallas Diesel's main diesel-engined rivals in Britain are the Audi Avant L 5D (£7,504), the Peugeot 604 D Turbo (£9,508), and two Mercedes-Benz models which we have not tested in their latest form, the 200D (£8,725) and 240D (£9,465). Of the large luxury saloons on the market powered by relatively small and economical petrol engines, perhaps the most competitive are the Rover 2600 (£7,784), the CX Athena 2.0 (£6,875), Volvo 244 GL (£7,674) and the Ford Granada 2.3 GL (£8,023).

The present 2,500 cc iron-block, alloy-head engine in the Pallas Diesel is a development of the C35 light utility vehicle power unit which first appeared seven years ago. Fractionally "over-square" (with a bore of 93 mm and a stroke of 92 mm), it has a compression ratio of 22.25:1. A CAV Roto-Diesel injection system is used, and the overhead valves are operated by pushrods; the camshaft is driven via an intermediate gear, unlike the chain system of Citroen's petrol engines.

This engine now develops 75 bhp (DIN) at 4,250 rpm, with peak torque of 111 lb ft (DIN) at a mere 2,000 rpm. These are highly respectable figures, and they make the Pallas D (no lightweight at 26.6 cwt) the quickest diesel-engined car we have tested.

Our lap speed of MIRA's banked circuit at an average of 96.3 mph compares with the 94.9 mph of the turbocharged Peugeot and 91.0 mph of the Audi, and the 0-60 mph time of exactly 16 sec leaves the other two trailing 0.6 sec behind. Even more impressive is the performance in 4th and 5th gears: the Citroen covers the 30-50 mph increment in 4th gear in 8.9 sec, a time which puts it on a par with many petrol-engined rivals, and 50-70 mph in top gear takes 14.0 sec, nearly one second less than the time of the four-speed Audi, and more than three seconds faster than the five-speed Peugeot.

In outright performance, of course, the CX Diesel is no match for a rival such as the Rover 2600, which is more than 20 mph faster and takes 7 sec less to reach 60 mph from rest. Nevertheless, the Citroen is never embarrassingly slow on the public road, and we are also very impressed with the advances the French company has made with this car in noise reduction and general refinement.

After the usual waiting period before the glow-plugs warm up (about 30 sec when the engine is cold), the CX fired up first time without problems during its time in our hands, and with none of the smoke and barely a trace of the knocking which characterises the public image of the diesel engine. So long as gear changes are made just before the governor restricts engine speed, there is scarcely any audible indication that this is a diesel engine; cruising at almost 90 mph is comfortable and fuss-free.

The five-speed gearbox has evenly spaced ratios, permitting full use of the engine's torque characteristics; Citroen claim that the governor cuts in at 4,900 rpm, which would give maxima of 25, 43, 63 and 84 mph, but our test car's engine seemed reluctant to go beyond 4,700 rpm. The top two gears are both overdrive, and top gear gives 22.2 mph/1,000 rpm.

The clutch is rather sharp, and the spring-loading of the gear lever is slightly awkward, but once mastered, the gearchange is acceptably rapid if a little clonky.

Performance which is superior by diesel standards has in no way been achieved at the expense of high fuel consumption. Overall, we recorded 33.4 mpg with the CX 2500D, and we estimate that 40 mpg would be within the reach of the average owner. This compares with the Audi's 32.2 mpg overall and estimated 38 mpg touring, and the Peugeot's disappointing figures of 26.4 mpg overall and 33 mpg touring. The petrol-engined Athena returned 25.3 mpg overall and 29.9 mpg touring, so a 2500D buyer can justifiably look forward to cheaper motoring. A practical range of well over 550 miles is attainable on a full 15-gallon tank of DERV.

The CX is unlike any other car to drive. Citroen, with Gallic self-assurance, sincerely believe that their suspension, steering and braking systems are not only more technologically advanced, but also better in practice than those of other manufacturers. Whether or not this is so would require a dissertation beyond the scope of this road test, but it is our opinion that a lot of learning time is required before it is possible to drive a CX smoothly; once the driver has completed his "training course", he will find that the car is very safe and has commendable reserves of roadholding, but is not at all sporting.

The VariPower steering of the CX is operated by hydraulic reaction; at high speeds the steering is made heavier by a centrifugal regulator which applies extra pressure to a cam which is linked into the system to provide "feel"; however, this is not real feel, and the front wheels can slide on a slippery road without transmitting any sensation to the steering wheel. The speed-sensing circuit also gives a self-centring effect, even when the car is stationary. Making small corrections to the steering without inducing sudden body roll — almost a "wobbling" sensation — requires a lot of practice.

In tight bends, the CX tends to understeer mildly, to the accompaniment of plenty of roll; in faster curves the car is more neutral, with even a suggestion of oversteer. Though it is rarely put off line by unevenness of surface through a bend, such bumps and hollows can cause diagonal pitching, a tendency which is also noticeable in crosswinds encountered at high speed.

The brakes — ventilated discs at the front and plain discs at the rear — are fully power-operated. The brake pedal has such short travel that it is more like a button. Somewhat oversensitive on light applications, it also has a heavy, lifeless feel during hard braking from high speed. However, the system is very powerful indeed, and we have never detected any trace of fade, nor any tendency to lock rear brakes.

While we continue to harbour a few reservations about the CX as a driver's car, there is no doubt that it is highly favoured by passengers, for it provides plenty of legroom in both front and rear, and headroom is also good (though a very tall back-seat passenger may find his hair lightly brushing the roof lining). The seats are well shaped and padded in the soft French style, but do not provide as much lumbar support as we would like. There is 10.2 cu ft of luggage space in the boot,

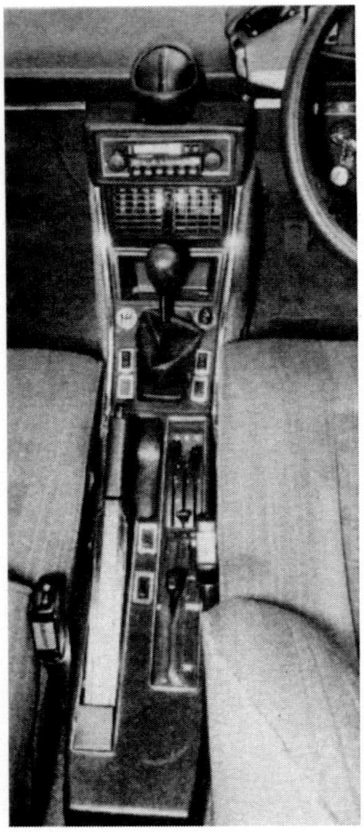

The heater controls are sited awkwardly ahead of the ride height lever. The two central vents are directly linked to the heater temperature setting, but may be closed off

rather less than average for this size of car, but internal stowage space is excellent, with a lockable glovebox, two angled cubbies in the facia, a bin and a pocket in each front door, pockets in the backs of the front seats and a very large rear parcel shelf.

Ride quality is in most circumstances of the highest standard, the hydropneumatic suspension soaking up most bumps and hollows before they can be transmitted to the interior of the car, but badly broken surfaces can cause quite firm jolts. There is also a small but noticeable amount of float over large-amplitude undulations.

With the exception of the imperfect lumbar support, the driver's seat which is height-adjustable will make people of all shapes and sizes comfortable, and all the major controls are well laid out. Whether or not you like Citroen's minor controls, which are arranged around the instrument pod for fingertip control is largely a matter of taste, but there are two specific criticisms we would make: the indicators do not self-cancel, and the heater controls (between the front seats) are poorly located.

The curved bonnet of the CX drops away to such an extent that parking is more hazardous an operation than is usual even in such a large car. Otherwise, all-round visibility is excellent, though we would prefer a larger interior rear-view mirror to complement the excellent remotely-controlled door mirror. The headlights are powerful on dip as well as main beam.

Citroen's instrument display provokes mixed reactions. We are not particularly fond of the speedometer, a revolving cylinder behind a glass window, and in this diesel version there are only two other gauges — for water temperature and fuel level, except for the oil-level check, which only operates when the engine is switched off.

Apart from the siting of the controls, the heater works well, giving good progression and a powerful flow. The fan boost is acceptably quiet on the lowest of its three settings. The ventilation is less impressive: not only is the driver's side eyeball vent poorly sited, but the air temperature from the outer vents is dependent on the heater setting, so that it is not possible to get cold air to the face and hot footwells simultaneously.

We have already complimented the 2500D for the refinement of its engine, and overall noise levels are extremely low. Wind roar is noticeable on a gusty day, but virtually absent in still air conditions, while road roar is moderate, though there is some suspension noise over badly broken surfaces.

The CX is pleasantly finished, and the seat upholstery in particular appears to be of high quality. The carpet in our test car was already, at a relatively low mileage, showing signs of fluffing up, and the roof console (housing a map light and light switches) had come loose.

For its price, the 2500D Pallas is well equipped. Original equipment, apart from the advanced mechanical specification already detailed, includes an electronic clock, electrically-operated front windows, an aerial and twin door speakers, Jersey cloth upholstery, tinted windows, a laminated windscreen, and adjustable and removable head restraints. Our test car was fitted with two extras — side sun visors and rear sun blinds.

As we have pointed out, the CX 2500D should be cheaper to run than a petrol-engined car in the same price bracket, but we should mention that the major service interval is at every 9,000 miles (as opposed to the 10,000 of Citroen's petrol models), and the high-detergent oil must be changed every 3,000 miles. The engine compartment is well laid out and all major service items are within easy reach.

The powerful, economical and refined 2,500 cc diesel engine is neatly installed

MOTOR ROAD TEST NO 33/80

● CITROEN CX 2500D PALLAS

PERFORMANCE

CONDITIONS

Weather	Wind 10-20 mph
Temperature	45°F
Barometer	29.5 in Hg
Surface	Dry tarmacadam

MAXIMUM SPEEDS

	mph	kph
Banked Circuit	96.3	154.9
Best ¼ mile	97.8	157.4
Terminal Speeds:		
at ¼ mile	66	106
at kilometre	83	134
at mile	92	148
Speed in gears (at 4900 rpm):		
1st	25	40
2nd	43	69
3rd	63	101
4th	84	135

ACCELERATION FROM REST

mph	sec	kph	sec
0-30	4.5	0-40	3.3
0-40	7.5	0-60	6.6
0-50	11.2	0-80	11.0
0-60	16.0	0-100	17.0
0-70	21.7	0-120	24.7
0-80	31.9	0-140	40.4
0-90	46.7		
Stand'g ¼	19.7	Stand'g km	36.8

ACCELERATION IN TOP

mph	sec	kph	sec
20-40	12.1	40-60	7.8
30-50	12.3	60-80	7.4
40-60	13.5	80-100	9.0
50-70	14.0	100-120	10.3
60-80	18.8		

ACCELERATION IN 4th

20-40	8.5	40-60	6.8
30-50	8.9	60-80	5.7
40-60	10.1	80-100	6.7
50-70	11.3		

FUEL CONSUMPTION

Touring*	40 mpg 7.1 litres/100 km
Overall	33.4 mpg 8.5 litres/100 km
Govt tests	31.8 mpg (urban) 46.3 mpg (56 mph) 34.9 mpg (75 mph)
Fuel grade	Derv
Tank capacity	15.0 galls 68.2 litres
Max range	600 miles 965 km
Test distance	1960 miles 3154 km

*Consumption midway between 30 mph and maximum less 5 per cent for acceleration (estimated).

NOISE

	dBA	Motor rating*
30 mph	63	9.5
50 mph	67	13
70 mph	72	18
Max in 2nd	72	18

*A rating where 1 = 30 dBA and 100 = 96 dBA, and where double the number means double the loudness

SPEEDOMETER (mph)

Speedo	30	40	50	60	70	80	90
True mph	27	36	46	56	66	76	86

Distance recorder: 1.5 per cent fast

WEIGHT

	cwt	kg
Unladen weight*	26.6	1351
Weight as tested	30.3	1539

*with fuel for approx 50 miles

Performance tests carried out by Motor's staff at the Motor Industry Research Association proving ground, Lindley.

GENERAL SPECIFICATION

ENGINE

Cylinders	4 in line
Capacity	2500 cc (152.4 cu in)
Bore/stroke	93/92 mm (3.66/3.62 in)
Cooling	Water
Block	Cast iron
Head	Light alloy
Valves	Pushrod ohv
Cam drive	Intermediate gear
Compression	22.25:1
Induction	Roto-Diesel injection
Bearings	5 main
Max power	75 bhp (DIN) at 4250 rpm
Max torque	111 lb ft (DIN) at 2000 rpm

TRANSMISSION

Type	5-speed manual; front-wheel drive
Clutch dia	9.0 in
Actuation	Cable
Internal ratios and mph/1000 rpm	
Top	0.73:1/22.2
4th	0.94:1/17.2
3rd	1.25:1/12.9
2nd	1.83:1/8.8
1st	3.17:1/5.1
Rev	3.15:1
Final drive	4.54:1

BODY/CHASSIS

Construction	Unitary all-steel
Protection	"Cataphoretic" dip, Tectyl underbody spray, silicon cavity injections

SUSPENSION

Front	Ind by equal-length double wishbones with anti-dive geometry; hydropneumatic spring/damper units with automatic self-levelling and constant (manually-adjustable) height control; anti-roll bar
Rear	Independent, by trailing arms hydropneumatic spring-damper units with automatic self-levelling and constant (manually-adjustable) height control; anti-roll bar

STEERING

Type	Rack and pinion
Assistance	"VariPower" hydraulic reaction varying assistance

BRAKES

Front	Disc, 10.2 in dia
Rear	Disc, 9.2 in dia
Park	On front wheels
Servo	Yes
Circuit	Dual
Rear valve	Yes
Adjustment	Automatic

WHEELS/TYRES

Type	Steel, 5½J
Tyres	Michelin 185 SR 14 (front); 175 SR 14 (rear)
Pressures	30/30 psi F/R

ELECTRICAL

Battery	12V, 88 Ah
Earth	Negative
Generator	Alternator 84A
Fuses	5
Headlights	
type	Quartz Halogen
dip	110 W total
main	120 W total

Make: Citroen
Model: CX 2500D Pallas
Maker: Automobiles Citroen, 133 quai Andre Citroen, 75747 Paris Cedex 15, France
UK Concessionaires: Citroen Cars Ltd, Mill St, Slough, Berks SL2 5DE. Tel: Slough 23808
Price: £6,541.00 basic plus £545.08 Car Tax plus £1,062.91 VAT equals £8,148.99

The Rivals

Other potential rivals include the Mercedes-Benz 200 D (£8,725), which we have not tested, and the 240 D (£9,465), which we have not tested in its latest form. There are also several other economical petrol-engined alternatives

CITROËN CX 2500 D PALLAS — £8,149

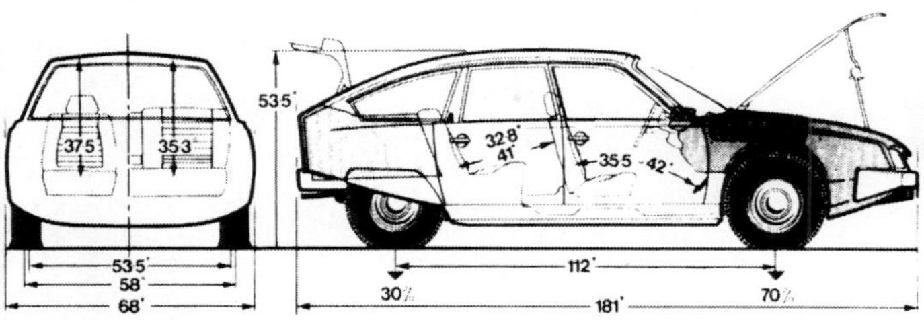

Power, bhp/rpm	75/4250
Torque, lb ft/rpm	111/2000
Tyres	185 SR 14 (front) 175 SR 14 (rear)
Weight, cwt	26.6
Max speed, mph	96.3
0-60 mph, sec	16.3
30-50 mph in 4th, sec	8.3
Overall mpg	33.4
Touring mpg	—
Fuel grade, stars	Diesel
Boot capacity, cu ft	10.2
Test Date	August 23, 1980

The quickest and most economical big diesel we have tested, the CX Diesel is also remarkably refined. In Pallas form, it is luxuriously appointed and well equipped. In other respects, it is similar to the rest of the CX range, so many of the comments we make about the petrol-engined Athena, which has a considerably lower purchase price, apply equally to this car. The CX Diesel is also available in Estate and Familiale forms.

AUDI AVANT L 5D — £7,504

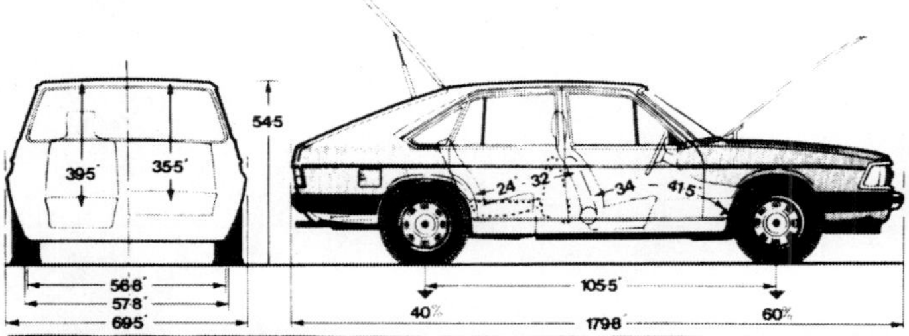

Power, bhp/rpm	70/4300
Torque, lb ft/rpm	91/3000
Tyres	185/70 SR 14
Weight, cwt	23.0
Max speed, mph	91.0
0-60 mph, sec	16.6
30-50 mph in 4th, sec	11.9
Overall mpg	32.2
Touring mpg	—
Fuel grade, stars	Diesel
Boot capacity, cu ft	10.9
Test Date	February 2, 1980

Five-cylinder two-litre version of Audi's executive class hatchback is a fast and economical diesel (though not quite a match for the CX) as well as impressively refined. Nice to drive with pleasant gearchange, excellent handling, good control layout, powerful brakes. Comfortable and roomy, but ventilation remains a weak point of the Audi 100 range as a whole.

CITROËN CX ATHENA 2.0 — £6,875

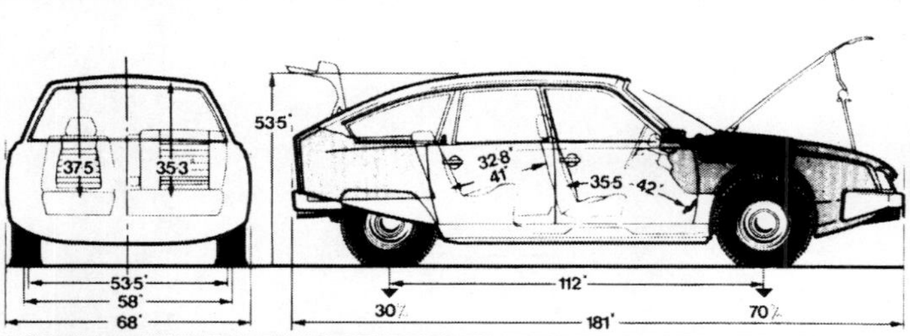

Power, bhp/rpm	100/5500
Torque, lb ft/rpm	122/3250
Tyres	185 HR 14 front, 175 HR 14 rear
Weight, cwt	24.2
Max speed, mph	106.3
0-60 mph, sec	11.8
30-50 mph in 4th, sec	8.8
Overall mpg	25.3
Touring mpg	29.9
Fuel grade, stars	4
Boot capacity, cu ft	10.2
Test Date	September 15, 1979

The Athena and Reflex models are now fitted with the 2-litre Douvrin-built all-alloy engine as used in the Renault 20 and the Peugeot 505. Performance is almost unchanged, but fuel consumption and refinement have improved dramatically. Other CX virtues including a comfortable ride, spacious interior and good high-speed cruising, remain, as do faults — poor instruments, unpleasant steering and brake feel.

PEUGEOT 604 D TURBO — £9,508

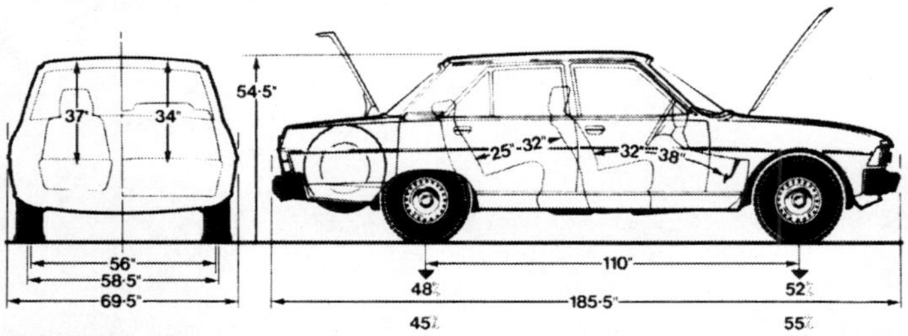

Power, bhp/rpm	80/4150
Torque, lb ft/rpm	130/2000
Tyres	175 HR 14
Weight, cwt	2[illegible].2
Max speed, mph	94.9
0-60 mph, sec	16.6
30-50 mph in 4th, sec	10.4
Overall mpg	26.4
Touring mpg	—
fuel grade, stars	Diesel
Boot capacity, cu ft	12.6
Test Date	February 18, 1980

Europe's first turbocharged diesel car, the Peugeot 604 D Turbo, is a strong contender in the prestige diesel market. Good performance and refinement, by diesel standards, from 'blown' version of Peugeot's 2.3-litre four-cylinder diesel but the CX diesel is faster, yet uses less fuel. Usual 604 attributes of excellent accommodation, steering, handling and ride spoiled only by poor driving position, bland interior and over complicated heating system.

ROVER 2600 — £8,084

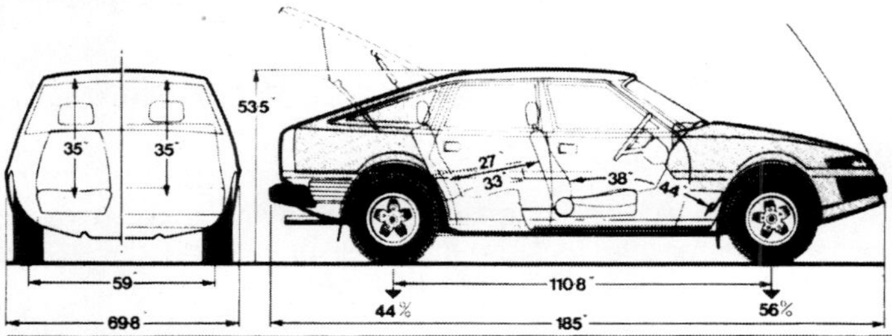

Power, bhp/rpm	136/5000
Torque, lb ft/rpm	152/3750
Tyres	175 HR 14
Weight, cwt	25.6
Max speed, mph	117.8
0-60 mph, sec	9.0
30-50 mph in 4th, sec	8.4
Overall mpg	20.5
Touring mpg	27.8
Fuel grade, stars	4
Boot capacity, cu ft	12.7
Test Date	October 22, 1977

An excellent car fitted with the new Leyland in-line six. Performance is nearly as good as that of the manual 3500. Economical for its size and performance. Like the Audi Avant, a hatchback rather than a saloon. Steering and handling excellent despite live rear axle. Ride at times jiggly, brakes unprogressive, door sealing poor. Quality control was a weak point, but appears to be vastly improved.

VOLVO 244 GL — £7,674

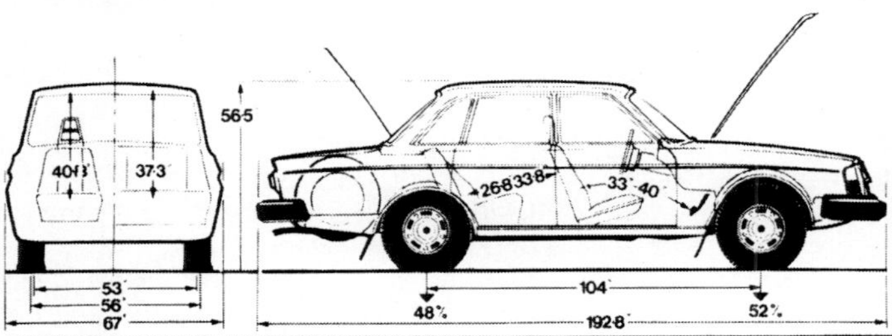

Power, bhp/rpm	100/5250
Torque, lb ft/rpm	125/3000
Tyres	175 SR 14
Weight, cwt	25.2
Max speed, mph	98.0
0-60 mph, sec	12.6
30-50 mph in 4th, sec	10.2
Overall mpg	22.3
Touring mpg	26.8
Fuel grade, stars	3
Boot capacity, cu ft	13.1
Test Date (244 DL)	July 30, 1977

We have not tested the 244 in this form, and the GL, with slightly more power and overdrive as standard, should have better performance and give better economy than is suggested by the figures of the 244 DL which we publish here. With notable improvements made in recent years, and a competitive price, the 244 range's strongest points are its quality, great solidity and in-built safety.

CX2500D

Citroen's answer to oil shortage

It really was extraordinary, really — drive out all the way from England, right into the heart of Switzerland, and have to stop only once for fuel. The car I was driving proved readily capable of covering 650 km on a tankful of fuel, in spite of being laden down with holiday luggage, including all the bulky apparatus necessary for water ski-ing, with an inflatable boat on the roof. The explanation of such remarkable performance lies in one single word: diesel.

Nothing is remarkable about that, of course. There have been diesel cars for years, and the greater efficiency of the diesel engine accounts for its use by nearly all forms of commercial transport on land and sea. But what is impressive is the way in which the diesel car has been so developed and improved over the years. The drawbacks of diesel motoring are scarely sufficient, any more, to discourage one from having a diesel car.

The one which I was testing on this Continental journey was the Citroen CX 2500D, and it's a far cry from the first Citroen diesel, which was notable for its sluggishness and poor hill climbing. In spite of its huge estate car body, its performance is surprisingly lively, and a good five-speed gearbox enables one to make the best of the power available. In fifth gear, it cruises along in very relaxed and no-fuss fashion at speeds around 135 km/h (84 mph).

It is not only the engine that has been improved since the days of the early and much more clumsy diesels: ease of driving is also much better. It used to be almost impossible to drive a diesel smoothly; now, by clever provision of a throttle over-ride, to prevent too abrupt a drop in engine speed during gear changes, the former jerkiness and snatch have been eliminated.

The "death rattle" of the diesel is still plainly audible from outside, and you get a lot of teasing. "I thought it was some

CX2500D

sort of tractor arriving to mow the grass" — that's the sort of comment you hear, but the smiles fade away and are replaced by looks of astonishment and envy when they hear how relatively inexpensive the diesel car is to run.

Noise suppression inside is very effective, so that the noise level for the occupants is not much worse that with an equivalent four-cylinder petrol engine.

The former complex stop and start controls have long since given way to ordinary key operation on all diesel cars, and cold starting pre-heat is much quicker. Only about 15 seconds with the glow plugs working is now necessary before the engine can be started from cold in mild weather, and there are no embarrassing clouds of blue smoke on starting up.

So, if the drawbacks have been eliminated, what of the advantages? Increasing the engine capacity to 2500 cc has made it not quite as economical as it used to be, but I was well content with consumption around 33 mpg. Having this much more modest thirst, with the same size of fuel tank as in the petrol model (68 litres) results in the impressive fuel range mentioned earlier.

In some countries on the Continent, notably France and Italy, there is a further benefit — diesel fuel costs much less than petrol. And again you score in having such a big fuel range that you can fill up in countries where it is cheap, and buy as little as possible in the ones such as Germany, where it is expensive.

Its diesel engine is only part of the overall package that makes this Citroen such an impressive car. Its body shape is aerodynamically excellent, and its hydropneumatic suspension system provides outstanding comfort. Its central pressure system serves as the power source for the brakes, thus getting over one of the drawbacks of a diesel — that there is not enough engine vacuum to work a conventional brake servo.

Citroen steering takes a little while to familiarise, being very light, high-geared and ultra sensitive. At first, you tend to make much larger steering corrections than are needed, but after further experience the lightness and accuracy of the steering can be enjoyed. The steering is power assisted towards the central position, and when the car is parked and the steering is released, the wheel turns automatically until the road wheels are pointing dead straight.

Front wheel drive is becoming established on big-engined cars, but is no novelty for Citroens which have always put the power through the front wheels. So it is not surprising that they achieve it without any misbehaviour — no tugging at the wheel in acceleration, and no snatch on corners. The Citroen is not an easy car to handle, because the driver always has to allow for the huge wheelbase; otherwise, the back wheels take the short cut over the pavement on tight corners. But the power-steering makes it light to handle, and the all-round view is excellent.

Two estate versions are offered, an ordinary five-seater model with vast load space, and the one I tried — the Familiale. This one has three rows of seats, to take a total of eight people. Outer seats on each side of the middle row fold bodily forward to give access to the back bench, which also can be folded for extra luggage space.

By combining the low fuel costs of this Citroen diesel with the ability to transport up to eight people, the result must be one of the lowest cost-per-km figures in the business. I can certainly think of no other way to carry eight so cheaply and at the same time in such comfort

A wise move

JOHN BOLSTER drives the Citroën CX Athena, named after the Goddess of Wisdom. He found it a worthy successor to the DS19.

Above: The Athena has a beauty of line unequalled among production saloons. Inset: Citroën's traditional double chevron badge. Below: As its name implies, the CX has a low drag coefficient figure.

It seems almost incredible, but it was a quarter of a century ago when the Citroën DS19 made all other cars seem old-fashioned. With its fully-powered steering, brakes, and self-levelling independent suspension, all fed by an engine-driven pump and accumulators, the DS gave riding comfort that had never been approached, and its advanced aerodynamics offered economical high-speed cruising and remarkable stability in side winds.

In those days, there were those who thought that the design was too clever by half, but the proof of the pudding is that the CX, which followed the DS, still has all these features. It's shorter yet even more spacious, because the engine is now transversely mounted, and the Varipower steering gives reduced assistance as the speed increases. Because the public will now accept a steeply raked windscreen, the CX, as its name implies, has an even lower drag factor than its illustrious predecessor and this functional shape gives it a beauty of line that is unequalled among production saloons.

The subject of the present test is the Athena, which is the up-market version of the 2-litre model, having a 5-speed gearbox and some extra equipment, compared with the 4-speed Reflex. Although Citroën are still using their own traditional pushrod engine in their 2.4-litre models, the Athena and Reflex have the Douvrin unit, which also appears in Renaults and Peugeots of equivalent size. Comparisons are odious, but it would perhaps be fair to remark that the Citroën has the highest maximum speed of the three and the greatest interior space.

The new engine gives a small increase in power and torque, but nothing spectacular, and it also saves a little weight, being largely of light-alloy construction. Its main advantages over the pushrod job, however, are greater refinement and, especially, remarkable fuel economy. The Athena looks a surprisingly big car to have only a 2-litre engine, but it is by no means difficult to achieve 30mpg on a run.

There is ample space for five people to ride in comfort and the seats are the ultimate in luxury. The personal opinions of a test driver should seldom be expressed, but while some people seem to like hard seats, I greatly prefer soft ones. The boot is large and has a flat floor, for ease of loading in the luggage.

The very soft suspension gives a ride of the magic carpet variety, though a thump can be heard when a wheel passes over a hole in the road. There is a considerable concentration of weight on the front wheels, but balanced handling is achieved by employing tyres of larger section at that end; there is some understeer but this is not excessive. The absence of wheelspin is exceptional for a front-drive car, though it is possible to spin the wheels deliberately when taking performance figures.

While the car certainly rolls when cornered at its very high limit, it is seldom advisable to drive as hard as that on the road and this effect is not annoying during normal fast travel. The steering is quite unusual, being rather like that of a racing car or a vintage sports car, with high gearing and very quick action, plus powered self-centring. Most modern cars have low-geared, unresponsive steering and people who have grown accustomed to this will find the Citroën very disconcerting at first. It is infinitely worthwhile to persevere, for suddenly one gets the message and then no other steering seems half as good.

To some extent, the same applies to the brakes, which are phenomenally powerful but may seem over-sensitive until the driver has learned to enjoy

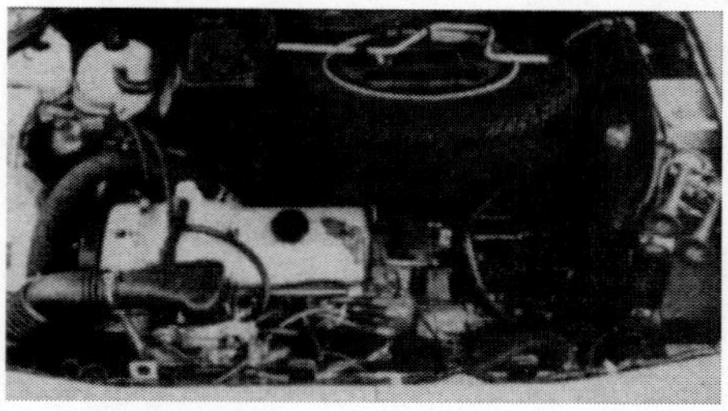

Renault's 2-litre ohc engine is a smooth power unit, finally giving the CX a motor to match its general refinement.

them. Special praise must be given to the handbrake, which really stops the car and will hold it on any gradient.

The gearbox is easy to handle, though it is best not to snatch at the lever. Fifth is a real overdrive and at the maximum speed of 110mph the rev-counter is just below 5000rpm, which is 500 revs under peak. Fourth is a splendid gear for winding roads, with a 103mph maximum. The engine is remarkably quiet, except when pressed towards its limit, and 100mph is an easy and effortless cruising speed. Indeed, it is in refinement that this car excels earlier Citroëns, rather than in performance alone.

While the placing of all the various control switches is truly excellent, one wonders why cars of this make don't have self-cancelling indicators and I cannot grow to love the monocular speedometer and rev-counter. This is by no means a small car, but the high-geared steering is a Godsend when parking in a confined space and the powered self-centring returns the wheels to the straight-ahead position, even when the car is stationary. The last few inches of the nose are not in the driver's view, however.

The Citroën Athena is a worthy successor to the dear old DS19. For space, comfort, and refinement it is outstanding and its appearance is delightful. Above all, it is supremely economical, even at high cruising speeds. The truly modern design of the car is at last equalled by that of its engine and after driving it one is inclined to wonder if there is much point in going above the 2-litre class nowadays.

CITROËN CX ATHENA
£6,875

Specification

Cylinders, capacity	4 in-line, 1995cc
Bore x stroke	88 x 82mm
Compression ratio	9.2:1
Valve gear	Belt-driven single overhead camshaft
Carburettor	Weber twin-choke downdraught
Power	106bhp DIN at 5500rpm
Torque	122lbf ft DIN at 3250rpm
Clutch	Single dry plate clutch
Gear ratios	0.733, 0.939, 1.250, 1.833 and 3.166:1
Final drive	Helical spur gears, ratio 4.54:1
Steering	Fully powered by high-pressure hydraulic system
Brakes	Fully powered discs by high-pressure hydraulic system
Suspension (F)	Hydropneumatic self-levelling, equal-length parallel transverse links, anti-roll bar
(R)	Hydropneumatic self-levelling, trailing arms, anti-roll bar

Dimensions

Wheelbase	112ins
Track (F, R)	58, 53.5ins
Length	182.25ins
Width	68ins
Weight	24.2cwt

Performance

Max in 5th	110mph
Max in 4th	103mph
Max in 3rd	77mph
Max in 2nd	53mph
Max in 1st	31mph
0-30mph	3.7s
0-50mph	8.1s
0-60mph	11.6s
0-80mph	22.5s
40-60mph in 5th	13.8s

Fuel

56mph	39.8mpg
75mph	31.4mpg
Urban cycle	23.3mpg
Test	25-32mpg

Above: The shape of things to come? Inset: An essay in ergonomics, all controls within easy reach. Below: The revolving rev counter and speedometer are not easy to read, though the battery of warning lights is comprehensive.

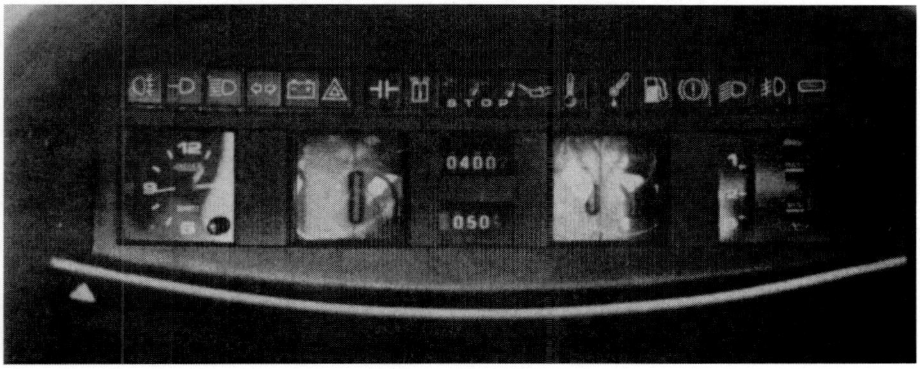

Brief Test

CITROËN CX PALLAS AUTO

Citroën have filled a long-standing gap in their otherwise comprehensive CX range by producing a fully automatic option for the Pallas and Prestige models. We test here the cheaper of the two automatic saloon versions.

WITH THE C-Matic (semi-automatic) versions of the CX accounting for a disappointingly small proportion of total CX sales, Citroën have finally succumbed and now offer a conventional 3-speed automatic as an option on the CX Pallas and Prestige. The subject of this test is the Pallas automatic, which at £9,559 stands towards the top end of the extensive CX range — it starts with the Reflex, priced at £6,179, and is completed by the luxurious Prestige automatic costing £12,290.

The CX Pallas automatic utilises a ZF epicyclic gearbox, coupled through a Fichtel and Sachs torque converter to the fuel-injected 2.4 litre version of the Citroën four-cylinder petrol engine. Apart from this the specification remains the same as that of the last Pallas (a diesel) we tested in August 1980.

Similarly, the suspension is unchanged, featuring equal-length parallel links with anti-dive geometry at the front and trailing arms at the rear, with springing and damping provided by Citroën's hydro-pneumatic system. This is designed to maintain a constant ride irrespective of load. Its setting can be adjusted by a lever between the front seats, allowing increased ground clearance for driving on rough terrain or easy changing of a wheel.

Anti-roll bars are fitted at each end. Steering and braking are both powered by the same central hydraulic system which supplies pressure for the suspension.

The latest CX Pallas automatic is considerably more expensive than the superseded C-Matic version, and it must compete in a highly competitive sector of the market. More expensive rivals to the CX are the Audi 100 CD 5E automatic (£9,861) and the Opel Commodore 2.5 Berlina CD automatic (£9,663); less costly competitors are the Saab 900 GLE automatic (£9,240) and the Ford Granada 2.8 GL automatic (£8,897) — though the more fully-equipped Granada Ghia automatic costs £10,219. The Datsun 280C appears to be the bargain of our selected rivals at £8,050, but in our experience it does not quite reach the standards of ride/handling, performance and economy expected although it does have a high level of standard equipment. Obvious rivals not tested by us in automatic form are the Renault 30 TS automatic (£8,839) and the Rover 2600 automatic (£8,983).

With Bosch L-Jetronic fuel-injection and an 8.75:1 compression ratio, Citroën's pushrod ohv, 2347 cc four-cylinder engine produces 128 bhp at 4,800 rpm and gives 145 lb ft of torque at 3,600 rpm.

The Pallas's performance is above average for the class. Its top speed of 112.4 mph is not bettered by any of our selected rivals, while the 0-60 mph time of 11.4 sec is beaten only by the Ford's 11.2 sec. Overtaking performance is also of a high order, 4.4 sec being required for the 30-50 mph increment when utilising the kickdown facility of the automatic gearbox. The Audi (4.1 sec) and the Ford (4.2 sec) are the only cars, amongst our selected rivals, which can better this time.

Noise and vibration from the engine are not intrusive below 5,000 rpm, but you are always aware that there is a large four-cylinder unit working under the bonnet rather than a more refined six-cylinder device which is more common in this class of car. Road noise is about average, but we were disappointed with a degree of wind

Above: auto selector lever is pleasant to use and is sensibly arranged; indicator lights are located along bottom edge of instrument pod. Finger-tip ergonomics work well but 'rotating drum' dials look ugly and are slow to respond — minor dials are scattered

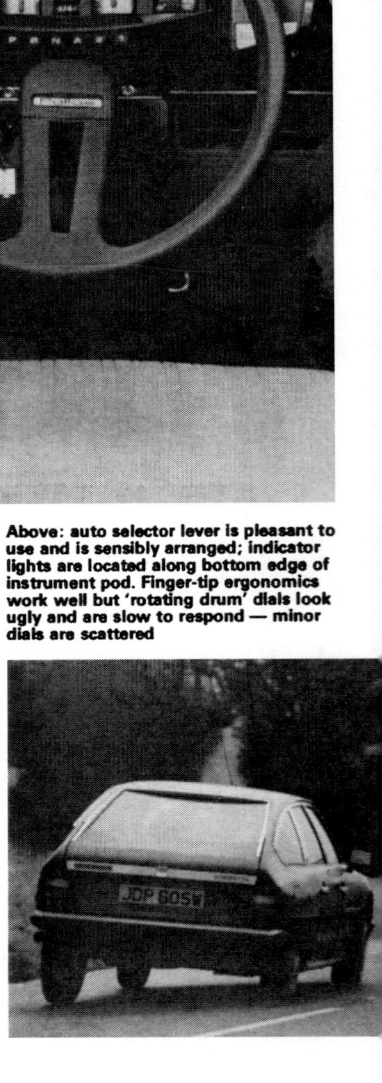

noise which was noticeable even at moderate speeds and worse than in previous CXs we've tested.

Fitting an automatic transmission to an engine usually has an adverse effect on fuel consumption. In the case of the Pallas automatic, however, we managed to achieve an excellent overall figure of 22.0 mpg which is superior to the 20.1 mpg of the 5-speed CX GTi which we tested in 1978. The fuel-injection system prevented the use of our fuel measuring equipment to determine steady-speed consumption figures and so computing a touring fuel consumption figure. However, a day-to-day consumption of 25 mpg would seem well within the reach of the Pallas, giving a useful range of 375 miles on its 15 gallon tank.

The ZF automatic gearbox is well matched to the Citroën engine and still provides an option for manually selecting the gears, (the main feature of the clutchless C-Matic transmission was manual, but clutchless, gearchanging) while also offering fully-automatic operation. With the gear lever left in automatic, upward gearchanges are smooth, even when accelerating hard. Change-up points are also well chosen if maximum acceleration is required, and there is little to be gained by holding the lower gears manually. When manual selection is preferred, the selector lever is pleasant to use and correctly arranged. There are no detents to prevent selection of lower gears, but one is provided where it is needed — to prevent inadvertent selection of neutral when changing up from "2" to "A". There is responsive part-throttle kickdown into second and full throttle kickdown to first is available up to 40 mph, and to second up to 65 mph. It does require a firm push of the accelerator pedal, however, and is slow in response, while the downward gearchanges obtained are not particularly smooth. The generally good control of the automatic system can be upset if the accelerator is released suddenly after hard acceleration, when the gearbox will change up with a jerk.

Citroën's hydraulically-powered steering, braking and suspension endow the CX with unique driving and handling characteristics. In particular, the steering requires considerable acquaintance before it can be controlled with the same competence as a "normal" power-assisted system. It is very direct and has artificial "feel" which varies with increasing speed; you can get an uncomfortable driver-induced "lurch" if steering lock is not smoothly unwound after a turn. Braking is powerful and much more progressive than in early cars, so that there is now little problem in achieving smooth braking. When used from high speed, though, the brakes feel rather heavy and "dead".

There are strong reserves of roadholding and the handling is always poised and safe, with understeer being kept well in check despite the fact that 70 per cent of the car's weight is over the front wheels. Roll becomes considerable with increased cornering speed and can inhibit full exploitation of the car's cornering potential. Ride continues to be a strong point of the CX, being excellent over a wide range of surfaces and speeds and only being caught out over severe road irregularities.

In other respects the Pallas automatic is similar to other CXs, our views on which have been well documented. Apart from the modest boot and poor headroom in the rear, the car is very roomy; the driving position is good (there is a height/tilt adjustment for the driver's seat) and the unusual layout of the indicator, light, horn, and wipe/wash switches is logical and effective (some switches such as those for the hazard lights and the rear fog lights may remain undiscovered without consultation of the handbook, however). Instrumentation is as before, with the exception of the addition of the automatic gearbox mode indicator which has been positioned underneath the revolving-drum speedometer and rev-counter which are still difficult to read behind their reflective covers. Ventilation is still, unfortunately, inextricably linked with the only passably-efficient heater.

The Pallas has a pleasant, accommodating interior and has the equipment specification that is to be expected from this class of car except for the absence of a radio/cassette fitted as standard (Citroën provide the necessary wiring and speakers, but leave the choice — and cost — of the unit to the prospective purchaser). Original equipment includes electrically operated front windows, centralised door locking, tinted windows, and a laminated windscreen.

MOTOR ROAD TEST 9/81 ● CITROËN CX PALLAS AUTO

PERFORMANCE

CONDITIONS

Weather	Wind 5-20 mph
Temperature	43°F
Barometer	29.7 in Hg
Surface	Dry tarmacadam

MAXIMUM SPEEDS

	mph	kph
Banked Circuit	112.4	180.8
Best ¼ mile	116.8	187.9
Terminal Speeds:		
at ¼ mile	77	124
at kilometre	98	158
Speed in gears (at 6000 rpm):		
1st	51	82
2nd	85	137

ACCELERATION FROM REST

mph	sec	kph	sec
0-30	4.1	0-40	3.2
0-40	5.8	0-60	5.3
0-50	8.5	0-80	8.4
0-60	11.4	0-100	12.1
0-70	14.8	0-120	17.0
0-80	19.7	0-140	24.5
0-90	26.5	0-160	35.0
0-100	35.4		
Stand'g ¼	18.2	Stand'g km	33.3

ACCELERATION IN KICKDOWN

mph	sec	kph	sec
20-40	3.4	40-60	2.1
30-50	4.4	60-80	3.1
40-60	5.6	80-100	3.7
50-70	6.3	100-120	4.9
60-80	8.3	120-140	7.5
70-90	11.7	140-160	10.5
80-100	15.7		

FUEL CONSUMPTION

Overall	22.0 mpg 12.8 litres/100 km
Govt tests	21.1 mpg (urban) 31.4 mpg (56 mph) 25.2 mpg (75 mph)
Fuel grade	97 octane 4 star rating
Tank capacity	15.0 galls 68.0 litres
Max range*	375 miles 603 km
Test distance	1651 miles 2657 km

*Assuming touring consumption of 25 mpg.

NOISE

	dBA	Motor rating*
30mph	61	8.5
50 mph	65	11
70 mph	72	18
Max revs in 2nd (1st for 3-speed auto)	75	23

*A rating where 1 = 30 dBA, and 100 = 96 dBA, where double the number means double the loudness.

SPEEDOMETER (mph)

Speedo	30	40	50	60	70	80	90	100
True mph	29	38	48	58	68	78	88	98

Distance recorder: 1.8 per cent fast

WEIGHT

	cwt	kg
Unladen weight*	25.5	1296
Weight as tested	29.2	1485

*with fuel for approx 50 miles

Performance tests carried out at 2600 miles by Motor's staff at the Motor Industry Research Association proving ground, Lindley.

GENERAL SPECIFICATION

ENGINE

Cylinders	4 in line
Capacity	2347 cc (143.1 cu in)
Bore/stroke	93.5/85.5 mm (3.68/3.37 in)
Cooling	Water
Block	Cast iron
Head	Alloy
Valves	Pushrod ohv
Cam drive	Toothed belt
Compression	8.75:1
Fuel system	Bosch L-Jetronic injection
Bearings	5 main
Max power	128 bhp (DIN) at 4800 rpm
Max torque	145 lb ft (DIN) at 3600 rpm

TRANSMISSION

Type	ZF 3-speed automatic with torque converter
Internal ratios and mph/1000 rpm	
Top	1.00:1/21.0
2nd	1.48:1/14.2
1st	2.48:1/8.5
Rev	2.08:1
Final drive	3.49:1

BODY/CHASSIS

Construction	Unitary steel
Protection	Cataphoretic dip, Tectyl underbody spray, silicon cavity injection

SUSPENSION

Front	Independent by equal length parallel transverse links, anti-roll bar, self-levelling hydropneumatic spring/damper units
Rear	Independent by trailing arms, anti-roll bar, self-levelling hydropneumatic spring/damper units

STEERING

Type	Rack and pinion
Assistance	"VariPower" hydraulic reaction varying assistance

BRAKES

Front	Disc, 10.2 in dia
Rear	Disc, 8.8 in dia
Park	On front wheels
Servo	Fully powered by engine-driven hydraulic pump
Circuit	Split front/rear
Rear valve	Yes
Adjustment	Automatic

WHEELS/TYRES

Type	Steel 5½J
Tyres	Michelin XVS 185 HR 14
Pressures	30/32 psi F/R

ELECTRICAL

Battery	12V, 70 Ah
Earth	Negative
Generator	Alternator 1.1 kW
Fuses	6
Headlights	
type	Halogen
dip	110 W total
main	120 W total

COMPARISONS

	Capacity cc	Price £	Max mph	0-60 sec.	30-50 sec.	Overall mpg	Touring mpg	Length in.	Width in.	Weight cwt.	Boot cu. ft.
Citroën CX 2400 Pallas Auto	**2347**	**9559**	**112.4**	**11.4**	**4.4**	**22.0**	**—***	**181**	**68**	**25.5**	**10.2**
Audi 100 CD 5E Auto	2144	9861	109.8	11.5	4.1	22.2	—*	179.8	69.5	24.5	10.9
Datsun 280C Auto	2753	8050	104.4	11.9	4.9	15.7	21.8	189.5	67.5	27.4	13.2
Ford Granada 2.8 GL Auto	2792	8897	105.5	11.2	4.2	18.1	21.0	187	70.5	26.1	13.2
Opel Com'dore 2.5 Berlina CD Auto	2490	9663	106.9	11.7	4.5	19.2	22.5	186	68	24.6	12.9
Saab 900 GLE Auto	1985	9240	102.0	13.9	5.4	21.3	—*	186.5	66.5	24.6	11.4

** fuel injected, so not measured*

Make: Citroën
Model: CX 2400 Pallas Automatic
Maker: Automobiles Citroën, 133 quai Andre Citroën, 75747 Paris Cedex 15, France

UK Concessionaires: Citroën Cars Ltd, Mill St, Slough, Berks SL2 5DE.
Tel: Slough 23808
Price: £7,673.00 basic plus £639.42 Car Tax plus £1,246.86 VAT equals £9,559.28

12,000 Miles On

Comely and comfortable

Individuality appears to be the cornerstone of the Citroën Athena's personality, as we found when we first road-tested the car: some of our testers liked it, some loathed it. But what's the Athena like over the course of a year? Roger Bell has been finding out

I DO not go along with the handy cliche of labelling the enigmatic Citroën CX a love-it or hate-it car, though it's certainly not one that can be regarded with total indifference. My guess is that even the most ardent fanatic could not be so enraptured by its magic as to be totally blind to its faults. I am certainly not, but I have to confess that I became ensnared by its charms.

But let's get down to facts. The Athena, and its lesser four-speed Reflex twin, both powered by France's co-op 2-litre (also used by Peugeot and Renault), superseded the old-nail pushrod 2000 here in August, 1979, giving the base CX models a new lease of life with a modern light-alloy overhead cam engine worthy of the advanced chassis that carries it. Advanced? Well, the CX was launched in 1974 (yes, as long ago as that) and its running gear, notably the unique hydropneumatic self-levelling suspension, was developed from the long-running DS it supplanted. Whether a design that's now basically a quarter of a century old can still be termed advanced, especially as it's never been flattered by imitation, is open to argument; but different and unconventional it undoubtedly remains. Just as important in this age of look-alike car clones, it imparts, along with other Citroënesque idiosyncrasies, an individualistic character quite unlike that of any rival.

This ingenious amalgam of Gallic flair and engineering eccentricity — purity, some might call it — is encapsulated within a body shell of profound beauty and elegance, notable for its wind-cheating properties and capacious cabin. These reasons alone should ensure the Athena's inclusion on the short list of anyone in the market for a prestige 2-litre, high in class and charisma. Indeed, there are strong grounds for putting it at the top of the list, as we shall see.

ON DELIVERY

★★ ★★ *Motor's* CX was a St Valentine's delivery, the second best I got that February 14. If it was a ruse by Citroën to capture my undying affection with sentimental claptrap, it largely succeeded. Putting aside matters of the heart, though, there were a few discordant notes during early courtship, not least those made by shutting the doors and bonnet. I'd never really noticed before that the CX has a rather tinny-sounding body. Those ample panels, which yield and shudder a bit under pressure, must have something to do with it. Yet beneath that seemingly thin skin, clearly a tougher hide than it looks, there's more quality and protection than meets the eye — or greets the ear when you slam a door — judging by the car's service record and immunity from rust. Moral: don't gauge a car by the thickness of its tinware.

Apart from the dismal radio reception, there were no delivery faults that I could find, nor any unwelcome surprises. But then I knew what lay in store, which is more than can be said of an acquaintance who took delivery of a company Athena at about the same time. His first impressions are really more valid than mine. Conditioned by a string of humdrum Cortinas, he was initially so thrown by the almost telepathic response of the exceptionally direct steering that he zig-zagged back to the dealers within 48 hours, asserting that the thing was undriveable. I guess they knew the patter because he was sent forth to try again. Bit by threepenny bit, he eventually did manage to drive in straight lines and smooth arcs after developing the necessary degree of delicacy and finesse.

LIFE WITH AN ATHENA

★★ ★★ If you normally drive solo on short-haul urban journeys, you don't really need a big Citroën. Some of its attributes will shine through no matter how or where you drive, but only when all of them are fully exploited is the Athena at its brilliant best. And to savour that you really need a full complement of four or five people, a heavily laden boot and a destination 400 miles away against the clock, preferably in the dark (to utilise the fine lights) over fast but indifferently surfaced roads. Only when playing the role of long-haul personnel express does the CX show its true colours.

Self-levelling suspension keeps

MOTOR LONG TERM TEST ● CITROËN CX ATHENA

Total mileage: 12,200
When acquired: February 14, 1980
Price when new: £6,578
Value now: £4,000 (see text)
Overall mpg: 30.2
Touring mpg: 28.9
Days off road: none
Extra visits to dealer: none

Make: Citroën. **Model:** Athena
Maker: Automobiles Citroën, 133 Quai André Citroën, 75747, Paris, France
Concessionaires: Citroën Cars Ltd., Mill Street, Slough SL2 5DE.
Price: £6,875 including car tax and VAT

★★★★ **excellent** ★★★★ **good** ★★★ **average** ★★ **poor** ★ **bad**

everything on an even keel, so there's no fear of bottoming out or blinding on-coming drivers. The handling, roadholding and ride — the best you can get over undulating surfaces, if not sharply pocked ones — are unaffected by a heavy load. And anyone who's wallowed their way across the Continent on holiday will appreciate what a boon that is. You tend to take it for granted, to assume it's quite normal in the CX. Of course it isn't. It's a very special and valued quality. Front seat passengers can stretch out without cramping occupants in the back, and the car's easy loping stride gobbles up miles without fuss, undue noise or incurring hefty fuel bills. Good economy, of which more later, and mechanical refinement are among the car's strongest suits. Of the three French manufacturers that use the 2-litre Douvrin co-op engine — Peugeot in the 505, Renault in the 20TS and Fuego TX/GTX, and Citroën in the Athena/Reflex — it's Citroën who have muted it the most effectively. Extended to high revs, there is a little booming, but driven normally it's an agreeably peaceful and smooth engine.

The ultra-sharp steering, fully powered by the central hydraulic system which also energises the hydropneumatic suspension and touch-sensitive brakes, calls for less physical effort than mental concentration if you're always to pick a clean and accurate line. If I'm feeling sharp and keyed up for driving, I love it: smooth, fluid inputs reap rewarding results. But a weary approach causes a ragged response. In the hands of an innately clumsy driver, passengering in a CX can be sheer misery, especially for people with queasy tums. Make no mistake: on narrow, twisty roads you can steer this big car with pinpoint precision — and steer it you must, because fine placement adjustments cannot be made by lifting the throttle to tighten your line. Ultimately, inherent and utterly predictable run-wide understeer is curbed by backing off, of course, but unlike most front-drive cars — and many rear-drive ones for that matter — the cornering line of a CX is largely unaffected by throttle opening. This gives the car impressive stability to add to its good roadholding and viceless handling. Talking of tight lines, you can cut the apex unusually fine in a CX: despite its long wheelbase, the rear track — appreciably narrower than that at the front — allows you to clip the verge without fear of hopping the back wheels over it. A nice Citroën subtlety, this.

It is hard to imagine getting into trouble with a CX short of doing something unbelievably silly. If you're going to skid, it's far more likely to be caused by slamming on the sensitive brakes too heavily in an emergency — I've done it once in 12,000 miles — than by over-exuberant cornering. With the steering I do have a certain love-hate relationship: I hate it most for automatically self-centring at rest, which can be very irritating when waiting to dive into a main road from a side turn. Its lack of genuine road feel (all resistance is quite artificial) is a bone of contention too. The brakes, or rather the *feel* of the brakes, I have never much liked. Whatever else they've got right, flying in the face of convention, Citroën have in my view got this bit wrong. True, at speed the brakes are firm and response progressive: but you have to feather the pedal on and off with tiresome delicacy to avoid head-snapping jerks in give-and-take driving. It need not be so: the similarly fully-powered setup of the Citroën GS is far less severe. Braking performance, mind, is beyond reproach, the car's stopping power quite remarkable.

You will gather by now, as if you didn't already know, that living with a CX is not like living with any other car, so let's run through all the other idiosyncrasies. The permanently illuminated rolling drum speedometer and rev counter, the brightness of which is thoughtfully rheostat controlled, are to me no substitute for a good pair of dials, and in daylight they pick up every distracting reflection going (they're crystal clear at night). Clarity and ergonomics apart, they give the compact instrument panel a strong and rather sparse appearance, alleviated by the battery of 17 colourful and useful warning lights, which include ones for worn brake pads and low fuel. The CX is also one of the very few cars around with an oil *level* gauge. The unusual one-spoke steering wheel gives a totally unobstructed view of the instrument nacelle, but how I miss those absent spokes at 3 and 9 o'clock on which to hook my thumbs on long motorway runs. The latest fashion for four-spoke steering wheels has a lot to be said for it.

In my last Running Report I said that the switchgear was "as inspired as it was unusual" and I don't retract that. But subsequent experience with the latest GSA's satellite setup, based on the Visa's, convinces me that the CX arrangement is the lesser of two masterful designs — which puts me at odds with a colleague who recently asserted otherwise. The one major flaw of the CX's switchgear is its double-sided symmetry, which to my mind is ergonomically unsound — as I frequently prove by flashing the lights when I want the horn, or switching on the wipers when going for the lights. The later satellite arrangement may not be aesthetically so neat, but there's little risk of making a wrong move. Even on the Visa and GSA, though, Citroën have perpetuated the irritation of non-self-cancelling indicators. And they still haven't got the ventilation sorted out properly, as warm air gushes from the central vents when the heater's on. Nor are the heater controls between the seats well placed, though given time you do learn to operate them "blind".

The single centre-pivot wiper blade works well, leaving no serious murky wedges for drivers of average height: tall ones will complain, though. It's the view aft that's more likely to be impaired in heavy rain — not by sprayback but by roof water channelling down the centre of the concave

Above left: the CX's ergonomics are unusual but convenient. The front seats, however (above right), are initially comfortable but lack lumbar support, and rotating drums (above) are no substitute for a decent pair of dials. Right: in the back, generous legroom is partly offset by limited headroom.

rear window due to some aerodynamic quirk. Visibility is not normally a problem, though, despite the long, invisible snout: you soon get the measure of the car for tight parking. The long wheelbase is a handicap only when negotiating, say, the ramps of tight multi-storey car parks, some of which are best avoided.

Not everything about the Athena is advanced or unconventional. It's surprising, but no doubt pleasing to many people, to find a manual choke (with a red-alert light in the knob so you can't forget to push it home) which needs careful setting to avoid over-revving or stutter and stall. Starting, hot or cold, has never been a problem, but warm-up takes rather a long time. The gearchange is undistinguished, easy enough to slot around but a mite imprecise and clonky. What's more, synchro clash after a cold start, particularly into second, is difficult to avoid without easing the lever through very carefully. The most satisfying change, which I frequently use when hurrying, particularly into roundabouts, is from fifth to third — a simple spring-assisted back and forward motion accompanied by an extended blip on the throttle. Normally, I tend to keep the revs down by hanging on to fourth or even fifth, and the cornering speed up, exploiting the secure roadholding, sharp-edged handling and strong mid-range torque. It's a technique that must have something to do with the car's excellent fuel consumption. I rarely exceed 85 mph, but make no mistake about the CX's long-league boots in 5th. It will cruise at 100 mph with consummate ease, and given favourable conditions will wind itself up to over 115 mph long before it runs out of revs at 6000 rpm. High gearing (22.1 mph/1000 rpm) tends to create the impression of a rather leisurely performance, but fully extended the Athena's no sluggard, as the 0-60 mph time of 11.0 seconds confirms. It's more at home — and to me more rewarding to drive — on open country roads than in town, where the rather heavy clutch and slightly snatchy drivetrain, among other things, can be a mite tiresome. On the other hand, the steering makes very light work of back doubles and manoeuvres. The big elephant-ear door mirror, with its vague internal joystick adjuster, is a boon, but why the penny-pinching absence of one on the passenger's side too? Citroën have gone overboard the other way with sun visors, the normal (twistable) front ones being supplemented by a side pair in the back and pull down see-through rear window blinds. The glass is tinted and the screen has an upper anti-glare zone too, so you're unusually well protected from the sun.

Even though comfort is one of the car's biggest attractions, the seats could and should be better than they are. When you first sink into the soft, spongey cushions, they feel marvelous. But a long stint at the wheel gives me (and others) backache because of inadequate lumbar support. Firmer

Underbonnet layout is generally untidy, but major service items are accessible

padding in the small of your back, and better side location at shoulder level, would be welcome.

RELIABILITY

★★★★ Trouble? What trouble? Reception of the excellent Blaupunkt radio (an extra) was not so much improved as discovered by re-routing the aerial down the left-hand screen pillar from the rooftop antenna, away from the instruments on the right. On left-hand drive cars, the aerial is where it should be, but on right hookers it's not. According to the importers, reception in some cars is perfectly OK, in others it's not, though they don't seem to know why. Citroën did this work themselves during a visit to their Slough HQ, when they also carried out a minor carburetter mod to prevent icing, which once brought the car to a brief halt after stuttering for a mile or so belching black smoke — a sure sign of excessive enrichment. By the time I'd lifted the bonnet to investigate, engine heat had melted the ice, leaving no trace of trouble. The problem has not recurred.

The only other fault has been a failed choke-out warning light, replaced under warranty. Bodily, the CX is in fine shape. It shouldn't be otherwise, of course, but it's a rare car that doesn't have some blemishes and rust stains on it after a year. The rear window trim and driver's door keyhole, gouged out with chisel and hammer, still bear the marks of some thieving vandal's attempt to force an entry, presumably to nick the radio/tape player. The only other signs of wear and tear are inside, where the skimpy flock-coating Citroën use on the lower part of the facia and cubby lid is going bald. The car is worthy of better trim — which it has elsewhere.

SERVICING

★★★★ Citroën have 260-odd dealers (with more to come), which is quite a healthy number for a modest importer but meagre compared with, say, Ford's 1250 or Austin Morris's 1900. I mention the figures because they underline the chore and inconvenience confronting many "minority marque" owners of taking their car, be it a Citroën or anything else, to another town — as I have to — just to get it serviced, perhaps as often as once a month for the high mileage user. It's a problem that I would not dismiss lightly, especially if there's no handy transport back to base. And from rural Herts where Middleton Motors, ostensibly of Potters Bar, are located, there isn't. As to the servicing itself, I have no complaints: Middleton's have done it efficiently and without hassle, though the frequency (every 5000 miles) is too often, and the costs rather high. If a Metro can go 12,000 miles without maintenance, so too should a Citroën.

COSTS

★★★ *Motor's* road test (September 15, 1979) on the Athena reported "radically improved fuel consumption" (compared with the old 2000), an "impressive" touring figure and "startling" steady speed economy in fifth. I had no doubt that I'd improve on the test team's 25.3 mpg overall, but I didn't expect to exceed 30 mpg — 30.2 mpg, to be exact, over 12,000 miles — with long-distance spot checks of up to 33 mpg. True, I don't drive as hard as some *Motor* testers, but I cover the ground pretty quickly, so these are not unrealistic pussy-foot figures. In fact a Citroën spokesman was quite disparaging about them: "Is that *all*?" he queried with a hint of disgust. Even though his claimed 35 mpg does seem too good to be true, the message is nevertheless unequivocal: for a big and reasonably swift car, the Athena is remarkably frugal thanks to its high gearing, clean aerodynamics and, if you exploit it, good mid-range torque.

As I have never added any oil between routine maintenance, the only other outlay so far has been on servicing. The first two, the 600-mile "freebie" (which actually cost £11.09) and that at 5000 miles (£15.35), were very reasonable. It was the 10,000-mile service, costing £92.56, that hit the wallet, or rather my Access card as Middleton's wouldn't accept a cheque, much harder than expected. The time allotted by Citroën, clearly indicated in the service manual so the cost shouldn't have been a surprise, is 5¾ hours, which seems an awfully long time for the listed check and adjust jobs: at £10 an hour (more in London) that accounts for £57.50 of the bill, over £66 with VAT. Lubricants and parts accounted for the rest. Hmm. The technical editor's Peugeot 505STi cost a total of £59.43 for the 10,000-mile service, and the labour charge for a Granada 2000's 12,000-mile service is only £34.

It's a pity that hefty service charges,

COSTS

	(for 12,000 miles)	£
PETROL	397 gallons at £1.30 per gallon	516.10
OIL	none added between services	—
SERVICING	at 600 miles	11.09
	at 5,000 miles	15.35
	at 10,000 miles	92.56
TYRES	front: 60 per cent worn, £46 per tyre	55.20
	rear: 35 per cent worn, £41 per tyre	28.70
ROAD FUND LICENCE	for 12 months	60.00
TOTAL	for 12,000 miles	779.00
BASIC COST PER MILE		6.50 pence

PERFORMANCE

CONDITIONS

Weather	Wind 5-15 mph
Temperature	45°F
Barometer	30.5 in Hg
Surface	Dry tarmacadam

MAXIMUM SPEEDS

	Staff car mph	RT car mph
Banked Circuit	107.0	106.8
Best ¼ mile	109.5	112.5
Terminal Speeds:		
at ¼ mile	75	75
at kilometre	94	94
at mile	99	100
Speed in gears (at 6,000 rpm):		
1st	31	31
2nd	53	53
3rd	78	78
4th	103	103

ACCELERATION FROM REST

mph	Staff car sec	RT car sec
0-30	3.6	3.8
0-40	5.5	5.7
0-50	8.0	8.2
0-60	11.0	11.8
0-70	15.4	15.8
0-80	21.0	21.6
0-90	28.7	29.5
Stand'g ¼	18.0	18.1
Stand'g km	33.6	33.5

ACCELERATION IN TOP

mph	Staff car sec	RT car sec
20-40	13.2	13.6
30-50	12.7	13.0
40-60	13.0	13.4
50-70	13.0	13.4
60-80	14.7	15.1
70-90	18.5	19.2

ACCELERATION IN 4th

mph	Staff car sec	RT car sec
20-40	8.7	9.1
30-50	8.5	8.8
40-60	8.9	9.3
50-70	9.2	9.5
60-80	10.9	11.2
70-90	13.7	14.[illegible]

FUEL CONSUMPTION

	Staff car	RT car
Touring*	28.9 mpg	29.9
	9.8 litres/100 km	9.5
Overall	30.2 mpg	25.3
	9.35 litres/100 km	11.2
Govt tests	23.3 mpg (urban)	
	39.8 mpg (56 mph)	
	31.4 mpg (75 mph)	
Fuel grade	97 octane	
	4 star rating	
Tank capacity	15 galls	
	68 litres	
Max range	452 miles	
	725 km	
Test distance	12,000 miles	
	19,308 km	

*Consumption midway between 30 mph and maximum less an allowance of 5 per cent for acceleration.

NOISE

	dBA	Motor rating*
30 mph	60	8
50 mph	66	14
70 mph	72	18
Max in 2nd	81	34

(1st for 3-speed auto)
*A rating where 1 = 30 dBA and 100 = 96 dBA, and where double the number means double the loudness

SPEEDOMETER (mph)

Speedo	30	40	50	60	70	80	90
True mph	29	38	47.5	57	66	76	86

Distance recorder: 2 per cent fast

WEIGHT

	cwt	kg
Unladen weight*	24.2	1229
Weight as tested	27.9	1417

*with fuel for approx 50 miles

Performance tests carried out by Motor's staff at the Motor Industry Research Association proving ground, Lindley.

COMPARISONS	Citroen Athena	Alfa 2.0 Giulietta	Ford Ghia Cortina 2.0	Princess 2000 HLS	Renault 18 Turbo	Vauxhall Carlton
Max speed, mph	**107.0**	112.0	102.6	98.5	111.4	106.6
Max in 4th	**103**	103	102.6	98.5	105.0	106.6
3rd	**78**	78	85	75	77	94
2nd	**53**	54	59	51	50	59
1st	**31**	32	32	32	28	35
0-60 mph, secs	**11.0**	9.5	10.3	13.1	10.1	11.4
30-50 mph in 4th, secs	**8.5**	7.0	9.0	10.8	7.0	11.8
50-70 mph in top, secs	**12.7**	10.3	9.0	12.1	9.8	11.8
Weight, cwt	**24.2**	22.2	20.3	21.8	19.7	22.2
Boot capacity, cu ft	**10.2**	9.5	11.3	12.4	11.8	12.9

*mean of left and right

IN SERVICE	Citroen	Alfa	Ford	Princess	Renault	Vauxhall
Price, inc VAT & tax, £	**6,875**	6,090	6,002	6,178	6,589	6,288
Insurance group	**6**	7	5	4	—	5
Overall mpg	**30.2**	23.9	24.3	23.0	23.8	22.0
Touring mpg	**28.9**	27.0	30.9	27.2	30.4	26.7
Fuel grade (stars)	**4**	4	4	4	4	4
Tank capacity, gals	**15.0**	11.0	12.0	16.0	11.7	14.3
Service interval, miles	**5,000**	6,000	6,000	6,000	6,000	6,000
No of dealers	**260**	130	1240	1900	480	650

Citroën performance and economy figures relate to long-term test car, others to normal road test cars.

and reputedly pricey spares and repairs (not that we've had any), should to some extent offset the advantage of low fuel bills. The 185 section front tyres are 60 per cent worn and should last for another 8000 miles: the slightly smaller 175 section rear covers should be good for 42,000 miles at their present wear rate. There's plenty of life left in the original brake pads, too.

As a Group 6 car, fully comprehensive insurance is not cheap — typically around £250 for a low risk driver with a good no-claims bonus. Heavy depreciation is the CX's Achilles heel, largely because motor traders pass on their misguided distrust of anything they don't understand to the public. The trade (Citroën dealers apart of course) tend to equate the unconventional with trouble despite strong evidence (as here) to the contrary. The suspension, backed by a two-year 65,000-mile guarantee and devoid of conventional dampers to wear out, is arguably the area of least concern, certainly for the first few years of the car's life. Be that as it may, big Citroëns don't hold their value well, though the Athena/Reflex twins should do better than the superseded 2000 or 2400 which, after two years and around 30,000 miles, are likely to be worth only about 30 per cent of their original value. That puts them near the top of the list for used-car bargain hunters, but not for anyone looking for high residual values. Pity. The big Citroën is worthy of better things but like many other upmarket imports, a high resale value is not something the original owner should bank on. Our Athena (priced £6,578 when new, but now £6,875 ignoring any discount) would probably realise about £3,250 at auction. Low-mileage V-registered Athenas have recently been advertised by Citroën dealers in *Motor* for between £4,995 and £5,750, though I've seen an "immaculate" 10,000-miler advertised elsewhere by a non-franchised trader at £4,350. So there seems to be considerable spread in prices, even among cars of similar age and mileage.

READER FEEDBACK

Not enough Athena/Reflex owners responded to our questionnaire (in fairness, we didn't give them much time) to make the sample as statistically meaningful as we'd like. But those owners who did respond certainly get around, their average mileage being 33,000 even though the oldest car (with 45,000 miles behind it) had been on the road for only 25 months.

The ratings below clearly endorse our own findings in most departments, high marks being given to cruising, road-holding, ride and seat comfort, noise, fuel consumption, reliability and styling. The poor ventilation scored the lowest marks.

Owners' ratings*

Acceleration	5.8
Cruising ability	10.0
Steering	6.4
Roadholding	8.3
Handling	5.8
Braking	7.0
Gearchange	4.6
Clutch action	3.8
Gear ratios	7.6
Ride comfort	9.4
Seat comfort	8.8
Driving position	8.2
Heating	6.0
Ventilation	2.8
Noise at 70 mph	8.2
Instruments	7.6
Minor controls	7.6
Fuel consumption	9.4
Tyre wear	6.6
Visibility	7.0
Lights	7.0
Boot space	4.8
Reliability	8.2
Paintwork	4.8
Rusting	5.0
Styling	9.4

*Owners were asked to rate from "Excellent" to "Bad". The scores are based on giving "Excellent" 10, "Good" 7, "Average" 4, "Poor" 2, and "Bad" 0.

Listed engine and transmission faults were minimal: one oil leak and one iced carburetter (like ours). There were no obvious weak spots elsewhere either, no two owners listing the same faults — what very few were mentioned. Only one car had been off the road (at 35,000 miles, to have a rectifier replaced) other than for routine servicing, generally rated as fair or good. Rust was noted by only one respondent who was awaiting a Citroën report.

None of our respondents said they'd not buy another similar Citroën, which suggests that all were pretty satisfied with the car. That was certainly the overriding message we got from our small sample.

SECOND OPINION

Roger's experience with the CX makes a persuasive argument for the big car's virtues: its "elegance", comfort, space, economy/performance balance, load-compensating suspension and relaxed motorway cruising are all, I agree, absolutely splendid. That his car has been so reliable also neatly pulls the carpet from under the feet of those who would assert that the complex technology used in the design is inherently troublesome.

Why is it, then, that after re-acquainting myself with the *CX experience* — in its Athena form, at any rate — I'm still not convinced that the sleek Citroën eclipses its peers? I suppose it all comes down to the driving, as it usually does when a CX is being discussed. More specifically it comes down to the steering and the brakes, both of which draw assistance from the high pressure hydraulics which serve the suspension.

In practice, ultra-high geared, no-feel steering and super-sensitive, no-travel brakes aren't as bad as they sound. Once the requisite degree of delicacy of hand and foot has been learned, the CX can be conducted, in most circumstances, with acceptable smoothness. But for me, the essentially fingertip and tip-toe nature of these controls is, ultimately, frustrating — whatever the initial satisfaction to be had from raising your level of finesse.

The major irritation with the steering is its complete lack of feel — maybe not so important on dry roads where the CX's impressive reserves of grip can be taken for granted, but absolutely crucial in slippery conditions where lack of forewarning of the front wheels losing their grip can be disturbing to say the least. It's also a bind to have to keep making small course corrections when driving on long, straight sections of road or when trying to maintain a smooth line on a long, sweeping curve: though I will admit that the high gearing and automatic self-centring which cause these effects are no problem on tighter bends.

Likewise the brakes can be unnervingly abrupt and demand a high degree of dexterity to avoid locking the wheels in an emergency when the going is slippery; that they are powerful is beyond doubt. **David Vivian**

MANUFACTURER'S COMMENT

We gave Citroën a copy of Roger Bell's report on the CX Athena and asked for their comments on the points raised in this article. Unfortunately, owing to the absence of their Press spokesman at the Geneva Motor Show, they have been unable to do so. Comments will appear in a later issue.

CONCLUSION

First and foremost, the Citroën Athena is *different*, a car of great aesthetic beauty and engineering integrity. No rival has such character or individuality, few outrank it on sheer road ability. Whether you like the way it *feels* and *behaves* is a matter of personal taste. Some of *Motor*'s testers do, others don't. What is beyond dispute is the Athena's comfort, even allowing for the poor lumbar support of the front seats and the feeble ventilation; its excellent performance/economy balance for a big, roomy car that can cover the ground deceptively swiftly and peacefully; and, if our sample is typical, its excellent reliability and freedom from rust.

That said, it is not likely to be a cheap car to own, despite its frugal thirst for fuel. Ironically, the central hydraulic system that energises the unconventional suspension, steering and brakes, those parts which give the car its unique disposition and appeal, is also largely responsible for its heavy depreciation. Distrust born of ignorance is something that the Citroën buyer must live with, however misguided. It's an interesting thought that a CX with metal springs and conventional steering and braking might well be a more successful car commercially. But it probably wouldn't be so good, and it certainly wouldn't be a Citroën. Long may the oil continue to course through its veins.

Auto TEST Citroen CX 2500 D Familiale

Load carrier extraordinary

Citroen CX 2500 D Familiale
Estate version of the Citroen CX range with eight-seater capacity on three rows of seats. Choice of 2347 c.c. petrol or 2500 c.c. diesel engine, each with four- or five-speed gearbox; diesel five-speed tested here. Familiar Citroen layout of front wheel drive and hydraulic power system for suspension, steering and all-disc brake operation. Four-door body with one-piece tailgate extending down to low platform unencumbered by spare wheel.

PRODUCED BY:
S.A. Automobiles Citroen,
133 Quai Andre Citroen,
75747 Paris 15,
France

SOLD IN THE UK BY:
Citroen Cars Ltd., Mill Street,
Slough, Berkshire SL2 5DE

DIESEL motoring is rather like being in a secret society. When you travel abroad, meet other holiday makers from Britain and hear them complaining about the expense of petrol, there is an evident air of disbelief when you reveal how relatively little the diesel car has cost to cover the same distance. Equally surely it can be presumed that the general motoring public are quite unaware of how much more civilised and practical the modern car diesel engine has become, as exemplified by Citroen's CX 2500 D.

Citroen offer the 2500 diesel engine for the saloon with Super or Pallas trim, and for both versions of their estate car. The Safari estate is the big load carrier of the range, with a folding bench rear seat, behind which there is immense space for luggage.

For this test, though, we have used the Familiale model, in which the rear bench is replaced with three individual seats. The outer one on each side readily tips forward bodily to allow easy access to a third row of seating. This comprises a folding bench farther back in the car. The car is thus designed to seat eight: two in front, and three on each of the rear rows of seats.

Taking advantage of its carrying capacity and economy, the Familiale was used for an extended Continental tour through six countries and covering nearly 3,000 miles. Although the car was very heavily loaded it coped with the weight and the added drag of a well-stacked roof rack with impressive ease, and climbed without apparent effort over the Grimsel, Furka, Gotthard, Plocken and Gr. Glockner passes. In a different sort of motoring – sustained high-speed cruising – it also proved outstandingly good, covering 628 miles in 8¼ hours, to give an average running speed of more than 76 mph.

Over an unusually extended test distance, the Citroen CX 2500 D Familiale had its load area packed to the roof, and carried a lot more on the specially tailored roof rack. The car is seen here at Heiligenblut, at the foot of the Gross Glockner pass, and opposite at the top of the pass, which it romped up in spite of the load

Performance
Much quicker than the figures suggest

Just to look at the performance figures of the Citroen may give a wrong impression that the car is not very quick, with a time of 17.2 sec to get from rest to 60 mph. But in ordinary long journey driving there is no suggestion of sluggishness at all; much more to the point is the impression that this diesel seems to cover the ground swiftly and in deceptively eager and relaxed manner. The nature of the engine, coupled with a cheerful lack of concern as to how much fuel it consumes – it's economical even when driven hard – lead one to use much more of the available power than one would with an equivalent petrol car.

Citroen actually offer the estate diesels with only a four-speed gearbox, but although the five-speed version is some £140 dearer it would be false economy not to specify the extra ratio. Not only does it benefit the already impressive economy, it gives much more refined fast cruising. Indeed, as one makes the change up to fifth, the low-revving note of the engine becomes as relaxing and unobtrusive as the background throb of the engines in a big boat.

The gear change doesn't like to be hurried too much, tending to go through with a dull thud if it is, but it is delightfully smooth and easy to use if the change is made in slightly more leisurely fashion. In moving off, there is sometimes a trace of clutch judder, but this can be avoided by a little care in feeding it in progressively with the right amount of engine revs. The spacing of the gears is ideal, giving maxima of 22, 40, 58 and 76 mph. As with all diesels, engine speed is limited by a governor, and it says much for the choice of gearing and the adequacy of the performance that we never once reached the governor limit point on the road, even when storming over mountain passes.

In fifth gear, the acceleration is quite acceptable so that it is not always necessary to change down to fourth to regain speed on a motorway, though fourth is often valued to cope with some of the fairly steep gradients sometimes experienced on German motorways. Maximum speed in fifth gear is 94 mph, which is by no means slow for a 2.5-litre car of this size. Although there is a feeling of "unburstability" about the diesel, which gives the impression that it would go on for ever at full throttle, the car tends to settle down happily to cruise a little slower than this, with 90 indicated in the window of its strange speedometer – a true 85 mph.

Although the engine note is certainly audible all the time, it is not obtrusively loud. There is much more noise outside than is heard within, and the steady clatter of the engine at tickover proclaims the car as a diesel to all around.

Economy
Almost too good to be true

In this extended test, with a great amount of weight on board for most of the distance, the 2500D Familiale returned almost exactly the same consumption as the 2500D Super saloon – 30.5 mpg, against the Super's 31.5 mpg. In spells of light running, economy improved to 34 mpg, and in contrast, sustained fast motorway cruising gave the lowest figure returned during the distance – a still very creditable 27 mpg.

The fuel warning light begins to flash when the level is down to the last two gallons, and remains on continually for the final gallon. The fuel gauge is quite accurate, and its very low rate of decline is a reassuring confirmation of the low rate of fuel consumption.

Such economy is rare in a car big enough to house a 15-gallon fuel tank, and results in a truly magnificent fuel range. On one occasion, the CX diesel covered 460 miles (true distance, not mileometer reading), without refuelling, and it is quite normal to run 400 miles on a tankful, resulting in a substantial saving of time. This massive range also enables one to take full advantage of the big difference in diesel costs on the Continent, filling up in places like France and Italy where it is cheap, and over-driving others like Switzerland and Austria where it is expensive. Sadly Italy has imposed a limit on the amount of diesel that can be exported, but enforcement of this seems fairly lax for cars.

The Citroen engine seems to have a fair thirst for lubricating oil, averaging 1,000 miles per litre. An oil level warning light is connected to a sensor in the dipstick, readily unplugged when the level is to be checked.

On the road
Immense capacity

As you load up the Citroen, lying almost in contact with the road like a great basking shark, its immense capacity encourages one to put more and more in; then, when the engine is started, it pumps its suspension back up to the normal ride height and the behaviour of the car is almost the same when very heavily laden as when empty. The comfort of the ride in these conditions, without any tail sag or pitching, is phenomenal and makes the Citroen estate a load carrier of quite outstanding ability.

The oleo-pneumatic suspension swallows up undulations and bumps impressively well, giving a level and very well-damped ride that enhances the overall comfort of travel. Little road noise is transmitted and there is a minimum of jolt or thud on bumps. When the car is fully laden, with a lot of weight on the roof, there is noticeably more body roll on corners and the driver learns to help the car round by trying to be under acceleration through a corner rather than braking, thus reducing the understeer. Even with a full load, it corners in very manageable fashion and is no concern when tackling the hairpins of a mountain pass. Early tyre squeal gives warning if the cornering limits are approached.

With its powered self-centering, the steering is like that of no other car. Release the wheel after stopping and switching off, and the steering automatically centres itself. The system is high-geared and exceptionally sensitive. At first acquaintance, the reaction of the car to movement of the wheel is a little unnerving, but with familiarity it makes the car a pleasure to handle, not least for the ease with which an arrow-straight course is held on a motorway. Considering the length of the wheelbase, the turning circle at 36ft is commendably tight, and the car is impressively easy to park or manoeuvre, thanks to the ease with which the steering is turned and the excellence of the all-round visibility.

Disc brakes are fitted all-round, and all four discs are internally ventilated. The system is fully power operated, rather than just power assisted, and there is slight lack of sensitivity so that a sudden application may be a little more abrupt than was intended; but braking response is always excellent, and a substantial safety factor for the car. No fade was experienced, either in our rather severe tests at MIRA or in hurried mountain descents. The handbrake operates the front discs, which means that it is much more effective than usual when applied as an emergency brake. Pulled on hard, it holds securely on a 1 in 3 test gradient.

The diesel engine is inclined forward and positioned to the right of centre. Although the space is well filled, access for attention is surprisingly good. A moulded tray in the spare wheel houses the jack, wheelbrace and toolkit, and has space for the standard Continental one-litre oil can

Behind the wheel
Remember the length

Good visibility and a very comfortable, relaxed driving position, go a long way towards making this big car very much more controllable than one might expect. Because of this, it is important not to get lured into forgetting just how long it is. The rear wheels are a long way back from the front ones, and on corners they take the short cut, like a trailer. Well-placed mirrors give a good view along the sides but they are not adjustable from inside by remote control.

A Citroen feature is the use of a huge centre-mounted windscreen wiper, which very effectively clears a large-diameter single arc of the windscreen. It is swtiched on by a trigger switch to the left of the instrument nascelle, pulled rearwards to operate the very effective screenwashers. Intermittent wipe is now provided, in addition to slow and fast speeds. At first acquaintance, the controls seems slightly unfamiliar, but any awkwardness is quickly forgotten and instead one is appreciative of the convenience of having everything within reach without taking the hands off the steering wheel.

A large centre console houses the radio – a big improvement on the original mounting of the radio on its side – and extends down to embrace the gear change and includes a cubbyhole which can house a few cassettes. Electric window lifts are standard for the front windows but not the rear ones; and they operate quickly provided the electrics are switched on by the column lock (which would be the ignition switch on the petrol model). Farther back is a switch for the interior lamp and, on the other side, a wash/wipe switch for the rear window. When the switch is given a touch, the wiper functions about five times and then switches itself off. In rain, when continuous action is needed to cope with the swirl following the car, constant run rear window wiping would be appreciated.

Living with the Citroen Familiale

Ready provision is made for removing the rear bench seat, making the Familiale temporarily only a five-seater, and this facility may encourage some buyers to opt for the Familiale even if the full seating capacity is not needed. However, the middle row of three individual seats are positioned rather upright in order to provide adequate legroom for those in the third row. The seating position is thus not very comfortable for a long journey – like sitting on a dining room chair – and so the Safari is to be recommended instead unless the extra capacity of the Familiale really is needed.

Front seats, in contrast, are sumptuously comfortable with soft cloth covered upholstery and adjustable backrests. Headrest are provided for the front seats, with detachable soft pads so that they can serve as true headrests, rather than just head restraints, if the passenger wishes to recline the seat and sleep in the car. The headrests are readily removable to give a better forward view for those in the back.

Since the Citroen CX estate first appeared, the ventilation has been greatly improved, with cool air outlets now added to the centre console in addition to the eyeball outlets at each end of the facia. But even with the addition of these, the through-flow is rather limited and the car tends to get rather warm inside on a hot day if speeds are too high for windows to be opened. At more modest speeds, the front windows can both be fully down without causing unacceptable wind noise. Heating is effective and controllable, and the regulators for ventilation are conveniently positioned between the seats.

An impressive line-up of tell-tale indicator lights caps the instruments, but their functions are soon memorised and related to the pictorial symbols. Finger-tip switches for horn, wiper, washers and indicators are on the left side of the nascelle abutment, and on the right are the headlamps dip and flash switches, and the main lighting control. There is a cubby-hole recess to the right of the steering column, and another in the centre console

The indicators do not self-cancel, but the audible clicking when they are on, and the easy reach from the wheel to the indicators rocker switch, make this no inconvenience. Light controls at the other side of the instrument nascelle give the convenient arrangement of main or dip, and dip or side, when the dipswitch is touched, according to position of the main lighting switch. There is a separate headlamp flasher switch matching that for the horn on the other side. First pressure on the horn button gives a gentle beep, but harder pressure brings in some purposefully penetrating air horns.

The highly unusual instrument layout comprises five windows, housing a clock, fuel gauge and an indicator for the level of the fluid in the power system to be checked before switching on. The fourth window houses the speedometer, in which the speed figures are seen through a lens, and this is illuminated all the time when the engine is running. The fifth would be the rev counter on the petrol model, but on the diesel it just has the Citroen chevron. This is also illuminated, and the brightness of both is regulated by a little thumb wheel rather difficult to find, below the control block on the right.

Above the instruments is a formidable array of warning telltales, but all are clearly marked, and include a positive "STOP" warning for failure of the power system. Above the radio at the top of the console is the cricket ball ashtray, readily removed by twisting for emptying.

One of the big advances of diesels has been the simplification of start and stop controls to an ordinary control like a petrol car's ignition switch. After no more than ten seconds' pre-heat, usually just the time taken to get comfortable and fasten the seat belt, the engine never once failed to start first time. Indeed, the starting of this diesel is a joy, and there is never any problem with fuel vaporisation on such occasions as when starting up again after a temporary halt during a mountain climb or a spell of high-speed running.

In conclusion on the convenience and satisfaction of running the Citroen CX diesel, we can say without any reservations that it is an admirably efficient car to live with and should prove a most rewarding purchase, the more so if there is hard work to be done. The only drawback is that derv is a messy fuel; owners need to keep a pair of rubber gloves in a plastic bag in the car for occasions when they have to fill up at a self-service fuel station. Because the CX2500D Familiale has only one real rival – the Peugeot 504 diesel family estate – we have omitted our usual page of comparisons in this test.

Legroom both front and rear is exceptionally good. The front seats are luxuriously comfortable, but the middle row have their backrests a little too upright for comfort and would be much better if recline adjustment was provided

The CX range

With the recent addition of the cheaper Reflex and Athena models, Citroen now offer no fewer than 19 CX models. The only diesel engine offered is the 2,500 c.c. four-cylinder, and in the saloon, Super or Pallas, it has a five-speed gearbox. The estates come with Super trim, and with choice of four-speed or five-speed gearbox. Because of the stepped roof of the estate there is no sunroof option, but air conditioning can be added.

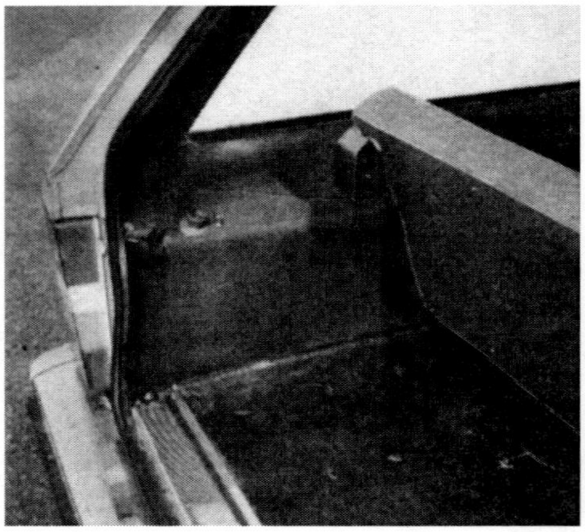

The outer one of the central row of seats on either side tips forward for access to the third row. The back seat in turn can be folded down, cushion to squab, and then rotated through 90 deg to stand vertically giving extra luggage space – or it is readily removed altogether. A filler for the rear window washer is on the side panel

HOW THE CITROEN CX 2500 D FAMILIALE PERFORMS

Figures taken at 10,850 miles by our own staff at the Motor Industry Research Association proving ground at Nuneaton, and on the Continent

TEST CONDITIONS:
Wind: 0-5 mph
Temperature: 18 deg C (61 deg F)
Barometer: 29.8 in. Hg (1010 mbar)
Humidity: 80 per cent
Surface: dry asphalt and concrete
Test distance: 2,969 miles

MAXIMUM SPEEDS

Gear	mph	kph	rpm
Top (mean)	**94**	151	4,250
(best)	**95**	153	4,300
4th	**76**	122	4,400
3rd	**58**	93	4,500
2nd	**40**	64	4,550
1st	**22**	35	4,350

ACCELERATION

FROM REST

True mph	Time (sec)	Speedo mph
30	**5.3**	33
40	**8.4**	44
50	**12.2**	55
60	**17.2**	66
70	**24.2**	76
80	**36.8**	86
90	–	95

Standing ¼-mile: 20.4 sec, 64 mph
Standing km: 38.0 sec, 81 mph

IN EACH GEAR

mph	Top	4th	3rd	2nd
10-30	–	–	6.8	4.3
20-40	12.0	8.6	6.6	5.5
30-50	11.7	8.8	6.9	–
40-60	13.4	10.0	–	–
50-70	15.9	12.4	–	–
60-80	20.7	–	–	–

FUEL CONSUMPTION

Overall mpg:
30.5 (9.3 litres/100 km)

Constant speed:

mph	mpg	mph	mpg
30	57.1	70	37.2
40	51.9	80	31.7
50	45.7	90	26.1
60	41.8		

Autocar formula; Driving and conditions: Hard 27.5 mpg; Average 33.6 mpg; Gentle 39.7 mpg

Grade of fuel: Derv
Fuel tank: 15 Imp. galls (68 litres)
Mileage recorder reads 2.7 per cent long

Official fuel consumption figures
(ECE laboratory test conditions; (not necessarily related to Autocar girues)

Urban cycle: 34.4 mpg
Steady 56 mph: 42.8 mpg
Steady 75 mph: 32.1 mpg

OIL CONSUMPTION

(SAE 20W/40) 1,000 miles/litre

BRAKING

Fade *(from 66 mph in neutral)*
Pedal load for 0.5g stops in lb

	start/end		start/end
1	26/30	6	38/65
2	28/35	7	38/60
3	30/40	8	40/50
4	35/45	9	40/50
5	35/55	10	40/50

Response *(from 30 mph in neutral)*

Load	g	Distance
10 lb	0.20	150 ft
20 lb	0.43	70 ft
30 lb	0.59	51 ft
40 lb	0.82	37 ft
50 lb	0.97	31 ft
Handbrake	0.42	72 ft

Max. gradient: 1 in 3

CLUTCH

Pedal 28 lb; Travel 6 in.

WEIGHT

Kerb, 28.7 cwt/3,213 lb/1,458 kg
(distribution F/R, 66.2/33.8)
Test, 30.6 cwt/3,423 lb/1,554 kg
Max. payload 1,422 lb/645 kg

DIMENSIONS

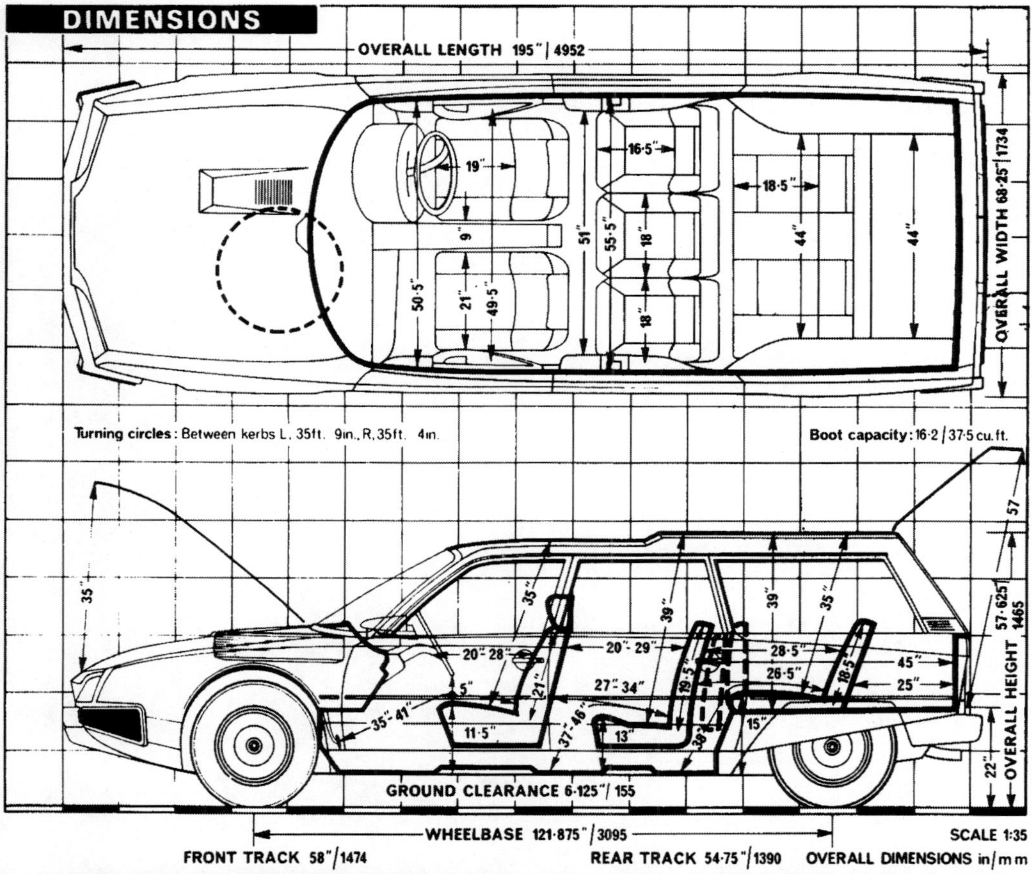

PRICES

Basic	£6,418.00
Special Car Tax	£534.83
VAT	£1,042.93
Total (in GB)	**£7,995.76**
Seat Belts	Standard
Licence	£60.00
Delivery charge (London)	£105.80
Number plates	£14.00
Total on the Road (exc. insurance)	**£8,175.56**
EXTRAS (inc. VAT)	
Metallic paint	£107.15
*Tinted windows	£138.29
Air conditioning	£664.03
**Fitted to test car*	
TOTAL AS TESTED ON THE ROAD	**£8,313.85**
Insurance	Group 5 or 6

SERVICE & PARTS

Change	Interval 3,000	6,000	9,000
Engine oil	Yes	Yes	Yes
Oil filter	No	Yes	Yes
Gearbox oil	No	No	Yes
Air cleaner	No	No	No
Total cost	£13.35	£19.90	£76.68

(Assuming labour at £11.50/hour inc. VAT)

PARTS COST *(including VAT)*

Brake pads (2 wheels)–front	£25.10
Brake pads (2 wheels)–rear	£19.82
Exhaust complete	£75.05
Tyre–each (typical)	£51.01
Windscreen	£129.64
Headlamp unit	£48.25
Front wing	£51.12
Rear bumper	£127.73

WARRANTY

12 months/unlimited mileage

SPECIFICATION

ENGINE	
	Front, front-wheel drive
Head/block	Alloy/Cast iron
Cylinders	4, bored block
Main bearings	5
Cooling	Water
Fan	Electric
Bore, mm (in.)	93 (3.66)
Stroke, mm (in.)	92 (3.62)
Capacity, cc (in³)	2,500 (152.5)
Valve gear	Ohv
Camshaft drive	Chain
Compression ratio	22.25-to-1
Injection	CAV Roto Diesel
Max power	75 bhp (DIN) at 4,250 rpm
Max torque	111 lb ft at 2,000 rpm

TRANSMISSION

Type		Five-speed manual
Clutch		Diaphragm spring
Gear	Ratio	mph/1000rpm
Top	0.73	22.07
4th	0.94	17.1
3rd	1.25	12.9
2nd	1.83	8.8
1st	3.2	5.1
Final drive gear		Helical spur
Ratio		4.54-to-1

SUSPENSION

Front – location	Independent, double transverse arms
springs	Hydropneumatic
dampers	Incorporated in springs
anti-roll bar	Yes
Rear – location	Ind., trailing arms
springs	Hydropneumatic
dampers	Incorporated in springs
anti-roll bar	Yes

STEERING

Type	Rack and pinion
Power assistance	Yes
Wheel diameter	15 in.
Turns lock-to-lock	2.5

BRAKES

Circuits	Two, split front/rear
Front	10.2 in. dia. ventilated disc
Rear	8.8 in. dia. ventilated disc
Servo	Power hydraulic system
Handbrake	Centre lever, operating front discs

WHEELS

Type	Pressed steel disc
Rim width	5½in.
Tyres–make	Michelin
–type	XZX
–size	185 SR 14
–pressures	F30 R32 psi (normal driving)

EQUIPMENT

Battery	12V 88Ah
Alternator	84A
Headlamps	120W/110W
Reversing lamp	Standard
Electric fuses	5
Screenwipers	2-speed
Screenwasher	Electric
Interior heater	Air blending
Air conditioning	Extra
Interior trim	Cloth seats, PVC headlining
Floor covering	Carpet
Jack	Screw pillar
Jacking points	2 each side under sills
Windscreen	Laminated
Underbody protection	Tectyl

AutoTEST Citroen CX2400 Pallas

Aerodynamic automatic

Citroen CX Pallas

Revised CX range now provides ZF automatic transmission as standard on Pallas model. Also available with diesel engine and five-speed manual gearbox, and GTi continues with manual transmission only. Long wheelbase Prestige model comes with choice of automatic or manual, and ZF automatic is also available for Safari and Familiale estates.

PRODUCED BY:	SOLD IN THE UK BY:
S.A.Automobiles Citroen, 117-167 Quai Andre Citroen, Paris 15, France.	*Citroen Cars Ltd., Mill Street, Slough, Berkshire SL2 5DE.*

Standard equipment on the CX Pallas now are fuel injection for the engine, and automatic transmission. The aerodynamic styling of the car remains unaltered

CITROEN policy, dating back half a century or more, has always been to establish a sound and very futuristic basic design, and evolve the theme with refinements and model developments within the original basic package, over a period of many years. This was the approach with the original DS19 of 1955, and with the Light Fifteen before it; and since the CX made its spectacular arrival on the market in 1974 there have been many additions to the model line-up turning it into a now very extensive range.

Throughout Citroen history, though, there has never been a fully automatic model until recently. That original DS of 25 years ago had a semi-automatic transmission leaving the driver to select the appropriate gears with a hydraulic control lever mounted on the column; and subsequently came the C-Matic, which was effectively a manual gearbox linked to a torque converter and automatic clutch. Again, it was "semi-automatic".

Last year, the range in Britain was widened with introduction of the CX2400 Prestige – the long-wheelbase luxury model; and for the first time a fully automatic transmission was available as an alternative to C-Matic. Citroen adopted the ZF automatic and, as we shall see, have done an excellent job of adapting the unit to the characteristics of the 2,347 c.c. four-cylinder engine with fuel injection.

Not everyone, though, wanted the great length, luxury and formidable price of the Prestige, while sales were still being lost for lack of a fully automatic version of the saloon. Introduction of the Pallas with fuel injection engine, as first launched on the five-speed GTi model, and with the same ZF automatic transmission as standard, was the result. It is this new model which is the subject of this Autotest. More recently automatic has become available on the Safari and Familiale. The five-speed GTi, of course, continues.

Side and indicator lamps are built into the front bumper. The single windscreen wiper remains a Citroen feature, and now incorporates very effective screenwasher jets adjacent to the blade.

Central locking is standard, but does not include the boot, which has a lockable push button

Performance
Smooth and forceful

Citroen reason that anyone who chooses the automatic model will not be looking for the more sporting concept represented by the GTi, and will be seeking refinement and comfort though still with responsive performance. The Pallas injection meets this specification very well indeed, and all who drove it during our test were unanimous about its excellent response, smoothness and good matching of transmission to the engine.

In comparison with the GTi, there is inevitably quite a marked performance penalty. The Pallas took 11.6 sec to reach 60 mph from rest, against the GTi's impressively quick 10.1 sec, and it was not quite able to get up to 100 mph on the one-mile length of our test straight, even with a fast run-in. But the impression formed all the time is that the Pallas performs very well indeed, with sustained power where it is needed. In particular, it has a very smart getaway without any drama, which makes it invariably the first car away after any traffic halt.

Change-up points are well chosen, and at full throttle first gear is held right up to 50mph, and second gear to 80. A sure sign that Citroen have got it right is that we were not able to improve on the times obtained just by putting a foot firmly down on the accelerator, when using the manual over-ride. With less throttle opening, in more normal driving, the upward changes occur progressively earlier, but without robbing the car of that impression of smooth, vigorous power pulling it along.

A lot has been written lately about automatic transmission selectors and the dangers of accidental movement beyond the Drive position and into Neutral, or even worse, Reverse; but with the Citroen layout there is no possibility of any confusion. The control moves in a straight line and is a smoothly shaped hand grip with the detent release as a lift-up pad beneath the curved top. Between Drive and second gear positions the lever is simply pulled back with light action and no need to use the release. Moving it forward, to go back into Drive, it comes to a positive block; and as the detent release never has to be used while on the move there is absolutely no risk of ever getting into an unwanted gear. We always knew exactly where we were with it on the relatively few occasions when it is helpful to over-ride the automatic control. This happens particularly when needing engine braking and extra throttle control to take the car through a fast corner or taking a roundabout at speed, and sometimes on a gradient when the automatic would tend to leave the transmission in top, causing rather a lot of churning through the torque convertor.

Pulled farther back, beyond the clearly felt second gear position, the selector moves into first gear position, again without any need to use the detent release. It is a movement that could never be made inadvertently but if it was, first gear does not engage above 44 mph. Full throttle kick-down changes can be made into first gear at up to 37 mph, and into second at up to 68 mph.

Changes, either going up or down, occur delightfully smoothly. The only jolt experienced is occasionally in traffic on very light throttle, when top gear sometimes comes in with a thud at about 20 mph. There is no jerk on engaging Drive to move away from rest, nor any engine surge if the lever is put into Neutral during a prolonged traffic halt to avoid holding the car back on the brakes. Fairly pronounced creep occurs at tickover with Drive engaged. The only possible criticism of the ZF in this application by Citroen is an occasional pronounced delay in assessing that extra throttle opening at fairly low speed, perhaps accelerating on about two thirds accelerator opening from 30 mph, is calling for a change down to second.

Indication of what gear has been selected is given by coloured boxes which light up the appropriate key letter across the lower part of the facia panel. "A" for automatic is used instead of the more familiar Drive, and lights in green; amber is used for the second and first gear positions, and blue for Park and Neutral. R for Reverse lights up in red. With such a positive and well-gated selector control there is little need for this refinement, but it is sometimes helpful in finding Reverse at night.

Main penalties of choosing an automatic Pallas instead of a manual one are added fuel consumption and less relaxed high speed cruising. It maintains a 90 mph cruising pace without too much fuss, but does not give the leisurely feeling of wafting along in a very high gear that is experienced with the five-speed model, although the overall gearing in top is not much lower than the GTi in fifth.

Injection for the engine more than compensates for the power losses of automatic, and the top speed of 115 mph is slightly more than the manual Pallas returned, and is only 3 mph behind the maximum for the GTi.

Noise
Very subdued

All the advantages of the CX body for good wind flow and lack of wind noise are unaffected, and the only difference is a rather more busy drone from the engine at speed. As the car accelerates away through the gears and reaches about 60 mph in top one begins to feel the need for another change up into a cruising overdrive gear, as would be made with the five-speed model. By about 75 mph the engine is making itself rather noticeably audible, but the noise level does not get much worse at higher speeds and could not be called tiresome or making the occupants talk loudly to be heard above it. It's just that it is not as good as the five-speed model.

At lower speeds, and around town, the noise level is much lower and very refined. There is sufficient slight throb from the engine to reveal that it has four, not six, cylinders, and quite a lot of tyre thud is heard on bumps and coarse surfaces.

Economy
Good for an automatic

It is normal to expect quite an economy penalty when a five-speed manual gearbox is traded for a three-speed automatic, but surprisingly the Pallas with this ZF transmission has returned fractionally better consumption than the GTi gave. The overall figure of 21.9 mpg is very fair indeed for such a roomy car with its swift performance, high top speed and automatic transmission

Refuelling is quick, and the 15

gallon capacity of the tank gives a range of nearly 300 miles. Among the row of tell-tales on the facia panel there is an amber fuel warning light which begins to flash when the level is down to the last two or three gallons.

Road behaviour
Superbly comfortable

It seemed a little strange that passengers commented about the impressive way in which the Citroen went round corners. No Citroen owner, we suspect, would venture this as one of the car's main attributes, but it is felt that what they appreciate is the way in which the Citroen leans gently into a corner and wafts round disguising the lateral forces; and with this and the way in which the seats so perfectly locate their occupants it almost gives the impression that all roads are straight.

Access for minor engine service is better than the crowded under-bonnet appearance would suggest. In this view the air horns, which are standard, can be seen. Space is provided in a shaped carrier inside the spare wheel for locating tools and a standard litre can of oil

When we weighed the car, we could scarcely believe the weighbridge read-out, showing that more than twice as much weight is carried by the front wheels as by the rear ones; and with very nearly a ton at the front it is inevitable that there should be very strong understeer. This is disguised to a great extent by the very responsive power steering. They is a lot of roll, but there is no tendency for the front end to plough on when taking a corner too fast – at least in the dry. On wet roads, rather more caution is needed. Tyre squeal gives ample warning before breakaway occurs at the front, and tyre grip on slippery surfaces is impressively good.

Citroen's steering characteristics have to be re-learnt every time one drives a CX. It has high response so that not much turning of the wheel is necessary, and has powered self-centring action so that even when the car has been parked and the engine switched off, the wheels return automatically to the straight ahead position as soon as the wheel is released. At first acquaintance, after driving other cars, the tendency is to turn the wheel too sharply, and to put on more lock than is needed. With familiarity the steering is soon mastered, and the high level of response for small movement of the wheel proves very convenient, making the car restful to drive. Little effort is called for in parking or turning the car, and manoeuvring is easy in spite of the fairly big turning circle of over 35ft.

On the straight, too, the car feels a little uneasy at first, because there is a very slight tendency to wander. If the driver concentrates on just holding the wheel steady, the Citroen keeps to a very good course indeed, but the initial temptation to try to correct small deviations off-line make it follow a rather wandering course. Directional stability, apart from this slight deviation, is excellent, and the car is wonderfully immune to cross winds.

For soaking up undulations and bumps, the suspension is very impressive indeed, seeming to float over the surface, yet with firm damping and without any tendency to wallow. A suggestion of firm resistance to small wheel movements is given by the rather harsh reaction over cat's eyes, manhole covers and other sharp bumps. Not everyone is equally happy with the Citroen ride, some finding it slight "queasy-making", but the general reaction is that it is outstandingly comfortable. The suspension "deflates" during prolonged parking, and there is sometimes a slightly joggy ride for the first hundred yards or so in the morning as normal pressure and ride height are recovered.

Large disc brakes are fitted all round, and they are operated by the power hydraulic system, instead of the more normal vacuum servo. Response is very high for relatively light pedal loads, a mere 50 lb effort on the pedal giving the maximum 95 per cent efficiency. A little care has to be used on the pedal, because travel is short, and it is quite easy to press rather harder than intended, giving an unwanted abrupt stop. The balance is very good and in all conditions we experienced no tendency for the wheels to lock up when braking, even on slippery surfaces. Resistance to fade is very good, and there was only a small increase in pedal load during our series of 10 stops at 0.5g from 75 mph. The handbrake operates on the front wheels, and as well as holding easily on the 1 in 3 test hill, it also works unusually effectively when used on the move as an emergency brake.

Behind the wheel
Ergonomic layout

Almost every minor control can be reached without taking a hand from the steering wheel, and the layout, once mastered, works very well. The nacelle before the driver has a push-in switch at each end, a rocking switch at the top at each end, and a lever control protruding beneath on each side. The left push sounds the horn, giving a discreet beep at light pressure and then bringing into effect powerful air horns when pressed harder. The matching switch on the other side is for the headlamp flasher.

The left rocker switch controls the indicators which in usual Citroen fashion, are not self-cancelling; but they have a prominent warning tell-tale and give a pronounced clicking sound so that there is never any occasion for forgetting to reset the indicators switch after use. The matching switch on the right gives main or dipped beam alternately when the main lighting switch is in the headlamps position, and gives dipped or side lamps alternately when it is at the sidelamps position. This is very convenient in town when there is need to alternate between dipped and side lamps according to the street lighting intensity, and movement of the master switch from side lamps to head lamps position

The new automatic transmission selector has straight to and fro movement, and need to lift a release pad on the under-side safeguards against accidental movement beyond the D position when moving the selector forward; there is sensibly free movement between D and 2. A formidable row of warning tell-tales extends across the top of the instrument nacelle, all with reasonably easily understood symbols. Instruments are a clock, "Swinging figures" digital speedometer and rev counter, and a vertical reading fuel gauge. Beneath the nacelle is a temperature gauge, left of the steering column

Seats are sumptuously comfortable, although rather short in the cushion at the rear. Front doors feature an open oddments bin, elasticated map wallet, and loudspeakers, and there is provision for two more door-mounted loudspeakers to be fitted to the rear doors

can be done without altering the lighting – if they are on and dipped, they remain so, and just alter to the other phase.

One huge windscreen wiper blade clears the big panoramic screen, and works at slow or fast speed, or intermittent with about a five-second delay. To work the washers, the wiper is turned on first and then the switch is moved towards the driver. Water is then spread across the screen from outlets linked to the wiper blade, and we certainly found this system very effective in clearing the glass in dirty weather.

Softly sprung and upholstered in cloth, the seats are luxuriously comfortable, giving good support in the small of the back and under the thighs, as well as excellent lateral support. A lift bar at the front is raised for to-and-fro adjustment, and a lever beside the seat cushion allows the back or front of the seat to be raised, either to adjust the cushion angle or to give height adjustment. As headroom is a little marginal, drivers need to set the cushion carefully to the correct height. Backrest adjustment is in notches, with another lever at the side of the seat to release it.

Seat head restraints are fitted, which also have clip-on cushions to turn them into headrests if there is occasion for a snooze in the car. The restraints are readily removed if required, aiding all-round visibility and improving the view from the back.

Living with the Citroen Pallas

So much thought has gone into the whole layout and detail finish of the Citroen that it should give lasting pleasure to its owner. We certainly liked the car all the time we had it on test. Typical thoughtful provisions are the really bright interior lamp in the centre of the roof, lit by opening any of the four doors, and supplemented by individual spot lamps to the rear compartment and bya forward map light, also roof mounted, which tilts to left or right serving driver or passenger, and switching on automatically as it is tilted.

Switches for the heated rear window and for the main interior light are also roof-mounted, forward of these units. The only possible drawback of the arrangement is that it might make it rather complicated to fit an opening sunroof, but this is available as an extra.

Central locking is standard, and when the key is turned in the driver's door a green light on the driver's door window sill lights to confirm that the electric lock at each door has operated. About 10 seconds later, the green light automatically goes out. The light still comes on when locking up even if one door has been imperfectly closed, but we found that even when locked on the first catch only, the door is completely secure.

Central locking does not secure the fuel filler, which is separately lockable, or the boot, which has a lockable push button release. The boot is easily loaded, having no sill for luggage to be lifted over, and although not very deep, the compartment extends well forward. A light in the boot comes on automatically when the lid is opened, and is independent of the sidelamps.

The rear seat is as comfortable as in the front, with ample legroom to stretch out, and a folding armrest turns the seats into comfortable armchairs when only two are to be carried in the back.

As invariably the case with fuel injection, the system compensates for cold weather ideally, so that engine behaviour is exactly the same whether stone cold or fully warmed up, and there is never any stalling or hesitance during warm-up. Tickover is even, at about 850 rpm, and the tickover point is marked by a red line on the rev counter. Speedometer and rev counter comprise figures swinging past an illuminated window with lens, and with a little searching one soon finds the thumb wheel below the right hand side of the nacelle for adjusting the brightness of these two instruments, which are lit day or night, whenever the engine is running.

Other refinements include a quartz analogue clock with constant run sweep second hand, a lockable glove box on the left of the facia as well as two open cubby holes, pull-up sunblinds for the rear seats on either side, and electric front window lifts which function swiftly and quietly, provided the ignition is switched on.

Big improvements in ventilation have been made by Citroen since the CX was first introduced. Originally a crude water valve affair, the heater is now a very effective air blending unit giving very good response to its temperature control, with good output and quick warm-up. There are cool air outlets in the console, as well as bleeds from the heater at either end of the facia for side window demisting.

Another big improvement since we last ran a Citroen in our fleet is provision for a loudspeaker to be fitted in each door.

It's good to find a car that, like the CX, has been so greatly developed since its first introduction. It should prove a very satisfactory car to live with in all respects, and there has certainly been little about it to fault in this test.

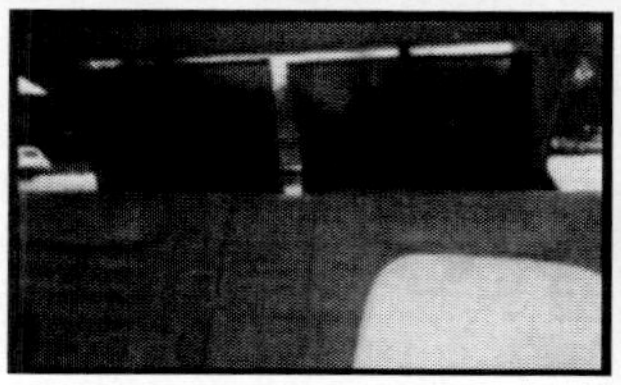

Unusual features to be appreciated in sunny countries are individual pull-up blinds behind the rear seats, and flip-down side visors over the doors

A light comes on automatically in the boot when the lid is lifted. Although the opening is not very deep, the compartment is quite spacious and extends well forward. The boot floor is carpeted

The Citroen CX Range

Basic models in the CX range are the more sparsely equipped Reflex, with four-speed gearbox, and the five-speed Athena. More luxurious upholstery and various extra fittings such as the front electric windows and improved sound damping come with the Pallas, which also has the 2,347 c.c. engine instead of the 1,995 c.c. unit of Reflex and Athena. The Pallas is now fitted as standard with ZF automatic and the injection engine. The range includes the Safari estate car, and the Familiale with estate body and three rows of seats, and both of these are available with four-speed or five-speed gearbox, as are the 2,500 c.c. diesel versions – saloon, Safari and Familiale. Other models are the GTi – a sporting version with injection engine and five-speed gearbox – and the luxury Prestige with long wheelbase body and choice of five-speed manual or three-speed automatic. The Prestige also gets the injection engine.

HOW THE CITROEN CX PALLAS PERFORMS

Figures taken at 3,300 miles by our own staff at the Motor Industry Research Association proving ground at Nuneaton.

TEST CONDITIONS:
Wind: 15-20mph
Temperature: 12 deg C (51 deg F)
Barometer: 30.0in. Hg (1016 mbar)
Humidity: 102 per cent
Surface: damp asphalt and concrete (dry for brake tests)
Test distance: 1,335 miles

MAXIMUM SPEEDS

Gear	mph	kph	rpm
Top (mean)	115	185	5,450
(best)	116	187	5,500
2nd	80	129	5,600
1st	50	80	5,900

ACCELERATION

FROM REST

True mph	Time (sec)	Speedo mph
30	4.4	32
40	6.0	42
50	8.1	53
60	11.6	64
70	15.7	73
80	21.9	84
90	29.5	93
100	–	103
110	–	114

Standing ¼-mile: 18.2sec, 77 mph
Standing km: 32.4sec, 92 mph

IN EACH GEAR

mph	Top	2nd	1st
10-30	–	6.3	2.5
20-40	–	6.7	3.0
30-50	–	9.7	3.5
40-60	–	–	–
50-70	–	–	–
60-80	–	–	–
70-90	13.7	–	–

FUEL CONSUMPTION

Overall mpg:
21.9 (12.9 litres/100km)

Constant speed:

Autocar measuring equipment not compatible with fuel injection

Autocar formula: Hard 19.7 mpg
Driving: Average 24.1 mpg
and conditions: Gentle 28.5 mpg

Grade of fuel: Premium, 4-star (98 RM)
Fuel tank: 15 Imp. galls (68 litres)
Mileage recorder reads: 1 per cent long

Official fuel consumption figures
(ECE laboratory test conditions, not necessarily related to Autocar figures)
Urban cycle: 21.1 mpg
Steady 56 mph: 29.7 mpg
Steady 75 mph: 25.2 mpg

OIL CONSUMPTION

(SAE 20/50) negligible

BRAKING

Fade *(from 75 mph in neutral)*
Pedal load for 0.5g stops in lb

	start/end		start/end
1	25/25	6	40/50
2	30/35	7	40/50
3	35/40	8	40/50
4	35/40	9	40/55
5	40/50	10	40/55

Response *(from 30 mph in neutral)*

Load	g	Distance
20lb	0.35	86ft
30lb	0.55	55ft
40lb	0.72	42ft
50lb	0.95	32ft
Handbrake	0.45	67ft

Max. gradient: 1 in 3

CLUTCH

WEIGHT

Kerb, 28.5 cwt/3,190lb/1,450kg
(Distribution F/R, 68.4/31.6)
Test, 32.3 cwt/3,610lb/1,639kg
Max. payload 1,124lb/510kg

DIMENSIONS

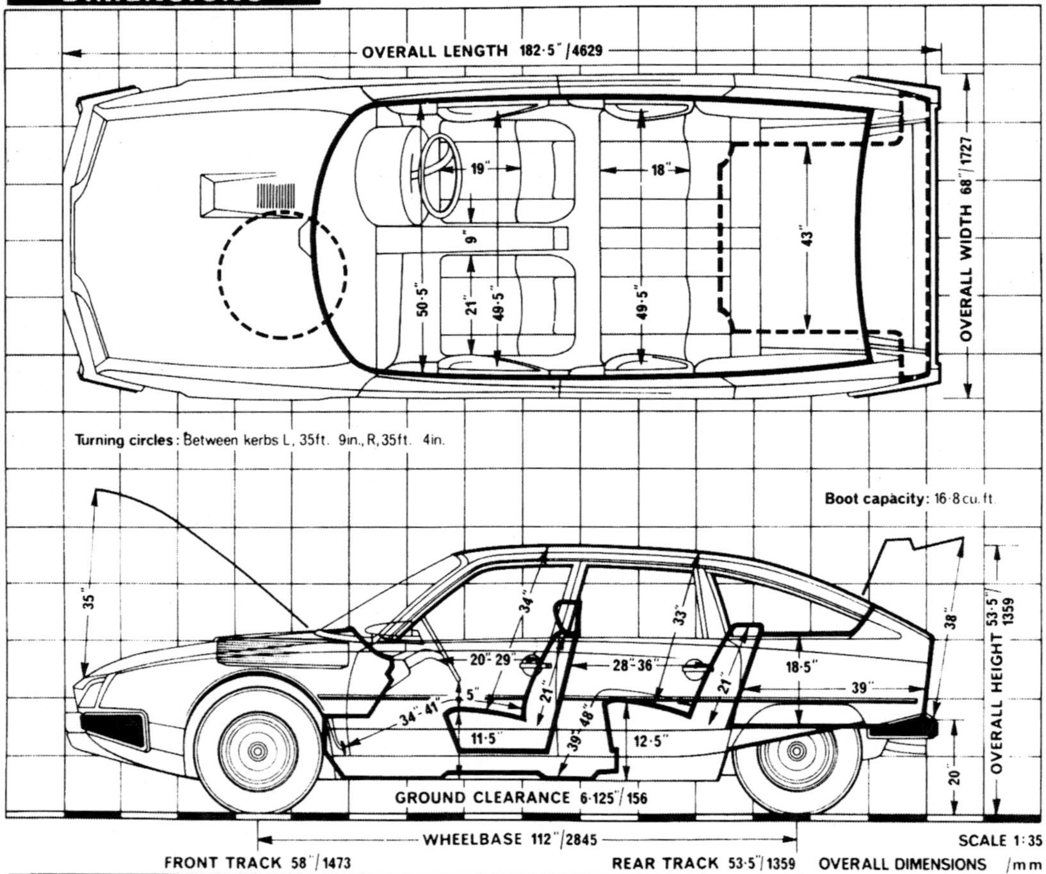

PRICES

Basic	£7,673.00
Special Car Tax	£639.42
VAT	£1,246.86
Total (in GB)	**£9,559.28**
Seat Belts	Standard
Licence	£70.00
Delivery charge (London)	£105.80
Number plates	£15.00
Total on the Road (exc. insurance)	**£9,750.08**

EXTRAS (inc. VAT)*

Metallic paint	£190.61
Electric sunroof	£421.10
Air conditioning	£546.92
Leather upholstery	£655.30

**Not fitted to test car*

TOTAL AS TESTED ON THE ROAD **£9,750.08**

Insurance .... Group 7

SERVICE & PARTS

Change	Interval 5,000	10,000
Engine oil	Yes	Yes
Oil filter	No	Yes
Gearbox oil	No	No
Spark plugs	No	Check
Air cleaner	No	Clean
Total cost	£13.86	£109.78

Assuming labour at £11.50/hour inc. VAT)

PARTS COST *(including VAT)*

Brake pads (2 wheels) – front	£26.11
Brake pads (2 wheels) – rear	£19.73
Exhaust complete	£75.37
Tyre – each (typical)	£66.33
Windscreen	£143.90
Headlamp unit	£53.57
Front wing	£61.82
Rear bumper (3 sections, total)	£102.17

WARRANTY

12 months/unlimited mileage
Suspension: 24 months/65,000 miles

SPECIFICATION

ENGINE

	Front, front-wheel drive
Head/block	Alloy/cast iron
Cylinders	4 in line, wet liners
Main bearings	5
Cooling	Water
Fan	Electric
Bore, mm (in.)	93.5 (3.68)
Stroke, mm (in.)	85.5 (3.37)
Capacity, cc (in³)	2,347 (143)
Valve gear	Ohv
Camshaft drive	Chain
Compression ratio	9.1-to-1
Ignition	Electronic, breakerless
Injection	Bosch L Jetronic
Max bhp	128bhp (DIN) at 4,800 rpm
Max torque	145 lb ft at 3,600 rpm

TRANSMISSION

Type: ZF automatic with torque converter

Gear	Ratio	mph/1000rpm
Top	1.0	21.04
2nd	1.48	14.24
1st	2.48	8.5

Final drive gear: Helical spur
Ratio: 4.77-to-1

SUSPENSION

Front - location	Independent, double wishbones
springs	Hydropneumatic units
dampers	Integral
anti-roll bar	Yes
Rear - location	Independent, trailing arms
springs	Hydropneumatic units
dampers	Integral
anti-roll bar	Yes

STEERING

Type	Rack and pinion
Power assisance	Yes
Wheel diameter	15.0in.
Turns lock to lock	2.5

BRAKES

Circuits	Two, split front/rear
Front	10.2 in. dia. disc
Rear	8.8 in. dia. disc
Servo	Central hydraulic pressure system
Handbrake	Centre lever operating front discs

WHEELS

Type	Pressed steel disc
Rim width	5½J
Tyres - make	Michelin
-type	XVS radial tubeless
- size	185 HR 14
- pressures	F31 R32 psi (normal driving)

EQUIPMENT

Battery	12V 60Ah
Alternator	79A
Headlamps	110/120W Halogen
Reversing lamp	Standard
Electric fuses	4
Screen wipers	2-speed, plus intermittent
Screen washer	Electric
Interior heater	Air blending
Air conditioning	Extra
Interior trim	Cloth seats, cloth headlings
Floor covering	Carpet
Jack	Screw pillar
Jacking points	Two each side under sills
Windscreen	Laminated
Underbody protection	Tectyl

HOW THE CITROEN CX PALLAS COMPARES

Citroen CX Pallas £9,559

Front engine, front drive

Capacity
2,347 c.c.

Power
128 bhp (DIN) at 4,800 rpm

Weight
3,190lb/1,448 kg

Autotest
28 March 1981

Audi 100 5E CD £9,861

Front engine, front drive

Capacity
2,144 c.c.

Power
136 bhp (DIN) at 5,700 rpm

Weight
2,632 lb/1,194 kg

Autotest
6 August 1977

Mercedes-Benz 230E £10,116

Front engine, rear drive

Capacity
2,299 c.c.

Power
136 bhp (DIN) at 5,100 rpm

Weight
3,038lb/1,378 kg

Autotest
not yet published

Opel Commodore Berlina £9,663

Front engine, rear drive

Capacity
2,490 c.c.

Power
115 bhp (DIN) at 5,200 rpm

Weight
2,849 lb/1,295 kg

Autotest
1 November 1980

Rover 2600S £8,983

Front engine, rear drive

Capacity
2,597 c.c.

Power
136 bhp (DIN) at 5,000 rpm

Weight
2,954 lb/1,340 kg

Autotest
22 October 1977

Volvo 264GL £9,954*

Front engine, rear drive

Capacity
2,849 c.c.

Power
155 bhp (DIN) at 5,500 rpm

Weight
lb/1,361 kg
2,998lb/1,361 kg

Autotest
10 January 1981 (265 GLE)

Manual car tested. Price shown for automatic model

MPH & MPG

Maximum speed (mph)	
Rover 2600S	117
Citroen CX Pallas (A)	115
Mercedes-Benz 240E (A)	112
Volvo 264 GL	111
Audi 100 5E (A)	109
Opel Commodore	109

Acceleration 0-60 (sec)	
Mercedes-Benz 230E (A)	10.4
Rover 2600S	10.7
Volvo 264 GL	10.8
Citroen CX Pallas (A)	11.6
Audi 100 5E (A)	11.8
Opel Commodore	12.2

Overall mpg	
Audi 100 5E (A)	23.3
Rover 2600S	22.4
Citroen CX Pallas (A)	21.9
Mercedes-Benz 230E (A)	21.1
Opel Commodore	20.2
Volvo 264GL	18.7

Ideally we would have liked to compare all automatic cars with this new Citroen, but unfortunately some of the models that are obviously direct competitors have so far been tested only in manual form. The choice of cars to pit against the Citroen includes the latest Mercedes 230E – a slightly unusual step as we have not yet published the test on this model. However, measurement has been completed, and the 230E test is due for publication in a couple of weeks. We have also had to use figures of the Volvo 265 GLE as a saloon has not yet been tested with the larger 2.8-litre engine; a 264 GL might have been able to put up a better showing. However, if even with the advantage of overdrive as tested, the Volvo could not better 20 mpg, it makes a rather poor comparison with the Citroen CX Pallas automatic, and the same can be said of the Opel Commodore which also proves slowest of the group.

The Citroen, on the other hand, comes out of it very well, proving to be, as it seems on the road, a good performer, and yet still able to weigh in with an acceptable mpg figure. The Audi 100 with five-cylinder injection engine offers a good compromise of performance with economy, and so does the rather faster Mercedes. But in general it stands out that the Rover is best all-rounder, offering best top speed, second-best acceleration and also near the top of the batch for economy. Certainly it had the advantage of being tested in manual form, with its very high fifth gear, but it gains much – like the Citroen – from its good body shape and an automatic one would not be expected to be much slower or to use a great deal more fuel.

ON THE ROAD

In one respect at least, the Citroen is without rival in this or indeed in much wider groups, and that is the matter of ride comfort. Its ability to swallow up bumps and undulations without reaction is most impressive. The nearest rivals in this particular group for ride and seating comfort are the Mercedes and the Audi, with the Volvo and Opel about equal behind. Ride comfort, although very adequate, is not one of the outstanding features of the Rover. In terms of handling, the Citroen is easily manageable, and goes round corners much better than its enormous weight bias to the front wheels would lead one to suspect, but in ultimate cornering its strong understeer needs to be predicted and allowed for. To a lesser extent, the Audi 100 is in much the same category, and higher standards are set by the Mercedes, with its feeling of near-neutral balance, the Rover marred only by its tendency to axle hop on a poor surface, and the Opel Commodore. There is also a lot more roll with the Citroen than with most rivals.

As a new addition to the range of cars available with fully automatic transmission, the Citroen offers a very refined system, with good throttle response, smooth changes, and an excellent transmission selector. The Rover 2600S and the Mercedes 230E are equally good, with the Audi almost but not quite in the same league. Not so good in these respects are the Volvo and the Opel Commodore.

SIZE & SPACE

Legroom front/rear (in)	
(Seats fully back)	
Volvo 264GL	40/42
Audi 100 5E	42/39
Mercedes-Benz 230E	43/38
Opel Commodore	40/41
Citroen CX Pallas	41/39
Rover 2600S	40/40

Only an inch here or there separates the dimensions of most of these cars, which are all spacious five-seaters. A little extra legroom is offered in the rear of the Volvo, while the Mercedes is best for maximum legroom in front. The Citroen Pallas seems and is a roomy car, but gives an immediate impression of being very low and squat on the road. This is accentuated by the suspension drop which takes place while the car is parked. Luggage loading is easy into the Citroen, due to lack of any rear sill over which luggage would have to be lifted, and scores here over all its rivals, but the space in the boot is not a match for the big capacity of the other models, notably the Audi, Mercedes, Opel and Rover. None of the group, of course, can match the Rover's load space versatility, with removable back shelf and folding seat squab.

VERDICT

In general, the Citroen makes a very good comparison in this rather elite group, offering a high level of comfort, reasonable space, and a good blend of performance with economy. It is hotly rivalled, especially by the front-drive Audi 100 and the rear-drive Rover, and although these do not match the Citroen for suspension comfort, they have more to offer in terms of low noise level especially at speed. Rover manage to do all this and be substantially the cheapest car of the group – enough said. □

test | Citroën CX Prestige, Automatic

ACCELERATION

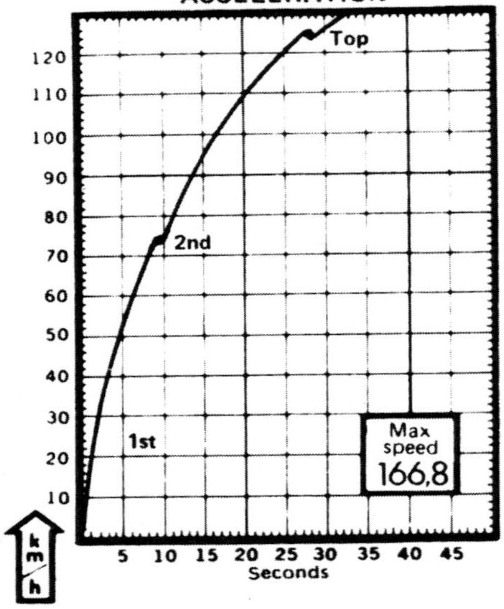

ENGINE SPEED

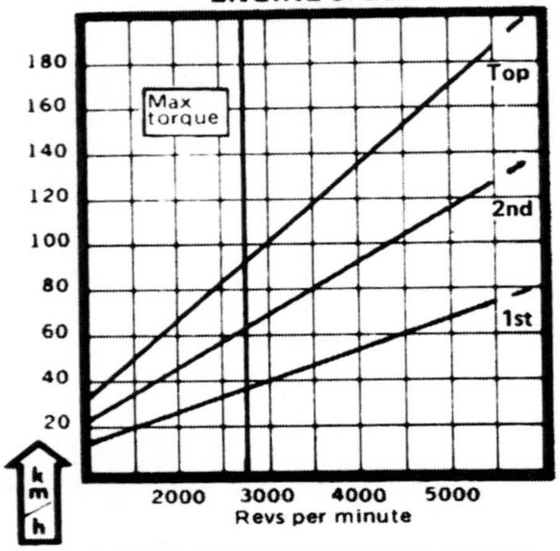

PERFORMANCE

PERFORMANCE FACTORS:

Power/mass (W/kg) net 61,7
Frontal area (m^2) 2,38
km/h per 1 000 r/min (top) . . . 33,9

INTERIOR NOISE LEVELS:

	Mech	Wind	Road
Idling	51,5	–	–
60	67,0	–	–
80	70,0	73,0	74,5
100	74,0	77,0	78,0

Average dBA at 100 76,3

ACCELERATION (seconds):

0-60 6,9
0-80 10,7
0-100 15,9
1 km sprint 36,4

OVERTAKING ACCELERATION (A/T):

40-60 2,9
60-80 3,5
80-100 6,0

MAXIMUM SPEED (km/h):

True speed 166,8
Speedometer reading 179
Calibration:

Indicated:	60	70	80	90	100
True speed:	54	63	72	81	90

FUEL CONSUMPTION (litres/100 km):

60 7,46
70 7,73
80 8,10
90 8,62
100 9,25

BRAKING TEST:
From 100 km/h

Best stop 3,7
Worst stop 4,3
Average 3,94

GRADIENTS IN GEARS:

Low gear . . . . 1 in 3,1
2nd gear . . . . 1 in 7,4
Top gear . . . . 1 in 16,4

GEARED SPEEDS (km/h):

Low gear 75,1
2nd gear 126,0
Top gear 186,2
(Calculated at engine power peak – 5 500 r/min.)

TEST CONDITIONS:

Altitude . . . . at sea level
Weather . . . . fine and mild
Fuel used . . . . 98 octane
Test car's odometer . . . . 7 293 miles

WARRANTY:

12 months.

TEST CAR FROM:

Sigma Motor Corporation, Silverton, Pretoria.

IMPERIAL DATA

ACCELERATION (seconds):

0-60 14,8

MAXIMUM SPEED (m-p-h):

True speed 103,6

FUEL ECONOMY (m-p-g):

50 m-p-h 34,7
60 m-p-h 31,3

BRAKING DISTANCES

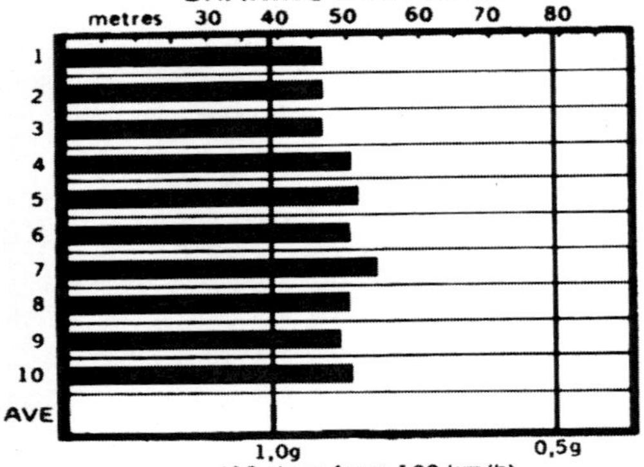

(10 stops from 100 km/h)

GRADIENT ABILITY

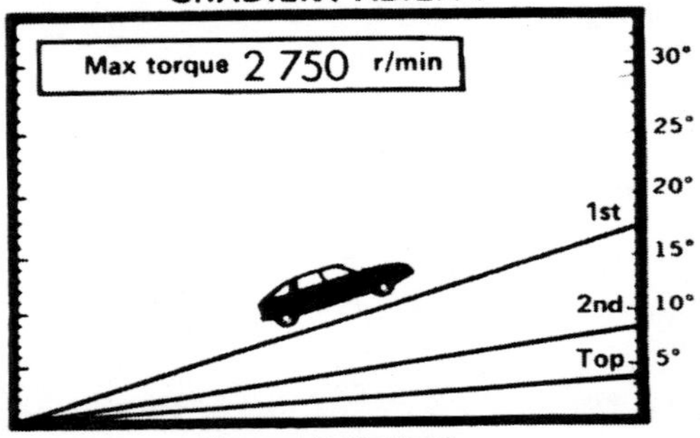

(Degrees inclination)

NOISE VALUES

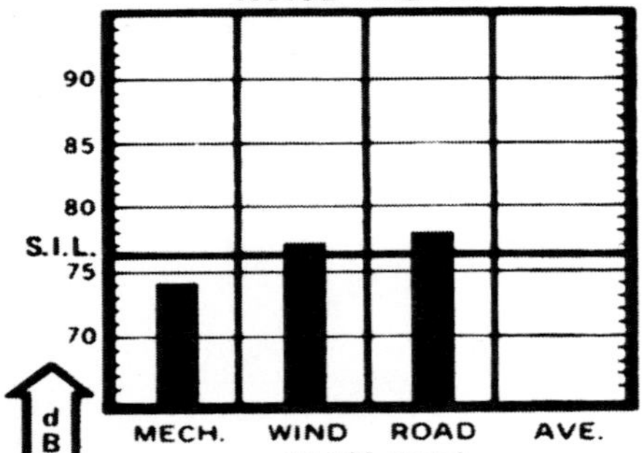

(at 100 km/h)
S.I.L. = Speech interference level

CRUISING AT 100

Mech. noise level . . . . 74,0 dBA
0-100 through gears . . . . . 15,9 seconds
Litres/100 km at 100 9,25
Optimum fuel range at 100 . . . 735 km
Braking from 100 . . . . . . 3,94 seconds
Maximum gradient (top) . . . . 1 in 24,4
Speedometer error . . . . 10% over
Speedo at true 100 110
Odometer error . . . . 2,1% over
Engine r/min at 100 . . . . 2 950

CALCULATED FUEL RANGE
(km)

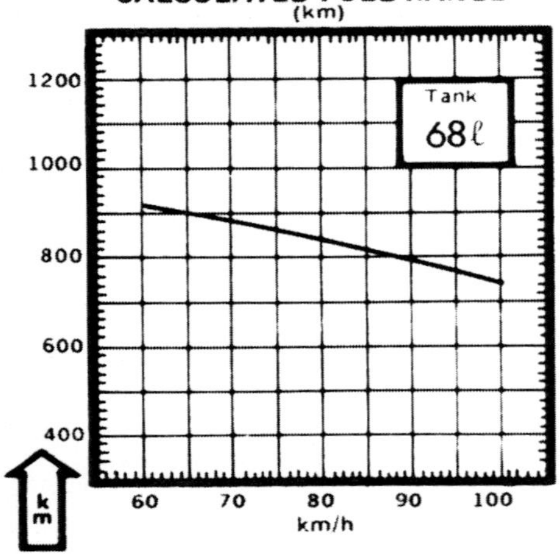

STEADY-SPEED FUEL CONSUMPTION
(litres/100 km at true speeds)

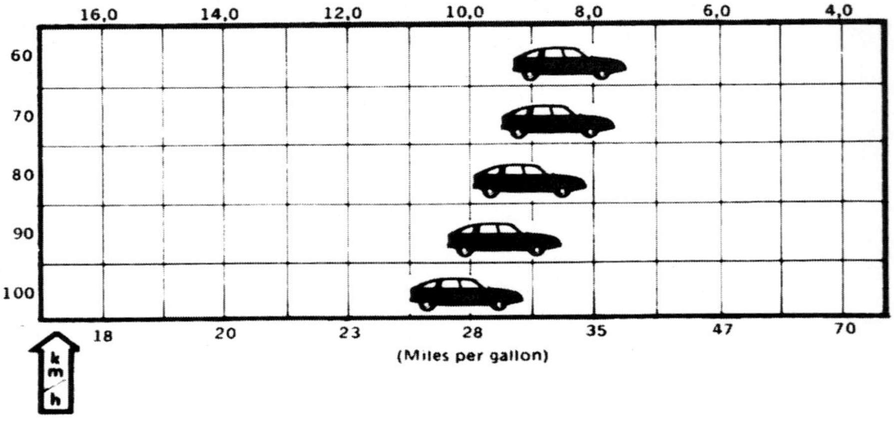

(Miles per gallon)

Citroën CX 2400 Prestige Automatic

The most luxurious and expensive Citroën ever—with superlative comfort and a character of its own

For sheer comfort – both stationary and on the move – there's hardly anything on four wheels to compare with the top Citroën: the new CX 2400 Prestige.

It flows over even the most rugged terrain, with its occupants cossetted in super-spacious and super-comfortable tailored chairs (they are just too luxurious to be called "seats"!), and with only a whisper of sound to show that it is moving, under power. This is the chosen limousine of French Cabinet Ministers, and it did not achieve that select status without considerable merit.

In other respects, though, it tends to be unreal – possibly more of a space capsule than a road car. Its instrumentation and controls are splendidly exotic, and it feels quite unlike any other car, to drive.

LONG WHEELBASE

In its essentials – basic shape, engine, drive train, brakes, and hydraulic (hydropneumatic) suspension – the CX Prestige is not all that much different from the Citroën DS models of recent memory. Trim and equipment are very much different, however, and it is set on the long-wheelbase platform of the Safari estate car to give it limousine-style rear seating, with so much legroom that it borders on being embarrassing – rear seat passengers feel almost too remote and exposed, with their legs at full stretch!

The interior spaciousness and standard of seating comfort are superlative: these are among the most delightful seats we have ever sat in, inside or outside a car. This is the most sumptuous Citroën ever offered to motorists, and both upholstery and trim feature a chamois-style cloth which looks and feels magnificent.

INSTRUMENTATION

The instruments are housed in a futuristic module which looks something like one half of a flying saucer, and while the layout looks spectacular, it uses the obsolete revolving-drum system for both speedometer and tachometer, which are prone to flutter and inaccuracy.

In acceleration tests, for instance, the digit-bearing drums rocked back and forth at each gearshift to make it difficult to take meaningful readings. And while the odometer was overreading by only 2,1 per cent, the rev-counter overread by 5,2 per cent and the speedometer by an excessive 10 per cent.

The instrumentation is also only semi-metric (obviously produced for the British market) with m-p-h predominating and distances in miles, with a small km/h supplementary lettering.

Finally, the tiny electric clock is badly placed, crowded into a corner of the instrument binnacle where only the driver can see it.

KEY FIGURES

Maximum speed	166,8 km/h
1 km sprint	36,4 seconds
Terminal speed	149,5 km/h
Fuel tank capacity	68 litres
Litres/100 km at 80	8,10
Optimum fuel range at 80	840 km
*Fuel Index	10,53
Engine revs per km	1 770
National list price	R38 000

(*Consumption at 80, plus 30%)

SPECIAL EQUIPMENT

Nothing is omitted on this top model. It has full air-conditioning, and for this reason has poor natural ventilation: fan boosting is needed to get any worthwhile flow. The heating of the interior is excellent, and there are electric windows all round, with individual control buttons at each door.

The rear passengers are particularly well provided for, with individual footrests, fold-down centre armrests, cigarette lighter, ashtrays and loudspeakers in the rear compartment. The side windows have sunvisors, and there is a see-through sunblind at rear to help keep the interior cool in summer.

The driving seat is adjustable for height as well as leg length and rake.

MAGIC HYDRAULICS

We are always intrigued by the Citroën system of hydraulics, which incorporates steering, braking and suspension and produces almost magical properties. The hydropneumatic suspension is the most obvious: the car settles low when stationary with engine off, and rises gently to its normal riding height when the engine is started, automatically levelling itself to allow for varying loads.

This fluent suspension allows a ride which is not unlike a floating sensation: the wheels follow the road contours – whatever these may be – but the car's body maintains a steady flow of motion without any trace of roughness or jolting.

Two side benefits of this specialised suspension are that the car's riding height can be raised for rough-terrain work merely by operating a lever alongside the driving seat, or the car can be jacked up altogether for wheel-changing – or to extricate itself from mud or sand. (We found this useful during test, when one front wheel dropped into a wet clay ditch, and the car was able to hoist itself out by hydraulic power.)

HANDLING AND BRAKING

The power steering has a variable ratio for light and responsive control via a rack and pinion system. The steering becomes progressively firmer with rising speed, and gives outstanding directional stability, as well as eliminating front-wheel drive feedback. The car is very swerve-sensitive, however, with suspension sway exaggerating the steering response in a slalom-type test.

The foot brake is the traditional Citroën hydraulic-boosted unit, giving very light control. But braking tends to be insensitive and not easy to graduate, particularly in an emergency.

Hydraulic failure on these cars can be serious, as it affects all aspects of handling and ride, but it is unlikely to occur under normal conditions because the system is robust and refined.

ENGINE AND TRANSMISSION

The four-cylinder, 2,4-litre engine of the CX is mounted transversely and drives the front wheels. It has been uprated to produce 88 kW and 196 N.m, with usable range of 5 500 r/min, or 6 000 in short bursts.

Test car was the automatic (the only version available in South Africa), using a new ZF three-speed automatic gearbox, with a generous measure of over-gearing for smooth and economical performance and cruising.

PERFORMANCE

The front drive of the CX Prestige is well-mannered, though the car's performance is modest in relation to its price.

It pulls gently from rest, without wheelspin, and takes 10,7 seconds to reach 80, and 15,9 to 100. Responsive enough for normal purposes, though, with good overtaking ability when the kickdown is employed. The transmission is somewhat over-sensitive, and tends to

(Left) The instrumentation is in a futuristic module with revolving-drum system for speedometer and tachometer. **(Right) Engine is a 4-cylinder 2,4 litre, mounted transversely and driving the front wheels.**

With hydropneumatic suspension the car settles low when stationary and engine off and automatically levels to riding height — according to load — when the engine is started.

SPECIFICATIONS

ENGINE:
- Cylinders . . . . 4 in line
- Fuel supply Weber 34 DMTR 35/250 twin-choke carburettor
- Bore/stroke . . . . . . 93,5/85,5 mm
- Cubic capacity. . . . . . . 2 347 cm^3
- Compression ratio. . . . . . 8,75 to 1
- Valve gear . . . . o-h-v, chain-driven o-h-c
- Ignition. . . . . . coil and distributor
- Main bearings . . . . five
- Fuel requirement . . 98-octane Coast, 93-octane Reef
- Cooling. . . . . . . .water; 12,3 litres

ENGINE OUTPUT:
- Max. power I.S.O. (kW) 88
- Power peak (r/min) 5 500
- Max. usable r/min. 6 000
- Max. torque (N.m) 196
- Torque peak (r/min) 2 750

TRANSMISSION:
- Forward speeds . . . three, ZF Auto
- Selector . . . . console
- Low gear . . . . 2,478 to 1
- 2nd gear . . . . 1,478 to 1
- Top gear . . . . direct
- Reverse gear . . . . 2,080 to 1
- Final drive . . . . 3,49 to 1
- Drive wheels . . . . .front

WHEELS AND TYRES:
- Road wheels . . . . pressed steel discs
- Rim width 5,5J
- Tyres . . . . 185 HR 14 radials
- Tyre pressures (front) . . . . .220 to 240 kPa
- Tyre pressures (rear) . . . . . .200 to 240 kPa

BRAKES:
- Front. . . . . . . .260 mm ventilated discs
- Rear . . . . .224 mm discs
- Pressure regulation . . . dual circuits, proportioning valve
- Boosting . . . . .hydraulic assist
- Handbrake position. . between front seats

STEERING:
- Type . . . . rack and pinion, variable power assistance
- Lock to lock. . . . . 2,5 turns
- Turning circle . . . . . . .11,8 metres

MEASUREMENTS:
- Length overall . . . . .4,916 m
- Width overall . . . . .1,734 m
- Height overall . . . . .1,375 m
- Wheelbase . . . . .3,095 m
- Front track . . . . .1,514 m
- Rear track . . . . .1,360 m
- Ground clearance . . . . . . .0,155 m
- Licensing mass. . . . . 1 429 kg

SUSPENSION:
- Front. . . . . independent
- Type . . . .hydropneumatic, variable height, anti-roll bar
- Rear . . . . independent
- Type . . . .hydropneumatic, variable height, anti-roll bar

CAPACITIES:
- Seating . . . . four/five
- Fuel tank. . . . . .68 litres
- Luggage trunk . . . . . . 475 dm^3 net

hunt between 2nd and top on gradients: we found it best to select 2nd manually to prevent this. The strong engine torque shows up in good gradient ability, and 100 km/h cruising involves an easy 3 000 revs.

Noise levels are particularly low on this well-insulated car: the engine is almost inaudible at steady speeds up to 100, and both wind and road noise are exceptionally low.

ECONOMY AND BRAKING

Citroën cars have a well-deserved reputation for fuel-efficiency, and this big-engined flagship maintains that tradition. We recorded 8,10 litres/100 km at a steady 80, and 9,25 at 100, giving a Fuel Index of 10,53 and a range potential of 600-plus km. In just under 400 km of test driving, we logged 11,14 litres/100 km overall.

The brakes are discs all round, ventilated at front, giving a good reserve of stopping power, and the Michelin XVS radials gave plenty of grip. This is 1,5 tons of car, though, and it took an average of nearly 4 seconds to stop it 10 times in succession from a true 100 (110 indicated). The pads became smoking hot from the 5th stop, but there was no serious fade.

SUMMARY

Like snails in garlic butter, or Camembert cheese, the Citroën cars are typically French and are an acquired taste. But once that taste is acquired, it can become a passion!

The CX Prestige, in particular, has such a strong individual character as to be almost overwhelming, and we imagine most people will either rave about it, or find it quite unappealing. It's difficult to be neutral!

Like all special imports, the mandatory 100 per cent excise duty makes it prohibitively expensive by ordinary standards — and also ensures that with its low volume, it will become something of a collector's item in this country. ■

Big, bigger, biggest

We compare three massive estates and find which really can carry the largest loads

For most buyers their car, however grand or humble, represents something of a status symbol. But there is a sizeable minority who look to a car as an object simply of sheer practicality.

Estate car buyers are typical of those who want a car to do a job of work rather than simply look pretty or go fast and there is a hard core of estate users who have always sought out the biggest, toughest, most durable models; machines almost truck-like in their abilities.

It's not a massive market, but big enough for a select group of manufacturers to want to ply their wares. Traditionally three companies carved up most of the sales between them: Citroen with their big CX Safari, Volvo with their 240 and 260 estates, and Peugeot with their 504. Always on the fringe were Ford with their Granada while newcomers with tremendous style, of not ultimate carrying capacity were Mercedes Benz.

It was inevitable, then, that when Peugeot's long serving 504 was pensioned off in favour of the 505, estate models would eventually follow the new saloons. Their arrival has taken longer than expected, but Peugeot make bold claims for the newcomers, saying that they are the biggest estates on the British market.

It was natural, then, for us to

decide to compare the 505 estate with two rivals which could previously claim that title and to repeat our unique capacity measurement tests that accompanied our last test of big estate cars. In that test we found the Volvo 244 to be handily larger that both Ford Granada and Mercedes T-series, while the Citroen CX, tested separately only in Family estate guise, showed the potential for being larger still.

So we chose the Citroen CX Reflex two-litre and Volvo 245DL to compare with the 505GR estate in what is a test of three massive but popularly priced estates.

THE CARS

The 505 estate is more than just a modified version of a saloon, claim Peugeot who say three years' development went into the model. Repeating the successful formula of the old 504, there are both conventional estates and 'Family' models that use the extra length to install a third row of seats.

At present the estates just use the old overhead valve 504 engine of 1971cc and not the newer 1995cc overhead camshaft, injection engine seen in the STi saloon, along with the 2.4 litre diesel unit. The petrol engine produces 82 bhp in the single choke GL guise and 96 bhp in the GR and Family models which use a twin-choke carburettor. An odd line-up of gearboxes sees the two petrol estates getting four-speed boxes while the diesel estate and the two Family models (petrol and diesel) have five gears. Brakes are front discs and rear drums.

Suspension is by front struts, while the independent rear end of the saloons has been replaced by a sturdier live axle (again following 504 precedents). Steering is rack and pinion; power assisted on all but the base GL model. Price of the GR estate is £7875.

The Volvo follows a similarly conventional design path to the Peugeot. Its 2127cc overhead camshaft engine develops 107 bhp in the DL model which is carburettored (the GLE uses the fuel injected 123 horsepower engine and the GL the larger 2.3 litre power unit that develops 112 bhp on carburettors). Gearbox is four-speed, with the option of an overdrive, while suspension is like the 505's, with front struts and a coil sprung live rear axle. Steering is rack and pinion with power assistance, and brakes are all discs.

The 245DL at £7885 represents the base model of a four car range of 240 series Volvo estates.

The CX Safari retains Citroen's ingenuity of design even within the formula of a practical estate car. The small engined Reflex model features the alloy 1995cc ohc engine that Peugeot also use in the 505 (though not, as we said, in the estate). With a twin choke carburettor it develops 106 bhp and is linked to a five speed gearbox. In contrast to the other two, the CX power unit is mounted transversely in the engine bay and drives the front wheels.

But the real points of difference are, of course, in the unique hydropneumatic suspension system, inter connected front-rear and self levelling – a useful asset in a load carrying estate car. Steering, too, is unique in having Citroen's Vari-Power system of assistance to the rack and pinion mechanism, and so too are the brakes which have high pressure hydraulic assistance to the all wheel disc braking.

There's now a six car range of CX estates, including three Familiale models similar to the Peugeot, and powered by the 2.4 litre ohv fuel injection engine and 2.5 litre diesel as well as the 2.0 engine. The 2.0 Reflex at £7695 is cheapest.

The three cars compare closely in overall dimensions: the CX is actually the longest at 194 ins, the 505 comes to 193 ins and the Volvo is shortest, at 188 ins. Overall widths are all within an inch of each other but the front drive CX runs on substantially the longest wheelbase (122 ins) compared with the 114 ins of the Peugeot and 104 ins of the Volvo.

Manufacturer claimed luggage capacities, give the 505 39.2 cu ft with seats up and 78.4 with them folded flat, the Volvo 42.1 and 75.3 cu ft and the CX 41 and 75 cu ft.

PERFORMANCE

Out-and-out performance in these big cars is less significant in itself than as an indicator of how they will behave when loaded up. The CX, with its modern overhead cam engine feels lively and even when being worked hard doesn't have quite the same slightly strained air as the Peugeot. The two's 0-60 mph times are identical but the more powerful CX does start to leave the 505 behind above this speed. The Peugeot's power deficit doesn't handicap its mid-range pull; its torque is almost the same as the Citroen's and its acceleration figures in each gear are actually slightly better, demonstrating that while it may lose out on top speed and acceleration to the slippery Citroen, it doesn't lose anything in sheer lugging ability.

The Volvo trails in third place. It has a hard, gruff engine that sounds very noisy when stretched and in this DL model the whole car becomes very boomy at speed – one certainly notices the absence of an overdrive.

Performance is down on the other two as well. The Volvo takes 14.2 secs for the run to 60 mph and its relative lack of top end pull shows in the comparative 50-70 mph times: the Volvo takes 12.9 secs in fourth gear, the Peugeot 10.3 secs and the CX 10.4 secs. The Volvo develops its sizeable peak torque (best of the three) at very low revs so it does have good initial take off and bottom end bite

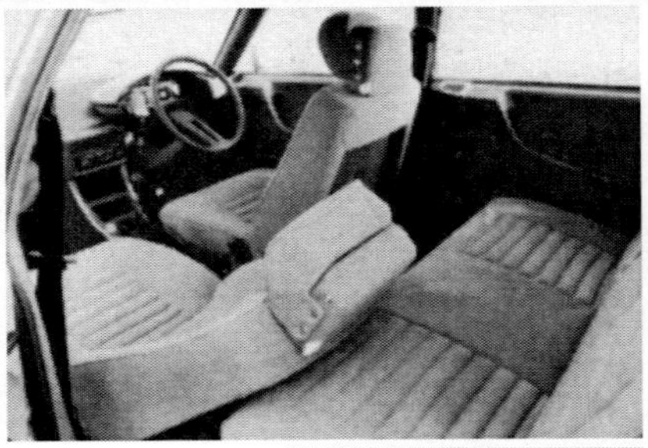

Even in estate car form the Citroen is still a stylish, good looking car. Its suspension ensures an always level ride and the big, square sectioned boot is remarkably roomy. Large interior has soft seats and unique facia with fingertip switchgear

CITROEN CX REFLEX

Group test: Citroen CX Reflex, Peugeot 505SR, Volvo 245DL

– useful for towing.

The Citroen, with its good aerodynamics, has the best top speed, pulling to 103 mph, while neither Peugeot or Volvo can quite manage 100 mph. The CX's five gears give it a useful overdrive top which quietens the quite noisy engine on motorways but the manual change is poor, having a sloppy, vague feel about it.

The Peugeot's change is good but it misses the fifth gear of the Family models for it feels low geared at speed and can be pretty noisy. The Volvo as we have said, badly needs the optional overdrive but the change itself is good.

HANDLING AND RIDE

All the cliches about the Citroen's 'magic carpet' ride have been repeated so many times, yet travelling in it remains a unique sensation and, of course, it is remarkable to find such comfort in an estate car – usually a vehicle beefed up on stiff springs for the heavy loads it takes.

The CX's hydropneumatic suspension creates this aircraft like sensation of detachment from road sensations that is so uncanny. It's a smoothness that some passengers (particularly children) find unpleasant but there is no doubting the car's comfort. An important secondary asset of the suspension system is that it is self levelling and the ride height remains constant whatever the load, so that the car feels virtually as comfortable and the same to drive laden as unladen. The car also settles down low on its suspension when the engine is switched off making loading up easier.

Handling needs some mastering to make the most of the smoothness; it will roll a lot in corners and can understeer strongly but responds well to smooth, sympathetic driving and its roadholding is surprisingly good. The VariPower steering adds to a driver's initial qualms; it is high geared and has strong self centring but once mastered the high gearing makes the driver's life easy. It has shortcomings when manouevring, though, when it can make the car jerky and awkward to handle.

From a thoroughly conventional design, Peugeot have managed to produce a car which can almost live with the CX's comfort. It hasn't that car's ultra-smoothness or perfect high speed stability but it still manages to rate as comfortable by any standards and exceptional by estate standards. Things get a bit firmer when the car is loaded and it jolts more over bumps but it is still a very effective set-up.

It's an easier, more natural car to drive than the CX, too. The power assisted steering is geared at three-and-a-third turns between locks and is well weighted to give a good degree of driver feel without excessive effort. Roadholding is good, and there is less body roll than in the Citroen, but the Pegueot can become bouncy when pressed hard over poor surfaces.

The Volvo feels quite a contrast to these two French cars. It is altogether much tauter and crisper in its handling, which can make it feel easier and quicker to drive but it has the traditional hard springing of an estate car and its ride is much too jolting when empty. It gets more controlled, though it is still noticeably harder than either of the others, when loaded.

The power steering has a firm feel about it, though there is still sufficient assistance and the Volvo has a usefully small turning circle, with a four feet advantage here over its rivals that also helps make it feel more manoeuvreable in town use.

With less body roll and tauter suspension than the French cars it can be hustled along pleasantly enough, but the rear end hops about easily on bumps and slides rather too easily on wet corners so roadholding is not as good as the handling.

PEUGEOT 505SR

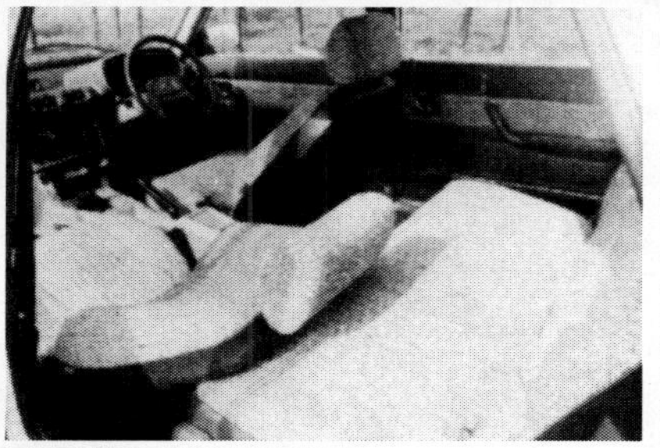

Big new Peugeot estate certainly looks the part with huge overhanging rear boot that has massive capacity and also usefully wide loading entrance. Details like underfloor spare wheel are sensible. Smartly trimmed interior is spoiled by indifferent facia

ACCOMMODATION

The Citroen is not quite such a big car inside as its exterior lines suggest; passengers sit down low and feel quite enclosed by the car. Front seats are big and soft; occupants sink comfortably into them like living room armchairs. They are superb on a long run and give quite good support against the body roll forces in cornering. Seat height adjustment is provided on the driver's side but for the tall driver there is always something of a compromise needed between tightish headroom and limited clearance between his knees and the over-close steering wheel rim.

The Peugeot's smart tweed cloth trimmed seats are not as sumptuous as the CX's but they are still relatively soft and they give very good long distance comfort by virtue of sound design. Peugeot passengers sit higher and the car feels airier and bigger than the Citroen, a sensation that isn't completely borne out by measurements with the tape.

The Volvo is narrower than the other two but its seats are high set and its interior light and airy so it still feels spacy inside. Its front seats are firmest of all but the Swedish company's famed attention to seating design ensures complete driver comfort. Both front seats have lumbar adjusters built in and the added bonus of heating and height adjustment on the driver's side.

The Volvo is smallest of the three for rear seat space, if only by a small margin; but its headroom is good and legroom certainly adequate. It is also the only one of the group to have rear seat belts fitted as standard. The CX's extra inches of wheelbase give it some legroom advantage in the back but the Peugeot scores on headroom and a more comfortable seat.

But the real question about these

cars is more how much luggage they will carry. As we have said before, we take manufacturers' carrying capacity claims with a large pinch of salt since our own tests have demonstrated that they can bear precious little relation to real load volume. (Manufacturers use different tests; some even use a computer to predict the volume of water the car will hold which is, of course, a far cry from trying to load solid objects into a boot.)

Our own test, used for our special estate car issue last year, involves loading each car with quantities of plastic crates, each approximately one cubic foot in volume. It has its limitations; notably that the size and shape of the crates means they can't be squeezed into every nook and cranny but it is a practical test and fair comparison.

How did the results work for these three cars? Firstly with the rear seats in place (and crates loaded just to top of seat level) it proved what the eye could readily tell, that the Peugeot with its long tail overhang clearly could carry the most. It held 19 crates, compared with 16 for the Volvo (one more than in our last year's test Volvo, which we put down to better packing) and only 14 for the CX, which has a short, shallow boot.

With seats folded down to give maximum load space, the Volvo has to give best to the two French cars. The Swede's seat folds in the conventional estate car manner: cushion tipping forward and seat back dropping down to form the floor. That allows it to carry 44 crates (again two better than we managed last time).

But the longer French cars extend their boots by tipping the seat cushion right over and folding the seat backrest down so that both act as elements of the extended boot floor. That extra length – the Citroen's maximum load length is 80 ins compared with the Volvo's 74; the Peugeot's a giant 92 ins – is translated into substantial extra load volume.

However our crates test didn't show the Peugeot as the outright winner its advertisers claim: it held 52 crates while the CX packed in 54. A word of interpretation about these results is needed, however. The CX's square sectioned body proved ideal for loading our crates, while the wider, slightly lower Peugeot was harder to fill and in the end a noticeable air space was left between crates and roof. We would be inclined to call the contest an honorable draw.

By coincidence we were also able to put the three cars through a second practical test of their capabilities, moving a large Victorian wardrobe. Here the Peugeot won handsomely for the extra width of its rear hatch made it the only one that would look at carrying the item; the Volvo nearly accepted it but the CX, with a narrow, upright opening failed hopelessly. It was a test that proved luggage capacity isn't everything.

LIVING WITH THE CARS

The Volvo may not have quite the space of the others but it scores well on practical design points; there are removable rubber mats on the boot floor, built in luggage ties, an easy folding rear seat, a rear hatch that opens from inside as well as out and a useful cubby hole under the boot floor.

For an estate which claims three years' development, we weren't overly impressed with some of the Peugeot's detailing. A carpeted boot isn't the most practical, the rear seat folding catches look flimsy and one broke during our time with the car. Worst of all, once the seat is folded the backs of the front seats are exposed to items being carried so there is nothing to stop them being damaged by sharp objects, or more dangerously, nothing to stop items sliding through to the front between the seats.

That's a contingency Citroen have covered well; the CX has a liftable metal end plate built into the back of the rear seat cushion. The CX boot also comes with sensible rubber matting and protective metal ribbing.

The Peugeot has a facia control to alter headlamp height when loaded up, the always level CX doesn't need one and the Volvo lacks this very necessary feature. The Volvo otherwise has a workmanlike interior; its dashboard is laid out in an orderly, functional way leaving little to complain of. Heating and ventilation are strong points; plenty of fresh air is available and the heater is easy and accurate to control. Rev counter and outside temperature gauge are included in the instruments. It's an easy car to drive, with a high driving position that gives a good view of all four corners of the straight sided body. The base DL model comes reasonably well equipped now, having central locking and headlight wash/wipe.

The Peugeot has the slightly disappointing facia of the 505, with too many bits of chrome trim and fussy detailing. Instruments are limited to the strictly necessary – speedometer, fuel and water temperature gauges. The heater hasn't the accuracy of the Volvo's super system and the ventilation is relatively modest in its efforts.

But it's another car that's easy to drive, belying its length with a commanding driving position, well placed controls and plenty of all round visibility. Equipment is quite modest – no central locking or headlamp wash/wipe for instance, though a radio/cassette is fitted.

The Citroen can be tricky to drive, particularly in tight town traffic, when the steering system, high pressure touch sensitive brakes, poor gearchange and relatively poor all-round visibility all conspire against the driver.

The CX interior is as futuristic as

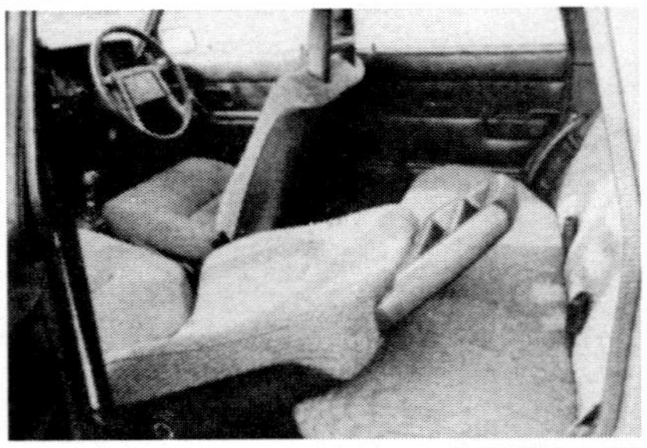

Volvo's familiar chunky lines have a certain timeless appeal. But boot is less roomy than French rivals', though trim is practical. Interior is well planned with especially good seats. Rear belts and headlamp wash/wipe are standard

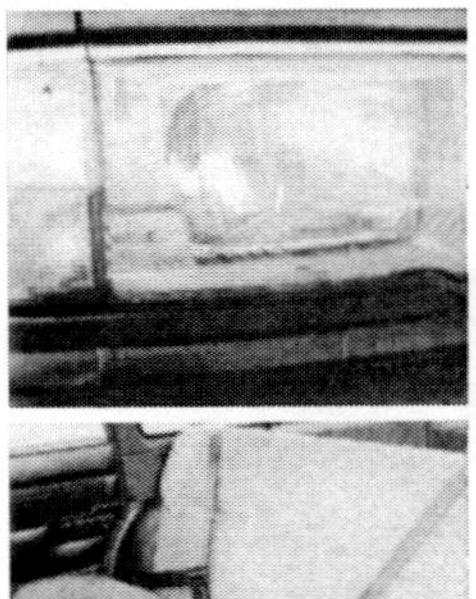

VOLVO 245DL

CITROEN CX REFLEX SAFARI

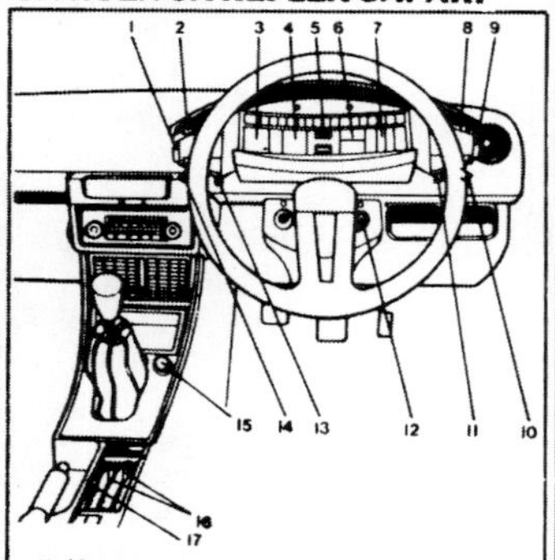

1. Horn
2. Indicators
3. Clock
4. Speedometer
5. Mileometer
6. Rev counter
7. Fuel gauge
8. Headlamp dip/main
9. Headlamp flash
10. Lights
11. Rear fog lights
12. Choke
13. Hazard warning
14. Wipers
15. Lighter
16. Heater controls
17. Heater fan

PEUGEOT 505GR ESTATE

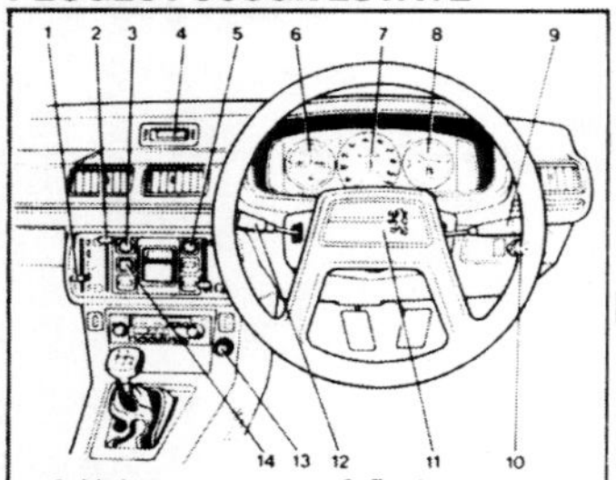

1. Lighter
2. Heated rear window
3. Hazard warning
4. Outside temperature
5. Clock
6. Rev counter
7. Speedometer
8. Temperature
9. Fuel
10. Rear fog
11. Lights
12. Horn
13. Fan
14. Heater controls
15. Overdrive (optional)
16. Indicators
17. Wash/wipe

VOLVO 245DL

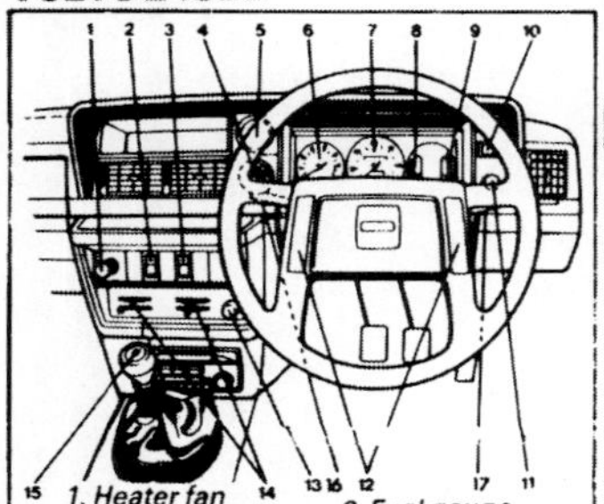

1. Heater fan
2. Heater controls
3. Hazard warning
4. Digital clock
5. Heated rear window
6. Temperature
7. Speedometer
8. Fuel gauge
9. Wipers
10. Headlamp leveller
12. Indicators/dip/flash/horn
13. Lighter
14. Rear fog lights

CAR	Citroen CX Reflex Safari	Peugeot 505GR Est	Volvo 245DL
PRICE	£7695	£7875	£7885
Other models Price span	7 sal., 5 est. £6794-11,850	4 sal., 2 est. £7078-8857	3 sal., 3 est. £6998-10,134
PERFORMANCE			
Max Speed (mph)	103	99	98
Max in 4th (mph)	100	—	—
Max in 3rd (mph)	78	80	81
Max in 2nd (mph)	53	56	53
Max in 1st (mph)	31	27	30
0-30 (sec)	3.9	4.0	3.5
0-40 (sec)	5.9	6.1	6.1
0-50 (sec)	8.6	8.5	9.3
0-60 (sec)	12.2	12.2	14.2
0-70 (sec)	16.3	18.2	19.2
0-80 (sec)	22.6	24.4	30.5
0-400 metres (sec)	18.8	18.8	19.3
Terminal speed (mph)	75	71	71
30-50 in 3rd/4th/5th (sec)	6.9/9.6/14.5	6.5/10.5	7.4/9.7
40-60 in 3rd/4th/5th (sec)	7.2/9.9/15.6	5.5/9.2	8.5/11.0
50-70 in 3rd/4th/5th (sec)	8.1/10.4/16.4	6.6/10.3	9.6/12.9
SPECIFICATIONS			
Cylinders/capacity (cc)	4/1995	4/1971	4/2127
Bore x stroke (mm)	88x82	88x81	92x80
Valve gear	ohc	ohv	ohc
Induction	2 choke carb	2 choke carb	2 choke carb
Compression ratio	9.2 to 1	8.8 to 1	9.3 to 1
Power/rpm (bhp)	106/5500	96/5200	107/5500
Torque/rpm (lbs/ft)	122/3250	119/3000	125/2500
Steering	PA/rack pin	PA/rack pin	PA/rack pin
Turns lock to lock	2.5	3.3	3.5
Turning circle (ft)	35.8	36.8	32.2
Brakes	P/Di(v)Di	S/DiDr	S/DiDi
Suspension front	IHP	IMcP	IMcP
rear	IHp	CTA	CTA
COSTS			
Test mpg			
Govt mpg City/56/75	23.3/36.2/28.8	24.8/38.2/28.5	20.6/35.3
Tank galls (grade)	15.0(4)	12.5(4)	13.2(4)
Major service miles (hours)	10,000(3.2)	10,000(2.75)	6000(2.6)
Parts costs (fitting hours)			
Front wing	£63.31(0.9)	£50.00(4.25)	£93.27(2.8)
Front bumper	£48.57(2.2)	£95.25(0.5)	£85.04(0.2)
Headlamp unit	£46.58(0.6)	£40.50(0.5)	£53.84(0.5)
Rear light lens	£24.69(0.2)	£15.30(0.25)	£32.67(0.3
Front brake pads	£19.85(1.2)	£20.60(1.0)	£16.29(0.7
Shock absorber	£52.18(0.5)	£31.00(3.75)	£34.63(0.9
Windscreen	£98.50(2.5)	£51.94(2.0)	£73.89(2.1
Exhaust system	£57.49(4.0)	£83.50(2.25)	£74.98(0.9
Clutch unit	£61.45(11.8)	£50.45(5.5)	£72.98(2.8
Alternator	£69.57(0.9)	£58.74(1.0)	£80.39(0.4
Insurance group	6	6	7
Warranty	12/UL + 24/65,000 Susp	12/UL + extra care	12/UL
Anti-rust	6 year	6 year	No
EQUIPMENT			
Automatic choke	No	Yes	No
Automatic transmission	No	No	£514
Five-speed gearbox	Yes	No	O/D £361
Electronic ignition	No	No	No
Central locking system	No	No	Yes
Load-adjustable headlights	Yes	Yes	No
Electric windows	Yes	No	No
Power Steering	Yes	Yes	Yes
Radio/cassette	No	Yes	No
Seat height adjustment	Yes	No	Yes
Rear seat belts	No	No	Yes
Rear wash-wipe	Yes	Yes	Yes
Headlamp wash-wipe	No	No	Yes
DIMENSIONS			
Front headroom (ins)	37-39	36	39-41
Front legroom (ins)	34-40	33-40	36-43
Steering-wheel-seat (ins)	11-18	11-19	12-18
Rear headroom (ins)	37	34	37
Rear kneeroom (ins)	29-36	26-35	28-35
Length (ins)	194	193	188
Wheelbase (ins)	122	114	104
Height (ins)	68	60.6	57.5
Boot load height (ins)	19	25	25
Boot depth (ins)	47-80	55-92	44-74
Boot height (ins)	16-56	15-35	15-39
Boot width (ins)	44.5-51.5	44-51.5	41-47
Overall width (ins)	68	68	67
Int. width (ins)	58	54	55
Weight (cwt)	24.6	25.0	27.6
Towing weight (cwt)	25.5	29.5	13.4
Payloads (lbs)	1521	1555	1204
Boot capacity (cu.ft)	41/75	39/78	42/75

KEY. Valve gear: *ohc, overhead camshaft; ohv, overhead valve.* **Steering**: *rack/pin, rack and pinion; PA, power assistance.* **Brakes**: *Di, discs; Dr, drums; S, servo assistance; P, power assistance.* **Suspension**: *I, independent; C, coil springs; Tor, torsion bar springs; ½E, semi-elliptic springs; Hg, Hydragas; Hp, Hydropneumatic; Wi, wishbones; McP, MacPherson struts; Ta, trailing arm location.*

the rest of the car; it has bags of style but a few shortcomings. Worst, certainly, is the ventilation which is extremely dificient. The facia itself is a love it or hate it affair, with ingenious fingertip switches and drum instruments.

COSTS

There is precious little to choose between the three in purchase price – less than £200. Differences start to emerge when considering fuel consumption. The Volvo didn't fare particularly well, averaging 19.7 mpg for the test period with highs of 22 mpg on occasions. The Citroen proved marginally superior, averaging 20.7 mpg overall, a figure which the car seemed consistently to return on intermediate checks. The Peugeot was left as the most economical by a distinct margin, with a 23.9 mpg overall average backed up by a high of 25.5.

The Citroen represents a rather terrifying mechanical proposition; whether that is translated into higher running costs is open to some question. Certainly its spares costs are not shown up as high.

Spares costs for the three are in fact broadly similar; the Volvo being slightly the most expensive. Though Volvo still talk in terms of 6000 mile service intervals for their cars, the difference in servicing time between them and the two French cars, which go for longer 10,000 mile breaks, is actually minimal over 30,000 miles. The Volvo needs 14.4 hours, the CX 13.55 hours and the 505 13.25 hours. Both the French cars have intermediate services.

Insurance ratings are group six for the CX and Peugeot, group seven for the Volvo. All three companies have a relatively modest dealer spread, with none having more than 300 nationwide.

VERDICT

This is a special test, to find the biggest estate as well as the best, and on that score the Volvo must be ruled out. It simply can't hold as much as either the Citroen or the Peugeot. Even if it could, it would still have to be rated third, for its rough, tough virtues can't make up for its lack of comfort and refinement where it is shown up badly.

So, Citroen or Peugeot? The Citroen has a tremendous amount going for it. It has the perfect suspension for an estate; level, smooth and unaffected by loading. It offers airline comfort over long distances, chic styling and yet a very practical load compartment. But against all this must be set its dismal ventilation, poor gearchange and the sheer awkwardness of the beast around town.

The Peugeot is a much more conventional machine; easier to drive and yet almost as comfortable. It has a remarkably good load volume, particularly when all the seats are in use, and a usefully wide rear entrance. It also demonstrated a worthwhile advantage in economy over the other two. We were disappointed by some of the detailing but, overall, the 505 must come out on top of the group.

The manners and style of our LTT Citroen CX Diesel weren't at issue; we aimed to test the promised economy and decide whether a slogging diesel was tolerable for 20,000miles. It was more than that . . .

CX Economique

FUEL PRICES EBBED AND FLOWED SO much during our 20,000miles of Citroen CX2500D motoring that on some occasions we were able to laugh contemptuously at drivers paying up to 30p per gallon more for petrol than we were paying for diesel. At worst we were able to produce the self-satisfied smirk of those who know they are winning in the £/mile race. The Citroen was never less than handsomely economical, and that rose to wonderful frugality much of the time. It had the other advantage of convincing us that diesel engines in passenger cars are now perfectly acceptable alternatives to the admittedly faster petrol-fired units. We used the CX in England, Wales and Scotland, we took it to Geneva and later to Turin; it was driven extensively during one of the worst winters of the century and suffered but one starting problem, due to operational ignorance rather than malfunction. And at the end of it all the 2500D emerged as one of the most popular and liked cars ever to pass through our hands. It had its imperfections, of course, but none of sufficient significance to warrant hands-in-the-air despair.

Because our Long Term Test of the old Peugeot 305GLD (see *CAR* May 1980) was a rather joyless affair, we approached the 2500D (now called the 25D) with reservations. Could we tolerate the noise, for example, and would it have enough real performance to satisfy us petrol-propelled addicts, in normal day-to-day conditions? And, indeed, would it realise the fuel economy standards that were promised?

Two minus-points seemed to be the fact that the 2500D would need a service every 3000miles and require the pre-heat in the combustion chambers to be activated for an irritatingly long time when starting from cold. So said the instruction book which we read as a first resort rather than the last. As delivered, the CX was in basic trim, and lacked some of the adjuncts of the '80s such as electronically-operated external mirrors, electric windows and central locking (electric front windows and central locking are standard on '83 spec cars). Nonetheless, the basics were there: good quality cloth trim and carpets, plus typical Citroenry such as self-levelling suspension, power steering, power brakes and five-speed gearbox. Less obvious were the under-bonnet sound-deadening materials that help suppress the cold-start racket.

Initial faults were minimal, however. The pre-delivery inspection had obviously been carried out by someone who cared about such things in all but one respect. On dipped beam, the headlamps were set just a fraction too high so that oncoming drivers tended to become slightly annoyed – a fault we decided we could live with and others would have to live with – until the first service. Meanwhile, we set about becoming accustomed to the way the 2500D worked, getting used to the big four-cylinder diesel's characteristics, knowledge of which is fundamental to achieving satisfactory results. Initially, we found ourselves changing gear far too frequently, for example, as we tried to shake off petrol-engine driving habits; accepting that there is so much torque so low down in a brisk-performance car is a large pill to swallow for the first couple of thousand miles. Also, the engine felt stiffer than a petrol unit of comparable mileage.

Likes and dislikes were beginning to manifest themselves by 1000miles. Our log book noted a wish for an internally-controlled exterior rear vision mirror and a courtesy light for the rear compartment, and recorded that the side windows were picking up far too much dirt, blown onto them from the single wiper's sweep. We also observed at the time that the screen washer, an integral part of the wiper arm, was outstandingly efficient and very economical on water/cleaner. We continue to wonder why such a straightforward, sensible system has not been more widely adopted. The clutch-pedal throw angle was widely disliked and that, coupled to the jerky throttle pedal, made town driving a slightly untidy affair. But if it had no other purpose it at least forced upon the diesel's drivers the desirability of using the copious torque rather than the revs. With a fuel tank capacity of 15gal, we were regularly running the CX close to 500miles between refills: on long motorway journeys that made such a huge difference to average speeds that we were able to cover the ground faster than hotshoes in performance cars, glugging their way through a tankful of petrol every 220miles. Regular consumption checks showed that the 2500D was giving around 35 to 36mpg on typical commuter work to and from London, running at averages that matched those of potentially much faster cars. A psychological problem that presented itself in driving diesel CX was in the realisation that while it was a large, comfortable saloon capable of cruising at high speeds, the actual overtaking performance tended to be limited in relation to the car's other capabilities. Once that point was recognised, and overtaking planned around the available acceleration, we were able to cover the ground – quickly – in that unique big Citroen style.

Our routine for starting the CX from cold differed slightly from the handbook's recommendation. When the starter key is turned to its first position it activates the combustion chamber pre-heaters and, when the warning light extinguishes some 20-30seconds later, the driver turns the key all the way and engages the starter. Our technique differed only in the time scale: turn key to first position, get comfortable and put on the seat belt by which time the handbrake-warning light is winking; engage starter. That ensures virtually instantaneous starting whereas the handbook's way frequently results in some rather ponderous cranking of the engine before it became self-supporting.

Only once did the engine fail us – in conditions of such stunning early morning cold (about – 15degC) that it hurt to breathe. The diesel started then died the moment the accelerator was touched. We repeated the performance three or four times, each with the same result. The fuel had clearly waxed in the extreme temperature and was blocking the micro-filters. After the temperature rose later in the day, and the injectors had been re-primed (simple once you have read the handbook) the CX sprang back into action as if nothing had happened. However, had we read the handbook with greater diligence we would have known that in very low temperatures it is wise to add a couple of gallons of two-star petrol to a tankful of diesel. Paraffin will do just as well but the Excise people become notably unpleasant if they catch you at it because it is not taxed as a motor vehicle fuel and they lose their cut.

There were some other minor difficulties. The driver's side door lock had shown signs of stiffness since new but one day (at 900miles) it simply grabbed the key and would not let go. It was quickly fixed under warranty. Colliers Garage in Islington, inner London, did the first service with great alacrity and little cost but completely blew their attempt to adjust the headlamps: they so mixed up high and low beams that when we switched on the lights on the motorway, low beam was not visible from the driver's seat and high beam was throwing for fully two car lengths. Without tools it was impossible to make roadside adjustments so the journey continued at a snail's pace, a nightmare in pouring rain. In fairness to Colliers Garage, it was the only time they have ever let us down, although we have been dealing with them, anonymously as always, for years.

We finally got the headlamps adjusted as best we could. Since the handbook was of absolutely no help, we had to do it ourselves against the garage doors and by trial and error on the road. Next morning we loaded the CX with four people and luggage pointed the nose south, towards Geneva. Interestingly, we went from Norfolk to London, thence to just south of Paris on the one tankful of fuel and did not refuel again until we got to Macon on the return journey. Because diesel fuel was cheaper in France than England, we topped up in Calais before crossing the Channel and returning to London. Geneva-London was a relaxed one-day trip and our fuel consumption, cruising at an indicated 85mph with a few bursts to 90 plus, was around 34mpg. We had expected it to be slightly better but some of the way we were battling strong winds, the car was heavily laden and the speed substantial. We took it in turns to sit in the rear. None of us had cause for real complaint but thought rear headrests would have been nice and that there was insufficient foot room under the seat in front; the former are optional, the latter has since been rectified. The accommodation arrangements proved to be exceptionally agreeable and the low noise level allowed normal-tone front-to-rear conversation. Ventilation, even in cool weather, was no better than marginal.

Our final reckoning on that trip was that we had covered the ground as fast as we would have in a thirstier petrol-engined car but we had used about 25percent fewer gallons of a fuel costing 25percent less – a notable saving in direct running costs even if the engine did have a thirst for oil.

We were less than pleased with the 6000mile service, carried out by Cooper City in their final Citroen-dealing days. They are basically BMW people and their charges reflected that: £18.50 an hour for labour. The actual service cost only £16.80 for labour and £9 for oil. A brake squeal problem cost £36.40 for fix and headlamp adjustment £3.50. Unhappily, labour at £18.50 an hour does not mean a job well done: they, too, adjusted the high beam down to an approximation of low beam and in their enthusiasm wrecked the plastic adjusting nuts which ended any prospects of an emergency DIY fix. Rather than risk another foul-up we sent the CX to BWB Motors in Clapham, who seem to have a profound understanding of Citroens in general, who got the headlamps finally sorted out, and who carried out subsequent service work for us.

The next serious journey was from London to the Lake District over the Easter period Purely leisure this time and that reflected in the consumption figures which hovered around the 37-40mpg mark, but the trip was marred by impact damage to the nearside wheel and tyre, caused by a pothole of unprecedented proportions. The wheel had to be changed on the spot (easy jacking and wheelchanging, our logbook recorded) but there had to be subsequent juggling because the front tyres are a different size to those on the back (185SR-14 and 175SR-14 respectively). A wheel trim was also lost during the pneumatic scuffling.

Straight after the 9000mile service, the Citroen was pressed into use once more as a European transporter, taking an editorial trio from London to Turin. Again, it proved its worth over long distances, providing the comfort, economy and speed as before. It should go without saying that the excellent Blaupunkt Paris stereo radio/cassette player was stolen from the CX within eight or nine hours of our arrival in Italy. Using the skill and daring for which Italian car-radio thieves are renowned, the baddy broke into the (locked) Citroen without doing any damage, but had to hack the central console around to remove the Blaupunkt. Nonetheless, he did no more damage than was absolutely necessary and even left the interior light fitting and bulb neatly together on the facia so that we could replace them with the minimum of inconvenience. Back home, we fitted a new radio, but it took time to get all the centre console parts since some of the more obscure bits had to be ordered from France.

Although it had been virtually submerged in salty slop during the worst of the winter, regular and thorough examinations of the CX revealed no signs whatsoever of corrosion and the high level of mechanical reliability continued unabated. In fact, the engine loosened up quite abruptly as the odometer rolled through the 12,000mile zone, which improved the acceleration and the fuel consumption to the point that it never gave less than 35mpg and frequently nudged 40. Servicing at 3000mile intervals had more nuisance value than financial hardship and although our log shows that the 2500D had all its services, not all were on schedule: some were as much as 1000miles behind simply because pressure of use prevented us from getting it to the garage. However, we meticulously checked the oil level and kept it topped, adding perhaps a litre between services.

More worrying was the paintwork. A small patch of the top coat lacquer peeled off a front wing at around 3500miles and by 6000miles we had it recorded on the service document for future reference. For no apparent reason and in no obvious sequence, other sections lifted as the miles wore on, marring what was otherwise an immaculate metallic silver finish. Citroen themselves were intially mystified by the problem and called in their technical people, who blamed the top lacquer coat's lack of adhesion on inadequate preparation when the car was painted. Apparently at assembly, the clear lacquer coat goes on when the under-paint is still wet; it seems that our car's paint was a little too dry when the clear coat went on. Citroen assure us that the problem is very rare and is the kind that would surface within a year if it was going to. Thus it can be rectified under warranty.

When we wound up our Long Term Test of the diesel CX at 20,000miles we yet again found ourselves in awe of the product. It was so light on cheap fuel that our wallet went into deep shock at having to buy petrol at as much as 30p per gallon more, especially when we realised that we were getting 15mpg fewer miles for every gallon over exactly the same routes covered in the same time. Economy was not something we set out to achieve: it was thrust upon us, provided as part of the car.

Of course, all the usual Citroen attributes applied equally to the 2500D. The self-levelling suspension proved itself still to be a major plus by any standard and the fully powered brakes and steering were excellent as always. We never failed to be impressed by the speed and ease with which the CX negotiated B-roads and how accurately it could be placed in tight conditions. However, the hydropneumatic suspension was found wanting over the humps and jumps in the Lake District but that was predictable; it really is about time that Citroen made the suspension more agreeable to stomachs on roads surfaced with successions of abrupt vertical bends.

We have always liked the CX around town and its virtues were enhanced by the tractability, the sheer lugging power, of the diesel engine. Rarely did we use all five gears; most of the time we would by-pass at least one ratio and sometimes two, slipping from second direct into fifth on any road where gravity was working in our favour. In dense moving traffic third and fourth were normally just fine, giving strong acceleration and an easy gait. But in stop-start work first (just for getting the CX moving) and second were ideal, the engine-braking effect virtually eliminating the need for the third pedal. If only the clutch pedal had had an angle more compatible with the human ankle and the accelerator pedal a less jerky action, driving the 2500D would have been like riding a silken carpet in a cloudless sky. Although it is an awful cliche to say it, the CX diesel is probably the car most missed from our fleet: it educated us, it made us comfortable and secure and, because of its economy, never once made us feel guilty about driving.

Familiar lines *of CX Diesel are enhanced by recent chrome-reduction, judicious black paint*

Italian car thieves *removed Blaupunkt radio by cutting dash away; parts were hard to replace*

Comfortable interior *has soft, low-mounted seats that do much to make CX Diesel a great tourer*

Diesel engine, *big 2.5litre four, was frugal yet propelled car at quiet, smooth 90mph cruise*

Low lip, *uncluttered interior characterise CX boot, pressed into service for long Euro-tours*

Make and model: Citroen CX 2500D
Engine: Transverse 2500cc four cylinder diesel, water-cooled with single overhead camshaft and fuel injection; producing 75bhp at 4250rpm with 111lb ft at 2000rpm, driving front wheels through a five-speed manual gearbox
Average fuel consumption: 36.7mpg
Performance: 100mph; 15.7sec 0-60mph
Mileage covered: 20,056
Total service and replacement costs excluding new radio, wheel and tyre: £280.22
Faults: Driver's door lock seized solid with key inserted; succession of headlamp alignment problems associated with uncomprehending servicing; slight ticking sound from speedometer head; wiper-rubber separated from mount in heavy rain and had to be replaced; excessive squeal from front brakes; instrument panel bulb blew; some interior-trim vibration when pulling hard from low speeds in high gears; excessive vinyl bleed onto inside of windows, specially steeply raked screen and rear window; radio stolen in Italy but long delay in replacing obscure centre-console parts; one instance of fuel waxing in extremely cold conditions; top layer of lacquer peeled off in patches
Comments: Exceptional economy on lower-cost fuel and unexpectedly high performance from smooth, quiet engine. Long-legged cruising with 15gal tank ensuring safe 475miles between fuel stops. Occasionally difficulty obtaining diesel fuel which is not as widely available as petrol but is not a factor entering into the final reckoning. At 3000miles, servicing intervals inconveniently frequent and often difficult to schedule on time. Usual Citroen CX virtues provide comfort, good cabin accommodation and excellent road behaviour with self-levelling suspension also ensuring dive-free braking. In our experience the CX is strongly resistant to corrosion, has good finish and is well made. However, with the current £653 price difference between the CX20 and the 25D, only high mileage drivers or those spending a lot of time travelling in Europe could justify opting for the diesel over the cheaper, faster and still reasonably economical petrol model.

CITROEN CX 1E SAFARI

It is hard to believe sometimes that the Citroen CX has been with us all of eight years as its wind-cheating shape is still rather more dynamic looking than current contenders to the crown of low-drag cars such as the Sierra and the Audi 100. That its 0.3 Cd was achieved that many years ago and without the aid of flush-fitting glass speaks volumes about Citroen's talent for aerodynamic achievement.

Mechanically, the CX has also been, like a good wine, improving with age. The lumpy tractor-like 2000 and 2200 pushrod engines, direct carryovers from the DS series cars, were the only really disappointing traits of the new car then and in 1976, the 2400 engine finally gave the CX the kind of urge that this heavy car needed. It remained however, not the nicest of power units and was rather frantic when rewed out towards the red-line while not exactly being over-endowed with torque at the other end of the scale.

The answer to all these criticisms came in 1978 when Citroen installed Bosch fuel-injection in a sporty model designated the CX GTi. That this engine has found its way into all the 2400cc engined CX's speaks volumes for its popularity. Now for 1984, there is a big-bore 2500cc engine available with 10 bhp more over the 128 bhp (DIN) 2400 and surprise, surprise, it is actually smoother.

In the meantime, the CX IE Safari continues to be available with the 2400 Injection engine and we had one of these capacious long-distance haulers through recently to see just where the CX stands eight years on.

At 16ft 3in in length, the CX Safari is an imposing vehicle and one has to watch it when manoeuvring in confined spaces or parking and this is when the Citroen Varipower steering comes in. Unique to the CX, when it was introduced and still so today, the steering provides maximum assistance when the vehicle is stationary (with the engine running) and tapers off until at speed there is no assistance, which helps to reduce the 'sneeze factor' of conventional power-assisted systems. What alarms most first-time drivers of the CX though is the fact that the steering flicks back to the straight ahead when you let go of the wheel, so such action is not recommended and this safety factor in the event of a high-speed blow-out is best dealt with by palming the steering wheel as opposed to grabbing it. Once you are used to this, the CX can literally be thought around corners.

Early CX instrument panels with their roller-drum speedometer and rev counter had black lettering on a yellow background, the whole unit being illuminated from behind. This was rather glaring at night and the latest cars now have orange lettering on a black background which has a soft orange lighting. The fact is, though, that the multiple lettering on the UK speedometers (which have both mph and km/h calibrations) remains harder to assimilate than a conventional unit.

Gone is the constant battery-wearing churning of the carburettor cars and the Bosch-injected engine starts at the turn of the key each time and every time and idles smoothly at 900 rpm. Moving off, the car displays adequate torque to move its large self through the air at a brisk pace and flooring the throttle at 70 mph in fifth gear brings instant response and a strong surge forward. The Safari IE would cruise effortlessly at the ton and with the magic carpet ride of the hydropneumatic suspension, it just seems to glide along gracefully. To another driver following a CX, the body of the car appears to remain totally unperturbed by bumps while the wheels move up and down following the road surface as opposed to the heaving motions shown by other cars on the road.

That hydropneumatic suspension is also the key to the eminent suitability of the CX for its role as an estate car with the haulage of heavy loads in mind. The handling of most other vehicles is prejudiced by uneven weight distribution acting on their rear suspensions and causing handling problems. These have to be dealt with by such remedies as stiffer springs and shocks which destroy the ride of the vehicle when it is in an unladen state, but the Citroen suspension merely increases its hydraulic pressure to maintain not only the ride height but also the ride quality — something hard to achieve even with a self-levelling strut on a conventional spring system.

With 75 cubic feet of load space with the rear seat folded flat, the Safari is certainly the ideal car to move house in and even as a five-seater.

Auto TEST Citroen CX25 DTR

£10,862 □ Max: 100 mph □ 0-60 mph: 14.1sec □ 29.8 mpg overall

STAND on the pavement in almost any town or village on the Continent and you will hear the familiar notes of a diesel engine. But unlike Britain, there will be a far higher proportion in ordinary family cars. In Italy, for instance, 40 per cent of new cars sold have diesel engines under their bonnets.

The reason is simple – and is called taxation. Petrol and diesel cost the same to produce, within a matter of pence. But what we pay at the forecourt pumps depends very much on the attitude of the government. This has meant that until recently, there has been very little price advantage in running a diesel-engined car in Britain. Indeed, in some places, diesel fuel was much more expensive than petrol. It now seems that the scene has changed, with diesel – or Derv, which stands for nothing more complicated than Diesel-Engined Road Vehicle, to distinguish it from fuel used for tractors or in marine diesels – at a distinct price advantage. On the Continent, diesel is generally very much less expensive than petrol, so that despite the higher road tax many countries levy to make up the revenue, it is still cheaper to run a diesel car. The main exception is Switzerland, where the high cost of diesel ensures that a major proportion of freight is carried by the State railways system.

Diesel engines have a reputation of being noisy, smelly and slow. But they are slowly winning the battle – and a car like the CX25 DTR Turbo shows just how refined a diesel can be, although to the newcomer the combination of the turbocharged engine's characteristics and what can only be termed Citroen's unusual approach to car design can initially be a little off-putting.

When cold a diesel engine needs some assistance to raise combustion chamber temperatures, and this is done with preheater plugs. On most modern engines, these need to run for just a few seconds before the key can be turned to operate the starter. On the CX25 DTR it took close to 30sec for the warning lamp to go out finally. In practice, we found that the engine would start quite happily when the plugs had been on for around 10sec. Until it warms up, a diesel engine is noisy – and the Citroen is no exception. On the other hand, when out on the open road, it really is quite difficult to pinpoint what sort of engine there is under the bonnet.

With peak power being developed at just 3,700 rpm, a change in driving pattern has to be used. The CX25 DTR has a rev counter, a curious rotating drum affair, matching the speedometer. But do not expect to see figures like 6,000 or even 5,000 rpm appear on it. It comes to an end at 4,500 rpm, and that is more cosmetic than any practical use, for the governor cuts in at 4,200 rpm, which is way above the speed at which you would normally have changed gear. This is an engine where torque plays an even more important part in performance than power.

Moving the CX25 DTR off the line quickly calls for no great skills. With such a broad power and torque spread, the clutch was fed in at around 2,500 rpm, which produced a brief note of protest from the fat Michelin TRX front tyres. The difficult part from then on was to get the gear changes in as rapidly as possible. Allow the revs to exceed around 3,900 rpm and the power falls right off: run

Turbo

TURBOCHARGED version of Citroen's 2.5-litre CX diesel, introduced in October. There is also the Safari estate model, with virtually identical specification

MODEL TESTED: Citroen 25DTR Turbo four door saloon, 2.5-litre 4-cyl turbocharged diesel engine; 95 bhp (PS-DIN) five-speed gearbox

FOR:
- *Long-legged cruising*
- *Good performance*
- *Comfortable seating*

AGAINST:
- *Mechanical complexity*
- *Dated steering*

right up to 4,200 and the car will almost lurch into the governor.

The 3,900 rpm change point gave speeds of 23, 40, 60 and 83 in the four lower gears: at 4,200 rpm, the speeds were 29, 43, 65 and 82 mph. With a flurry of gear-changes before the 60 mph mark was reached, the CX25 DTR took 14.1sec to get to that speed, with 70 coming up in 20.3sec and 80 mph in 27.2sec. In practice, it is very much easier to get the best from a diesel-engined car than from a petrol-engined one. The main thing to remember is to make gearchanges early rather than late.

Where the CX25 DTR shines is in its performance in the gears. The flat, fat torque curve means that the car will pull very strongly from very low crankshaft speeds. For instance, it will haul away from 10 mph in fourth – a mere 210 rpm. Admittedly, it does not

Technical focus

TURBOCHARGERS have been around for much longer than many people realise, although their appearance on ordinary passenger cars is very much more recent. One of the first appearances in *The Autocar* was in 1940, when it was recorded that the Wright Cyclone engines in the B-17, the Flying Fortress, were turbocharged. The reason here was to ensure that the engines would perform well at high altitudes, where the air is thinner.

Among diesel-powered trucks, turbochargers have been used for many years. Unlike a petrol engine, a diesel engine has no carburettor. Instead, the engine speed and power output is controlled simply by the amount of fuel supplied to the injectors. Air is drawn in through plain ducting by the action of the pistons – and this is the limiting factor. If the fuel-air mixture gets too rich, clouds of black smoke, made up of partially burned diesel oil, errupt from the exhaust pipe. So the engine is governed to prevent this over-rich mixture occurring. In fact, a diesel engine will not come to much harm if it is taken over the governed speed. What does occur is a drastic increase in noise levels with very little more in the way of power or torque.

But what happens if you can pack in more air? The answer is that more fuel can be burned, so that from an engine of a given capacity, there are major increases in power and torque outputs. In the case of the Citroen, the normally aspirated 2,500 c.c. diesel engine develops 75 bhp (PS-DIN) at 4,250 rpm and 111 lb. ft. torque at 2,000 rpm. Add the Garrett AiResearch TO3 turbocharger, running at a maximum boost of 8.5 psi (0.6bar) and dramatic things happen. The power jumps nearly 27 per cent, to 95 bhp, but this is now developed at only 3,700 rpm. Even better is the improvement in torque, up by over 43 per cent, to 159 lb. ft., still at 2,000 rpm.

Because diesel burns at a slower rate than petrol, which in turn means that pick-up response is slower when the accelerator pedal is pressed, any lag in the turbocharger speeding up is masked. The improvement in power and torque outputs also allows the CX25 DTR Turbo to utilize very much higher gearing, with top pulling a leisurely 27.7 mph/1,000 rpm.

At speed, the CX25DTR remains very stable even in blustery cross winds. Roll is limited and pitch virtually non-existent

Inset: To aid high-speed stability, the rear spoiler normally seen only on the CX GTi is used on this model. The boot lid hinges down to the top of the bumper moulding, with no sill

sound very happy doing this, but it does exhibit the car's amazing flexibility. The turbocharger effect is felt more as a gentle but powerful push than a punch in the back. The driver soon gets used to letting the torque do the work, so that much driving out of town is done simply in top and fourth, with third being needed really only for the sharper corners.

Well over half the test distance was done on a fast run to and from southern Germany, which meant that the CX25 DTR was being cruised flat out for most of the time. The long-legged top gear gave a mean maximum speed of 100 mph on the high-speed circuit at MIRA, equivalent to 3,600 rpm. On the *autobahn* the car would head towards the 110 mark on the downhill stretches, but speed was not knocked off too much by the up gradients.

Below: Diesel engine service is best left to the experts, and the battery is tucked away, low down below the right-hand headlamp unit

Economy

When the car had completed its test mileage in this country, the overall consumption worked out at 32.8 mpg, with a worst brim-to-brim figure of 26.8 mpg, recorded during the MIRA test session. By the time the car had come back from Germany, the overall had dropped by 10 per cent to 29.8 mpg. These figures compare well with the 31.5 mpg we achieved with the normally aspirated CX2500, (*Autocar,* 7 July 1979) which was considerably slower – 0-60 mph in 17.0sec – and 102lb lighter.

Diesel engines are not at their most economical when working flat out, and this is shown up by the 24.7 mpg recorded on one 270-odd mile leg on the *autobahn* where the speedometer was rarely below the 100 mph mark. By contrast, a fairly gentle run to the West Country, keeping off motorways for much of the time, gave a figure of close to 37 mph. The tank on the CX25 DTR holds 14.9 gallons, which means that allowing a gallon in reserve, the car can cover over 400 miles between refills even when being driven very quickly. A good feature is that the wide filler neck means that frothing and blowing back, the main curse of so many diesel-engined cars, is reduced to a minimum.

Refinement

Putting a turbocharger in the exhaust system goes a long way in reducing noise levels almost at source. And as we have said, once the diesel engine has warmed up, there is little evidence of knock, even at idle. It is *just* possible to hear the turbocharger winding up, but at speed it is inaudible.

Despite its appearance, with smooth, flowing lines, the CX bodyshape it not as aerodynamically efficent as might be thought at first. The drag figure of 0.36 is good but not outstanding by some of today's more modern cars. To some extent this is borne out by the blustering wind noise which is generated at speed, and an annoying hissing whistle, on the test car at least, from the front passenger door seal.

Road behaviour

The high-pressure, engine-driven hydraulic pump in the CX25 DTR serves the suspension, steering and braking system, all of which are hallmarks of this model, and take time to get used to. With its extra power and speed, this car runs on low-profile 190/65HR-390 Michelin TRX tyres. The damping has been modified and a slightly thicker – 24 against 23mm – anti-roll bar is used at the front.

Rather than using conventional steel springs, the CX has oleo-pneumatic units for each wheel, supplied from the high pressure system. This not only gives the car an in-built self-levelling capability, but also allows the car's ride height to be raised when the going becomes difficult. Over the years, the system has been refined considerably, and gives a good, smooth ride which can cope with amazing ease with broken, indifferent surfaces. There are times when it can be caught out – hump back bridges taken fast are a classic case – when the car will find itself in the position of the suspension still on its way down when the road surface is coming rather more rapidly upwards. Generally, however, the car copes well, with little roll and virtually no pitch.

When the CX was launched nine years ago, its VariPower steering was by any standards unusual. Steering wheel movements are fed to the front wheels hydraulically, although there is a mechanical rack and pinion system there in case of pump failure. The system is speed-related, so that when parking or driving slowly round town, effort needed at the rim is relatively low. As the speed builds up, so the amount of servo effect is reduced, making the steering feel heavier. The VariPower system is also different in that it provides for power self-centring of the front wheels, even when the car is at a standstill. The system is also very high-geared, with just 2½ turns from lock to lock, which gives a fairly good turning circle, for the size of car, of about 35½ft.

One result of the power self-centring is that the car has to be steered positively both into and out of corners. Allow the wheel to run back quickly through your hands, as you might on a car with a more conventional system, and you will find that the front wheels will return to the straight-ahead position very quickly. This could mean that to the unwary, the car could suddenly lurch across the road. It does not take long to get used to the need to steer the car every inch of the way.

Any feel in the steering is artificially generated and lacks the true touch which feeds so much information back to the driver's hands. This and the need for constant, small corrections to be made, leads to the car cornering at high speed in what one driver called a "three-penny bit" manner, rather than in a smooth curve.

With over 70 per cent of the weight carried over the front wheels, the CX25 DTR might be thought to have a lot of understeer. Surprisingly, it is not anything like as marked as this figure would imply. Lifting off in the middle of a fast corner will send the front tucking in on a smooth line. Blustery cross winds hardly affect the car's stability, which always feel superb.

As with the suspension and steering, the brakes too rely on the high pressure hydraulic system. Applying pressure to the pedal gradually opens a valve in the system (which runs at around 2,000 to 2,500 psi). A spring bias in the pedal gives a degree of feel to it, but one still needs to be fairly feather-footed to prevent the wheels from locking up. Just 10lb pressure produced 0.35g, 50lb gave 0.92g. The all-round disc brake system – the front ones are ventilated – came through our tough fade tests very well, with pressures rising from 20/20lb for the first of the 10 0.5g stops to just 28/33lb at the end. The handbrake works on the front discs through a conventional cable system and gave a very good 0.5g. On the 1-in-3 test hill, the CX25 DTR held easily and moved off up again without a hint of trouble.

Behind the wheel

Citroen's unusual approach to things continues inside the car, although the layout is now looking a little dated. The instruments are deeply recessed within an elongated oval pod, which carries the assorted switchgear on "horns" adjacent to the wheel rim. The rotating drum speedometer and rev counter are rather difficult to interpret, while the other gauges – fuel tank and oil level – have vertical scales, with horizontal pointers. A Veglia digital clock, which kept anything but the correct time, is tacked on as something of an afterthought alongside the ignition key hole. The instruments are lit whenever the ignition is switched on.

The finger-tip controls on the horns are really very easy to use, once their locations have been memorized. As usual, the indicators are not self-cancelling, but there is a loud repeater to make sure that you don't leave them switched on. Two horns are fitted: first pressure produces a polite note, while second

Database

CITROEN CX25DTR TURBO

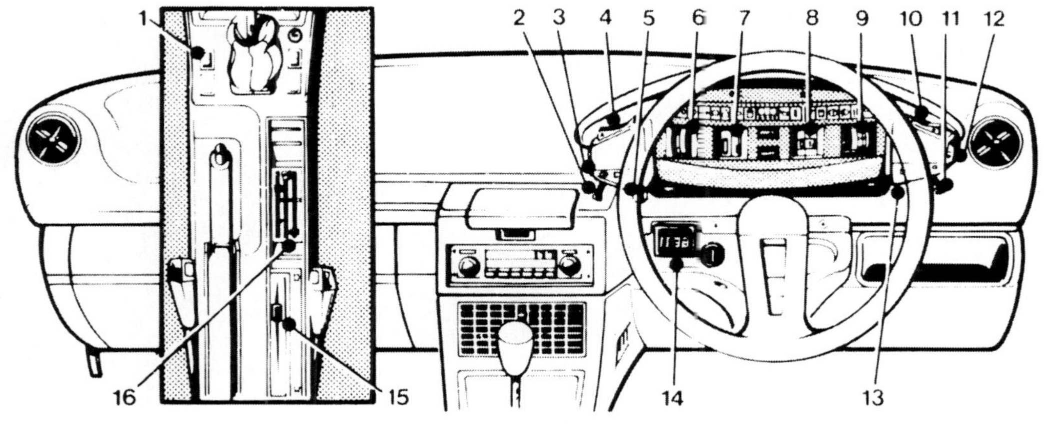

1. Electric window lifts, 2. screen wipers and washer, 3. horns, 4. indicators 5. hazard warning, 6. turbo boost, 7. speedometer, 8. rev counter, 9. oil level, 10. headlamp dip, 11. lamps switch, 12. headlamps flash, 13. instrument light dimmer, 14. digital clock, 15. ride height control, 16. heater controls, with heated rear window switch on roof console

SPECIFICATION

ENGINE
Transverse front, front-wheel drive. Head/block Al. alloy/cast iron. 4 cylinders in line, bored block, 5 main bearings Water cooled, electric fan.

Bore 93.0mm (3.66in.), stroke 92.0mm (3.62in.) capacity 2,500 c.c. (152.6 cu.in.). Valve gear ohv, toothed-belt camshaft drive. Compression ratio 21.0 to 1 CAV Roto-Diesel DPC injection. Garrett TO3 turbocharger, boost pressure 8.5 psi (1.6 bar).

Max power 95 bhp (PS-DIN) (70 kW ISO) at 3,700 rpm. Max torque 159 lb.ft. at 2,000 rpm.

TRANSMISSION
Five-speed manual. Single dry plate clutch, 9.0in. dia.

Gear	Ratio	mph/1,000 rpm
Top	0.67	27.7
4th	0.88	21.2
3rd	1.21	15.5
2nd	1.83	10.2
1st	3.17	5.9

Final drive gear helical spur, ratio 3.81.

SUSPENSION
Front, independent, twin wishbones, oleopneumatic spring and damper units, anti-roll bar. Rear, independent, trailing arms, oleopneumatic spring and damper units, anti-roll bar.

STEERING
Rack and pinion, VarioMatic hydraulic power assistance. Steering wheel diameter 15in., 2.5 turns lock to lock.

BRAKES
Dual circuits, split front/rear. Front 10.2in. (259mm) dia ventilated discs. Rear 9.3in. (236mm) dia discs. High pressure hydraulic servo.

WHEELS
Light alloy, 6in. rims. Michelin TRX tyres, size 190/60HR-390, pressures F35, R29 psi (normal driving).

EQUIPMENT
Battery 12V 88Ah. Alternator 80A. Headlamps 110/120W. Reversing lamp standard. 5 electric fuses. 2-speed, plus intermittent screen wipers. Electric screen washer. Air-blending interior heater; air conditioning extra. Cloth seats, cloth headlining. Carpet with heel mat/floor covering. Laminated windscreen. windscreen.

DIMENSIONS

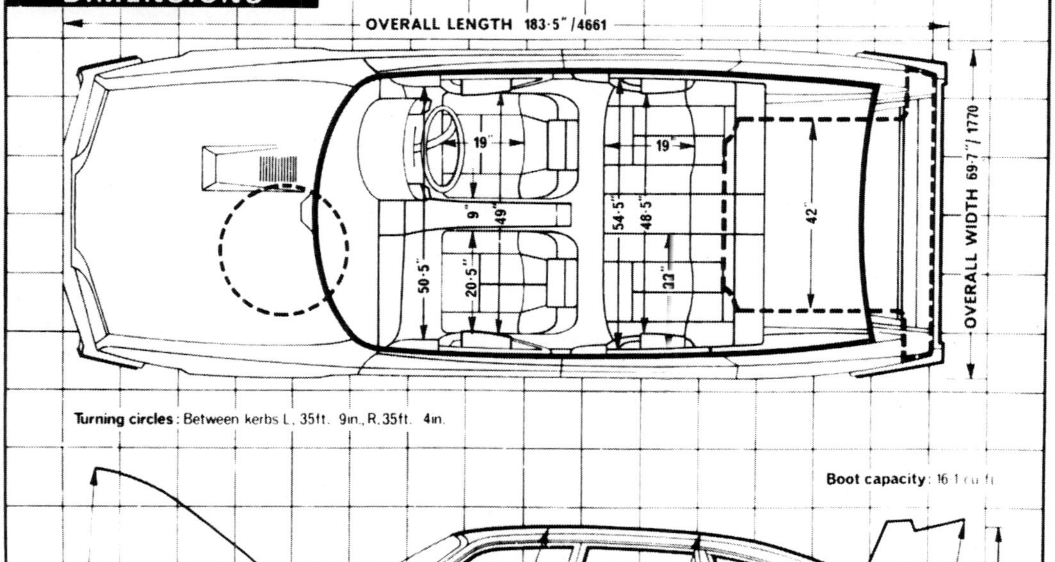

Performance

CITROEN CX25 DTR TURBO

MAXIMUM SPEEDS

Gear	mph	kph	rpm
Top (mean)	**100**	161	3,600
(best)	**102**	164	3,680
4th	**82**	132	4,200
3rd	**65**	105	4,200
2nd	**43**	69	4,200
1st	**25**	40	4,200

ACCELERATION

FROM REST

True mph	Time (sec)	Speedo mph
30	**4.2**	31
40	**6.5**	41
50	**10.2**	51
60	**14.1**	61
70	**20.3**	72
80	**27.2**	82
90	**41.4**	92
100	–	103

Standing ¼-mile: 19.6sec, 69 mph
Standing km: 36.3sec, 87 mph

IN EACH GEAR

mph	Top	4th	3rd	2nd
10-30	–	14.9	8.2	4.7
20-40	18.1	10.3	6.3	4.4
30-50	14.4	8.6	6.0	–
40-60	12.7	9.0	7.2	–
50-70	13.6	10.2	–	–
60-80	16.7	12.7	–	–
70-90	23.5	–	–	–

FUEL CONSUMPTION

Overall mpg:
29.8 (9.5 litres/100km) **6.55** mpl

Constant speed
Autocar *constant speed fuel consumption measuring equipment not compatible with fuel injection.*

Autocar formula: Driving and conditions — Hard 26.8 mpg; Average 32.8 mpg; Gentle 38.7 mpg

Grade of fuel: Derv.
Fuel tank: 14.9 Imp. galls (68 litres)
Mileage recorder reads: 2.0 per cent long

OIL CONSUMPTION

(SAE 15W/40) 1,300 miles/litre

BRAKING

Fade *(from 69 mph in neutral)*
Pedal load for 0.5g stops in lb

	start/end		start/end
1	20-20	6	24-26
2	20-20	7	28-28
3	20-24	8	26-32
4	20-22	9	28-32
5	24-28	10	28-32

Response *(from 30 mph in neutral)*

Load	g	Distance
10lb	0.35	86ft
20lb	0.45	67ft
30lb	0.65	46ft
40lb	0.80	37.6ft
50lb	0.92	32.6ft
Handbrake	0.50	60ft

Max. gradient: 1 in 3

CLUTCH

Pedal 28lb; Travel 4½in.

WEIGHT

Kerb, 27.3cwt/3,052lb/1,387kg
(Distribution F/R, 70.6/29.4)
Test, 30.6cwt/3,427lb/1,558kg
Max. payload, 1,100lb/500kg

TEST CONDITIONS:

Wind: 7-8 mph
Temperature: 15.4deg C (60deg F)
Barometer: 29.8in. Hg (1,011 mbar)
Humidity: 87 per cent
Surface: dry asphalt and concrete
Test distance: 2,614 miles

Figures taken at 1,870 miles by our own staff at the Motor Industry Research Association proving ground at Nuneaton and on the Continent.

pressure brings in a pair of strident air horns.

The CX25 DRT has a thermostatically controlled heating system with a temperature sensor mounted on the roof, just aft of the screen rail. Slider controls between the front seats control temperature setting, direction and fan speeds. Alongside these controls is the one for ride height.

Our taller drivers found that front seat legroom was a little limited and that the seats themselves did not provide quite the sort of support expected, especially on long journeys.

Living with the CX25 DTR

Passengers in the rear seats of the CX have plenty of room for legs and heads, and in sunny weather, they can cut down glare with sun blinds across the rear window and visors above the side windows. The car probably has one of the most comprehensive internal lighting systems around. The main roof lamp is really big, so that one does not have to fumble about in semi-

Above: Taller drivers would have appreciated a little more front-seat legroom; the driving seat can be adjusted for cushion angle. The headrest padding can be unclipped or adjusted for height with press-fasteners

Above left: Pods within finger tip reach of the steering wheel rim are a Citroen feature. This left-hand one controls indicators, horns, screen wash/wipe and, underneath, hazard warning lamps

Below left: Rear seat passengers can cut down the sun's glare with pull-down blinds; there are also vizors for the rear side windows

Comparisons

FOR MANY years diesel-powered cars have had a slightly worthy, taxicab image, shunned by the vast majority of ordinary motorists. Now that image has changed, and the competition, once very limited, is now wide open. Just about the only major European manufacturer without their own, modern in-house diesel are Austin Rover.
diesel are Austin Rover. A newcomer on the scene, and one which we have yet to drive, is Ford's own 1.6-litre diesel unit, which will be first seen in the Fiesta.

By turbocharging their 2.5-litre diesel, Citroen have been able to rejoin the ranks of the high-performance cars in the compression-ignition class – but way out in front are Audi, with their delightful 80 Turbo which can run rings round every other model in terms of acceleration; it also sits at the top of the fuel consumption league, with the Vauxhall Cavalier.

The larger turbocharged models – Citroen, Rover SD, Peugeot 505GRD and 604SR – all have engines in the 2.3- to 2.5-litre size. The 604SR is a big car, and this pays the penalty in both performance and consumption. The smaller, lighter 505, on the other hand, is a real match for the Citroen. *Autocar* figures for the superseded 505SRD model gave it a 0-60 mph time of 14.3sec, a mean maximum of 99 mph and an overall consumption of just 30.4 mpg. In terms of carrying capacity, there is little to choose between this and the Citroen. A major plus for the Peugeot must be its mechanical simplicity when compared to the complexity of the Citroen.

Although the Rover SD Turbo is still something of a rarity in Britain, it has become very popular on the other side of the Channel, and in Italy in particular. A combination of the Italian-made VM turbo diesel and British *chic* seems to have caught on. The 100 mph plus cruising is combined with a fuel consumption close to 30 mpg – and you get the advantage of the hatchback facility.

Mercedes have always been in the forefront of passenger car diesels, but the 300D, the only model in the current range we have tested, is lagging way behind in performance. This was not helped by the fact that the car had automatic transmission. The 300D, at £12,280 with a manual gearbox, is also expensive. The 240D (£10,660) is the smaller version. Mercedes do, of course, have that enviable reputation for quality – and a 120 bhp (PS-DIN) turbocharged version of the 300D is on sale on the Continent.

Ford's diesel image has been improved recently with the addition of the 2.3-litre Peugeot-engined Sierra. This is the normally aspirated engine, but in Britain, the model does have the advantage of being available in a far wider range of bodies and trims than most of its

SPECIFICATIONS FROM Autocar BUYERS' GUIDE

	£ Price	Insurance Group	Doors	Seats	Engine Capacity (c.c.)	Driven Wheels	Engine Position and Type	Bore and Stroke (mm)	BHP at RPM	Torque (lb. ft.) at RPM	Valve Position
Citroen CX 25 DTR Turbo Diesel	10,862	-/-	4	5	2,500	F	F4Tr	93.0x92.0	95/3,700	159/2,000	O
Audi 80 Turbo Diesel	8,107	4/4	4	4/5	1,588	F	F4IL	76.5x86.4	70/4,500	98/2,600	Ohc
100 Turbo Diesel	11,245	-/-	4	5	1,986	F	F5IL	76.5x86.4	87/4,500	126/2,750	Ohc
Citroen CX 25 D Safari Diesel	9,776	5/6	5	5	2,500	F	F4Tr	93.0x92.0	75/4,250	111/2,000	O
Ford Sierra 2.3GL Diesel	7,185	3/3	5	4/5	2,304	R	F4IL	94.0x83.0	67/4,200	102/2,000	O
Granada 2.5L Diesel	8,579	4/4	4	5	2,498	R	F4IL	94.0x90.0	69/4,200	109/2,000	O
Mercedes-Benz 300D Diesel	12,280	6/OA	4	5	2,998	R	F5IL	90.9x92.4	88/4,400	126/2,400	Ohc
Peugeot 305 GR Diesel	5,945	3/4	4	4/5	1,905	F	F4Tr	83.0x88.0	64/4,600	88/2,000	Ohc
505 GRD Turbo Diesel	9,095	5/5	4	5	2,304	R	F4IL	94.0x83.0	79/4,150	136/2,000	Ohc
604 SRD Turbo Diesel	11,395	6/7	4	5	2,304	R	F4IL	94.0x83.0	79/4,150	136/2,000	O
Renault 18 TD Diesel	5,575	4/4	4	4/5	2,068	F	F4IL	86.0x89.0	67/4,500	93/2,250	O
Rover 2400 SD Turbo Diesel	10,899	6/6	5	5	2,393	R	F4IL	92.0x90.0	90/4,250	142/2,350	O
Vauxhall Cavalier 1.6 L Diesel	6,314	3/3	4	4/5	1,598	F	F4Tr	80.0x79.5	54/4,600	70/2,400	Ohc
Volvo 760 Turbo Diesel	13,649	6/7	4	5	2,383	R	F6IL	76.5x86.4	109/4,800	151/2,400	Ohc

ABBREVIATIONS ● = standard equipment or optional at no extra cost, ○ = optional at extra cost. **Engine:** F = Front, M = Mid, R = Rear, Ro = Rotary, S = Supercharged, T = turbocharging. **Gearbox:** * = overdrive standard, A = Automatic transmission. **Brakes:** † = anti-lock standard,

darkness when getting into or out of the car. To the front of this is a map-reading spot lamp for use either by driver or passenger (we found its beam was aimed a little too far forward) while at the rear of the main lamp unit are individual reading lamps for those in the back seats. Also up on the roof console is the switch for the heated rear window.

Boot room is generous, but as one of our testers found, it is awkwardly shaped, so that squeezing in a carry-cot chassis proved tricky. The CX25 DTR comes with electric front window lifts and central locking; this has a green indicator lamp, which stays on for five seconds, on the inside door capping to show that the locks have operated.

Under the bonnet, which has a self-latching prop, the layout is neat, with all the points which need regular attention reached easily. A point worth noting is that the engine needs an oil change every 3,000 miles, but this is the sort of job which could be carried out quite easily by a competent DIY owner.

What it costs

CITROEN CX25DTR TURBO

PRICES

Basic	£8,719.00
Special Car Tax	£726.58
VAT	£1,416.84
Total (in GB)	**£10,862.42**
Licence	£85.00
Delivery charge (London)	£129.95
Number plates	£15.00
Total on the Road (exc. insurance)	**£11,092.37**
EXTRAS *(inc. VAT)*	
Electric sunroof	£488.37
*Metallic paint	£219.27

**Fitted to test car*

TOTAL AS TESTED ON THE ROAD	**£11,311.64**
Insurance	Group 6

SERVICE & PARTS

Change	Interval 3,000	6,000	12,000
Engine oil	Yes	Yes	Yes
Oil filter	Yes	Yes	Yes
Gearbox oil	No	No	No
Air cleaner	No	No	Yes
Total cost	£30.79	£53.33	£70.84

(Assuming labour at £16.10/hour inc. VAT)

PARTS COST *(including VAT)*

Brake pads (2 wheels) – front	£23.59
Brake pads (2 wheels) – rear	£20.39
Exhaust complete	£82.09
Tyre – each (typical)	£103.32
Windscreen (laminated)	£122.98
Headlamp unit	£58.16
Front wing	£79.05
Rear bumper	£66.79

WARRANTY

12 months/24 months suspension, unlimited mileage; 6 year anti-corrision

PRODUCED BY:
SA Automobiles Citroen
64 Boulevard Victor Hugo
92208 Neuilly-sur-Seine
France

SOLD IN THE UK BY:
Citroen Cars Ltd.,
Mill Street
Slough
Berkshire SL2 5DE

competitors. The new 2.5-litre diesel Granada has shown itself to be far faster off the mark than the previous 2.1-litre model, but its 17.5sec 0-60 mph time is still lagging behind the Citroen's 14.1sec.

Renault's 18 is available both as a saloon and estate – and it will be interesting to see if and when this model will get the 85 bhp (PS-DIN) turbocharged diesel which is used in the 20 in Europe. The non-turbo version does not hang about, and with more power the 18 diesel would be even better.

The car which started the current fashion in diesels, the Golf, is not currently available in Britain: sales of the new models are expected to start in the New Year. The only VW diesel listed at present is the Jetta C, at £5,840. Two relative newcomers in the small diesel range are the Renault 9 (£5,195) and the 2.0-litre Peugeot 305GLD and GRD saloons and estates, which range between £5,495 and £6,445.

TESTERS' SHORT LIST

Citroen CX25 DTR Turbo
100 mph; 0-60 mph 14.1sec; 29.8 mpg

Renault 18 TD
95 mph; 0-60 mph 14.6sec; 38.2 mpg

Audi 80 Turbo Diesel
96 mph; 0-60 mph 12.8sec; 37.3 mpg

Rover SD Turbo Diesel
104 mph; 0-60 mph 14.3sec; 29.6 mpg

Ford Granada 2.5D
87 mph; 0-60 mph 17.5sec; 27.5 mpg

Vauxhall Cavalier LD
87 mph; 0-60 mph 17.8sec; 38.2 mpg

VERDICT

People who are thinking of buying a diesel car are probably far more concerned with economy in terms of fuel consumption and running costs than they are of performance. But the Audi 80 Turbo Diesel is a car which combines all the advantages of diesel running – 37.3mpg – with the sort of performance which would be most acceptable with a petrol-engined car. Its price, at £8,106 also adds to the attraction.

Both the Renault 18TD and the Vauxhall Cavalier LD are cars in a similar mould, although at just £5,575, the French car is £871 less expensive than the Cavalier. It is also very much faster – 14.6sec against 17.8sec to 60 mph. The Cavalier we tested had only a four-speed gearbox; a five-speed one is now standard, as with the Renault. This would probably mean that the Vauxhall's top speed would be comfortably higher than the quoted 87 mph. Both cars achieved 38.2 mpg, topping the six-car league.

As with these two cars, the Rover and Citroen are similar in what they set out to achieve – a large car with good performance and ample room. There is very little to chose between them when it comes to performance, economy or price. But the Citroen is starting to show its age, and many would find it hard to come to terms with some of the car's more idiosyncratic ideas. By contrast, the Rover is almost a model of practical commonsense. Yet despite this, our choice for those looking for a diesel car would be between the Audi and the Renault.

Carburettors or Fuel injection	Gearbox Speeds 4	5	A	Tyre size (in.) and Type	Brakes: D = Disc, Dr = Drum, S = Servo, P = Power Hydraulics,	Power Steering	Fuel Tank (galls)	Wheelbase in.	Overall Length in.	Width in.	Height in.	Boot Luggage Capacity cu. ft.	Maker's Unladen kerb Weight lb	Maximum Payload (luggage + passengers) lb	Main service (,000 miles)		AUTOTEST PERFORMANCE DATA: Legroom front/rear (fully back) in.	Maximum speed mph	0-60 mph sec	Overall fuel consumption mpg	When tested
iT	–	●	–	190/65HR-390	DP	●	14.9	112.2	183.5	69.7	53.5	16.1	3,307	1,521		**Citroen CX 25 DTR Turbo Diesel**	41/39	100	14.1	29.8	3/12
iT	–	●	–	165SR-13	DDrS	○	15.0	99.9	172.6	66.2	53.7	17.8	2,249	1,014	10	Audi 80 Turbo Diesel	40/38	96	12.8	37.3	11/82
i	–	●	○	185/70HR-14	DDrP	●	17.5	105.8	188.7	71.4	56.0	20.0	2,756	1,102	10	100 Turbo Diesel	–	–	–	–	–
i	–	●	–	185-14	DP	●	14.9	121.9	194.9	69.7	57.7	41/75	3,230	1,543	6	Citroen CX 25 D Safari Diesel	–	–	–	–	–
i	–	●	–	165SR-13	DDrS	○	13.2	102.7	173.5	67.7	53.6	12/51	2,677	1,014	12	Ford Sierra 2.3GL Diesel	–	–	–	–	–
i	–	●	–	185SR-14	DDrS	●	14.3	109.0	182.2	70.5	54.3	14.3	2,745	1,195	12	Granada 2.5L Diesel	41/40	87	17.5	27.7	7/83 (2.5D Estate)
i	●	○	○	175SR-14	DS*	●	14.3	110.0	186.0	75.2	56.6	17.7	3,197	1,146	12	Mercedes-Benz 300D Diesel	43/38	90	20.8	27.2	12/76 (Auto)
i	–	●	–	155SR-14	DDrS	–	11.6	103.2	167.8	64.4	55.5	16.4	2,227	1,025	15	Peugeot 305 GR Diesel	–	–	–	–	–
iT	–	●	–	185/70-14	DDrS	●	15.3	108.0	180.3	68.4	56.4	18.5	2,932	1,169	12	505 GRD Turbo Diesel	42/38	99	14.3	30.4	Autocar figures
iT	–	●	–	190/65-390	DS	●	15.4	110.2	185.8	70.0	56.7	17.6	3,296	1,113	12	604 SRD Turbo Diesel	41/39	94	17.0	27.7	4/80
i	–	●	–	165SR-13	DDrS	–	11.6	96.0	172.5	66.2	55.3	14.0	2,237	959	4	Renault 18 TD Diesel	39/35	95	14.6	38.2	4/81
iT	–	●	–	175HR-14	DDrS	●	14.5	110.8	185.0	78.5	54.4	11/35	3,296	1,036	12	Rover 2400 SD Turbo Diesel	40/40	104	14.3	29.6	11/82
i	–	●	–	165SR-13	DDrS	○	13.4	101.3	171.9	65.9	53.6	18.0	2,293	1,113	9	Vauxhall Cavalier 1.6 L Diesel	39/39	87	17.8	38.2	7/82 (4-speed)
iT	●*	–	–	195/60HR-15	DS	●	18.0	109.1	188.4	68.9	55.5	17.1	2,932	1,080	9	Volvo 760 Turbo Diesel	–	–	–	–	

IL = In Line, Tr = Transverse, V = Vee, HO = Horizontally opposed, * = Air cooled. **Valve Position:** O = Overhead, Ohc = Overhead camshafts per cylinder bank. **Carburettors:** Figure = number of carburettors, i = fuel injection.
* = anti-lock optional at extra cost.

BriefTest

CITROËN CX 25 DTR

Now equipped with a turbocharger, Citroën's big diesel is once again the fastest diesel we've tested — and one of the best, too

AS THE UK diesel car market grows to significant levels home buyers are able to take advantage of the intensive development ploughed into car diesels over the years for the much more receptive European market. The latest diesel cars have all but dispelled the slow, clattery, smelly image and shown that diesel car economy can be combined with more than respectable levels of performance, as well as comfort and refinement which is every bit the equal of petrol-engined rivals.

Citroën have been at the forefront of diesel car design for some while and back in 1980 the CX 2500 diesel was notable for being both the quickest *and* the most economical large diesel saloon tested by *Motor*. Since then a number of rivals have appeared to challenge the Citroën (in terms of performance, if not always economy), not the least of which is our own home-grown (but Italian VM-powered) Rover 2400 SD Turbo. Keen to regain their position at the top of the pile Citroën have added a Garrett turbocharger to their well-proven 2.5-litre engine and claim not only a significant boost in performance but also improved economy and refinement as well.

In its normally aspirated form Citroën's 2,500 cc diesel (still available in the CX Safari) develops 75 bhp (DIN) at 4,250 rpm and 111 lb ft (DIN) of torque at 2,000 rpm. With the help of the turbocharger, used simply to pump more air into the cylinders in diesel engines, power goes up to 95 bhp at an exceptionally low 3,700 rpm, while torque gets an even bigger hike up to 159 lb ft at 2,000 rpm. To cope with the extra power and torque the engine has been generally beefed up by strengthening the crankcase, crankshaft, connecting rods, pistons and cylinder head, and in an effort to reduce engine noise levels the gear drive for the camshaft, which operates the valves via pushrods and rockers, has been replaced by a toothed belt.

The turbo engine is available in the CX saloon and in the Safari estate (to special order only). Both models boast trim to the luxurious Pallas level, and are fitted as standard with alloy wheels shod with low profile Michelin TRX tyres, the saloon sporting a spoiler on its rump similar to that fitted to the petrol CX GTi. The torquier engine has allowed higher gearing to be specified, arrived at by revised internal ratios and a taller final drive ratio, giving an exceptionally long-striding 27.7 mph/1,000 rpm in fifth gear. To cope with the sprightlier performance there is also a thicker front anti-roll bar (the rear one remains unaltered) and the damper settings incorporated in the CX's hydropneumatic suspension have been altered.

Otherwise the CX specification reads much as before with a transversely-mounted engine driving the front wheels through a five-speed gearbox, all-round independent suspension by double wishbones at the front and trailing arms at the rear, and springing and damping by Citroën's self-levelling hydropneumatic system which can be set at different ride heights. Both the rack and pinion steering and the disc brakes (ventilated at the front, solid at the rear) are fully powered, drawing on the same high pressure hydraulic power source as the suspension.

At £10,862 the Citroën CX DTR turbo diesel saloon tested here is competitively priced for the executive diesel car market. The closest rivals in terms of size and concept are the Audi 100 TD (£11,245), not yet tested by *Motor*, and the Rover 2400 SD Turbo (£10,899), while similarly sized, but mainly slower, competitors include the Ford Granada 2.5 D (£7,574), Mercedes 300 D (£12,280), Peugeot 604 SRD Turbo (£11,395) and the Volvo 760 GLE Turbo diesel (£13,649).

Despite poor testing conditions the CX 25 DTR comfortably lived up to Citroën's assertion that it is one of the fastest (and most economical and responsive) diesels on the UK market, if not quite equalling their claims of a top speed of 108 mph and a 0-100 kph time of 13.3 sec. Nevertheless a maximum average speed of 106.3 mph around MIRA's banked circuit means that a Citroën is once again the fastest diesel tested by *Motor* while the 0-60 mph time of 12.5 sec (0-100 kph in 13.7 sec) also earns it the fastest diesel sprinter title.

Of the executive diesel rivals which *Motor* has tested only the Rover 2400 SD Turbo comes close (102.9 mph maximum speed, 0-60 mph in 14.2 sec) and surprisingly, considering its significantly lower gearing, it is also marginally inferior to the Citroën in terms of pulling power in fourth and fifth gears. The CX 25 DTR manages the crucial 30-50 mph increment in fourth and 50-70 mph in fifth in 7.7 and 12.9 sec, respectively, while the corresponding times for the Rover are 8.0 and 14.6 sec. Both cars, however, are comfortably better than the class average in this respect.

In fact the Citroën's performance is on a par with some (lower capacity, non-turbo) petrol-engined rivals, though, as ever, equivalent performance doesn't equate to similar price — diesel owners have to claw back the higher purchase price of their cars through lower fuel costs.

They don't have to suffer any traditional diesel bugbears in the process, however, because the DTR's engine noise suppression is well up to the high standards of the executive car class and the only time it's audibly obvious that you're sitting behind a diesel is at idle and when starting up. The engine also performs very sweetly, revving smoothly to peak revs (according to Citroën the engine governor takes effect at 4,625 rpm but on our test car the tachometer came to a virtual standstill at an indicated 3,800 rpm) with no discernible turbo lag, or any sudden surge as the turbocharger comes on boost. The low rev limit (exaggerated on our test car by an under-reading rev counter) is no problem in practice because the turbo diesel unit pulls strongly from low revs and once the driver is accustomed to changing up with no more than about 3,500 rpm showing on the rev counter it is actually rather impressive how such brisk performance is delivered with so little evident mechanical stress or commotion. Starting is prompt from cold, after waiting for the glow plug warning lamp to go out after 10 sec or so, and the warm-up period is reasonably fuss-free.

Citroën claim that their CX turbo diesel is more economical than the normally aspirated model and the improved Government fuel figures (32.9, 49.6 and 38.7 mpg in the urban cycle and at 56 and 75 mph, respectively, for the DTR compared with 31.7, 46.3 and 34.9 mpg for the 2500 D) would seem to bear this out. The determination of our testers to exploit the DTR's performance advantage to the full, however, probably accounts for its overall consumption being 2.1 mpg down on the CX 2500 D, at 31.3 mpg. Nevertheless it is still an excellent result and usefully better than the 29.6 mpg recorded by the Rover 2400 SD Turbo. Most owners should find little difficulty in returning fuel figures around the 38 mpg mark, at which rate of consumption the generously-sized 14.9 gallon fuel tank offers a theoretical range of more than 550 miles.

The ratios of the five-speed gearbox are evenly spaced and well matched to the characteristics of the engine. From cold the first to second gearchange can be notably stiff and notchy but, apart from this, the cogs can be shifted swiftly and easily with well-judged spring loading easing the lever through the dog leg gearchanges. The clutch is moderately weighted and engages smoothly.

As ever the CX is a unique experience to drive with its hydraulically-powered suspension, steering and brakes. There is no doubting the safety and stability of its handling which, with the assistance of the TRX tyres, offers strong grip in the wet and dry and remains utterly fail-safe under the serverest provocation. The suspension does allow above average body roll,

Left: no change to the switchgear and instrumentation. Below left: rear seating area is spacious and very comfortable.

Right: big diesel 'four' is extensively uprated and now has toothed belt camshaft drive

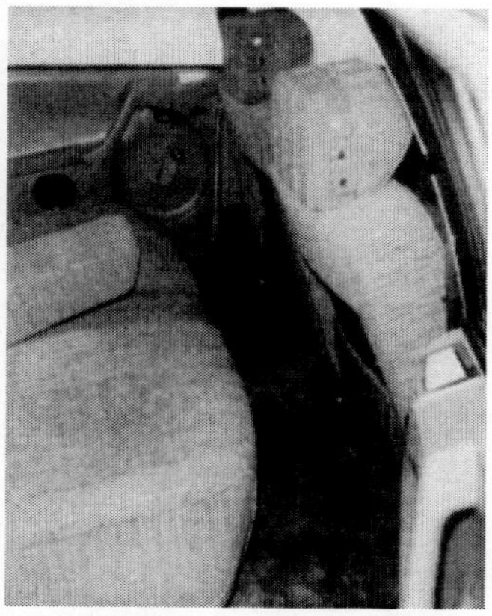

Soft but supportive front seats have rather crude height/tilt adjustment

however, and the VariPower steering is very direct and lacks any real feel, making it difficult to steer the CX smoothly. Similarly, the brakes are very powerful, show little tendency to fade, and infallibly pull the car up in a straight line — but they are oversensitive to light applications and the minimal pedal travel makes it hard to feather the brakes on and off smoothly.

Where the hydraulics do score full marks is in helping to provide ride comfort which is among the best available for any price. Minor quibbles are its uncharacteristically stiff reaction to severe disturbances such as potholes and a tendency to be caught out by large humps taken at speed. These minor failings are highlighted, though, by its uncannily efficient absorption of virtually every other type of surface.

In most other respects the DTR differs little from the other CX models discussed extensively in *Motor* since its launch in 1975. The soft seats and driving position are generally comfortable, although the coarse recline/tilt/height adjustment for the driver's seat is of little practical value. Accommodation is generous for passengers but slightly below average for luggage and all-round visibility is good, though marred slightly by the lack of a passenger door mirror. The pod-mounted switchgear and revolving drum instruments are long-standing Citroën idiosyncracies, the former working quite well (although the non-self-cancelling indicators are still irritating) and the latter not so well, being rather unattractive reflective and difficult to read at a glance. They are, however, adequately comprehensive. The heating system works well but the controls are rather inconveniently sited in between the front seats, and it's not easy to get a comfortable supply of face level fresh air independently of the heater.

Cruising refinement is generally excellent, thanks to the very low level of engine noise, but our test car had an unusually high level of wind noise which we have not encountered previously in the CX range. Inside the DTR is suitably plush and well equipped, though the sweeping curves of the facia continue to jar a little.

Despite its age the CX remains a very competitive and technically advanced car. In turbo diesel form it is a particularly attractive proposition with its combination of class-leading performance, excellent fuel economy and superb comfort and refinement. As ever, the deciding factor for many prospective buyers will be whether they can live with the more idiosyncratic aspects of its design.

MOTOR ROAD TEST No 58/83 **CITROËN CX 25 DTR**

PERFORMANCE

WEATHER CONDITIONS

Wind	5-12 mph
Temperature	41°F/5°C
Barometer	29.7 in Hg/1005 mbar
Surface	Damp tarmacadam

MAXIMUM SPEEDS

	mph	kph
Banked circuit	106.3	171.0
Best ¼ mile	107.1	172.3
Terminal Speeds:		
at ¼ mile	72	116
at kilometre	91	146
Speeds in gears (at 4,200 rpm):		
1st	25	40
2nd	43	69
3rd	65	105
4th	89	143

ACCELERATION FROM REST

mph	sec	kph	sec
0-30	3.7	0-40	2.8
0-40	5.9	0-60	5.3
0-50	8.9	0-80	8.9
0-60	12.5	0-100	13.7
0-70	17.8	0-120	20.6
0-80	24.2	0-140	30.6
Stand'g ¼	19.0	Stand'g km	35.5

ACCELERATION IN TOP

mph	sec	kph	sec
20-40	—	40-60	10.0
30-50	14.5	60-80	8.7
40-60	12.9	80-100	7.7
50-70	12.9	100-120	8.9
60-80	14.4	120-140	11.7

ACCELERATION IN 4TH

mph	sec	kph	sec
20-40	10.2	40-60	6.2
30-50	7.7	60-80	4.7
40-60	8.0	80-100	5.3
50-70	9.1	100-120	6.3
60-80	12.3	120-140	10.5

FUEL CONSUMPTION

Overall	31.3 mpg 9.0 litres/100 km
Govt tests	32.9 mpg (urban) 49.6 mpg (56 mph) 38.7 mpg (75 mph)
Fuel grade	Diesel
Tank capacity	14.9 galls 68 litres
Max range*	566 miles 911 km
Test distance	1,200 miles 1,931 km

*Based on an estimated consumption of 38 mpg at touring speeds.

NOISE

	dBA	Motor rating*
30 mph	65	11
50 mph	71	17
70 mph	76	24
Maximum†	75	23

*A rating where 1=30 dBA and 100=96 dBA, and where double the number means double the loudness
†Peak noise level under full-throttle acceleration in 2nd.

SPEEDOMETER (mph)

Speedo	30	40	50	60	70	80	90	100
True mph	28	37	47	57	67	77	87	97

Distance recorder: 2.2 per cent fast

WEIGHT

	cwt	kg
Unladen weight*	26.9	1,367
Weight as tested	30.6	1,554

*with fuel for approx 50 miles

Performance tests carried out by Motor's staff at the Motor Industry Research Association proving ground, Lindley.

GENERAL SPECIFICATION

ENGINE

Cylinders	4 in-line
Capacity	2,500cc (152.4 cu in)
Bore/stroke	93/92mm (3.66/3.62in)
Cooling	Water
Block	Cast iron
Head	Aluminium alloy
Valves	Pushrod ohv
Cam drive	Toothed belt
Compression	21:1
Fuel system	CAV Roto-Diesel injection, Garrett TO3 turbocharger
Bearings	5 main
Max power	95 bhp (DIN) at 3,700 rpm
Max torque	159 lb ft (DIN) at 2,000 rpm

TRANSMISSION

Type	5-speed, manual
Clutch dia	9.0in
Actuation	Cable
Internal ratios	and mph/1,000 rpm
Top	0.674:1/27.7
4th	0.882:1/21.2
3rd	1.207:1/15.5
2nd	1.833:1/10.2
1st	3.166:1/5.9
Rev	3.154:1
Final drive	3.81:1

BODY/CHASSIS

Construction	Unitary, all steel
Protection	Cataphoretic immersion, Tectyl underbody spray, wax cavity injection

SUSPENSION

Front	Independent by double wishbones with anti-dive geometry; hydropneumatic spring/damper units with automatic self-levelling and adjustable height control; anti-roll bar
Rear	Independent by trailing arms; hydropneumatic spring/damper units with automatic self-levelling and adjustable height control; anti-roll bar

STEERING

Type	Rack and pinion
Assistance	"VariPower"

BRAKES

Front	Ventilated discs, 10.2in dia.
Rear	Discs, 8.8in dia
Park	On front wheels
Servo	Fully powered
Circuit	Dual, split front/rear
Rear valve	Yes
Adjustment	Automatic

WHEELS/TYRES

Type	Alloy, 150 TR 390
Tyres	Michelin TRX 190/65 HR 390
Pressures	35/29 psi F/R

ELECTRICAL

Battery	12V 88Ah
Earth	Negative
Generator	Alternator, 90A
Fuses	5
Headlights	
type	Quartz halogen
dip	110 W total
main	120 W total

COMPARISONS

	Capacity cc	Price £	Max mph	0-60 sec	30-50* sec	Overall mpg	Length in	Width in	Weight cwt	Boot cu ft
Citroën CX 25 DTR	**2,500**	**10,862**	**106.3**	**12.5**	**7.7**	**31.3**	**183**	**69.8**	**26.9**	**10.2**
Mercedes 300 D Auto	2,998	12,995	88.4	18.5	7.8	24.2	186	70.3	28.7	14.2
Peugeot 604 SRD Turbo	2,304	11,395	94.9	16.6	10.4	26.4	186	69.5	29.2	12.6
Rover 2400 SD Turbo	2,393	10,899	102.9	14.2	8.0	29.6	185	69.8	28.3	12.7

*In kickdown for Mercedes 300 D; in 4th for others

Make: Citroën. **Model:** CX 25 DTR
Maker: Automobiles Citroën, 133 quai André Citroën, 75747 Paris, France.
UK importer: Citroën Cars Ltd, Mill Street, Slough SL2 5DE. Tel: Slough 23808
Price: £8,719.00 plus £726.58 Car Tax and £1,416.84 VAT equals £10,862.42.

CX 25 TRI SAFARI
THE THINKING MAN'S ESTATE

The CX25 TRI Safari submits to the scrutiny of Philip Llewellin who votes it a "sophisticated cocktail of grace, speed, comfort, convenience, economy and versatility"

ESTATE CARS USED TO LOOK LIKE a cross between the baker's van and Anne Hathaway's Cottage. Quite a few still have the elegance of a sumo wrestler. The Citroën Safari, in sharp and delightful contrast, might have been created for *Star Wars* or one of the other big-budget sci-fi epics. It will look good at the turn of the century when its 1984 rivals appear as quaint and dated as the old timber-framed dinosaurs do today. But that's typical. Citroëns in general, and big Citroëns in particular, have never been anything if not futuristic.

The sleek, shark-like styling is not just an eye-catching exercise in automobile cosmetics. It envelops a bumper bundle of appropriately advanced technology combined with the luxury of a five-seater limousine and a small truck's ability to swallow loads. A week with the latest CX25 TRI 5-speed variation on the Safari theme left me with no doubts about its right to be hailed as the thinking man's estate car. Where else can you exchange just under £11,000 for such a sophisticated cocktail of grace, speed, comfort, convenience, economy and versatility?

Just over four years had passed since I last gripped the single-spoke wheel that is one of the character-packed Safari's many unusual features. That was a 2500 Diesel Super which covered 2,092 English and French miles laden with five Llewellins – two adults and three teenagers – plus what a neighbour described as enough luggage for a full-scale action replay of the D-Day landings. We like to camp in comfort. That means a big tent, airbeds, chairs, a table and a "portable kitchen" in addition to sleeping bags, clothes, emergency

rations, books, maps, snorkels, flippers and father's bulky bag of camera equipment.

We had sampled several other big estate cars on previous holidays, but were invariably obliged to supplement internal space with a roof rack. That's bad news under several headings. Noise levels increase, fuel consumption suffers, security becomes a major problem and there are nasty visions of your goods and chattels slipping off into the scenery. The only challenge posed by the Safari was what to do with the space that remained when all the customary kit had been stowed. My wife's answer was to pack our huge Martini parasol and its equally king-sized base.

The man next door raised his eyebrows so high they almost went into orbit. But there was an element of told-you-so triumph in his voice as

Plenty of mid-range muscle, well-spaced gear ratios, razor-sharp steering and completely trustworthy brakes

he studied the Safari's tail, which was within an inch or two of the road; "Great," he said. "Only trouble is, there's no way you can drive the thing with so little clearance."

He knew as much about Citroëns as I know about nuclear physics. But not for long. Just start the engine and, as if by magic, the self-levelling, all-independent hydropneumatic suspension does its stuff. That, of course, is the Safari's greatest asset. Load your common or garden estate car to the limit and its nose-up attitude recalls a hard-charging powerboat. Citroën's solution automatically keeps you on the level even when, in the case of the new CX25 TRI, the payload's right up to its 1,543 lbs maximum.

The Llewellins camped in *real* style that summer – and the Safari's fuel consumption was just as astonishing as the kit-carting facet of its character. Initially convinced that the fuel gauge set new standards for optimism, I came to terms with the carefully-checked fact that we were averaging 38 mpg and could indeed cover the thick end of 600 miles before patronising the next diesel dispensary. Performance was not exactly dazzling on give-and-take roads with heavy traffic – a reminder that you can't have your *gateau* and eat it – but we cruised French motorways at 80 mph with quite a few healthy horses left in the stable.

Driving the newcomer was like greeting an old friend who had just been given a heart transplant. The most muscular Safari is fast – faster than quite a few so-called sports cars and allegedly hot little hatchbacks. Lift the bonnet and you find a very efficient 2.5-litre engine whose four cylinders, fed by a high-precision fuel injection system, develop a crisp 138 bhp at 5000 rpm allied to 155 lbs/ft of torque exactly 1000 revs lower down the scale. You tend to associate that sort of punch with engines quite a lot bigger.

But performance has not been achieved at the expense of smoothness, flexibility and the other down-to-earth characteristics essential for relaxed driving. In heavy, slow-moving traffic you can trickle along in fourth or fifth gear at no more than a sedate, economical 1000 rpm. When the situation improves, whipping down to second or third is like giving a thoroughbred a touch of the spurs.

Although standing-start times are really of little more than academic interest, they generally give a fair indication of a car's overall performance. It would have been unfair to pit the CX25 TRI against the stopwatch – it had barely 800 miles to its credit at the start of the week – but Citroën claim 0-100 kph in just 10.2 seconds. Switch to the more traditional, non-metric British yardstick and you can think in round-figure terms for the 0-60 mph dash. Swift indeed.

Top speed, unlike acceleration, is something that cannot be checked without resorting to a test track or Germany's limit-free motorways. Be that as it may, Citroën's figure of 121 mph must be in the right ballpark. It coincides almost exactly with the power curve's highest point if you are in the long-striding fifth gear which gives 23.9 mph for every 1000 rpm. The three-speed automatic, incidentally, provides 21.6 mph in top.

My first outing in the TRI was a reminder that the big Citroëns really are *different* in more ways than one. Styling sets them apart from the rest of the herd and is matched by characteristics that seem downright eccentric to complete strangers. Frank Sinatra's *My Way* would be the perfect theme song.

Let's put that into some sort of perspective. One aspect of my work involves driving more cars in a year than most people sample in a lifetime. This week's Rolls-Royce is exchanged for a 2CV which might be replaced by literally anything from a 150 mph showstopper to a mud-plugging monster with four-wheel drive. Each has its own distinct personality, but it rarely takes more than a mile or three to figure out what's what. Boil it *right* down to the bare bones and you realise that 99 per cent of the world's cars have a great deal in common from the driver's viewpoint. Citroën provides the most notable exceptions.

The unique VariPower steering, for instance, is almost certainly the most advanced system available, regardless of price. Although very light at low speeds – something you bless when wriggling in and out of tight parking spaces – its hydraulic circuits provide just the right amount of feel for fast, safe and effortless driving on the open road. It absorbs bumps and, unlike conventional power-assisted systems, reacts with the speed and precision of an Olympic fencing champion. You get the best of both worlds. But the way in which that single-spoke wheel self-centres does make it all feel somewhat strange until novelty gives way to familiarity. That is underlined by the fact that Citroën's PR department sends its road-test cars out complete with details about how the CX steering works.

In other words, potential buyers sampling a Safari for the first time should insist on more than the traditional quick spin round the block. It takes more than a couple of miles to get the hang of the system. When you do, the brilliance of Citroën's solution to the steering problem shines forth like a lighthouse.

Much the same can be said for the brakes. The rubber "mushroom" of the DS has given way to a conventional pedal, but activating the four powerful discs still involves pressure rather than two or three inches of movement. A gentle touch is all that's needed, not the hefty push that experience with other cars has probably programmed into your reactions.

One thing that grabs your attention even before the engine starts is the "flying saucer" housing the instruments and minor controls. I prefer conventional dials and needles to the revolving-drum speedometer and tachometer, but love the way Citroën's ergonomic experts put horn, lights, wipers and indicators within finger distance of the steering wheel's padded rim. In the words of my golf-mad younger son, it's as convenient as having the first tee on your front lawn. One thing the Safari does need, however, is a full-time wiper for the tailgate window, not one which rewards each press of the button with just four sweeps. In adverse conditions the glass gets mucky in a matter of only a few minutes.

My first two days with the CX25 TRI involved nothing more exciting than brief sorties in town traffic. Some cars feel bigger than they look and shred the nerves in such circumstances. The Safari "drives small" and belies its impressive overall dimensions with delightful agility. That was particularly good news when a five-star idiot left his vehicle a few feet behind me on a car park's no-go area. Getting out looked like a job for a heavy-duty helicopter, but the Safari was on its way home after a few twirls of the steering wheel.

So far, so good. But a car's true character is revealed on a long journey – ideally undertaken solo without the obligation to maintain a conversation. That's why I tiptoed from the house at seven o'shivering clock on a Saturday morning to drive from the border of North Wales to near Norwich and back by late afternoon. The main reason for the trip was simply to provide *Citroën* magazine with a realistic review of the CX25 TRI. Taking coffee with friends in rural Norfolk was nothing more than a bonus.

The warmth and comfort of the cloth-covered seat was swiftly supplemented by the lusty heater whose temperature lever, mounted between the front seats, goes right up to a toe-toasting 30 degrees Centigrade. Overtly comfortable seats often fail to impress after an hour or two, because the luxury is superficial. Speaking as one who has been living with a dorsal disaster area since 1965, I am well aware how quickly a spine can sag without proper support. Citroën's seats lived right up

The CX25 TRI Safari "drives small" and belies its impressive overall dimensions with truly delightful agility

to expectations, just as they had during that 2,000-mile holiday fortnight in 1979.

A lanky driver might like to slide his seat back another couple of inches, but yours truly – just on six feet tall, with short legs and a long body – had no complaints. The classic "sit behind yourself" check was equally satisfactory with about four inches of horizontal and vertical clearance.

Incidentally, the Safari also provides the versatility of a back seat whose folding options cater for one, two or three full-sized adults. Cutting the human element down to just the driver and a single passenger expands the superbly "clean" boot from 41.1 to 76.7 cubic feet. In the words of that old Eartha Kitt song about dreams of avarice, the Citroën is big enough to have a bowling alley in the back. Space allied with space-age suspension explains why so many Safaris are used as ambulances in their native land.

Powerful and long-striding, the TRI made light work of the outward run. So much so, in fact, that I lingered over an unscheduled breakfast and still arrived a good 30 minutes earlier than expected. It performed superbly on motorways, where 70 mph had the engine purring away at barely 2900 rpm, and would doubtless have been equally at ease going 50 per cent faster for hour after hour. On lesser roads, plenty of mid-range muscle, well-spaced gear ratios, razor-sharp steering, completely trustworthy brakes and Michelin TRX tyres made the going just as easy – and a lot more fun. You don't expect a capacious holdall to reward enthusiasm with such crisp, predictable handling.

The home-to-home average, including all stops, was exactly 49 mph. More miles on the clock, and a little less pressure on the accelerator pedal, would doubtless have spread each and every gallon over several more miles, but 26.16 mpg was excellent in the circumstances. It combined with a lot of stop-start running to give an overall figure of 22.41. Even more significant, in its own way, was the fact that packing 441 miles into 540 minutes left me feeling as fresh as the proverbial daisy. Fresh enough, if the truth be told, to enjoy a *very* prolonged and convivial dinner party that night.

A car that cossets you to that extent is worth its weight in gold. □

The sleek, shark-like styling is not just an eye-catching exercise in automobile cosmetics. It envelopes advanced technology, the luxury of a five-seater limousine and a small truck's ability to swallow loads

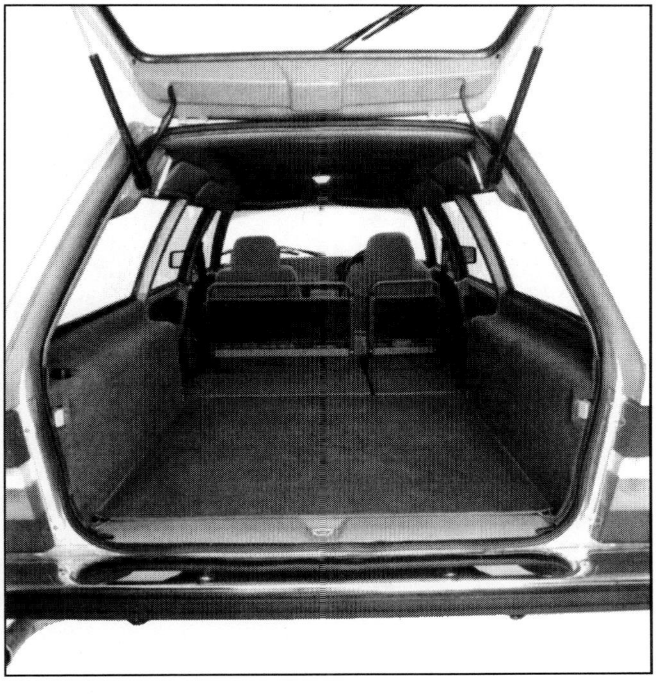

High roller

READERS' SURVEY

It's said that Citroens are bought only by Citroen fanatics, and to a large extent our survey bears this out, for just under 70 per cent of the replies came from drivers who had owned Citroens previously.

But the stereotyped owner was not quite so much in evidence; our drivers, mostly married and with two or three children were in a broad range of occupations, and there was not a single antique dealer in sight, and only one advertising man.

Clearly though, our drivers bought their CXs through their hearts rather than their heads because style, looks and design were by far the most important reasons for buying. The amount of interior space (in the case of the Safari models) was next on the list, and, interestingly, quite a few respondents bought a CX because they got a good deal on the car, though this alone confirmed their intention rather than being the sole reason for choosing Citroen.

That the CX is an excellent high mileage motorway car is also borne out in the mileage our drivers covered – a huge average of just under 27,000 miles per year from their Citroens.

Our file of readers prepared to take part in the survey stretched back to 1979, and although a number of readers no longer drove CXs, some returned their forms nevertheless – Citroen motoring is clearly not something you can give up easily!

Only 50 per cent of our readers bought their cars new, but at the same time coming on for 60% of the cars were bought by companies. The overwhelming majority of readers had their cars serviced and repaired by authorised agents, though a few brave souls were prepared to tackle the fearsome mechanics of the CX armed only with their own DIY skills.

NEARLY 70 PER CENT SAID THEY WOULD DEFINITELY BUY ANOTHER CITROEN CX

Citroen dealers generally fared reasonably well, though value for money did not rate highly in our readers' view, and neither did the poor spread of dealers, which was mentioned by a few respondents when asked how the Citroen network could be improved.

Our readers managed to return an average of 26 miles per gallon which seems pretty good compared to what we achieved, though inevitably the high of 32 miles per gallon was returned by a driver with a diesel powered CX.

We are pleased to report that despite the mechanical complexity which undoubtedly puts a lot of people off CXs, our readers' cars were on the whole pretty reliable, and the survey contained hardly any disgruntled owners who took the chance to air their grievances. With cars having covered over 100,000 miles (the highest was 154,000 miles, and another at 114,000 miles though on a replacement engine), there were the inevitable wide selection of faults, but not enough to build up a picture of any common trouble. We were particularly interested to find out how the suspension hydraulics fared over high mileages, and only one fault was recorded in this respect.

In our survey we asked readers to rate out of 10 various aspects of the car, and scoring notably high were 'Styling' (9.0), 'Ride Comfort' (9.6), 'Reliability' (8.8), and 'Brakes' (9.3). With 7-8 being about the average score from past survey experience, 'Ventilation' (5.1), and 'Gearchange' (6.7) were poor scores.

But perhaps the most telling response is that to the question: 'Would you buy another?' Nearly 70 per cent said they would definitely buy another CX which goes part of the way to bear out that motorists fall in love with Citroens once they are bitten with the bug. 18 per cent said definitely not, while 12 per cent were still undecided.

COSTS

Price	
List price, August 1981	£9559
Radio/cassette	£241
Sunroof and vinyl roof (fitted 1983)	£247
Delivery, plates	£100
Total	£10,147
Resale value, July 1984	£2400
Depreciation	£7747
Fuel consumption	
50,000 miles at 22 mpg, 4-star	£4007
Oil: negligible between services	
Servicing and repairs	
600, 5000 & 10,000 miles	£136
15,000 & 20,000 miles	£275
25,000 & 30,000 miles	£192
35,000 & 40,000 miles	£299
45,000 miles	£64
Tyres (three), plus one inner tube	£201
Brake pads (two sets)	£88
Radio repair	£56
Removal of body rust	£140
Light lens	£25
New number plate	£12
Standing charges	
Road tax (36 months)	£235
Insurance (36 months)	£445
Cost per mile over 50,000 miles	**27.8p**

PERFORMANCE

Max speed (mph)	109
0-40 mph (sec)	6.7
0-50 mph (sec)	8.8
0-60 mph (sec)	11.5
0-70 mph (sec)	14.3

Insurance is for 35-year-old married man living in medium risk area, clean licence, full discount, insured and spouse driving only. Quote supplied by Taylor Price & Co, London WC1.

Is Citroen's reputation as a maker of big, expensive cars still justified? We spent three years with their top of the range CX to find out for ourselves

Ever since the revolutionary *Traction Avant* made its appearance just over 50 years ago, Citroen have had a reputation for adventurous engineering and technical sophistication. Their often lovably eccentric creations have gone off at a complete tangent to mainstream motoring design thought, and have in the process gathered a particularly devoted and die-hard following.

But Citroen's very different approach to design has more often than not resulted in cars which have been mechanically very complex, and therefore *very* expensive to run. It was with this knowledge that six years ago *What Car?* decided to run a couple of big Citroens; firstly a CX Safari, and then after it a CX Pallas Injection saloon. Were they reliable? Were they as expensive as people had predicted they would be?

The first machine did in fact prove to be reliable though certainly not cheap to run; every time it went into a garage for the slightest attention the bill was almost enough to keep a Mini Metro running for a year, and the huge beast had an unquenchable thirst for fuel, giving us a best of only 18 mpg overall.

Our second CX has now covered 50,000 miles since we bought it in August 1981 at a cost of £9559. It too, has proved very reliable. We went for the then newly announced Pallas Injection auto, as the availability of a genuine automatic transmission promised relief from two fairly awful CX characteristics: a heavy vague clutch with too quick an engagement, and a terrible gearchange. This transmission, fans of the marque would no doubt contend, was far too 'conventional' for Citroen, as it replaced the previous 'C-Matic' arrangement, a system where the clutch was electrically disengaged as soon as the top of the gear lever was touched.

A total of 50,000 miles has certainly proved that we made the right choice in going for the automatic version instead of the five-speed manual, as it is much easier to drive in town where our CX covers much of its mileage. Getting used to Citroen's Vari-power steering does not take long, but we know from extended use of other CXs that the manual clutch and gearchange do not really become second nature, and are a real bind in stop-start traffic.

Moreover, the big four-cylinder engine of 2347cc, fuel-injected to give 128 bhp, is well suited to an auto box. It pulls smoothly and strongly from low revs ('a lusty beast', as its owner describes it), and the box tactfully changes up a gear before the top-end harshness can ever become apparent. This engine has since then been enlarged to 2.5 litres, 138 bhp.

Hydropneumatic suspension is of course a Citroen innovation, and a feature which so delights enthusiasts of these cars. Fed by high pressure hydraulics, the system is self-levelling and each wheel is independently sprung, giving a marvellous ride which is also a very even one. The CX rides well even on bad surfaces; on good roads the ride is very nearly as good as an airliner.

But the CX is not simply a boulevard cruiser with no roadholding. Wind it up into tight bends and it grips the road surprisingly well, with even a slight 'chuckable' feel to it. The long suspension travel however, results in a fair degree of body roll.

We find that the saloon, with its wheelbase shorter than the Safari's, seems to have slightly better handling, feeling generally more stable on the road – particularly at high speeds. And, having had two CXs now, our owner is a fan of the hydropneumatic suspension: "It makes more sense to have Citroen's system than any other," he declares without hesitation.

Steering and brakes are interconnected to the suspension system, running off the same hydraulics. The steering, as the Vari-power name suggests, has variable assistance. At parking speeds the steering is finger light, while on the move the amount of power assistance decreases until at motorway cruising speeds there is hardly any at all. Gearing is very high; at less than three full turns lock to lock it can lead to a sharper than anticipated cornering action until the driver becomes familiar with the car.

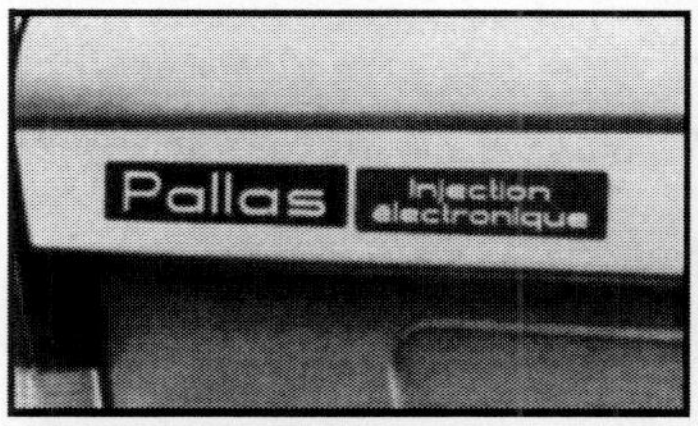

Injection engine (above) is well matched to three-speed automatic: roadholding is good but body roll can be disturbing to passengers

Likewise, brakes require getting used to and it's fair to say that they are not ideally weighted for a variety of road conditions. In town the four discs require merely a brush on the pedal to make the 25 cwt car stop on near enough a sixpence, though one can soon become used to this. What's a little more tricky is stopping, or even simply slowing down a little from high speeds. The tendency is to apply too much pressure to the pedal, causing driver and passenger to rocket forward, straining against seat belts, and giving the driver in the car behind a worrying moment.

Volumes have been written on whether or not the unique configuration and design of the CX is better or worse than more conventional cars, but it's a pointless argument; those who don't like it will not have a CX as a gift, while others will drive nothing else. Our driver is among the latter, and now that *What Car?* is about to sell the CX and replace it with something else (and less adventurous), it's an interesting time to take a look back and see how the CX has fared against rivals since its introduction almost 10 years ago.

The hydropneumatic suspension, shared with the GS, has stood the test of time well, and in fact is a feature which gives few reliability problems on CXs; ours has been perfect. The car rides better than most modern rivals, though automotive development costs have meant that most manufacturers have now gone for as simple a system as possible, struts and torsion axles for example, rather than follow Citroen's example. Only companies such as Mercedes-Benz have invested a fortune to develop a sophisticated suspension system.

AT 50,000 MILES THE CX IS IN GOOD FETTLE: WE KNOW THERE IS NOTHING NASTY LOOMING ON THE MECHANICAL FRONT

Aerodynamics? Citroen certainly showed the way back in the early '70s, though again other manufacturers have gone off in a different direction. The cigar-shaped CX (with a drag factor of 0.37) has given way to initially rather odd looking wedges such as the Audi 100, Ford Sierra, and even the Mercedes-Benz 190.

We always praised the facia arrangement of the CX with its well placed controls which can be touched without lifting either hand off the steering wheel. This seems to be one area where few competitors have dared to tread; they prefer to play safe and avoid designing a facia which is ergonomically advanced but might put off buyers on looks alone.

On the other hand we have always said that the CX's instruments are difficult to read, and rather ironically some of the most up-to-the minute electronic dashboards around at the moment frankly are little improvement. But not to be deterred from their path, Citroen have persevered with the rotating-drum units for their most recent BX model.

Although automatic, our CX has shown a more modest appetite for fuel than its predecessor. Whereas we never saw 20 mpg on the Safari, we have very rarely dropped below the 20 mpg mark in the Pallas and generally count on obtaining between 20 and 27 mpg, depending on whether the car is being driven in town or country conditions. This improvement is no doubt thanks largely to the greater precision in the fuelling from the Bosch injection system.

It would be putting it too strongly to say that our CX Pallas still feels like new after 50,000 miles and three years on the road, but the car is still in very good shape. Apart from a couple of little rust spots (which we will come to later) and a driver's door which, after being swung back too forcibly on its hinges on a couple of occasions, opens and shuts with a spine-jarring crack, there is little to mention.

The steering wheel has become a little shiny and none too pleasant to hold, and there are a few scuff marks here and there which cars inevitably gather over time. But the soft seats have lost none of their posture and remain as comfortable as ever.

Our car was fitted with a slide-back fabric sunroof relatively recently; this was a worthwhile investment of £250 because writing this report in the height of summer reminded us of just how poor the ventilation is, and sliding back the roof is a much better way of obtaining fresh air. Weather permitting, the generally wide and long opening of the sunroof also makes the rather claustrophobic interior of the CX feel a little more airy. Buffeting is rarely a problem.

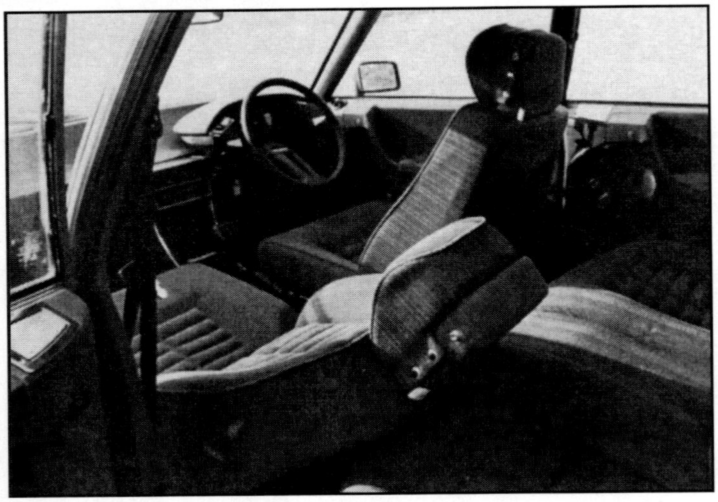

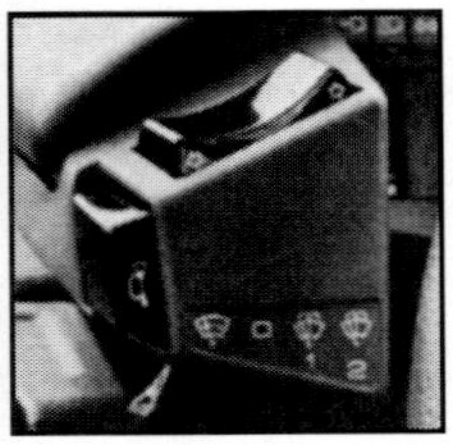

Ride is superb but interior feels less spacious than rivals; outlandish dashboard works well. Dismal ventilation was helped by sunroof fitment

SERVICING, RELIABILITY

The file on our CX contains 23 assorted invoices and statements. That's how many times the car has been in for servicing and repairs in its 50,000 miles with us, though in fact it has only let us down once when a fuel metering component blocked, a part which was replaced under warranty.

The Citroen's service schedule consists of a major stop at 10,000 miles and an intermediary oil change at 5000 miles. Roughly speaking our car has paid about one visit to a garage in between these scheduled stops. All our regular servicing has been satisfactorily performed by E.S. Motors of Ashford, Middlesex, though they surely recognise our car by now, after our six years of custom!

In garage visits alone, we have paid out £2091 to keep our Citroën running, though £241 for an elaborate Pioneer radio/cassette can be knocked off, as can a further £247 which we paid for the full-length fabric sunroof plus a matching vinyl roof.

The initial 600 mile service cost us £13.94, and the following 5000 mile service was £17.42. At that time, and naturally under warranty, we asked E.S. Motors to look into why the engine stalled when idling in reverse. There was also a squeak and an oil leak from the engine plus rattles from the dash, and a door trim cover not fitting properly. All this additional work was carried out satisfactorily, though to this day the engine is a little lumpy when idling in anything apart from neutral, giving the impression it is just about to stall.

By 9000 miles the CX had eaten its way through a set of brake pads – first of five sets to date. This job set us back £47.67.

The 10,000 mile service was a straightforward affair totalling £104.50 (labour rates £12.50 per hour); labour and parts costing £84.12, lubricants £6.75 and the rest VAT. Just over two months later the car was back at E.S. Motors for another set of front brake pads which this time were fitted for £40.64.

THE CAR HAS NEVER LET US DOWN APART FROM THE TIME THE FUEL INJECTION PLAYED UP DURING THE WARRANTY PERIOD

At 15,000 miles another intermediate service was carried out and the total came to £90.40. But £50 of this is accounted by the purchase of a child's safety seat. Still under warranty, the failed horn was fixed.

Next stop was Tyreservices Great Britain who sold us a front tyre and balanced it for £54.10. Rather than buy a pair and throw away the other tyre which had about 1000 miles left on it, we fitted the brand new spare to match the one we bought and slung the old one under the bonnet.

By the time the next major service stop was due at 20,000 miles, the CX was ready for brake pads set number three, plus a replacement set for the rear discs. Otherwise the service was routine, yet we picked up a bill of £184.83. That's more like the bills one associates with CXs we thought, though in fact service bills since then have been more.

After a few months it was time to have a 25,000 service, and we asked for the brake pads to be checked. But we were lucky; they still had some life in them. The total was £32.91, which included adjusting the handbrake. After a trouble-free 5000 miles (apart from the need to replace a light lens, costing £24.55) it was once again 30,000 major service time, and yes, once again time for some more new brake pads, plus a set of handbrake pads. Total cost was £159.

The next service at 35,000 miles, which included adjusting the handbrake again, cost £102.47, but that amount included £66 for fitting rear inertia seat belts – a lesson to us all!

More tyres were needed so we decided to boost Tyreservices' profits a little more. This time there was no spare to use, so we had to buy a pair.

Soon after this came some attention which was the first sign of middle age for our Citroën. Around the bottom of all four doors were areas of rust which by this time, almost two years to the day after we bought the car, were beginning to look worrying. We took the patient to Goodwins, an engineering concern in Enfield who wire brushed the rust, resprayed the metal and renewed the lower door seals. This work cost us £140, but we are sorry to report that only eight months later the rust appears to have re-invaded the door.

The 40,000 service brought us our all time peak bill of £197.70, and looking back over the records there is no extra work save the inevitable front brake pads, which knocked up the total. Parts alone came to £73.90 and labour was £86.80. The rest was made up of lubricants and VAT.

Prior to the 45,000 service there have been a number of small points on the CX which have needed attention; headlamps out of adjustment, a tendency to pull to the right, a new electrical regulator (cost £63.35), and the radio not working. Shortly before service time we bought another tyre at a cost to our budget of £58.26.

Low sill allows boxy boot to load easily

The last service we have had to date (the 50,000 service being too late for inclusion here) was the 45,000 attention which would have passed off quietly and cheaply had it not been for the driver's door lock bearing. The barrel of the lock failed and we needed a replacement plus, of course, a new key. We paid £64 for this work plus the service, and now, irritatingly, have two separate keys for the two front doors, though central locking means it is not a problem.

Our CX will have had its 50,000 service as you read this, and with a slightly dead feeling brake pedal the last time we drove it, we are willing to bet that a new set of brake pads will be needed. However, the CX's hunger for brake pads is understandable – an automatic 25 cwt car is not an easy beast to slow.

The second part of this section – 'reliability' is a very short one simply because the car has not let us down apart from the time when the fuel injection played up during the warranty period. The car has always been a good starter, hot or cold, and unlike some, has showed no tendency to go off tune in between services.

At this stage in the CX's career, just as it is about to go and spend its middle years with a new (and hopefully well-heeled) owner the Citroën is in good fettle. We know there is nothing nasty looming on the mechanical front, and apart from that door rust, and a couple of small scrapes on the body, it looks clean.

CONCLUSION

We have enjoyed driving our Citroën very much for the last three years, but had it not been run through a company then it is doubtful whether the driver would have derived so much pleasure. Apart from the bank-breaking bills, a look at second-hand prices reveals rather horrifyingly that our £9559 purchase of three years ago is now worth less than £3000 and could fetch even less than £2000.

Compare this to the much higher prices that an equivalent Mercedes-Benz or BMW of the same year would fetch, and the clear message is that you have to really enjoy driving a Citroën CX to justify the purchase.

It's also difficult not to look at more recent executive cars we have run – an Audi 100 CD for example – and just compare the running costs. The Citroën has very much big-car running costs while the Audi can be run for almost the cost of a more modest machine.

That, however, is the coldly logical approach to assessing executive cars, and we prefer not to stick to it too strictly. Even after almost a decade the CX still has a lot going for it, and those who are prepared to pay the inevitably high running costs should enjoy colourful and character-filled motoring, something of a rare treat these days.

THE FASTEST MAN ON FOUR WHEELS

Citroën magazine salutes **Thrust 2**, *latest in a long line of British-built four-wheeled vehicles to bring home the land speed record. Richard Noble's amazing 630+mph, exceeded that of the last British holder, Donald Campbell in* **Bluebird**, *by over 200mph.*

Although Citroën had no part to play in either of these record breaking feats, it's interesting to note that **Bluebird**, *the 1964 world-beater, had hydropneumatic suspension not dissimilar to Citroëns. Even more interesting are the unique parallels between* **Thrust 2** *and current Citroën models, particularly GSA and CX, factors which play a significant part in their superb straight-line stability. Long wheelbase, for instance. The GSA and CX wheelbases are longer than those of competitive models.* **Thrust 2's** *rear wheels are actually mounted behind the body and the front wheels as far forward as possible. The centre of gravity in* **Thrust 2** *is well forward similar to that in the GSA and CX. Vital for good aerodynamic stability. But perhaps the most striking common feature is the rear wheel location geometry. The trailing arm rear suspension used in* **Thrust 2** *is, as its designer John Ackroyd confirmed, identical to that used on all current Citroën models. This means that absolutely no bump steer is generated through suspension movement – very important, especially for Richard Noble: for the faster the vehicle travels obviously the more serious the effects of bump steer would be.*

It seemed like a good idea to invite this speed-hero of the moment to test drive the newest addition to the CX range, the CX DTR. A challenge he accepted with the kind of enthusiasm and style "England expects" from the fastest man on four wheels.

RICHARD NOBLE TESTS THE CX25 DTR TURBO

I WAS REALLY SORRY TO HAND back the DTR Turbo, as I grew to like the car. In fact I had been looking forward to testing it because, never having driven a Citroën or a diesel before, I wanted to experience Citroën's advanced and original engineering for myself.

First, a quick preflight check. This DTR is beautifully finished in Neptune Grey, a green/grey metallic – and I could find no sign of paint flaw or orange peel. The tyres are the wide Michelin TRX 190/65HR 390s and they do a good job, for I couldn't spin the wheels, even in the wet. The sculptured alloy wheels are pleasantly attractive and functional. There are well-placed toe points at the front and rear. Under the surprisingly light and well insulated bonnet, the 2500cc diesel is mounted transversely ahead of the driveline with the 5 speed gearbox to its rear and right.

The turbocharger is an AiResearch unit, mounted forward of the engine, thus shielding the driver and passengers from the turbo whine. An 88 amp/hour battery provides plenty of reserve for those cold morning starts – but I found that the engine always started with the first twist of the key. The engine layout is very neat and clean, with excellent accessibility for such a complex installation.

Next, into the driving seat, which is superbly comfortable with good leg room provided. The brake and clutch pedals are small and neat (just as I like them) – but the accelerator is positioned too high and too far to the right for me to heel and toe. The standard of finish inside is exceptional, with excellent rear seats, good leg room all round and considerable comfort. A great deal of original thinking has gone into the design, particularly with the interior lights and the beautifully engineered heater/temperature controls which are light and simple to operate, being positioned where an airline pilot might find his throttles. I also like the neutral grey interior colour which is relaxing and not distracting.

The engine starts immediately, even with very heavy frost all over the car, and there is little sign of diesel chatter, rattle or smell after the engine has warmed. The speedo and the rev counter are of the vertical drum type, which take a lot of getting used to. With needle and dial-type indicators, a quick glance gives the needle positions and readings – but with drums you have to read the figures, which takes longer. Most cars today are fitted with the column stalk type indicators – the DTR has rocker switches which take some getting used to. But, I am sure that it is the better system because the switch is always to hand and to actuate it you don't have to remove your hand from the wheel.

As I am over 6ft tall, I tend to find many driving positions uncomfortable – but the Citroën accommodated me well. My only criticism is that with the seat correctly adjusted, I found the gear lever throw too long, putting 1st, 3rd and 5th at the limit of my forward reach. Also the driver's armrest is mounted some 6" too low on the door, thus failing to provide good elbow location – something I discovered to be vitally important on *Thrust 2*.

Driving the DTR takes quite a bit of personal adjustment. Basically the engine develops max Torque at 2,000 rpm and max bhp at

RICHARD NOBLE TESTING THE CX25 DTR TURBO

▶ 3,700. In practice, I found it best to use the rev range of 2000 to 3,250 RPM, which gives plenty of power and acceleration, but does require frequent gear shifting. The shift was tight and fatiguing initially, especially as I found it difficult to make a clean change from 2nd to 3rd – but during the test either it or I loosened up and it became more acceptable.
Considering that driving the turbo diesel requires more gear changing, I would have preferred a small, light gear stick with which one could flick through the gears, keeping the engine revs between 2,000 and 3250 rpm.
Driving extensively and hard in London, I found I could out-accelerate almost all but the most determined traffic, but I found it difficult to gauge the car's width due to the high window/body waistline, and length because of the invisible nose. The rear spoiler helps with high speed adhesion, but I felt that it slightly reduced rearward vision. All this meant that I couldn't thread the car through the London traffic with quite the agility of my MG Metro – but then the DTR is more of a high speed/ comfort tourer.
The brakes are excellent and well-matched to the tyres. I was never able to lock a wheel in the wet and the brake pedal always had a good solid feel – which I believe is artificial, but that

"I am amazed that Citroën has been able to get such performance from a diesel – achieved not only with excellent mpg figures (49.6mpg at 56mph) – but without any diesel rattle"

doesn't matter for it was backed up with good brake efficiency.

All modern cars have a self-centering action built into the steering geometry – but with the Citroën this is an hydraulic function, which is very powerful. In fact, I like the Varipower steering's artificial feel which kept pace well with speed.

Overtaking required a special technique, which was simple in essence. It is most important to have 2,000 rpm on the clock before pulling out, otherwise you will waste time changing gear on the far side of the road. The tremendous surge of power at this rpm ensures overtaking is smooth and speedy.

The large central wiper which also includes the washer fluid jet shows the rest of the motor industry the way to go. One wipe with the water applied over the whole screen is sufficient to clean it, and there are no tiny high pressure jets to clog. Another well-thought-out feature is the lamp which lights the ignition keyhole – just switch on the sidelights and the keyhole is well illuminated.

Due to my rather chaotic lifestyle at the moment, I was not able to get the DTR onto a track to test high speed adhesion – but travelling fast on a wet and winding road, despite the Citroën roll, the car held the road like a leech – and gave me tremendous confidence. In fact I found it difficult to break away either front or rear wheels, though this could be done with a more vicious manoeuvre than I was prepared to try on the road.

Incidentally, at speed there was no evidence of noise or rattle from the body, an indication of the high quality build standard.

I am amazed that Citroën has been able to get such performance from a diesel – achieved not only with excellent mpg figures (49.6 mpg at 56 mph) but without diesel rattle. If you do hear a rattle – it's the truck in front of you!

So quiet is the engine that you wouldn't even know that it is a Turbo, since there is no compressor whine at all. It makes it just that little bit harder to remember to idle the engine for a few seconds before switching off – just to ensure that the turbocharger is well lubricated.

This week, I've just heard that the Guild of Motoring Writers has awarded the 1983 Top Car Award (the Guild's accolade of excellence) to Citroën for the BX which is praise indeed from the many critical writers who drive just about everything on four wheels.

As for the DTR, it took a bit of getting used to, but I enjoyed it and like the motoring writers, have learned a great deal from Citroën. □

Photographs Nigel Arter

Colour matched bumpers and alloy wheels distinguish the Turbo version from lesser models

Fastest Citroen CX to date

Description and driving impressions of the new 136 mph CX GTi Turbo which Andrew Kirk has been testing on the French and German highways and byways

Citroen's most powerful version of the long serving CX, the GTi Turbo, is to be launched in the UK at the Motor Show and is likely to go on sale soon after. We were fortunate enough to sample the cigar shaped projectile on a recent trip to Bavaria. In simple terms Citroen engineers have fitted a turbocharger to the current production 2.5 litre engine, but in reality there are a number of other modifications that have been made to make the car more able to handle the extra power safely.

In full turbo dress, the exterior changes include discreet badges on front wings and boot, plus the addition of a not-so-discreet 'T' badge on the bonnet bulge. An unusual design of rear spoiler with two clear plastic sections — to aid rear visibility — is fitted, along with semi-flush fitting alloy wheels shod with low profile Michelin TRX tyres that carry 210/55 VR 390 dimensions. These are the widest tyres fitted to any production Citroen, but they certainly do not look out of place. Both the wider footprint rubber and large door mirrors are effective in raising the drag co-efficient, but the addition of the rear spoiler has brought the figure down to Cd 0.36 — the same as for the normally aspirated CX.

Under bonnet urge comes via the reworked four cylinder engine that now benefits from a Garrett turbocharger combined with Bosch fuel injection. Power output has gone up from 138bhp of the previous GTi to 168bhp for the Turbo and, with it, an impressive maximum torque figure of 217 lb.ft at only 3,250 rpm. This figure is only marginally less than that of the V8 engined Rover Vitesse and understandably Citroen are very proud of the fact that their 'four' has the pulling power of an 'eight'. It clearly shows the benefits that can be had from forced induction and is a point that has been so clearly demonstrated in Formula 1 racing.

Deceptively quick

Performance is deceptively quick. Acceleration is slightly better — at least on paper — than its nearest rival the Audi 200 Turbo, with 0-60 mph taking only 8 seconds. This is coupled to an impressive top end speed of 136 mph — again better than the Rover, but not quite as good as the Audi's 142 mph.

The Garrett T3 equipped engine features a reduced compression ratio to 7.75:1, has modified combustion chambers and is fitted with flat crowned pistons with reduced surface area to give benefits in cooling. These constitute the major internal changes while other tweeks have included reducing the size of the inlet manifold in an attempt to improve engine response and thereby reduce turbo lag. The maximum boost pressure of 8psi is controlled by

Left: Engine cut-away Cast iron block with alloy head are modified to handle turbo installation. Compression is reduced from 8.75:1 of the GTi to 7.75:1

Right: Turbocharger installation 1. spring, 2. valve, 3. exhaust gas directed to turbocharger, 4. exhaust by-pass channel, 5. turbine housing, 6. turbine wheel, 7. diaphragm, 8. compressor, A & B, boost pressure control via adjustable wastegate

New

Citroen CX GTi Turbo

a conventional wastegate arrangement that also allows the pressure to rise at lower engine speeds to give increased torque. A knock sensor is responsible for controlling detonation and retards the solid state electronic ignition system accordingly.

No intercooler

Oddly, by current trends, the turbocharged engine is not intercooled. There are two main reasons why this has not happened, the first due to a lack of underbonnet space and the second that the engine is not stressed to a point whereby detonation is a problem for the knock sensor to handle. This more complex system is preferred to a simpler pressure retard distributor since it is quicker acting and has the capacity to detect detonation and adjust the ignition accordingly within one power stroke.

The engine conversion appears to work well and the power comes in smoothly in one long surge right up to maximum revs. As one might expect with so much power going through the front wheels, caution is required in the wet when applying the throttle as wheelspin is easily provoked when the turbo comes in. Keeping the car under control in such a situation is made worse by the lack of feel through the power assisted steering.

Accelerate hard in fifth gear and you are immediately aware of the impressive torque characteristics of the big four. It will pull from under 20 mph in this gear up to the maximum speed. We managed 130.1 mph on a deserted stretch of autobahn, and Citroen's 136 mph claim appears realistic enough given a longer run up. It gets to the maximum 6,000 rpm in the first four gears without too much problem whilst our maximum in fifth corresponded to 5,510 rpm — just over peak power of 5,000 rpm.

Twin exhaust pipes and distinctive rear spoiler are other GTi Turbo trademarks. Spoiler has clear plastic sections to aid rear visibility

Motorway cruiser

The engine characteristics make it ideally suited to fast motorway cruising and this is where the Citroen really felt at ease, but the more highly stressed engine has had a marked effect on fuel economy. We could only muster 19.6 mpg overall after our three hour stint behind the wheel, whilst certain other lead footed journalists recorded a meagre 14 mpg. Citroen's claim of 20.2 mpg for the urban cycle ought to be possible driven at a more leisurely pace, but even so this is still quite a thirsty machine.

The CX Turbo scores more points with its beautifully stable behaviour at speed. This particular aspect is no doubt aided by the good aerodynamics, low centre of gravity and the parallel suspension layout that allows all four wheels to rise and fall vertically without any camber change. There is precious little wind noise even when pushing the maximum speed and engine noise has been slightly reduced over the previous GTi by a slight change in the gear ratios to allow the engine to turn at lower revs. Road noise is perhaps more noticeable as a result of the excellent sound insulation overall.

The ride is typically soft; the car wallows a fair bit, but it is impressive how the bumps are soaked up before reaching the interior, and once accustomed to the cushioning effects of the gas suspension, there is little to better Citroen's Hydropneumatic system. Thicker front and rear anti-roll bars feature on the Turbo version, as do revised damper rates, though the car still rolls a fair amount when cornering hard.

The ultra-sensitive power steering is something uniquely Citroen and takes considerable time to adjust to. The wheels turn for only the slightest steering action and this particular aspect, combined with a remarkable lack of feel, can leave the driver guessing as to which way the wheels are pointing. The power steering has built in self centring which also works when the car is stationary and even with the ignition off due to the remaining pressure in the system.

Sensitive brakes

This same over-sensitive feel is also apparent with the four-wheel disc brakes. The fronts are ventilated and the system has little difficulty in slowing the 3,053 lb motor car from any chosen speed, but the amount of pedal pressure required to achieve full deceleration is very light and pedal movement at most is only around ¼in. Inevitably you adjust your driving style in time but in a panic stop and especially in the wet, locking is all too easy.

Inside, the overall layout is similar to the normally aspirated CX and as such is very neat and well thought out. Six conventional style pointer type gauges in a revised dashboard layout are responsible for the important engine functions and lights, indicators and wipers are grouped at either side of the wheel — in typical Citroen fashion — and within reach of your fingers.

The interior trim, in dark grey and black is a little claustrophobic, but echoes the restrained sports image that the Turbo certainly conveys. Seats are velour trimmed, have armchair styling, give similar armchair location and are very comfortable over long distances, but do lack lateral support.

Citroen's GTi Turbo is obviously aimed at the top end of the market and providing the price is right — still to be announced but expected to be around £12,500 — stands to take a fair number of customers away from Audi, Rover and other makes in this sector of the market.

On paper the Citroen looks a worthy adversary and after our brief drive it struck us as an ideal motorway car. It is less happy on country lanes due to rather cumbersome proportions and the fact that the power comes in when you don't want it to as a result of the inevitable turbo lag, but on the open road, the big Citroen is as impressively quick as it is quiet and refined

Michelin TRX low profile radials are standard fitment. Turbo badges feature on front wings

CX SLICK

Citroën's new CX GTi Turbo bows in as the swiftest car from the Paris-based purveyors of the double chevron since the Maserati-engined SM. With a claimed top speed of 136 mph and acceleration to match, it's hunting in Audi 200 Turbo territory. David Vivian went to Bavaria to drive it

CITROËN ONCE made a supercar. Powered by a 2.7-litre Maserati quad-cam V6, assisted by high-pressure hydraulics of formidable technical complexity and capable of outrunning a Jensen Interceptor on the *autobahn*, it was the most extravagantly-specified car ever to wear the double chevrons. If it was a surfeit of sophistication that killed off the SM (some say prematurely), its memory is significant: with a top speed of around 137 mph for the later injected model it has remained, by a wide margin, the swiftest Citroën ever made.

That it should remain so *in memoriam*, however, is not in the current Citroën script. Although the executive car sector has contracted in recent years, it remains a lucrative pocket of trading for car makers with the models to exploit it. Upmarket contenders include Audi's 200 Turbo, Renault's R25 V6 Injection, BMW's 528i and Opel's Senator in whose company Citroën's seven-year-old executive express (the 120 mph CX GTi) is simply out of its depth. Aspirations to compete effectively in the upper echelons of this class demanded a new Citroën flagship which would have given the old SM a run for its money.

The CX GTi Turbo makes its international debut at the Paris Salon this month. Essentially the logical turbo development of Citroën's fleetest CX, the big news is under the bonnet, where the installation of Garrett's widely-used T3 turbocharger boosts power by 22 per cent (168 bhp against 138 bhp) and torque by an impressive 40 per cent at a lower engine speed (217 lb ft at 3,250 rpm against 155 lb ft at 4,000 rpm). The performance claims are equally big-league: 136 mph and a sub-8 second 0-60 mph time.

Engineered for optimum mid-range flexibility rather than ultimate power — 144 lb ft of torque is available at a mere 1500 rpm — the boost pressure curve peaks (0.57 bar) relatively low in the rev range at 3250 rpm, which coincides with maximum torque. Boost pressure drops progressively thereafter so that at peak power (5000 rpm) it has already fallen to 0.43 bar. As with the normally aspirated version of this 2.5-litre "four", fuel is supplied by Bosch L-Jetronic injection which also limits the maximum engine speed to 6000 rpm by cutting off the fuel supply. A sensor on the turbocharger does the same thing if boost pressure builds too high through a wastegate failure, while the solid-state electronic ignition system is fully mapped and incorporates a knock sensor which alters the timing at the onset of detonation.

The Hydropneumatic suspension common to all CX models has been uprated to cut down body lean in fast cornering by stiffening the damping and increasing the diameter of the front and rear anti-roll bars. For sharper steering responses and better grip 210/55 VR 390 Michelin TRXs on new 150 TR "run-flat" alloy wheels are fitted, the latter incorporating larger air scoops on the front for improved brake cooling.

Appearances count for a lot in this market, and Citroën has spared no effort in seeking to endow the familiar but still modernistic CX shape with a "new identity" in keeping with its elevated class position. The rather ugly rubber tailgate spoiler is at least distinctive and, according to the wind tunnel boffins, helps to compensate for the GTi Turbo's wider wheels, maintaining the drag factor at a respectable 0.36. More successful aesthetically are the disc-type alloy wheels, the colour-keyed bumpers, the black window trims and the discreet "Turbo" badging. Inside, black velour is the over-riding theme but, more remarkable, is an instrument display composed

SM QUICK

Above: Shock horror — a host of conventional dials clearly marked and easy to read

entirely of conventional dials and gauges, clearly marked and easy to read. The reasoning behind this recant is rooted in the desire to give the more "sporting" driver likely to buy the GTi Turbo a level of information incompatible with Citroën's usual style of avant-garde instrument presentation. It sounds like a sell-out to me, but the conventional approach will suit most people just fine.

The seats are comfortable and supportive in the soft and all-enveloping way that has become a CX hallmark; they are particularly effective at absorbing what few vertical disturbances slip through to the cabin after the superbly supple and controlled Hydropneumatic suspension has effectively flattened the worst of the bumps. The GTi Turbo may have more roll stiffness than its normally-aspirated stablemate — which, incidentally, it will sell alongside rather than replace — but its overall standards of comfort remain among the very best.

On the other hand, the GTi Turbo's handling — while surefooted and predictable — doesn't seem notably crisper than that of the ordinary GTi. The artificial-feel power steering still needs smooth handling if the car isn't to lurch untidily through a bend, and understeer is the predominant characteristic in tighter turns. What the modifications have wrought, however, is a much more neutral cornering balance in fast medium-radius bends: ultimately this Citroën will oversteer, and on the drenched twisting roads of Bavaria chosen for our test drive you needed to be finely attuned to this fact if progress wasn't to be punctuated by a series of tail wriggles.

My particular test car had covered only 3,500 km and was obviously still a little tight. Even so, it didn't feel anything like as quick as Citroën claim. While endowed with bags of mid-range urge for overtaking — as, indeed, you would expect with 217 lb ft of torque at 3250 rpm — its top-end urge was disappointing, the engine running out of breath well before the 6000 rpm red-line and simply refusing to push the Citroën along any faster than 204 kph (127 mph) on the flat. In fact, our best downhill reading of 132 mph was still 4 mph adrift of Citroën's top speed claim. While I'm willing to believe that my test car would have been faster with more miles under its belt, I think it unlikely that it would improve by the required amount.

No matter. The GTi Turbo will keep up 120 mph-plus averages on the autobahn with so little effort that the ulimate lack of Audi 200 Turbo chasing ability seems less than crucial.

Citroën plan to make 5000 GTi Turbos in 1985, of which 50 per cent will be exported. It goes on sale in France on October 1 for 137,000 francs (£11,913).

The distinctive Citroen CX gains a fuel injected 2500cc engine to add polish to the prestige. But it's still a car that demands the driver's familiarity as we discovered with the CX 25 GTi.

FAMILIARITY BREEDS CONTENT

With a seemingly never-ending stream of new arrivals, motorists would appear to be virtually swamped for choice in almost every class of vehicle. And with similar thought processes determining the development of rival vehicles they tend to offer 'packages' that are so similar that determining which is preferable often boils down to 'nit picking'. For attempting to satisfy the widest possible market means playing safe. Few manufacturers want to go out on a limb and offer a 'love it or hate it' car.

Citroen would seem to be one of this select group, with their CX range being arguably their most daring offering of recent years. Familiarity with the CX's distinctive form has dulled the model's visual impact, it is true. But more detailed study quickly reveals the extent to which the CX differs from the norm. It is an oddball — and proud of it!

Stepping down into a Citroen CX is the starting point in a process of re-education. For with the hydropneumatic suspension only activated once the engine is running, the car sits low and dead when not in use. Start the front mounted four cylinder engine and the hydraulic accumulator is set in motion. The steering and brakes are brought to life. The suspension is awoken from its deep slumber and the car begins to rise.

One's astonishment with the long-lived French executive saloon is compounded as one moves under way. The steering seems incredibly light, emitting strange hydraulic noises as it gleefully returns itself to straight ahead. The all-disc brakes seem wildly over-enthusiastic, while the driving controls seem too bizarre to comprehend. Indeed, one cannot help but pity the unfortunate salesman faced with the task of impressing a first-time CX driver, for there are so many wild differences from conventional saloons that one suspects that many motorists simply flee in terror!

Though such a feeling of disorientation among newcomers is easily understandable, a brief test drive is perhaps the cruellest fate. For only when one has become accustomed to the idiosyncracies of the CX can one evaluate it fairly. That's not to say that once understood the CX is *bound* to be loved (it's far too peculiar for that!) but rather that the CX has its own distinct personality that one must come to terms with. Like a person with a strong character, the CX genuinely demands 'Love it or hate it' — and for one member of our testing team at least, it was definitely the former.

The CX's distinct nature is revealed most clearly inside its unusual passenger compartment. Few could take exception to such delightful details as the sun visors above the rear windows, the rear head rests, the soft (if perhaps too short) cushioning, the individual map reading lights, the retractable rear screen slats and the superb provision of a light and spacious environment for rear seat passengers. Few could dislike the extensive sophistication of the front compartment, either. On the roof they will find a marvellous central light, a swivelling map reading light and a push-button switch for the heated rear window. In the central seat divider they will find fore and aft rocker switches for the (all) electric windows, together with the ventilation controls and a lever which can command the suspension to let the car rise or fall to suit specific needs. But all these details are totally over-

Bosch fuel-injection gives 138 bhp to the latest GTi, boosting top speed to 130 mph.

Sleek lines and spoilers give the CX GTi a Cd of 0.31.

shadowed by the avant-garde styling of the CX's interior — and in particular the instrument binnacle.

Minor changes have been made to the car's instrumentation over the years, but it remains as distinctive/peculiar as ever. Central to this (in more ways than one!) are the horizontally-revolving barrel-like gauges indicating both engine and road speeds. Surrounding these fractionally inconspicuous gauges can be found the trip meter, mileage recorder, fuel gauge, oil gauge, water temperature gauge and no less than seventeen warning lights. And as if this array were not confusing enough for first-time CX motorists, the various controls are laid out in a fashion which only now is beginning to be mimicked by other (predominantly Japanese) manufacturers. Organically-shaped pods contain elegant switches for all the secondary controls — lights, wiper, horn (rather effeminate in tone) and the distinctively Citroen non self cancelling indicators. It all takes a fair bit of getting used to!

But only once one is truly familiar with the wildly unusual system can one really drive the Citroen CX with confidence and evaluate it objectively — and sadly many potential customers never get to this point. Presuming that one can travel this far down the course and cross the hurdle of unfamiliarity, to what extent is one likely to be impressed?

In certain respects the shapely French saloon is beginning to show its age, with noisy electric windows, a poorly positioned digital clock, less than comprehensive seat adjustments, a manually-adjusted exterior mirror (and only on the driver's side at that) and a below-par Blaupunkt Melbourne M21 stereo radio/cassette leaving the CX slightly behind the pack. One cannot help but take note of the extensive use of moulded plastic, the non height-adjustable steering wheel, non-lockable fuel cap and many conspicuous Phillips screw heads. Coupled with seats in need of greater under-thigh support and oddments stowage space with the emphasis on style rather than volume, one is faced with a car that falls short of perfection in a significant number of respects.

But maybe this shortfall is only significant because the CX is so outstanding in so many others. In many respects, and in particular ride comfort, the Citroen CX GTi feels like a £15,000 limousine, while various various small details make it feel to be worth only half as much.

Given the model's price tag of £11,503, the CX GTi can therefore only be rationally evaluated in the light of the purpose which it is intended to serve. This purpose is perhaps mildly confused by the letters GTi — albeit for the wrong reasons. The transverse 2500cc four cylinder engine is helped to a respectable 138bhp and commendable 155ft lbs of torque by the use of fuel injection, it is true, and there are few cars preferable for a 'Grand Tour' of Europe. But the GTi badge has come to be associated with models that put out-and-out performance top of their list of priorities. With a 0-60 time of 9.2 seconds and a claimed maximum speed of 125 mph, the CX GTi is creditable in its performance, but hardly outstanding. Once accustomed to the controls, an enthusiast will find it well balanced, giving fine grip with its 190/65 Michelin TRX tyres and good, safe handling at high speeds. But the CX GTi is not an out-and-out performance

Much the same as when it was launched in 1976, the interior of the latest CX is odd at first acquaintance, but grows on you.

car, rather a luxury limousine with the capacity to transport four adults at high cruising speeds in tremendous comfort, as a high speed journey of 550 miles with three passengers proved quite emphatically.

In the context of such journeys, the CX GTi has few peers. With the Varipower steering system reducing the power assistance as speed builds up, the single-spoke wheel feels pleasantly weighted, while the gearing (with both fourth and fifth gears being overdrives') and soundproofing combine to cut the engine noise down to pleasant levels. First rate straight line stability and truly outstanding ride comfort make the injected saloon a very tempting proposition for those who regularly cover long distances. The good, but unexceptional, luggage capacity means that load lugging is not the CX's forte (though the suspension system will compensate for increased loads) and the sheer size of the car prevents it being driven as aggressively on B roads as the hordes of smaller GTi's. But if one was required to drive across Europe with passengers tomorrow, the CX GTi is a car which one would be glad to take.

CX fans in search of greater load carrying capacity can plump for the Safari or Familiale models. And as we discovered in the 'Estate Express' they can opt for even greater power too . . .

A 'sleeper' by definition (apart from being an unactivated Soviet spy) is a car that is outwardly standard and preferably innocuous looking, but goes like the clappers when prodded. Standard production cars that fall into this category are the VW Jetta GLi, the BMW M535i (without its optional spoilers) and the old 6.9 litre S-class Mercedes-Benz to name but a few. In the case of these cars, dyed-in-the-wool enthusiasts would soon twig on to the reason for their rapid departure from sight, but when a sedate-looking family holdall picks up its skirts and leaves cars with recognised sporting pretensions floundering in its wake, there is more than enough cause for interest to be aroused.

If at this point you are thinking that the Citroen CX 2400 RS injection Turbo, to coin its lengthy appellation, was developed with blowing the doors off the fast hatchback brigade in mind, you'd be wrong. You will be surprised to learn that the conversion was actually done with a view to endowing the estate car version of the CX with substantially more torque to give it effortless performance when moving with a full complement of people or goods, a move better suited to Citroen than perhaps any of its rivals in view of the handling and roadholding balance maintained by the hydropneumatic self-levelling suspension even with a full load. And when you learn that most of these conversions are done on three-speed automatic versions of the car, then the raison d'etre becomes self evident.

There were mutterings when the CX was launched in 1976 that the outgoing DS23EFI was perhaps the best of the big Citroens. Certainly its fuel-injected 2.3-litre engine endowed it with a 120 mph plus top speed and a 0-60 performance in the low nine second bracket, a performance envelope that was the envy of the more modern CX until the debut of the CX 2400 GTi, a car with more overtly sporting pretensions. The pushrod 2000 and 2400 engines were, in a word, agricultural; in carburettor form, they were dogs. Hard to start, rough, unwilling to rev and noisy, they were the worst aspect of a brilliant motorcar that even today, nearly a decade on, is in many ways ahead of the pack. Filtering the Bosch fuel-injection through to the rest of the CX's fitted engine effected a cure, and now in 2500cc with the rest of the CX's fitted with the 2400cc engine effected a cure, and now in 2500cc fuel-injected form, the current CX range is a veritable Audi 100 basher, with 138bhp pushing its top speed up towards the 125 mph mark. But new cars are expensive, the current top end of the CX range being well into five-figures. Market forces that prevail have pegged fairly late second-hand CX's at more affordable prices, and it would now be fairly easy to buy a good 1983 car, have the turbo conversion done and still make a saving. The gap will be even greater soon as the factory have been threatening to release their own turbocharged version sometime this year and this car (which has exactly the same power output as our test car) will not be cheap.

RSL (Racing Systems Ltd) Tuning have until now kept a fairly low profile on the production car scene. Their forte was building engines for Formula One, which they did for 8 years, specialising in the Cosworth unit. Towards the end of the '70s, they realised that the writing was on the wall for the Cosworth, which was reaching the end of its development potential, and not wishing to go down the Formula ladder (ie to formula 2 or 3) the company diversified into modifying and tuning road cars, particularly BMW, Mercedes-Benz and Citroen; RSL do a 142 bhp conversion for the Mercedes 190E for under £900 as well as undertaking the mechanical part of the Hartge conversions for Autosport + Design. Early work on Citroens consisted of fitting fuel-injection to CX2400 Safaris as until last year, only the saloons had the injection fitted, and also preparing the engines and gearboxes for Chris Sclater's Visa rally car. "We initially had problems with Citroen Cars Ltd," said RSL's German director, Peter Haas. "There was someone there at the time who was ultra conservative and frowned on what we were doing." Since then, internal changes at Slough have brought about a very acute market awareness of the requirements of avid Citroenists, and the organisation now endorses what RSL are doing, even to the extent of pointing customers who want cars modified in their direction.

"The first CX Turbo was done over a period of nine months," Peter explained. "It started off as a fairly low priority project with work being done in fits and starts as information and parts were gathered." Notes were compared with Dr Schrick in Germany who was developing camshaft profiles for the CX and it was agreed that there was a gap in the CX market, particularly for the estate cars. "It was particularly interesting at the end of the day to compare the Schrick Turbo CX with ours," Peter went on, "as our installation was developed with the possibility of air-conditioning the car in mind." This is something not taken into

Original Citroen parts have been used in the Turbo conversion. The air filter for instance, comes from the CX diesel.

The familiar innocuous shape of the CX Safari hides the hot-hatchback beating potential of the turbocharged engine.

account by Schrick and is rather more than a moot point as the steeply raked front and rear glass on the CX makes air-conditioning almost a must in the long hot continental summers. "Ventilation on the CX is not very good to start with," says Peter, "and it is even worse on the RHD cars with the more constricted aid duct trunking. Even little things like this are important to us."

Early on in the game, it was impossible to get hold of a Garrett AiResearch T3 turbocharger with an integral wastegate

Subtle badge on the rear of the Safari is the only clue to the swift performance of the car.

as these were only being supplied by OEM equipment or to specialists. So the project went through its first few months with a separately wastegated unit. Enter Turbo Technics. Six months into the project, TT came on the scene and shared premises with RSL, giving the latter access to a T3 with an integral wastegate.

Four and a half pounds of boost is all that is applied to the fuel injected CX engine, which remains virgin in the course of the conversion. "We did not want to lose low speed torque and drive-ability," Peter explained, "so the compression and camshaft remain standard and we settled for a moderate boost pressure and an electronic management system to control ignition retardation and provide over-boost protection." This device also acts as a rev- limiter as there might otherwise be a chance of blowing the large inlet valves on this rather old-fashioned engine. While the boost pressure may seem rather tame when even 6 psi is considered mild, the end result is a staggering 163 bhp at 4,750 rpm and 183lb ft torque at 3,450 rpm against 128 bhp at 4,800 rpm and 135lb ft at 3,500 rpm with the standard engine.

A standard CX produces quite high underbonnet temperatures and has a large but thin radiator spanning the front end of the engine bay. Due to the need to site the air-to-air intercooler up front as well, a rad of smaller profile but greater depth has been fitted allowing the inter-cooler to slot neatly in next to it on the offside. Two big electric cooling fans sit up front, one of which is standard and the other which is normally fitted to cars with air-conditioning. On the nearside, but in front of the radiator sits the oil cooler, a squat looking device that RSL had to scout around for in view of the limited space available should an air-conditioning evaporator be fitted in front of the radiator. Elsewhere, original Citroen parts are used wherever possible and the new air-cleaner assembly comes from a CX diesel.

The CX Turbo starts up like a normal car and idles smoothly and quietly, the turbo installation making the engine even more muffled than usual. Slipping the transmission into D and moving off, the difference is immediate and staggering. The engine revs smoothly and picks up momentum faster than normal, but what is immediately evident is the tremendous smooth surge of torque available at a touch of the right foot.

It is hard to believe that there is a big-banger four up front, as the absence of a screaming, straining engine and a glance at the speedo to check the rate of knots being gathered actually seems to imply the presence of a torquey V8. Given the boot, the modified three-speed ZF transmission still allows the car to reach 60 mph in 9.4 seconds from a standing start and the standing quarter mile is covered in 16.9 seconds. While these figures show a brisk performer, it should be remembered that with the auto box, the CX is actually undergeared and tops out at only 115 mph. A higher final drive is available and with the turbo fitted to a five-speed manual car, a second could easily be chopped off the 0-60 time and top speed raised to 130+ mph. But these figures do not readily illustrate the flexibility of the Turbo, and it is accelerating in the intermediate gears where the car really scores, the 40-60 mph and 50-70 mph increments being carried out in 4.5 seconds and 5.4 seconds respectively.

The fact that no suspension modifications are necessary speaks volumes for the excellence of the Citroen's chassis. The standard Michelin XVS tyres squeal a lot in hard cornering however, and the car does generate a fair amount of roll, so press-on drivers may want to fit the thicker anti-roll bars and TRX wheel/tyre assemblies from the GTi. A partial solution to ameliorating understeer which we have proven to work in the past is adjusting the front/rear tyre pressures to 31/25 for normal running, obviously raising the rears to compensate for heavy loads in the Safari.

The CX2400 RSinjection Turbo installation is as versatile as the CX. In the GTi or even the Prestige, it produces a very refined and truly high performance saloon with arguably the best ride comfort (barring an XJ6) that money can buy. In the Safari, these same virtues are combined with almost unrivalled load carrying ability. If circumstances dictated that we could only have one vehicle and had £2,400 to spend on top of the price of a good low-mileage Safari, we know what we would do . . .

Citroën blows hot

The Editor samples the fastest Citroën ever made... the new turbocharged CX GTi... it re-writes the meaning of the initials that stand for Grand Turismo...

CITROËN were in a blunt mood when they addressed their press conference at the unveiling of their new turbocharged version of the CX. "The GT initials have been de-valued, we are setting out to revive the true meaning." It caught the party of journalists somewhat off-guard... perhaps it was the champagne, caviar and high-life travel of arriving in a specially chartered Mystere executive jet... or perhaps it was the plain fact that no-one really associates Citroën with GT sporting cars.

But the occasion was to witness the unveiling of a significant development for Citroën. Germany, followed by Britain, has a significant market for the "executive express", and the charts on the wall setting out the new Citroën's performance showed where Citroën want to go... there for comparison were the performance figures for BMWs, quick Mercs and Rovers... Citroën now want a slice of this action.

The new image-booster is their hefty four-lunger engine of 2,500cc – one of the biggest four-pots on the market – now given a 22 per-cent power charge from a Garret T3 turbocharger, lifting torque by an impressive 40 per cent, and hiking up the power from 138 bhp to 168 bhp. Top speed from its five-speed box is claimed to now be 136 mph, with standstill to 62 mph in eight seconds.

Much firmer suspension settings from the traditional magic-carpet ride of the CX match the new power, even to the extent of firmer seats, along with heftier anti-roll bars.

Brakes are improved with additional cooling scoops, and tyres are now 210/55 VR TRXs on new alloy wheels. A distinctive spoiler at the rear is said to improve the car's already superlative stability, and slots have been filled in across the back of the spoiler with clear perspex panels – no Citroën could possibly be introduced without some form of extrovert aerodynamic oddity.

The Citroën CX was introduced as far back as 1974. It has stood the test of time well, for the shape is only two-thirds through its projected life, Citroën reckoning that it will be well past 1990 before it is changed.

We recently had our Citroën education extended (we can admit to running a Citroën 2CV as a runabout – nice car, hideous spares costs) when the Slough Press office of Citroën told us it was time we learnt how to drive a CX. We accepted an invitation to drive a turbo diesel, quickly followed by the GTi, and we came to the conclusion that the diesel turbo was the better of the two – which surprised us. 'Learning' was the right word, because there is an art to hustling these cars quickly. The ultra-light power assisted steering takes some getting used to, so to does the hydroneumatic suspension which can 'rock' disturbingly if you give it any rough treatment. These cars are designed to "flow", requiring a light, deft touch, and once you can restrict the more normal 'heavy-handed' technique, the CX can be an impressive mile-burner.

So we had some idea of what to expect when it came to driving the latest GTi, plus turbo. Quick it certainly is. Incredibly stable at romping down motorways, and now more capable on its firmer settings for a cross-country fling on twisty roads. Put through its paces on clear roads in the Bavarian Black Forest, the CX was in its ideal world.

The Turbo is smoother, markedly so. Not, as Citroën claim, as smooth as a V8... but ranking with some big sixes.

With no speed limits to worry about, we swept down autobahns with just a commendable swish. It was pelting Bavarian cats and dogs at the time, which restricted most scribes to doing no more than a ton. But we were able to relax, appreciate our earlier CX experiences, and exploit rather more confidence in this quick Citroën's capabilities. We recorded a top whack of 124 mph in the rain on the black-box computer which had been specially installed to monitor journalists efforts – enough to score a 'fastest-time-of-the-day', which drew comment from a motor-notor of *Fast Lane* that he was bloody glad he had decided not to share a car with *Sporting Cars*.

But we were there to sample the fast lanes, earlier over a private breakfast with the Managing Director of Citroën UK, we learnt that the previous day he had clocked over 140 mph on the "revolutionary" non-digital, traditional, *very* round instrument panel.

Surprising people, these Citroën types.

Philip Young

NEWCOMERS

TURBO POWER PROMOTES LATEST CX GTi TO SUPER SALOON STATUS

Citroën see the 136 mph CX GTi Turbo as the valid successor to the SM, their short-lived Maserati-powered flagship that created such a memorable impression during the early seventies. Like the SM, the new GTi Turbo is being promoted as a quality Grand Touring machine – and far more than a simple bolt-on conversion job. Its introduction puts Citroën into a new performance bracket that the existing GTi could never quite reach but only 250 are targetted to come to Britain next year.

Using hardware derived from the diesel DTR, the GTi Turbo uses the 2.5-litre version of Citroëns' in-line four cylinder engine, but now develops 168 bhp at 5000 rpm. There's Bosch L-Jetronic fuel injection with fuel cut-off and a knock sensor, solid state electronic ignition and a Garrett T3 turbo set up to deliver peak pressure at a low 3250 rpm, co-inciding with maximum torque of 217 lb.ft.

Transmission, five-speed manual with higher gearing than the 138 bhp GTi, offers a loping 25.2 mph per 1000 rpm in top with evenly-spread lower ratios. The CX's assisted rack and pinion steering remains the same but the damping rates of the hydropneumatic suspension have been raised and the front and rear anti-roll bars increased in diameter. The ventilated

GTi Turbo gets big tail spoiler, new wheels and, inside, round facia dials for the sports market

CITROËN'S CRUISE MISSILE

front discs are now served by larger air scoops – the rear discs are unchanged – and low-profile Michelin TRX tyres are standard issue.

Aerodynamic alloy wheels and a distinctive rear spoiler are GTi Turbo trademarks. The spoiler, not perhaps the most stylish of appendages, isn't there just for show; despite the CX's outstandingly smooth outline, it's needed to ensure composed high speed cornering and compensate for the increased drag brought on by the wider tyres and passenger door mirror. The GTi Turbo is quoted as having a 0.36 cd which slightly betters that of the GTi. Colour-coded bumpers, tinted windows, twin exhausts and small Turbo badges are further changes.

Inside, the big news concerns the un-Citroën-like instrument panel with round dials replacing the idiosyncratic revolving drum arrangement of other CXs. The layout, with prominent speedometer and tachometer and four minor supporting gauges, is utterly conventional and very attractive. A small turbo boost gauge nestles at the foot of the rev counter, the steering wheel and gear lever knob are leather-covered and throughout the interior the finish is predominantly black and sporty. But why the change to round dials? Because, say Citroën, market research has shown that buyers in this class expect full instrumentation and that means lots of dials and gauges. But Citroën traditionalists may be relieved to learn that there are as yet no plans to chop the existing CX 'cyclops eye' set-up in the interests of rationalisation.

Straight-line stability coupled with the ability to deliver 136 mph performance safely were two of the engineers' main targets with the CX Turbo. Engine flexibility especially from low down was an important consideration too. This explains the unusually strong torque curve which shows a 144 lb.ft reading at just 1500 rpm. In practice the CX GTi Turbo will pick up cleanly from as low as 1000 rpm and be pulling strongly by 2000 rpm. The boost, shows minimal lag and the blower itself is quiet.

Stability *is* first rate: the car runs arrow-true irrespective of speed and

THE NEW CX GTi TURBO IS IDEALLY SUITED TO HIGH SPEED MOTORWAY DASHES FROM ONE AREA OF THE COUNTRY TO ANOTHER

seems unaffected by side winds. Fully extended, the GTi Turbo will manage 136 mph but when we tried the car on the autobahn recently, 110 mph appeared a natural cruising speed. Citroën's claimed performance times of 0-62 mph in 8.0 secs and 0-400 metres in a shade under 16 secs have a realistic look to them. And this will put the Turbo ahead of some notable opposition such as BMW's 528i, Renault's 25 V6 and the Volvo 760 Turbo. According to official figures, fuel economy isn't penalised too heavily either the GTi Turbo averaging 28 mpg; yet during our driving spell which took in both autobahn and twisty rural routes our CX averaged slightly over 19 mpg.

If the CX GTi Turbo is ideally suited to high speed motorway dashes from one area of the country to another, it's less at home along testing minor roads where its bulk and soft suspension make it rather unwieldly to drive until full acclimatisation has set in.

For all its suspension stiffening, the GTi Turbo still leans heavily around corners and dips back and forward during gearchanges. Other CX characteristics – such as the zero travel brakes and the light, assisted steering with its strong self-centring action – remain.

The new instrument arrangement works well; the information provided is clear and easy to read but there's the suggestion that perhaps the two main dials are just a shade small. But at least Citroën have shown that they're just as capable of coming up with a neat dash as say, BMW.

The CX GTi Turbo is a fast, exciting addition to Citroën's burgeoning CX line-up. It has arrived just in time to cash in on the current performance boom but is no boy racer machine, more of a refined motorway cruiser – ready to take on any hard charging executive saloon that comes its way. No price had been announced as this went to press but at an envisaged £12,250 it should give rivals plenty to think about.

MODEL: CITROËN CX 25 GTi TURBO

DATE ON SALE:	October '84
ENGINE:	2500cc, 168bhp
PERFORMANCE:	136mph, 0-62mph 8.0 secs
MPG:	20.2-35.5
ESTIMATED PRICE:	£12,250

Citroen joins the high performance executive saloon battle with a 135mph turbocharged CX GTi and – probably – a very competitive price tag/Peter Newton

In France it costs the Franc equivalent of £11,900 and Citroen representatives told us that it wasn't expected to cost much more than that in Britain when we were recently given a chance to view the long awaited CX GTi Turbo in Germany during early September.

All of which puts the new high performance addition to Citroen's CX range at the lower end of the price scale in the performance executive saloon market. From Citroen's point of view it's perhaps unfortunate that this market segment isn't as price-sensitive as some, but in all probability it will represent extremely good value in relation to some of its obvious competitors – the Rover Vitesse, the Audi 200 Turbo, the Mercedes 280E, Opel Senator, etc.

Citroen sees the car as a valid successor to the quirky Maserati engined SM on three main counts; acceleration, stability and maximum speed. Citroen claims a maximum speed of 137.5mph for its new car, rather more than the carburettor SM but slightly less than the injected version.

On an officially corrected speedometer we achieved 132.8mph *after* a downhill section of a German autobahn – albeit on a wet and blustery day – conditions were difficult, to put it mildly.

In terms of stability the CX, as anyone who has had any past experience of the marque will testify, has never been a problem. The equal length driveshafts, suspension arms and steering links ensure that geometry changes don't take place under load – everything remains in parallel, and the drag coefficient for the CX – 0.36 – has not been compromised despite the fitment of the widest section tyres (210/55 VR 390) ever fitted to a Citroen. This is mainly due to the compensatory effort of a new rear spoiler. In view of the car's still classic shape, that drag coefficient may sound quite high. Citroen will only tell you that the way it carries out its wind tunnel tests may not be quite the same as other manufacturers – it won't be drawn any further. Suffice to say that the addition of wing mirrors, wipers or passengers in the car, (ie: with the car in a fully loaded state), can make a big difference. And besides, it's high speed stability that's important for a car of this nature, and on a very windy day, flat-out on the autobahn, this car performed superbly – one couldn't ask for more. Roll stiffness has been increased front and rear via uprated dampers and thicker anti-roll bars – 1mm bigger at the front and 2mm at the back.

Strange that that new rear spoiler, which one might have imagined would be hollow, is in fact filled-in with perspex centres! Apparently it produced better figures in the latter state.

Acceleration in a CX is always deceptive, and in pouring rain on flooded roads it's difficult to get a true picture of the car's potential. However, the traction afforded by the massive Michelin TRX tyres is phenomenal, although their propensity to aquaplane in standing water needs careful watching. Citroen claims 8.0 seconds for the 0-60mph sprint for its new car, as against 9.2 seconds for the standard CX GTi, and figures like 7.7 seconds for the Rover Vitesse and 8.2 seconds for the Audi 200 Turbo.

In other words, the new car is very much on the pace in terms of figures, but the CX, like the Audi 200T, is a long distance car, not a traffic lights sprinter, and during flat-out acceleration runs even the addition of a turbocharger can't disguise the ancient ancestry of this four cylinder engine, which can be traced back to the DS and beyond.

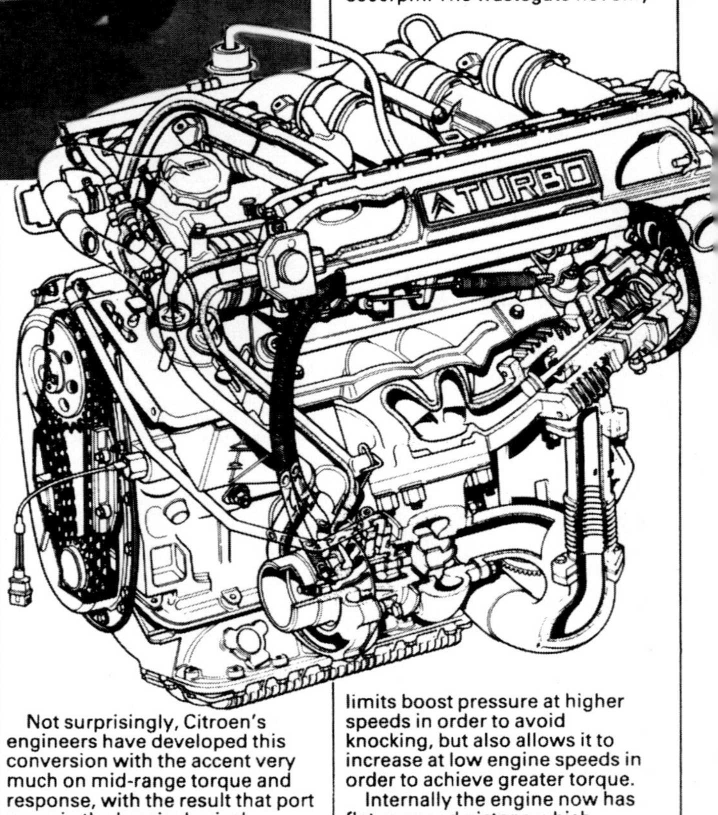

Not surprisingly, Citroen's engineers have developed this conversion with the accent very much on mid-range torque and response, with the result that port areas in the hemispherical combustion chamber, alloy head have been reduced to advantage, in order to speed up gas flow; and a suitably revised camshaft is fitted – the modifications restricting maximum RPM to 6000.

The cast iron cylinder block, with its steel crank and connecting rods, is the same as that of the turbo diesel – in other words the thickness of the bore walls has been increased, while the ignition system is totally solid state – there are no moving parts in it at all.

The ratios of the five speed gearbox remain the same as for the GTi but the final drive has been slightly raised.

The car uses the same Garrett T3 turbine as the diesel, but with a separate wastegate supplied direct by Audi, for whom the French company has the highest respect in these matters.

Maximum boost pressure is set at 8psi, with 6.4psi available at 5000rpm. The wastegate not only limits boost pressure at higher speeds in order to avoid knocking, but also allows it to increase at low engine speeds in order to achieve greater torque.

Internally the engine now has flat crowned pistons which reduce surface area and thus temperature; a reduction in compression ratio from 8.75:1 to 7.5:1 to reduce both temperature and pressure in the combustion chambers; and the existing asbestos head gasket receives an interlayer of stainless steel.

A revised sump provides an oil

return line from the turbocharger, and the cylinder block has a repositioned crankcase vent attachment and provision for a knock detector.

The inlet valves (as already mentioned) have been reduced in diameter from 47mm to 42mm and the output of the oil pump has been increased by 15 percent.

A water/oil radiator has been fitted, and the engine is fed by a Bosch L-Jetronic fuel injection system including a cold start injector controlled by a time delay thermostat.

The clutch gets a reinforced pressure plate and operating fork; the exhaust system is suitably strengthened and the gearbox gets heavy duty bearings.

All these modifications support Citroen's claim that this is not a bolt-on turbocharger conversion, but a totally revised package, and one would not have expected this company to do the job by halves. The result is a 22 percent increase in power over the CX GTi from 138bhp to 168bhp at 5000rpm, and a massive 40 percent increase in torque, up from 156 lb. ft to 217 lb. ft at 3250rpm – which puts the car firmly in the Rover Vitesse category. Indeed, on the road mid-range response is not unlike that of a big V8 – it's most impressive. And when you look at the torque curve, you can see why. Torque of 145 lb. ft is developed as low as 1500rpm and doesn't fall below 202 lb. ft between 2000 and 4000rpm. Citroen engineers are to be congratulated.

Citroen claims an average fuel consumption figure of 27.9mpg for the car, which may be possible with sympathetic use. Suffice to say that on our short acquaintance, which was not unnaturally a go-for-it affair, we managed to reduce that figure to 14.8mpg!

Citroen claims an engine design life of at least 93,000 miles which must be reassuring to many people, and it's well protected against driver-generated hooliganism – the fuel supply is cut-off if either the boost pressure exceeds a certain value or if the engine speed rises above 6000rpm.

The essential factor still remains however. You either love a Citroen or you hate it. The modifications to the suspension haven't significantly altered the nature of the ride or the way in which the car handles. Obviously its roadholding limits are now much higher, and those who hated Citroen's quirky instruments will be relieved to know that the car is equipped with a full set of round dials – explained away by the company as not so much a change of heart, more a matter of marketing requirements.

But when all's said and done, a Citroen is a very personal purchase. It takes time to get used to – the steering especially, which we think is marvellous but others hate! And it's not the sort of mass market executive car that, say the Audi 200T, a topline Ford Granada or the Opel Senator could be.

If I lived in Paris and drove long distances in France, I wouldn't hesitate, and recent experience with a GTi leads me to think that I'd probably grow to love a turbocharged version. Yet finer feelings suggest that turbocharging one of these superb machines is somehow to ignore its primary purpose, but that's another story.

What *is* important for Citroen is that after Germany, the UK is its second most important export market for high performance executive saloons, and the company expects the new car to take 14 percent of total CX sales in this country next year – that'll be over 250 GTi Turbos. It certainly represents an attractive deal.

CITROEN TURBO RECALLS SM

The long wait for Citroen's 140mph-plus CX GTi Turbo has been worthwhile. In many ways the car reigns supreme/LJK Setright

FIRST THINGS FIRST. IN ITS new turbocharged form, the Citroen CX has the finest roadholding of all production cars. We are not talking about Ferrari GTO or Porsche Group B extravaganzas, of course, but the term 'production car' may still be interpreted pretty widely without them and their likes intruding; and in all such reasonable company, this CX is supreme. That is my opinion; it is also maintained as verified fact by an industrial source (*not* Citroen) which, very competently and for its own publicity-shy purposes, tries them all. Thus, with its prodigious and almost incomparable ride, roadholding, steering and braking, the CX is supremely fit to manage even more power than it has now been given.

Even more torque, for that matter; it is this that is remarkable in the CX Turbo. The power is merely 168bhp, which is not at all exceptional for a turbocharged 2.5litre engine – though its availability at only 5000rpm (with another 1000 to go before the fuel is cut off by the electronic injection system) is already a clue to the steamy urge of this rugged big four. The torque, on the other hand, makes all other turbocars in this bracket look a bit spindle-legged: if you recall that the CX25GTi developed 155lb ft at 4000rpm, what do you make of the Turbo which gives 144 at a trifling 1500 – and then inflates itself to a peak bmep of 214lb in^2 to develop 217lb ft at 3000rpm? What you make of it is a king among cars, and the more difficult the road conditions, the more regal is its superiority.

Conditions were bad when I tried the car, over a three-figure mileage in Bavaria. The heating and ventilation systems disposed quickly of the first difficulty, which was that the air was chilly enough to make all the windows of a four-seater saloon mist up as soon as its lone occupant had drawn a couple of breaths. The next was ever present, a dismal unrelenting rain which kept the roads awash, defying the gusty wind ever to dry them. With the first third of the route consisting of very winding and narrow roads in the hill country, the prospect of finding the behavioural limits of a high-performance car was far from attractive. Yet, despite the CX being a car reputed to need time for familiarisation (and I had not driven one of any kind for a couple of years) I was very soon reassured.

The availability of ample and immediate boiler pressure to be tapped by my right foot was evident when I had scarcely emerged from the car park: here was a turbo with no problems of delayed response. The response of the car to all other control inputs was just as prompt and unfailing: the suspension and running gear of the CX Turbo have been uprated to match its speed. Those nitrogen-bubble springs are unchanged, but the damper assemblies beneath their spheres have been altered, and the anti-roll torsion bars have been thickened by a millimetre at the front and by two at the back – increases which should equate stiffening of 8.5 and 24percent respectively. Finally, the Turbo wears the widest tyres ever fitted to a Citroen, 210/55VR390 Michelin TRX with enough drainage even for these conditions and lots of bite in all directions. Whether they would be as good on British road metal I do not yet know, but on Bavarian *Bahnstoff* they were excellent.

I am not saying that they never lost their grip. On one occasion they all did – or I did! – quite comprehensively. I was storming into one of a succession of bends on a glistening asphalt backroad when the surface suddenly assumed a slipperiness redolent of old London's tramlines and woodblocks and high-gloss bitumen. What to do? When to do it?

There is something about a CX which encourages a cool rational contemplation of circumstances that in any other car would have one thrashing in a lather of ill-conditioned reflexes. Sitting there and mentally extrapolating the prevailing rates of slip and yaw, I estimated that if I did nothing the car would recover its grip and proceed in the desired direction just at the last possible second; so nothing was what I did, and thanks to this least treacherous of cars nothing, with one or perhaps two inches to spare, proved to be the right thing to do.

When this dream of a car brought me safely out of the agricultural twisties into the second leg of the route, it was to encounter heavy and sullen traffic on major and secondary roads linking and piercing some minor towns. Here was the time to relish the frustration-defying comfort, the dark cool privacy, the ergonomic perfection, and the musically rich reproduction of radio and tape, in that hushed and peculiarly secluded cabin. Not much has changed in there from the GTi, except that the velour is new and the binnacle's gauges are all of circular-arc analogue type. Not much had needed changing: with the coming of the GTi, CX seats reconciled softness and support in a way which seems strangely beyond emulation by others.

I had even begun to like the old Citroens' Cyclops-eye speedometer, which could be read very precisely though not very fast. In this car, an auxiliary electronic recording speedometer (of demonstrated accuracy) had been fitted for the purposes of the test, and on the third leg of the course – a two-lane autobahn– I hoped to verify the claimed DIN maximum speed of 136mph. When checking the route, a dry day or two earlier, the firm's UK managing director had recorded 143mph (the car is very high-geared), but Setright was doomed not to match nor even approach that figure. Jupiter Pluvius had with his sluice-gates achieved what none of us might have thought possible, having cowed even the Germans into driving slowly, even on the autobahn. Picking their way carefully from lane to lane, and pondering long before indicating their next moves, they never gave me enough room to reach more than 133mph – at which speed, of course, the CX felt just as competent and controllable as at any other. And in the prevailing conditions such stability was all the more praiseworthy.

The foundations of this imperturbability are laid in the self-levelling suspension. Because of this, the springing can be so very progressive that, despite the vast wheel travel available, actual wheel motion over the road has very little amplitude. Because of that, the geometry of wheel motion (determined by double equal parallel wishbones at the front, purely trailing arms at the rear) can impart purely vertical displacement limited to only one plane. This means a complete absence of changes in camber, and that

Citroen have left the exterior of the CX GTi largely untouched in its Turbo transformation. The oddly designed but very effective rear spoiler is the most obvious new feature. In fact the elegant body could do with an aerodynamic tidy-up to bring the CX drag factor down

means freedom from gyroscopic precessions inducing spurious deflections. Thus there are no parasitical steering effects induced by suspension movement: however fast a CX might be made to go, it would not be tempted to wander.

Nor does it pitch; the anti-dive anti-squat suspension sees to that too. Yaw and litt are ruled out by the aerodynamics: the drag coefficient of the CX is no longer as low as those of some rivals (the car needs a good clean-up, in fact, especially underneath) but with the aid of a newly efficaceous if weird-looking tail spoiler the Turbo is aerodynamically stable at all times – and of course the self-levelling assists in this, too. When will the rest of the industry recognise that suspension is more than mere bump-softening?

If they are taking a long time to emulate Citroen's control of wheels and wind, Citroen took a long time to bring out their turbo car. I do not know why they took so long; we have been awaiting it for years. Maybe they could not afford to do it earlier; maybe their masters would not let them; maybe they just needed a long time to develop their turbocharging system until it was as good and as simple as it is now. It is so good that it is not detectable in the cabin, unless one watches the boost gauge; it seems always to be working, as though it were a mechanically driven supercharger. Yet the plumbing looks simple, without any intercooling – not because it is undesirable, but because there is no room for it. But the usual wastegate is unusually controlled: not only positive pressure in the inlet manifold but also negative pressure in the compressor inlet are tapped to act upon the aneroid which opens the wastegate. Only Audi employ similar circuitry, but the settings are different, as are the results. In the Citroen, the turbine is driven from 1000rpm to reach maximum boost pressure (0.56bar,

about 8.0lb^2/in) when the engine reaches its 3250rpm torque peak; beyond, the cumulative suction and pressure upstream and downstream of the compressor act to open the wastegate progressively, reducing the boost pressure to 0.44bar (6.0lb/in^2) at the 5000rpm power peak, so as to avoid detonation. The result is a wonderfully fat torque curve, fit to propel the car on with extra urgency whenever you require it.

Detonation is held at bay electronically anyway, just to be safe. This engine has a brace of ignition systems like that superb one which graces the Visa two-cylinder engine; I doubt if any other system works better at high speeds, and no other works so well to induce a start at absurdly low cranking speeds. Added to this lovely arrangement is a knock-inhibition circuit, retarding the spark at the behest of a detecting accelerometer and restoring it at a safe rate, with further fail-safe logic built into the ingition computer lest the detector go wrong.

What else? Nothing unusual, for the engine had already been massively reinforced from July 1983 when it grew to its present displacement. Flat-crowned pistons to reduce heat input face extensive squish bands to enhance internal turbulence, a reduction of 12percent in the inlet valves' diameter further fattens the torque curve, and the rest are trivia. I told you this was a simple installation.

It leads to a simple conclusion. This is a car which is really quick on ordinary roads, wonderfully safe and controllable, eminently civilised, decently economical, and overwhelmingly desirable. It deserves the lightening and aerodynamic cleansing which would keep it the world's most modern car for another 11years; but it is already so functionally beautiful that it deserves to be as successful commercially as it is technically – if only that were possible. We can hope, at least.

Turbo installation on 2.5litre four (above) is relatively simple. There is no inter-cooler because of lack of room. Torque rather than power is the unit's forte; no less than 214lb ft at 3000rpm gives dynamic performance. Roadholding is excellent

DIFFERENT STROKES

Traction Avant has been part of the Citroen formula seemingly since time immemorial. Now the French manufacturer has discovered the performance car phenomenon. We recently put the CX 25GTi Turbo, and the BX 19GT through their paces, and found them to be very different

CITROEN CX 25 GT TURBO

Mentioning Citroen and performance may well seem odd to anyone brought up to chuckle at the sight of a 2CV rolling its chicken shack way along Gallic highways. In fact a previous Citroen generation, the DS 19, predicted the current obsession with aerodynamics amongst major car manufacturers with a sleek shape in the sixties. Citroen scored a number of major, sometimes controversial, World Championship rally victories. In 1985 Citroen plan to enter a 405 horsepower, turbocharged BX with 4-WD in top class rallies.

The BX and CX tested in this issue contrast an almost conventional front drive performer (1.9 BX) with the true taste of French character and individuality found in the CX GTi Turbo.

The recipe

The essential ingredients in the Citroen CX recipe were established in the August 1974 CX 2000 and 2200, but it should be remembered that the unfashionable pushrod valve (rather than today's more common overhead camshaft cylinder head design) four cylinder traces back to even earlier Citroen designs. Front drive, *traction avant*, has been a Citroen feature since the thirties and continues throughout the range.

Thus we find a rugged iron block four mounted across the engine bay. It drives the front wheels via a five speed gearbox that is better known for its role in exotica such as the current Lotus Esprit and the 142mph Citroen Maserati SMs of the past.

Around that big four cylinder are today's high tech representatives from Bosch and Garrett AiResearch: L-Jetronic fuel injection and a T3 turbo. The UK-built turbocharger is set to provide 0.57 bar/8psi boost at peak torque (217 lb.ft at 3250rpm), dropping to 0.43 bar/6psi at 5000rpm, the 168 horsepower maximum power point. The bias is toward mid range and considerable internal engine strength. Our figures demonstrate fourth and fifth gear pulling power that is considerably fleeter than the 2.8i Capri.

Perhaps the most controversial aspect of CX motoring, aside from ever learning to drive the unique switch gear(!) is the use of high pressure hydraulics and air systems (hydropneumatic) to power-assist brake, steering and suspension components.

For the Turbo models, the mechanical suspension elements, such as dampers and roll bars front and rear, have been uprated, but the pressure within Citroen's unique spheres remain at 1100 psi front and 600 psi rear. Overall the suspension, cooperating with the widest tyres Citroen have ever fitted — 210/55 VR TRX on unique 5.9 in wide by 15.3 in diameter alloy wheels — is the most successful aspect of the power assistance devices offered. The brakes are extremely effective four wheel discs, but few liked the degree of power assistance offered. The quick — 2.5 turns lock to lock — power steering was disliked by all of the half dozen testers who drove this, or the identical CX GTi, rack and pinion layout.

Externally the GTi Turbo is distinguished from other CX's by a new rear spoiler. Unusually, what look functional ducts in the black back wing are actually blanked off with perspex panes "because this was found best for the aero factor," explained a Citroen technician. The drag factor is a competitive 0.36 Cd with a noteable gap between front TRX tyre and wheelarch.

Other Turbo decoration includes colour coded bumpers, a rather naff T planted upon the bonnet bulge, profuse badgework and even the use of the emotive turbo ID on the wheels. Functional changes externally include a twin pipe exhaust, efficient double reflector headlamps with H4 and H1 bulbs, plus electrically heated twin mirrors that tended to dry dirt over their surfaces and become useless in typically grimy British use.

Standard equipment at £12,990 provides most of the features expected in a class that extends to more expensive alternatives in front drive turbo power from Saab (the aerodynamically bodied 16 'S' is £14,090 in 3-door style only) and Audi. The latter charge just over £17,000 for their 182bhp 4-door that can reach 140mph.

The test Citroen listed only metallic paint as an option, but the company — like most West German importers — actually only fit radio speakers and aerial rather than the in-car entertainment unit itself. So you could spend anything from £150 upward on a unit to complement the car.

The test CX had a very satisfactory Philips 760 radio/cassette stereo unit installed. It should also be noted that the test was carried out on a production vehicle as opposed to a pre-production model with prototype engine management map given to some of the weekly motoring magazines.

Inside story

The equipment supplied for the Turbo CX, such as Chevron-emblem cloth seating, leather rim for most of the one-spoke steering wheel's circumference and six round dials of analogue instrumentation all performed well, although the speedometer's registration of nearly 140mph whilst travelling at a true 126mph did not endear itself.

Unsatisfactory to all UK users seemed to be switchgear. It is laid out with Gallic logic and includes two main pods, rather than steering column levers. This means the flashers do not automatically cancel, which leads to obvious and dangerous misunderstandings between a new operator and the outside world.

The lighting is a nightmare for strangers. The three position light switch is fair enough, but to get main beam demands operation of a third switch, separated from the dip and main light switch.

As with every other aspect of the car, you seem to be asked to pass an initiation test before you can operate the car safely. . . Speaking of which the fog light location could actually cost lives: it is tucked away *under* the main instrument pod and one of our number had to stop and find the owner's manual to illuminate the car correctly when encountering sudden Northern fog. He was not the only one to be baffled in that manner either.

Aside from the usual oil pressure and water temperature functional readouts found in many performance cars, CX Turbo included an oil temperature dial, the pressure gauge incorporating an oil level indicator. An induction of oil temperature proved useful and could extend the 2½ litre's life by allowing sympathetic driving from a cold start. The tachometer has a 5500rpm limit, but the engine does not cut out until 6100 revs are attained. The speedo speaks of 150mph, but the kilometre equivalents expire at a figure corresponding to 136mph (220km/h).

At first sight it seems impossible that Citroen could offer a sunroof option, for there is an enormous roof light layout, along with the rear screen heater element push button (that's Citroen logic. . .!) Yet you can specify an electric sunroof (£518.27), or there is air conditioning for a further £688.94.

Action

The starter gasps asthmatically, wheezing the big four into life slowly and bringing the dashboard illumination along for the ride, whether the sidelights are on or not.

First impressions are dominated by the fiddle to get the ignition key working, the strange location of an LCD clock beside the steering column — read it in motion and the car ahead is in for the free trip of a lifetime! — and the panting of that strange steering as you manoeuvre from lock to lock.

Because it is such an abrupt, almost mechanical, transition from straight ahead to a deliberate build up in effort as lock is increased, you tend to treat the steering with initial suspicion and progress may be as erratic as that of a classic drink driving suspect. None of our half dozen liked the system, but the writer did enjoy the faster lock to lock response, compared to any other production car. Ultimately you can push the car just as hard as any rival without disaster.

The brakes divided testing opinion neatly. With practice you come to appreciate a firm pedal and startling, instant, response. All the driver's felt the assistance offered was too powerful and a promising World Class rally driver commented that it was very difficult to progressively adjust the braking effort required, leading to the danger of locking up wheels on slippery surfaces. We agreed about the "on/off" nature of the brakes, but two of us did over 250 miles each, one including performance tests, without locking a wheel, even under real stress.

The final power-aided system, that of the suspension, left the most favourable memories. All of the team commented on comfort as a primary attribute of the CX and the way in which its long wheelbase goes striding over B-road bumps is an object lesson to all but Jaguar. The seats play a part here, but those with Germanic taste for unyielding cushions may find Citroen's soft comforts simply decadent.

Although the Citroen is a totally different mechanical layout to the current Jaguar, cornering character is similar. Cosseted by the ride you turn in and benefit from considerable roadholding abilities rather than any desire to push the car into a corner as far as it will go. Like the Jaguar, a long travel suspension allows more body roll than Audi, BMW and Mercedes traditionally provide. Draw into the equation an engine that is at its best between 2000 and 4000rpm, driven briskly rather than revved to the rather low limit, and you get the picture of pampered comfort whilst travelling effortlessly. Push hard, in the manner that the badgework frills might suggest, and you will end up with disastrous fuel consumption: two of the journalists recorded 15mpg figures at the official launch and we got under 10mpg in performance tests. Harder use simply makes the car feel ungainly, and there is no hiding the fact of its considerable girth on narrower roads.

Thus the CX is at its best using mid-range overtaking ability that is in the V6 league, and long-striding comfort, as its premier attributes. Oddly enough, luggage capacity is not good in practical terms for such a long vehicle, the boot more like a cave, built deep into the rear end.

Detail annoyances include having to jack the car up on ride height, or shift it forwards if the tyre valves come to rest within the rear spats when you want to check the pressures, and the lack of a rear wiper for that concave back screen. Sure, it clears at speed, but in traffic there are just a collection puddles to view. Even effective ventilation, controlled by a handy three stalk layout between driver and passenger, cannot overcome the wet weather vision aft.

Performance

Accelerating from rest or belting with perfect stability around the Millbrook bowl at 126mph, the CX Turbo failed to match the ambitious claims of the makers. We do not think there was any deficiency whatever in the test car: it ran perfectly with the recommended exhaust tinge in the twin pipes. The light gearchange with uprated clutch provided all the cooperation we could have desired in making a speedy progress.

At the German launch two UK journalists recorded 132mph maximum speeds, but only as the high point of more than a mile downhill! At the time we felt a 125mph honest maximum was likely and, in almost still weather, we recorded both average and top speeds within a one mph band of each other, for our UK full test procedure.

From a standing start an average of 8½ seconds to 60mph is about what we would have expected from such a weighty 168bhp device, with 0-100mph also in a similarly predictable 25 to 26 seconds. For comparison the respected 2.8i Capri returned a rounded off 8.3s and nearly 27 seconds for the same routine in December's issue. Citroen claim 0-60mph in 7.9s and one of our respected rivals did manage a better figure than that, using the prototype RHD CX mentioned earlier.

In the middle rpm range the Citroen's conscientious turbo development has returned the right results: we returned less than 7 seconds for every 20mph fourth gear increment between 30 and 80mph, a sure indication of superior passing performance in owner's hands rather than the tyre squealing, headline-grabbing, 0-60mph act. Even in fifth gear the big four seater outlugs the bigger-engined, lighter, Capri 2.8. In fact Citroen virtually halved the sporting Ford's 70-90mph time of 20.51 seconds in fifth, returning 10.43 seconds.

On the road you can see that full boost as reported by just 2200rpm, rather than the more normal 3000rpm of turbo power plants. The result is superb fourth and fifth gear performance with the flexibility to chug around town at just 1000rpm in third and fourth, and still accelerate extremely smoothly.

Cruising at 70mph demands just under 2800rpm, and the car will be returning close to 30mpg. Watching the boost gauge carefully and excluding performance testing from our measured tank figures returned 19 and 20mpg with the overall figure shown. By class standards it is not particularly good.

Summary

Given the performance/mpg superiority of rear drive designs with straightforward fuel injection, and the fact that many drivers prefer rear drive with higher power outputs, we must see the potential CX customer coming from existing Citroen ranks. Or a potential buyer of powerful front drive turbo technology from Saab or Audi — with a wider choice from Renault (25 Turbo), Lancia (Thema, ie Turbo 2000) and SAAB (9000 Turbo 16) on the way.

Existing Citroen customers, already used to the quirks of the breed, will love the CX GTi Turbo for its grace and suspension suppleness. However, BX customers will not automatically love the bigger CX, for the smaller BX Citroen is the nearest this strongly French company have come to providing a normal car: one that a Sierra or Cavalier buyer could consider. For traditional Citroenists the CX Turbo's virtues in speed, if not economy, will be welcome.

Treated in an overall market context, remember the £12,990 price tag, for that may well sell the car against an opposition that is mostly more expensive. Our turbo front drive recommendation in this sub-£13,000 group would go to the superb Saab 900 4-door at £11,890; if its 145bhp was not enough, then the Turbo 16 without the aero panelling modifications can be had in 4 door style from £13,490.

The writer did enjoy using the CX Turbo for its individual interpretation of restful speed, but our testing panel voted 5-1 against and one even described the handling as that of "a flat bottom boat!"

Jeremy Walton

Less than a decade ago turbocharging spelt high performance and exclusivity, but it was also synonymous with dubious reliability. The few models around came with a degree of turbo lag that had to be experienced to be believed. But while the early turbos may have been raw and unrefined they were also highly exciting cars to drive, and as Saab discovered with its classic black-only 99, there was a tremendous amount of prestige associated with the 'turbo' badge.

Now everybody is turbocharging and the reasons are easy to see: for a relatively small investment an existing engine's power output can be dramatically increased, in the short term bypassing the need to build a new engine, and, because of the amount of development which has gone on over the years, the turbo is now perceived by the buying public to have sufficient reliability.

It's arguable that few other cars could be as well suited to a turbo adaptation as the two we look at here. Both cars, in normally aspirated form, rely on four-cylinder engines which must surely have very nearly reached the end of their development potential.

Saab in particular have done an excellent job in developing turbo technology on an existing engine. From a slanted single overhead camshaft engine of 1.85 litres which once powered a rear-driven Triumph the Swedes have produced a front-drive two-litre intercooled, turbocharged engine which in 1982 gained the benefit of automatic performance control, an ignition system allowing it to run on any grade of fuel.

But even more exciting than this was the recent introduction of the same engine with double overhead camshafts plus four valves per cylinder, increasing the already respectable power output of 145 bhp to 175 bhp at 5300 rpm, and marginally improving government fuel figures in the process. Torque is a healthy 201 lbs ft at 3000 rpm.

Citroen do not have the same turbo experience as Saab, but this hasn't stopped the French company making a supreme effort to freshen up the look of the CX.

The big four-cylinder 2.5-litre engine (which sits transversely, unlike the Saab's) nevertheless bears some similarity to the Saab in having a Garrett T3 turbocharger bolted on, plus an intercooler and Bosch fuel injection, and produces 168 bhp at a slightly lower 5000 rpm. Torque is marginally more than the Saab; 217 lbs ft at 3250 rpm. Both cars employ five-speed transmissions.

There are three different versions of the Saab Turbo 16 – the three-door, four-door, and the exceptionally racy-looking three-door 16S, which we test here. Its running gear is the same as other 900s – wishbones at the front and a dead axle on coils at the rear – though springs are tougher and alloy wheels are shod with fat 60-series tyres. Steering is by a power-assisted rack and pinion system.

Extra equipment also includes side 'skirts' integrated with a front spoiler, plus a rear deck spoiler. Inside there is cruise control, central locking, electric windows, and a sunroof. All this results in a £14,090 price tag, an extra £600 over the normal Turbo 16 three-door.

The Citroen's running gear is the usual hydropneumatic suspension and Vari-power steering, though for the turbo model bigger anti-roll bars are used and damping rates are changed. The high pressure hydraulic brakes now have larger front air scoops, and the 55-series tyres run on alloy wheels. In its appearance the Citroen looks positively low key alongside the Saab. Only the wheels, a rear bootlid spoiler, and some discreet badging sets it apart from other CXs. But inside there has been a pretty drastic change by Citroen standards – the adoption of a conventional facia panel bearing six round dials. The much praised fingertip controls remain, however. Central locking and electric windows are included in the specification. The CX 25 GTI Turbo is £12,990.

PERFORMANCE

SAAB	●●●●
CITROEN	●●●●

By just about any standards the performance of both cars is utterly thrilling; abundantly quick for even the still unrestricted German autobahns, and providing acceleration which remains breathtaking no matter how often sampled.

Yet neither, we feel, can go all the way to five marks in this category. Essentially, the Saab's performance edge is flawed just a little by that age-old turbo characteristic – the lag before power pick-up. The engine has to be working at around 2500 rpm before too much happens in the way of boost, and although the new double cam unit feels more flexible than either the APC eight-valve or the predecessor to that, there's still a very slight hesitation before the needle on the boost gauge hurls itself into the all-systems-go sector.

Possibly the slight lag is exaggerated by gearing which is a shade high for a car of this performance

Turbo

How do the Citroen CX and Saab Turbo shape up now they have extra firepower?

potential, for third and fourth gears necessarily keep the engine around 2000 to 3000 rpm at normal road speeds. If, for example, you want to blast away from 25 mph, a quick change down to second is advisable.

But as soon as the Saab gets into its stride, it's just unbelievably quick. Once the boost gauge is in the go section the eerie turbo whistle can be heard rising in pitch, and the ensuing quickening of pace makes everything in the rear view mirror shrink away rapidly. And there seems hardly any top end limit to the rocketship acceleration; even at 90 to 100 mph in top full throttle sends the Saab surging forward, the steering momentarily lightening as it does so.

It should be clear by now that the Saab's performance is at its best on motorways. Working at higher revs than would be used around town, say 3500 to 4000 rpm in fifth, a mere brush of the shoe on the accelerator pedal is sufficient to produce enough passing power for virtually any circumstances.

On paper the Saab's figures cannot fail to impress: a standing 60 mph is reached in 8.2 secs, while 100 mph comes up in 24.3 secs. The eight-valve APC turbo achieved 0-60 mph in 8.9 secs when we tested it in May 1983. Even though there is still a slight degree of turbo lag, pick-up times are excellent: in fifth 50 to 70 and 70 to 90 mph come up in 8.5 and 6.0 secs respectively.

Back down to earth, the Saab displays no sign at all of any temperament, and the improved breathing of twin cams and more valves reduce the slight harshness of the normal turbo when revved. The gearchange is acceptable rather than sporty; it has a reasonably precise movement but a dead feel to it.

Despite the CX's extra three cwt over the Saab, plus a marginal power disadvantage, it provides acceleration figures which are broadly similar to the Saab, and at the crucial 0-60 mph time it actually beats the Saab by a fraction.

By giving the GTi slightly lower gearing, Citroen have managed to almost completely disguise any turbo hesitation, and the result is an instant pick-up not available from the Swede. Add to this that the turbo begins to spin well below 2500 rpm, and the overall effect is that Citroen's turbo installation is arguably a more usable one for most road conditions.

Performance is certainly tremendous compared with any other CX we have tried in the past; 60 mph is covered in only 8.0 secs, and 100 mph is seen in 22.3 secs. Fifty to 70 mph and 70 to 90 mph in fifth are covered in 7.9 and 7.4 secs.

As with the Saab, the CX is in its element in high-speed motorway dashes. Again only the slightest pressure on the throttle is enough to provide all the acceleration one could wish for, and the high speed at which the CX responds swiftly to instructions from the right foot is impressive. What the CX's turbo also does is to disguise the rather tired and asthmatic note of the 'big banger' four-cylinder engine; the rousing note of the turbo induction mostly covers the harshness which is present at high revs. Another welcome effect is that because the turbo tap starts to run at low revs, the engine feels immensely torquey – second gear becomes virtually redundant in town-speed traffic.

But at very low speeds the CX begins to shed marks left right and centre. The gearchange has a stiff, notchy movement which can be described as good only in comparison to previous CXs.

The respective top speeds of these cars are somewhat academic, so we have left them to the end of this category. But for the record, the Saab will achieve 125 mph, and the Citroen 131. Few owners will attain such speeds, but nevertheless they cannot fail to impress.

twosome

HANDLING AND RIDE

SAAB	●●●●
CITROEN	●●●

The two cars could hardly be more different in this respect; the Saab is firmly sprung with a taut feeling at all times, whereas the CX is more luxuriously compliant. Considering just how old is the Saab's heritage, there's a surprising amount of roadholding in its chassis. And in this uprated version, Saab engineers have wrung even more grip out of it. The low-profile tyres cling to every corner with stubborn grip and the big car really is a joy to hurl through a series of tight bends.

What's more, the Saab always feels very safe indeed; there is no sting in the tail if the driver goes too far, for the amount of understeer simply gets more and more marked. The rear beam axle defies the usual front-drive trait of sliding out of line if power is taken off midway through a corner. It's a pity, though, that the steering does not have more weight to it, because while taking speedy bends the system feeds back little of what is happening under the front wheels. This latest Saab has more weight to the steering than previous 900s, but a little more still would be welcome nonetheless.

But at low speeds and in parking the Saab's steering is a dream; a tight parking spot can be negotiated with one hand, and for cornering at normal town speeds the gearing of just over 3.5 turns is ideal.

But if the Saab impresses with its sporty handling, its ride lets it down in a big way. Already firm on the standard 900, the 60-series tyres and tougher springs harden it more.

Initially the CX's handling feels a disaster, for the Vari-power steering, with only 2.5 turns lock-to-lock, plus on-or-off brakes, leads to some pretty ragged driving at first. But persevere with the Citroen, learn its idiosyncrasies, and it becomes a car with good handling capabilities.

If there is any real criticism of the high power brakes it's not that one tends to accidentally stop on a sixpence in town, for one soon gets used to the delicate pressure, but that at speeds above 60 mph it can be tricky to reduce speed marginally.

At high speeds on smooth roads the CX is wonderfully even and confortable; but what shows the car's age is that large bumps catch the system out.

CITROEN CX 25 GTi TURBO

GTi version looks similar to other CXs; only alloy wheels and spoiler tell it apart. Turbo installation is very good with little lag. Seating is luxurious but those in front fare less favourably than those in rear in terms of space. Boot is small and cramped – not a CX strength

ACCOMMODATION

SAAB	●●●●
CITROEN	●●●●

Equal marks here, but once again the two cars are completely different. The front seats of the Saab can only be described as excellent – they would alone be capable of selling the car. They offer perfect support along with an ideal driving position, and allow better adjustment than those of the Citroen. As previously mentioned, the front seats go a long way to compensating for the poor ride. Welcome in winter are the heater elements for the front seats, but unwelcome at any time is the poor rear visibility from the driver's seat.

In the rear, occupants have well shaped seats and the slanting rear roofline does not restrict headroom as much as might be expected. But an area in which the Saab shows its age is in the narrowness of the cabin; three adults in the rear is out of the question, and broad-shouldered front occupants may find themselves brushing the door trim. Access to the rear seat is good enough despite only two doors, but rear passengers would doubtlessly prefer to travel in the four-doored 900.

As mentioned, our Saab came with leather seating; this we cannot recommend, for it's a little slippery, especially under cornering, and many will see it as out of keeping with Saab's sporty but sensible image for the up-market 16S.

Rather unusually it's the rear seat passengers who get the better deal in the CX. A big soft bench seat is almost as comfortable as that favourite armchair at home, and three occupants have plenty of head and legroom, as well as more doors to get in and out of.

But in the front the Citroen is disappointing. The seats are not a patch on the Saab's, with back portions sadly lacking in support and being too soft. All but the smallest of drivers will find the steering wheel too close to the knees, the headlining brushing the scalp, and pedals too small and too close together. Finally, seat adjustment is poor: the backrests recline by means of levers and cannot be finely adjusted, and the seat height adjustment does little for comfort. Whereas the Saab has poor rear visibility, it's the frontal extremities of the CX which can be hard to see at times.

If the CX offers rear doors, the Saab replies with an immense boot and opening tailgate. This part of the Saab is one of its best, for despite the streamlined tail of the body the cargo area is truly massive – from almost 100,000 miles with our trusty long-term test 900 we can vouch for this. A further useful feature is the massive tailgate offering a low sill, and that huge rubber bumper doubles as a support when loading heavy objects. No split-rear seat is offered on this model, which is a pity.

The CX is one of the few cars with a 'two-box' shape which does not offer a hatchback and the result is a boot with an irritatingly small opening. No way could large objects be loaded in, and retrieving a small object from the back of the boot requires gymnastics.

LIVING WITH THE CARS

SAAB	●●●●●
CITROEN	●●●

Until now, few points have separated the two, but it's here the Saab pulls strongly ahead for its sheer practicality and thoughtfulness of design. The Saab's dashboard couldn't be clearer; there isn't a vast amount of instrumentation but what there is is well presented in plain yellow on black, meaning that information can be assimilated at a glance.

Heating and ventilation is also very good indeed, with a versatile capability, including a fiercely powerful demister and centre vents which give cool air independently of the heater. Instead of using a conventional steering column lock, Saab position the ignition key down by the gear lever so that it can only be withdrawn when the transmission is in reverse.

High gearing reduces noise levels on the Saab, so at 70 mph-plus things are quiet and relaxed; there's no need to turn up the radio. Under the boot floor there's a neat compartment which houses the tool kit . . . plus a 'space saver' spare wheel. Durability has always been a strong point on Saabs, and while only time can tell how they perform over the years, items such as big bumpers, mud flaps and a general toughness of build will help maintain the car's condition in the short term.

SAAB 900 TURBO 16S

Side skirts and alloy wheels dramatically brighten up otherwise dumpy Saab. Twin cam engine is ultra quick, but still shows some turbo lag. Seating is very comfortable, though optional leather is not to everyone's taste and is expensive. Boot space is excellent and load bay is massive

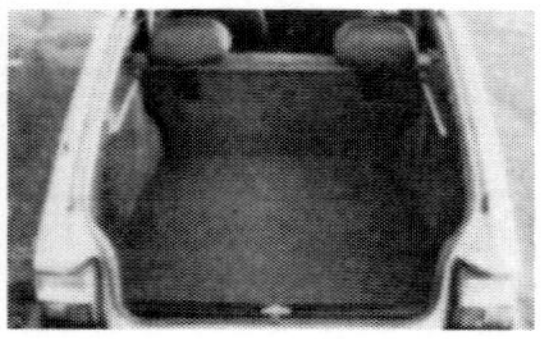

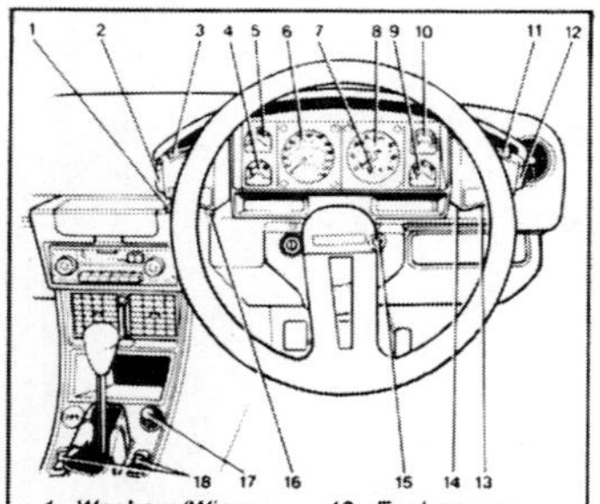

1. Washers/Wipers
2. Horn
3. Indicators
4. Water temp
5. Oil temp
6. Speedometer
7. Boost gauge
8. Rev counter
9. Oil pressure
10. Fuel gauge
11. Dip/main
12. Headlamp flash
13. Lights
14. Rear fog
15. Rheostat
16. Hazard warning
17. Lighter
18. Window lifts

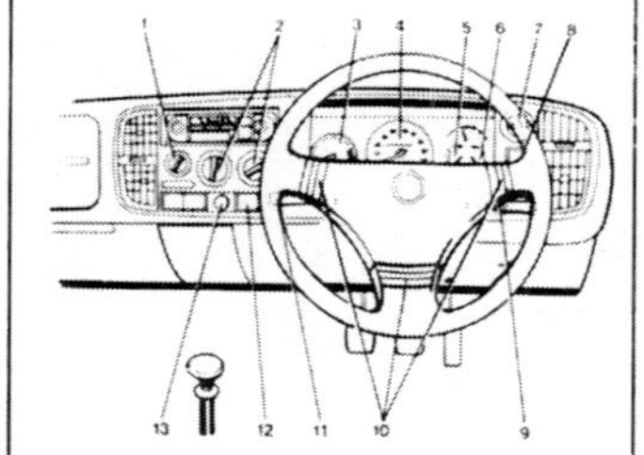

1. Heater fan
2. Heater controls
3. Rev counter
4. Speedometer
5. Fuel gauge
6. Water temp
7. Lights
8. Rear fog
9. Washers/wipers
10. Horn
11. Heated rear window
12. Hazard
13. Lighter

The biggest change to the CX for many a year has been the fitting of a conventional instrument panel to nestle among the company's traditional fingertip controls. Whether this arrangement is a better one is an impossibly subjective judgment, but it's certainly crammed with information – perhaps too much for instant clarity.

The rest of the facia is good; those controls work very well once you get used to them and the non-cancelling indicators are, on balance, a good thing. But it's annoying that a cheap-looking digital clock has been thoughtlessly slapped on near the ignition switch. On a roof console are mounted the interior light and heated rear window switches.

Low marks are due to the CX's poor heating and ventilation. For a start, even at full blast, the heater puffs out precious little heat despite a noisy fan. It's also a pity that there is no independent fresh air supply.

Noise levels are higher in the CX than the Saab, but there's still little cause for complaint. At speeds up to 100 mph the Citroen is still civilised in this respect. Most testers liked the luxurious looking but restrained interior trim of the CX – more so than the Saab's leather.

COSTS

SAAB	●●●
CITROEN	●●

There can't be a winner here, for both cars are not only thirsty on petrol but will cost a lot in general running costs too. Government fuel figures show the Saab to be marginally more economical than the CX – 22.4/39.8/29.7 at urban 56 mph/75 mph compared with 20.2/35.3/28.5. But in practice both cars are likely to return fuel consumption well below 25 mpg, and if the turbo is used too liberally, under 20 mpg. Our CX gave us 22 mpg under normal driving, slipping to 18.5 after our test session, while the Saab returned 22 mpg and 21.1 mpg under similar conditions. A best of 25.8 mpg was worthy of praise.

Servicing takes place at 12,000 miles for the Saab, with an oil change at 6000 miles, while the CX needs attention at 10,000 miles with a lubrication halfway. Citroen score better on the number of dealers with 270; Saab only have 146. But when it comes to workshop repairs the Citroen's mechanical complexity scores against it – some jobs normally straightforward on other cars take many hours, even although parts are not that expensive. A clutch change for example, needs 14.4 workshop hours.

Mechanical guarantees for both cars are 12 months and an unlimited mileage, and Citroen additionally offer a separate warranty on the suspension. Citroen also issue a six-year anti-rust guarantee.

VERDICT

SAAB	●●●●
CITROEN	●●●

The Saab is the logical winner here – add up the points both have scored in the course of the contest and it's the Saab that wins the match. Despite its age the Saab is still a stunner, with phenomenal performance. Best of all it combines the enjoyment of driving with a high degree of practicality.

But even although the Saab is a highly desirable car, we feel we must withold that extra blob which would have given it a full house. Thrilling performance apart, the turbo engine needs more thrust lower down.

With its comfort bias, the CX chassis is possibly not the best car to try to turn into a sportster, but Citroen has done an excellent job and the result is a huge improvement over previous sporty CXs.

What is particularly good about the CX is just how well the turbo suits the engine and what it does for the drivability of the car. It rejuvenates a rather tired old engine and injects that indefinable quality into the CX – driving pleasure.

The dynamic qualities of the Citroen are a little behind those of the Saab, but it's really in terms of practicality and how well you could live with the CX which finally lets the Saab win through.

HOW THE CARS COMPARE

CAR	CITROEN CX 25 GTi TURBO	SAAB 900 TURBO 16 S
PRICE	£12990	£14090
Other models	4 saloons 6 estates	7 h/backs, 5 saloons
Price span	£8450-£16367	£8315-£14090
PERFORMANCE		
Max in 5th (mph)	135	125
Max in 4th (mph)	105	109
Max in 3rd (mph)	85	87
Max in 2nd (mph)	58	55
Max in 1st (mph)	33	29
0-30 (sec)	2.5	2.7
0-40 (sec)	4.2	4.9
0-50 (sec)	5.7	6.4
0-60 (sec)	8.0	8.2
0-70 (sec)	10.2	11.4
0-80 (sec)	13.2	13.9
0-90 (sec)	17.6	18.2
0-100 (sec)	22.3	24.3
0-400 metres (sec)	16.3	16.9
Terminal speed (mph)	86	87
30-50 in 3rd/4th/5th (sec)	4.0/5.6/10.9	4.4/8.1/13.0
40-60 in 3rd/4th/5th (sec)	3.8/5.0/8.9	3.8/6.6/10.6
50-70 in 3rd/4th/5th (sec)	4.4/5.2/7.9	3.6/5.7/8.5
60-80 in 3rd/4th/5th (sec)	5.6/5.5/7.4	3.4/5.7/8.5
70-90 in 4th/5th (sec)	9.9/9.3	5.7/6.0
SPECIFICATIONS		
Cylinders/capacity (cc)	4/2500	4/1985
Bore x stroke (mm)	93 x 92	90 x 78
Valve gear	ohv	dohc
Induction	inj/turbo	inj/turbo
Compression ratio	7.8:1	9.0:1
Power/rpm (bhp)	168/5000	175/5300
Torque/rpm (lbs/ft)	217/3250	201/3000
Steering	PA/rack/pin	PA/rack/pin
Turns lock to lock	2.5	3.6
Turning circle (ft)	38.5	34.0
Brakes	P/Di(v)/Di	S/Di/Di
Suspension front	I/Hp	I/Wi
rear	I/Hp	DA/C
COSTS		
Test mpg	18.5-22.3	21.1-25.8
Govt mpg City/56/75	20.2/35.3/28.5	22.4/39.8/29.7
Tank galls (grade)	15.0(4)	13.9(2-4)*
Major service miles (hrs)	10,000 (2.4)	12,000 (3.0)
Parts costs (fitting hours)		
Front wing	£79.19 (6.0)	£83.50 (4.1)
Front bumper	£144.20 (2.4)	£160.00 (0.4)
Headlamp unit	£56.05 (1.0)	£77.50 (0.4)
Rear light lens	£41.33 (0.1)	£45.50 (0.1)
Front brake pads	£22.73 (1.2)	£26.50 (0.7)
Shock absorber	£51.52 (0.5)	£35.56 (0.3)
Windscreen	£118.54 (2.3)	£72.94 (1.2)
Exhaust system	£175.57 (1.4)	£162.50 (1.0)
Clutch unit	£95.81 (14.4)	£77.50 (2.1)
Alternator	£73.05 (1.2)	£80.00 (1.5)
Insurance group	8	8
Warranty	12/U	12/UI
Anti-rust	6 yr	none
EQUIPMENT		
Cruise control	no	yes
Petrol cap lock	no	no
Leather upholstery	£957	£600
Rear seat belts	£51	yes
Heated front seats	no	yes
Sunroof	£523	yes
Headlamp wash/wipe	no	yes
DIMENSIONS		
Front headroom (ins)	33-35	36
Front legroom (ins)	33-41	36-40
Steering-wheel-seat(ins)	10-17	12-18
Rear headroom (ins)	32	35
Rear kneeroom (ins)	32-40	26-33
Length (ins)	183	186
Wheelbase (ins)	112	99
Height (ins)	52	56
Overall width (ins)	70	66
Int. width (ins)	58	54
Weight (cwt)	27.3	24.8
Towing weight (cwt)	25.6	29.5
Boot capacity (cu ft)	16.1	21/56

KEY. ***Valve gear:*** *ohc, overhead valve; dohc, double overhead cam.* ***Steering:*** *rack/pn, rack and pinion;* ***PA:*** *power assistance.* ***Brakes:*** *Di, Discs; (v), ventilated; S, servo; P, power assistance.* ***Suspension:*** *I, independent; C, coil springs; Hp, hydropneumatic; DA, dead axle; Wi, wishbones.*
**Saab runs on any fuel grade.*

CITROEN CX GTi

Attractive alloy wheels are standard fitting on GTi and suit car's lines well. A drastic change for GTi is conventional dials to replace previous unusual rotating drum instruments of before

SAAB 16S

Saab's profile is complemented by alloy wheels, a simple yet pleasing design. A sunroof is standard, unlike the CX. Badge on tailgate tells the Saab's story; 16 valves and double overhead cams give tremendous performance potential

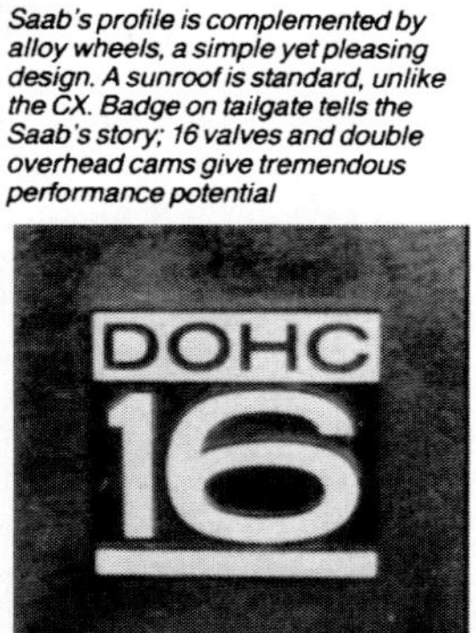

Citroën CX25 GTi Turbo

A special appeal

FROM THE point of view of a road tester, assessing any Citroën model is a task fraught with more hazards than usual. The word *idiosyncratic* might have been coined specifically with the respected French marque in mind. Truly, owning and driving a Citroën is not only a way of life, it is also a state of mind. Devotees are incredibly loyal to the company, if not necessarily fanatical motoring enthusiasts. It can be argued that Citroën's name and reputation was founded not on the production of an invigorating, high performance sporting saloon, but on levels of ride comfort and accommodation which the buyer would find impossible to find elsewhere on the market, at any price.

Citroën owners are loath to change their marque loyalty. On the other hand they seem more than content to buy a succession of variations on a single model, a factor which must surely have accounted for the longevity of the Light 15, and the DS and the CX range — the three large saloons which have served this manufacturer so effectively since the Second World War. It is over 10 years since the CX range finally supplanted the DS, but there is obviously still plenty of life in Citroën's current big saloon yet as our recent experiences with the CX25 GTi turbo definitely indicate.

Free-revving, long-legged performance has always been a hallmark of Citroën CX behaviour, the earlier models being relaxed and reassuring at high speed although they had to be rowed along quite energetically to get them up to speed in the first place. The advent of the CX25 GTi turbo changes all this, endowing this capacious four door saloon with a top speed in the region of 135 mph and 0-60 mph taking around 9 sec.

The 93 × 92 mm, 2,500 cc four-cylinder engine is equipped with a Garrett T3 turbocharger which boosts its output to a very respectable 168 bhp (DIN) at 5,000 rpm, and the incorporation of new integrated electronic ignition has helped contribute to significantly improved torque figures of 217 lb/ft (DIN) at 3,250 rpm which makes the car more flexible, less frantic and altogether a more relaxed proposition in traffic.

Although the engine performs well enough, and revs quite freely, it is not the smoothest engine in its class. But it has been matched to its turbocharger extremely effectively and there is no obtrusive throttle lag to make life tedious: in fact, there is only a slight whine from the turbine to indicate that this is not a normally aspirated machine, even though the performance very definitely suggests otherwise.

Few people would deny that the Citroën CX has an attractive, wind-cheating profile which set standards of aerodynamic excellence in the mid-1970s that many other cars have even yet failed to match. Lack of wind noise and impressive directional stability are aspects of this Citroën's behaviour which prove hard to dislodge from one's memory, but there are other features of its road manners (dare I say *quirks?*) which require a little more acclimatisation.

In terms of interior equipment, the CX has grown up considerably since its arrival on the market. The velour-trimmed seats are supportive and unquestionably luxurious, offering splendid levels of comfort although, with energetic cornering in mind, we would have appreciated a little extra lateral support. The fascia is dominated by a single spoke steering wheel of distinctly Citroën style, while the old digital instrumentation has given way to a neatly laid out

DESPITE injection trunking and a turbocharger, there is still room for the fat spare tyre to nestle behind the transverse block.

selection of legible circular dials for speedometer, rev counter, turbo boost, water and oil temperature and oil pressure functions. Tinted windows are standard all round and the whole interior is re-styled in predominantly black trim. At each outer extremity of the instrument binnacle immediately in front of the driver are a selection of controls which can easily be reached by the fingertips when the driver has his hands at the traditional ten-to-two position. I confess that I remain totally bewildered that such a well-equipped car comes with flashing indicators that have to be manually cancelled, although, having said that, they are no hardship.

The gearchange controlling the five-speed 'box feels a little rubbery at first acquaintance, but once you learn to utilise the full length of clutch travel, selection of the individual ratios becomes no problem at all. Dramatic, tyre-burning starts invoke a measure of sudden torque reaction from the front-wheel-drive configuration, but once on the move the legendary Citroën stability takes over and progress is confident and reassuring. Strangely, the CX25 GTi turbo does not feel particularly quick off the mark, but when its progress is checked against the stopwatch there can be no questioning its competitiveness.

Citroën's excellent hydropneumatic suspension system incorporates height correctors all round, enabling the suspension to maintain constant ground clearance no matter what load is being carried by the vehicle. In the case of the GTi turbo, the specification includes stiffer anti-roll bars and dampers all round and the result is a ride sufficiently firm to complement the car's performance but not harsh enough to detract from the inherent comfort provided by the hydropneumatics system. The manner in which this Citroën suspension soaks up the bumps never fails to amaze some and a trip up a local farm track which connects two sections of tarmac lane could be accomplished in comfort at around 40 mph in conditions where 15 mph is a spine-cracking affair in a Capri 2.8i.

Initially, trying to drive energetically whilst getting used to the variable feel, rack and pinion power steering demands a great deal of concentration. Once on the move the steering is finger light, increasing in feel as the speed builds up, but there is an inevitable temptation to use excessively large wheel movements at first acquaintance. The problem is that one tends to grip the wheel too tightly and it takes quite a time before you realise to relax and feed in just the most gentle input with one hand whilst steadying the rim with the other. Once this technique has been mastered — and it *does* take some time — the GTi turbo can be thrown into corners with a reassuring degree of confident abandon, understeering progressively and rolling quite considerably, but sustaining high levels of ultimate adhesion thanks to its 210/55 VR390 Michelin TRX radials mounted on wide alloy rims, the trims of which are of a flat design for low drag.

The braking performance is well in keeping with the rest of the car's performance with discs all round, ventilated at the front, solid at the rear. There is a powerful servo which tends to catch out the unwary: one barely needs to *brush* the brake pedal in order to unleash the most generous decceleration. What is more, because maximum rear brake pressure is controlled via the suspension system, the GTi turbo maintains normal braking performance under all load conditions.

A week in the company of this top-of-the-range Citroën brought me to the stage where I was just feeling confident and familiar with its very particular handling qualities. It is not a car like a high performance BMW or Ford where one hops in and feels safe and secure, well able to get the most out of it, within a few miles. It is one of the few cars left in which one has to consciously adapt one's technique to produce the best of its character. Drive the Citroën GTi turbo like any other large saloon car and progress will be ineffective, possibly disappointing. Concentrate hard, make the effort and the experience becomes rewarding — not to mention relaxing and highly efficient.

With a 15 gallon fuel tank, the GTi turbo is capable of covering somewhere around 430 miles on one fill-up, an average consumption of just below 30 mpg which is clearly quite feasible on a lengthy run. Ducking and diving in and out of London's rush-hour traffic, mixing a smattering of Motorway cruising with some acrobatics through tiny rural lanes, the GTi turbo returned an average of 25.9 mpg during its time at Standard House. That seemed impressive enough to us, bearing in mind the ease in which this oh-so-very French performer can cruise for mile after mile in the region of 110/115 mph.

Bear in mind, also, that this is a very well equipped high performance saloon. Standard equipment includes electric windows front and rear, front and rear head restraints, central door locking, laminated windscreen, front brake pad wear warning light, rear sun blinds, tinted windows, rear spoiler, height adjustable driver's seat and front driving lamps. All of which adds up to a quite impressive package with a price tag of £12,990, taxes paid, particularly for those with a life-long devotion to this manufacturer of technically sophisticated French cars. — A.H.

CITROEN CX25 DTR TURBO £11,929

Ten years ago, when the Citroen CX was new, people said the same things about it as they did only a year ago about the BX middleweight – that it wasn't different enough for a Citroen, that it erred too much toward the mainstream of buyers' tastes, that it would age far faster than the DS models that had gone before. They even said it 'wasn't far enough ahead of its time', which was one of the ironies of the '70s.

Why? Because the Citroen CX is only truly realising its potential a decade after its launch. In the past 12months, the two best versions of the car – the two that suit its style and function best of all – have been launched, and have taken it onto a new plane of sophistication and desirability. These are the CX GTi Turbo (launched a couple of months ago at £12,990) and the CX25 DTR Turbo (new this time last year, selling now at £11,929). Each confers a new performance capability on the CX, and each is one of the best turbo applications available in Europe today. That is probably because each uses a relatively large engine, mildly pressurised, so that the step between boost-on and boost-off is not the usual insurmountable step; the words 'throttle lag' rarely pass the reviewers' lips.

Our favourite of the pair is the DTR Turbo because of the remarkable mix of qualities it has. The petrol turbo GTi is merely a fast car made quicker (it will touch 140mph on a good day), whereas the turbo diesel is a quick car which has the supreme lack of fuss of a diesel, amazing flexibility while supporting a gearing which is about the most relaxed (highest) of any car in the class – and it has the ability to deliver 35mpg under really tough conditions, and better than 40mpg when the going is easy. That is a feat which seems to break all conventional rules when you consider that the machine needs practically no gearchanging when driven in town, can sprint from 0-60mph in around 13sec, a respectable time, is even more competitive with petrol opponents in its passing acceleration times – say, 60-80mph – and has a true top speed approaching 110mph. That means it'll cruise all day at 100mph with a little over 3500rpm on the clock! Those who have considered the low wear rates and the fuel savings of this car are the ones who are ordering it up in numbers the dealers can barely handle.

original concept. Even now, people see it as futuristic, something which throws mud very firmly in the eye of the critics of '74.

The CX package itself stands up extremely well. It's no secret that there will be a facelift for the shape – the first for 10years

– in 1985, but even now it's hard to imagine just what will be changed for the better. The interior is in for alteration, of course, but that is easy enough to foresee when you consider just how much the inside of, say, a family Ford has come in a decade. But it is still an even bet that the '85, changed, CX will be different rather than better, and that fact speaks volumes for the beauty of the

On the road, the CX shows its age but little. The low-speed bump-thump which now exceeds that of a comparable Volvo or Ford Granada, has been tamed to an extent by the fitment of Michelin TRX tyres, but it's still there. The wind noise is a little

'It is an even bet that the changed CX will be different rather than better'

out of court. The high-geared, fully powered steering now lacks the sensitivity of more conventional power arrangements, though its sharpness is still a virtue to those of us who have taken the time to learn it well.

The car's suspension advantages, barring some 30mph thumps, shine as brightly as they did in 1974. The remarkably relaxing gait, the brilliance of the self-levelling quality, the refusal of the car to nose-dive under brakes; these things are as striking as they were in '74 – and that makes you wonder just what has been achieved by the steel spring brigade in 10years.

CITROEN CX 25 FAMILIALE

CITROEN CX FAMILIALE

Price	£9222-£11,833
●●●●	
Engine cc/bhp	petrol 1995/106, 2500/138 diesel 2500/75
Gearbox	5-sp man, 3-sp auto
Max speed (mph)	petrol 103, 112 diesel 94
MPG	petrol 23-26 diesel 28-32
Length (ins)	195
Boot cap (cu ft)	16/38
Headroom front/centre/rear	37/37/33
Max Legroom front/centre/rear	42/36/26
Seat width centre/rear	53/42
Rear seat belts	no
Power steering	yes
Central locking	no

Streamlined Citroen uses hydropneumatic suspension to provide very good ride laden and unladen; centre row of seats is not comfortable and entry into rear can be awkward. Injection car is a capable fast cruiser but is not so happy when performing tight manoeuvres

Citroen, past masters at the estate art, spared no effort with the CX, giving it not just an extended wheelbase but a raised roofline too. Though it has been out for almost a decade now, the CX still rates as an original, eccentric and semi-space-age estate design, with the boxy cargo end contrasting starkly with the streamlined nose.

The transversely mounted front wheel drive four cylinder engine has crept up in power over the years: now it is a mighty 2.5 litres and gives 138 bhp thanks to its fuel injection. Two-litre carburettor fed versions are also available, as is a diesel. Suspension is independent by high-pressure hydraulics which also power the steering and the brakes.

Seating plan in the CX is similar to the Peugeot's except that the centre row of seats is split into three, with the centre portion fixed and only the side seats tipping forward for access to the back. Comfort in the centre is nowhere near as good as the Peugeot's, though life is better at the very back. Ventilation is very poor indeed, especially for those in the rear, and many's the passenger who has fallen foul of the soft, floaty suspension and the unreal feel of the CX's airliner-like ride.

For an estate, the hydraulic suspension is ideal: it allows the car to be loaded up to the hilt yet still maintain the same ride height, headlamp beam setting and handling behaviour. Steering, braking and interior design are as unusual as only Citroen can make them: suffice it to say that as many love the cars as loathe them.

With the fuel injection engine the CX's performance is now distinctly rapid, high-speed motorway cruising being the Familiale's true forte. It's less happy around town or in tight mountain work where its length makes it hard to manage. Though the CX may have been made to look over complex and tricky by the Peugeot 505, for many it's the only estate they will ever seriously consider.

French flyer

Citroen CX 25GTI Turbo

Price as tested: £13,594

We have no hesitation in rating this turbo installation as the best there is.

It seems hard to believe (time flies when you are having fun), but the Citroen CX has been around for 11 years. Proof of just how advanced the car was when we were boys!

For while the CX today does not look quite the same space-age machine it surely once appeared to be, it still manages to look as though it possesses a wind-cheating shape. In terms of accommodation it may now be only class average, but in many other respects it still leads the field.

Lemon aids

A year after its launch, in 1975, the CX was voted Car of the Year by 49 journalists from 14 European countries. At the Geneva motor show, it won the supreme 'Award Style Auto' for its design, and the French motoring press gave it the safety award 'Prix de la Securité'. Citroen can still boast that no other vehicle in the world has won all these three awards.

Mind you, that was ten years ago and times change. Is the CX now in the twilight of its life? Well, the hand-on-heart word from Citroen is that there is plenty of life in the old dog (if that's the right word) yet and further models are in the pipeline. With petrol engines, diesel engines (some turbocharged, some not) and saloon and estate variants, you wonder what could possibly be next. Your guess might just be as good as ours but an interior face-lift is surely overdue.

Meanwhile the CX sits in a sector of the market which is losing ground as many drivers decide to 'buy down' into a different class. Not many could 'buy down' to a Citroen CX.

That said, dealers found themselves able to order the latest Citroen CX 25GTI Turbo towards the end of October and by mid-January they had collected over 100 cars. Clearly, the garage boss could drive nothing else.

An educated guess puts total sales for 1985 in the UK at about 300 turbo cars — making them a pretty exclusive form of transport. The car — as tested here — is fitted with a fuel-injected, four-cylinder engine of 2500cc capacity which develops 168bhp at 5000rpm and a truly remarkable 217lb ft of torque at a very modest 3250rpm. Without the 'blower' this big-banger would give just 138bhp and 155lb ft of torque at 4000rpm.

How it goes

Citroen claims that the turbo's torque figure is the best in its class — we can believe that. And performance claims are designed to impress — a top speed of 136mph and a 0-62mph acceleration time of 8sec. It would take a test track to show just how honest the claims were, but on the road the car's tremendous flexibility at mid-range ensures that nothing leaves you behind. We have no hesitation in rating this turbo installation as the best there is, with the possible exception of the Lotus Esprit Turbo.

With so many cars, the turbo just isn't suited for the use to which the car is likely to be put. Screaming power is all very well at the test track where you make a determined effort to use it all, but on the road such cars can have power gaps in all the wrong places. Some turbos are so biased to producing top-end power that they can be driven for miles and miles without being called upon to blow at all.

Nevertheless, we did wonder if a turbo that blows from just 2000rpm like that would make you pay for your pleasures by visits to filling stations. Our hard driving, which included many short trips in freezing weather, produced an overall return of 18mpg. Most buyers we reckon would be sure to improve on that figure but not necessarily by much. After all, why pay for power if you don't plan to use it?

And use it we did. There's no trace of turbo lag (the delay while you wait for the turbo fan to accelerate to its phenomenal speed) as the car leaps off with breathtaking urge. Indeed, the CX is much better on the road than it is on the test track — and it isn't bad there, by any means.

First reaction to the CX 25GTI Turbo was far from unbridled enthusiasm, however. Like escargots, a CX is an acquired taste but, like snails, it turns out to be a taste worth acquiring.

One thing Citroen has never done is to copy other manufacturers, thus ensuring that familiarisation with the interior is a job which demands the use of the handbook. DRIVE's tester spent 10 minutes in the dark searching for the heated rear window switch, to discover it, eventually, set into the roof lining. Fog lamps are standard at

the front, as well as the usual high-intensity foglamps at the back — but try finding the switches ... We eventually located them buried under each side of the instrument pod, completely out of sight. Other controls are grouped on two pseudopodia and nothing lights up to help you.

A newcomer to Citroen's hydraulic steering system discovers little of the legendary stability because even a small steering input can rock the car off-line and lead to wobbly over-compensation. That's why you hear tales of sea-sick Citroen passengers. The idiosyncratic, variably-powered set-up has just two turns from lock to lock and its action is unlike anything you have ever experienced before.

A demonstration of how well it works can be arranged by placing a brick in your drive and gently driving over the obstruction with your hands off the wheel. The steering wheel refuses to be deflected.

A useful feature? Well, hit a puddle at very high speed or burst a tyre and you'll have no problems in a CX. That steering system which feels unnerving at first proves to be very safe.

We were less impressed by the way the big, one-spoke steering wheel rubs along the top of thighs — even slender ones like our tester's. The steering wheel position cannot be adjusted to compensate, either.

And the brakes could have been more impressive, too. Like everything else on the CX they rely on the principles of pressurised hydraulics and respond as if operated by an on-off switch rather than a brake pedal. We estimated that the total travel was probably less than one inch — not a lot. It is difficult at first to be smooth on the pedal but there can be no question about the stopping power. Out on the test track, the brakes pulled the car up time and time again from close on 120mph with contemptuous ease. The pedal in those circumstances feels as though it is connected to an anti-locking system, but it isn't. As you pull up with no hint of nose-dive, the pedal oscillates gently under foot.

The Garrett T3 turbocharger fitted under the CX's long bonnet has been under development for many years and its pressure curve has been carefully defined to give lots of torque at low engine speeds. The transition from the normally-aspirated phase is excellent, with power pouring in with creamy smoothness as the turbo starts to whistle. Fuel supply is by Bosch electronic injection, with sensors to ensure good engine management with no risk of over-revving. Surprisingly for an injected car, the big Çitroen didn't start at a touch and our car chuntered slowly to life on the bitterly cold mornings that prevailed through the test. Power delivery was not always perfect, either, with the occasional 'fluff' under hard acceleration. Not severe enough to be called a flat-spot but noticeable even so.

Our test track visit was on one of those days that Citroen stability was necessary to preserve a normal heart beat. The banked high-speed circuit had been cleared of ice except for a widish strip right at the top — which was just where we needed to be. Our aim had to be to run

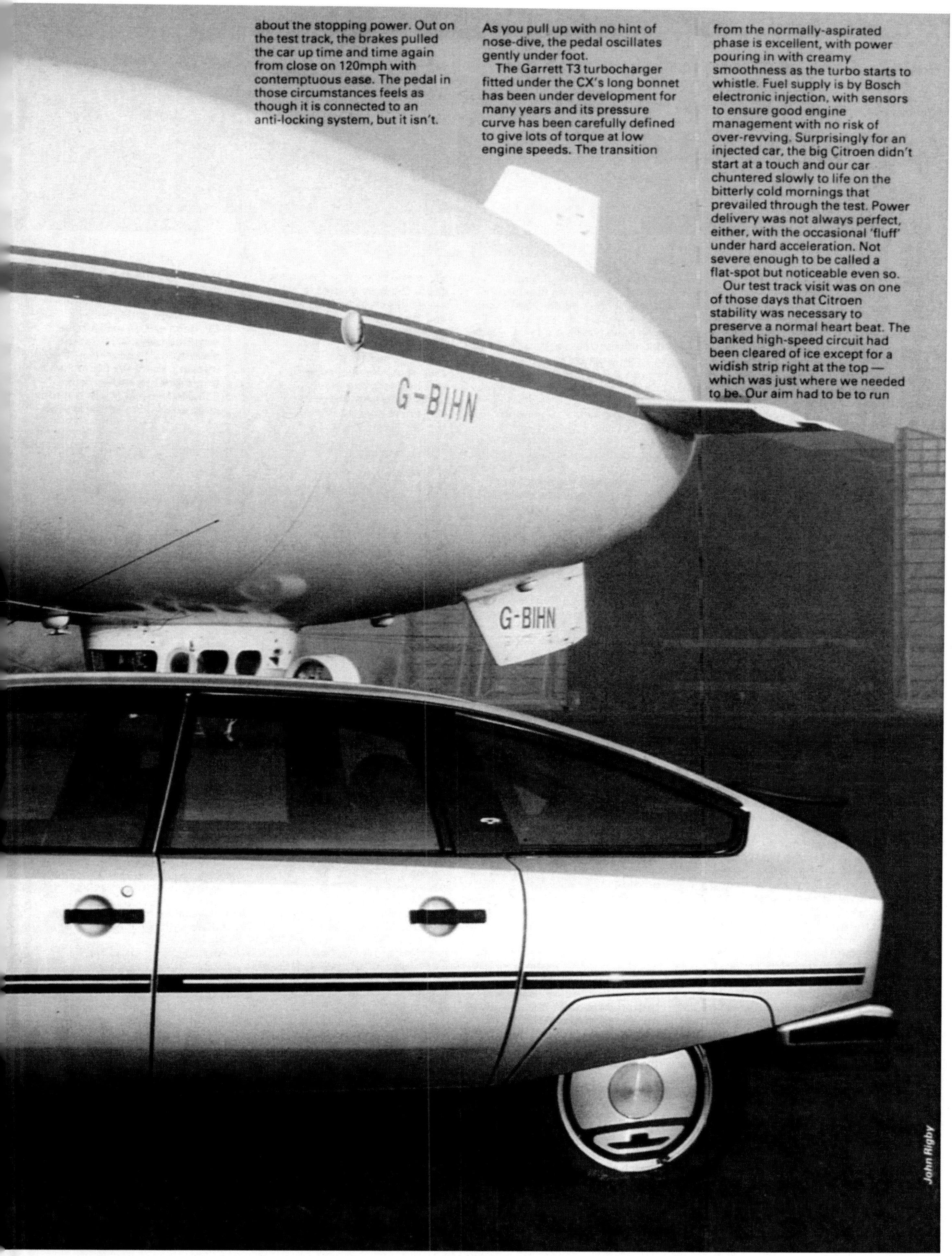

John Rigby

Neat dials are conventional, but small

Big Michelins are standard

Kneeroom's not specially good

Seats are softly sumptuous

close to the ice but not to touch it.

The car was pushed flat out and the watch started. And as each mile post went by, the car went a little faster. By the end of the six-mile blast the speedometer was touching an indicated 140mph but, as usual, the instrument was being less than honest. The stopwatch revealed our true speed to be 128½mph — some way behind the Citroen claim of 136.

A slipping clutch slowed us down when we came to take acceleration figures, but happily it was a problem which manifested itself only at the track.

Ice on the Millbrook steering pad prevented us from measuring maximum sideways G-force, but a spell on the handling course showed that the mighty Michelins had a lot of grip to offer. Bags of power and front-wheel-drive aren't often a recipe for excitement and while a tail-slide is out of the question, the big Cit turns out to be a very satisfying car to hustle. Keen drivers would like a little feel at the steering wheel but the trade-off is the system's speed and responsiveness.

How comfortable

A CX's ride is arguably the best there is. Certainly, it is in the Jaguar bracket and we'd say that a Mercedes can't even approach the magic-carpet quality of the French limousine. The system can be caught out by the occasional hump but it is always extremely impressive.

In turbo form, big tyres and a screwed-down suspension have knocked a lot of the softness out of the system but it remains the best in its class. Seating has been criticised by some magazines because you sit in the seats rather than on them, so making you hot and sticky on a long trip. We don't agree — the seats are as comfortable as they look. However, for such a large car, legroom is not exceptional and pushing the front seats well back leaves rear occupants wondering what's coming. We found the rear seat cushion was set rather low, forcing one to sit doing the knee's-up.

The boot may not be top of the class for space when measured in cubic feet but it is a very practical size with no sill problems. In terms of accommodation, though, the CX is still a saloon with a boot and that means the back seat can't be adjusted to accommodate the occasional large load. Nothing wrong with that, you might say, but somehow the CX just looks as though it ought to have a hatchback's versatility. Every driver, for instance, went looking for a rear wash/wipe system that didn't exist.

Headlamps were fine on main beam but feeble on dip.

It took us a week to familiarise ourselves with the switchgear and we could still find mental blocks when it came to switching off the wiper or flashing the headlamps. On the left-hand pod are indicators (which don't self-cancel — and no one else agrees with Citroen's thinking about that), a strident horn and the wipers. On the righthand pod are light switches, including the dipper and flasher. None of the switches lights up at night.

At least the instrument dials are conventional on this Turbo car. The speedometer is graduated up to 150mph but the small dial makes it difficult to take precise readings. The rev counter offers a broken red line from 5000 to 5500rpm, beyond which a cut-off prevents engine damage. Minor dials include water temperature, oil temperature, fuel gauge and a combined oil-level/oil-pressure indicator. The myriad of warning lamps are not all clearly marked — notably the orange one which signalled a knock-sensor failure and had our puzzled tester checking underbonnet fluid levels because the handbook was of no help.

The effective heating is thermostatically controlled but ventilation is, quite simply, not good enough. Standard equipment includes central locking, electric windows and head restraints all round — but no rear seatbelts. And the AA would not approve of the space-saver tyre housed next to the engine.

VERDICT

The quickest Citroen to date remains the legendary SM with its Maserati connections, but even that ball of fire couldn't match the mid-range acceleration of the CX Turbo.

Given a country which would allow you to do it — Germany is about the only place left — the car would sit happily at 120mph and simply devour those autobahn miles — along with the old four-star, that is.

In those circumstances the car's remarkable arrow-like stability would leave you wondering why anyone would buy anything else. However, before you made a decision to buy it would be worth considering the car's fairly dismal rate of depreciation. Big Citroens are, as we said, an acquired taste. While some people don't know what they are missing, there are others who don't want to know. Your £13,000 bargain might not look such an asset at trade-in time.

PERFORMANCE

Maximum speed 128mph mean/130mph best in 5th, 104mph in 4th, 78mph in 3rd, 50mph in 2nd and 30mph in 1st (at 5500rpm)

Acceleration from rest

true mph	time (sec)	indicated mph
30	2.8	33
40	4.6	43
50	6.0	53
60	8.5	64
70	10.7	74
80	13.9	85
90	17.3	96
100	23.1	107
110	30.8	118
120	38.2	129

Acceleration in gear

	4th (sec)	5th (sec)
20-40	6.4	11.5
30-50	5.0	8.3
40-60	4.9	7.0
50-70	5.1	7.4
60-80	4.9	7.5
70-90	5.8	7.7
80-100	9.3	10.9

Standing ¼-mile 16.2sec
Terminal speed 87mph

ENGINE
Type and size front-mounted 4-in-line, transversely-mounted driving front wheels; 2473cc, water-cooled, cast iron block, aluminium alloy head
Compression ratio 7.75:1
Valve gear pushrod ohv (chain-driven)
Fuel system Bosch L-Jetronic fuel injection with Garrett T3 turbocharger (boost pressure 8psi)
Ignition electronic
Max power 168bhp (DIN) at 5000rpm
Max torque 217 lb ft (DIN) at 3250rpm
TRANSMISSION
Gearbox five-speed manual. Ratios: 1st 3.167:1, 2nd 1.833:1, 3rd 1.207:1, 4th 0.882:1, 5th 0.674:1, final drive 4.2:1
Mph 1000rpm in 5th 25.2, in 4th 19.2
CHASSIS
Suspension Front: independent by equal-length parallel transverse links with anti-roll bar and hydropneumatic self-levelling. Rear: independent by trailing arms, hydropneumatic springs and anti-roll bar
Steering rack and pinion with 'Varipower' hydraulic assistance. 2½ turns between locks
Wheels aluminium alloy 6in rims, with Michelin TRX 210/55 VR390 tyres
Brakes ventilated discs front, plain discs rear, handbrake acting on front discs

The thinking-man's fast Estate

When it came to a long-distance haul, Philip Llewellin reckoned there was just one Estate fit for the job – the Citroen CX Safari

WHAT, you may well ask, is a big, diesel-engined estate car doing in a magazine dedicated to machinery of the sporting ilk? The simple answer is that there are times when even the most enthusiastic driver accepts the need for a sophisticated, spacious and economical holdall.

Nearly two years ago, Mrs Llewellin and I spent a few days in France with a Fiat X1/9. The mid-engined midget was great fun and fairly frugal. But this exercise included two junior Llewellins – Philippa, aged 21, and Magnus, two years younger – plus all the personal and professional kit needed for a comfortable week in a *gite* a few miles south of Caen. Equally important was my determination to return home with a vast quantity of bargain-price beer in addition to our quota of duty-free wines and spirits, plus all manner of French goodies for the pantry.

Transport had to be big enough to guarantee long-distance comfort for the party's human element. In view of the return load, it also had to maintain its equilibrium with a great deal of weight in the back. I thought hard for all of five seconds before putting in a request for a Citroen CX 25DTR Safari.

Stretching the tape to an impressive 16.25 feet, the sleek, shark-like Safari maintains a constant six inches of ground clearance thanks to its unique hydropneumatic suspension. There is no danger of the tail striking sparks from the tarmac or the lights dazzling low-flying aircraft. You can maintain crisp cruising speeds on rural roads whose humps and bumps would otherwise dislodge your fillings. At rest, a fully-laden Safari fools folks who don't know their cars into thinking you must be right out of your tiny little mind. But switch on, wait a few seconds and it raises itself like a well-trained camel.

Another camel-like characteristic is an ability to cover huge distances without pausing to replenish essential fluids. The tank holds 14.9 gallons and we averaged 31.7 mpg while covering just over 1,500 miles. All of which indicates that a 25DTR, driven with a modicum of restraint, can stretch the distance between pumps to 500 miles or more. That is good news, because it has to be said that diesel is smelly stuff that clings to your hands unless you travel complete with a rubber glove. Brimming is a problem, because the fuel froths and foams like a bubble bath, and pumps are often out in the open, in Britain if not in France where, incidentally, diesel is not the bargain it used to be.

Under the bonnet, almost hidden by pumps and plumbing for the suspension, brakes and steering, is a 2.5-litre engine whose four cylinders – slightly bigger in bore than stroke – have their diet boosted by one of Mr Garrett's excellent TO3 turbochargers. The combination delivers 95 bhp at 3,700 revs, losing interest in the proceedings after that point is passed, while the torque curve's 159 lb/ft peak represents only 2,000 rpm.

You ride on 190/65HR TRX Michelins and drive reaches the front wheels through a five-speed gearbox. The top cog gives 28 mph per 1,000 revs, so you need nearly 3,800 to reach the 106 mph maximum claimed by Citroen. This is not a car for startling stopwatch statistics, but it hits the 60 mph mark 13.5 seconds after the clutch starts earning its keep.

Switching from one car to another is easy enough when a typical year embraces almost everything from off-roaders and superminis to the likes of BMW's 158 mph M635CSi. But big Citroens are the exception to the rule. Varipower steering always feels very wierd at first, triggering all manner of ungainly lurches before you speedometer and tachometer, plus minor gauges that are even more difficult to read. If the one for the turbo twinkles into life, drive slowly to your nearest Citroen dealer.

Fortunately, I covered about 250 miles in the Safari before setting out on the first leg of the drive to Normandy. That was more than enough to reconfirm my long-standing faith in the big Citroen as the thinking man's estate car. Here's a potted account of what happened.

Friday: Heavy traffic on the A5 underlines the lack of punch for overtaking, but the M54, M6 and M1 reveal B137 **Saturday:** Magnus, over six feet tall and lanky with it, commends back seat's comfort during 80-minute run through rain to Townsend Thoresen's berth in Portsmouth. Straight aboard *Viking Venturer* and up to dining room where big, £4.45 breakfasts herald a diet-devastating week. Ferry crowded with excited schooldchildren whose energy dissolves when ship clears Isle of Wight and encounters heavy seas. Break out the paper bags, Mr Christian! Llewellins stiffen upper lips and retain their breakfasts. It's a reminder that *mal de* flowers, central heating, big garden, several large-scale maps of the area.

Nip down to Thury Harcourt where Philippa's excellent French – spoken in a Marseille accent, for some inexplicable reason – delights sundry shopkeepers. Supplies include claret, Muscadet, the Calvados without which no Normandy holiday would be complete, and a hyper-pungent cheese said to be the subject of a special by-law forbidding its carriage in Paris taxis.

Sunday: Joke about paper boy failing to deliver *The Observer* before organising a

tune yourself to its unique feel. The same applies to the brakes. The old rubber button has given way to a more conventional pedal, but the system still depends more on pressure than travel. Forget about its sensitivity and you have visions of being brained by the back bumper, or standing the Safari on its shapely snout.

The minor controls take a little learning, but are basically superb. But the instruments can only be described as a joke if you find the bizarre amusing. Presumably designed by someone with a penchant for fairground rides, they include revolving drums for the

EBL to be an excellent cruiser with praiseworthy pose in the wet. Despite motorway morons, average 68 mph from Castell Llewellin to Swiss Cottage. It takes almost as long to find a parking space in the West End, where we met Philippa for a late dinner in Melange, a splendid little Covent Garden restaurant.

Joined by the most senior Llewellins – in London for the weekend – the team quaffs considerable quantities of wine. Yours truly sticks to mineral water and emerges, sober as a judge, to do battle with taxi drivers. Spend night at daughter's house in Dulwich, dreading six o'clock start.

mer has two distinct stages. First, you think you're going to die. Second, you hope you're going to die.

Just under five hours to Cherbourg – a commendable crossing in good weather – then off down Liberty Highway towards our Gites de France cottage in a sleepy hamlet above the River Orne's deep, wooded valley. Citroen's all-disc braking efficiency proved when a lunatic local, presumably filled to the gills with strong waters, overtakes a truck on a corner. Average nearly 60 mph to cottage which exceeds even our most optimistic expectations. Stone walls, beamed living room with log fire, fresh

post-breakfast recce to the nearby Auberge du Pont de Brie, a stone's throw from the Orne, which gets a 'good average' rating in Michelin's invaluable 1985 guide to France. Plaque on wall recalls fact that Manchester Territorials, part of Monty's 59th Division, saw action here towards the end of the Battle of Normandy in 1944.

Return a couple of hours later for five-course lunch. Cost per head is about £13 including aperitifs, two bottles of wine and immense glasses of hard stuff to go with the coffee. Decide to take long walk before slotting self back behind Safari's two-spoke wheel. Mrs Llewellin, first name on list of in-house chefs, later serves inevitably superb evening meal. Contemplate putting masking tape over bathroom scales.

Monday: Along quiet rural roads to a Caen hypermarket, then down to Pegasus Bridge where Major John Howard's glider troops started the ball rolling a few minutes after midnight on D-Day. Alas, the cafe that was the first building in France to be liberated was shut. When the Brits landed in '44, its proprietor went into the garden and excavated the eight cases of champagne buried just before the Nazis arrived five years earlier.

Decide to brim tank, having covered nearly 430 miles since leaving home. It takes a squirt over 13 gallons, so we're averaging virtually 33 mpg despite plenty of pressure on the loud pedal. Like all diesels, the engine does a good impression of Marley's chain-rattling ghost when ticking over, but is perfectly civilised once you get rolling. Handbook recommends wait of 25-60 seconds before firing her up, depending on ambient temperature. Jumping the gun, first thing in the morning, produces more smoke signals than Custer's Last Stand.

Down the Orne Canal to the coast, then back inland following the road taken on D-Day by the King's Shropshire Light Infantry. They went closer to Caen than any other Allied troops, but long and bitter fighting preceded the city's fall. We had almost as much trouble with its traffic before locating the abbey where William the Conqueror was buried before hostile elements tossed his bones into the nearby river. Philippa takes credit for five-star evening meal followed by a well-lubricated *Trivial Pursuits* marathon.

Tuesday: Drive to Bayeux, where father and son discover traditional French *pissoir* from which passers-by can be greeted. Explore narrow, olde worlde streets before visiting majestic cathedral and famous tapestry embroidered to commemorate Battling Bill's trip to Hastings in 1066. Back at base, meal cooked by Magnus paves way for serious assault on the liquid refreshments. Wish my offsprings were as abstemious as the Safari.

Wednesday: Time for the Citroen to stretch its legs on a longish, cross-country run to Mont St Michel and back. Twisty bits draw attention to the five-speed's shift, which is reasonably precise but on the slow side, while long, fast corners highlight the big car's inherent stability. On the straights it cruises at a majestic 80-90 mph and lives up to Citroen's magic-carpet reputation over poor surfaces. Short, sharp crests can catch the suspension out, but that's about all.

Pile a posse of Canadian hitch-hikers into the back, then join a million tourists at Mont St Michel. Despite the crowds, despite the shops selling over-priced junk souvenirs, it cannot fail to impress. My turn to cook tonight, so we dine at the Auberge du Pont de Brie.

Thursday: Along quiet, sun-blessed rural roads to the quaint old port of Honfleur where tall, timber-framed buildings overlook the inner harbour. A couple of beers in the open air, a big picnic, then a stroll through the narrow streets before the Safari gets another bundle of miles under its belt.

Friday: Lots of rain, so off to another Caen hypermarket for the end-of-week shopping The load includes two cases of wine, 400 quarter-litre bottles of beer, four bottles of firewater and all manner of solids rated as good buys by the ladies. Our trusty steed has averaged 30.2 mpg over the previous 391 miles.

Saturday: Bid a reluctant farewell to the cottage, then make tracks for the D-Day beaches. First to Arromanches, where the Mulberry harbour was built, then to Omaha and the last resting place of 10,000 Americans. Finally to Pointe du Hoc whose cliffs were scaled by US Rangers with ropes and grappling irons. Spend the night in Carentan.

Sunday: Down to Omaha Beach, posing the Safari with a Sherman tank in the background, then spend a good, in every sense of the term, three hours making our way through a five-course, £7 lunch at the France et Fuchsias in the fishing port of St-Vaast-la-Hougue. Discovered during the 1983 trip, the restaurant now ranks high amid our all-time favourites.

A calm, uncrowded crossing, complete with Sunday papers, and *Viking Venturer* reaches Portsmouth right on schedule. But there's a long night ahead. We could rest the bones in London, but I have to be back at the typewriter first thing tomorrow morning. So it's up the road to Dulwich, followed by the prospect of nearly 200 miles of serious route-frapping twixt there and Castell Llewellin. But the long-striding Safari, in its element on deserted, late-night motorways, covers the distance in little more than three hours.

The only problem, when we reach home, is finding space to store all that beer.

Safari on Mont St Michel causeway.

Photography by Kent Mears

Oh so French

The CX 25 continues Citroen's distinctly Gallic and slightly eccentric approach to luxury motoring.

by David McKay

LET ME DECLARE my bias right away. I have been an admirer of Citroen ever since my first sighting as a school boy when a friend's parents turned up one weekend in the "Traction Avant" model. The year was 1934 and the car had a streamlined integral all-steel body, no running boards, torsion bar suspension, four independently suspended wheels, hydraulic brakes and front-wheel drive.

I have many fond memories of Citroen – the pale green "Big Six" in the 1950 Bathurst race; the unveiling of the DS19 at the Paris Salon in 1955; the D Super driven by Lucien Bianchi and Jean Claude Ogier that almost took out the 1968 London to Sydney Marathon (but for a runaway Mini that took out the Citroen at a control); the Ogier-driven 2.1-litre DS that won the 1970 Ampol Trial; the Maserati four-cam-six engined SM I drove in France.

It was no surprise when in Stuttgart with Daimler-Benz in the mid-1970s Citroen came up over dinner. I was asked which car had impressed me most during the past 25 years of road testing and I replied Citroen. Yes, of course, said the DB director, "but of the ordinary cars which one?" Praise indeed.

My latest encounter with a Citroen was when I had the chance to drive a CX 25 electronically injected automatic on a longish country run. Being an automatic the CX was no fire cracker around town. But if stirred along manually, it developed into a worthy traffic carver.

Of course, its forté is highway touring. I don't know of another car which gives a better impression of flying. It is so silent, the seats so comfortable and roomy that you expect a hostess to waft by with a little something before she serves dinner.

The interior of the CX reflects the luxury one expects from Citroen. The cloth trim in the model I drove is the standard fitment and leather is available as an option at $1000.

I gave the CX a fairly storming run down the south coast of NSW and up into the highlands using the automatic box like a manual till the tyres were squealing in protest. Under this handling the car's fuel consumption was 14 litres per 100 kilometres.

There were only two minor points of contention: The wiper blade intrudes into the front seat passenger's line of vision, and the instrumentation looks fussy and old fashioned – particularly in a car otherwise so sleekly designed.

CITROEN CX25 PALLAS IE
2.5-litre, three-speed auto

ENGINE

Location .... Front, longitudinally mounted
Cylinders/cooling .... Four, in-line/water cooled
Bore x Stroke .... 93.0 x 92.0 mm
Capacity .... 2500 cm^3
Induction .... Electronic fuel injection
Compression Ratio .... 8.75 to 1
Fuel Pump .... Electric
Valve Gear .... Cog-belt drivein single OHC
Claimed Power .... 103 kW at 5000 rpm
Claimed Torque .... 210 Nm at 4000 rpm
Maximum Recommended Engine Speed .... 6000 rpm
Specific Power Output .... 41.2 kW/litre

TRANSMISSION

Type .... Three-speed automatic
Driving Wheels .... Front

Gearbox ratios

Gear	Ratio	km/h 1000 rpm	Max Speed	At (rpm)
First	2.478	14.5	87	6000
Second	1.478	24.3	146	6000
Third	1.000	35.9	194	5400

Final-Drive Ratio .... 3.14 to 1

SUSPENSION

Front .... Independent, hydropneumatic self-levelling
Rear .... Independent, hydropneumatic self-levelling
Wheels .... Alloy
Tyres .... 185 RA XVS Michelin

BRAKES

Front .... ventilated discs
Rear .... discs

STEERING

Type .... rack and pinion
Turns, Lock to Lock 2.5
Turning Circle .... 11.5 metres

DIMENSIONS AND WEIGHT

Wheelbase .... 2845 mm
Front Track .... 1514 mm
Rear Track .... 1360 mm
Overall Length .... 4657 mm
Overall Width .... 1770 mm
Overall Height .... 1360 mm
Ground Clearance .... 155 mm
Kerb Weight .... 1370 kg
Weight to Power .... 13.3 kg/kW

CAPACITIES AND EQUIPMENT

Fuel Tank .... 68.0 litres
Cooling System .... 12.3 litres
Engine Sump .... 5.3 litres
Battery 12V 60AH

CHECKLIST

Alloy Wheels .... Yes
Adjustable Steering .... No
Air-conditioning .... Yes
Central door locking .... Yes
Clock .... (digital led) Yes
Intermittent Wipers .... Yes
Petrol-filler lock .... Yes
Power Steering .... Yes
Power Windows .... Yes
Radio .... Yes
Tape Player .... Yes
Remote outside mirror adjustment ... (two, manual) Yes
Tachometer .... Yes

FUEL CONSUMPTION

European City/Highway .... 12.2/9.2 litres/100 km

ACCELERATION (claimed)

0-100 km/h .... 11.7 seconds
Standing 400 Metres .... 18.2 seconds

LIST PRICE $34,950
PRICE AS TESTED $35,400
Includes options: Spoiler, black window trim and door handles $450

The Citroen certainly stands out, a rare beauty among our every day conveyances. For anyone wanting a very special car and who's prepared to learn her very French ways, I'd recommend the CX 25.

The return of the chevron

CITROEN is one of a number of European marques which slid into limbo in Australia as a result of bartered import quotas and stringent emission controls. But the Government's new policy on vehicle imports combined with the adoption by several European countries of emission control laws similar to Australia has meant it has once again become economically viable to import these cars.

According to Sydney Citroen dealer Ian Robinson the French car maker had been unwilling to produce an engine specially modified for Australian design rules. But now that the Swiss and Swedes required similar emission controls, Citroen was making the necessary modifications. As a result the CX 25 is available in Australia – though in very limited numbers.

In addition to the CX 25 Pallas IE automatic a few performance GTi models are also being imported. Although the first to arrive were pre-sold, there should be more of these exciting new cars by around August.

The GTi sports a five speed manual transmission and while it has the same power and torque figures as the EI, it has a claimed top speed of a little more than 200 km/h, can go from 0 to 100 km/h in 9.2 seconds and do the standing 400 metres in 16.6 seconds. It also has beefed up suspension with stiffer shock absorbers and anti-roll bars.

When the GTi does arrive, it will be priced around $36,500.

Individual expression

WHILE CITROEN's unique design makes the cars quite distinctive, our test CX had a few touches added to set it apart even from its brothers. The spoiler at the rear was added as were the black window trim and the black door handles. Normally these are chrome plated stainless steel. All these touches add about $450 to the list price. The only option available on the CX apart from leather trim is metallic paint ($450).

The car sound system for the CX has been added in Australia. The top-of-the-range Alpine with a four speaker system was chosen and is included in the price. □

FUJICHROME BY PETER WEARING SMITH

CITROEN SAFARI — UNE VOITURE FORMIDABLE

We were not looking forward to the trip. After a sixteen hour flight from Hongkong the prospect of eight hours of driving in English traffic didn't exactly appeal.

However, the CX 25 TRi Safari was delivered to us at Heathrow airport, and we were underway. A brief stop to drop a Hongkong friend and fellow passenger in nearby Beaconsfield, then we were off to the first available Marks and Spencers store for some of their delicious, creamy — and disgustingly fattening — meringues. An interview in Coventry was next, followed by the drive up the Motorway to Leeds.

Our fears of succumbing to fatigue proved to be unfounded, however, thanks to the superb comfort of the Citroen's velour covered seats and the excellent driving position we were able to attain.

When the Citroen DS19 was launched in 1955, many reviewers described the design as being twenty years ahead of its time. They were almost right. In fact, some three decades later, the DS design is still recognisable in the CX — itself more than ten years old. It now looks less

FUJICHROME BY PETER WEARING SMITH

outlandish than it did because, with the increasing importance of aerodynamics, other cars are beginning to look more like Citroens.

But if the CX is beginning to look, well, conventional, there is still plenty of technical novelty under the surface. Like the self centreing "VariPower" steering

FUJICHROME BY PETER WEARING SMITH

which can be quite disconcerting if one parks and then switches off with the front wheels still turned. Even with the engine switched off there is still sufficient pressure in the hydraulic reservoir to return the wheels to a straight ahead position.

Then there are the brakes. Citroen brakes used to be operated by a large button instead of a brake pedal. Now, the button is still there, but as a concession to conventional practice, a pedal is provided which pushes against the button, but care must be taken, especially when braking from slow speeds, as the action can be very sudden. From higher speeds, however, the power-assisted four-wheel disc brakes are both firm and progressive without a trace of fade after a series of heavy applications.

The Citroen's ride is superb and the handling likewise. The CX Safari is, by any standards, a large vehicle, but we found it could be thrown around with all the verve of a sports car. It was also very forgiving. If a corner was entered too fast, throttle-off understeer would scrub speed off very quickly indeed. The fully independent suspension utilises double wishbones in front and trailing arms in the rear, anti-roll bars at both ends, and hydropneumatic springing and damping assuring a smooth and level ride, no matter how heavy the load, or how irregular the road surface. For really rough going, ground clearance may be increased by means of a lever mounted on the centre console alongside the handbrake lever.

Long legs were another of the wagon's many virtues. With a top speed of more than 200km/h, the ideal cruising speed seemed to be around 160-170km/h, with the controllability of the car giving a feeling of tremendous confidence. Road and wind noise were such that at these speeds a conversation could be carried on in normal tones.

The five ratios of the manual gearbox in the test vehicle were well spaced, and second and third were particularly useful. Fourth and fifth gears are both overdrives, so high-speed cruising proved remarkably economical, requiring only 11.2 litres per 100km for sustained running at the old 100mph. However, in the heavy traffic of London, the manual gearbox was a pain, coupled as it was with one of the heaviest clutches we have experienced on a road car. Automatic transmission is definitely essential for mainly city or urban use.

The big, 2½ litre, four cylinder engine is mounted transversely and is equipped with Bosch L-Jetronic fuel injection. It produces a respectable 101kW at 5000 r/min and feels virtually indestructible. Maximum torque of 113Nm is developed at 4000 revs, which is surprising because the wagon pulls remarkably well from low engine speeds. Accessibility is good, with the large, rear hinged bonnet lifting well clear for regular maintenance and checks.

We have already commended the seats, but instrumentation and general visibility are also essential factors in safety and comfort. All-round visibility is good, with few blind spots. Despite its size, the Citroen is easy to park, although care must be taken with the very long nose.

Although somewhat way out for our liking, instrumentation is clear, grouped in a binnacle which is well shaded. The speedometer and tachometer are both revolving barrels and there are gauges for fuel, oil pressure and coolant temperature. Above these instruments is an array of warning lights which would do justice to an airliner. On either side of the binnacle is a cluster of switches — direction indicators and wipers/washers to the left and light switches to the right. Also in the left hand group is the button for the two-tone horn. This last should be immensely popular in Asia, as a light touch sounds a polite toot, but heavy pressure unleashes a pair of powerful airhorns, the blast from which would shift even the most obtuse bus or taxi driver.

Load carrying capabilities are prodigious. With the rear seats folded forward, a full 2050mm x 1124mm flat-bed is available. The wide opening rear hatch allows loading of objects up to 900mm in height and one metre in width. Total payload is no less than 700 kg. To secure loads there are six load anchoring points. The "Familiale" version has additional fold-down seating for three passengers in the rear, and with the stepped roof, even these seats afford sufficient headroom for adult passengers.

Altogether, the Citroen is truly *une voiture formidable* and it is hardly surprising that it has attracted a worldwide coterie of devoted followers. Of course, with a vehicle which relies so heavily on electrical and hydraulic systems, expert servicing is essential and any potential buyer in Asia should satisfy himself that adequate servicing facilities are available.

If they are, the Citroen CX 25 TRi Safari is one of the finest and most versatile station wagons on the market.

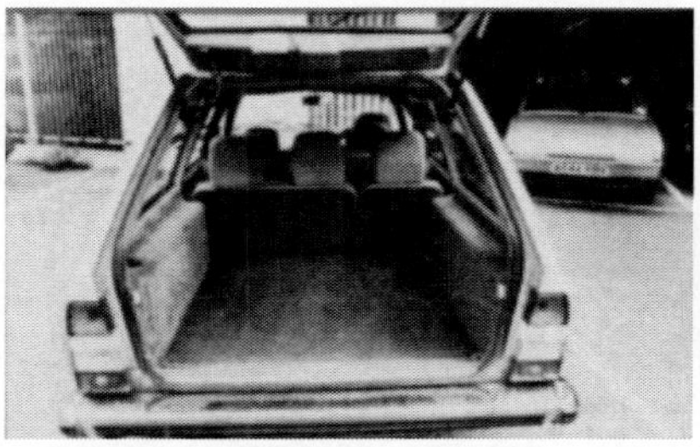

AVANT GARDE REVISITED

Citroën's big CX has been revised inside and out, and a new engine introduced to the range. Camilla Herrmann tried the new CXs and found them almost as idiosyncratic as ever

IN ANY road test of a Citroën, you'll find words like "idiosyncratic", "eccentric", "avant garde" or "controversial" scattered freely among the adjectives. With the absorption of Citroën into the giant PSA empire, its more recent products, the BX and the Visa, aren't quite as Citroën-esque as you might expect. It's left to the 2CV and — at the other end of the scale — the CX, to maintain the standards of individuality.

The Citroën CX first went on sale in 1974, and although it was ahead of its time in some ways, that makes it pretty well obsolete by the existing standards of most major manufacturers. Indeed, PSA engineers are currently working on its replacement, being designed in tandem with the replacement for the Peugeot 604, and due for launch late next year. In the meantime, Citroën has announced major revisions to the CX range. ABS braking becomes available for the first time; there's a new 2.2-litre model; and there are some external revisions and a complete redesign of the interior.

The new models, which go on sale here this week, have been available in France since mid-summer — though, in fact, this is the soonest after the French launch that Britain has ever had a new Citroën model, since Citroën Cars managed to get Type Approval through in record time.

Externally, the new models still maintain the characteristic "basking shark" appearance of the older cars. Colour-coded plastic bumpers, as already seen on the BX, are the major change, along with black plastic sill trims. The door mirrors have been redesigned to cut down the wind noise, which is one of the areas where the CX is showing its age. Aerodynamics, where the CX was once well ahead of the crowd, now rate only as average, with a Cd range from 0.34 on the Prestige to 0.37.

The most obvious changes lie inside the CX, where Citroën has finally decided to do away with the "Cyclops Eye" speedometer, already outlawed on the GTi Turbo, replacing it with conventional dials throughout. The control pods, designed to put lights, indicator and wiper controls within fingertip reach, are in fact extensively redesigned, but probably only the regular CX driver or dedicated Citroën fan would notice the differences, since the set-up is still a long way from a standard two-stalk arrangement. Indicators are now on the left — still non-self-cancelling, although that's something that will be done away with in the near future — and wipers are on the right.

Imaginative use is made of the central console behind the gear lever, where the radio is now mounted. It's evidently intended strictly for the driver's use, however, or for passengers who can read upside down, as the radio is mounted sideways. Gone from the same site is the heating distribution slide, which used to give you the option to move air from the little Citroën man in his trilby hat to the Citroën foot. Instead, the heater controls are all mounted in the centre of the facia. Temperature is thermostatically controlled, with a turn-wheel marked in degrees Centigrade complementing similar controls for heater fan and air intake. Air distribution cannot be adjusted at all, the only possible variations being windscreen demist or complete cut-off of air intake, controlled by push-buttons.

The remaining area on the facia is occupied by three small cubby-holes, covered by flaps which require a sharp blow to open them and a fair amount of force to close. The right-hand one can't open all the way because it's baulked by the instrument pod. The centre cubby contains coin-holding slots; the left-hand one, on the GTi Turbo, conceals the controls for the on-board computer.

The only completely new model in the CX range is the 22 TRS saloon. It uses the Douvrin "four", already utilised in the 2-litre CXs, in its longer-stroke 2165 cc form. The same engine is also used in the Renault 25 GTX, among other applications. In Citroën's carburetted form it produces 115 bhp at 5600 rpm, with 131 lb ft of torque at 3250 rpm. It runs on such a lean mixture that an electric heater has been installed in the inlet manifold to eliminate cold running problems; this should mean that the (manual) choke won't be needed for long even on a cold morning.

ABS, the Bosch designed anti-lock braking system, is now standard on the GTi Turbo and Prestige saloons and available ass a £995 option on all other 2.5-litre models.

On the road

It is always necessary to allow time and miles to get used to any Citroën, making it an exceptionally difficult car to assess in only a few hours. Chief among the CX's quirks, and unchanged in its new guise, is the very strongly self-centring steering. The first input in any steering manoeuvre always goes towards overcoming the self-centring; when nothing appears to happen you turn the wheel a little more; whereupon the power assistance takes over, and you go all over the road. The end result is what is known to CX devotees as "cornering on a 50p piece" (or, for the incorrigibly pre-decimal, "on a threepenny bit"). Given that you understand the problem, the tendency is soon overcome; the trick is not to use any sharp or sudden movements but to let the car do the work. After a little practice you find that the CX can be an immensely relaxing car to drive, with an excellent combination of handling and ride.

The hydropneumatic suspension throughout the CX range has now been stiffened to the same specification as the old normally-aspirated GTi. This eliminates any tendency to wallow, making the CX a pleasure to drive on swooping bends. Ride is, as always, excellent under most circumstances and the CX can take bumps in its stride.

The new 2.2-litre engine successfully fills the gap in the old range between the 2.0 and the 2.5, being a smooth and willing performer which pulls the CX's big body efficiently. Unfortu-

Above: Newcomer to the range, the 22 TRS, in action. Left and below left: Smooth-acting "pod" controls are complemented by modern conventional dials. Below: The whole facia has a more contemporary look. Seats are supportive and comfortable

nately, the example we tried had only 25 miles or so on the clock, making exuberant driving impossible, although there was still plenty of performance to be had.

At the upper end of the range is the GTi Turbo, topped on price only by the long wheelbase Prestige, with its extra rear legroom, air conditioning and leather seats. The Turbo does, however, now feature such little luxuries as heated exterior mirrors, a trip computer and a series of temperature displays. Its performance when we tested it in the old form last November was phenomenal, closer to a supercar than any car in the £13,000 bracket has a right to be. It's impressive to drive, though the performance doesn't kick you in the back; instead the speedo needle just swings rapidly and effortlessly upwards.

Brakes are, of course, the other Citroën idiosyncrasy; the difference between the lightest of check braking and an emergency stop is about half an inch of pedal travel. Those who might have feared locking up the brakes and sliding into the car in front now have their fears assuaged with the fitment of anti-lock braking, which means that you can stop with the customary Citroën efficiency in the wet or if, say, a tractor pulls out in front of you. We only had the opportunity to sample the ABS in the dry; the 10 pulses per second were all but undetectable and stopping efficiency was impressive. Anti-dive suspension compensates for the worst effects of sharp braking in the CX, so even an emergency stop isn't too uncomfortable.

Driving position is good, with excellent wraparound seats and height adjustment on the driver's side. There's not a lot of headroom for a tall driver, however, especially if the optional electric sunroof is fitted. The pod-mounted minor controls take a little getting used to but are smooth and efficient in action.

There are areas where the CX still cries out for improvement; chief among these is ventilation. On a no more than mild September day, with the temperature control set on minimum and fan boost on its somewhat noisy mid-range, fresh air supply simply wasn't adequate; open windows or a sunroof (a £553 option), or perhaps even air conditioning (£736) were really needed. On the driver's side, output from the face-level fresh-air vent is diverted round the control pod and barely brushes your ear.

It's hotter, of course, in an all-black trim GTi Turbo with velour seats. However, the lighter versions don't have it all their own way, since the beige trim creates problematic internal reflections in both windscreen and rear window.

Quibbles aside, the CX is an autoroute cruiser par excellence. It's not really a town car, but its inability to be deflected by bumps makes country driving a pleasure too. It's still remarkably good value. The six-saloon, seven-estate car range starts at £8453 for the 20 RE and £9435 for the 20 RE Familiale seven-seater estate, rising to £13,350 for the GTi Turbo and £16,549 for the long-wheelbase Prestige.

REFORMED CHARACTER?

Facelifted outside, rearranged inside, the Citroen CX has a fresh look after 11 years. How well does it shape up to its modern rivals?

CITROEN CX 22TRS

FOR:

PERFORMANCE

ERGONOMICS

AGAINST:

REFINEMENT

VENTILATION

Almost exactly 11 years have passed since Citroen launched the CX model as the successor to the famous ID and DS series cars. It has worn remarkably well, its distinctive aerodynamic shape remains largely undated, and Citroen is now reaping the benefit of a long production run by being able to offer CX customers very good value for money.

When the giant PSA company was forged from Peugeot, Citroen, and Chrysler Europe/Talbot, it was pledged that Citroen would remain autonomous as far as possible, retaining the individuality that had won it firm fans over the years.

It remains to be seen if the new big Citroen already in the pipeline will continue the slightly maverick streak or be forced to be more conformist.

So far, the PSA influence upon Citroen has succeeded in resolving some of the more extreme idiosyncrasies in the car, thereby extending the appeal without alienating loyal customer who buy them because the cars *are* different from the crowd.

The latest CX series clearly reflects this trend, especially with the new interior, control, and instrument layout. Externally, the only differences are new composite bumpers front and rear, wheelspats, side protection panels and door mirrors.

There is also a new engine, fitted to the 22TRS test car, in the form of the 2.2-litre carburettored version of the Douvrin-produced four-cylinder alloy engine already used in the Renault Espace people carrier.

The fitment has been designed to answer criticisms that the 106bhp, 2-litre unit lacked the muscle to provide the CX with respectable performance. The extra nine bhp from the 2165cc engine, plus a similarly modest hike in torque, may be enough to silence the critics.

The 1986 CX still has hydropneumatic suspension, self-centring steering, and the powerful but sudden brake system so disconcerting to Citroen newcomers.

Inside, the CX has really cleaned up its act, however. Traditional analogue instruments replace the odd collection of dials and 'cyclops eye' speedometer, and the control and switch grouping now appears to have some order to it. The twin-pod switchgear arrangement is retained in modernised, colour-keyed form. Unfortunately, Citroen's excellent anti-lock braking system is not available on the 22TRS or the base car. ▶

TECHNICAL FOCUS

The French Douvrin factory, a co-operative between manufacturers Citroen, Peugeot/Talbot and Renault, is a design school for engines that gained recognition following development of the 2.5-litre V6 six-cylinder unit which was to find its way into the Renault 30, Peugeot 604 and Volvo 760 models. The most recent developments, however, concern the four-cylinder power units currently employed by all the PSA partners and the J6T A 500 engine in particular, which is now slotted in under the bonnet of the Citroen CX to produce a suitable gap filler between the 2.0 and 2.5 litre models.

The engine is also used in the Peugeot 505 GTi and Renault 25 GTX, although fuel injection is incorporated. In the case of Citroen, only the larger engined CX 25 has the improved fuel metering. The CX 22 TRS breathes through a single Weber twin-choke DMTR carburettor. As a result power output is slightly down, but the four cylinder overhead camshaft engine still produces a creditable 115bhp at 5600rpm and 131lb ft torque at 3250rpm.

Engine construction is of light alloy for head, block and sump. Wet liners are fitted along with light alloy pistons and forged connecting rods. Compression ratio is set at 9.8:1 and four star fuel is therefore necessary.

The five main bearing crankshaft drives via a single-plate cable-operated clutch to a five-speed all-synchromesh gearbox (mounted 'end on') equipped with five forward gears.

The 'Varipower' steering system common to the CX range is developed from the high-performance Citroen SM. It features a unique self-centring ability to aid stability.

PERFORMANCE

The adoption of the 2165cc engine into the CX range has broadened its appeal no end. No longer is it necessary to be content with the slightly leisurely response of the 2-litre version; the CX22 TRS performs very well for a car which weighs 1.25tons.

It moves off the line from a standing start gracefully and without fuss — no excessive torque-steer which normally accompanies front-wheel drive cars — to reach 30mph in 3.5secs and 60mph in a very respectable 10.8secs. The welcome lack of torque-steer is perhaps partially due to the 67.3 per cent front-biased weight distribution. To reach 60mph, however, does require two gear changes, due to the 58mph top speed in second gear, which just keeps the time the wrong side of the 10secs mark: not of monumental importance, but some people do regard 10secs as some sort of psychological barrier.

The CX22 TRS achieves its mean maximum speed of 111mph in fifth gear at 5000rpm — at the beginning of the red cross-hatching on the rev-counter. The best recorded speed was 113mph. The top speed, reached in fourth gear on the solid red line of 5500rpm, turned out to be 87mph, which shows fifth gear to be a partial overdrive for providing economy motorway cruising. There is still enough reserve power to get a driver out of trouble at motorway speeds.

The incremental in-gear times suggest a relatively flat torque curve over the speed range in the gears which explains the evident eagerness of the CX22 to 'pull' across the mid-range in all gears — something which is missing in the 2-litre models. The CX 22 was reluctant, however, to pull away from 10mph in fourth gear; it did manage it, but was not happy about being asked.

Fast gearchanging is not that easy in the CX range and the 22 TRS is no exception. With practice it can be accomplished smoothly but as the car is not a 'performance' model, the fairly long throws of the gearchange are unlikely to deter the average owner.

ECONOMY

The CX22 TRS returned an overall average consumption figure of 26.2mpg during its time with us; about what could be expected from a car weighing 1.25 tons and powered by a carburettored 2.2-litre engine.

The worst figure of 24.9mpg included the test session at MIRA, but an average motorist should be able to achieve nearer 30mpg for normal day-to-day driving. Based on the overall figure, the 15-gallon tank should allow a range of 390 miles.

The tank fills quickly and easily right to the top and there is no need for a locking fuel cap as the flap is an integral part of the central locking system.

REFINEMENT

The CX certainly looks the part as a smooth, quiet and comfortable means of transport. Supple, self-levelling suspension, and the clean aerodynamic shape of the bodyshell, suggest above average levels of refinement. Unfortunately the promise is not completely kept.

Wind noise intrusion is certainly less than on the previous model, the reduction aided by the redesigned door mirrors. However, we noticed a sharp increase in wind roar from 80mph and above, supplemented by an aeolian whistle from the A-pillar.

Road and tyre noise is audible but too intrusive up to the legal limit, but again the level appears to rise sharply when the car is pressed to higher speeds.

The ventilation system provoked the greatest mutterings of discontent. Despite its bright new packaging the system is still below par. Ram air supply is at a premium, and at any speed below 50mph needs help from the fan to achieve a reasonable airflow. During the recent spell of warm weather we found that the fan needed to be used on the upper and noisier levels of its settings to cool the interior.

Mechanical noise intrusion is commendably low. At motorway cruising in the overdrive fifth gear, the engine is turning over at a modest 1575rpm. Heavy acceleration produces some harshness at the upper rev limit, but in general the engine performs smoothly and quietly. Transmission noise is minimal.

ROAD BEHAVIOUR

Idiosyncratic is the adjective most commonly used to describe the general driving behaviour of the CX range. The latest addition to the UK model range is no exception. Those testers unfamiliar with big Citroens found that it took longer than usual to become acclimatised to the controls; particularly the steering and the brakes.

You either love or hate the self-centring power-assisted steering. Either way, it does feel very strange at first, but does not take too long to get used to. This self-centring function is at its most valuable and relaxing when driving at speed in a relatively straight line, but both hands have to be kept on the steering wheel to avoid straying off course due to the ease with which minor movements of the wheel occur. The sensitivity of the steering, combined with only 2.5 turns lock-to-lock, can be a little unnerving.

Take your hands off the wheel with the CX22 stationary, some steering lock applied, and even with the ignition turned off, the wheel smoothly returns itself to dead centre, accompanied by the hiss of the hydraulic power assistance. The only time this habit becomes a little annoying is when parking on an incline and one wishes to leave the front wheel turned into the pavement — it just keeps returning the wheels to the straight ahead position.

The hydropneumatic suspension system effortlessly provides a very smooth ride and a constant ride height. Citroen has had more than 20 years to perfect its hydropneumatic system, and it is now well tried.

The ride height is constantly maintained via the built-in self-levelling, regardless of the number of passengers or any load in the boot. For such a big car the CX handles very well, with understeer as the predominant factor when cornering hard. Take the power off in mid-corner, however, and the rear can be provoked to break away. This happens smoothly and progressively and is easy to control. The suspension does all the work, keeping the car level, and a slight steering correction is all that is needed to pull the tail back into line. The CX feels generally solid and safe at all times, even when being driven vigorously.

Like the steering, the brakes require some driver adjustment. Pedal travel is less than one inch and pedal effort at a bare minimum, with 50lb of pressure producing over 1g of deceleration. As with the steering, sensitivity is the watchword. The fully powered split-circuit, all-disc system passed the harsh 10-stop fade test with flying colours.

Full application of the handbrake provoked a remarkable 0.5g of stopping power without locking-up the front wheels, and the 1-in-3 test slope was handled easily in both directions.

The CX is a strange beast to drive for the first time, but acclimatisation does not take an inordinately long time — just a little longer than with other, more conventional cars. A quick spin around the block is simply not enough to get used to the CX.

AT THE WHEEL

The 1986 CX models have received substantial revisions to the interior (changes that make the instrument and switchgear layout more conventional than ever before) but which, at the same time, enhance the considerable ergonomic advantages always enjoyed by CX drivers.

Most obvious change is in the main facia panel, the glass of which is now convex instead of concave and incorporates a vee-shaped centre console housing the revised heat/vent controls and some subsidiary controls, including the ride height adjuster, which is now electronically-operated from a small switch set below the ashtray. The space between the seats, vacated by the manual lever and the heater slides on the old model, is now occupied by a sideways-located radio.

The main control binnacle still has the twin switch pods either side of the instrument display which now features traditional analogue instruments including a round dial speedometer to replace the old 'cyclops eye' rolling drum, plus strip warning lamps as in the BX, and an illuminated diagram of the car to show up any open doors.

The switches on the binnacle 'horns' have been rounded off and finished in colour-keyed plastic with a raised dot surface for better grip. Curiously, the functions of lights and wipers have been switched, with the paddle switch for the wipers now on the right and that for the lights on the left. Headlamp flasher is on the outside of the left pod and horn on the right. Rocker switches for indicator and intermittent windscreen wash/wipe are on top of the left and right pods respectively.

Hazard flash, rear foglamp switch and choke pull are located in a stepped switch section down by the driver's right knee. An LED clock is set in a centre facia panel, below which are three flaps covering a pair of cubby holes and a coin tray.

Switches for the standard front electric window lifts are in the doors, but the door mirrors are adjusted manually by a remote joystick in the door panel.

New tweed-covered seats are comfortable — for a while. Longer journeys reveal the beginnings of what bad back sufferers call the 'soft mattress syndrome' with lack of lumbar support becoming evident. In warmer weather they can become hot and uncomfortable. There is a lever control rake adjuster and cushion tilt as well as the usual fore and aft slider.

Door layout is much neater and cleaner, although we could see little point in the somewhat tacky wood strip insert in the top moulding. A light on the driver's door illuminates to signify that the central locking system has been activated.

CONVENIENCE

Although certainly less quirky than it used to be, the revised CX still displays some illogical touches — the three hidden lockers on the facia front, for example. The centre coin tray could well be justified, but what are the others for? In any case, the lid on the right hand one cannot open fully because it fouls the binnacle pod. On the subject of storage, the door pockets are extremely shallow, as is the perch shelf above the drop-down glove locker. ▶

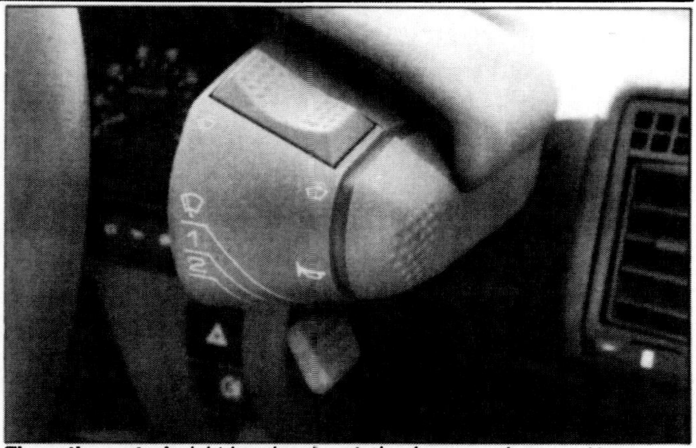

Fingertip control: *right-hand pod controls wipers, washers, and horn*

Restyled interior: *new facia still retains many elements of the old*

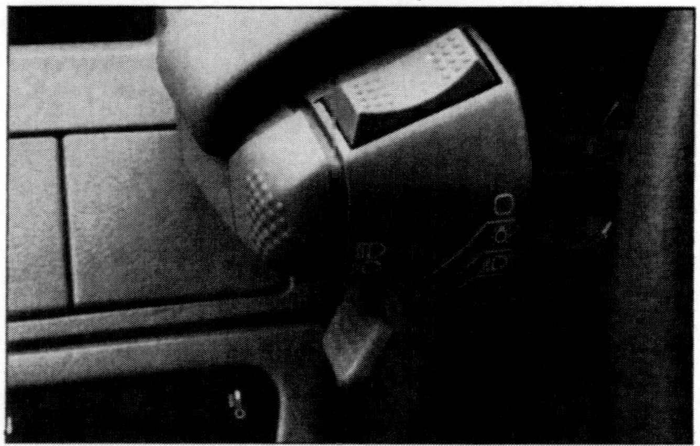

Instrument cluster: *on the left are the indicators, lights, and dipswitch*

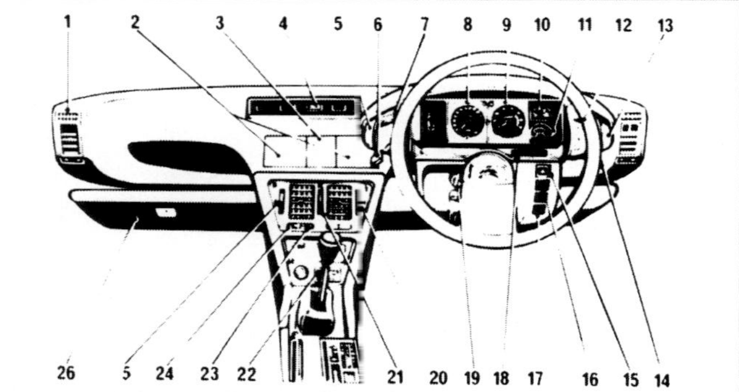

1 Air vents, 2 Cubby holes, 3 Coin tray, 4 Clock, 5 Headlamp flasher, 6 Light switch, 7 Indicator switch, 8 Speedometer, 9 Rev counter, 10 Fuel gauge, 11 Oil level/temperature, 12 Wash/wipe, 13 Horn, 14 Wiper switch, 15 Hazard flasher, 16 Rear fog lamp, 17 Choke, 18 Warning lamps, 19 Ignition lock, 20 Vent/temperature control, 21 Fresh air control, 22 Ride height adjuster, 23 Recirculating air switch, 24 Demist switch, 25 Fan speed, 26 Glove locker

ROAD TEST — CITROEN CX 22TRS

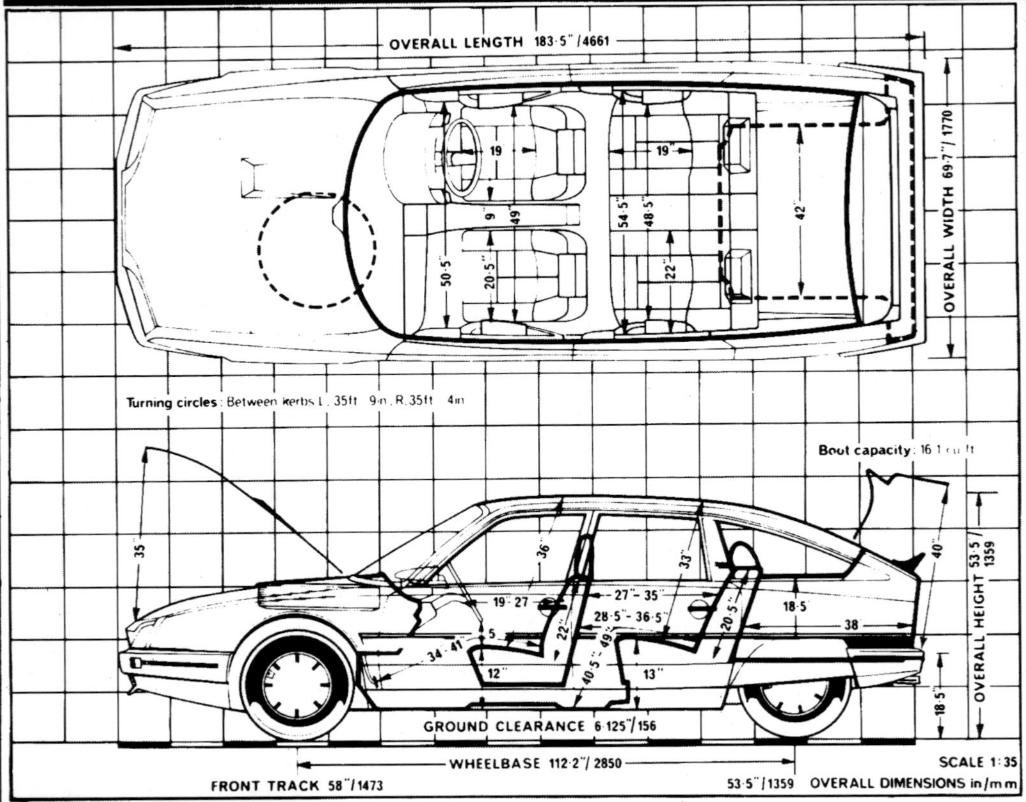

SPECIFICATION

ENGINE

Transverse front, front-wheel drive. Head/block al. alloy. 4 cylinders in line, wet liners, 5 main bearings. Water cooled, electric fan.

Bore 88mm (3.46in), **stroke** 89mm (3.50in), **capacity** 2165cc (132.2 cu in).

Valve gear ohc, 2 valves per cylinder, toothed belt camshaft drive. **Compression ratio** 9.8 to 1. Electronic ignition, Weber 34 DM TR 110/100 carburettor.

Max power 115bhp (PS-DIN) (86kW ISO) at 5600rpm. **Max torque** 131lb ft at 3250rpm.

TRANSMISSION

5-speed manual. Single plate and diaphragm spring clutch 8.5in dia.

Gear	Ratio	mph/1000rpm
Top	0.733	22.51
4th	0.939	17.57
3rd	1.250	13.21
2nd	1.834	9.00
1st	3.168	5.21

Final drive: helical spur, ratio 4.36.

SUSPENSION

Front, independent, transverse steel arms forming parallelogram, hydro-pneumatic damping, anti-roll bar.

Rear, independent, trailing arms, hydropneumatic damping, anti-roll bar.

STEERING

Rack and pinion, hydraulic power assistance. Steering wheel diameter 15in, 2.5 turns lock to lock.

BRAKES

Dual circuits, split front/rear. **Front** 10.2in (260mm) dia ventilated discs. **Rear** 8.9in (225mm) dia discs. Hydraulic servo. Handbrake, centre lever acting on front discs.

WHEELS

Steel, 5.5in rims. Tyres (Michelin MXL on test car), size 195/70R 14 front, 185/70R 14 rear, pressures F32 R31 psi.

EQUIPMENT

Battery 12V, 33Ah. Alternator 72A. Headlamps 55/60W. Reversing lamp standard. 13 electric fuses. 2-speed, plus intermittent and flick wipe screen wipers. Electric screen washer. Air blending interior heater; air conditioning not available. Cloth seats, preformed headlining. Carpet floor covering. Screw pillar jack; 2 jacking points each side. Laminated windscreen.

PERFORMANCE

MAXIMUM SPEEDS

Gear	mph	km/h	rpm
OD Top (Mean)	111	179	4930
(Best)	113	182	5020
4th	97	156	5500
3rd	73	117	5500
2nd	50	80	5500
1st	29	47	5500

ACCELERATION FROM REST

True mph	Time (sec)	Speedo mph
30	3.5	32
40	5.4	42
50	7.6	52
60	10.8	61
70	14.4	71
80	19.4	81
90	26.0	91
100	36.3	101

Standing ¼-mile: 17.6sec, 77mph
Standing km: 32.9sec, 97mph

TEST CONDITIONS

Wind: 3.2mph
Temperature: 15deg C (60deg F)
Barometer: 27in Hg (1007mbar)
Humidity: 68per cent
Surface: dry asphalt and concrete
Test distance: 532 miles

Figures taken at 1751 miles by our own staff at the Motor Industry Research Association proving ground at Nuneaton.

IN EACH GEAR

mph	Top	4th	3rd	2nd
10-30	—	9.7	6.7	4.1
20-40	12.4	8.5	5.8	3.8
30-50	12.1	8.2	5.5	4.2
40-60	12.1	8.0	5.8	—
50-70	12.3	8.5	6.6	—
60-80	13.3	9.9	—	—
70-90	15.9	12.0	—	—
80-100	22.3	17.0	—	—

CONSUMPTION

FUEL: Overall mpg: 26.2 (10.8 litres/100km) 5.8mpl

Constant speed

mph	mpg	mpl	mph	mpg	mpl
30	50.5	11.1	70	32.4	7.1
40	46.2	10.2	80	28.5	6.3
50	41.3	9.1	90	23.8	5.2
60	36.2	7.9	100	18.9	4.2

Autocar formula: Hard 23.6mpg
Driving and conditions: Average 28.8mpg, Gentle 34.1mpg

Grade of fuel: Premium, 4-star (98 RM)
Fuel tank: 15 Imp galls (68litres)
Mileage recorder: 0.01 per cent
Oil: (SAE 15W/40) negligible

BRAKING

Fade (from 77mph in neutral)
Pedal load for 0.5g stops in lb

	start/end		start/end
1	20-20	6	20-32
2	20-30	7	20-42
3	20-30	8	20-38
4	20-35	9	20-38
5	20-38	10	20-50

Response (from 30mph in neutral)

Load	g	Distance
20lb	0.52	57.9ft
30lb	0.75	40.1ft
40lb	0.92	32.7ft
50lb	1.02	29.5ft
Handbrake	0.50	60.2ft

Max gradient: 1 in 3

Clutch Pedal 22lbs; Travel 7in

WEIGHT

Kerb 25.3cwt/2836lb/1283kg (Distribution F/R, 67.3/32.7)
Test 28.9cwt/3236lb/1464kg
Max payload 1113lb/503.6kg

COSTS

Prices

Basic	£7457.00
Special Car Tax	£621.42
VAT	£1211.76
Total (in GB)	**£9290.18**
Licence	£100.00
Delivery charge (London)	£149.50
Number plates	£15.00
Total on the Road (excluding insurance)	**£9554.68**
Insurance Group	6
EXTRAS (inc VAT)	
Electric sunroof	£553.15
Metallic paint	£252.91
Total as tested on the road	**£9554.68**

SERVICE & PARTS

Change	Interval 6000	12,000	18,000
Engine oil	Yes	Yes	Yes
Oil filter	Yes	No	Yes
Gearbox oil	No	No	No
Spark plugs	No	Yes	No
Air cleaner	No	No	Yes
Total cost	£25.99	£59.55	£39.65

(Assuming labour at £17.00 an hour inc VAT)

PARTS COST (inc VAT)

Brake pads (2 wheels) front	£26.79
Brake pads (2 wheels) rear	£22.33
Exhaust complete	£92.92
Tyre—each (typical) front/rear	£63.54/£54.57
Windscreen	£102.87
Headlamp unit	£71.65
Front wing	£82.39
Rear bumper	£86.25

EQUIPMENT

Ammeter/Voltmeter	N/A
Automatic	N/A
Cruise control	N/A
Economy gauge	N/A
Electronic ignition	●
Five speed	●
Limited slip differential	N/A
Power steering	●
Rev counter	●
Steering wheel rake adjust	N/A
Steering wheel reach adjust	N/A
Trip computer	N/A
Headrests front/rear	●/●
Height adjustment	●
Lumbar adjustment	N/A
Rear seat belts	●
Seat back recline	●
Seat tilt	N/A
Split rear seats	N/A
Door mirror remote control	●/●
Electric windows (front)	●
Heated rear window	●
Interior headlamp adjust	N/A
Tinted glass	●
Headamp wash/wipe	N/A
Tailgate wash/wipe	N/A
Alloy wheels	N/A
Central locking	●
Childproof locks	●
Fog lamps (rear)	●
Internal boot release	N/A
Locking fuel cap	●

● Standard ○ Optional at no extra cost N/A Not applicable † Part of option package DO Dealer option

WARRANTY

12 months/unlimited mileage, 6-year anti-corrosion

PRODUCED BY:

Automobiles Citroen,
62 Boulevard Victor-Hugo, 92208
Neuilly sur Seine, France

SOLD IN THE UK BY:

Citroen Cars Ltd, Mill Street,
Slough, Berkshire SL2 5DE

THE OPPOSITION

AUDI 100 CD — £12,498

The car which, more than any other, lent impetus to the present automotive aerodynamics race. Test figures revealed just how a low drag figure, and generally efficient design, can translate into truly impressive performance and economy. The Audi is also commendable for its superb high-speed stability, predictable handling and roomy cabin

Tested	November 1982
ENGINE	2144cc
Max Power	136bhp at 5700rpm
Torque	133lb/ft at 4800rpm
Gearing	28.6mph/1000rpm
WARRANTY	12/UL, 6 anti-rust
Insurance Group	7
Automatic	£587
5-Speed	●
Radio	●
Sunroof	£642.85
WEIGHT	2675lb

TOP SPEED	128mph	MPG	29.4mpg
0-60mph	9.5sec	Range	517 miles

BMW 520i — £10,950

Even though the body styling is showing signs of its age by the rather upright appearance, this big saloon offers a great deal in terms of room and performance. The injection 2-litre engine is very smooth, giving reasonable economy. comfortable ride and predictable handling, although it can get a little tail happy in wet conditions

Tested	N/A
ENGINE	1990cc
Max Power	125bhp at 5800rpm
Torque	125.3lb/ft at 4000rpm
Gearing	18.4mph/1000rpm
WARRANTY	12/UL, 6 anti-rust
Insurance Group	7
Automatic	£640
5-Speed	●
Radio	DO
Sunroof (electric)	£635
WEIGHT	2696lb

*TOP SPEED	117mph	**MPG	28.7mpg
*0-62mph	11.4sec	Range	442 miles

FORD GRANADA 2.0GL — £9196

The shape is becoming more familiar now — and it is very different from the previous Granada. Power from the 2-litre engine is not outstanding, but performance is deceptive, really coming into its own on fast, open roads. Plenty of room, well appointed and more than ample space for luggage. Good ride and safe handling are features

Tested	N/A
ENGINE	1993cc
Max Power	105bhp at 5200rpm
Torque	116lb/ft at 4000rpm
Gearing	N/A
WARRANTY	12/UL, 6 anti-rust
Insurance Group	6
Automatic	£583
5-Speed	●
Radio	●
Sunroof	£360
WEIGHT	1185lb

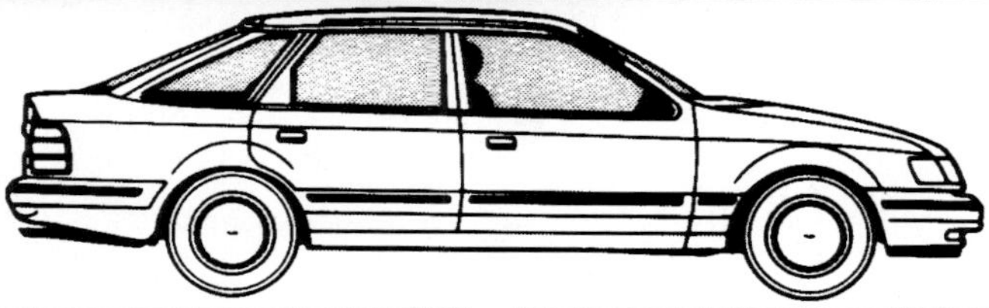

*TOP SPEED	117mph	*MPG	31.8mpg
*0-60mph	10.7sec	Range	490 miles

RENAULT 25 GTX — £10,865

The north-south engine layout is retained, driving the front wheels. The 2.2-litre engine supplies ample power for this big, elegant hatchback. Superb handling and very good ride, typical of the *marque*. Generous amount of interior room, with comfortable seats. Very good fuel economy. Power steering standard, but Renault's automatic an extra

Tested	N/A
ENGINE	2165cc
Max Power	123bhp at 5250rpm
Torque	133lb/ft at 2750rpm
Gearing	22.1mph/1000rpm
WARRANTY	12/UL, 5 anti-rust
Insurance Group	7
Automatic	£410
5-Speed	●
Radio	£375
Sunroof	£380
WEIGHT	2619lb

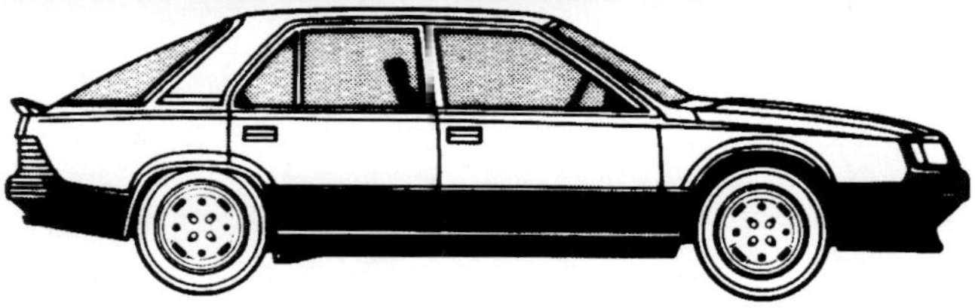

*TOP SPEED	121mph	**MPG	30.9mpg
*0-62mph	10.3sec	Range	454 miles

VAUXHALL CARLTON 2.2 CDi — £10,568

With its front engine, rear drive layout, plus a live rear axle and three-box shape, the Carlton is something of a 'senior citizen' among the increasing number of front drive cars. Nevertheless, it is a worthy one, well worth considering when it comes to space, performance and value for money. Injection 2.2-litre engine gives good economy

Tested	30 Jan 1985
ENGINE	2197cc
Max Power	115bhp at 4800rpm
Torque	134lb/ft at 2800rpm
Gearing	24mph/1000rpm
WARRANTY	12/12,000 miles
Insurance Group	6
Automatic	£448
5-Speed	●
Radio	●
Sunroof (manual)	●
WEIGHT	2661lb

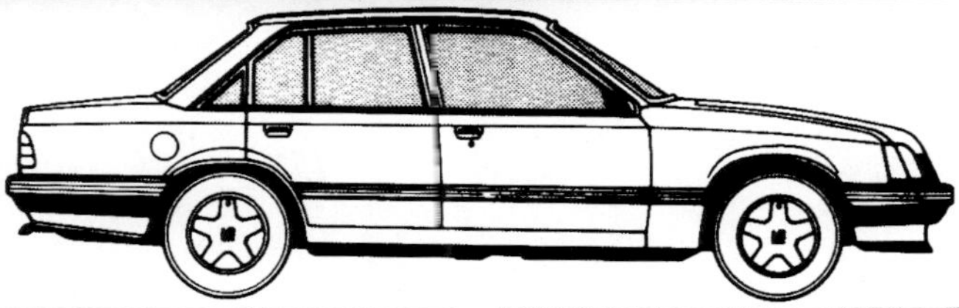

TOP SPEED	115mph	MPG	25.8mpg
0-60mph	10.6sec	Range	369 miles

VOLVO 740 GL — £9700

Big, comfortable car, but slightly awkward appearance, with sloping bonnet lines and near-vertical rear window. The latest 'low friction' engine gives surprising performance allied with very good economy for such a large car. Sensible driver control layout, but ventilation indifferent. Well-balanced and very good ride qualities

Tested	N/A
ENGINE	2316cc
Max Power	114bhp at 5200rpm
Torque	141lb/ft at 2500rpm
Gearing	N/A
WARRANTY	12/UL
Insurance group	OA
Automatic	£620
5-Speed	●
Radio	DO
Sunroof	£464
WEIGHT	1260lb

*TOP SPEED	109mph	**MPG	29mpg
*0-62mph	12sec	Range	383 miles

● Standard ○ Optional at extra cost ONC Optional at no extra cost N/A Not applicable DO Dealer Option * Manufacturer's figures ** European Legislative Average

Locating the radio between the seats is a neat solution, but we suspect a not entirely safe one because button pushing or tape changing on the move might require looking away from the straight ahead. The storage slot behind the radio can be used to house further hi-fi gear such as equalisers.

Heating and ventilation is better, but still not good. Fresh air throughput is only effective when the fan is on its noisier setting. Ram effect air from the two central vents is not strong enough in warm conditions and the right hand vent at the end of the facia is badly masked by the binnacle end.

The fat section front seats restrict rear kneeroom and the thick cushions also leave little space between the driver's thighs and the steering wheel rim. Tall drivers may find headroom slightly lacking.

Underbonnet access for routine checks is good, the bonnet strut locks automatically and there is a bulb for illumination. Boot space is deep with a flat floor and no lip, although it can be hard to reach right to the very back of the compartment and the absence of handholds makes the L-shape lid awkward to lift.

SAFETY

Launched in 1974 and awarded the 'Prix de la Securite' or Safety award by the French press in 1975, the CX range comes with notable safety features incorporated in its advanced for the time aerodynamic-design.

Citroen's adoption of hydro-pneumatic suspension and the unique self centring steering system are the two key features in providing the CX with remarkable straight stability at speed, so that fast cruising feels both safe and relaxed. This point is further emphasised by the self-levelling suspension, which helps maintain the optimum angle of attack.

The high speed cruising potential is further aided by four-wheel disc brakes and built-in anti-dive front and anti-lift rear geometry.

New to the CX range are anti-glare exterior mirrors (except on 20RE models) and improved driver information display in a revised instrument layout. Most controls are now illuminated and there are dash-mounted warning lights to indicate open passenger doors, bonnet or luggage compartment.

VERDICT

As we said at the outset, the revised CX is a successful attempt to broaden the appeal of the big Citroen by removing some of the worst eccentricities, specially on the inside. It still remains very different from the crowd and requires a fair amount of effort and dedication in order to learn to drive the car well.

Once you have this ability, the CX rewards by delivering smooth and effortless long-distance progress, a virtue enhanced by the fitment of the 2.2-litre engine with its extra power and flat torque curve for improved mid-range performance.

The new interior is a major step forward. We had no complaint with the previous excellent pod arrangement for main controls, which is retained, but the more logical and ergonomic grouping of the other switchgear is very welcome.

Heating and ventilation remains a disappointment, and as far as we can see the new controls and facia layout conceal an unchanged arrangement underneath.

Assessed on value for money, the CX does well, being cheaper than any rival in our comparison panel, although we feel that an extra £553 for a sunroof might be regarded as an essential investment. ■

New looks: *subtle restyling has brought the CX bang up to date*

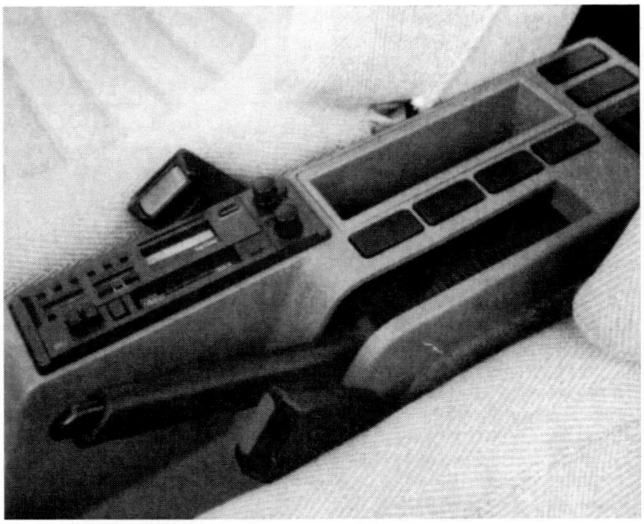

Repositioned radio: *easy to reach but difficult to see to retune*

New engine: *endows CX with 111mph top speed and 0-60mph acceleration in a respectable 10.8secs. Economy is average for class*

CITROEN CX SERIES 2

IN BRIEF	
Make	Citroen
Model	CX GTi Turbo
Price	£13,350
Type & Passenger Doors	S4
Seats	5
Engine Size (cc)	2500
Max Power (bhp/rpm)	168/5,000
Max Torque (lb ft/rpm)	217/3,200
Max Speed (mph)	136
0-62mph (secs)	8.0
Mpg Urban Cycle	20.2
Boot Capacity (cu ft)	17.9

After eleven years of production, Citroen have finally given their CX range a much needed facelift. When the car was introduced in 1974, it was at the forefront of aerodynamic design, but the opposition have steadily caught up until the CX was no more than a mid-field runner in the increasingly important drag coefficient stakes. The latest Series 2 cars now have tidied-up fronts, spats over the wheels, side protection strips and new door mirrors. However, the improved air penetration increases performance and aids economy whereby, according to Citroen, the new Cd factor is a realistic 0.34.

New for the '86 model year is the CX 22 TRS, which features a 2.2 litre version of the Douvrin four-cylinder motor. The biggest change, however, concerns the new interior, where there are few components which have been used on the older cars; out have gone the 'bathroom scales' instruments in favour of normal dials. Perhaps when the GTi Turbo was launched last year thus equipped and Citroen said drivers of that class of car preferred those dials, this was just a toe in the water in a move against art for art's sake? Now as well as new dials, there is an efficient new heating system with servo switches and plenty of vents; a great improvement over the older cars. Still remaining are the characteristic (and now copied) satellite switches and the non-cancelling indicators. However, those who have driven Citroens for a couple of hundred miles or so, will probably go along with company philosophy that they are more of a help than a hindrance. Anti-lock braking is now standard on the GTi Turbo and long-wheelbase Prestige, optional on the Diesel Turbo and other fuel-injected models.

Strangely for the overall production of the new CX line-up, the French company anticipate the diesel being marginally the more popular of the range, taking some 51% of sales. With 80% of sales for 1986 being for saloon variants, the full breakdown is as follows: CX 20 and CX 22 19%; fuel-injected petrol versions 20%; turbocharged petrol versions 10%; diesel at 17% and turbo diesel at 34%. For the quirky British market, the GTi Turbo is again expected to be the best-selling model.

On the road

The new CX range may look tidier and more modern than its predecessors, but they are exactly the same to drive. Not having piloted one for about a year, the high-powered brakes and strong self-centring steering took a good few miles to get used to again, but thereafter they proved no trouble at all. The CX 22 TRS version is a welcome addition to the range, for it provides a good top speed of 115mph, or so, and reasonable acceleration with a long-striding fifth gear, making for relaxed motorway cruising.

In the light of some very competent opposition, the CX now feels a little dated when pressed really hard into corners, and if the steering is relaxed a little when turning the car hard into a fast bend, the body bucks away from the desired direction as the self-centring steering takes over.

We also had a brief drive of the GTi Turbo which, although for some reason wasn't as quick as the 'Mark One' example driven on that model's launch, nevertheless gave an impressive turn of speed. Its ABS braking also saved the day on one occasion when one myopic patron of the Queen's Highway nudged out from a side turning when he wasn't meant to.

With just a few changes, Citroen have moved their large saloon back on par with the opposition who have themselves improved dramatically over the years. If anything, the *avant garde* French manufacturer has compromised a little with its new cars' interiors to try and win t more friends without in any way losing their high-tech dynamics. The CX range is not the most popular in conservative Britain, but the Series 2 versions can only improve on those circumstances.

Laurie Caddell CC

CITROEN'S IDIOSYNCRATIC CX HAS JUST BEEN GIVEN THE BIGGEST OVERHAUL IN ITS 11YEAR LIFE. A PARTLY RESTYLED EXTERIOR AND A NEW INTERIOR RAISE ITS APPEAL BUT, AS GEORG KACHER LEARNS, THE CAR'S CHARACTER IS UNCHANGED

SURVIVAL KIT

FOR ITS ELEVENTH BIRTHDAY, the Citroen CX was given a thorough facelift. Even after a decade there was nothing wrong with the basic shape of the car, but the detailing definitely needed attention. Chief designer Carl Olsen, the man who transformed the Visa from an ugly duckling to quite a pleasant looking runabout, came up with one of the most successful restyling jobs seen for a long time. He replaced the steel bumpers with rugged, wraparound impact-absorbing section, painted to match the body colour. Then he swapped the chromed screw-on rocker panels for more aerodynamic designs in black plastic. The body rubbing strips were widened and mounted higher up, the panel which covers the rear wheel opening was enlarged, new air deflectors were fitted front and rear, and the car was given new, low-drag hubcaps, faired door mirrors and a body-colour grille went onto some models.

Thus the CX series two – due in Britain at the end of September – is virtually a new car below the beltline but the glasshouse remains largely unchanged. The windows are by no means flush-fitting, the sizable dripails protrude as if they had never seen a wind tunnel, and the single-arm wiper sticks out proudly, too. But despite these things, the drag coefficient of the new CX is reduced from 0.37 to 0.35. As far as its practical virtues are concerned, the body shape of the big Citroen has barely aged at all. The large, wide-opening doors give easy access to a roomy cabin which seats five adults in style and comfort. The well lined and uncluttered boot has a low loading lip and is roomy, but there is no doubt that a hatchback option would enhance its appeal even further. On the debit side, the car has poor visibility (the nose drops out of sight), and the rear view is impaired by the big spoiler, wide C-posts and reflections in the rear window, as well as the cabin's tendency to heat up quickly on a warm day.

To complement the exterior revisions, the CX receives a completely new interior which is both more functional and better looking. Take the seats, for example, which are now covered in a rugged yet tasteful tweed cloth. They are even more comfortable than the previous ones, they offer better lateral and lumbar support, and they are fully adjustable in reach, rake and height. The restyled, cloth-trimmed door panels accommodate up to four loudspeakers, a joystick operating the door mirror and the switches for the electric window winders which are unfortunately placed much too low. Although the shape of the instrument binnacle and the position of the steering wheel were taken over unchanged from the previous model, the new dashboard looks fresh, modern and more purposeful.

The bathroom scale-type gauges have in all CX models given way to round instruments as used in the GTi Turbo since September 1984. They are certainly more conventional, but they are also relatively small and poorly calibrated, so it remains debatable whether the legibility has actually improved. In line with other PSA cars, the new CX now boasts a so-called check control panel which warns the driver of burned out lamps and of the bonnet, bootlid or a door left ajar. CX drivers will be pleased to hear that the satellites on both sides of the instrument panel are still there, but they will not like the fact that the headlamp and wiper controls have changed ends. The two pods are now somewhat easier to understand and operate since certain secondary controls have been relocated.

The top end of the unusually wide V-shaped centre console houses the digital clock and the display of the on-board computer which is standard on the GTi Turbo and optional on the long wheelbase Prestige. The hydropneumatic suspension is not controlled through a lever between the seats any more. It is now activated by an electric motor instead, which receives its orders from a small glide switch planted between the ashtray and the gearlever. In true SM and GS fashion, the radio was moved from the dashboard to an opening next to the handbrake. This may be a

traditional solution for Citroen, but it is not a very practical one since most radios are designed for horizontal instead of vertical installation and operation. In this car, cassettes can only be handled by persons with a well developed sense of touch.

To improve handling and roadholding, the Citroen engineers have stiffened the suspension settings (all models are now virtually identical in rate with the GTi Turbo), and have fitted fatter anti-roll bars to reduce the lean through fast corners. The brakes have a more efficient ventilation system, a la GTi Turbo, and all fuel-injection and turbodiesel models are now available with a Bosch ABS system. This sophisticated and very efficient anti-lock device is standard on Turbo and Prestige.

Two of the 16 CX versions are newcomers to the range. To close the gap between the CX20 and the CX25, Citroen have introduced the CX22TRS which is powered by a 2.2litre edition of the familiar Douvrin alloy four. This sohc engine, which develops 115bhp at 5600rpm and 128ft lb at 3250rpm is coupled to a five-speed gearbox, to accelerate the 2772lb CX22TRS in 10.6sec from 0 to 60mph and on to a top speed of 116mph.

The CX25 Prestige Turbo is the new PSA flagship. Its 168bhp engine accelerates the long-wheelbase saloon in 8.0sec from 0 to 60mph and propels it to a maximum speed of 138mph. The all-in space cruiser returns 26.4mpg, according to the makers. The price of all '86 models CXs will reportedly increase by about three percent.

The new 2.2litre engine is lively, flexible and economical – but quiet and refined it is not. Starting from cold is a hassle since the manual choke is buried low down in the facia (should one reach it through the steering wheel, or around it?). To keep the engine alive, you must constantly fiddle with this sticky control, and even when the 1.2gal of lubricant have reached their working temperature, throttle response is sometimes hesitant and pick-up slow. This version of the Douvrin four is a torquey performer, but

Biggest change to new CX is completely new interior, which works better and looks better. Seats are even more comfortable than old model's, with better support. New dashboard looks more modern. Old bathroom-scale instruments are replaced by conventional but small round dials. Hydropneumatic suspension is now activated by electric switch

it feels and sounds rough from about 3000rpm to the 6000rpm cut-out. The engine of our test car also suffered from distinct booms, and it set up unnerving vibrations which pervaded the entire driveline.

'I must admit that this engine is not quite as civilized as it should be,' concedes a Citroen spokesman, 'but our top priority was not smooth running. We wanted to achieve the best possible compromise between performance and fuel economy, and I think we've succeeded. You see, in the CX22TRS you can cruise all day at about 100mph and still better 28mpg.' The five-speed box that goes with the engine is still not particularly quick or precise, but its ratios are well spaced and invites you to change up early. The CX22TRS will happily potter along at 50mph in fifth, and when you put the foot down, those horses are ready to gallop all the way to the warning sector at 5500rpm, which is 115mph.

There is no doubt that one can learn to live with this shirt-sleeved engine, just as one can learn to live with the CX's peculiar ergonomics or the avant-garde body style – but how about the ultra-quick steering and those hyper-sensitive brakes? Even when you know what to expect, the CX always needs a few dozen familiarisation miles. Once you've come to grips with the car, it's hard not to like its brisk handling qualities and its eagerness to react to tiny inputs. I often used to wonder whether all big saloons should feel like a CX, but now that the competition has caught up, I know that above average results do not always require such radical technical solutions as in the CX.

Take the steering, for instance, which is very light and extremely direct: it is why the big Citroen is one of the quickest-handling full-size saloons on the market. Unfortunately it can also be a rather nervous, sometimes twitchy machine. Instead of being nicely progressive and full of road feel, the power steering has a strong, artificial self-centring action by trying to pull back to the straight-ahead position. It sheds natural steer-

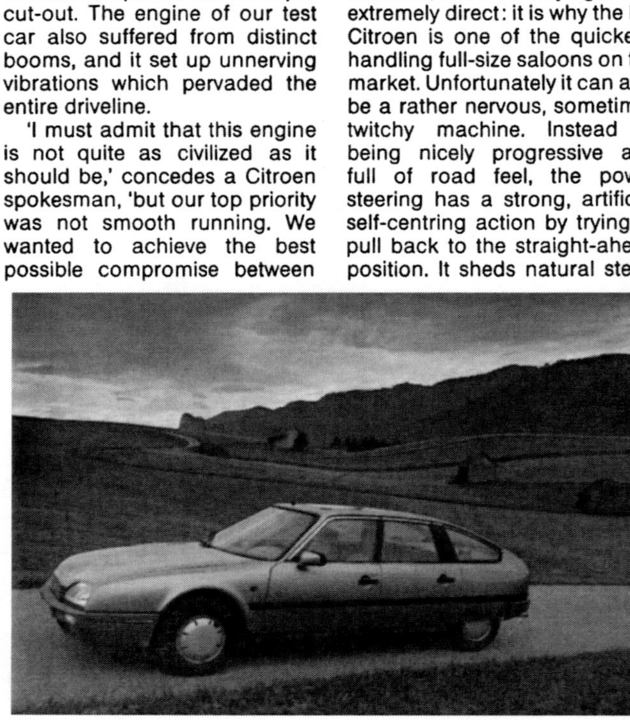

ing feel in favour of something built in, and is uncommunicative.

Take the brakes, which are extremely powerful, virtually free from fade and very responsive: they give the Citroen deceleration practically second to none. Unfortunately these power-assisted brakes are not progressive either. Modulation is by pedal pressure instead of pedal travel. Hit it hard, and there is a good chance that the wheels will lock. True, Citroen are now offering anti-locking for the CX, but it is not available in the 2.0 and 2.2litre versions. All you can really do is train your right foot to treat that brake pedal with care, especially in a panic stop.

One advantage the CX still has over its rivals is its elaborate, maintenance-free and well proven hydropneumatic suspension which is as attractive as ever. While others are playing around with electronically controlled ride-height and suspension setting adjustment devices, Citroen have the most sophisticated and most efficient solution which enables the car's ground clearance to be varied (there are four positions to choose from) and has a four-wheel self-levelling system. The CX does squat and dive quite a bit when accelerating and braking, and body roll is also still a prominent feature, but the revised calibration of the hydropneumatic suspension, together with the bigger anti-roll bars, has improved the car's dynamic qualities. Straightline stability is still excellent.

On a fluid, fast road, the Citroen CX is a wonderfully relaxed high-speed cruiser. The car retains its composure through 60mph-plus bends, but when the radius tightens, understeer can cut in and the whole thing becomes more ponderous. The CX is no friend of fast S-bends which require brisk changes of direction, but although it leans and lurches like a steamer, it does remain sure-footed. This balance can only be upset by sudden weight transfers close to the limit when the CX will tilt from power-on

CX still looks wonderful after 11 years, and is improved by '86 mods like new bumpers and body rubbing strips. Drag factor is reduced from 0.37 to 0.35, with straight-line stability as good as ever. Douvrin 2.2litre engine is new CX offering, while control satellites have been simplified with some of the minor controls moved onto the dash

understeer to power-off oversteer. In the case of the 168bhp GTi Turbo, it is even possible to provoke oversteer under power. But it takes only a dab of opposite lock to bring the CX back on course.

Although the hydropneumatic suspension is occasionally caught out by transverse ridges or humpback bridges, it still beats most conventional steel systems when it comes to ironing out potholes, grooves and other deficiencies of our road network. As far as sheer ride comfort is concerned, the CX's excellent suspension, long wheelbase and very good seats defends its leading position. In terms of overall comfort, however, it loses several points because of totally inadequate ventilation, its harsh engine and substantial wind and tyre noise.

The build quality of the CX has improved dramatically over the past 11years, but despite having a fully satisfactory paint job the big Citroen is still not nearly as well made as its German competitors. On our test car, we noticed that the door hinges and certain folds and welding seams were only painted instead of sealed, that the carpets and seat covers were fitted carelessly and that two of the exterior clip-on plastic panels had already come adrift. The glovebox opened but would not shut again, there were three unidentified screws and washers rolling about in the rear passenger compartment, and the dashboard was almost as squeaky as a coffin lid in a Hammer

thriller. Little things, perhaps, but in the long run poor finish can cost real money.

So what's the verdict? The CX22TRS is a roomy, comfortable and well equipped family car which is easy on fuel and relatively cheap to buy. Since the build quality is still not up to standard, though, the resale value is likely to remain uninspiring. If its dramatically different steering and brakes appeal to you, the big Citroen can nevertheless be a good buy. After all, the '86 model CX is the best CX there ever was. It remains a car which only suits those who are prepared to cope with its particularities. Yet even after 11years there are important areas where it still beats its more modern rivals.

FAMILY AFFAIR

FOR:
- CONVENIENCE
- REFINEMENT

AGAINST:
- ECONOMY
- PERFORMANCE

Although first launched more than 12 years ago, the Citroën CX remains basically unchanged. Most versatile of the range is surely the big estate, the Familiale, tested with fuel-injected engine and in automatic form

The glossy Citroën CX brochure proclaims proudly "... improved, but not beyond recognition." Perhaps the most remarkable thing about this statement is how true is the latter part, bearing in mind the

CX range first appeared in the UK as long ago as 1974. And, apart from a few aerodynamic alterations, the shape of the CX remains basically the same. This says a great deal about the wisdom of the initial concept.

With a wheelbase of 112ins and an overall length of 183ins, the saloon versions of the CX are 'big' cars, but add 9ins to the wheelbase and 12ins to the overall length and the result is a really *big* car, the Familiale. By increasing the length of the bodyshell, Citroën is able to equip the Familiale with a third row of seats, while still retaining 16.2cu ft of luggage space at the rear. This endows the Familiale with the enviable capability of carrying seven adults and an amount of luggage.

Only three Familiale models are available, and two of these are to special order only. The base version is the CX20RE, which is powered by a carburettored 1995cc engine, while the two special-order CX25Ri models use the fuel-injected 2473cc unit. There are two versions because an automatic transmission is available as well as a five-speed manual gearbox. The test car was fitted with the Borg-Warner three-speed automatic gearbox.

The engine in the CX25Ri Familiale is the same 2473cc unit as found in the CX25 saloons, producing a maximum power of 138bhp at 5000rpm and developing maximum torque of 155lb at 4000rpm. The big Citroën took about two laps of ▶

Special order *CX25Ri Familiale has 2473cc, 138bhp engine*

TEST UPDATE

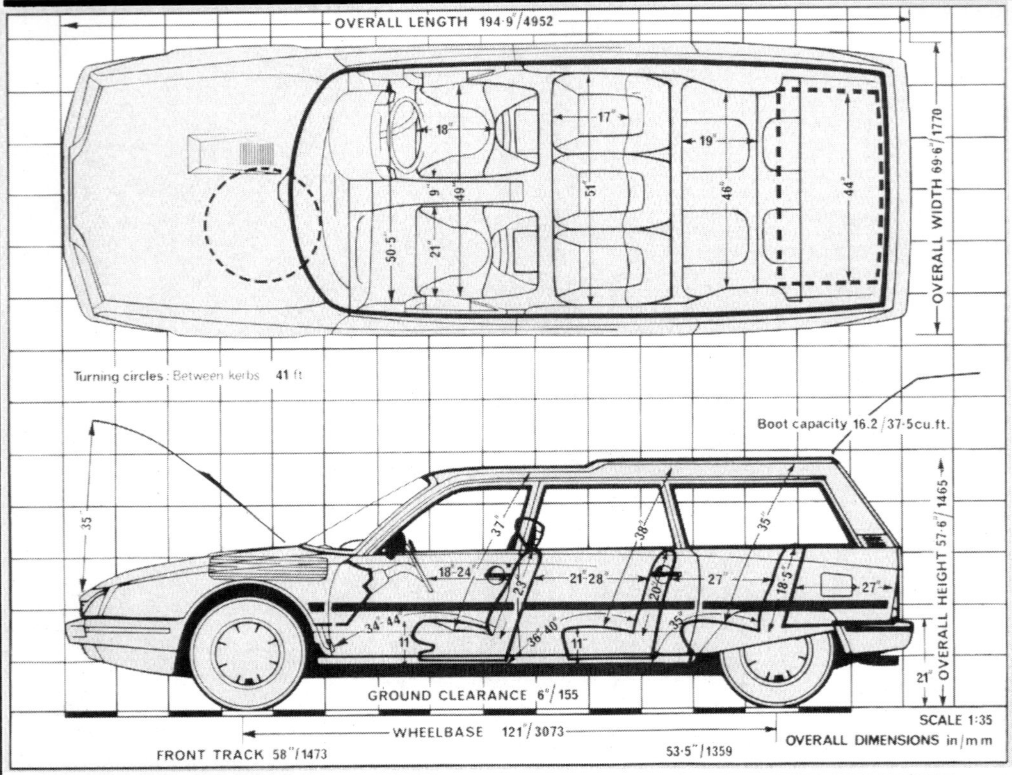

MODEL

CITROËN CX25Ri FAMILIALE AUTO

PRODUCED BY:
Automobiles Citroën S.A.
62 Boulevard Victor Hugo
92208 Neuilly sur Seine
France

SOLD IN THE UK BY:
Citroën UK Ltd
Mill Street
Slough SL2 5DE.

SPECIFICATION

ENGINE
Transverse front, front-wheel drive. Head/block Al.alloy/cast iron. 4 cylinders in line, wet liners, 5 main bearings. Water cooled, twin electric fans.

Bore 93mm (3.66in), **stroke** 92mm (3.62in), **capacity** 2473cc (151 cu in).

Valve gear sohv, 2 valves per cylinder, chain camshaft drive. **Compression ratio** 8.75 to 1. Breakerless electronic ignition, electronic fuel injection.

Max power 138bhp (PS-DIN) (102kW ISO) at 5000rpm. **Max torque** 155lb ft at 4000rpm.

TRANSMISSION
3-speed automatic, Borg Warner, Type 35. Torque converter, max converter ratio 2.17.

Gear	Ratio	mph/1000rpm
Top	0.691	21.79
2nd	1.022	14.73
1st	1.712	8.78

Final drive: Helical spur, ratio 4.77.

SUSPENSION
Front, independent, transverse steel arms forming parallelogram, hydropneumatic damping, anti-roll bar.

Rear, independent, trailing arms, hydropneumatic damping, anti-roll bar.

STEERING
Rack and pinion, hydraulic power assistance. Steering wheel diameter 15in, 2.5 turns lock to lock.

BRAKES
Dual circuits, split front/rear. **Front** 10.2in (259mm) dia ventilated discs. **Rear** 9.3in (236mm) dia ventilated discs. Hydraulic servo. Handbrake, centre lever acting on front discs.

WHEELS
Alloy, 5.5in rims. Tyres (Michelin MXV on test car), size 195/70R14ins, pressures F34 R27 psi (normal driving).

EQUIPMENT
Battery 12V, 60Ah. Alternator 93A. Headlamps 110/120W. Reversing lamp standard. 13 electric fuses. 2-speed plus intermittent screen wipers. Electric screen washer. Air blending interior heater. Cloth seats, cloth headlining. Bottle jack; 2 jacking points each side.

PERFORMANCE

MAXIMUM SPEEDS

Gear	mph	km/h	rpm
Top (Mean)	113	182	5200
(Best)	116	187	5325
2nd	81	130	5500
1st	48	77	5500

ACCELERATION FROM REST

True mph	Time (sec)	Speedo mph
30	4.5	32
40	6.3	43
50	8.7	52
60	11.9	63
70	15.8	73
80	21.1	84
90	29.1	95
100	41.2	104

Standing ¼-mile: 18.7sec, 76mph
Standing km: 34.9sec, 92mph

ACCELERATION IN EACH GEAR

mph	Top	2nd	1st
10-30	—	—	3.4
20-40	—	—	3.6
30-50	—	—	4.2
40-60	—	6.5	—
50-70	—	7.1	—
60-80	—	8.9	—
70-90	13.9	—	—
80-100	19.7	—	—

CONSUMPTION
FUEL
Overall mpg: 20.4 (13.9 litres/100km) 4.5mpl

Autocar constant speed fuel consumption measuring equipment incompatible with fuel injection

Autocar formula: Hard 18.4mpg
Driving and conditions: Average 22.4mpg, Gentle 26.5mpg
Grade of fuel: Premium, 4-star (98 RM)
Fuel tank: 15 Imp galls (68.2 litres)
Mileage recorder reads: 0.1 per cent long
Oil: (SAE 15W/40) negligible

BRAKING
Fade (from 76mph in neutral)
Pedal load for 0.5g stops in lb

	start/end		start/end
1	13-15	6	24-27
2	17-17	7	29-31
3	19-20	8	24-35
4	19-24	9	24-37
5	21-24	10	24-31

Response (from 30mph in neutral)

Load	g	Distance
10lb	0.39	77ft
20lb	0.78	39ft
25lb	0.81	37ft
30lb	0.90	33ft
Handbrake	0.31	97ft

Max gradient: 1 in 3

CLUTCH Pedal 24lb; Travel 4.9in

WEIGHT
Kerb 28.4cwt/3182lb/1440kg (Distribution F/R, 67.5/32.5)
Test 31.9cwt/3569lb/1615kg
Max payload 1534lb/700kg

COSTS

Prices	
Basic	£9431.00
Special Car Tax	£785.92
VAT	£1532.53
Total (in GB)	**£11,749.45**
Licence	£100.00
Delivery charge	£157.55
Number plates	£20.00
Total on the Road (excluding insurance)	**£12,027.00**
Insurance group	OA
EXTRAS (fitted to test car)	
Philips 760 stereo radio/cassette	£228.11
Total as tested on the road	**£12,255.11**

SERVICE & PARTS

Change	6000	12,000	24,000
Engine oil	Yes	Yes	Yes
Oil filter	Yes	Yes	Yes
Gearbox oil	No	Yes	Yes
Spark plugs	No	Yes	Yes
Air cleaner	Yes	Yes	Yes
Total cost	£57.95	£117.65	£135.65

(Assuming labour at £18.00 an hour inc VAT)

PARTS COST (inc VAT)	
Brake pads (2 wheels) front	£27.87
Brake pads (2 wheels) rear	£25.15
Exhaust complete	£113.82
Tyre—each (typical)	£78.10
Windscreen	£106.99
Headlamp unit	£74.51

WARRANTY
12 months/unlimited mileage, 6-year anti-corrosion

EQUIPMENT

Ammeter/Voltmeter	N/A
Cruise control	N/A
Economy gauge	N/A
Electronic ignition	●
Limited slip differential	N/A
Power steering	●
Rev counter	●
Self-levelling suspension	●
Trip computer	N/A
Headrests front	●
Heated seats	N/A
Height adjustment	●
Rear seat belts	●
Seat back recline	●
Seat cushion tilt	●
Electric front windows	●
Heated rear window	●
Tinted glass	●
Headlamp wash/wipe	N/A
Tailgate wash/wipe	●
Central locking	●
Child proof locks	●
Locking fuel cap	●
Luggage cover	N/A
Metallic paint	£360.38
Door mirror remote control l/r	●
Radio/cassette	DO
Speakers	DO
Aerial	●

● Standard ONC Optional at no extra cost N/A Not applicable † Part of option package DO Dealer option

TEST CONDITIONS
Wind: 9-15mph
Temperature: 19deg C (67deg F)
Barometer: 29.5in Hg (1000.3mbar)
Humidity: 74per cent
Surface: dry asphalt and concrete
Test distance: 903miles

Figures taken at 2805 miles by our own staff at the General Motors proving ground at Millbrook.

◀ the Millbrook high-speed bowl to reach its mean maximum speed of 113mph with a wind-assisted best of 116mph recorded over the fastest flying quarter-mile. These speeds correspond to 5200rpm and 5325rpm respectively, just over the 5000rpm power peak.

The standing start acceleration runs proved to be a fairly sedate experience, but this was not unexpected; with a test weight of just over 1.5 tons, the CX25Ri Familiale is no lightweight. The benchmark 60mph was reached in 11.9secs with the quarter mile distance covered in 18.7secs at a terminal speed of 76mph. The kilometre post was reached in 34.9secs at a speed of 92mph.

These figures were achieved shifting the transmission manually on the red-line of 5500rpm, this technique proving to be fractionally faster than leaving the gear in automatic mode. In automatic, with the right foot to the floor, the change-up points correspond to 44mph—first to second—and 74mph — second to top. These both relate neatly to the 5000rpm peak power point.

Despite the less-than-impressive performance, the CX25Ri Familiale Automatic also returned a rather less than impressive overall fuel consumption figure of 20.4mpg during its 900 miles with us. Taking the calculated *Autocar* average consumption of 22.4mpg as a more representative figure, a 'normal' motorist might expect to achieve close to 22mpg, which, combined with the 15 gallon fuel tank, will give a range of just over 300 miles.

The main reason for the poor performance and fuel economy is the power-to-weight ratio, combined with the Cd factor. A ratio of 86.5bhp/ton laden is not particularly impressive, and combined with a Cd factor of 0.37 and an automatic gearbox, it is not an ideal combination. The result is mediocre performance and, by today's standards, poor fuel consumption for an injected engine.

Climb in behind the steering wheel and the alterations to the interior become obvious immediately. The controls for the wipers, lights and non self-cancelling indicators are still sited to the right and left of the binnacle within fingertip reach while the driver's hands remain on the steering wheel, and the remainder of the facia is now similar to that seen in the rest of the CX range. The centre console is angled steeply away from the front-seat occupants and gives a far greater impression of space than in the previous models.

Gone is the manual adjustment lever for the suspension height in-between the two front seats; this is replaced by an electric switch set in front of the gearstick on the facia, below the heater and ventilation controls. With the facia raked away from the driver, there is nowhere to fit a radio-cassette player which is accessible while driving, so the Familiale retains that strange Citroen feature of a vertically mounted player fixed into the console which runs between the front seats.

This sounds like a good idea in theory, but in practice it proves difficult to operate as it requires too much looking away from the road for the driver and the machine is upside-down as far as the passenger is concerned, once again making operation difficult.

One very neat feature on this automatic is the position of the gear indicator, to the right of the steering wheel and clearly visible at all times —a much better position than next to the gear stick.

The front seats are typically Citroen: supportive, fully adjustable for position, but perhaps a little over-cushioned for some tastes. They do, however, remain comfortable over long motorway journeys and, combined with the excellent ventilation, make the Familiale an ideal long distance cruiser as far as passengers are concerned.

Driving a Citroën CX of any type for the first time is a strange experience. The steering and controls do take some getting used to, requiring a slightly different driving technique from more conventional cars. Once used to them, though, they become easy and relaxing. With only 2.5 turns lock-to-lock, very sensitive power-assisted steering which is automatically self-centring and a 15ins wheel, straight-line progress can be initially difficult for the CX novice. The classic driving-school 'shuffle' is the only way to ensure smooth steering.

Front-wheel drive, front-mounted engine and a front/rear weight distribution of 67.5/32.5 per cent make for a car which naturally understeers, especially when combined with the hydropneumatic suspension. This is, of course, a safe and reassuring system in the main, but it does tend to feel a little soggy and inaccurate at times, especially as speed rises. The suspension, however, takes pot-holes and road surface irregularities in its stride. The only time it seems to be caught out is over a long series of regular undulations, where it begins to 'boat', front to rear.

One advantage of hydropneumatic suspension on a car like the Familiale is that it is self-levelling, so that it maintains the correct attitude no matter how much the car is loaded or not, as the case may be. This is especially important when carrying uneven heavy loads.

Large *rear door for easy access*

From all angles, *the Familiale is a truly large car*

Revised facia *gives greater feeling of space than before*

Seven seats, *but without a split on the third row*

The Familiale, however, is not just a simple estate car; it is a large and comfortable people-carrier courtesy of its third row of seats. Access to the rear seats is via large, wide-opening doors and once in the middle row of seats there is sufficient room for three adults. The rear seats are not quite so spacious as far as legroom is concerned, but there is adequate headroom due to the roof height extension which begins above the centre row of seats. There is sufficient room left behind the seats for a reasonable amount of luggage, but if seven people are going on holiday a roof rack will be necessary.

As a people-carrier, the Citroën CX25Ri Familiale fulfils its task admirably and will appeal especially to those drivers who prefer the more conventional looks of an estate car to those of 'tall-vehicle' alternatives.

Refinement levels are up to Citroën's usual excellent standards with good all-round sealing and insulation, but the car is let down to a certain extent on the performance and economy fronts. It is one of those cases where, say, a V6 engine might have been a more appropriate way of improving the power, flexibility and fuel economy of what is basically a very accomplished motor car. ■

CITROËN
French Connection Part II

By Mark Ewing
Photography by Earl Whited

I had a neighbor once who owned Citroens, mostly DS21s. The cars had driving lights mounted on the rear of the tall roof that to my super-heated imagination resembled sucker fish on a whale's back. There was a small, mushroom-shaped button on the floor for the brakes instead of a real honest-to-God-and-Henry-Ford pedal. And though the cars did not have velvet tuck-and-roll upholstery or murals of Aztec warriors across their flanks, the local lowrider contingent envied the cars' sophisticated hydraulic suspension. In a neighborhood full of Galaxie 500s and Dodge Coronet wagons, Mr MacEwan's Citroens were like something out of Rube Goldberg's worst nightmare.

Mr. MacEwan wasn't exactly the average guy on the block either, which I suppose made him the stereotypical Citroen owner. He went to his monthly highland clan meetings wearing a kilt. Do-it-yourself home improvements were a specialty, and he eventually knocked out most of the interior walls in his house. He even built a sail boat in his backyard one year and towed it to Newport Beach behind his red and white DS21. In short, he was a bit much for suburbia.

Which is exactly the problem Citroen always had in this country. The cars Citroen brought here in the 1950s and 1960s were too different for a mainstream America obsessed with chrome-coated two-ton cars with hulking V-8s. Citreons and their sometimes eccentric owners were the frequent butts of neighborhood jokes. A former publisher of a major auto magazine once named a Citreon car of the year as a cruel joke on management.

After years of frustrations and limited success, Citreon pulled out of the U.S., its last model being the Citreon-Maseriti SM. The year after the pull-out Citreon introduced the CX series to the European market, where it has sold steadily ever since. And now for those like Mr. MacEwan, who for the last 13 years have had to satiate their appetites for the eccentric with Peugeot diesels, Citreon CX25s are available in North America through Citreon Importers of North America here in Atlanta. The only disappointment ahead for those long-time Citreon afficianados is that in a world now accustomed to Mercury Sables and Audi 5000s, the CX25 just doesn't seem all that strange.

The CX25 should remain in production at least two more years and French management being what it is, probably till the end of the decade, when it will be superceded by the DX now in development that Citroen may itself market in the U.S. The CX25 follows patterns set by previous Citroens: it has front-wheel drive, a distinctive and aerodynamic shape, and a hydraulic suspension that gives it one of the smoothest rides of any car produced. Citroen first started building cars like this in the late 1930s, when the Traction-Avant models were a favorite with French resistance fighters because they could outrun the BMWs and Mercedes of the Nazi occupation forces, at least in the labyrinth of Paris.

Our test car was a CX25GTi Trubo, which has the standard 2.5 liter fuel-injected, four-cylinder engine, with the addition of a Garrett AiResearch turbo. The engine, mounted transversely and canted forward to allow for the low, sloping hoodline, delivers its 168 E.P.A.-certified horsepower through a smooth five-speed gearbox that was only a little notchy in our test. The base engine produces 138 horsepower. The car is covered by a limited 5 year/50,000 mile warranty.

The CX has four-wheel discs with ABS that are particularly good. Gone is the mushroom pedal of old, replaced by something that at least resembles a brake pedal. At first try, the brakes are grossly oversensitive, but after some time behind the wheel tailgaiting on the freeway becomes good sport because there's seemingly not much on the road that can outbrake the CX. That's how much confidence, and stopping power, the brakes generate.

The CX's interior drew high marks from everyone on the staff. The leather was beautiful, though the same cannot be said for all of the cloth patterns available. The seats are like modern Italian lounge chairs with the lateral and lumbar support of Recaros. Deep and well bolstered these seats have enough thigh support even for the long legged. The general fit and finish of the interior, as well as the rest of the car, was high. This is partially a result of Eurocar's policy of importing CXs from the German Citroen distributor, who sends back to the factory any car that does not meet the standards required of the German market. We hope that if Citroen does choose to reenter the American market, they will match these high standards.

The dash is a flat plane steeply raked away from the driver, which adds to

the car's feeling of spaciousness. The tach and speedometer gauges, housed in a panel that projects out of the raked dash, are mercifully not gee-whiz digitals but superb analogs. Gone are the gauges of the ID19 that worked like the revolving dial on a bathroom scale. In the center portion of the upper dash there are digital readouts for oil and water temperature, and a third screen that can, with the touch of a few buttons on a keyboard under a flap on the console, compute average time of arrival, rate of fuel consumption, and perform a number of other useful functions. Two control clusters projecting out of the instrument panel to within fingertip reach of the steering wheel contain controls for wipers, lights, turn indicators, and those wonderful Fiamm horns.

Because it is such an integral part of the Citroen mystique, the hydraulic system deserves some mention. The basis of the system is six elastomeric spheres that are divided by a steel diaphragm. The upper half of each sphere is filled with hydrogen gas, the lower with hydraulic fluid pumped to 1100 lbs. of pressure by a pump that runs off an output shaft. At each corner there is a sphere, with a fifth to handle steering and braking and a sixth serving as a reservoir. All six are interlinked. At the flip of a console-mounted switch the amount of fluid in the spheres at each wheel can be greatly reduced, lowering the car to the ground a position only suitable for parking lot entertainment or more fluid can be pumped into the spheres to lift the car up for that occasional foray onto a dirt road. Under heavy braking the front spheres are pumped with fluid to reduce nose dive, and under hard acceleration the rear spheres conpensate in much the same way to reduce squat. This system produces a smooth ride and has its other uses. But the most fun is had in bumper-to-bumper traffic, where surrounding drivers can be entertained by raising the car up and then dropping it to the ground. This game is of particular fun with gas station attendants, not the jaded sort indiginous to Southern California, but the variety found in the Mayberrys and boroughs of this region.

The system's only drawback is the exaggerated sense of body roll that comes in anything other than a gentle curve. The car actually doesn't lean as much as the driver feels through the seat of his pants, but the sensation is that you're cornering on the door handles. Or lost in a ten-foot lifeboat on a rolling sea. In spite of that feeling, the car is well suited to dodging through congested traffic, and its handling is confidence-inspiring once the yaw of the suspension is accepted and understood.

The Citroen's reason for being is not slaloming, however. It's meant for high-speed touring on open highways. In the short time we had the car, it was taken on an all-night trip through the North Georgia mountains into the Carolinas. The Blue-ridge highway doesn't have the cut-and-slash, cliff-hanging roads of Southern California's Angeles Crest highway; instead, it's like a snake coiling and uncoiling through the lush green forests of Appalachia. As we came within 40 miles or so of the Carolina border the heat lightning began flashing with more intensity and the

fog grew thicker. On those sections where the road opened up we took the car to 115 m.p.h. with enough left on the tach to break 120 if it were really necessary. But the car was most comfortable at 95 or 100. Wind noise at these speeds was minimal and a little jazz coming through the excellent Alpine stereo created the perfect atmosphere for conversation.

When the road began to coil up the car was stable in the corners, asking only for a little respect. This is no a canyon charger. At no time, either on high-speed straights or in the winding roads that lead into the Carolina upcountry, did the car not do what it was asked. It was a silent and willing partner that inspired the kind of confidence you wish you'd had with that first love.

So, you might ask, have Citroens changed enough to make it in the U.S. on a second go-round? Well, yes and no. The cars are competent when kept within their limits, well made, and distinctive. They offer touring capabilities to match those of almost any other four-door available in this country, with a dash of Gaullish charm. And even in the high-stakes hangouts we went to, where the BMW roundel is your badge of courage, the car drew attention like none other in the lot. The design has been proven by twelve years of success in Europe, where it is a favorite among salesmen for its smooth ride, long legs, and living room interior. Some might say that there are plenty of sedans that can go much faster and do so in equal silence, but most will cost far more than the $ 28,000 entry into a CX turbo.

And the American public's mindset has been irreversibly altered by cars like the Sable and Taurus, which has made the aerodynamic look accessible to the average buyer. With Fords looking as futuristic as Citroens, there should be much less resistance to the car's appearance. So, if you want one and are concerned that people will point and stare when you're driving around town, you should be. But they won't be laughing this time.

SPECIFICATIONS

Year/Model: 1986 Citroen CX25 GTi Turbo
Manufacturer: Citroen Automobile S.A.

GENERAL DATA

Vehicle Type: Four-door sedan
List Price: $24,675
Body/Chassis: Unitized body, subframe
Fuel Economy: 20 city/35 Hwy

ENGINE

Type: OHC Turbocharged inline four cylinder
Displacement: 2500 cc
Bore/Stroke: 93 x 92mm
Horsepower: 168 @ 5000 rpm
Torque: 217 lbs. ft. @ 3250 rpm
Compression Ratio: 7.75:1
Fuel System: Bosch motronic
Fuel Required: 87 octane unleaded

DRIVETRAIN

Transmission: 5-speed manual
Gear Ratios: 1st:3.166:1; 2nd:1.833:1; 3rd:1.206:1 4th:0.882:1; 5th:0.673:1
Final Drive Ratio: 4.214:1

PERFORMANCE

0-60: 7.8 sec.
¼ Mile: 16.2 sec.

DIMENSIONS/CAPACITIES

Wheelbase: 9' 4"
Overall Length: 15' 2"
Overall Width: 5' 8"
Overall Height: 4' 4"
Curb Weight: 3053 lbs.
Fuel Capacity: 14 gal.

CHASSIS

Suspension: **F:** Hydropneumatic independent
R: Hydropneumatic independent
Steering: Type: Rack-and-pinion
Brakes: **F:** 10.5-in. ventilated discs
R: 9.0 solid discs
Wheels: Cast alloy
Tires: 210/55 R390 RX

Citroën CX25 GTi

Weird styling, strange steering, funky brakes, and deep knee bends, too.

• When André Citroën decided to break into the automobile business at the end of World War I, he did so not to satisfy a passion for motorcars or a lifelong dream to mobilize the masses but simply to keep his ammunition factories working. Peace would destroy the company he had built unless he could adapt it to a high-volume product whose manufacture would require the sort of precision machinery he already owned. Cars seemed a promising choice, but Citroën might just as well have gone into tractors or electric motors.

That André Citroën brought no preconceived notions to the car business was perfectly clear in the products of his new enterprise. The original Citroën, the 1919 Type A, was one of the first inexpensive cars in France, introduced at a time when most carmakers were building lavish chariots for the rich. The company has continued to go its own way ever since. In 1934, a year before André Citroën died, it unveiled the technically exotic Traction Avant, with front-wheel drive, a unitized body-and-chassis structure, torsion bars in the rear suspension, and a short-stroke engine. After World War II, the company swung toward the opposite extreme with the 2CV, the French answer to the VW Beetle. This basic-transportation workhorse, powered by an air-cooled, 375cc two-cylinder engine and draped in homely but easy-to-manufacture body panels, has survived nearly 40 years of production. In 1955, Citroën dropped another bombshell on the world in the form of the DS19. This engineering tour de force employed an unusually streamlined body, hydropneumatic suspension, hydraulically assisted steering and brakes, and a single-spoke steering wheel. As a source of departures from the norm, Citroën is the company to count on.

The CX25 that has just landed on our shores is faithful to this proud tradition. Indeed, although the CX was introduced a dozen years ago, it remains farther removed from the automotive mainstream than any other production car you can name. Its body was shaped with as much attention to aerodynamics as any of today's slicksters. The CX's designers adopted a fundamental approach to low drag, shaping their top-of-the-line sedan as closely as possible to the teardrop ideal. It has a fat nose, a tapered tail, and considerable tumblehome, all blended together by smoothly curving lines. Aesthetic con-

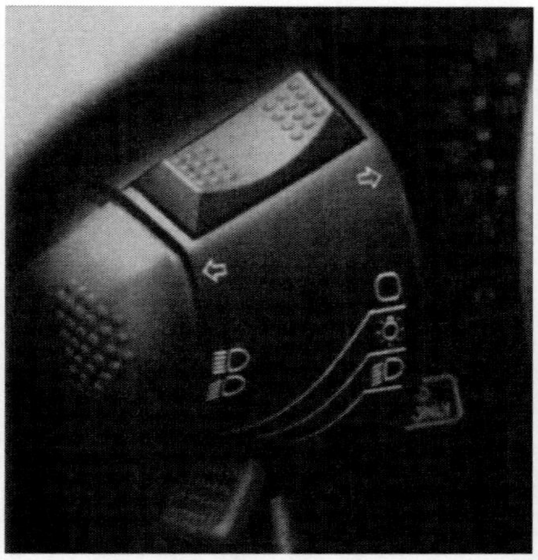

siderations, as usual, were given less emphasis. The CX looks right at home on the Champs Elysées, but it could make the denizens of Main Street think they're under rocket attack.

The CX's interior design is every bit as nonconformist as its exterior. The first time we glanced inside our test car, our eyes were assaulted by vast expanses of blue-and-gray herringbone upholstery. The view from the driver's seat is equally unnerving. The steering wheel has but one spoke, the column has no stalks, and on either side of the instrument cluster is a daunting pod of rockers, push buttons, and flip switches. The control layout works reasonably well, but it takes a while to climb the learning curve. The horn button is located on the side of the right pod. The turn-signal rocker switch is relatively convenient but doesn't cancel itself after a turn. Fortunately, all the gauges are absolutely conventional.

The steering wheel grabs your attention not only with its bizarre design but also with its unique self-centering action. We're not just talking about strong on-center feel here. If you turn the CX's wheel to full lock when the car is stationary and then relax your grip, the power mechanism will slowly wind the wheel back to dead center. On the road, this system produces excellent straight-line stability and feels quite reassuring; it also feels a bit artificial, especially in corners.

The CX's brakes are unusual as well. The energy-dissipating elements are conventional discs with anti-lock control. The weirdness presents itself in the special way the calipers operate and in a very different braking feel, almost free of travel. When the driver steps on the pedal, he is simply opening a valve that releases stored hydraulic pressure to do the work of applying the brakes. Further, the system responds primarily to the pressure the driver applies to the pedal, not to how far he moves it. Since the brake systems of many domestic models do little but hiss during the first inch of pedal travel, the CX's slack-free system can come as quite a shock to the uninitiated. The pedal is so firm and linear in its action, however, that a sensitive driver can quickly learn to apply the brakes smoothly. The only remaining irritation is a sloppy fluttering underfoot when the anti-lock is activated.

A third hydraulic peculiarity of the CX is its suspension system. Instead of springs, four hydropneumatic struts support the car's weight. The fluid in each strut is regulated by its own spherical reservoir, in which a flexible diaphragm separates hydraulic fluid on one side from compressed nitrogen on the other. As the suspension moves, the struts pump fluid into the reservoirs, compressing the nitrogen to provide springing. Damping forces are produced as the fluid flows through various calibrated orifices in the passageways between the struts and their reservoirs.

As the CX is loaded and it sinks on its suspension, mechanical sensors admit more hydraulic fluid into the struts from a storage reservoir that is pressurized by an engine-driven pump. This action lifts the car back to its normal height, increases the pressure of the compressed nitrogen, and raises the effective spring rate of the suspension. As a result, the CX can always maintain its proper ground clearance, level stance, and ride comfort. A cushy ride is possible because the spring rate is always keyed to the car's load. In contrast, conventional fixed-rate springs must be calibrated to deal with maximum loads, so they produce a relatively stiff ride when lightly burdened.

Of course, we forgot all about the sober

The four-position switch on the center console controls the CX's deep genuflections.

practical advantages of the CX's suspension system as soon as we discovered its four-position height control. The CX can be raised high enough to run harmlessly over a dog—well, at least a toy French poodle. The ostensible benefit of this ability is to permit tire changes without a jack: simply raise the car with the console-mounted switch, put a block under the appropriate corner, and drop it back down; the offending tire is now in the air, where it can easily be changed. Alternatively, the CX can be dropped so low that it almost drags on the pavement, thus permitting easier access to the engine bay.

The true value of the system, however, is to rivet the attention of those deadheads who might otherwise overlook the CX. To double its eye-catching index, simply set the suspension at one extreme or the other. (Citroën cautions against driving in the extreme positions, which lock the suspension against its limits and produce a brutally hard ride.) Cycling the car through its full range of travel before an assembled audience is also amusing; except in certain parts of East Los Angeles, cars that appear to be capable of levitation are a rarity. Dropping from high to low is the most startling trick of all: the CX drops its nose rather suddenly but settles its tail at a more leisurely rate, rather like a camel dropping to its knees for a drink.

Remarkable as it is as a rolling sideshow, the CX is just as good at its real purpose: comfortable transportation for five. For starters, it's extremely roomy. Citroën has long believed in locating a car's wheels as close to their respective corners as possible, and that principle, combined with a transverse engine and front drive, makes for a spacious interior. Shoulder room may be greater in full-size American cars, but the CX's headroom and legroom, both front and rear, are beyond reproach.

The CX feels quite sprightly, too, even though it has only a 2.5-liter four-cylinder to motivate its 3150 pounds. The engine is plenty torquey and responsive, and it suffers few ill effects from its conversion to American emissions standards. With the help of its slick-shifting five-speed, the CX reaches 60 mph in 10.1 seconds and tops out at 119 mph.

The CX is also satisfying when driven hard. Although it rolls prodigiously and has no more than 0.72 g of adhesion at the limit, it responds nicely to its controls. The CX can't outrun a serious sports sedan, but it never loses its aplomb.

If these virtues sound like the formula for an excellent large sedan, you've solved the equation correctly. The rub is high price. The CX is imported not by Citroën but by CX Automotive, an independent concern in Lebanon, New Jersey (201-236-2576). Only 2000 units will be offered in the 1987 model year, and as with many low-volume items, their prices will be high. The CX25 GTi is the cheapest model in the lineup, at $29,500. The turbocharged and limousine models range up to $44,000. For that kind of money you have a choice of any number of top-notch sedans—many with performance, reputations, and service networks that the CX can't hope to match.

The role of the CX in America, therefore, is that of an exclusive boutique car, one bought more for its distinctiveness than for its intrinsic value. In this case, however, rarity is not the only reward. Have you seen any other cars that can do deep knee bends? —*Csaba Csere*

Vehicle type: front-engine, front-wheel-drive, 5-passenger, 4-door sedan

Price as tested: $31,700

Options on test car: base Citroën CX25 GTi, $29,500; anti-lock brakes, $1700; freight, $500

Standard accessories: power steering, windows, locks, and sunroof, A/C, rear defroster

Sound system: Sony XR-57R AM/FM-stereo radio/cassette, 4 speakers

ENGINE

Type	4-in-line, iron block and aluminum head
Bore x stroke	3.66 x 3.62 in, 93.0 x 92.0mm
Displacement	153 cu in, 2500cc
Compression ratio	8.8:1
Fuel system	Bosch L-Jetronic fuel injection
Emissions controls	3-way catalytic converter, feedback fuel-air-ratio control
Valve gear	pushrods
Power (SAE net)	130 bhp @ 5000 rpm
Torque (SAE net)	150 lb-ft @ 4000 rpm
Redline	5500 rpm

DRIVETRAIN

Transmission	5-speed
Final-drive ratio	4.21:1

Gear	Ratio	Mph/1000 rpm	Max. test speed
I	3.17	5.3	29 mph (5500 rpm)
II	1.83	9.2	51 mph (5500 rpm)
III	1.25	13.5	74 mph (5500 rpm)
IV	0.94	18.0	99 mph (5500 rpm)
V	0.73	23.0	119 mph (5150 rpm)

DIMENSIONS AND CAPACITIES

Wheelbase	112.0 in
Track, F/R	59.9/53.9 in
Length	183.1 in
Width	69.0 in
Height	53.5 in
Ground clearance	6.0 in
Curb weight	3152 lb
Weight distribution, F/R	66.9/33.1%
Fuel capacity	18.0 gal
Oil capacity	5.6 qt
Water capacity	8.8 qt

CHASSIS/BODY

Type	full-length frame with rubber-isolated body
Body material	welded steel stampings

INTERIOR

SAE volume, front seat	51 cu ft
rear seat	46 cu ft
trunk space	18 cu ft
Front seats	bucket
Seat adjustments	fore and aft, seatback angle, front height, rear height
General comfort	poor fair good **excellent**
Fore-and-aft support	poor fair good **excellent**
Lateral support	poor fair **good** excellent

SUSPENSION

F:	ind, unequal-length control arms, hydropneumatic springs, anti-roll bar
R:	ind, trailing arm, hydropneumatic springs, anti-roll bar

STEERING

Type	rack-and-pinion, power-assisted
Turns lock-to-lock	2.5
Turning circle curb-to-curb	38.5 ft

BRAKES

F:	10.5 x 0.8-in vented disc
R:	9.3 x 0.3-in disc
Power assist	hydraulic with anti-lock control

WHEELS AND TIRES

Wheel size	5.9 x 15.4 in
Wheel type	cast aluminum
Tires	Michelin TRX, 190/65HR-390
Test inflation pressures, F/R	35/29 psi

CAR AND DRIVER TEST RESULTS

ACCELERATION	Seconds
Zero to 30 mph	3.1
40 mph	4.9
50 mph	7.1
60 mph	10.1
70 mph	13.6
80 mph	18.0
90 mph	25.2
100 mph	36.0
Top-gear passing time, 30–50 mph	12.2
50–70 mph	13.8
Standing ¼-mile	17.3 sec @ 79 mph
Top speed	119 mph

BRAKING

70–0 mph @ impending lockup	190 ft
Fade	**none** moderate heavy

HANDLING

Roadholding, 300-ft-dia skidpad	0.72 g
Understeer	minimal **moderate** excessive

COAST-DOWN MEASUREMENTS

Road horsepower @ 30 mph	6 hp
50 mph	15 hp
70 mph	33 hp

FUEL ECONOMY

EPA city driving	**16 mpg**
EPA highway driving	21 mpg
C/D observed fuel economy	**18 mpg**

INTERIOR SOUND LEVEL

Idle	57 dBA
Full-throttle acceleration	78 dBA
70-mph cruising	74 dBA
70-mph coasting	71 dBA

CURRENT BASE PRICE dollars x 1000

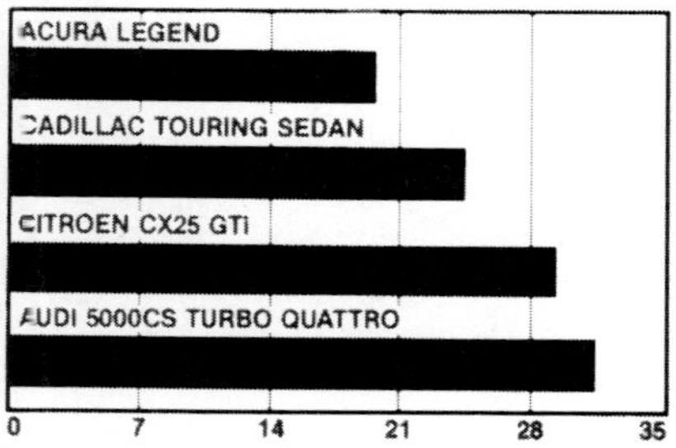

ACCELERATION seconds

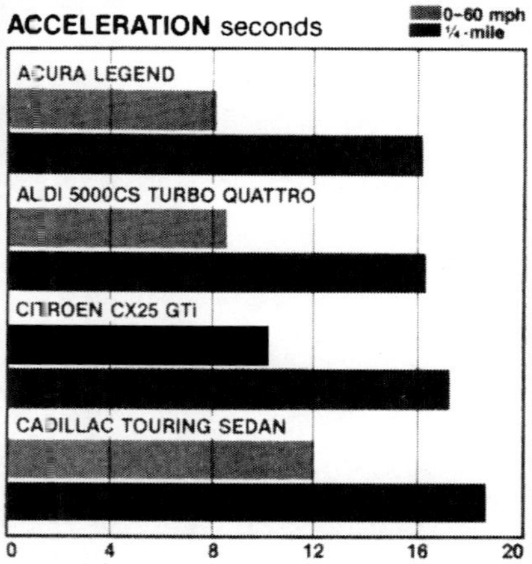

70–0 MPH BRAKING feet

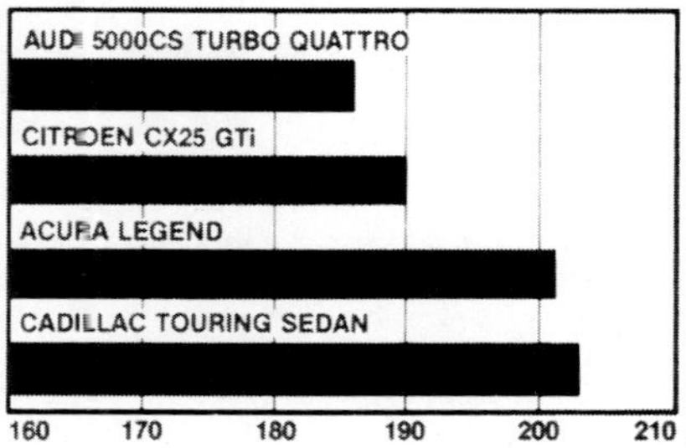

ROADHOLDING 300-foot skidpad, g

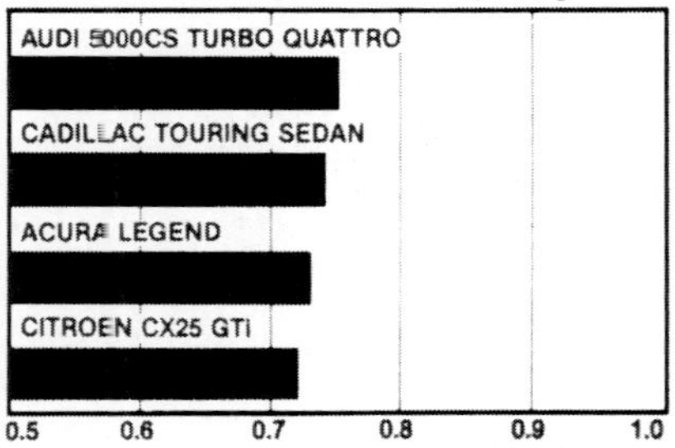

EPA ESTIMATED FUEL ECONOMY mpg

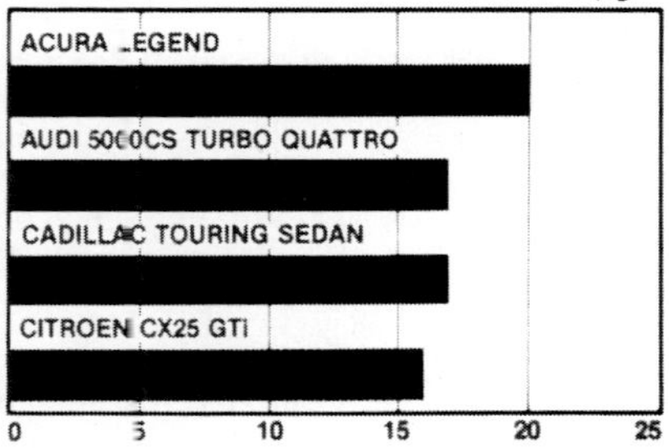

IMPRESSIONS

CITROEN CX GTi TURBO 2

● ***Those wanting a performance saloon with a great deal of character could find what they want in the Citroen CX GTi Turbo, which now gains an intercooler and ABS braking, if not much in performance terms. John Henderson has been driving the teenaged French turbo.***

Citroen's CX is 13 years old in August and a replacement is under development, but that does not mean that the 1975 Car of the Year has been left to retire quietly. The sporty CX GTi Turbo we first saw in October 1984 has gained an air-to-air intercooler and ABS to become the CX GTi Turbo 2.

An intercooler improves the volumetric efficiency of a turbo engine, which, put simply, means that you get more oxygen molecules in a given amount of cool air than in the same volume of warm air, in which they whizz about more. The 2500cc engine's output stays the same, with 168bhp at 5000rpm and a good 217lb ft torque at 3250rpm. But Citroen says that the intercooler gives better torque characteristics and saves fuel.

It also claims that top speed is up by 3mph, to 139mph, with 0-62mph (100kph) down from 8.0 to 7.8 seconds. Those are the sort of differences we might expect when taking the same car to the test track on different days. When we tested a CX Turbo in 1985, it did only 126.2mph and hit 60mph in 8.5 seconds.

If torque characteristics have been improved, there should also be improvements in fourth and fifth gear times, in which the original turbo proved competent. Even so, it is likely that only driving the Turbo and Turbo 2 back to back would show the difference.

Back in 1985, with a visit to the test track, the CX Turbo did 20.1mpg, while the Turbo 2, driven hard but without going to the track, managed 23.9mpg. The government constant speed figures show an improvement of about 1mpg.

On the road, the CX Turbo 2 retains a strong 'on-off' turbo action. It's off-boost performance is still respectable, but as the tachometer needle passes through the 2500 to 3000rpm sector the turbocharger's benefit is strongly felt. Smoothing out the effect of the turbo's arrival is not made any easier by a throttle pedal which feels as dead as a diesel Land Rover's.

Neither do the gear ratios help. The engine pulls well in the lower gears, but in fourth and fifth the turbo lag becomes annoying. There is also wide spacing between third, fourth and fifth ratios so changing up can leave you in turbo no-man's land. Fourth is high enough at 19.2mph per 1000rpm to lack flexibility for town driving below 40mph. The change is also slow and stodgy with a heavy and abrupt clutch.

For a performance saloon costing £14,995, the CX Turbo 2 is not very refined. We felt the engine was not as pleasant as the original CX Turbo's, which was no gem itself.

Though the high 25.2mph per 1000rpm fifth gear allows mechanically relaxed high speed cruising, the engine is gruff whenever it is worked. It can also sound rather diesel-like, particularly at town speeds when it contributes to an unpleasant boominess in the car. Poor roads also cause boominess.

Any CX fan coming to the Turbo 2 is likely to be disappointed by the ride. It still retains the amazing oleopneumatic ability to absorb impact with any hole that doesn't need bollards round it, yet without the high-speed float of other CXs. But it has been firmed up and combined with 55 per cent aspect ratio Michelin TRX tyres – so there is a constant patter through to the seats from small irregularities, particularly ridges.

In spite of the tightening up, body roll is still quite pronounced, though the suspension ensures that the wheels stay where they should be for good roadholding. But the tightening has also made the suspension seem a little slower to respond and high speed humps can unsettle the car. On some S-bends it does not quite settle back from one bend before having to take the next.

As with all CX's the steering is fully powered rack and pinion that is strongly self centring. Its feel is remarkably artificial: put the car on ice and turning the wheel requires the same effort as on wet tarmac! The CX's seat of the pants feel is also poor, leaving the driver strangely isolated from the road.

You get used to the amazing powered brakes, which on all CX's are discs all round, ventilated at the front. You eventually find out how to brush the brake pedal for a smooth stop and they are very efficient. ABS, which used to be an option, is now standard and reassuring.

Conventional instruments replace the Citroen drum-type ones in the domed binnacle. The tachometer is small but clear, as are the petrol and oil pressure/level gauges, but the speedo is fussy. A facia centre strip of four clear LCDs usefully displays oil, water and exterior temperatures, plus a readout for the trip computer.

Major switchgear is very well located. Instead of stalk switches there are rockers, push panels and tabs on the binnacle edges.

Minor switchgear is far less praiseworthy. A string of illuminated buttons runs down to the right of the steering column, with the hazard warning at column level and running down to a badly obscured front foglamp switch below knee height. The heated rear screen switch is in a roof panel and has no real warning light. The trip computer, under a neat facia flap, and handbrake are located for left-hand drive.

We can quite understand why people get hooked on Citroens. They are so refreshingly different and have such character that their faults are easy to forgive. But while we have enjoyed driving many cars of the double chevron, including other CXs, the Turbo 2 disappointed even our most ardent Citroen fanatic. Even with its new intercooler, the engine is not good enough, lacking refinement and response by most standards, while the firming up of the suspension has weakened one of the CX's strongest assets. ●

Likes: Relaxed cruising, major switches.

Dislikes: Lack of refinement, poor gearbox, turbo lag, handling feel.

Price: £14,995

SURVIVAL OF THE FITTEST

Our CX GTi Turbo was not a pretty sight after its argument with a bridge parapet, but it is a credit to Citroën's design staff that it survived at all. Dave Alexander reports on living a hectic life with the fastest production CX

So now it's time to say goodbye to the 'Black Beast.' With 24,000 on the clock and one major accident, our long-term Citroën CX GTi Turbo has returned to its maker. All in all, the members of the *Autocar* staff, including myself, have enjoyed the car immensely.

Its capacity for effortless, long-distance, high-speed cruising made the CX the staff's favourite transport when travelling any sort of mileage.

Around town its sheer size makes the CX fairly unwieldy, although it does help that the steering lock is only 2.5 turns from one extreme to the other. Time is needed to become familiar with Citroën's power-assisted steering though its self-centring effect is a great help in keeping the car pointing in the right direction at speed — it ploughs on as straight as an arrow whatever the conditions or speed. The steering does, however, have a dead feel when the car is driven very slowly if the wheel is turned from side to side suddenly.

If the steering is open to a certain amount of criticism, the suspension is less so. The CX hydropneumatic system has been retained but uprated in the Turbo to handle the increased power. Combine this with the wide-section, low-profile Michelins and the ride is exceptionally good although the system can be fooled by large deflections such as humpback bridges taken at speed. The ride height should be constantly adjusted via the built-in self-levelling, but as the miles have piled up the CX tends to sit higher at the back. Even with the engine running the car fails to return to level flight — this has been most noticeable since the Black Beast had its run-in with a bridge parapet.

The CX GTi Turbo is the most powerful CX in current production, the addition of a Garrett T3 turbocharger and relevant plumbing adding some 22 per cent to the power output of the 25 GTi to give 168bhp at 5000rpm and 217lb ft of torque low down at 3250rpm. The turbo installation is excellent. There is very little lag and the car, for its size, is exceptionally flexible, pulling away cleanly and quickly from low revs in the upper gears, making motorway overtaking manoeuvres a safe and easy exercise. Our long-term CX has never matched the performance figures claimed by Citroën, though.

In terms of maximum speed, the best that the CX has managed is 129mph. It has reached this speed on all the occasions that the car has been tested but has clearly had nothing more to give, denying us the 136mph claimed by the manufacturer. The best 0-60mph time that our road test team has managed to achieve is 8.2secs.

A problem we encountered at an early test session, when 9.3secs was the best 0-60mph time, was thanks to a fail-safe system incorporated in the CX. When the cylinder block sensor detects an irregular combustion sequence it immediately retards the system by eight or nine degrees. If the irregularity is not repeated, the system is designed to crank up the advances until the timing is normal again. There is, however, a more radical second stage to the fail-safe procedure in which event the ignition can go back as far as 18deg and provides no advance at all below 1200rpm. This is what happened to our car.

It was driven very carefully to Traffic Garage, at Walton-on-the-Hill, where both block sensor and computer were replaced under warranty. Operation completed, our CX was returned to rude health once more.

Most of the *Autocar* staff were impressed by the general performance levels of the CX, although the overall smoothness of the engine ▶

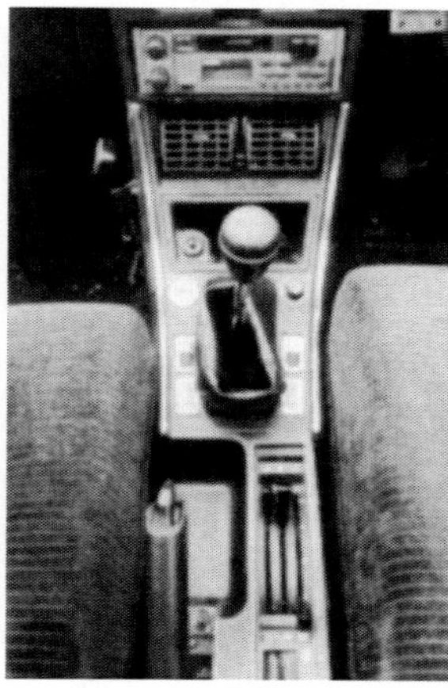

Block sensor *and engine computer were changed quite early in the life of the CX Turbo (far left)*
Gearchange *(left) was always baulky but deteriorated around the 20,000-mile mark*
A style all of its own: *the Citroën CX certainly stands out*

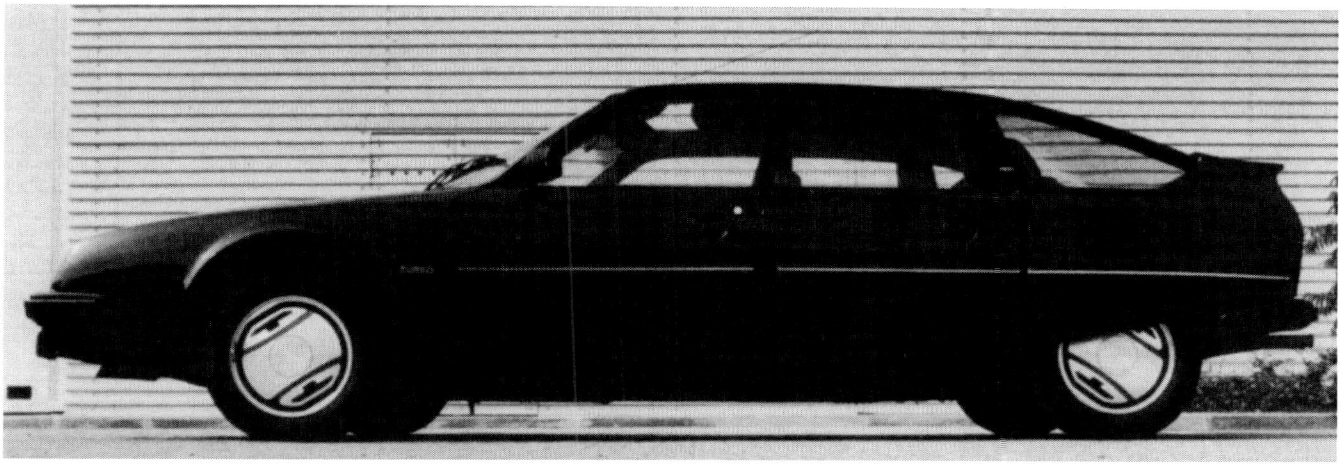

◀ deteriorated during the last 1000 miles that the CX was with us, the overrun becoming jerky, which we put down to the overrun fuel cut-off valve sticking and causing the engine to hunt.

The gearbox was always a little baulky but in the later stages of its time with us the change quality began to feel very tired; the syncromesh was still there but it had slowed right down, expecially on the lower three gears. Changing down in any sort of a hurry required double declutching.

There were two incidents in the life of the CX that highlight the safety factors that are a tribute to Citroën. The first occurred as one of our road testers was starting a maximum speed run on the high-speed track at MIRA. Noticing a shake in the steering he wisely decided to pull over and investigate the problem. To his horror he found that almost the entire outside band of tread on the offside front tyre had stripped off. The cover was still inflated but damaged beyond repair. The tyre was removed and sent to Michelin for comment and after assessment by the technical department, Michelin's technical liaison manager gave his verdict.

The incident had been our fault. Although the testers had followed normal practice and raised the tyre pressures before taking to the high-speed track, Michelin's advice was that we should have been running at least 10 psi above normal pressures (front 33.5psi, rear 22psi). The marked front weight bias of the car made it particularly sensitive in that situation and where we might have got away with it in a car with more even weight distribution, the high-speed banking, with all the loading that involves, caused the tyre to roll right over on to the side wall, generating enough heat to effectively carbonise the rubber tread.

The second incident was the argument with a bridge parapet. Picture the scene: night had just fallen and the drizzle had been falling for a couple of hours. I was proceeding with four passengers in an easterly direction down a quiet lane approaching an S-bend with a hump-back bridge in the middle. I had used the road many times before and knew it well. The problem with this particular bridge is that there is enough room only for one vehicle to cross at a time, so bearing this in mind, I slowed down and watched for the headlights of oncoming traffic. I could see none so pulled out to the centre of the road to cross the bridge.

Imagine my surprise and horror when a car appeared on the crest of the bridge displaying only side lights. Now, a driver who was perhaps more used to the CX wouldn't have made the mistake I did. He would have remembered the excellent, perhaps over-servoed, brakes. I took avoiding action, swinging the car to the left

Incorrect tyre pressure *caused the tread to strip (below)*
Accident damage *took the CX off the road for two months (bottom)*

CITROEN CX 25 GTi TURBO 2 COMPARED

Minor aerodynamic *changes lowered wind noise levels in Turbo 2*

It was in the autumn of 1985 — in this country anyway — that the effort to smooth out some of the worst quirks in the Citroën range caught up with the CX models.

Parent company PSA had already called in its connections with Peugeot and Talbot to sort out the BX. Much of the effort went into the interior, where changes such as rationalising the switchgear and introducing standard instruments to replace the famous 'cyclops eye' drum speedometer, greatly improved the broad appeal of the car.

The 'new look' CX — almost the last change to the current design before the new flagship appears — was little changed on the outside. Experiments had been conducted to improve the aerodynamics, especially to reduce levels of wind noise from window frames and screen surrounds, but the small benefits were more than outweighed, literally, by the extra poundage of panelling and cost.

In the end Citroën Style settled for an extra hit on the metal press forming the front wings to allow the fitment of a single unit front bumper undertray in composite material. There were new and more streamlined exterior mirrors plus composite aerodynamic covers for the rear wheels.

To a certain extent there was a reduction in wind noise levels but at the higher speeds achieved by the GTi Turbo, the 15-year-old design still suffered from progressively severe wind noise intrusion. The small changes to the body *did* raise the threshold at which the wind roar began to drown out the radio.

Inside, the 'new' CX is very different. Substantial changes to the facia design, instrument and switchgear layout and the seats, create an impression of space besides physically providing more room.

Main instrument grouping and the pod style switchgear follows the old system which was in fact ergonomically very efficient. The GTi had analogue instruments anyway and these are retained.

One of the complaints about the old car concerned the poor ventilation. Our old GTi, with its black exterior and interior, could be a real sweatbox in the summer and the sunroof was essential rather than an option.

On the new car the heat vent system is thermostatically controlled and there are more outlets than before so that a decent airflow can be achieved. Air conditioning is another useful addition to the specification on the top models.

The centre console houses much of the important switchgear including the selector for the ride height control. This electric slider switch replaces the manual lever system that was installed in the older car between the seat. The space there is now occupied by the radio.

Adding anti-locking braking helps to overcome the fears of a panic stab on the hair-trigger pedal instantly locking up all four wheels.

At the introduction of the revised CX, Citroën also announced that it would be fitting a new 2.2-litre, 115bhp engine to the 22TRS version. It was quicker than the old 2-litre, but still not as quick as the GTi turbo that claimed to offer a top speed of around 130mph, although we were never able to get ours up to that level.

But the GTi was not forgotten. Citroën had plans in the pipeline to give it more power by adding an intercooler to the turbo unit. The gain in absolute power was minimal because Citroën set up the system to concentrate on producing more torque for improved acceleration.

and at the same time giving the brake pedal an over-zealous stab. The brakes locked and the Citroën careered over the greasy road surface as straight as an arrow, into the bridge parapet. The crumple zones crumpled. Fortunately nobody was so much as slightly injured, although the oncoming driver might have been, had he bothered to stop . . .

The addition of anti-lock braking (see separate sidebar) came just too late to save me.

The CX really comes into its own at high speed where it will cruise effortlessly for hours on end. There is some tyre roar from the wide-section Michelins and the wind whistles round the front windows at anything over 70mph. Often opening and reclosing the front windows alleviated this problem.

Starting from cold is never any problem although I found the starter motor quite loud.

The instrumentation in the CX is easy to live with although some people don't like it on first acquaintance. Conventional gauges are placed in a compact group and the black-faced instruments with white numbers and orange points look purposeful and neat. Citroën has retained the familiar rocker switch arrangement for indicators and main beam, plus the finger-tip controls for horn and headlamp flash. These pods of switchgear allow the driver to keep both hands on the wheel in the correct position.

A 15ins diameter, leather-bound steering wheel is fitted, with the word 'Turbo' embossed in the centre section. I always wondered if the emblem was put there to remind the driver of the fact that a blown engine was fitted.

The large steering wheel necessitates a splayed legs driving position and the steering is sufficiently highly geared to allow a smaller wheel to be fitted.

There is only just enough legroom for average height drivers, a problem which could be sorted out if the front part of the seat had a tilt arrangement fitted. The rear of the driver's seat can be lowered to provide more headroom, a fact that drivers of 6ft or more will appreciate, especially when a sunroof is fitted. Another solution would have been to make the steering column adjustable. After 24,000 miles the seats are becoming rather tired and losing their firmness, although the fabric covering has stood up remarkably well to long-term wear.

So after 24,000 miles, 1053 gallons of fuel, 10 litres of oil and one major accident, which kept the car off the road for two months, it was time to wave farewell. I am missing the CX, surprisingly. It is an individual beast that, once you have become accustomed to driving, is hard to do without. ■

Seats *(below) went a little soggy but generally stood up well*
Citroën combines *four-seat comfort with versatility*

LONG-TERM DATA

WHAT IT HAS COST

Price new (July 1985)	£12,575
Price now (June 1987)	£14,995
Estimated trade-in value of our car	£5500

FUEL/OIL (Cost for 24,000 miles)

1053 gal, 4-star (£1.76/gal)	£1853.28
10 litres oil (£2.00/litre)	£20.00
Total	£1873.28

TYRES

Cost £126.50 (each)	
Life Front — 70% worn	£177.10
Rear — 50% worn	£126.50
Total	£303.60

SERVICE AND REPAIR RECORD
Faults on delivery: None noticed.

SERVICE

Distance	Date	
600	Jul 1983	£19.66
6000	Sep 1985	£35.15
12,000	Nov 1985	£63.86
18,000	Apr 1986	£35.12
24,000	Nov 1986	£148.00

REPAIRS

Distance	Date	
3500	August 1985, filler pipe leak	£9.20
4000	August 1985, replace fuel tank (Warranty)	
6000	September 1985, replace washer bottle (Warranty)	
Total		£9.20

TOTAL REPAIR AND SERVICE COSTS:	£310.99

EXTRAORDINARY ITEMS

Replaced tyre damaged while testing	£126.50
Replace front foglamp	£39.45
Total	£165.95

ANNUAL STANDING COSTS

Road tax	£100.00
Insurance premium (calculated)	£270.00

DEPRECIATION
(23 months, estimated) £7075.00

TOTAL RUNNING COSTS
(23 months, ex-depreciation) £3197.04

COST PER MILE
(including tax and insurance) 13.3p
(including tax, insurance and depreciation) 42.6p

*To put all our cars on equal footing for insurance costs, the figure given above is a typical quotation for a good-risk driver, with clean record, and car garaged in Oxfordshire, a middle-risk area. Full no-claims discount has been deducted, as has the saving for £25 excess. Source: Quotel Motor Insurance Service

SPECIFICATION

ENGINE
Transverse front, front-wheel drive. Head/block al. alloy/cast iron. 4 cylinders in line, wet liners, 5 main bearings. Water cooled, electric fan

Bore 93.0mm (3.66in), stroke 92.0mm (3.62in), capacity 2473cc (151.0cu in)

Valve gear ohv, 2 valves per cylinder, chain camshaft drive. Compression ratio 7.8 to 1. Electronic ignition, Bosch L-Jetronic injection. Garrett T3 turbocharger, boost pressure 8psi (0.57 bar).

Max power 168bhp (PS-DIN) (122kW ISO) at 5000rpm. Max torque 217 lb ft at 32500rpm

TRANSMISSION
5-speed manual, single dry plate clutch.

Gear	Ratio	mph/1000rpm
Top	0.67	25.2
4th	0.88	19.2
3rd	1.21	14.1
2nd	1.83	9.3
1st	3.17	5.4

Final drive: Helical spur, ratio 4.2.

SUSPENSION
Front, independent, transverse steel arms forming parallelogram, hydropneumatic damping, anti-roll bar.

Rear, independent, trailing arm, hydropneumatic damping, anti-roll.

STEERING
Rack and pinion, hydraulic power assistance. Steering wheel diameter 15in, 2.5 turns lock to lock

BRAKES
Dual circuits, split front/rear. Front 10.3in (261mm) dia ventilated discs. Rear 8.8in (223mm) dia discs. Hydraulic servo. Handbrake, centre lever acting on front discs.

DIMENSIONS, WEIGHTS
Length 183.5ins (4661mm)
Width 69.7ins (1770mm)
Height 53.5ins (1359mm)
Wheelbase 112.2ins (2850mm)
Weight 3107lb (1409kg)

PERFORMANCE

MAXIMUM SPEEDS

Gear	LT		RT	
Top (mean)	127	5000	126	5000
(best)	129	5020	128	5010
4th	115	6000	115	6000
3rd	84	6000	84	6000
2nd	55	6000	55	6000
1st	32	6000	32	6000

FUEL CONSUMPTION

Overall mpg:
LT 22.8 (12.4 litres/100km)
RT 20.1 (14.0 litres/100km)

ACCELERATION

From rest

True mph	Speedo mph LT	Time secs RT	RT
30	33	2.8	2.8
40	42	4.2	4.2
50	53	5.8	5.9
60	64	8.2	8.6
70	75	10.4	11.3
80	85	13.9	14.8
90	96	17.3	19.0
100	108	22.2	24.3
110	119	30.2	35.2
120	129	—	—

Standing ¼-mile: LT 16.5sec, 84mph
RT 16.7sec, 83mph
Standing km: LT 29.7sec, 107mph
RT 30.2sec, 106mph

In each gear

mph	Top		4th		3rd	
	LT	RT	LT	RT	LT	RT
10-30	—	—	10.4	11.3	6.5	6.5
20-40	12.7	13.6	8.1	8.2	5.0	4.8
30-50	10.1	10.9	6.2	6.7	4.0	3.9
40-60	8.6	8.6	6.0	5.7	4.0	3.9
50-70	8.6	8.4	6.0	5.9	4.6	4.7
60-80	9.6	9.8	6.4	6.5	—	6.7
70-90	10.4	10.8	8.1	7.5	—	—
80-100	11.4	11.4	11.0	9.2	—	—
90-110	—	15.0	—	—	—	—

RT denotes performance figures for CX GTi Turbo tested in *Autocar* of 24 October 1984.

CITROEN CX25 DTR TURBO 2 TEST UPDATE

Citroen's newest and most powerful turbo diesel engine is now available in a well equipped CX saloon body.

Perfomance to petrol engine standards joins comfort and economy in giving the ageing CX impressive new credentials.

PRICE *£14,995* **TOP SPEED** *112MPH* **0-60MPH** *10.1 SECS* **MPG** *30.1*
FOR *Performance, equipment, refinement* **AGAINST** *Steering*

THE CITROEN CX25 DTR TURBO 2 SALOON is claimed to be the fastest, most powerful diesel saloon on sale in the UK. There is no doubt that the latest oil-burning version of Citroen's big saloon is an impressive performer — if not quite as impressive as Citroen says.

Improvements to the new model are the result of incorporating an intercooler, which allows turbo boost pressure to be increased from 0.6 to 0.8 bar, liberating more power and torque from the 2500cc four-cylinder engine. Power is increased from 95bhp at 3700rpm to 120bhp at 3900rpm, and torque climbs from 158lb ft to 188lb ft at 2000rpm. The engine features a cast iron block, five main bearing steel crankshaft, forged steel connecting rods, light alloy pistons, a camshaft placed high in the block and driven by a toothed belt, reinforced light alloy cylinder head with two valves per cylinder and combustion turbulence chambers of the Ricardo Comet V type.

The turbocharger has been changed from a Garrett TO3 to the new, smaller TO25, the object being to improve response without affecting power. Boost pressure starts to make itself felt at about 1300rpm now, so there should be really usable power and torque at low engine speeds. At the same time, the overall gearing has been raised from 27mph to 28.9mph per 1000rpm in fifth gear, a change which takes advantage of the engine's improved efficiency.

As with the previous version, the CX turbodiesel is distinguished externally by a rear spoiler, similar to that fitted to the CX GTI, rubber overriders and airhorns. Inside, tweed upholstery, rear inertia-reel seatbelts and more comprehensive instrumentation are the main identifying marks.

With diesel cars now accounting for 5 per cent of all car sales in the UK, it was decided that a well specified saloon version of the CX DTR, originally launched as estate only early in '87, was necessary to help fill a developing gap in the fleet market. The saloon was introduced in August.

Improved performance is the *raison d'être* of this car, and it takes only a brief spell behind the wheel to find that its sprightly performance and responsive nature make it the equal of the majority of petrol-engined cars. At the test track, the CX DTR recorded a 0-60mph time of 10.1secs, which compares nicely with Citroen's 10.5secs 0-62.5mph claim. Mean maximum speed was disappointing, however: 112mph against the factory's alleged 121mph. The in-gear maxima were achieved by running the engine to the governor, the resultant speeds equating to 4150rpm, lower than the 4750rpm redline marked on the tachometer.

Subjectively, a diesel engine complements the CX's pleasantly eccentric nature well. The engine

Familiar CX shape *is sleek as ever in new DTR Turbo; rear spoiler identifies the model*
With intercooler, *the 2500cc blown diesel now gives 120bhp for 0-60 sprint in 10.1secs*

CITROEN CX25 DTR TURBO 2

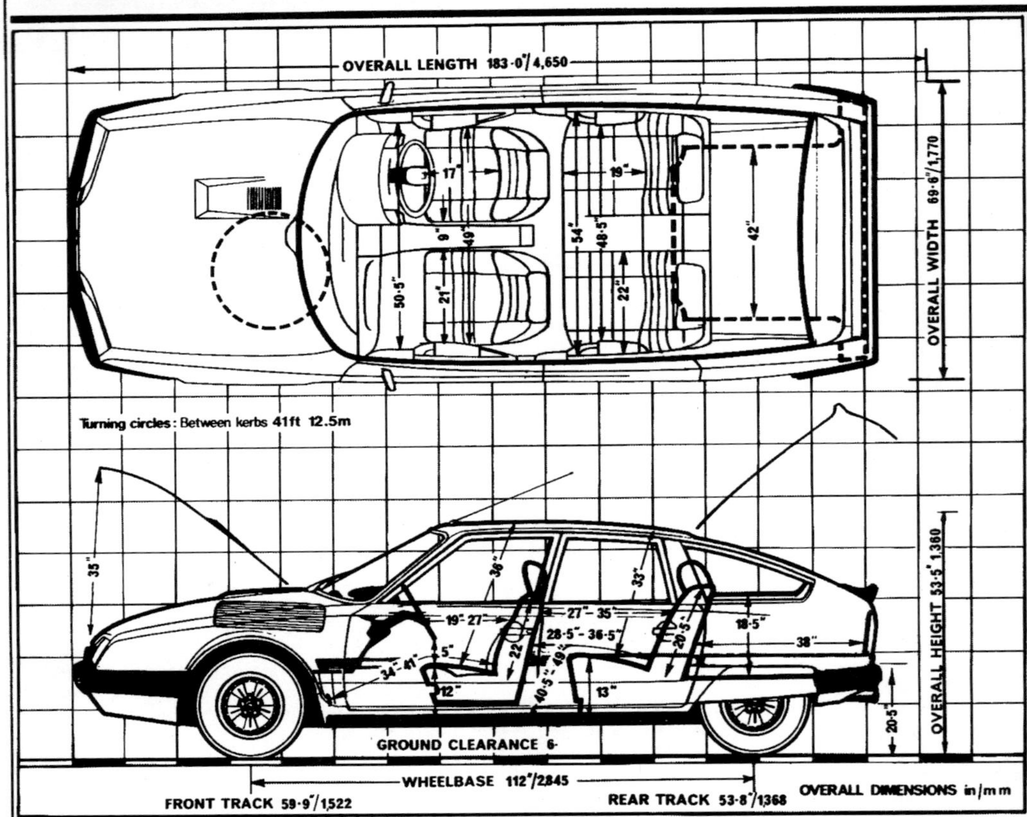

MODEL

CITROËN CX 25DTR TURBO 2

PRODUCED BY:
Automobiles Citroën SA,
62 Boulevard Victor Hugo,
Neuilly-sur-Seine,
F-92208 Paris, France

SOLD IN THE UK BY:
Citroën UK Limited,
Mill Street,
Slough SL2 5DE.

SPECIFICATION

ENGINE
Transverse, front, front-wheel drive. Head/block al. alloy/al. alloy. 4 cylinders in line, wet liners, 5 main bearings. Water cooled, electric fan.
Bore 93mm (3.66in), **stroke** 92mm (3.62in), **capacity** 2473cc (151 cu in).
Valve gear ohv, 2 valves per cylinder, chain camshaft drive. **Compression ratio** 21.0 to 1. Lucas fuel injection. Garrett T03 turbocharger, boost pressure 8.5psi (0.6bar).
Max power 120bhp (PS-DIN) (89kW ISO) at 3900rpm. **Max torque** 188lb ft (277Nm) at 2000rpm.

TRANSMISSION
5-speed manual, single dry plate diaphragm spring clutch, 9ins dia.

Gear	Ratio	mph/1000rpm
Top	0.674	28.94
4th	0.882	22.10
3rd	1.250	15.60
2nd	1.945	10.03
1st	3.418	5.70

Final drive: helical spur, ratio 3.688.

SUSPENSION
Front, independent, transverse steel arms forming parallelogram, hydropneumatic damping, anti-roll bar.
Rear, independent, trailing arms, hydropneumatic damping, anti-roll bar.

STEERING
Rack and pinion, hydraulic power assistance. Steering wheel diameter 15in, 2.5 turns lock to lock.

BRAKES
Dual circuits, split front/rear. **Front** 10.3in (261mm) dia ventilated discs. **Rear** 8.8in (223mm) dia discs. Antilock standard. Hydraulic servo. Parking brake, centre lever acting on front discs.

WHEELS
Al alloy, 6in rims. Radial ply tyres (Michelin MXV on test car), size 195/70R14, pressures F36 R33 psi (normal driving).

EQUIPMENT
Battery 12V, 88Ah. Alternator 80A. Headlamps 110/120W. 2-speed plus intermittent screen wipers. Air blending heater; air conditioning extra. Cloth seats, cloth-covered headlining. Carpet with heel mat floor covering. Screw pillar jack; 2 jacking points each side.

PERFORMANCE

MAXIMUM SPEEDS

Gear	mph	km/h	rpm
OD Top (Mean)	112	180	3850
(Best)	113	182	3900
4th	92	148	4150
3rd	65	105	4150
2nd	42	68	4150
1st	24	39	4150

ACCELERATION FROM REST

True mph	Time (sec)	Speedo mph
30	3.2	31
40	4.8	41
50	7.3	52
60	10.1	62
70	13.9	72
80	18.5	82
90	24.3	93
100	33.9	103
110	—	113

Standing ¼-mile: 17.8sec, 78mph
Standing km: 32.8sec, 98mph

ACCELERATION IN EACH GEAR

mph	Top	4th	3rd	2nd
10-30	—	—	6.9	3.6
20-40	15.6	9.0	5.0	3.2
30-50	12.2	7.0	4.5	—
40-60	10.3	6.9	5.1	—
50-70	10.1	7.6	—	—
60-80	11.0	8.4	—	—
70-90	13.2	12.2	—	—
80-100	17.8	—	—	—

FUEL CONSUMPTION
Overall mpg: 30.1 (9.3 litres/100km) 6.6mpl

Autocar formula: Hard 27.1mpg
Driving Average 33.1mpg
and conditions Gentle 39.1mpg
Grade of fuel: Derv
Fuel tank: 15 Imp galls (68 litres)
Mileage recorder: 1.1 per cent long
Oil: (SAE 10W/30) negligible

BRAKING
Fade (from 78mph in neutral)
Pedal load for 0.5g stops in lb

	start/end		start/end
1	20-25	6	35-40
2	20-25	7	35-45
3	25-30	8	35-45
4	30-35	9	40-40
5	35-35	10	40-35

Response (from 30mph in neutral)

Load	g	Distance
10lb	0.15	201ft
20lb	0.30	100ft
25lb	0.60	50ft
30lb	0.62	48ft
35lb	0.85	35.4ft
Parking brake	0.30	100ft

Max gradient: 1 in 3
CLUTCH Pedal 30lb; Travel 6.5in

WEIGHT
Kerb 2978lb/1351kg
(Distribution F/R, 68.8/31.2)
Test 3338lb/1514kg
Max payload 1102lb/500kg
Max towing weight 2866lb/1300kg

COSTS

Prices

Basic	£12,117.00
Special Car Tax	£1009.75
VAT	£1969.01
Total (in GB)	**£15,095.76**
Licence	£100.00
Delivery charge (London)	£230.00
Number plates	£28.75
Total on the Road	**£15,454.51**
(excluding insurance)	
Insurance group	O.A.

SERVICE & PARTS

Change	Interval 5000	10,000	15,000
Engine oil	Yes	Yes	Yes
Oil filter	Yes	Yes	Yes
Gearbox oil	No	No	Yes
Glow plugs	No	No	Yes
Air cleaner	No	No	Yes
Total cost	£37.60	£37.60	£133.52

(Assuming labour at £23.00 an hour inc VAT)

PARTS COST (inc VAT)

Brake pads (2 wheels) front	£30.81
Brake pads (2 wheels) rear	£25.68
Exhaust complete	£209.54
Tyre—each (typical)	£80.83
Windscreen	£118.27
Headlamp unit	£82.36
Front wing	£99.72
Rear bumper	£99.16

WARRANTY
12 months/unlimited mileage, 6-years anti-corrosion option

EQUIPMENT

Ammeter/Voltmeter	N/A
Automatic	N/A
Cruise control	N/A
Economy gauge	N/A
Five speed	●
Limited slip differential	N/A
Power steering	●
Tachometer	●
Self-levelling suspension	●
Steering rake adjustment	N/A
Steering reach adjustment	N/A
Trip computer	●
Head restraints front/rear	●
Heated seats	N/A
Height adjustment	●
Lumbar adjustment	●
Split rear seats	N/A
Air conditioning	£859.63
Door mirror remote control	●
Electric windows F/R	●
Heated rear window	●
Interior adjustable headlamps	N/A
Sunroof (electric)	£642.85
Tinted glass	●
Headlamp wash/wipe	N/A
Tailgate wash/wipe	N/A
Central locking	●
Childproof locks	●
Fog lamps	●
Internal boot release	N/A
Locking filling cap	●
Luggage cover	N/A
Metallic paint	£295.26
Radio/cassette	DO
Aerial	●
Speakers	●

● Standard N/A Not applicable
DO Dealer optional

TEST CONDITIONS
Wind: 2-7mph
Temperature: 7deg C (45deg F)
Barometer: 30.0in Hg (1017mbar)
Humidity: 82per cent
Surface: dry asphalt and concrete
Test distance: 865miles
Figures taken at 3800 miles by our own staff at the General Motors proving ground at Millbrook.

◀ starts easily from cold once the glowplugs have warmed up, and pulls cleanly to the governor thereafter. There's evidence of the power and torque improvements in the way the engine is happy chugging along at 1000rpm in fifth, despite the higher gearing. The only side effect here is a distinct blue haze in the rear view mirror under hard acceleration.

Considering the performance, our overall fuel consumption figure of 30.1mpg is reasonable. It will yield a range of well over 400 miles thanks to the generous and easily filled 15-gallon fuel tank. In the course of the test, we recorded figures ranging from 28.8mpg to 31.3mpg, and it is conceivable that a more gentle driving style could produce a consumption figure closer to the *Autocar* calculated average of 33.1mpg.

A diesel engine's distinctive rattle is definitely present on the CX DTR, but on balance it classifies as a refined engine, with noise and vibration levels well within acceptable limits. Even so, the engine is the main noise source at urban speeds with some pronounced thumps and bumps coming through from the tyres on poor surfaces. As speed builds to the motorway limit wind noise takes over, although it's well controlled. Road noise is apparent, its level dependent on the coarseness of the surface, while at higher cruising speeds the engine note subsides to a quiet hum. In that respect, the Citroën is a relaxing car in which to cover long distances.

Dynamically the DTR is like any other CX, the most noteworthy item on initial acquaintance being the self-centering, power-assisted steering. In theory, it should help keep the car tracking straight at speed, although having the wheels automatically revert to the straight-ahead position, with the engine running or not, can be a hindrance when parking. Despite being high-geared — 2.5 turns from lock to lock — there's a dead feel to the steering at times, as well as a nervousness at high speeds which means the driver can't completely relax. First-time CX drivers will find the sensitive steering often results in corners being taken in a series of lurches, but familiarity overcomes this.

On most surfaces, ride quality is both supple and absorbent, but the DTR exhibits one longstanding Citroen weakness when you take longer frequency bumps at speed. Here, there can be a very harsh reaction on the rebound when the car's hydraulics don't seem able to react quickly enough.

Ride height is constantly adjusted through the built-in self-levelling system and, for a big saloon, the CX handles well. Like any car with a nose-heavy weight bias, understeer is predominant when cornering hard, the rear end being provoked into gentle breakaway only by shutting the throttle mid-corner. Even then, the car stays predictable and easy to control.

The brakes also take getting used to. Pedal travel is minimal and servo assistance such that a pedal pressure of only 35lb produced the maximum deceleration of 0.85g on a dry tarmac surface before ABS was activated. The four-wheel disc brakes also handled the fade test without drama: the pedal pressure needed to maintain 0.5g of braking force over 10 stops building slowly until stabilising by the seventh stop.

The facia is similar to previous CXs tested by *Autocar*, the only notable change being the addition of an external temperature readout with two other LEDs showing coolant temperature and time. When the numerals start to flash, the outside temperature has fallen to between +3deg C and –5deg C and there is a risk of ice forming. The position of these displays, in the centre of the facia, makes them reflect distractingly off the windscreen at night. So do the instrument lights on the driver's side window.

Heating and ventilation are controlled by three large wheels for booster fan speed, facia-level airflow and interior temperature. The airblending heater works quickly and effectively but airflow is poor with the fan off.

The instrument layout is straightforward with the binnacle containing clearly marked tachometer and speedometer, petrol and oil gauges and warning lights. The familiar rocker switch for the indicators and fingertip controls at either end of the binnacle for horn and headlamp flash, remain, so the driver can use them with his hands on the steering wheel. They are easy enough once familiarised.

There is plenty of seat adjustment but the position is too high, making it difficult for the driver to avoid rubbing his knees against the steering wheel rim. A smaller diameter steering wheel might help and would not significantly increase steering effort. The pedals are well placed for easy operation although the clutch has a comparatively long 6.5ins of travel and is quite heavy at 30lb.

The seats look impressive and supportive but they are far too soft for a car — you sit in, rather than on them — and can become uncomfortable on a long journey. The gearchange works well but feels rubbery and obstructive if hurried, particularly on the change from second to third.

Forward visibility is very good, with a large windscreen and sloping bonnet, though steeply raked windscreen posts create large blind spots. Rear vision is restricted by the sloped window and large headrests. This can be a problem when parking or reversing but the large door mirrors help considerably.

Citroën's CX range retains a lot of character. The CX DTR will appeal to the diesel fan looking for a large comfortable saloon capable of covering long distances with a minimum of fuss. Its combination of good performance and refinement with impressive standard equipment might win over previous petrol advocates. It provides Citroën with a strong luxury contender in the diesel fleet market.■

Ride height *is adjusted by self-levelling system* **Large** *steering wheel can cause problems for taller drivers. Seats may look comfortable but are far too soft for long-term comfort. Pedal layout is good but clutch heavy* **Gauges** *in binnacle give clear information outside temperature readout is new — and distracting* **Heater** *needs fan for good airflow*

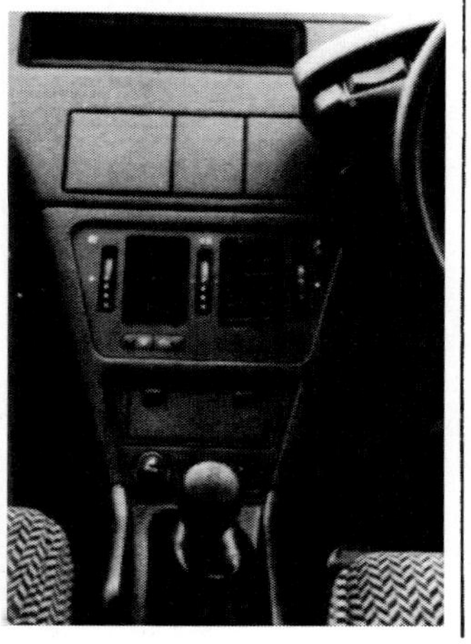

CITROEN CX 25DTR

British Leyland could have made a car like this but they would never have dared. Nevertheless, there is a tenuous connection between our state-owned bureaucracy (for bureaucracy it certainly was in the mid-1970s) and the then Michelin-owned Citroën. They connected in Italy and the styling house of Pininfarina.

There took shape in Turin an aerodynamic styling study based on a British Leyland 1100 platform, low, rounded, of two-box configuration and featuring a six-light side elevation and a cut-off Kamm tail. Although much admired by those who saw it at the Turin show, the design seemed destined to go no further. Until, that is, Citroën unveiled the GS.

It looked uncannily like the Pininfarina study. Citroën remained tight-lipped as to whether or not the resemblance was any more than coincidence and certainly would not admit to buying the design, but most people made the link between Turin and Paris. Meanwhile, British Leyland came up with their own Allegro, perhaps an unfairly maligned car but notably lacking in the flair that was the Citroën's keynote. It was an opportunity missed.

Both car companies timed their next arrivals contemporaneously too. Citroën's CX and British Leyland's revamped 1800/2200 broke together into a 1974 sedated by the energy crisis. The CX is still made. The 1800/2200, despite being converted to the hatchback Ambassador in later years, died in 1984. Significantly, the CX looked very much like a larger GS, the shape, in this case attributed to Citroën's Velizy design centre but not to one stylist, looking fresh and modern even today.

Compared with the BL car, the Citroën was the purer, more elegant, more thoroughly engineered solution in every way. Neither was destined to be a roaring sales success.

The CX was, like the DS before it, ahead of its time. The very name CX alluded to the car's low drag coefficient, a parameter sometimes termed Cx rather than Cd. A figure of 0.30 was claimed upon the car's launch, though the figure currently given for cars in normal road trim is a more believable 0.35, which is still very good for a car launched nearly 14 years ago.

In its frontal styling the CX set a trend not followed with conviction by rival manufacturers for another eight years. Yet nowadays it is almost the norm to find a low, rounded snout with a slim, slotted grille flanked by trapezoidal headlamps. Look at the products of Austin Rover, Ford, General Motors, Peugeot, Renault; the CX beat them all. Look a little closer at the big Citroën, though, and you will see that it is beginning to show its age.

In cross-section the doors are thick and bulbous, the windscreen surround retains a bright beading, and that intriguingly concave rear window is not incorporated into a hatchback despite the body shape's suggestion that it should be. The smaller GS was converted thus in later life but the CX remained as was. Ahead of its time though the CX originally was, nose treatment and large single wiper apart it set few trends. Rival manufacturers favoured instead a simpler, more accessible, more predictable approach over the Citroën's hydraulic complexity and *avant-garde* ergonomics. Who can blame them, in the face of consumer conservatism?

You do not see many CXs on British roads unless you look for them specifically. If you are driving the CX with which *Motor* and Citroën between them broke 21 speed and endurance records last August, achieving a 117.64 mph average over 24 hours on the track, you cannot help but be in a state of CX hyper-awareness. There are more around than you thought.

The whole point of the record attempt is that it was a stack of *diesel* records we were aiming to demolish. As probably the then world's fastest diesel car (the Mercedes-Benz 300D turbodiesel is likely to usurp that throne), the CX was the car for the job. We did not learn much else about the CX 25DTR Turbo 2 through simply circulating around Millbrook for 1391 laps, which is why we have now tried the same car – completely standard, remember – in its more natural highway habitat.

In our insular fortress, the CX never caught on in a big way. Yet, even in 1988, it has merit still, merit enough for the Citroën to hold its own pending the arrival of its replacement in a couple of years' time. This is likely to be named DX and there is a planned GS-size car to slot in between the BX and AX in the future, so how Citroën will solve the nomenclature problem will be intriguing.

The CX's merit is the greater for the existence of the turbodiesel. Here perhaps is the optimum CX, flowering late. This late bloom is because only now does it have an intercooler, which boosts the output of the 2473 cc iron-block, aluminium-head, fractionally oversquare pushrod four-pot to a useful 120 bhp/3900 rpm and an even more useful 188 lb ft of torque at 2000 rpm. It sounds like a recipe for extremely relaxed progress, especially when you realise that fifth gear gives 28.9 mph/1000 rpm. Truly seven-league boots.

This engine's ancestry can be traced right back to 1965, when the ID/DS range got new powerplants with five-bearing crankshafts. Its cast-iron block contained wet cylinder liners and over the years it grew from its original 1985 cc to 2473 cc in which form it appears, now mounted transversely, in the extremely rapid CX 25GTi Turbo 2. Smaller-engined CXs, however, have used ohc engines from the Douvrin co-op since 1979.

In the interests of the greater block stiffness required by a diesel with its high compression ratio (21.25:1 in the DTR Turbo 2's case), and accepting the weight penalty involved, the

TURBO 2

TEST REVIEW

"dieselised" version of the 2473 cc engine has a closed-face, fully bored block. When you consider the combustion pressures involved, particularly with a turbocharger and inter-cooler, this re-engineering comes as no surprise.

In this car, the lethargy often associated with a diesel is not a problem. The figures prove the point. At a windy Millbrook, without the benefit of 24 hours of warm-up, the CX reached 116.2 mph. We know, and Citroën know, that it can go faster because we proved it in August. It will accelerate from a standstill to 60 mph in 10.0 sec, from 30 to 70 mph in 10.4 sec. In fourth gear it covers the 40-60 mph increment in 7.0 sec, with 7.8 sec required for the 30-50 slot and 7.7 for the 50-70. Tackle this last segment in fifth gear instead and despite the long, long gearing only 10.5 seconds are required.

Point made? These figures mean that, on the road, this CX will leave an old-style BMW 318i or a Mercedes 190 for dead, ditto a 190E in the higher gears, and give an Alfa 75 Twin Spark, an Austin Montego 2.0Si and Vauxhall Cavalier SRi a hard time, to name but a few. It's all done with a minimum of effort on the part of the driver, who will never need, or indeed be able, to rev the engine beyond 4000 rpm and who will enjoy the knowledge that Derv is consumed at just 33.2 mpg even when going hard. With a gentle approach, easy in this machine, a touring consumption of 41.7 mpg is on offer.

The engine has a languid low-speed punch like few others and suits this second-fastest of CXs perfectly. You can forgive the taxi-like clatter at tickover, for once under way this diesel is as smooth as any even if you have to be travelling at motorway speeds before the compression-ignition sound is finally swamped. All you have got to do is learn to love the rest of what makes the CX a CX, the last – 2CV excepted – of the pure pre-PSA Citroëns.

Think hydraulic. Instead of being flummoxed by the way a CX feels so different from anything else currently made, try to understand why it is the way it is. Open your mind. And think hydraulic, because it is only through the medium of mineral-based hydraulic fluid that you connect with the road when you drive a CX.

A BX has oleopneumatic self-levelling suspension and fully powered (rather than merely servo-assisted) brakes. In the CX, the steering too is fully powered, the force coming from the same central hydraulic pump that powers the suspension displacers and the immensely powerful, all-disc braking system. Dubbed "Vari-power", the steering differs from normal power-assisted designs in that it constantly tries to return the steering rack to the straight-ahead position even when the car is stationary. The faster the car travels, the stronger the self-centring becomes, thus increasing the perceived steering weight. The feel given by the system is an en-

tirely artificial one, making it hard to assess when the front wheels are about to relinquish their grip but, as some compensation, the system cancels out torque steer before the driver even feels it.

High gearing – 2.4 turns lock-to-lock – plus the lack of conventional feedback mean that the first-time CX driver will progress up the road in a series of gentle swerves. Soon, though, the necessary lightness of touch is learned and the advantages of quick gearing can be enjoyed. Large car though the CX is, it can be threaded through gaps and flicked around urban junctions with singular ease and economy of movement, to the accompaniment of hisses and swishes from the steering which remind you where the effort is coming from. Sudden, jerky inputs, forgiven by some cars, punish the CX driver with a twitch and a lurch. Kid-glove gentleness, to go with the similarly clad iron fist of the engine's torque, is the key to CX satisfaction.

The ride, of course, is superb. Firmer than in some CXs past, and better damped in roll than in the Safari estate version, the DTR Turbo 2 floats along without introducing the queasiness of passenger the term usually implies. Sharp humps used to be the CX's undoing but they don't worry this one. Road roar is as well suppressed as ever. That the front and rear subframes are linked by side members to form a perimeter chassis to which the body is rubber-mounted at 16 points, is why.

The other difference between this car and other CXs we have driven over the years is that it will edge into oversteer on a fast, tightening bend. It does this very gently, so gently that it would never catch you unawares, but this trait and the decisive turn-in with which it is probably linked make for a car whose chassis agility now comes close to its steering alacrity. Tyres are 195/70 R14 Michelin MXV all round. Only the 22TRS now has larger tyres at the rear than at the front. The front suspension, incidentally, is unusual in having equal length wishbones which cause the camber change to equal the body roll angle and allow the steering to retain true centre-point geometry throughout the range of wheel travel.

About three years ago the CX gained a minor facelift. As well as colour keying for the grille, the bumpers and the door mirrors and black anodising of the previously bright side pillar finishers, the interior was remodelled. Nothing too drastic, mind. Items likely to be an ergonomic hindrance even to the most ardent CXophile were out but other features combining individuality with utility remained. Thus we lost the bizarre rotating-drum speedometer and tachometer, gaining instead conventional instruments (of corporate PSA style) unusual only in that they are lit whenever the ignition, perhaps a misnomer for a diesel, is switched on.

Turbodiesel engine (above) gives effortless and deceptively strong performance, undiminished by 24 hours of flat-out driving en route to 21 world endurance records. Interior (right) could only be Citroën. But why did they put the radio between the seats?

The switchgear pods either side of the single-spoke steering wheel, which were sadly sacrificed in the BX to the need to gain conquest sales, remain virtually unaltered in the CX. As with so much else in this car, learn about them – it is not hard – and their logic is indisputable. Naturally the indicators don't self-cancel but the complete control you are thus given is ample compensation. It encourages the discipline of thinking about what you are doing.

Curves were the keynote of the first CX facia and in this the current one is little different. The poor ventilation remains and it seems odd that the new dash couldn't have included the radio (which is situated sideways, with breathtaking stupidity, on the centre console by the driver's left elbow) and the ceiling-mounted heated rear window switch within its confines. Instead, the most prominent centre-facia position is occupied by three storage cubbies. Citroën logic can be very fallible.

Earlier CXs were cursed with a sometimes obstructive gearchange and an awkwardly angled clutch pedal with a heavy action. Nowadays the change is slicker thanks to a steeper synchromesh cone angle meaning that gearwheel speed synchronisation takes place over a shorter lever movement and a clutch release bearing in constant contact with the diaphragm spring to eliminate free play. The reduced release bearing movement has allowed a shorter pedal travel and an increased mechanical advantage and thus a lighter action.

The design priority of today's CX is untainted, the ease of driving enhanced. When powered by a potent turbodiesel, it is a family-carrying express of great efficiency and great honesty, a convincing alternative to the mainstream. Soon this monument to the pre-PSA Citroën will die. When it does, a little bit of Citroën's creative independence will die too, with just a loyal band of CX drivers left to appreciate among themselves what once was. That there are not more of them is sad. Our record breaker, meanwhile, is about to start a new career as a Lucas-CAV diesel research vehicle. I would have liked it to be preserved in a museum for posterity, for this must be the most important CX ever made.

CxAuto CX 25 GTI Turbo 2

FRENCH IMPRESSIONS

How stumbling around a dark riddling room in search of the Magic Voiture leads to discovery of a basic truth: Less is not always More

BY T C BROWNE

PHOTOS BY BRIAN BLADES

IT SEEMED so probable. Here was this spectacular French luxus automobile, levitating and then reclining itself every so often, as if eager to be off; then there was the 1804-kilometer test loop to California's beckoning Wine Country; finally, an irresistible logic: With the current outbreak of French Champagne producers buying or establishing vineyards and constructing facilities to produce sparkling wines from California grapes, what could be more appropriate than to let this enchanting carriage convey us thither?

When designers lock themselves away from the marketing guys, they can actually produce coachworks slick enough (0.34 C_X) to make big cars (112.0-in. wheelbase, 183.0-in. overall) go fast (140 mph) with small engines (2.5 liters). And there's no wind noise to disturb your composure or mask that beguiling soft passage in "Poet and Peasant."

The engine cooling fan is another matter altogether. If current technology has produced one louder than this, it has escaped the attention of your humble servant. And, notwithstanding our choice of the GTI Turbo (or hot rod) version of what may be the world's most desirable high-speed touring sedan for this exposition, it is elegant, soft transportation,

■ A typically Gallic blend of the luxurious and the weird, the GTI Turbo's interior has all sorts of visual (single-spoke steering wheel) and sensory (auto-pulse brake pedal) amusements. Seats are biased toward comfort, not lateral support.

not all-out high-performance driving, that this car is about.

Outward vision for the driver is ample, in spite of a thick A-post that threatens to intrude and never does. The windshield is large and window area is quite generous in this low (53.0 in.), 7-window sedan. The front half of the passenger compartment obtains an unusual spaciousness by the simple expedient of having the cowling and dashboard shoved far forward, while the rear occupants slide back on their shoulders for truly imperial indifference to the world outside and a blithe uncertainty as to their distance from the front seats.

Ah, the seats! Here is what French automotive ambiance is all about. Just try pronouncing "Recaro" with a French accent and it will be revealed why the CX's chairs are so opulent, at the apparent expense of function. Never mind. There is more to automotive life than 9/10s cornering, 1.0g side loading, and getting through the slalom quicker than Hector. These seats come from the society that invented luxury. The longer you sit in them, the more welcoming they seem.

That earlier reference to lowness must be explored to cover this particular vehicle. The heights of the cars of which the GTI is a family member depend on 1) whether the engine is running and 2) in which of the four notches the operator places the lever in the center of the console, a control designed to raise (according to the conditions of the road surface) or lower (in order to use the unique automatic jacking feature). What the height does *not* depend on is the load inside the car, or the end in which it is stowed. Hence, no headlights pointing skyward because the trunk is full of wet sand, no change in height/attitude resulting from the family wolfhound deciding to leave the car while it is underway. Automatic leveling is an additional benefit of the high-pressure, oleo-pneumatic suspension, also unique to Citroën. This closed complex of pumps, hoses, seals, valves and regulators also supplies the power to operate steering and brakes, each of which takes a little getting used to.

Arbitrary judges will label the steering lifeless and too quick, the brakes too abrupt and difficult to modulate. All this moderates with familiarity. That doesn't mean everyone will grow to like these features. Some people never do. But it's comforting to know that if you're condemned to man the driver's position while waiting for someone to join you, you can always put the single-spoke steering wheel over to one lock or the other, release it, and watch it slowly center itself.

Tiring of that, one can enjoy the brake control's built-in Magic Fingers. Curiously, this attraction isn't

PHOTO BY STEVE SNYDER

even mentioned in the equipment list. Here's how it works: As you dawdle at the signal that takes forever, give the brake button a tiny stab and quick release. Do it just right and the little mother will begin oscillating against the bottom of your foot; subtle pressure is required to keep it bouncing. French Massage will continue until the green light when you can reposition your foot on the throttle pedal, which, alas, has no additional recreational benefits.

Another quality built into Citroëns for at least the last 35 years is continued admirably in the CX series. The operator is provided with levers, buttons and switches controlling turn signals, parking and headlamps, horn, windshield washer and wipers, all easily governed by hands that never need leave quarter-to-three on the steering wheel. It is hard to imagine an automobile easier to drive, not just because of power this, automatic that, but rather because of the logical arrangement of controls that make drivers' duties complementary rather than challenging.

So the windows are up and you want to lock the car. Point this little red key-fob thing at the center of the ceiling inside the car from any position outside the car and squeeze it. With a great mechanical glonk, all the doors lock. A similar squeeze unlocks everything. The ignition key works the locking system in the conventional way.

While it may be inappropriate in a hard analysis of a mechanical device like a car, I feel moved to unburden myself of something not noticed when gathering impressions of other automobiles. In reviewing tapes I recorded en route to California's better half in the CX GTI, I discovered a tendency to fumble around in philosophical explorations concerning man and his environment, why I was having a good time, what it all means, etc. Was it because I liked the car so? Maybe. Did the car require so little monitoring that the mind could wander while the car did the work? Probably. Upon reflection, however, I believe it had something to do with compatibility, with user-friendliness. Drive a couple of hundred miles in a CX and you will have a good time whether you like it or not. The car was so suited to the task that

PHOTO BY STEVE SNYDER

I could not help being impressed with how well I was being treated.

The 100-mph trudge up I-5 went off without event, except, of course, the passage through the vapors of Fat City. Yes, you can smell it before you can see it. No, the sparrows are not so healthy that they chase cats.

Without a stop, 305 miles seemed about enough for the fuel tank, although for the driver it was a stroll in the woods. At 100 mph, 20 miles per gallon is real economy.

During 450 miles in seven hours, the car performed flawlessly; I felt as if I'd been driving a living room, which is to say a space in which a person would like to spend some time because it is elegantly and logically furnished. Is it worth $46,000? I dunno. The longer you live with it, the less relevant becomes the price.

As a warmup for visiting the palaces of sparkling wine (in California, it is seldom called "Champagne" unless it *comes* from Champagne), local winery guide Alan Selby and I stopped by Chateau St. Jean. The tasting room was manned by Dave Rose and the attractive lady who works at the bank during the week and wears cute boots and pours sipping samples on weekends. We tasted sparkling Blanc de Blanc and departed for the legendary lunch at Domaine Chandon.

The Oakville-Trinity Grade provided its usual ration of steep climbs and deceptive bends and the CX

SPECIFICATIONS	
Curb weight	**3180 lb**
Wheelbase	112.0 in.
Track, f/r	60.0/54.0 in.
Length	183.0 in.
Width	69.7 in.
Height	53.0 in.
Fuel capacity	18.0 gal.
ENGINE & DRIVETRAIN	
Type	ohv **inline-4**
Bore x stroke	93.0 x 92.0 mm
Displacement	**2500 cc**
Compression ratio	8.8:1
Horsepower (SAE)	**150 bhp @ 5000 rpm**
Torque	**156 lb-ft @ 4000 rpm**
Fuel injection	Bosch LE-Jetronic
Transmission	**5-speed manual**
CHASSIS & BODY	
Layout	**front engine/front drive**
Brake system, f/r	**vented disc/disc;** power asst, ABS
Wheels	cast alloy, **14 x 6**
Tires	**195/70R-14**
Steering type	**rack & pinion,** power asst
Suspension, f/r	**upper lateral links, lower A-arms,** oleo-pneumatic spring-shocks, anti-roll bar/**trailing arms,** oleo-pneumatic spring-shocks, anti-roll bar
PERFORMANCE	
Acceleration:	
0–60 mph	8.6 sec
0–1320 ft (¼ mi)	16.5 sec @ 84.5 mph
Braking:	
Minimum stopping distance	
From 60 mph	162 ft
From 80 mph	285 ft
Overall brake rating	very good
Handling:	
Lateral acceleration	0.73g
Slalom (700-ft)	58.0 mph

managed all without embarrassment.

The restaurant at Domaine Chandon was closed so we made a strategic withdrawal to Ristoranti Piatti where the wine list includes a depressing 16 examples of local Chardonnay and I'm not sure how I feel about ravioli stuffed with pumpkin, squash and brown butter-sage sauce.

The Taittinger new construction in Carneros is enormous, impressive, almost pompous. Eileen Crane is the managing director and she will have Domaine Carneros up and running this summer.

Domaine Mumm, the other sparkling wine production center under construction when we were in the Napa Valley, should also be receiving visitors as you read this. Located on the Silverado Trail, near Rutherford, this facility is jointly owned by the French producer best known to Americans and Seagram Classics.

PHOTO BY STEVE SNYDER

Piper Sonoma, now entirely owned by Piper Heidsieck, is in most attractive surroundings near Healdsburg, provides an agreeable reception area for weddings, etc., and bottles Brut, Blanc de Noirs, Reserve and Tête de Cuvée.

While the first four French-owned sparkler producers are bunched in the Napa-Sonoma area, Roederer is at Philo, in breathtakingly beautiful Anderson Valley, 115 miles north of San Francisco. Theirs is the smallest, most automated, most sophisticated operation of them all. Everything is computer-controlled or robotized except those things that can only or best be done by human hands. In *méthode champenoise* production, there is blessed little of that, and Michel J. Salgues, Roederer Winery manager, tolerates only the irreducible minimums. Mechanical riddling (turning of the bottles as the wine ages) has become common in California but Roederer now has machines that place the foil and align upper and lower labels regardless of how they come down the conveyor. Is the wine any good? I hope to kiss a pig. But how much of a factor was the ride up in the world's best sedan, and how much was the spectacular scenery surrounding the winery? Take your picnic along and see what you think.

The ride home had its entertainments, but they don't match this story; the ride up provided the profundity. But the most profound experience of the enterprise came when I got home to my own car. After 1500 miles in the CX GTI Turbo, I discovered my Alfa GTV 2.5 had the stiffest clutch, spongiest brakes, most square-cornered gearbox, harshest coal-cart ride, most positive steering, and hardest seats I had ever encountered!

On the trail of the Dragon

Martin Hodder reports on a drive along the A5 through North Wales, accomplished in the superb luxury of a Citroën CX 2400 Pallas **Photos by Martin Hodder**

FEW roads can take you to such fascinating places as the A5, which, after passing into North Wales, twists its way through some of the most fabulous scenery in Britain. Like the A1 and A4, it is a classic road, well worth exploring.

But I have painful memories of A5 drives in the fifties and sixties, when the long stretch through the Midlands was a stop-start crawl amid the asphyxiating fumes of badly maintained lorries. Even the scenic drive through the mountains was a drag at times, because the road was so narrow and twisting that, inevitably, you ended up in a long, slow snake attached to the rear of a Foden lorry or Eccles caravan.

In the fifties, the A5 was the only real link between London and the industrial might of the West Midlands, and was once Europe's busiest road. For the most part it has now reverted, to the relief of everyone, to the pleasant thoroughfare it must have been in the thirties and forties, thanks to the M1, M6 and M54.

Some time ago I planned to drive the A5, but in comfort, if only to assuage those old memories. And which is one of the world's most comfortable cars? Yes, the Citroën CX.

The CX, in fact, is a giant among the great cars of France, improving considerably on the DS, and continuing a line of fine,

Estate version of CX, above, could seat up to eight people

technically advanced vehicles which began in the thirties. Today, the CX probably doesn't get the recognition it deserves from the classic movement, perhaps because it is too modern, but its day is sure to come. In my view, the CX is every centimetre a classic, especially so the earlier ones, with their abundance of chrome.

When I suggested pursuing the trail of the Welsh dragon in a CX to Roger Bradford of the CX Centre in St Ives, Cambridgeshire, he offered me the pick of his showroom. Roger, one of life's great enthusiasts, didn't so much as blink when I opted for an as-new 1979 Pallas. 'Keep it is as long as you like,' he said. The man clearly doesn't know me.

Thankfully, I picked the car up in daylight. Even with a car that has done only 30,000 miles from new and has clearly been cherished by its one owner, you need time to acclimatise. Well, you do if it is a Citroën CX.

Fine cars they are, but they are also idiosyncratic. There's the unique, floating feel of the hydropneumatic suspension, the powerful self-centring action of the steering (stop the car with the steering turned, and it pumps itself round to the straight-ahead position), the small brake pedal with its half-inch movement, the most unusual instruments and the ash tray which looks like an air freshener.

However, by the time I had driven to my A5 starting point at first light the next morning, each one of the car's unusual features had endeared itself to me... well, apart from the brake pedal. I was already totally in love with this car; not only was I going to enjoy this particular drive, I knew this was a car I could enjoy driving to the end of my days.

I joined the A5 at the Roman town of Lactodorum, more commonly known as Towcester. I was to concentrate on the long Welsh section of the road, but, to put the whole thing in perspective, didn't want to miss out on the bit through the Midlands.

The Citroën wafted me northwards on the old Roman road, Watling Street, crossing the Fosse Way to the south-east of Hinckley. I passed the home of Reliant at

Llangollen station and Horseshoe pass were among places visited by Hodder

SPECIFICATION	
Citroën CX 2400 Pallas	
Engine	4-cyl, ohv
Capacity	2347cc
Max power	115bhp @ 5500rpm
Steering	Rack-and-pinion with VariPower assistance
Suspension	Hydropneumatic, all wheels independent
Transmission	5-speed manual
Brakes	Discs
Length	15ft 2.5in
Width	5ft 8in
Max speed	112mph
Fuel cons	25mpg

Interior is superbly wacky – note circular door pockets – but also very comfortable

Above, multilingual traffic light instructions are an A5 feature; below, beside Eliseg's Pillar

Tamworth, and couldn't help draw comparisons between uncomfortable three-wheelers I had driven years ago and the magic carpet qualities of the CX. And this particular CX, on sale for £3000, is about the same price as an average used Reliant. Makes you think.

At Cannock I cheated, diving off to the left to pick up the M54, wanting to make up some time. I took the CX into Shrewsbury, hoping to find a camera shop for a much-needed battery for my classic Canon. I went off that idea rather quickly: have you tried parking in Shrewsbury lately?

Passing Chirk, now thankfully into Wales, I resisted the temptation to stop while I looked at the castle. But I did stop at Llangollen, to photograph the station and its resident Thomas the Tank engine, before striking north for a while to pit the Citroën against the Horseshoe Pass.

The CX oozed past the ruins of what looked like a Norman abbey, and then Eliseg's Pillar, dating from the 9th century and honouring King Eliseg of Powys. Then the climb began. My car's 2347cc sideways-mounted, front-drive, four-cylinder motor shrugged off even the most difficult bit, where a tight, climbing turn forced me down into second. Full throttle for a while, and I changed to third for the rest of the climb.

Reversing direction at the visitor centre just past the summit, the brakes were put to the test on the run back down to Llangollen. Apart from some squealing there were no problems. Now for Snowdonia, and the real magic of the trip.

From Corwen, the A5 became more the road I remembered from years back, although there was plenty of evidence of bends having been opened out. However, there were moments of surprise, with corners only showing their true colours when I was half-way round and doing about the twice the speed I should have been.

Situations like this provide a perfect opportunity to put a car's roadholding and stability to the test, let alone the brakes, steering and your own resistance to heart attacks. Add in the fact that, carefully hidden at regular intervals, were traffic lights installed by diligent Welsh road workers. To be fair, all the lights – and I have never seen so many outside central London – were given advance warning boards marked clearly in Welsh and English. How wonderful to see an ancient language in everyday use Well done Wales.

The Citroën carried me ever northwards and westwards. I marvelled at the comfort, the best I have ever experienced, and had to keep reminding myself that this was a 1979 car, not something fresh out of the factory, so impressive was its overall competence.

In Betws-y-Coed I wondered at the number of visitors on this cold February day, and only just managed to drive past a fish-and-chip shop without falling into temptation. The electric sunroof, opened earlier to make the most of afternoon sun, drew in the magic smell, then, seconds later, also sucked in the clattering of a military helicopter as it passed overhead. ▷

'I marvelled at the comfort, the best I have ever experienced'

Left, the grave of Gelert, the dog killed in error by the Welsh king 700 years ago

Below, outside the Nazareth post office, far away from the warmth of the Holy Land!

CLUB

Citroën Car Club, PO Box 348, Bromley, Kent BR2 8QT

At Capel Curig I should have remained on the A5, but turned off left for a memory lane trip. Back in 1952 or '53 I had spent a most enjoyable fortnight under canvas as a member of the 2nd Soham Scout troop, a holiday which gave me a love for camping and the outdoor life which, today, burns as strongly as ever. I had to see if the camp site at Beddgelert was still there.

The village gets its name because it was the burial place of Gelert, the favourite hunting dog of the 13th century King Llewellyn, who slew the animal when he thought – wrongly, it turned out – that it had killed his son. With the Citroën parked beside Beddgelert's fast-flowing river I walked across the fields to the dog's grave, just as I had done as a 12-year-old boy. I had never dreamed in those days that I would be driving around in swanky cars like the CX.

My camp site was still there, larger and better equipped than in the early fifties. Sweet memories of my scouting days came flooding back as I drove slowly around it; I shall return as soon as possible, with tent and sleeping bag.

Looking for somewhere to spend the night, but with more facilities than my little tent, I headed first for Caernarfon, stopping for a quick look at the remains of the Roman fort, then went south down to Porthmadog where I found the excellent Sportsman's Hotel. The management thoughtfully provided some entertainment in the form of the local fire brigade attending to the lounge bar chimney fire while I downed a couple of welcome pints.

Next morning, after non-stop rain throughout the night, I drove the short distance to Black Rock, a lovely stretch of beach I had first come to know during a motorcycling camping trip to the area with wife Sylvia in 1960. It provided an excellent setting for some photographs of the Citroën, its smooth, aerodynamic lines contrasting beautifully against the waves rushing across Tremadog Bay.

On the way up to Caernarfon I literally screeched to a halt when I saw a sign to Nazareth, putting to a test the famed anti-dive characteristics of this fine product of the Gauls. I just had to have a look, if for no other reason than to convince myself I hadn't wandered a couple of thousand miles off course. I hadn't, although some Middle East warmth would have been welcome on this cold winter's day.

After rejoining the A5, I took the new bridge, built on top of the original railway construction, over the Menai Strait, then steered the trusty CX across the Isle of Anglesey, following the signs to Holyhead. Much as I would have enjoyed putting the car onto a ferry and heading across to Ireland, I had reached journey's end with the termination of the trunk road. Well, not quite, because I had to come back to the office to write this story.

Highlight of the return trip was chatting to an engineer brought out of retirement to take charge of some maintenance work on the old Menai Bridge, built by a certain Mr Thomas Telford. My friendly engineer not only explained how the bridge was constructed, but asked me if I had felt the earthquake the night before. It seems there was a sizable 'quake centred on that particular area, but I never was able to feel the earth move!

Chasing the Welsh dragon was a superb experience, renewing my knowledge of the supreme beauty of this part of the Principality. And just as enjoyable was the sheer pleasure of driving the incredible CX, which performed faultlessly and enthusiastically throughout, heightening the whole experience considerably.

If I had had any doubts about the Citroën's classic eligibility, I have them no more. The CX deserves to go down in history as one of the great saloons of all time, and I am pleased to play a small part in seeing that this happens. ■

BUYER'S CHECKLIST

CITROEN CX

Cheaper than a DS and just as characterful, the CX makes a great daily driver, says Mark Dixon

Stylish, practical and affordable, the Citroën CX is a classic alternative to a newer car

A sign of a good car is when motoring journalists dig into their own pockets to buy one. On that basis, the Citroën CX must have something going for it, because British hacks seem to have bought more of these than any other used car.

So what's special about the CX? The space-age looks; the superb ride and handling; and the fact that you can pick up a CX for half the price of a decent DS. If you like big estates, you won't find a bigger one than a CX Safari. But remember that the CX saloon is just that, and not a hatchback, despite its shape.

Most people are put off old Citroëns by horror stories of fiendishly complicated hydraulic systems. The fact is, however, that CX hydraulics are very reliable and well-understood by a large number of small independent specialists across the country. Rust did take

We look at a Citroën CX for sale

The CX Centre is probably unique in that it operates from a modern Citroën dealership, where classic CXs and the odd Maserati-engined SM rub shoulders with new Xantias. Although briefly tempted by a GTi Turbo 2 (£5,995 in sexy black, with black leather interior) we finally plumped for this Series 1 Prestige.

Roger Bradford says the upmarket Prestige is less sought after than standard CX saloons – it's based on an estate floorpan, and the extra length puts off some buyers. In fact the difference is undetectable once you're behind the wheel, and the Prestige benefits from air conditioning and electric windows.

This example looks very smart following a respray by the CX Centre in its original metallic green and appears rust-free apart from some minor corrosion on the inner bottom seams of the front doors: there's some filling to the rear corner of the nearside front door, too. The offside rear was replaced with a new panel by The CX Centre.

Inside, the favourable impressions continue with a clean and original interior, complete with removable rear footrests in that palatial rear compartment. The only evidence of wear is some paint chipping on the dash binnacle, housing those unreadable but stylish rotating drum gauges. However, severe condensation on the inside of the screen and a moist glovebox suggest a slight screen weep, not helped by torrential rain just before our visit. The original service record is stamped up to 40,000 miles.

This CX performs well on the road, its automatic gearbox changing smoothly and kicking down easily. It's a relaxing car to drive, its super-light power brakes and power steering encouraging a laid-back approach. A slight pull to the left indicates the tracking needs adjustment – a common fault – confirmed by a worn shoulder on the nearside front tyre. There's plenty of tread all round, however, and the tyres are the correct Michelins.

Any problems will be sorted before the car is sold. Whoever buys it will also have the reassurance of a six-month unlimited mileage warranty.

Verdict: One of the more desirable classic CXs and a practical alternative to a modern car.

This CX Prestige has clean and original interior, and bodywork is generally very good

Interior	★★★★
Exterior	★★★★
Running gear	★★★★
Value	★★★★
Year produced	1983

For sale by: The CX Centre, Harding Way, Somersham Road, St Ives, Cambs PE17 4WR
Tel: 01480 492066

MoT Renewed when sold
Mileage 62,634

£3,250

Photography by Mark Dixon

Basic specification

1975-1991: 1,985-2,473cc four, 66-168bhp, petrol or diesel; front-wheel drive; four-door saloon, long-wheelbase saloon, estate and eight-seater estate. Max speeds 91-137mph, 0-60mph 20.8-7.7sec, 23-45mpg

Prices

£200-£300	Old nail Series 1 that may or may not be legal
£400-£500	Tatty Series 2 cars with some MoT still to run
£700-£1,500	Average high-spec S1 or low-spec S2 saloons
£3,000-£3,500	Decent GTi Turbo or good early Prestige

Mechanics

Engine: Petrol engines very reliable and capable of huge mileages, especially earlier DS-sourced units. These were of 1,985cc, 2,175cc, 2,347cc and 2,473cc capacities. All-alloy 1,995cc and 2,165cc units fitted to Athena, Reflex and 22-models not as unburstable but long-lived if properly serviced. Diesel engines more problematic – Turbo 2s suffer from porous blocks – and best avoided.
Gearbox: Early cars had four-speed manuals, gradually displaced by five-speed units across range. Rarely give any problems. Semi-automatic transmission called C-Matic optional until 1981 when replaced by conventional three-speed ZF auto. C-Matic featured conventional gearlever linked to electronically controlled clutch; worn oil seals can make gear selection difficult in later life.
Running gear: Contrary to myth, CX hydraulic system is neither unreliable nor expensive to repair. Gas-filled spheres lose their charge over time, which destroys the car's ride, but recharged units are cheap to buy. However, expect to pay £170 or so to replace rear spheres due to labour involved. Hydraulic pipes suffer from surface corrosion and are often an MoT failure but are thick-walled and respond to cleaning. Check rear wheels are vertical and not leaning inwards, which indicates suspension trouble. Handbrakes operate on front brake discs and need frequent adjustment; impossible if discs are worn thin. Rear discs corrode due to lack of use. Clutches should see 100,000 miles but cost £650 to replace.
Electrics: Not a strong point, so check everything works. ABS fitted to very late cars can be troublesome but faults are usually minor. Avoid steam-cleaning engine bays of late cars with ECUs!
Interior: Series 1 cars have tumbler gauges; Series 2 and all Turbos have conventional dial gauges. Trim in early cars disintegrates but later cars last better. Leather optional on some models; standard for '85-on Prestige.

Watch for rust bubbling on the rear hatch

1

Wings don't bolt on, so beware rust

2

Crusty door bottoms are typical of old CX

3

7

Estate CXs can rust along roof above hatch

8

Rear spats are expensive to buy if missing

9

Gas-filled spheres may need charging

Parts

Most parts are available new from Citroën at reasonable prices. The exceptions are rarely ordered components, which can be astronomically expensive – a GTi Turbo exhaust manifold costs £850! – but CX specialists can usually supply secondhand items. Prices are for genuine parts unless stated otherwise and are excluding VAT.

Recharged sphere:	£17
Front wing:	£100
Door skin:	£82
Door shell:	£280
GTi Turbo engine:	£1,966
Michelin TRX tyre for GTi Turbo:	£180
Michelin MXV tyre for saloon/estate:	£90
Headlight:	£132
Brake disc (pattern):	£30
Top engine mounting Series 1/Series 2:	£35/£52
Top or bottom front ball-joint (pattern):	£25

a hold on earlier cars, it's true, and gave the CX a bad name from which it never fully recovered, although Citroën got to grips with the problem from 1981 onwards with much-improved body protection. The range was completely restyled in late 1985 with colour-coded bumpers and so on but earlier cars have more classic appeal.

Now that used SMs are flooding the market, fewer CXs are being bought by the non-enthusiast although old CX estates (Safaris) and eight-seater estates (Familiales) are still sought after by Joe Public. The

***Pros:** unique looks; super ride; practicality; huge load space in estate versions*

BUYER'S CHECKLIST

Prices

£3,500-£4,000	Outstanding early GTi or Pallas; good estates
£5,000	Top whack for a mint Series 1 Prestige
£7,000	Upper limit for a superb GTi Turbo 2
£8,500-£9,000	Very late, H-plated estates in top condition

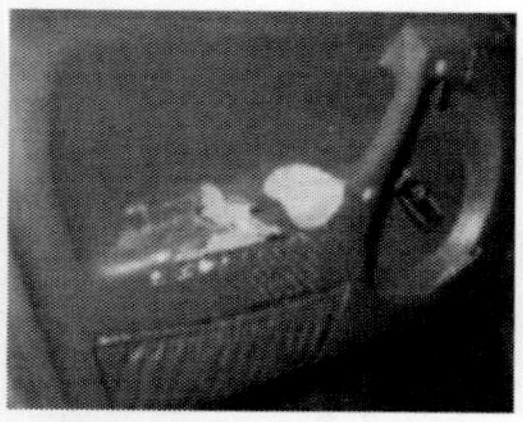

Early interiors are not as durable as late ones

4

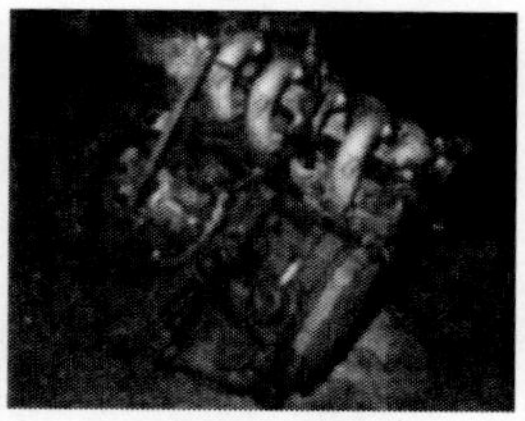

Petrol engines are capable of huge mileages

5

Headlight units cost £155 each inc VAT

6

10

Length of estate version means dents are likely

11

Upper ball-joint needs special extractor

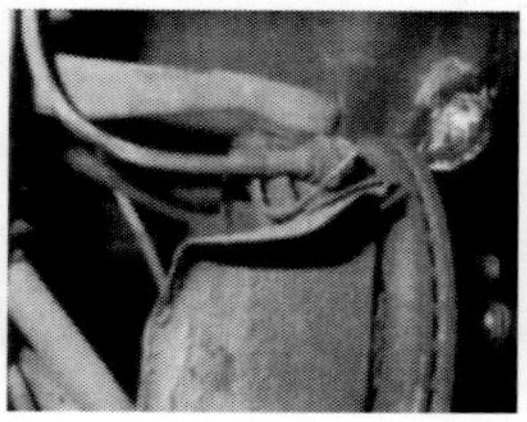

12

The correct Michelin tyres must be fitted

***Cons:** confusing range of models; hydraulics need specialist attention; rust in early cars*

Safari is the ultimate autojumbler's workhorse, but you won't get quite as much in a Familiale – only the back row of seats fold flat.

Although CX diesels can deliver up to 45mpg, they aren't as tough as the petrol models – Roger Bradford of The CX Centre, who supplied much of the information for this feature, stopped buying and selling diesels some time ago because of the grief they caused him. Roger's top tips for the most collectable CXs would be the Series 1 GTi Turbo or the long-wheelbase Prestige saloon.

CLASSIC CARS

Model evolution

June 1975:	CX launched in UK as 2000 and 2200.
April 1976:	CX2000 Safari estate introduced to UK.
Aug 1976:	2400 replaces 2200, 2400 Safari replaces 2000 Safari, and launch of 2200 Diesel (saloon and Safari) plus luxury Prestige.
Oct 1977:	Fuel-injected, 128bhp CX GTi launched.
April 1978:	2500 Diesel replaces 2200 Diesel.
July 1979:	Reflex and Athena economy models replace 2000 and 2400 Super.
Feb 1981:	Improvements include better rust-proofing, new paint colours and conventional auto.
Oct 1981:	All cars given flared wheelarches. 2000 Reflex estate launched.
Sept 1982:	CX20 replaces Reflex, CX25D replaces Reflex D, Athena axed, Pallas introduced.
Oct 1983:	CX25 estate replaces 2400; turbodiesels introduced as CX25RD and CX25DTR.
Sept 1984:	Super-quick CX25 GTi Turbo launched.
Oct 1985:	Series 2 introduced in UK. Colour-coded bumpers, grille etc plus round-dial instruments. CX22TRS joins range.
Aug 1986:	Intercooled CX25 GTi Turbo 2 introduced.
June 1987:	CX DTR Turbo 2 is launched as fastest diesel production car.
Nov 1989:	CX saloons discontinued. Estate production transferred to coachbuilders Heuliez.
Jan 1991:	Estate production ceases.

Selection of specialists

The CX Centre, Harding Way, Somersham Road, St Ives, Cambs PE17 4WR. Tel 01480 492066, fax 01480 492065. Sales, service, new and used parts.
Andyspares, Units 1/2, Gresham Way, Reading RG30 6AW. Tel 01734 452300. Mainly new parts, some used.
Andrew Brodie Engineering Ltd, 50 Sapcote Trading Estate, 374 High Road, Willesden, London NW10 2DH. Tel 0181-459 3725. Parts, service, restoration.
Citroëmech, Unit 3, Avenue Works, Eastheath Avenue, Wokingham, Berks RG41 2PR. Tel 01734 794204, fax 01734 892323. Servicing, bodywork, new/used parts.
Barry Coombes, Unit 3, Spring Court, Spring Lane South, Malvern, Worcs WR14 4AJ. Tel/fax 016845 66500. Servicing, parts, ECU repairs.
John Greaves, 4-6 Park Centre, Station Road, Horsforth, Leeds LS18 5NX. Tel 0113 2586131, fax 0113 2585791. Servicing, new and used parts.
M & C Lockwood, Unit B1, Enterprise Way, Idle, Bradford, W Yorks BD10 8EW. Tel 01274 621840, fax 01274 610673. New and reconditioned parts.
Pleiades, 20 Glatton Road, Sawtry, Cambs PE17 5SY. Tel 01487 831239. Hydraulic specialist, parts and fitting.
Southern Continental, 320A Coldharbour Lane, London SW9 8SE. Tel 0171-274 8233. Repairs, parts.

Clubs

Citroën Car Club: PO Box 348, Bromley, Kent BR2 8QT. Has a CX Register with 400-500 members from a total membership of 2,800. Costs £22 per year plus £5 joining fee. Offers insurance scheme and some CX parts; produces monthly magazine *The Citroënian*.

This is not just an early Series I CX, it is the oldest known survivor, chassis number 48. Roger Bradford had been looking for an early car for some time and when he had a call from a Citroën Car Club member telling him about this one, he had no idea of its significance. It is left-hand drive, but UK-registered, and it soon emerged that this was one of two cars sent to Britain from France as pre-production evaluation vehicles.

The car was near-derelict, but this information was all Roger needed to strike a deal, take his trailer down to Kent and pick it up. The undoubted expert on the CX in this country, Roger Bradford, proprietor of the CX Centre in St Ives, Cambridgeshire, was the ideal candidate to undertake the restoration of this historic Citroën.

As the full details of its origins were uncovered, he became more excited. This was the actual car which appeared on Citroën's Earls Court Motor Show stand in October 1974, and again in January 1975 at the Ulster Motor Show. It was seen at Earls Court by a Mr Oswald Jones, who insisted that he be allowed to buy it (he had previously bought the first Citroën DS imported to Britain, and the first SM). Citroën said that it wouldn't be on sale in Britain until the summer and he would have to wait. But wait he did, finally taking delivery of the show car, resprayed silver from its original gold, in July 1975.

That was about a year after the car had been made. CX production began in June 1974, with the official launch taking place in August. It was registered new in Britain in September 1974, a full 10 months before the CX's official UK debut. Roger now refers to it as 'Old Number One'.

Luckily, the car was virtually complete. In fact, it is lucky that it exists at all, because it had been disposed of in a very sorry condition in 1992, only to be rescued by Huw Rhys-Williams, a Kent Citroën specialist who eventually sold the car to Roger in June 1992 for £500 (part of which went as a contribution to the Citroën Car Club).

Although it was in running order, early CXs have a terrible rust record, and this example reinforces every tale of woe you've ever heard about them. Terminal rust was visible in the doors, front wings, rear wings, sill structures, rear crossmember, floorpan, rear wheel spats, under the front bumpers and inside the boot on the inner wheelarches.

"Early CXs are very rare nowadays," says Roger, "but it's still not

French revolution

Roger Bradford's CX starred on Citroën's stand at the 1974 Motor Show, but chronic rust almost consigned it to the crusher; Chris Rees reports on its rescue

worth investing in a ground-up restoration because they're virtually valueless when complete. But this was obviously a different story because it's a unique car.

"The restoration would have been a lot more difficult if the car hadn't been so complete. Being a pre-production prototype, it has a number of small differences over the standard car, and it would have been impossible to return it to its original state if parts had been missing. For instance, the concave hub caps are a unique feature and luckily all four were sitting in the boot. There was a pair of original French sidelights, too, but one got smashed, so I had to use UK-spec lamps."

Roger's first task was to strip the car to a rolling shell. Then the search for replacement body parts began,

Interior just needed tidying up, but Roger could not find new 'wood-look' headlining

New panels are readily available. Unlike those of DS they are welded, not bolted, into place

Early CXs suffer very badly from rust. This dissolving wheelarch is typical

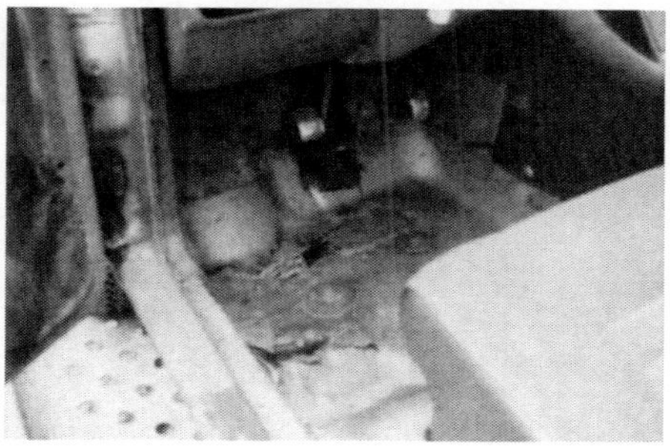

Tarmac was visible through holes in floorpan below pedals and around front inner wheelarch

Rear lower corners had disappeared. New side carpets for boot came from Citroën in France

Who can help?

Citroën Car Club, PO Box 348 Bromley, Kent; tel: 0992 700944. **CX Centre,** (Roger Bradford) St Ives, Cambs; tel: 0480 492066; **M & C Lockwood,** Bradford; tel: 0274 621840; **Doctor Chevron,** Ely, Cambs; tel: 0353 722 101; **Wolsey House Motors,** Diss, Norfolk; tel: 0379 642 718; **Pleiades,** Sawtry, Cambs; tel: 0487 831239; **Voiture Technique Services,** Warwick; tel: 0926 402101; **Citroëmech,** Wokingham, Berks; tel: 0734 794204

and Roger hit relatively few snags. Most panels are readily available from Citroën and those that are not are fairly easy to trace from specialists, despite the fact that there is virtually no demand from restorers.

The new nearside front and rear wings were bought from Wolsey House Motors; the nearside front and rear doors, also new, from Doctor Chevron; the sills from M&C Lockwood of Bradford and the rear crossmember and rear wheel spats direct from Citroën UK.

Being the man who runs the CX Centre certainly had its advantages during the restoration. One of those was the selection of parts available off-the-shelf from its own stocks: for instance, there were offside doors, a new offside rear wing and a rear bumper all sitting on the shelf.

The final source of parts was a 1977 CX 2000 purchased as a donor car. "This was absolutely invaluable," comments Roger. "I couldn't imagine doing the restoration without the donor car. It saved endless running about for tiny items."

Still with all the mechanicals fitted, the shell was sent to RJ Beeby

Roger's car shows us the CX as it was intended to look by its designers, its pure shape is stunning. Concave hub-caps are unique

of March (0354 53755) for a serious dose of surgery. Over 90 hours of welding was required to return the CX to its former unpeppered state, including fabricating and welding in a new chassis side longeron, repairing the inner front wings, wheelarches, floorpan and inner sills. The new panels were also welded into place: unlike the DS, with its beautifully simple removable panels, all the CX's metal has to be cut out and welded in.

From there, the shell went to a friend of Roger's, Phil Greaves, who stripped the bonnet, roof and boot (all were remarkably free of rust). He also fitted up some remaining bodywork items and prepared and primed the shell ready for spraying.

Robin Pinkerton (0860 644618) was given the task of respraying the car. First he prepared and fitted all the doors and located the recipe for the original colour used on the CX at the Motor Show. This is *Sable Cendre* (ash gold), a rare early gold colour which the original owner had had changed to silver by Citroën UK before being delivered. For the sake of originality, Roger decided that gold should be reinstated. The wheels were also sprayed the correct light grey, although only two of the wheels are the original 1974 type. "You just can't find them," explains Roger. Finally, the sills were sprayed up black, as original.

In this basic but presentable state,

Roger fitted new front undertray and refitted original bumper. Original 1974 wheels are unobtainable, so two are of later type

Bottoms of doors were rotten, Roger found two new and two second-hand replacements. Sills were sprayed black as original

Roger's costs

Purchase	£500
Donor car	£100
Bodywork welding	£1128
Bodywork preparation	£400
Paintwork	£1195
Hydraulics	£255
N/s doors (each new)	£150
O/s door (each s'hand)	£50
Front wings (each new)	£90
Rear wing (new)	£50
Rear wing (second-hand)	£30
Rear crossmember	£100
Front undertray	£10
Total	**£4348**

the CX was brought back to St Ives for a small launch party for the Citroën Car Club in June 1993. This first British CX was joined by the very last saloon to be registered in here for an 'unveiling ceremony'.

To finish the bodywork, Roger fitted a new front undertray, a new rear bumper from stock (with an end cap from Citroën UK) and refitted the original front bumper. The door handles came from the donor car. He says: "I also found some original Citroën rustproofing fluid and poured gallons of the stuff into the bodywork. There is no way this CX is going to rust again."

There was a minor problem with the unique hub caps. The bolts are

Both engine and gearbox were in excellent condition

This car feels remarkably 'normal' for a CX because it lacks the feather-light Vari-Power steering

different from the ones used on the production hub caps and special bolts had to made up in the Citroën dealer workshop of which the CX Centre is a part.

Roger was very lucky to have a complete interior in generally very good condition. Most of the trim is a startling shade of orange and, needless to say, finding serviceable trim in this colour is near-impossible. All the carpets were undamaged. CX door trims are notorious for cracking and coming adrift, but all four were in perfect condition. Like the rest of the interior, they only needed a good clean and polish.

The driver's seat had a hole in it and this required some professional attention. The head rests, which were a standard feature on all CXs, were missing, but luckily Roger obtained second-hand head rests in the correct colour from an early scrap car. And the headlining had completely disintegrated. Roger has just located a replacement headlining, although it is white, not the original, faintly bizarre, wood-effect finish. "Fitting it is not a job I'm looking forward to," he admits.

Another familiar early CX fault is poorly-bonded rear windows. On this example, both rear three-quarter windows and the concave rear window had virtually fallen out because of perished bonding. Rebonding them in place was undertaken by a professional.

As for the mechanical side, there has really been almost nothing to do. "This is typical," says Roger. "Bodily, the early CX was a disaster, but the mechanical side of things is unburstable. I haven't touched the engine (which is also fitted to the DS, albeit fitted transversely). It hasn't even had an oil change yet and it fires first time every time. Likewise, the gearbox is in perfect health. I'll service everything eventually."

Driving Old Number 48

Anyone who gets behind the wheel of a CX for the first time comments on the weird self-centring power steering. Not on this car. The earliest CXs didn't have power assistance and this is the strangest thing about driving the car: it feels normal. You can also park it with the wheels at an angle – when was the last time you saw a CX do that?

Being an early example, the suspension is also much softer than later CXs, almost coming up to the standard of the DS. The feeling inside is also one of comparative austerity: this was the poverty model, with the most basic trim ever seen in a Citroën CX. But you have to admire the pure and unadulterated sculptured interior surfaces.

The 1985cc engine gives the CX 2000 unexpectedly lively performance (*Autocar* recorded 112mph and 0-60mph in 12.2 seconds in 1975), but it doesn't feel refined by normal CX standards. The gearchange is smooth, but lever travel long.

Roadholding is in the highest category: this is one of the largest front-wheel drive cars ever made and has safe, predictable and enjoyable manners.

It may not have the sophistication of the later CX models, but this, the very earliest CX, is a rare delight in the flesh. It reminds you how far ahead of everything else the CX was in 1974 in terms of ride comfort, aerodynamics and sheer design brilliance. There has never been a car to match it.

Hydraulic system overhauled and new suspension spheres fitted

Luckily the huge concave rear window was in good condition

Just about the only new parts needed underneath were a new exhaust and a new brake valve. The latter had to be adapted because the car is left-hand drive.

The hydraulic system was treated to an almost complete overhaul as a matter of course. The suspension experts Pleiades replaced all five spheres, all the rear pipework and the rear ride-height corrector.

Not only is this the earliest CX on record, it must also be the most meticulously presented, if only because so few have been restored. Seeing it in its as-new condition, devoid of all the rubber strips and spoilers with which the CX was almost immediately adorned, reminds you just what a stunning car it was in its day.

Amazingly, just 55 CX 2000s are left on the road. This one has a busy calendar for 1994: it travels to France in May for the 20th anniversary celebration for the CX. Later that month, it will appear on the Citroën Car Club's stand at the NEC Classic Car Show, and it will be seen at the main Citroën Car Club event of the year in June. If you get a chance to see it – take it. ❑

1975–1991

CITROËN CX

Is this the world's most under-valued classic? We reckon it has to be. There aren't many about, but there are even fewer buyers. Tragic...

The Citroën CX was 1975's Car of the Year, with spaceship styling, advanced hydraulic suspension, equipment galore and dynamics that belied generous proportions. The very name summed it up – CX is derived from the French for 'drag co-efficient' on account of its ultra-slippery shape. However, while classic car fans fawn over the iconic DS, its successor is overlooked despite the fact it's a more capable car. By the time the classic car world truly cottons on to the CX, it may be too late – which is why you need to find yours while there are still some superb examples available for reasonable amounts of cash.

BODYWORK

Pre-October 1980 CXs used to rust as soon as they'd been built; cars made after this were painted and rust-proofed far better. However, the newest CXs are now 16 years old, and corrosion has affected most survivors.

Because the wings are welded on, replacing them is a pain – and there's a good chance they'll be rotten. The rear wings are especially rot-prone around the wheelarch lips as well as in the box sections at the rear. Other critical areas include the base of the windscreen pillars – once these have rotted it's very tricky to effect repairs. Even if the structure is fundamentally sound, you need to be on the lookout for less serious corrosion. Door bottoms dissolve, as does the leading edge of the bonnet. Floorpans also rot badly, while the inner and outer sills are usually pretty flaky. Most importantly, even if the car looks solid up top, check the state of the rear subframe. This is riveted to the longerons towards the rear of the floorpan, and replacement is a huge and expensive job. Estate tailgates suffer from rot, as does the trailing edge of the roof where the hinges are mounted. Once corrosion begins in these areas, it quickly takes hold and becomes a nightmare to eradicate – something that's also true for the lower edge of the bootlid.

All the above relates especially to those pre-October 1980 cars – later examples are tougher but far from immune. If you want to know when the car was built, post-October 1980 examples feature a console-mounted ashtray; CXs built in the preceding two years had a weird spherical unit in the top of the dash.

ENGINES

Three types of engine powered the CX. First were Citroën's petrol powerplants carried over from the DS, which encompassed 1985cc, 2175cc and 2347cc units. The latter option was expanded to 2473cc. Properly

SPECIALIST

Roger Bradford has specialised in CXs for 24 years, setting up the CX Centre back in 1990. Says Roger: 'The CX is so comfortable, and so fabulous to drive, yet largely forgotten. It's a far more usable car than the much more popular DS, but by the time the CX is properly appreciated, it'll be too late because already there are few early cars left. Now is the time to track down a superb example and squirrel it away. Values can only go up.'

THANKS TO

Keith Webb of the Citroën Car Club, Roger Bradford of the CX Centre and Shaun Lilley, owner of the car pictured in this feature.

HOTLINKS

- www.citroenz.com/CX/hist_cxcentre

SPECIFICATIONS

	CX2000	CX2400 estate	CX Prestige	CX25 GTi Turbo	CX25 diesel turbo estate
■ ENGINE	1985cc/4-cyl	2347cc/4-cyl	2347cc/4-cyl	2500cc/4-cyl	2500cc/4-cyl
■ POWER	102bhp@5500rpm	115bhp@5500rpm	128bhp@4800rpm	168bhp@5000rpm	95bhp@3700rpm
■ TORQUE	112lb ft@3000rpm	133lb ft@2750rpm	146lb ft@3600rpm	217lb ft@3250rpm	159lb ft@2000rpm
■ TOP SPEED	108mph	108mph	118mph	139mph	106mph
■ 0-60MPH	12.6sec	11sec	11.1sec	8sec	13.3sec
■ CONSUMPTION	28mpg	25mpg	26mpg	28mpg	35mpg
■ GEARBOX	4-speed manual	4-sp man/3-sp semi-auto	5-sp man/3-sp auto	5-speed manual	5-speed manual
■ LENGTH	15ft 3in (4.66m)	15ft 3in (4.66m)	16ft 2in (4.92m)	15ft 3in (4.66m)	16ft 3in (4.95m)
■ WIDTH	5ft 8in (1.73m)	5ft 8in (1.73m)	5ft 8in (1.73m)	5ft 10in (1.77m)	5ft 10in (1.77m)
■ WEIGHT	2789lb (1265kg)	3098lb (1405kg)	3252lb (1475kg	2723lb (1235kg)	3352lb (1520kg)

'All the petrol engines, including the all-alloy Douvrin family, will outlast most CX bodywork. Even the earlier diesels can clock up 150,000 miles'

maintained, these engines are amazingly durable; they'll easily outlast the bodywork of any car, racking up 300,000 miles without murmur.

The second type of engine is the all-alloy overhead-cam Douvrin family, introduced in 1995cc form in 1979, and 2165cc guise in 1985. They're more powerful as well as more economical than the earlier units, if not as durable – but they'll still outlast most CX bodyshells as long as the rubber timing belt is replaced every 40,000 miles or five years.

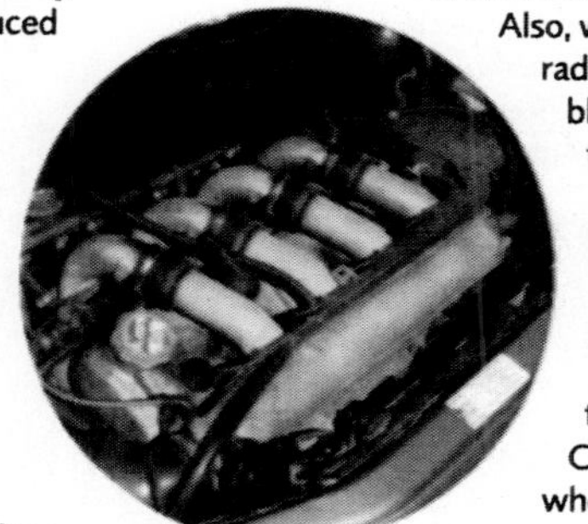

The final engine family is the diesels, starting with the now-extinct 2.2-litre unit that lasted until 1978. You're more likely to find the later 2.5-litre unit, which typically lasts at least 150,000 miles as long as the oil has been changed every 5000 miles or so. By far the most common oil burner is the turbodiesel – the Turbo I and Turbo II editions.

The first offers 95bhp, while the intercooled later version offers a healthy 120bhp and mountains of torque. Both units can suffer from a cracked cylinder head, so look for any signs of fracturing.

The later unit, known as the DTR Turbo 2 and current between 1987 and 1990, can suffer from a porous block. The symptom is water being used, but it's hard to check for this from a one-off inspection. Also, water can be used through a leaking radiator, perished coolant hose or blown head gasket, all of which need to be checked for.

TRANSMISSION

There were various types of gearbox fitted to the CX, ranging from four- and five-speed manuals to a semi-automatic unit called the C-Matic. This was available until 1980 when it was superseded by a conventional ZF three-speed automatic transmission. None of the manual boxes give trouble, aside from synchromesh wearing out at inter-galactic mileages. It's an easy check; just see if there's any crunching as you go up and down through the ratios. The C-Matic is best avoided as it's unreliable at high mileages and parts are hard to find. That leaves the ZF auto, which is tough but very costly to fix should things go wrong.

OWNER

Shaun Lilley is clearly a Francophile; he's owned several other CXs and also owns an SM as well as an ultra-rare GS Birotor. Says Shaun: 'I owned DSs for ten years, and while they're nice, the CX is much more refined, and effortless to drive over long distances. With an ultra-high spec that includes air conditioning as standard, the Prestige is a superb long-distance tourer as it's fast and astonishingly comfortable. This particular example has needed quite a lot of work doing in the the six years I've owned it, but now it's had some fresh panels and paint, I don't think there's much chance of me letting it go.'

➔

BUYING GUIDE – CITROËN CX

SPOT THE ROT

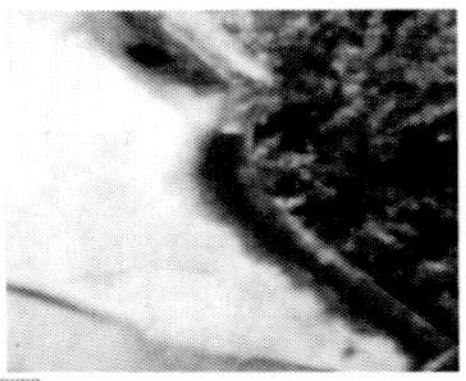

1 **All panels needs to be scrutinised closely for rot, especially hidden areas such as the bonnet underside.**

2 **The hydraulics frighten people, but they're simple and easy to both overhaul and maintain – and reasonably cheap.**

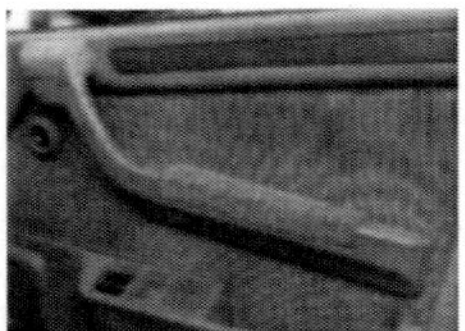

3 **Some interior trim can be sourced second-hand, but you won't find any new parts. At least the Series II trim is tougher.**

> 'Buyers view the hydropneumatic suspension with suspicion. It's actually simple and reliable'

Be wary of a clutch that's slipping, unless you're handy with the spanner set. The engine has to be removed on the earlier cars to facilitate clutch replacement. It's also worth checking the driveshaft gaiters, as they can split or become dislodged. Replacement typically takes two hours per side.

SUSPENSION & STEERING

One of the reasons why potential buyers view the CX so suspiciously is its hydropneumatic suspension. It's actually a very simple system that's both effective and reliable if properly maintained. The system is based around six gas-filled spheres (two for each end of the car plus two high-pressure accumulator units in the engine bay). These lose pressure over time but can be recharged cheaply and easily.

Switch the engine on and ensure the car's ride height lifts to the normal position within 15 seconds or so. If it's much slower than this, the fluid needs replacing (at £20 for the fluid plus an hour's work). The fluid should be bright green in colour and replaced every few years. It's also possible that the hydraulic pump is getting

NEED TO KNOW

PRACTICAL CLASSIC?
Yes, but you'll need to be a competent mechanic with a comprehensive toolkit to do your own maintenance.

WHAT ARE THEY LIKE TO DRIVE?
This is where the CX really scores, with its magic carpet ride, strong brakes and surefooted handling.

WILL I FIT BEHIND THE WHEEL?
No problem – and if you buy a Prestige or Safari you can hold a party in the back. Track down a Familiale eight-seater and you can hold several parties concurrently.

WHAT ARE THE KEY PROBLEMS?
- Corrosion
- Damaged trim
- Lack of maintenance

WHAT SHOULD I PAY?
Diesels and estates aren't sought after; it's petrol-powered saloons that everyone wants, with the Prestige being most valuable, followed closely by the GTi Turbo 2. Saveable CXs are worth £400-£1000 depending on condition, while usable cars are £1500-£2500. The few really good examples fetch anywhere between £3000 and £4500.

WHAT WILL INSURANCE COST ME?
Comprehensive cover for a £3000 1985 CX GTi is £93, based on a 5000-mile annual limit. Driver must be over 25 years with the CX being a

PRICE CHECK: MINT: £3000-£4500 | AVERAGE: £1500-£2500 | ROUGH: £400-£1000

weak; they're durable but do fail occasionally. A reconditioned unit is around £100. Also listen out for continuous clicking from the belt-driven pump that maintains pressure in the system; this indicates the main accumulator sphere needs replacing at £25.

Do a bounce test at each end; push down and see if the car quickly settles. If there's any bounce, the suspension needs some TLC in the form of recharged or replacement spheres; either route costs £25 per unit. Look particularly closely at the front suspension. With two-thirds of the car's weight in the nose, it's the front spheres that need renewing most often. Not all CXs came with power steering, but most surviving examples have it. Driven by the same spheres that 'power' the suspension and called VariPower, it's very unusual for problems to occur.

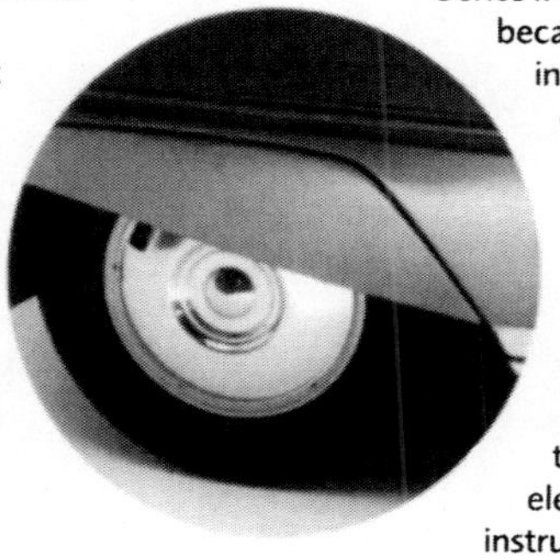

WHEELS & BRAKES

Most surviving CXs were fitted with alloy wheels, while many earlier examples featured pressed-steel units. The protective lacquer on the alloys will be a distant memory by now, but re-polishing them is easy enough.

The CX's brakes should be reassuring; there should be no need to push hard on the pedal for strong, progressive, fade-free deceleration. Don't worry about hissing from under the bonnet as they all do that, but if you're driving a late car with ABS, make sure it works. The electrics on these later cars were not great, with the ABS being one of the first things to pack up.

TRIM

Early cars had trim with the durability of rice paper, but Series II cars fare better – which is just as well because it's not easy tracking down any interior trim, new or used. Exterior trim is durable, and there isn't much of it. But if anything is missing or damaged, it could prove tricky to find.

ELECTRICS

Most electrical problems are caused by a lack of use – corroded terminals are likely. Some switches are also temperamental, such as those for the electric windows. The switchgear and instrumentation are reliable and easy to find used, although new parts have now disappeared. It's the same for the exterior lighting, but front indicators can be bought still in the box.

CONCLUSION

Buy on condition rather than specification. If you can find a long-wheelbase Prestige (as shown here) you'll have a proper limousine for peanuts. Track down a Safari and you'll have one of the most capacious and comfortable load-luggers ever made; find a Familiale and you can add a third row of seats to the mix. If you're a city dweller, the CX makes perfect sense because it's so easy to park. And with its suspension set at its lowest level, there isn't enough clearance to attach a wheel clamp...

WHICH IS WHICH

1974: CX announced in France.
1975: First 2000 and 2200 editions arrive in UK.
1976: Estate launched (2000 Safari), along with 2400 (also in LWB Prestige form) and the first diesels (badged 2200 D).
1977: All 2400 editions get five-speed 'box and Familiale estate arrives. Injected 2.4-litre GTi launched.
1978: A 2.5-litre diesel replaces the previous 2.2-litre unit
1979: Reflex and Athena replace the 2000.
1982: Cars are now badged 20 and 25.
1983: 25 DTR (turbodiesel) range arrives with five-speed gearbox. There's also a fuel-injected 2473cc engine for the 25 TRI Safari, 25 IE Familiale and 25 GTI LWB CX.
1984: 25 GTi Turbo brings 168bhp from 2473cc.
1985: Series II with redesigned interior, electronically adjustable ride height.
1986: GTi Turbo 2, 168bhp.
1987: 25 DTR 2 arrives with intercooled 2.5-litre diesel. All 2.5-litre cars get ABS as standard.
1989: Estate range rationalised and saloon killed off to make way for XM.
1990: All CXs to special order only, with the final car being built in 1991.

second car. Quote from RH on 01277 206 911.

WHO ARE THE SPECIALISTS?

- Roger Bradford (the CX Centre), Cambs. 01354 692634, 07716 064 889
- Andrew Brodie Engineering, London. 0208 459 3725, www.brodie.co.uk
- M&C Lockwood, Bradford. 01274 640590
- Chevronics, Beds. 01462 731733, www.chevronics.co.uk
- John Greaves, Leeds. www.citroenspecialists.com
- Citroën dealers

SPARES PRICES?

Prices are approximate and from M&C Lockwood

Brake pads	£30 set
Handbrake cable	£30 pair
Engine mounting	£60
Suspension spheres	£25 each
Clutch kit	£140
Alternator	£100
Starter motor	£100

ARE ANY PARTS HARD TO GET?

- Panels
- Interior trim
- Exhaust systems

CAN THEY COPE WITH UNLEADED?

Yes, without adjustment.

WHERE ARE THE IDENTIFYING MARKS?

There's an aluminium plate riveted to the offside inner wing – this contains the chassis number, which is also stamped into the offside wing flange.

WHICH OWNERS' CLUB SHOULD I JOIN?

- Citroën Car Club. 07000 248258, www.citroencarclub.org.uk

WHICH IS THE BEST BOOK?

- *CX Haynes Manual (petrol cars only, 1975-1988).* ISBN 9781850104490.
- *Citroën CX De Mon Père by Marc-Antoine Colin.* ETAI, ISBN 978-2-7268-84294 (French text).

They came from outer space

Sam Dawson has a close encounter with four generations of Citroën's outlandish big saloons: the ID/DS, CX, XM and C6

'Cat's eyes' came in for '67, white roof an ID constant; steering light but precise; grip strong. Flat-six wasn't sorted for launch so DS used Traction 'four'

Imagine that it's 1955 and you're looking for a new saloon car for between £1000 and £1500. You're probably about to trade in a facelifted pre-war design, something such as a Daimler Conquest or an Armstrong Siddeley Sapphire. Most likely, it had a separate chassis, rear drive, a huge 1930s-style radiator grille – complete with bonnet mascot – and either a vague suggestion of separate wings or half-hearted American-style tail-fins.

You could go for something sporty: maybe an Alfa Giulietta or a Jaguar Mk1. You could try to impress the neighbours with a Mercedes-Benz 180 'Ponton' or a Lancia Aurelia. Or you could recall a favourable comment a friend once made about Citroën's Traction Avant. You find yourself, perhaps an hour later, in a dealership, staring gobsmacked at a machine that you're not even sure is a car, but a form of transportation from the future that may well fly, float and take you into space as well. You're admiring a Citroën DS: artform, technical *tour de force*, cultural icon, philosopher's muse, and yours for £1400 at the time. Since that moment, the only cars whose appearance have caused comparable astonishment have worn the charging bull of Sant'Agata.

Flaminio Bertoni – Italian modernist sculptor, artist and designer – moulded the shape. Although he draughted the stylish if somewhat conventional-looking Traction Avant beforehand, you get the impression that the *Déesse* started life as a commissioned work to reflect the idiosyncratic beauty of Paris, rather than a car.

The doors, for example, are the shape of shopping bags from some swish Latin *couturier* in St-Germain-des-Prés. The swinging line they follow through the body suggests the jubilant walk of a Parisienne who's found a bargain. Then there's the elegant roofline, its spindly framework recalling Art Nouveau Metro stations and even the Eiffel Tower, with the wonderful high-level, cone-shaped indicators hanging over the bootlid like streetlights. At its launch, philosopher Roland Barthés decreed that the Citroën should be considered as a piece of art in the same light as a Gothic cathedral. I can't imagine nowadays, say, Alan de Botton being similarly moved by the interior plastics of the new Audi A6.

This otherworldly effect was played upon by Citroën's PR department, which often presented the car without wheels, floating on the Seine to illustrate the hydropneumatic suspension, or poised vertically and surrounded by a viewing gallery, like a rocketship. Photographer André Martin portrayed it as part of the French landscape, even with its wheels attached. It's tempting to think that Robert Opron took the same approach when he restyled the front end for '67. He produced the shape you see here, with the feline squint of the headlights echoing Toulouse-Lautrec's *Le Chat Noir* or SEV Marchal's logo. The famous steering inner lamps were optional on the ID, which began as a cheaper, simpler DS but gradually gained most of its equipment.

Once aboard this '69 ID20, the aeronautical sense is heightened. The glassfibre roof and curving, frameless glass are reminiscent of a glider, as are the easily removable body panels and supporting subframe. The notion is reinforced by a single-spoke wheel, similar to an aircraft's control column, and a clasp-fitting seat-belt. 1955-man might have found the firm action to operate the clutch, four-speed column change

ID stands for *Idée*, or idea; signature *cornet de frites* indicator; ID has a brake pedal, instead of the DS' famed 'mushroom' button; small hubcaps on most IDs

CX's variable-rate Diravi steering light but rock-solid on motorway; engine was transverse and canted 30° forward, which meant front discs went outboard

and the 'umbrella' handbrake familiar (the DS has a foot lever), but the rest of the driving experience would have been well and truly alien.

First, there's the suspension, raising the car with an almost imperceptible hiss as the engine fires up, readying it for take-off. Then there's the brake pedal, which is powered via the hydraulics and slams on the anchors with little effort. The steering works via the same system. It's solid and heavy when stationary, dissipating into creamy-smooth precision when moving, but still has enough weight to avoid the car feeling remote.

Once under way, with passengers perched on plump sofas that create support by allowing their occupants to sink into them rather than firmly bolstering them in, the car appears to be floating a foot or two above the road. Even the most severe of last winter's potholes fail to cause a shudder through the bodywork, merely creating a slightly bouncy ride. It almost feels as if you are piloting a low-flying aircraft over the countryside as you gently guide the single-spoke wheel – created so that the instruments would not be obscured while steering – and occasionally brush the brake pedal. Unfortunately, the illusion is tarnished – if not shattered – by the underpowered engine, derived from the '30s Traction Avant, roaring and clattering away up front.

If the engine is a car's heart, then the DS also has lungs, LHS or LHM blood coursing through a network of veins and arteries, as well as muscles to control its suspension. The car also has a

'IT DIDN'T JUST DEVELOP THE STRENGTHS OF THE DS: THE CX ELIMINATED ITS DRAWBACKS, TOO'

brain, manifested in a forceful character that snaps drivers out of their stubborn ways into a more intellectual method of driving. An air-cooled flat-six was mooted from the start but never developed, though the aged four-pots were at least offered with Bosch electronic fuel injection from 1970. Yet even this was never enough for a car that looked and felt as though it should probably run on compressed air.

Despite Citroën selling nearly 1½ million DSs, rival manufacturers remained sceptical of its radical technology, sticking to tradition in the form of rear drive, cliff-face aerodynamics and heavy mechanical controls. A few bravely ventured into its territory, most notably NSU, whose semi-automatic Ro80 cost significantly more and the unreliability of its rotary engine bankrupted the firm. Audi's 100LS and Lancia's Flavia were similarly refined, albeit otherwise conventional, takes on the front-drive saloon. Saab had always made much of its aviation links, and squared up to the DS from its makeover year with the quirky, slant-four-engined 99.

Closest to the DS recipe was BMC's 'Landcrab', combining Alex Moulton's Hydrolastic suspension for a similar ride with clever Issigonis packaging. Its looks never rivalled the Citroën, though, until the arrival of the 'wedge' Princess in 1975, but build quality had nosedived by then and the car that had looked so promising on paper turned out to be an embarrassment.

Against all of this – plus the oil embargo,

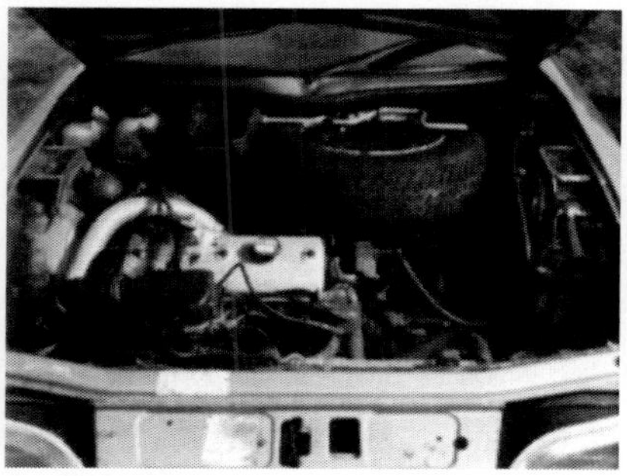

Super-stylish doorhandle; crosswise engine gives bigger cabin; moondisc-style hubcaps; wacky, rotating-drum gauges with magnifying lenses

which affected sales of all cars – Citroën could have ditched the costly if successful DS. The cheaper but similarly stylish GS was coming on stream, proving that the technology could work in a mass market. And few rivals threatened Citroën's mastery of ride quality; even Rolls-Royce had adopted André Lefèbvre's suspension design for the Silver Shadow by the late '60s.

But no. Citroën, crippled by the purchase of Maserati and the development of the SM – with its management well aware of impending doom and a potential Peugeot takeover in the offing – pressed ahead with '*Projet L*'. This later evovled into the 'CX' because Robert Opron's sleek and beautiful styling of the ultimate prototype boasted a drag coefficient ('CdX') of just 0.36. This car was intended to not only better the DS, but also to save Citroën as an independent entity. Failure was not an option, and no drawbacks in the design could possibly allow criticism other than from a few Philistines who didn't understand the French avant-garde.

The result is a four-wheeled Pompidou Centre. Relentlessly, unashamedly modernist, leftfield and Gallic, the CX didn't just develop the strengths of the DS, it eliminated its drawbacks. The driving position is snug and sporty, visibility is virtually uninterrupted through 360°, the 'Douvrin' engines – offered five years after the car's '74 launch – are smooth and fairly quiet, and wind noise is practically non-existent. The all-alloy 2-litre overhead-cam unit puts out just

'RATHER THAN FALLING FOR RETRO, THE C6 IS AS BOLD AS BIG CITROËNS HAVE ALWAYS BEEN'

106bhp, but makes the most of the long-legged gears – there's a standard five-speed 'box on this UK-market Athena, the plusher base model.

The CX looks bigger than the DS, yet it's 8in shorter and feels more compact. Its lower seating position affords the driver the confidence to treat the CX like a hot hatch until the narrow-set rear tyres start to squeal. When the car reaches a sharp bend, the loping nose bounces wildly into understeer. Dabbing the brakes to bring it back into line isn't advised while you're still adapting to their switch-like operation, so a carefully metered throttle lift is the way to do it. Once this is understood, the CX becomes a pleasure to drive, especially in mastering the long-throw gearbox. The clutch action is firm and its pedal travel excessive, but slotting the lever between ratios is like satisfyingly shoving an airliner's hand-throttle to 'maximum'.

There's more pleasure to be had in the CX's detailing, too. The seats, in electric-blue Jersey nylon – contrasting subtly with the dashboard and bodywork – are bold and daring. The dash-top ashtray looks like a miniature Aarnio 'Globe' chair and the jewel-like warning lights have you mischievously wondering what abuse you might have to inflict just to see their vibrantly coloured lenses illuminate. Best of all, though, is the sheer ergonomic pleasure. Controls for everything are clearly labelled and just a touch away. The speedo and rev-counter are vivid yellow revolving drums spinning behind stationary markers. They're not

Stunning C6 marked a massive return to form, with cleverly reworked suspension so that the car handles as well as it rides: a Sport mode – mon Dieu!

Cabin lacks eccentricity of the DS and CX, but it's beautifully detailed and loaded; 245/45s on 18in Atlantic alloys help with new-found agile handling

XM is a little gawky in this company yet it's hugely capable and almost as chuckable as a C6 – now a bargain, too; complexity tarnished its reputation

only fun to look at, but also extend the cerebral approach begun by the DS – prompting the driver to think about the numbers involved in acceleration, cruising and gearchanges, rather than a needle soaring towards a redline.

The CX eventually lost those dials in a facelift in which the chrome bumpers also went in favour of plastic ones. It was all part of the inevitable Peugeot cost-cutting and ensuing rationalisation that had followed the Maserati sale to Alejandro de Tomaso and the failure of a plan to joint-build a big saloon with Lancia. Still, Peugeot had no reasons to kill off the extraordinary CX and, like many charismatic mid-'70s designs (Ferrari 400i, Lamborghini Countach, Porsche 928), it stayed in production until the early '90s, and didn't look old even when it was retired.

In fact, you could say that the CX is one of the most influential car designs of all time. Look at the slashing curve of its window-line, the triangular light clusters front and rear and the way that they bisect the trapezoidal grille. These are all hallmarks of Ford's industry-changing 'edge' design, in particular the original five-door Focus, a car the world and his labrador attempted to copy. Today, it helps the CX to look both original and modern, even in chromed early form.

Replacing the CX was a daunting task, and one that the new Peugeot Société Anonyme (PSA) Group would not take lightly. The CX had been plagued with niggling build-quality issues and, in the '80s, a new 'executive' class of buyer had sprung up, one who was maybe more interested in the badge on the front than the substance under the skin. They would typically only keep a car for a year, too, ditching it for a new model as soon as possible, so 'residual values' – something Citroën buyers of old weren't bothered about – shot to the top of their wish-lists. These people invariably bought German, but many had been tempted by the blindingly rapid 168bhp CX GTi Turbo, which rekindled memories of the SM.

If Citroën was to be successful in this new, arguably slightly blinkered era, this was the kind of car that could do it. It would also bring a 3-litre V6 engine back to the range after 14 years. And Citroën would call it the XM.

After several consultations, styling was entrusted to American Art Blakeslee of Bertone, who concocted what must be the world's most subtle retro-design. Sure, there's the obligatory '90s 'floating' roof and straight waistline indentation, but look at the flat, thin nose and the upward kink towards the rear – they're all hallmarks of Opron's 1970 SM. Even the shape of the smoked glass of the rear reversing and indicator-light clusters pay homage to the SM's chromed rump. Behind the wheel, the black cabin seems slightly dour, but there are playful touches, too, such as the black strip of smoked plastic behind the wheel, from which warning lights emerge and vanish. A green digital glow in the middle of the rev-counter reminds you which gear you're in. It's all charmingly reminiscent of early kids' hand-held digital computer games.

Drive the XM and you'll find a confidence not always present in its ancestors. There's little understeer, the brakes are more conventionally controlled and the 2.1-litre turbodiesel unit has ample torque for cannoning the XM from bend to bend. The bump-eliminating suspension, by then called Hydractive, still features – you'll barely notice cattlegrids – but with it comes a firmness more orientated towards the sporting

Neat reversing lights in SM-style rear; sober cabin perhaps a reflection of PSA parent; single-spoke wheel was replaced with airbag-equipped version

C6 offers a nod to the past, with 'self-cleaning' concave rear screen like the CX, plus wonderful flowing light clusters. XM takes its cues from SM; script-type badges also featured on the Xantia

Athena and Reflex were first CXs with 'Douvrin' motors. Turning main beams optional on ID; lines aren't heating elements, but just a styling flourish

driver, accompanied by the usual clicking and hissing as sensors make calculations about the pressure exacted on the spheres and adjust load accordingly. With a V6, it would make for a brilliant four-door GT, and it's currently a two-grand bargain for anyone harbouring SM fantasies. No wonder the XM featured in the most notable movie car-chase since *Bullitt*, pursued through Marseilles by an Audi S8 in *Ronin*.

Sadly, executive buyers spurned the XM, which expired in 1999. PSA descended into dullness, with Citroëns offering little flair and Peugeots piling on the pounds while losing their frisky handling. But after pressure from Renault, revitalised under Patrick le Quément, Citroën threw caution to the wind and started exploring its roots once more. First up was the C4 in 2004, with its 'reinvention of the steering wheel' packing a fixed central boss with fingertip controls and clothing it all in strikingly French style. Sébastien Loeb took four of his seven WRC titles in C4s. Then came the C6 in '06.

This is, without doubt, the most accomplished luxury car Citroën has ever made, and thankfully shows deep understanding of the marque at PSA. The classic short tail is still there but, rather than falling into retro clichés (the CX window lines have been duplicated for visibility), it's as bold and original as big Citroëns have always been. Its rear lights drape delightfully over the wings like Dali's clocks. On the inside, the driver wants for nothing on this Exclusive – with even a head-up display on the 'screen so you don't have to take your eyes off the road. It's a sea of leather and slabs of Mukonto wood as far as the eye can see. What's most interesting, though, is how it drives. With the exception of the 240bhp from the brilliant joint PSA-Ford-JLR HDi V6 providing acceleration that would represent supercar performance to a DS buyer, the ride, handling and steering are familiar, across all these cars and all these years. What's new is a Sport button that switches from CX lope to XM corner-attack.

Yet what's most satisfying about this quartet of Citroën saloons is their intellectual appeal, their demand that you get to know the car's unique engineering ethos before you learn to drive them most smoothly. Too many luxury cars are either try-hards – of the genuine opinion that you live in fear of Mr Jones from next door coming round with a tape measure to compare 'shutlines' – or like a simpering Jeeves, scurrying around desperate to cater for your every whim.

A big Citroën, on the other hand, is like sinking into a favourite armchair for a deep and meaningful conversation with a philosophically inclined friend. They are places to think, and to contemplate the answer to the question that they all pose: just what is luxury, exactly?

Thanks to *Stephen Clements Gray for his ID, Sean Padden for his CX, Paul King of Paris Autos (0161 477 6030; www.paris-autos.co.uk) for his XM and Citroën UK for the loan of its C6*

CITROËN ID20

Sold/number built 1955-'75/1,455,746 (all ID/DSs) **Construction** steel monocoque punt, with steel outer panels, glassfibre roof **Engine** iron-block, alloy-head, ohv 1985cc in-line 'four', with single Solex or Weber carb; 103bhp @ 5500rpm; 101lb ft @ 3000rpm **Transmission** four-speed manual, driving front wheels **Suspension** independent, at **front** by twin leading arms **rear** trailing arms; self-levelling hydropneumatic spheres, anti-roll bars f/r **Steering** powered rack and pinion **Brakes** powered discs f (inboard), drums r **Length** 15ft 10½in (4839mm) **Width** 5ft 10½in (1791mm) **Height** 4ft 10in (1473mm) **Wheelbase** 10ft 3in (3124mm) **Mpg** 21 **Weight** 2811lb (1275kg) **0-60mph** 15 secs **Top speed** 95mph **Price new** £1399 (DSpécial, 1970) **Price now** £5-£10,000 (ID/DSuper)

CITROËN CX 2000 ATHENA

Sold/number built 1975-'91/1,042,300 (all CXs) **Construction** steel monocoque **Engine** all-alloy, sohc 1985cc in-line 'four', with Weber twin-choke carb; 106bhp @ 5500rpm; 122lb ft @ 3250rpm **Transmission** five-speed manual, driving front wheels **Suspension** (where different to DS) **front** upper and lower arms; interconnected front-rear **Steering** powered rack and pinion **Brakes** powered discs **Length** 15ft 2½in (4636mm) **Width** 5ft 8in (1727mm) **Height** 4ft 5½in (1359mm) **Weight** 2722lb (1234kg) **Wheelbase** 9ft 4in (2845mm) **0-60mph** 11.8 secs **Top speed** 104mph **Mpg** 24 **Price new** £3195 **Price now** £1500-£6000

CITROËN XM 2.1 TDSX

Sold/number built 1989-'99/329,388 (all XMs) **Construction** steel monocoque, with glassfibre bonnet and hatchback **Engine** iron-block, alloy-head, sohc 2088cc diesel 'four', with three valves per cylinder, mechanical injection and Mitsubishi turbo; 110bhp @ 4300rpm; 183lb ft @ 2000rpm **Transmission** four-speed auto **Suspension** Hydractive (hydropneumatic, with extra sensors and controlling electronics) **front** MacPherson struts **Steering** powered rack and pinion **Brakes** powered discs **Length** 15ft 5¼in (4705mm) **Width** 5ft 10½in (1791mm) **Height** 4ft 6½in (1384mm) **Wheelbase** 9ft 4¼in (2851mm)-**Weight** 3205lb (1455kg) **0-60mph** 9.6 secs **Top speed** 121mph **Mpg** 43 **Price new** £18,449 **Price now** £875-£3000

CITROËN C6 3.0 HDI EXCLUSIVE

Sold/number built 2006-date/722 (UK) **Construction** steel and aluminium monocoque **Engine** all-alloy, dohc-per-bank 2992cc diesel V6, high-pressure direct injection, twin turbos; 240bhp @ 4000rpm; 332lb ft @ 1600rpm **Transmission** six-speed auto, driving front wheels, with ESP and traction control **Suspension** Hydractive 3+ (with switchable modes) **front** double wishbones **rear** multi-link **Steering** speed-sensitive, power-assisted rack and pinion **Brakes** discs, with servo, ABS, EBD and EBA **Length** 16ft 1¼in (4908mm) **Width** 5ft 6in (1860mm) **Height** 4ft 9½in (1464mm) **Wheelbase** 9ft 6¼in (2900mm) **Weight** 4130lb (1873kg) **0-60mph** 8.9 secs **Top speed** 149mph **Mpg** 38 **Price new** £37,895 **Now** from £12,000 s/h

Printed and bound in Great Britain by
Marston Book Services Ltd, Oxfordshire